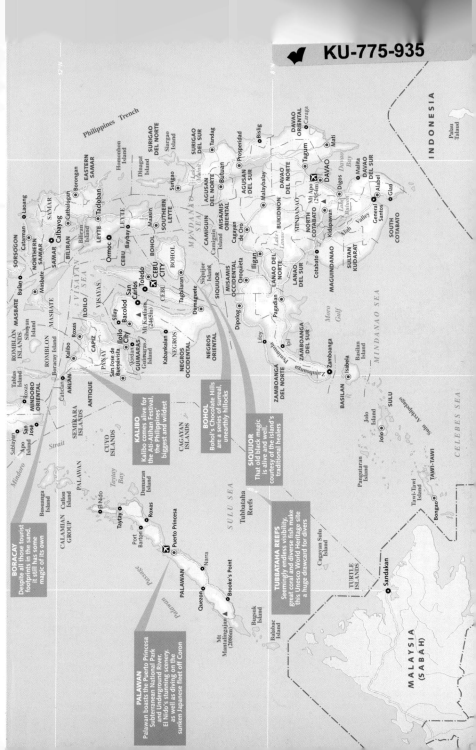

KU-775-935

BORACAY
Despite all those tourist footprints in the sand, it still has some magic of its own

KALIBO
Kalibo comes alive for the Ati-Atihan Festival, the Philippines' biggest and wildest

BOHOL
Bohol's Chocolate Hills are a series of surreal, unearthly hillocks

SIQUIJOR
That old black magic is alive and well courtesy of the island's traditional healers

TUBBATAHA REEFS
Seemingly endless visibility, great coral and diverse fish make this Unesco World Heritage site a huge drawcard for divers

PALAWAN
Palawan boasts the Puerto Princesa Subterranean National Park and Underground River, El Nido's stunning scenery, as well as diving on the sunken Japanese fleet off Coron

Philippines Trench

EASTERN SAMAR
NORTHERN SAMAR
SAMAR
SORSOGON
Catarman
Laoang
Catbalogan
Borongan
Calbayog
Homonhon Island
Dinagat Island
SURIGAO DEL NORTE
Siargao Island
Bislig
DAVAO ORIENTAL
Caraga
Mati
INDONESIA
Palau Island

MASBATE
Bulan
Masbate
Sibuyan Island
ROMBLON ISLANDS
Tablas Island
ROMBLON
AKLAN
Kalibo
Roxas
CAPIZ
ANTIQUE
PANAY
ILOILO
Iloilo City
Jordan
GUIMARAS
Guimaras Island
San Jose de Buenavista
NEGROS OCCIDENTAL
Bacolod
Silay
Kabankalan
Mt Kanlaon (2465m)
NEGROS ORIENTAL
Dumaguete

LEYTE
Tacloban
Ormoc
Baybay
SOUTHERN LEYTE
Maasin
BILIRAN
Biliran Island
CEBU
CEBU CITY
San Carlos
Toledo
BOHOL
Tagbilaran
Siquijor Island
SIQUIJOR

Surigao
SURIGAO DEL SUR
Tandag
Prosperidad
Butuan
AGUSAN DEL NORTE
AGUSAN DEL SUR
CAMIGUIN
Camiguin Island
Cagayan de Oro
MISAMIS ORIENTAL
Malaybalay
BUKIDNON
Mt Apo (2954m)
DAVAO DEL NORTE
Tagum
DAVAO
Davao
Digos
DAVAO DEL SUR
Malita
Lake Mainit

VISAYAN SEA
VISAYAS
Roxas
MINDORO ORIENTAL
SEMIRARA ISLANDS
CUYO ISLANDS
Cuyo Island
CAGAYAN ISLANDS

MINDANAO SEA

Dipolog
ZAMBOANGA DEL NORTE
Iligan
Oroquieta
MISAMIS OCCIDENTAL
LANAO DEL NORTE
Lake Lanao
LANAO DEL SUR
Pagadian
ZAMBOANGA DEL SUR
Ipil
High Valley
NORTH COTABATO
Kidapawan
Cotabato
MAGUINDANAO
SULTAN KUDARAT
Lake Buluan
General Santos
Alabel
SOUTH COTABATO
Glan
Moro Gulf

Zamboanga
Isabela
ZAMBOANGA
Zamboanga Peninsula
BASILAN
Basilan Island

MINDANAO SEA

SULU
Jolo
Jolo Island
Pangutaran Island
SULU ARCHIPELAGO
Cagayan Sulu Island

TAWI-TAWI
Tawi-Tawi Island
Bongao

CELEBES SEA

TURTLE ISLANDS
Sandakan
MALAYSIA (SABAH)

Mindoro Strait
Sablayan
Apo Island
San Jose
Busuanga Island
CALAMIAN GROUP
Coron Island
Dumaran Island
PALAWAN
El Nido
Taytay
Roxas
Port Barton
Puerto Princesa
Narra
Quezon
Brooke's Point
Bugsuk Island
Balabac Island
Mt Mantalingajan (2086m)
Palawan Passage
Tayay Bay

SULU SEA

Tubbataha Reefs

Philippines
8th edition – June 2003
First published – February 1981

Published by
Lonely Planet Publications Pty Ltd ABN 36 005 607 983
90 Maribyrnong St, Footscray, Victoria 3011, Australia

Lonely Planet Offices
Australia Locked Bag 1, Footscray, Victoria 3011
USA 150 Linden St, Oakland, CA 94607
UK 72-82 Rosebery Ave, Clerkenwell, London, EC1R 4RW
France 1 rue du Dahomey, 75011 Paris

Photographs
Many of the images in this guide are available for licensing from
Lonely Planet Images.
w www.lonelyplanetimages.com

Front cover photograph
Siargao island, Mindanao (John Borthwick)

Diving in the Philippines title page photograph
Coral and schools of fish, off Pescador island, Cebu (Grant Somers)

ISBN 1 74059 210 7

text & maps © Lonely Planet Publications Pty Ltd 2003
photos © photographers as indicated 2003

Printed through SNP SPrint Singapore Pte Ltd at
KHL Printing Co Sdn Bhd Malaysia

Philippines

Chris Rowthorn

Monique Choy   **Michael Grosberg**
Steven Martin   **Sonia Orchard**

LONELY PLANET PUBLICATIONS
Melbourne • Oakland • London • Paris

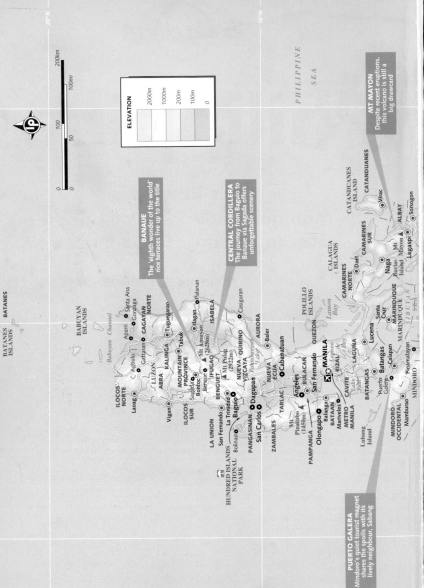

BATANES
The northern islands, a world away from party-down Boracay, are ideal for hiking and biking

BANAUE
The eighth wonder of the world' rice terraces live up to the title

CENTRAL CORDILLERA
The journey from Baguio to Banaue via Sagada offers unforgettable scenery

MT MAYON
Despite recent eruptions, this volcano is still a big drawcard

PUERTO GALERA
Mindoro's quiet tourist magnet shares the spoils with its lively neighbour, Sabang

ELEVATION

2000m
1000m
200m
100m
0

SOUTH CHINA SEA

PHILIPPINE SEA

BATANES

BATANES ISLANDS

BABUYAN ISLANDS

Babuyan Channel

ILOCOS NORTE
Laoag

CAGAYAN
Aparri · Santa Ana
Gonzaga
Abulug
Gattaran
Tuguegarao

KALINGA
Tabuk

ABRA

LUZON

MOUNTAIN PROVINCE
Sagada
Bontoc
Bangued

IFUGAO
Mt Amuyao
Mt Pulag (2928m)

ISABELA
Ilagan · Palanan

QUIRINO

BENGUET
La Trinidad
Baguio
Benguet

NUEVA VIZCAYA

ILOCOS SUR
Vigan

LA UNION
San Fernando

PANGASINAN
Bolinao
Dagupan
San Carlos

HUNDRED ISLANDS NATIONAL PARK

ZAMBALES

TARLAC

NUEVA ECIJA
Cabanatuan

AURORA
Baler
Casiguran

PAMPANGA
Angeles
San Fernando

BULACAN

MT Pinatubo (1745m)

BATAAN
Balanga
Mariveles

Olongapo

METRO MANILA
MANILA

CAVITE
RIZAL
Laguna de Bay

LAGUNA

QUEZON
Lucena

POLILLO ISLANDS

Lamon Bay

BATANGAS
Batangas

Lubang Island

MINDORO OCCIDENTAL
Mamburao

MINDORO
Puerto Galera
Calapan
Pinamalayan

Santa Cruz

MARINDUQUE

CALAGUA ISLANDS

CAMARINES NORTE
Daet

CAMARINES SUR
Naga

CATANDUANES ISLAND
CATANDUANES
Virac

Burias Island
Mt Mayon
Legaspi

ALBAY

Sorsogon

SIBUYAN

Contents – Text

MINDANAO & SULU 397

PALAWAN 437

LANGUAGE 460

GLOSSARY 468

THANKS 470

INDEX 472

MAP LEGEND back page

METRIC CONVERSION inside back cover

Contents – Maps

The Authors

Chris Rowthorn

Chris was born in England and grew up in the USA. After graduating from college, he worked a variety of less-than-stimulating jobs before deciding in 1992 to move to Kyoto, Japan. After a few years working as an English teacher, he became a regional correspondent for *The Japan Times*. This led to work with Lonely Planet, first on its *Japan* guide and then on titles such as *Kyoto*, *South-East Asia on a shoestring*, *Victoria* and *Read This First: Asia & India*. Chris is still based in Kyoto and travels whenever possible in Asia and the rest of the world.

Monique Choy

On Monique's travels she has sipped tea with a Templar knight on the Camino de Santiago in Spain, cast a line for barramundi with Yolngu people in Arnhem Land, Australia, and tussled with an angry ghost on a former 'island of the banished' in the Maldives. She now lives in the town of Cockatoo (near Melbourne), Australia.

Monique has contributed to Lonely Planet's *Aboriginal Australia & the Torres Strait Islands*, *Rajasthan*, *Tibet* and *Australia* guides.

Michael Grosberg

Michael was raised in the Washington DC area, studied philosophy in Michigan and Israel and then worked in business on a small island in the Northern Marianas. After a long trip through Asia and across the US he left for journalism and NGO work in South Africa. He has since returned to New York City, taken many random jobs, pursued graduate work in literature and currently teaches at university in between trips abroad. This is his first Lonely Planet assignment.

Steven Martin

A native of San Diego, California, Steven spent much of the 1980s living and travelling in the Philippines. Since 1989 he has used Thailand as a base while travelling and writing about Southeast Asia for various publications. Besides English, Steven speaks (in descending order of fluency) Thai, Lao, Tagalog and Spanish. In his spare time, Steven collects antique opium-smoking paraphernalia.

Sonia Orchard

Sonia has completed degrees in music, literature and biology; lived in Australia, Asia, Africa, Europe and America; worked as a cook, a marine educator, a diving instructor; and published a novel. She now lives on a property near Bells Beach (Australia) where she teaches music, writes, grows vegies, tries to surf and was recently attacked by a rooster.

FROM THE AUTHORS

Chris Rowthorn I'd like to thank all the kind people of the Philippines who helped me during my stay there. Special thanks are due to Virgilio Calaguian, for his tireless assistance, careful work and in-depth knowledge of Manila. Thanks are also due to Avette Guiverra, Cliff, Mister Ding, and the entire crew from Verukha Salt. Thanks to all the inhouse staff at Lonely Planet for their hard work on this book. Thanks also to the many readers who took the time to send emails and letters to Lonely Planet about the Philippines and to Joseph Bindloss for his Philippines briefing. I'd also like to thank Mrs. Shirley Diamond for letting me use her writer's cabin – I wouldn't have finished the book without that calm refuge! Lastly, I'd like to thank my coauthors Monique Choy, Michael Grosberg, Steven Martin and Sonia Orchard for their hard work on this book – you all did a great job!

Monique Choy Thanks to all the people who smoothed my way during research, including Cecilia Duran at Fernandos Hotel in Sorsogon, Adollo M Lazares in Boac, Jojo Villareal at Kadlagan Outdoor Shop in Naga, Vic and Richard at Halcon Mountaineers, Gilbert P Yulo in San José, the friendly folk in the Sablayan Eco-Tourism Office for the video show, Gerry M Jamilla in the Provincial Tourism Office of Marinduque, and tourism authorities throughout Mindoro and Bicol for their generous help. Special thanks also to all the readers who wrote in with tips and suggestions and to Chris Rowthorn and the team at Lonely Planet.

Michael Grosberg Thanks to Kinad in Bontoc for his knowledge and expertise; Kurt and Dixy Hensema in Solano for their hospitality; Chit Asignacion of Tam-awan Village and Brenda and Gloria Palispis in Baguio; Jessie Vicente in Hundred Islands National Park for a good day of kayaking; Antonio and Monavic M de Ubago in Tuguegarao for their kindness and assistance; Germy Singson Goulart in Vigan; Jan van der Ploeg for information on the Northern Sierra Madre National Park; and the folks at the DOT in Baler.

Steven Martin My most heartfelt thanks goes to Wilfredo Cruz, without whose friendship I would probably not have been introduced to the fascinating side of Manila to be found outside the confines of Ermita during my first trip to the Philippines back in 1981. A close second goes to the many Filipino friends in Malabon who, with patience and humour, taught me their language and culture: Erwyn; Rommel; Glenn De La Cruz and family; Jun Tolentino; Edgar Santos; Edgar Gonzales; Ronnel Velasquez; Bong-Bong Pineda; Venher Marron; Victor Vargas; Mang Monching and his daughters May, Fe, Daisy and Dolor; and about twenty or thirty others whose names escape me but who nonetheless left a positive and lasting impression. During the updating of this guidebook I was generously assisted by my *kumpare* Ronnel Velasquez, my godson Charlemagne, and the rest of the Velasquez family. Many thanks also go to Rosette Lerias, Rio Cahambing, Don Ramon Escanõ and the good folks of Southern Leyte, as well as Martin Oppus for pointing me in the right direction. Michael Newbill and Camille Purvis of the American embassy in Manila deserve special thanks for handy advice and a tantalising tour of Manila's hippest venues. A big thanks also to Kathleen McGowan of the US embassy in Bangkok for introducing me to Michael and Camille. Robert Gardner's informative website was a big help with understanding Philippine architecture. Last but not least, kudos to my travelling companion Dan Lovering for rising to the occasion and eating not one, but two, *balut* in order to appease my insistent *barkada* in Malabon.

Sonia Orchard

A huge thanks to both Stuart Green in Cebu (DENR) and Daisy Yanson in Iloilo, whose excellent research assistance and company contributed significantly to the Visayan odyssey. The Around Manila section was smoothly piloted by the very generous Joey Cuerdo. Many thanks also to the charming Art Tajanlangit; the helpful Boyz Jamandre; the knowledgable Jake Willis and Isabel Isherwood; the supportive Kristen Odijk, Jane Thompson, Chris Rowthorn (all from LP); Emmanuelle, the Alona Beach philosopher-raconteur boatman; and the relentless smiles of the Filipino people.

This Book

The first six editions of Lonely Planet's *Philippines* guidebook were written by Jens Peters. The 7th edition was thoroughly rewritten (and maps redrawn) by a team of writers that included Russ Kerr, Joe Bindloss, Virginia Jealous, Caroline Liou and Mic Looby. For this 8th edition a wonderful team of authors updated the entire book. Chris Rowthorn, coordinating author, updated the introductory chapters, and worked on the Manila chapter with the assistance of Virgilio Calaguian. Chris also wrote the 'Diving in the Philippines' special section. Sonia Orchard worked on Around Manila and co-authored the Visayas chapter with Steven Martin. Michael Grosberg updated North Luzon; Monique Choy updated the Southeast Luzon and Mindoro chapters; and Steven Martin worked on Mindanao & Sulu and Palawan. Along with Chris, Steven also contributed to the Language chapter.

FROM THE PUBLISHER

This 8th edition of *Philippines* was produced in Lonely Planet's Melbourne office by the coordinators Gina Tsarouhas (editorial) and Jacqueline Nguyen (cartography); it was briefed and commissioned by Mary Neighbour, Kristin Odijk and Jane Thompson. Gina was ably assisted by a fabulous team of editors and proofers that included Hilary Ericksen, Justin Flynn, Jennifer Garrett, Jocelyn Harewood, Nancy Ianni, Rebecca Lalor, Kristin, Tom Smallman, Sally Steward and Meg Worby. Jacqueline was assisted with mapping by Daniel Fennessy, Kusnandar, Tessa Rottiers and Jody Whiteoak. Pablo Gastar designed the lovely colourwraps and was in charge of the book's layout. Big thanks go to Sally Morgan and Indra Kilfoyle for assistance during layout. The gorgeous cover was designed by Brendan Dempsey, with Yukiyoshi Kamimura creating the artwork. Cheers to LPI for the fabulous images. The illustrations were drawn by the ever-talented Martin Harris. Special thanks go to Quentin Frayne for the language chapter, to Kus for the climate charts and to Simone Egger, Tegan Murray and Suzannah Schwer for editorial assistance during layout. Thanks also to production services for Quark support and to the very kind (and very patient) Pablo for answering a thousand-and-one Pilipino queries. Many thanks to Huw Fowles (project manager) who from the beginning took this baby by the hand and led it through production in a firm but steady fashion. And finally, the book could not have happened if it wasn't for the enthusiasm and dedication of the talented authors: Chris, Monique, Michael, Sonia and Steven – thank you!

THANKS
Many thanks to the travellers who used the last edition and wrote to us with helpful hints, advice and interesting anecdotes. Your names appear in the back of this book.

Foreword

ABOUT LONELY PLANET GUIDEBOOKS

The story begins with a classic travel adventure: Tony and Maureen Wheeler's 1972 journey across Europe and Asia to Australia. There was no useful information about the overland trail then, so Tony and Maureen published the first Lonely Planet guidebook to meet a growing need.

From a kitchen table, Lonely Planet has grown to become the largest independent travel publisher in the world, with offices in Melbourne (Australia), Oakland (USA), London (UK) and Paris (France).

Today Lonely Planet guidebooks cover the globe. There is an ever-growing list of books and information in a variety of media. Some things haven't changed. The main aim is still to make it possible for adventurous travellers to get out there – to explore and better understand the world.

At Lonely Planet we believe travellers can make a positive contribution to the countries they visit – if they respect their host communities and spend their money wisely. Since 1986 a percentage of the income from each book has been donated to aid projects and human rights campaigns, and, more recently, to wildlife conservation.

Although inclusion in a guidebook usually implies a recommendation we cannot list every good place. Exclusion does not necessarily imply criticism. In fact there are a number of reasons why we might exclude a place – sometimes it is simply inappropriate to encourage an influx of travellers.

UPDATES & READER FEEDBACK

Things change – prices go up, schedules change, good places go bad and bad places go bankrupt. Nothing stays the same. So, if you find things better or worse, recently opened or long-since closed, please tell us and help make the next edition even more accurate and useful.

Lonely Planet thoroughly updates each guidebook as often as possible – usually every two years, although for some destinations the gap can be longer. Between editions, up-to-date information is available in our free, monthly email bulletin *Comet* (W www.lonelyplanet.com/newsletters). You can also check out the *Thorn Tree* bulletin board and *Postcards* section of our website, which carry unverified, but fascinating, reports from travellers.

Tell us about it! We genuinely value your feedback. A well-travelled team at Lonely Planet reads and acknowledges every email and letter we receive and ensures that every morsel of information finds its way to the relevant authors, editors and cartographers.

Everyone who writes to us will find their name listed in the next edition of the appropriate guidebook. The very best contributions will be rewarded with a free guidebook.

We may edit, reproduce and incorporate your comments in Lonely Planet products such as guidebooks, websites and digital products, so let us know if you don't want your comments reproduced or your name acknowledged.

How to contact Lonely Planet:
Online: e talk2us@lonelyplanet.com.au, W www.lonelyplanet.com
Australia: Locked Bag 1, Footscray, Victoria 3011
UK: 72-82 Rosebery Ave, Clerkenwell, London, EC1R 4RW
USA: 150 Linden St, Oakland, CA 94607

Introduction

Start with an archipelago of more than 7000 islands strewn across a great stretch of tropical sea. Throw in one of the world's most diverse ecosystems. Add hundreds of ancient cultures and one very modern one. Steep it in a rich history at the crossroads of Southeast Asia. Top it off with soaring volcanos and serrated mountains, and voilá! You've got the Philippines.

Long bypassed by most travellers to Southeast Asia because of its location on the 'wrong' side of the South China Sea, the Philippines is a well-kept secret among those who have been there. These coral-fringed islands are home to wonders enough to stagger even the most jaded traveller: extraordinary rice terraces, tropical rainforests, underground rivers, soaring limestone towers, uninhabited 'Robinson Crusoe' islands, and cascading waterfalls. And that's just above the ocean surface! Below, the reefs and walls offer some truly memorable diving and snorkelling, and the wreck diving may just be the best in the world.

But more than just stunning natural scenery, it's the people of the Philippines that many visitors find unforgettable. From isolated hill tribes to hip urban intellectuals, Filipinos form a mosaic that reflects the islands' rich and varied nature.

Long governed by foreign interests, the Philippines inevitably bears the deep imprint of other cultures. But scratch a little deeper and you're bound to see something distinctly Filipino. With a calendar jam-packed with colourful festivals, there are ample opportunities to enjoy the natural warmth and vibrancy of Filipinos at their uninhibited best.

The best thing about travelling in the Philippines is the sense that there are still discoveries to be made, sometimes just around the next corner. With so many islands and so few visitors (at least in comparison to some other Southeast Asian nations), the Philip-

pines is one of the last great frontiers in Asian travel. For those who are willing to adapt to the challenges of travel here, there are plenty of rewards. So slow down, set your clock to Philippine time and keep your eyes open – somewhere among those 7107 islands there's a great adventure waiting to happen.

Facts about the Philippines

HISTORY
Way, Way Back

Thanks to 'Tabon Man', who left a bit of his (or her, according to some) skull in a cave in Palawan at least 22,000 years ago, a sliver of light shines into the deep, dark prehistory of the Philippines. The oldest known human relic of the islands, this bone suggests that the Tabon Caves helped early *Homo sapiens* survive the last ice age. Later generations left behind tools and terracotta jars, including the 3000-year-old Manunggul burial jar. Hailed as a masterpiece of ancient pottery, the jar depicts two people paddling a boat into the afterlife. To this day, the ocean and the boat remain powerful symbols in the Philippines. Even the word *barangay*, meaning a community or the basic Filipino social unit, is derived from the ancient *balangay*, or sailboat.

The longest-held theory on the origins of Tabon Man is based on distinct waves of migration. Assuming that much of modern-day Asia was linked by land bridges, this theory posits that around 250,000 years ago our earliest human ancestors simply walked over to what is now the Philippines.

Then, about 200,000 years later, in strode the nomadic Negrito groups from the Malay Peninsula, Borneo and perhaps even Australia. At the same time the sea was thought to be swallowing up low-lying land, forcing the nonocean-going groups to settle permanently in this new frontier. Today, their descendants include indigenous tribes such as the Bukidnon, Karolano and Ata on the islands of Mindanao, Panay, Guimaras, Negros and Masbate.

After an interval of roughly 2000 years, the Neolithic Age arrived in the form of the seafaring, tool-wielding Indonesians. The Indonesian groups brought with them formal farming and building skills.

It's fair to assume that this bunch was busily carving out the spectacular rice terraces of North Luzon at around the time Jesus Christ was making a name for himself in the Middle East. Modern-day descendants of these Indonesian master builders are thought to include tribes such as: Luzon's Ifugao and Kalinga; Mindoro's Mangyan; Palawan's Tagbanua; and Mindanao's Bagobo, Manobo and Mandaya.

With the Iron Age came the Malays. Skilful sailors, potters and weavers, they built the first permanent settlements and prospered from around 1st century AD until the 16th century, when the Spanish arrived. The wave migration theory holds that the Malays arrived in at least three ethnically diverse waves. The first wave provided the basis for the modern-day Bontoc and other tribes of North Luzon. The second laid the foundations for the most dominant of modern-day indigenous groups – the Bicolano, Bisayan and Tagalog. The third wave is thought to have established the fiercely proud Muslim Malays.

If this version of early Philippine history seems too tidy to be true, that's because it is – at least according to those who see wave migration as a Western colonialist fantasy. After all, there's no evidence to support *any* migration pattern before Tabon Man's existence, let alone a neat order of events based on a hierarchy of ethnic one-upmanship. Even terms such as 'Indonesian', 'Negrito' and 'Malay' are relatively recent European inventions. In short, Asia has long been more complex and subtle than its colonial masters have needed it to be, and Western theories on Eastern prehistory reflect this.

And so modern Philippine scholars have come up with a theory to try to plug the historical holes left by their predecessors. Their 'core population' theory has taken the wave migration concept and turned it into a less rigid model of prehistoric settlement. It suggests that the early inhabitants of Southeast Asia were of the same racial group (the Pithecanthropus group, to be exact), with more or less the same traditions and beliefs. Over time, divisions formed according to the demands of the environment – which may well have inspired Tabon Man to settle in a cave in Palawan all those years ago.

Trade

Defying their Confucian traditions, the Chinese became the first foreigners to do business with the islands they called MaI, as early as the 2nd century AD. Of course, the islands' tribal communities were trading among themselves long before then. Ancient gold coins have been found in several parts of the Philippines. Engraved with local dialect characters, these conical coins are thought to have been made by pouring molten metal into the folds of palm leaves.

The first recorded Chinese expedition to the Philippines was in AD 982. Within a few decades, Chinese traders were regular visitors to towns along the coast of Luzon, Mindoro and Sulu, and by around AD 1100 travellers from India, Borneo, Sumatra, Java, Siam (Thailand) and Japan were also including the islands on their trade runs. Gold was by then big business in Butuan (on the northern coast of Mindanao), Chinese settlements had sprung up in Manila and on Jolo, and Japanese merchants were buying shop space in Manila and North Luzon.

For several centuries this peaceful trade arrangement thrived. Despite the island's well-known riches, the inhabitants were never directly threatened by their powerful Asian trading partners. The key, particularly in the case of China, was diplomacy. Throughout the 14th and 15th centuries, the tribal leaders of the Philippines would make regular visits to Peking (Beijing) to honour the Chinese emperor.

By the late 15th century, a far less benign giant was awakening. Europe's aristocrats were rich and restless. The thrill of feudal tyranny had faded and they wanted more. One man who wanted more than most was Jakob Fugger, a phenomenally rich German banker with a sideline in Europe's newest obsession – spices. With a Muslim monopoly controlling the spice trade overland, Fugger longed to find an alternative spice route. Owed money by none other than King Charles I of Spain, Fugger had little trouble convincing the Spanish that sending a few ships into the unknown made good business sense. Ferdinand Magellan, denied funds by his native Portugal for him to sail westward, leapt at the chance to lead this Spanish fleet.

The Spanish Era

A triumphant Magellan set foot on Samar at dawn on 16 March 1521. He claimed the islands for Spain and named them the Islas del Poniente (Western Islands). Soon after, the Portuguese arrived from the east and declared them to be the Islas del Oriente (Eastern Islands). Undaunted, Magellan set about giving the islanders a crash course in Catholicism and winning over various tribal chiefs before fatally taking things one step too far on Mactan Island (see the boxed text 'Magellan's Last Stand' under Around Cebu City in the Visayas chapter).

Determined to press its claim, Spain sent four more expeditions; Ruy Lopez de Villalobos, commander of the fourth expedition, renamed the islands after the heir to the Spanish throne, Philip, Charles I's son. Philip, as King Philip II, sent a fresh fleet led by Miguel Lopez de Legazpi to the islands in the mid-16th century with strict orders to colonise and Catholicise. In 1565 an agreement was signed by Legazpi and Tupas, the defeated chief of Cebu, which made every Filipino answerable to Spanish law. The Filipinos' long and bitter servitude to foreign powers had begun.

Legazpi, his soldiers, and a band of Augustinian monks wasted no time in establishing a settlement where Cebu City now stands. First called San Miguel, then Santisimo Nombre de Jesus, this fortified town hosted the earliest Filipino-Spanish Christian weddings and – critically – the baptisms of various Cebuano leaders. Panay Island's people were beaten into submission soon after, with Legazpi establishing a vital stronghold there (near present-day Roxas) in 1569. The Spanish soon discovered that in their mission to divide and conquer, half their work was done for them. The Philippines was already divided: first by nature, and second by a mosaic of barangay.

Written Language

From the outset, Spanish colonisation removed more than the Filipinos' freedom – it systematically stripped much of their culture. There's little doubt that the Spanish caused the swift decline in written indigenous languages. Only fragments remain of the precolonial inscribed bamboo tubes and tablets once found throughout the islands. Of the dozen or so distinct systems of writing (based on a 17-letter alphabet known as *baybayin*), only two remain – Tagbanua on Palawan and Hanunuo Mangyan on Mindoro. Both defied extinction because Palawan and Mindoro were too remote for Spanish domination.

Mic Looby

As the indigenous islanders were no match for the Spanish and their firearms, the greatest threat to Spain was to come from an old enemy – Islam. To Spain's horror, the Muslims had a big head start: Islamic missionaries from Malacca had established towns in Mindoro and Luzon almost a century before the Spanish arrived. Legazpi finally succeeded in taking the strategic Muslim settlement of Maynilad (now Manila) in 1571, hastily proclaiming it the capital and building over the *kuta* (fort) of Rajah Sulayman. This was eventually to become Fort Santiago.

So began a 300-year-long religious war that still smoulders in Mindanao, the spiritual home of Islam in the Philippines. The Spanish recruited newly Christianised Filipinos to help fight the Moros (as Muslim Filipinos were dubbed), many of whom earned a violent living as pirates. Spanish forts were built during this period, paid for with taxes imposed on the Philippines' colonial subjects. Such forts are seen today on islands such as Palawan, Romblon, Cebu and Mindanao.

Spain's strategic colonisation meant it could woo the Filipinos' best trading partner, China. Throughout the 16th and 17th centuries, Spain's galleons – many of them built in Cavite near Manila – also specialised in taking spices, silk, porcelain and gold to the New World, and returning with Mexican silver. Moro pirates, who outsailed and outsmarted the Spanish right up until the advent of the steamship in the mid-1800s, dodged many a cannon ball to claim a share of these riches. The Moros also conducted bloody raids, making off with prisoners who were later sold on the East Indies slave market.

By the 18th century, Spain's grasp on the Orient was slipping. It was sharing its traditional trade routes with colonial rivals. It was at war with England and fast running out of friends and funds.

Before long, with a big shove from the powerful East India Company, Britain invaded Manila in 1762. Unaware that Spain was even at war, the authorities in Manila at first thought that the 10,000 invaders cruising into the bay were Chinese traders.

The British won few fans by violently ransacking the surrendered city, and under their freshly-installed government a passionate, Filipino-led resistance movement immediately began to plot.

Philippine national hero, Dr José Rizal

Less than two years later, the British were chased out of Manila Bay by homegrown forces.

From the earliest years of colonisation, revolts against the Spanish had come and gone, sparked by wholesale land grabs, cruel taxes, corrupt officials and religious thuggery, but by the 19th century, this rage was becoming more focused. With the Spanish humbled by the British and the British in turn humbled by the Filipinos, a united, nationalist spirit was forming. Anticolonial sentiment was reaching new heights as friars, acting as quasi governors, became tyrants of a most un-Christian order. Filipinos who failed to grovel at the feet of a friar risked being branded *filibusteros* ('traitors' or 'rebels', depending on your point of view), which meant being arrested, imprisoned, exiled or worse. Meanwhile, terms such as Indios, used by Spanish officials to identify 'inferior' dark-skinned Filipinos, were cutting to the core.

From these Indios emerged a powerful group of nationalist heroes. The greatest and most famous hero was Dr José Rizal, doctor of medicine, poet, novelist, sculptor, painter, linguist, naturalist and fencing enthusiast. Executed by the Spanish in 1896, Rizal epitomised the Filipinos' dignified struggle for personal and national freedom. Just before facing the Spanish firing squad, Rizal penned a characteristically calm message of both caution and inspiration to his people: 'I am most anxious for liberties for our country, but I place as a prior condition the education of the people so that our country may have an individuality of its own and make itself worthy of liberties.'

By killing such figures, the Spanish were creating martyrs. Biblical history was repeating itself and the irony – at least to the Filipinos – was as heart-rending as it was inspiring.

In the simmering build-up to Rizal's death, the Suez Canal opened, effectively bringing an enlightened Europe and the USA closer to the Philippines. It was in this heady atmosphere that a failed 1872 uprising by Filipino patriots in Cavite became an excuse for the nervous Spanish authorities to round up scores of Filipino patriots, including priests. A mockery of a trial saw three prominent priests publicly garrotted. These three greatly revered martyrs are today collectively referred to as Gomburza, after their surnames: Gomez, Burgos and Zamora.

The incident fired Rizal to found La Liga Filipina (The Philippine League) and launch a peaceful barrage of literature condemning the Spanish and calling for social reform. Silenced by Rizal's subsequent arrest and exile to Dapitan in Mindanao, La Liga Filipina was superseded by a far more aggressive movement led by Andres Bonifacio. The Kataastaasan Kagalanggalangang Katipunan ng mga Anak ng Bayan (Highest and Most Respected Society of the Sons of the Nation)

– better known as the Katipunan or KKK – secretly built a revolutionary government in Manila, with a network of equally clandestine provincial councils. Complete with passwords, masks and coloured sashes denoting rank, the Katipunan's members (both men and women) peaked at an estimated 30,000 in mid-1896. In August, the Spanish got wind of the coming revolution (from a woman's confession to a Spanish friar, according to some accounts) and the Katipunan leaders were forced to flee the capital.

Depleted, frustrated and poorly armed, the Katipuneros took stock in nearby Balintawak, a baryo (district) of Caloocan, and voted to launch the revolution regardless. With the cry 'Mabuhay ang Pilipinas!' (Long live the Philippines!), the Philippine Revolution lurched into life following the incident that is now known as the Cry of Balintawak.

The shortage of weapons among the Filipinos meant that many fighters were forced to pluck their first gun from the hands of their enemies. So acute was the shortage of ammunition for these weapons that some (many of them children) were given the job of scouring battle sites for empty cartridges. These cartridges would then be painstakingly repacked using homemade gunpowder made of saltpetre, sulphur and charcoal. Needless to say, shooting practice was not encouraged.

After three years of bloodshed, most of it Filipino, a Spanish-Filipino peace pact was signed and the revolutionary leader General Emilio Aguinaldo agreed to go into exile in

The Flag

Exiled Filipino revolutionary General Emilio Aguinaldo kept himself busy in Hong Kong by designing what is today the national flag of the Philippines. Made of silk, the flag was sewn by expat Filipina Doña Marcela de Agoncillo and her daughter.

The striking design includes a sun with eight sword-like rays, representing the first eight provinces placed under martial law by Spain. The three gold stars represent the three major island groups – Luzon, the Visayas and Mindanao. The background triangles symbolise equality and unity (white), peace and justice (blue), and valour (red).

Mic Looby

ERIC L WHEATER

Hong Kong in 1897. Predictably, the pact's demands satisfied nobody. Promises of reform by the Spanish were broken, as were promises by the Filipinos to stop their revolutionary plotting. The Filipino cause attracted huge support from the Japanese, who tried unsuccessfully to send money and two boatloads of weapons to the exiled revolutionaries in Hong Kong.

The American Era

Meanwhile, another of Spain's colonial trouble spots – Cuba – was playing host to an ominous dispute over sugar between Spain and the USA. To save face, Spain declared war on the USA; as a colony of Spain, the Philippines was drawn into the conflict. Soon after, an American fleet under Commodore George Dewey sailed into Manila Bay and routed the Spanish ships. Keen to gain Filipino support, Dewey welcomed the return of exiled revolutionary General Aguinaldo and oversaw the Philippine Revolution mark II, which installed Aguinaldo as president of the first Philippine republic.

The Philippine flag was flown for the first time during the proclamation of Philippine Independence on 12 June 1898.

After a bitter struggle, Spanish troops in Manila and outlying towns were crushed by allied American and Filipino forces and Spain's 400-year-long occupation came to an end. With the signing of the Treaty of Paris in 1898, the Spanish-American War ended and the USA effectively bought the Philippines, Guam and Puerto Rico for US$20 million. Filipino representatives in Paris weren't even allowed to witness this monumental, internationally approved betrayal of the country.

Back in US-occupied Manila, tempers were rising. Filipino revolutionaries were openly defying the Americans, and the Americans were antagonising the Filipinos. Any dreams of impending Filipino independence were shattered in 1899 when Malolos, the makeshift capital of President Aguinaldo's Philippine Republic, was captured by American troops – led by General Arthur MacArthur.

The US decision to take the Philippines was not made lightly, if the confessions of President McKinley to a group of clergymen (from 'Interview with President William McKinley' by General James Rusing; published in 1903) are anything to go by:

The truth is, I didn't want the Philippines, and when they came to us, as a gift from the gods, I did not know what to do with them. When the Spanish war broke out, Dewey was in Hong Kong, and I ordered him to go to Manila, and he had to; because, if defeated, he had no place to refit on that side of the globe, and if the Dons (the Spanish) were victorious they would likely cross the Pacific and ravage Oregon and California coasts. And so he had to destroy the Spanish fleet, and he did it! But that was as far as I thought then. When next I realised that the Philippines had dropped into our lap, I confess I did not know what to do with them. I sought counsel from all sides – Democrats as well as Republicans – but got little help. I thought first we would take only Manila; then Luzon; then the other islands, perhaps, also. I am not ashamed to tell you, gentlemen, that I went down on my knees and prayed to almighty God for light and guidance more than one night. And one night it came to me this way – I don't know how it was but it came: (1) That we could not give them back to Spain. That would be cowardly and dishonourable; (2) That we could not turn them over to France or Germany – our commercial rivals in the Orient – that would be bad business and discreditable; (3) That we could not leave them to themselves – they were unfit for self-government – and they would soon have anarchy and misrule over there worse than Spain's was; and (4) That there was nothing left for us to do but to take them all, and to educate the Filipinos; and uplift and civilise and Christianise them, and, by God's grace, do the very best we could by them, as our fellowmen for whom Christ also died. And then I went to bed, and went to sleep, and slept soundly, and the next morning I sent for the chief engineer of the War Department (our map maker) and told him to put the Philippines on the map of the United States; and there they are, and there they will stay while I am president!

By 1902 the first Philippine Republic was dead and buried and a succession of American neocolonial governors-general ensured it stayed that way. Like the Spanish, the Americans' main intention was to serve their own economic needs, and by 1930 they had engineered an industrial and social revolution, with two of the biggest booms coming from mining and prostitution.

Not until 1935, once it had firmly lassoed the country's resources, did the USA endorse the Commonwealth of the Philippines, along with the drafting of a US-style constitution and the first national election. On paper at least, democracy and freedom had at last

Mark Twain

The US government's role in the Philippines was condemned by many of its own people – including none other than the author Samuel Langhorne Clemens, better known as Mark Twain. Twain and his fellow anti-imperialists were convinced that Americans, if they knew all the facts, would have demanded an instant withdrawal from the Philippines. In an essay published in 1902 Twain described the situation thus:

We (the US) have bought some islands from a party who did not own them; with real smartness and a good counterfeit of disinterested friendliness we coaxed a confiding, weak nation into a trap and closed it upon them; we went back on an honoured guest of the Stars and Stripes when we had no further use for him and chased him to the mountains; we are as indisputably in possession of a wide-spreading archipelago as if it were our property; we have pacified some thousands of the islanders and buried them; destroyed their fields; burned their villages, and turned their widows and orphans out of doors; furnished heartbreak by exile to some dozens of disagreeable patriots, subjugated the remaining ten millions by Benevolent Assimilation, which is the pious new name of the musket; we have acquired property in the three hundred concubines and other slaves of our business partner, the Sultan of Sulu, and hoisted our protecting flag over that swag.

Mic Looby

come to the Philippines, but, as WWII was about to prove, they came at a terrible price.

When Japan bombed Hawaii's Pearl Harbor in 1941, US troops attacked the advancing Japanese Air Force.

The man who gave these orders was General Douglas Mac- Arthur, whose father had led the American charge into the Philippines 42 years earlier. Within two days, Japanese troops landed at Vigan in North Luzon, eventually driving the allied Filipino and US troops to the Bataan peninsula, opposite newly occupied Manila. From here, soldiers and civilians alike faced not only relentless bombardment but also hunger, disease and disillusionment.

MacArthur, holed up on nearby Corregidor island, made his now famous promise to return, and fled to Australia (for details see the boxed text 'I Shall Return' under Corregidor in the Around Manila chapter).

The Japanese Era

Ordered to maintain a 'holding action', MacArthur's abandoned troops soon fell to the Japanese with the unconditional surrender of around 76,000 people – 66,000 of them Filipinos. Those still able to walk began a 120km 'Bataan death march' from Bataan to San Fernando, and on to prison camps in Capas, Tarlac. As many as 20,000 people died along the way and another 25,000 died while imprisoned. This event is honoured with the annual Araw ng Kagitingan (Bataan Day) public holiday on 9 April. From 1942 to 1945, the Philippines endured a brutal Japanese military regime. Unlike the previous colonial forces, the Japanese actively encouraged Filipino languages as part of the Greater Asia Co-Prosperity Sphere, Japan's scheme of keeping Asia Asian. In 1944 MacArthur landed at Leyte, determined to dislodge the Japanese. The main battleground in this onslaught was Manila, whose defenceless residents suffered horrifically in the ensuing crossfire. By the time MacArthur marched into the city, at least 100,000 civilians lay dead or dying. In total, over 1.1 million Filipinos were killed during WWII.

In early 1946 Japan's General Tomoyuki Yamashita (see also the boxed text 'Gold-Diggers' later) was tried as a war criminal and hanged by order of MacArthur. In July of the same year, Manuel Roxas was installed as president of the Republic of the Philippines under the auspices of the USA, and the immense task of rebuilding a war-torn nation began. Far from free, the Philippines faced crippling high-interest loans in the form of US 'aid', and its society (and more than three-quarters of its schools and universities) lay in ruins.

The Marcos Era

First elected in 1965 under the seductive slogan 'This nation can be great again', the charismatic former lawyer Ferdinand Marcos became the first president to win two terms in office. By 1970, widespread poverty, rising inflation, pitiful public funding and blatant corruption triggered a wave of protests in

Gold-Diggers

It's more than likely that before General Tomoyuki Yamashita was captured and executed, he organised the burial of masses of gold plundered during WWII. This may have been done when the Philippines seemed a safe, Japanese-held storage spot, or it may have been done in desperate haste as American troops closed in – or perhaps it was a bit of both. In most cases, prisoners of war (POWs) were used to dig the often-complex tunnels and to set antitheft booby traps. These POWs, and sometimes even fellow Japanese officers, were executed after burying the treasure – the total value of which has been estimated to be around US$100 billion by today's standards.

The vast majority of this loot was almost certainly dug up years later by one of the nastiest treasure hunters of all time – Ferdinand Marcos.

In 1998 a group of middle-aged Philippine soldiers filed a claim in California and Zurich against the Marcos estate for their efforts in unearthing an estimated 60,000 tonnes of gold and gemstones between 1973 and 1985. A joint affidavit, signed by around 100 alleged diggers, accompanied the claim. These men were apparently members of 'Task Force Restoration', formed primarily to undertake 'massive diggings and excavations', while ostensibly fighting communist rebels. This in turn spawned a secret government industry involved in melting down the gold to remove all traces of its origin, all helped by Marcos' martial law.

Whether Marcos carried out his massive gold-digging in cahoots with other – possibly foreign – parties will probably remain a deeply embedded national secret. What is certain is that even this alleged grand theft by Marcos pales in comparison to the countless lives he stole during his time as leader.

As recently as 1999, 'Yamashita's Gold' claimed four lives in Lumban, near Laguna de Bay, southeast of Manila, when two treasure hunters were buried in a mine shaft they'd built. During the attempt to dig the men out, two emergency workers also died. Lumban, according to the recent revelations, was one of the first places Marcos's men struck gold. It seems that searching for lost treasure will always remain a popular activity.

Mic Looby

Manila. When several demonstrators were killed by police outside the presidential Malacañang Palace, Marcos' image as a political saviour died with them.

Citing the rise of leftist student groups and the New People's Army (NPA), Marcos imposed martial law on the entire country in 1972. Normally a constitutional last resort designed to protect the masses, martial law was declared by Marcos to keep himself in power (the constitution prevented him from running for a third term) and to protect his foreign business buddies. By this time, their formidable enemies included the anti-imperialist National Democratic Front (NDF) and the Islamic Moro National Liberation Front (MNLF) in Mindanao.

With martial law imposed, the Philippines was plunged into a darkness reminiscent of the Japanese occupation – only this time it was at the hands of a fellow Filipino. A curfew was imposed, the media was silenced or taken over by the military, international travel was banned and thousands of antigovernment suspects were rounded up and thrown into

military camps. An estimated 50,000 of Marcos' opponents were jailed, exiled or killed. Marcos then set about raising revenue by handing over great tracts of prime land to foreign investors and imposing heavy taxes on those who could least afford them.

When Marcos made a show of lifting martial law in 1981, to silence rising discontent, he reinvented himself and the constitution to form a sham of a democracy. Under this 'New Republic', Marcos won a mid-year election conveniently devoid of a free press or any real opposition.

In 1983, however, when thugs dressed as a military escort gunned down Marcos' political foe, Benigno 'Ninoy' Aquino Jr, within minutes of his return from exile, a new Filipino martyr was created. The two million mourners who poured onto the streets to accompany Aquino's funeral cortege in Manila began a steady march towards a new era.

By 1986 even Marcos's long-time supporters were publicly questioning him, as were many embarrassed foreign powers. Another rigged election saw Marcos beat

Ninoy Aquino's widow, Corazon 'Cory' Aquino, but this time the masses stormed the presidential palace. Within days, virtually all members of the nation's armed forces had sided with the masses, the Marcoses were airlifted out of the country by the US Air Force and Aquino was installed as president and national heroine.

Thus was the force of the 1986 'people power' movement, or EDSA (Epifanio de los Santos) Revolution. An account of this tumultu ous time can be found in James Fenton's *The Snap Revolution* (for more information on this book see History & Politics under Books in the Facts for the Visitor chapter).

Ferdinand Marcos died in exile in 1989 and his wife, Imelda Marcos, soon returned to the Philippines, where she somehow wriggled out of an 18-year jail sentence for graft. Evidence teased from Swiss bank accounts has her facing charges of stealing US$13.2 billion from the Filipino people. Yet, despite these charges, Mrs Marcos remains free and even ran for president in 1998 (she 'gave' the votes she garnered to the winner, Joseph Estrada, who in June 1998 asked the courts to give Marcos a presidential pardon; in October 1998 the Supreme Court acquitted Marcos of corruption charges).

A New Era

The cataclysmic eruption in June 1991 of Mt Pinatubo, northwest of Manila, ended another long chapter in Philippine history. Showered in volcanic ash and refused a new lease agreement, the US military bases at Clark and Subic Bay were closed down and US troops headed home. This left a sizable hole in the Philippine treasury. One of the biggest benefits of the US presence had been the money paid by the US government to occupy bases in the Philippines. Regarded as 'aid' by the USA and 'rent' by the Philippines, this much-needed cash was first paid in 1979 during Jimmy Carter's presidency, at a rate of US$500 million over five years. When this deal expired in 1983 a US$900 million five-year deal was struck.

By 1988 a two-year pledge of US$962 million was made, falling well short of the Philippines' new asking price of US$2.4 billion over five years.

In 1998 the Philippines celebrated its centennial of independence in typically festive fashion. But for many Filipinos, it wasn't until the US bases were closed – almost 500 years after Magellan landed at Samar – that the fight for independence was won.

Or was it? In March 1999 the Philippine Senate approved a controversial deal with the USA known as the Visiting Forces Agreement (VFA). A victory for the USA and a swift kick in the teeth for Philippine independence, the VFA – along with the Acquisition and Cross-Service Agreement (ACSA) and the Status of Forces Agreement (SOFA) – allows the presence of US armed forces in the Philippines.

As far as the VFA's extremely vocal critics are concerned, this allows for far more than war games, and it's a very one-sided agreement (in favour of the USA, of course). Critics range from women's and human rights groups to church elders and people within the Philippine Armed Forces – all of whom have presented strong, varied arguments against the VFA. Arguments *for* the VFA amount to vague hopes of economic and military benefits – none of which come close to being guaranteed in the agreement.

One of the first major troop deployments under the new scheme came in January 2002, when the USA sent 1200 troops to Basilan island to help local forces track down Abu Sayyaf Islamic militants. While the troops were originally slated to leave in July 2002, their stay has been extended indefinitely and another 2700 American troops have been added.

Despite frequent protests against their presence outside the American embassy in Manila, it looks as though the American troops are in it for the long haul, especially as the USA seeks new bases in Southeast Asia for its 'war on terror.'

For more information on recent Philippines history, see Government & Politics later in this chapter.

GEOGRAPHY

From north to south, the Philippines stretches some 1900km. From east to west it spans around 1110km. Three main islands or island groups – Luzon, the Visayas and Mindanao – divide the country into north, central and southern regions, respectively, though in everyday parlance Filipinos use 'southern Philippines' to cover anything beyond the Bicol region.

The 11 largest islands of the Philippines are as follows: Luzon (105,000 sq km); Mindanao (95,000 sq km); Samar (13,100 sq km); Negros (12,700 sq km); Palawan (11,800 sq km); Panay (11,500 sq km); Mindoro (9700 sq km); Leyte (7214 sq km); Cebu (4400 sq km); Bohol (3900 sq km); and Masbate (3300 sq km).

The most heavily forested island is Palawan. Deforestation and agricultural activities have denuded vast areas of other islands, in particular Leyte and Samar. Most islands feature volcanic mountains, several of which have been increasingly active since the 1980s. Strong earthquakes occur regularly. At around 10,000m deep, the Philippine Trench northeast of Mindanao is one of the world's deepest abysses.

Among the nation's 7107 islands, the three major island groups of the Philippines have mostly inland mountains, with peaks ranging from around 1000m to almost 3000m, and a total land area of 30 million hectares. While Mt Apo (2954m) in Mindanao is the country's highest summit, the country's most commanding mountains are volcanic, namely Mt Pinatubo on central Luzon and Mt Mayon on South Luzon.

There are almost as many theories about the origins of the Philippines as there are islands making up the modern-day nation. Some are scientific, some are mythical. One legend has it that the islands were created when a weary giant let a bare rocky ball of earth fall from his shoulders, causing it to shatter and form this fragmented land. Some geologists believe the islands rose from the sea in a massive volcanic eruption, one of many in the Pacific Ocean's 'Ring of Fire' volcanic region. The majority of scientists, however, favour the idea that the islands are the tips of a long-submerged land bridge that once allowed for one hell of a hike from China to Australia via Borneo, Indonesia and New Guinea. All the main islands of the Philippines have large rivers, many of which provide vital transport routes. The mightiest river on Luzon is the Cagayan, followed by the Abra, Chico, Pampanga and Bicol Rivers. Many rivers flowing through or near urban centres are partly or wholly degraded by industrial and domestic waste.

Limestone caves are found on many of the islands, with the best known being the St Paul Subterranean National Park's Underground River in Sabang, Palawan; those around Sagada in the mountainous region around the Banawe Rice Terraces in North Luzon; and the Callao Caves in the Cagayan Valley.

CLIMATE

The Philippines has two seasons: dry and wet. Generally, the dry season is from September to May and the wet season is from June to September, though weather patterns have become much less predictable.

By far the hottest month in lowland regions is May, when temperatures hover as

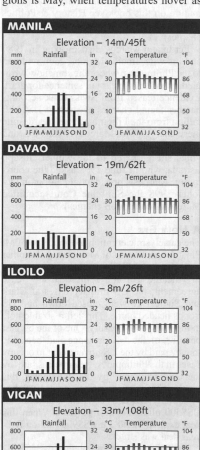

CLIMATIC ZONES

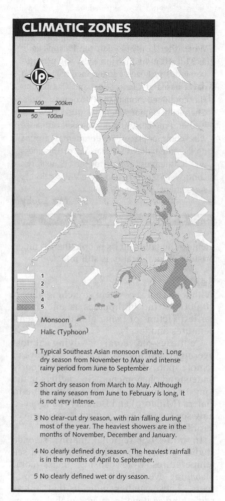

Monsoon
Halic (Typhoon)

1 Typical Southeast Asian monsoon climate. Long
dry season from November to May and intense
rainy period from June to September

2 Short dry season from March to May. Although
the rainy season from June to February is long, it
is not very intense.

3 No clear-cut dry season, with rain falling during
most of the year. The heaviest showers are in the
months of November, December and January.

4 No clearly defined dry season. The heaviest rainfall
is in the months of April to September.

5 No clearly defined wet or dry season.

An average of 20 typhoons, known as *bagyo*, whip across the Philippines each year. Striking mainly in Luzon and the Visayas, they bring heavy rains and strong winds and cause millions of dollars worth of damage. Although typhoons can occur at anytime, they occur most often in the rainy season, from June to September.

Like much of Asia and northern Australia, the Philippines has suffered the parching effects of the El Niño weather phenomenon and is now playing host to La Niña, which has brought unseasonal rainstorms and more flash floods.

In 1999 the combined impact of these weather patterns was blamed for a P7.5 billion loss in the vital Philippine fishing industry.

Recent research suggests this freakish brother-and-sister weather combination may become an increasingly frequent phenomenon thanks to global warming. For a country so dependent on crops and fishing for survival, this is a truly alarming prospect. It could mean more and more roads washing away without warning, telephone lines failing, drinking water becoming contaminated and increased incidence of cholera and other diseases.

ECOLOGY & ENVIRONMENT
Land

Before 1900 around two-thirds of the Philippines was covered with dense forest. Most estimates now put the total forested area of the Philippines at around 18%, only 3% of which is primary forest. Most alarmingly, the Philippines' remaining forests are vanishing at a furious rate – about 2700 sq km per year.

Environmentalists have noted bitterly that much of what's left of Philippine forests is too high up for loggers to be bothered with, or it's scrappy secondary forest yet to be eaten up by the ravenous Integrated Forest Management Agreements (IFMA, formerly the Timber License Agreements) that have allowed most of the damage.

This modern disaster has been caused by unregulated logging, massive farming expansion and a migrating lowland population. Throughout the 20th century, indigenous people's claims on upland regions were ignored and rich resources were plundered by a powerful elite. Poor lowland communities

high as 38°C. The cooler months are December and January, but unless you're high in the mountains, of 70% to 85% humidity levels tend to cancel out these 'low' 25°C temperatures.

Rainfall typically comes in sudden, heavy bursts, and flash flooding is now more common than it should be due to widespread deforestation and soil erosion.

One of the worst flash floods struck in November 1991 in Ormoc, Leyte. Fed by rains on newly bared mountainsides, Leyte's normally tame rivers burst their banks, killing approximately 8000 people and leaving 50,000 homeless.

headed for the hills, often to jobs clearing land, and the indigenous residents were pushed onto less and less fertile land.

In Mindanao in 1998, 100,000 families faced eviction from their small-scale farms to give way to the palm oil industry of Malaysia. Around the same time, families from the indigenous Manobo groups were forced to evacuate their traditional homeland and flee to Davao City due to regular military operations in the area.

Despite having an officially recognised ancestral domain claim on the area, the Manobo people found themselves at the centre of a bitter land dispute with the timber company Alcantara & Sons (Alsons). The government had allowed the company to log commercially there through the notorious IFMA.

The battle to save what's left of the upland forests has begun with indigenous land rights claims and new conservation policies, but there's still enormous pressure on the government from both domestic and foreign land interests. The Department of Environment & Natural Resources (DENR), the main environmental arm of the government, is entrusted with the task of wrenching the country's resources out of corporate hands and into community-based projects. Respect of ancestral domain rights and forest boundaries is seen as integral in this fight to retain what's left of Philippine forests.

Various attempts to rejuvenate degraded forests have been plagued by unchecked introduced species and poor management, and in some cases degraded forests have simply been degraded further. New strategies for these areas include localised sustainable management programmes, natural resource mapping and (at long last) taking the advice of indigenous experts.

Of course, the Philippines isn't alone in its tendency to talk rather than act when it comes to halting such degradation. Nor is it the only nation with a long history of exploitation by outside forces.

Rich in mineral, timber and marine resources, the Philippines has been beaten, raped and robbed as brutally as any developing nation on earth. As recently as 1995, a mining act was amended to effectively encourage the destruction of rich wildlife and tribal areas such as those around Sipalay and Hinoba-an (Negros province). It's a testa-

Toxic Bases

When the US military left the Philippines in 1991 it left more than just a thriving prostitution industry. Luzon's abandoned military and naval bases at Clark, Subic and Camp John Hay contained more than 30 toxic waste sites. Chemicals dumped here included solvents, lead and mercury, and unexploded ordnance was commonplace. Environmental groups drolly noted that the clean up of this mess was finished just in time for the US military's controversial return (under the Visiting Forces Agreement; VFA) in 1999.

Mic Looby

ment to the land and its people that so much pristine natural beauty is still intact.

Sea

With a coastal ecosystem stretching almost 20,000km, the Philippines is one of the earliest victims of rising global ocean temperatures and levels.

Centuries-old coral is dying almost overnight and it's no longer just divers in remote spots who are witnessing this poorly understood phenomenon. Snorkellers in the long-time tourist haunts around Puerto Galera (Mindoro) and Boracay (Panay) can now see for themselves what a coral graveyard looks like.

In mid-1999 regional marine science studies grimly reported that increased sea temperatures were causing 'mass coral bleaching events' in the world's best coral reefs. These studies indicate that unless something is done to reduce global warming, the Philippines' magnificent underwater world will be gone by around 2100 – along with Australia's Great Barrier Reef.

In the meantime, increasingly desperate fishing communities are robbing waters even of staple fish species. In many areas healthy coral reefs are being destroyed by dynamite, cyanide and chlorine fishing methods. Cyanide stuns fish so they can be caught live and sold for a higher price, but at the same time kills the coral. (For more information on destructive fishing practices, see the boxed text 'From Dynamite to Diving Fees' in the Bohol section of the Visayas chapter.)

Its value as a marine nursery disastrously underestimated, the mangrove ecosystem that once supported ocean life on the Philippine coast has more than halved since first monitored in 1918. Around 450,000 hectares of old-growth mangrove forest had dwindled to 140,000 hectares by the late 1980s. Of these, around 65% were in Palawan. An estimated 95% of the country's commercial saltwater fishponds are converted mangrove forest.

Equally underestimated is seagrass, which once sustained huge numbers of vegetarian marine creatures, such as turtles, sea urchins and dugongs. Seagrass also shielded smaller organisms from predators, produced oxygen, regulated salinity levels, filtered impurities and stabilised the sea bed. Vast swathes of this stuff have gone the same way as the old-growth mangrove.

Since the Philippines is still shovelling its research funds into the oil, gas and coal industries, it's up to the local coastal communities to save their own skins. Thankfully, there are people doing some good work in this area (see the contact information under Solutions later), and government projects such as the Coastal Environment Program (CEP).

Solutions

It's certainly not all bad news on the Philippine environmental front. The country's many environmental groups are passionate and vocal, and numerous local governments have put their weight behind the establishment of marine and wildlife reserves and have actively campaigned against destructive mining, development and energy projects.

One good-news story is the little island of Danjugan, off the coast of Negros. A victim of dynamite fishing, this coral wonderland is recovering nicely, thanks to the miracle-working Negros Forests & Ecological Foundation (NFEF) and the Danjugan Island Support Fund (DISF, under the auspices of the UK-based World Land Trust). One of the few small islands in the region that's managed to hold on to its rainforest, Danjugan came up for sale a few years ago and was bought by the environmental protection group World Land Trust (ⓦ www .worldlandtrust.org) using donations.

Recommended Philippine environmental groups include:

ASEAN Regional Biodiversity Centre for Biodiversity Conservation (ⓦ www.arcbc.org.ph) Provides for general information on protected areas and conservation activities in the Philippines and other Southeast Asian countries

Coral Cay Conservation (CCC) (ⓦ www.coral cay.org) Works to protect coral reefs and other marine environments

For excellent general information on Philippine environmental concerns, try the following websites:

International Marinelife Alliance (ⓦ www.marine .org) Includes information on sustaining the world's coral reefs

Negros Forests & Ecological Foundation Inc (ⓦ www.nfefi.org) Works to protect various Philippine habitats, focusing on Negros

One Ocean (ⓦ www.oneocean.org) Works to protect and manage Philippines coastal areas

Rainforest Action Network (ⓦ www.ran.org) Provides excellent general information on rainforests and rainforest conservation, with information on the Philippines

Silent Sentinels (ⓦ www.abc.net.au/science/ coral) Presents an Australian ABC Science forum about coral and global warming

FLORA & FAUNA

The Philippines is one of the earth's 'biodiversity hotspots', with an estimated 12,000 plant species, 1100 land vertebrate species, 560 bird species, and at least 500 species of coral. Perhaps more impressive is the number of species found only in the Philippines – some 6000 plant species, over 100 mammal species, and at least 170 bird species.

Unfortunately, the huge habitat losses of recent decades have put many of these species in danger.

Protected areas, like national parks and marine reserves, are the only hope for many of those remaining.

Flora

While the pretty yellow flowering *nara* is the national tree of the Philippines, the unofficial national tree must surely be the nipa palm, which lends its name and timber to the traditional nipa hut found in villages and tourist resorts all over the country.

The national flower of the Philippines is the *sampaguita*, a variety of jasmine. The orchid could also stake a claim as the country's national flower, with some 900 stunning endemic species, including the *waling waling*

(*Vanda sanderiana*) of Mindanao and the red-spotted star orchid (*Rananthera mautiana*).

Introduced crop species include tobacco and corn. One crop unique to the Philippines is the *pili* nut, which is sold in the form of cakes and sweets, ice cream and even soap. It's harvested from May to October, mostly around Sorsogon in South Luzon. *Abaca*, a native hemp plant used to make rope, is harvested in huge quantities in Mindanao. This island is also famous for its durians, a fruit as smelly as it is popular. And on the lovely little island of Guimaras, off Panay, rich red soil has produced what many swear are the sweetest mangoes in the world.

Fauna

The best-known Philippine member of the bird family is the *haribon* (Philippine eagle); only about 100 survive in their natural habitat on the island of Mindanao. Further south, the Sulu Hornbill of Sulu, Jolo and Tawi-Tawi is another amazing and elusive mountain-dwelling bird. The Palawan peacock pheasant is a remarkable bird: the males of this species have a metallic blue crest, long white eyebrows and large metallic blue or purple 'eyes' on the tail. Nearing endangered status, these ground-dwellers are found only in the deepest forests of Palawan.

Of the reptile family, Southeast Asia travellers will be most familiar with the gravity-defying, mosquito-chomping gecko and its raspy 'tap tap tap' mating call. More elusive scaled beasts include the sailfin dragon and the flying lizard – discovered by national hero José Rizal while he was exiled in Dapitan on Mindanao – and a wide variety of venomous and nonvenomous snakes, including pythons and sea snakes.

The Philippines is said to still be home to the sea cow, or dugong (known locally as the *duyong*), once found in great numbers in Philippine waters but now rare. You're more likely to spot dolphins, whales and, if your timing's just right, the magnificent whale shark (known to some locals as *butanding*) near Donsol in South Luzon.

The local tourism industry there is desperately hoping these plankton-feeding gentle giants will continue their present habit of surfacing from around February to May each year (for more information on these whale sharks, see Donsul in the Southeast Luzon chapter).

The common beast of burden in the Philippines is the *kalabaw*, a native water buffalo highly prized for its strength and vast patience as a plough-puller.

Endangered Species

Huge numbers of the Philippines' animal and plant species are in danger of extinction. Of the Philippines' animal species, 47 are critically endangered, 44 are endangered and 103 are vulnerable. Thirty-seven plant species are critically endangered, 28 are endangered and 128 are vulnerable.

Sadly, some species aren't listed as endangered when they should be. Philippine seahorses, despite a 70% population plunge, aren't on the list because there's too much money to be made from exporting them live or selling them dead and dried as souvenirs or aphrodisiacs.

Environmental groups warn that the seahorse may be wiped out within 10 years. At the other end of the biological spectrum is the equally endangered *tamaraw*, a stout little native buffalo (see the boxed text 'The Tamaraw' in the Mindoro chapter).

Many species of Philippine flora and fauna have been threatened by biological pollution in the form of introduced alien species. Along with feral cats and other vermin, introduced aquatic species have proven particularly damaging. These include the giant catfish, black bass, white goby, marine toad, American bullfrog, leopard frog, golden apple snail, water hyacinth and water fern. According to the DENR, of all these pests, only the white goby was accidentally introduced. Whether well-meaning, accidental or downright barbaric, the reasons for introducing such vermin are now irrelevant as, one by one, native species fall victim to the invasion.

One of the more humble Philippine creatures quietly facing extinction is a shellfish, which is known locally as *diwal* (literally 'angel wings'). The *diwal* was a popular menu item in many Philippine restaurants, but it proved to be too tender and juicy for its own good, and even seasoned veterans of oceanic study at the University of the Philippines have been shocked to discover how fast *diwal* numbers have declined.

Once widespread throughout Visayan waters, the *diwal* is now found only in pockets of the western Visayas. While overfishing and trawling have contributed enormously to

Something Fishy

An incredible 80% of tropical marine fish sold worldwide comes from the Philippines. A massive diversity of fish, combined with cheap labour and export-friendly air-freight costs, means a veritable rainbow of species pour out of Philippine waters and into aquariums around the world each year.

Apart from the obvious damage to local fish populations and ecosystems, many of these fish die from severe liver damage within days of being transported. Such damage is common in marine creatures poisoned by sodium cyanide – a chemical first introduced in the Philippines in the 1960s to stun fish and now widely used as an easy way to catch large numbers of fish for both domestic and foreign markets.

Mic Looby

STEVE ROSENBERG

its decline, it's thought that the *diwal* has been poisoned by chemicals from large-scale prawn farming. Sanctuaries are currently being sought to save the *diwal* before it's much too late.

On Bohol, beyond the town of Corella, near the village of Sikatuna, is the Tarsier Visitors Centre built in 1999. The Philippine tarsier is a small primate endemic to just a few of the country's islands and the centre gives hope for its survival. For details on the tarsier see Corella & Tarsier Visitors Centre under Around Tagbilaran in the Bohol section of the Visayas chapter.

The Haribon Foundation (w www.haribon .org.ph) provides information on endangered species in the Philippines and its efforts to protect them.

National Parks

Despite rabid opposition from various land developers, energy companies and sectors of the government, a large-scale project to protect the best of the Philippines' natural resources got underway in 1992. The aim of this project is to establish protected areas in eight distinct ecological regions of the Philippines. The project is known as the National Integrated Protected Areas Program (NIPAP) and it's funded by the European Union (EU).

A priority of this programme is to involve the indigenous people living in or around the protected areas in the management of the resources.

Northern Sierra Madre National Park (North Luzon) At 200,000 hectares, this is the Philippines' largest protected area, equivalent to 10% of the country's remaining primary forest. For information on hiking around here see Northern Sierra Madre National Park in the Cagayan & Isabela section of the North Luzon chapter.

Mt Isarog National Park, Camarines Sur (Bicol) Mt Isarog (1966m) is Bicol's second-highest volcano, presently dormant. The park and the volcano are one and the same, as Mt Isarog stands on its own. Malabsay Falls, near the park's entrance, is a popular picnic spot for city dwellers. For details on hiking here see Mt Isarog National Park in the Bicol section of the Southeast Luzon chapter.

Mt Iglit-Baco National Park, Mindoro Occidental (Mindoro) One of the last remaining grazing patches for the critically endangered *tamaraw*, Mt Iglit-Baco National Park is a vital – if seemingly unremarkable – expanse of steep grasslands comprising Mt Iglit and Mt Baco in central Mindoro.

The problem for the *tamaraw*, and the local indigenous Mangyan people, is that farmers encroaching into the area have caused a steady reduction in grasslands. See Mt Iglit-Baco National Park in the Mindoro Occidental section of the Mindoro chapter for information on visiting this park.

NATIONAL PARKS

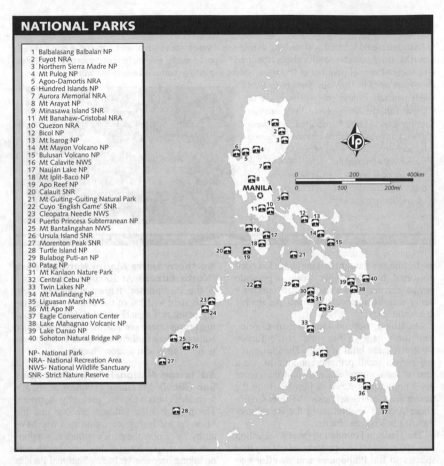

1 Balabasang Balbalan NP
2 Fuyot NRA
3 Northern Sierra Madre NP
4 Mt Pulog NP
5 Agoo-Damortis NRA
6 Hundred Islands NP
7 Aurora Memorial NRA
8 Mt Arayat NP
9 Minasawa Island SNR
11 Mt Banahaw-Cristobal NRA
10 Quezon NRA
12 Bicol NP
13 Mt Isarog NP
14 Mt Mayon Volcano NP
15 Bulusan Volcano NP
16 Mt Calavite NWS
17 Naujan Lake NP
18 Mt Iplit-Baco NP
19 Apo Reef NP
20 Calauit SNR
21 Mt Guiting-Guiting Natural Park
22 Cuyo 'English Game' SNR
23 Cleopatra Needle NWS
24 Puerto Princesa Subterranean NP
25 Mt Bantalingahan NWS
26 Ursula Island SNR
27 Morenton Peak SNR
28 Turtle Island NP
29 Bulabog Puti-an NP
30 Patag NP
31 Mt Kanlaon Nature Park
32 Central Cebu NP
33 Twin Lakes NP
34 Mt Malindang NP
35 Liguasan Marsh NWS
36 Mt Apo NP
37 Eagle Conservation Center
38 Lake Mahagnao Volcanic NP
39 Lake Danao NP
40 Sohoton Natural Bridge NP

NP- National Park
NRA- National Recreation Area
NWS- National Wildlife Sanctuary
SNR- Strict Nature Reserve

Mt Guiting-Guiting Natural Park, Sibuyan Island (Romblon)

This mountainous 16,000-hectare forest is a rare slice of living history in the Romblon group of islands and one of the finest natural wonders on offer in Asia. For thousands of years the spectacular slopes of 2058m-high Mt Guiting-Guiting have nurtured and protected a world that would have long ago been destroyed by human activity if not for its isolation. Geologically and biologically, Sibuyan Island is a relic from the ice age. Several quite bizarre species of fruit bats, more than 100 known bird species and large macaques live among the ancient teak trees of the park. The extremely well-organised ranger and the visitor facilities here don't make the climb up Mt Guiting-Guiting any easier, but if it's biodi-

versity you crave, it's well worth the effort. For more details see Mt Guiting-Guiting Natural Park under Sibuyan in the Romblon section of the Visayas chapter.

Coron Island (Palawan)

A prized diving area, Coron Island's beauty lies in the fact that it was left alone for so long. Managed properly, the island's virgin forests and stunning cliffs should stay just as they are. Coron Island is best accessed from nearby Busuanga Island.

El Nido Marine Reserve (Palawan)

The El Nido Marine Reserve is 430km from Manila but, like nearby Coron Island, it seems to be drifting a little closer every year, as transport routes proliferate. A wonderland of jagged cliffs (above and below sea level) and secret beaches, the reserve is in the Bacuit Bay area of El Nido and is home to several upmarket – and relatively low-impact – resorts. The town of El Nido is the unofficial caretaker of the reserve. For more details see El Nido under North Palawan in the Palawan chapter.

GOVERNMENT & POLITICS
The Political System
Based on a US-style constitution, the Philippines' national government is headed by a president and a vice-president who are elected directly by the people for a term of six years. The president's office constitutes the executive branch of government, while Congress, made up of a Senate (or Upper House) with 24 members and a House of Representatives (or Lower House) with 250 members, functions as the legislative branch. Like the president, the senators are voted into office in nationwide elections, but the members of the House of Representatives (usually called congressmen) are elected by the citizens of the districts they represent.

The nation's 78 provinces are grouped into 16 regions, including the National Capital Region (NCR) of Metro Manila. Each province is headed by a governor, a vice-governor and usually two board members, all elected on four-year terms. Provinces comprise cities and municipalities, which in turn are divided into districts, villages or communities called barangay.

The Philippine legal system, a Spanish and US hybrid, is headed by the Supreme Court, the highest legal forum in the land. This comprises a chief justice and 14 associate judges – all of whom are appointed by the president. The Court of Appeals acts as an intermediary between the Supreme Court and the municipal courts. Every city has a municipal court.

Politics
When democracy was 'restored' in 1987, Philippine politics once again became as lively and rambunctious as the nation's other obsession – show business. The new president at the time was Cory Aquino, the nation's first woman leader. Amid impossibly high hopes, the Aquino government drew up a new constitution, had it ratified by national referendum, and attempted to turn the country's fortunes around. In doing so, Aquino in-

curred the wrath of influential Marcos supporters. Several military coups to overthrow her came close to success and cost hundreds of lives. At the end of her six-year term, a reputedly relieved Aquino passed the reins of government to Fidel Ramos, her trusted defence secretary and a key player in the downfall of Marcos.

Despite his shaky credentials – including being a second cousin to the disgraced Marcos *and* a Protestant – Ramos won comfortably, supported by the powerful Lakas ng Edsa and the National Union of Christian Democrats (NUCD) political parties.

By 1998 Ramos had become something of a lame-duck president and his increasingly outspoken critics were baying for blood. With all the same old economic problems pretty much unchanged, Ramos' sober presidential term ended and a massive election win swept the populist politician and former vice-president Joseph Estrada into power. An ageing movie idol, Estrada immediately promised to redirect government funding to help the poor and fight for the rights of the long-neglected average Filipino. Sound like a movie script? Welcome to the Philippines.

The landslide election victory that catapulted Estrada into office in 1998 did so with such force that even the party faithful were surprised. The country's intelligentsia, along with the middle classes, looked on in horror and disbelief as Estrada revealed himself to be nothing but a latter-day Marcos bent on plunging the nation back into the darkest days of cronyism and shady deals.

Their fears were not groundless – less than three years after his election, an impeachment trial in the Philippine Senate showed the stunned nation just how badly Estrada had robbed state coffers. The trial gripped the entire nation, as one prosecution witness after another gave damning testimony about the leader's crimes. Glued to TV sets, the entire nation watched the trial – until that fateful night when half of the Senate vetoed a motion to open an envelope containing evidence fatal to Estrada.

That was the straw that broke the camel's back. In a spontaneous outpouring of frustration and anger, people gathered at EDSA Shrine (built to commemorate the first 'people power' revolution that had toppled the hated Marcos regime). Four days later, on 20 January 2001, Gloria Macapagal-Arroyo was sworn in by Chief Justice Hilarion Davide as the 14th president of the Republic of the Philippines, to the roar of a million people on the streets.

Troublespots

Both the Philippine and foreign media dutifully report on violence that is perpetrated by Islamic militants in Mindanao, but the background for the fighting is rarely discussed. Government moves to weaken and displace the Muslim majority, crush all resistance without question and offer what many see as token autonomy, only serves to fuel the resistance.

Thanks to its well-publicised kidnap-for-ransom activities, Abu Sayyaf has become the most infamous, of terrorist or bandit gangs operating in the Philippines. Abu Sayyaf is actually made up of two or three groups, each one under a different commander. One such group was behind the kidnapping of tourists holidaying in a resort on the island of Palawan. This incident saw the ruthless beheading of an American hostage and the fatal shooting of another. Several Filipino hostages were also put to death; the severed heads of some of them were sent by the Abu Sayyaf to the victims' grieving relatives.

In Mindanao and Sulu, residents and foreigners alike have fallen victim to kidnapping and other violent attacks – for more information see the boxed text 'Warning' at the start of the Mindanao & Sulu chapter.

The NPA is reported to be still active in rural and mountainous areas of North Luzon, Southeast Luzon and Mindoro. It's best to ask locals before heading off the beaten track in these areas.

For more information on dangerous areas of the Philippines, see the boxed text 'Safe Travel in the Philippines' in the Facts for the Visitor chapter.

ECONOMY

The main sectors of the Philippines' economy are agriculture, light industry, service industries and tourism. Agricultural products include rice, corn, bananas, sugar cane, mangoes, pork and fish. Industries include textiles, electronics, wood products and some chemical processing. The USA is the Philippines' biggest trading partner, accounting for one-third of the country's exports and around a quarter of its imports.

The GDP of the Philippines was estimated at US$310 billion in 2000. The GDP of the Philippines has been growing at a fairly rapid clip in recent years: almost 4% in 2000. This figure slipped to around 3% in 2001, in part due to a slowing world economy (exports, for instance, fell 26% in the same year).

Of course, any visitor to the Philippines will be struck by the astonishing poverty of the country, and the incredible gap between the rich and the poor. In 1997 it was estimated that about 40% of the population lived below the poverty line. More telling, perhaps, is the fact that in the same year, the wealthiest 10% of the population received around 40% of the national income, while the poorest 10% percent of the population received only 1.5% of the national income.

President Gloria Macapagal-Arroyo inherited a government bankrupted by the ineptitude and greed of Estrada and his cronies, but she is now instituting reforms that should bear fruit before she comes up for re-election (since she was not elected into office, she can run for president in the next election).

POPULATION & PEOPLE

In July 2001 the population of the Philippines was estimated at almost 83 million people. Around 60% of the populace lives in rural areas, although this figure is steadily falling as rural residents head for urban centres, such as Manila and Cebu City, and the urban sprawl eats up formerly rural areas. Metro Manila's population is thought to be growing at a rate of around 4% per year, while the standard of living appears to be steadily declining.

Mainstream Culture

Ethnologically, the vast majority of Filipinos are related to Malaysians and Indonesians. Culturally, they represent both East and West, having welcomed migrants from China, Vietnam, Taiwan, Japan, Korea, the USA, Europe and India. Just as profound has been the migration of Filipinos to all corners of the globe. Statistics show that around half a million Filipinos leave the country every year to take up employment or residence abroad. Those who decide to take up permanent residency in their adopted countries are called *balikbayan* (literally 'returnees to the home country') when they come back to visit or to stay.

Muslim communities are thought to make up about 5% of the Philippine population, with the vast majority living in Mindanao and the Sulu islands. Outside the mainstream Muslim population, five indigenous groups in this region are also Islamic (see the entry on the Manobo under Cultural Minorities later).

Since the earliest days of sea trade, Chinese migrants have settled in the Philippines. Today, around 1% of the total Philippine population is ethnic Chinese (the figure rises to 10% when Filipinos of mixed Chinese and Filipino ancestry are counted), with a disproportionate number of influential Filipinos claiming Chinese ancestry.

These include José Rizal, Cory Aquino and Cardinal Jaime Sin (the archbishop of

Manila; who held a key role in both the 'people-power' revolts).

Cultural Minorities

There are more than 100 cultural minority groups in the Philippines, as defined by their language. Of these, about half have been identified as unique linguistic cultures. The other half represent a blurred grouping of distinct cultures with common linguistic traits.

The Negrito Often referred to as the aborigines of the Philippines, the Negrito are represented by the Aeta, Ati, Eta, Ita and Dumagat peoples. Now thought to number as few as 20,000, the Negrito are generally the shortest, darkest and most racially victimised of the Filipino people. The Negrito

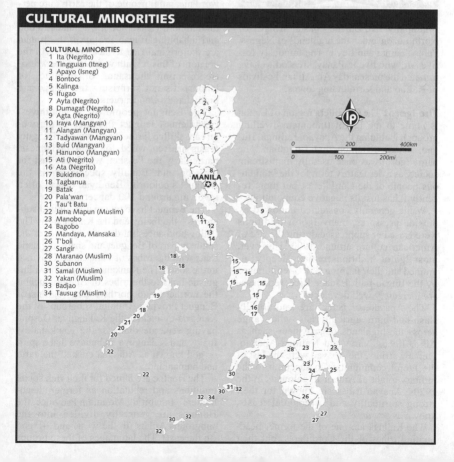

CULTURAL MINORITIES

CULTURAL MINORITIES
1 Ita (Negrito)
2 Tingguian (Itneg)
3 Apayo (Isneg)
4 Bontocs
5 Kalinga
6 Ifugao
7 Ayta (Negrito)
8 Dumagat (Negrito)
9 Agta (Negrito)
10 Iraya (Mangyan)
11 Alangan (Mangyan)
12 Tadyawan (Mangyan)
13 Buid (Mangyan)
14 Hanunoo (Mangyan)
15 Ati (Negrito)
16 Ata (Negrito)
17 Bukidnon
18 Tagbanua
19 Batak
20 Pala'wan
21 Tau't Batu
22 Jama Mapun (Muslim)
23 Manobo
24 Bagobo
25 Mandaya, Mansaka
26 T'boli
27 Sangir
28 Maranao (Muslim)
30 Subanon
31 Samal (Muslim)
32 Yakan (Muslim)
33 Badjao
34 Tausug (Muslim)

Negrito Royals

Although dismissed by successive colonial powers, there is a long history of 'royalty' among the Negrito people of Luzon and other islands. Until the 1970s, King Alfonso and Queen Mary were two such Negrito figureheads. Far from enjoying the red-carpet treatment, the royals and their people lived in houses made of scrap materials and survived off *basura* (garbage) from the nearby US military's Clark Airbase. Despite earning the honorary rank of US Air Force brigadier general, King Alfonso and his queen vanished some time after a low-land Christian group began competing for the Americans' garbage.

Mic Looby

principally live on the coastal fringes of North Luzon and in the highlands of Negros, Panay, Samar and Leyte. The famously festive Ati, who live in Panay, are said to have initiated the present day Ati-Atihan Festivals of Kalibo and surrounding towns.

The Igorot The Cordillera region of Luzon is home to the Igorot (mountain-dwelling groups), including the Apayao, Kalinga, Ifugao, Benguet, Bontoc, and Tingguian. The name Igorot was once used by mainstream society as a derogatory term for the indigenous people of the Cordilleras, but more recently it has lost its negative connotations.

While generally considered unbowed by outside pressures, many Igorot traditions were erased or suppressed during the rise of American culture around 1900. However, most Igorot traditions remain deeply ingrained and their farming skills – epitomised by the Ifugao-built Banaue Rice Terraces – are incredibly well developed.

The Apayao, or Isneg, are traditionally slash-and-burn agriculturists who range across the highlands of provinces such as Abra, Ilocos Norte and Kalinga-Apayao. Fierce warriors, the Apayao were the last of the Igorot communities to succumb to the military might of American colonists in the 1920s. Apayao tribes are known for their strong spirituality and ceremonial feasts, known as *say-am*.

The Kalinga are one of the former headhunting tribes of the Cordilleras, but their traditional penchant for finely woven textiles and age-old songs has proved a more enduring trait. Songs of the Kalinga include the *ading*, *wasani* and *dandanag*, all of which are likely to accompany the well-known *bodong* (peace rite) that is practised by various Kalinga subgroups, including the Tabuk, Tinglayan and Pinukpuk. The Kalinga are also known for their bead culture, an ancient form of currency using semiprecious stones as 'coins'. The most precious bead among the Kalinga is the colourful *adjongan*, thought to be a type of agate brought by traders to the Philippines around 1000 years ago. The tribe also takes its custodianship of the land very seriously (see the boxed text 'The Kalinga & the Outside' in the North Luzon chapter).

The Ifugao, whose name comes from a word meaning 'people of the earth', are perhaps the best-known of all Philippines cultural minorities. Numbering around 130,000 and inhabiting Ifugao Province, the Ifugao are the original rice terrace carvers. As the creators of this 'eighth wonder of the world' (representing thousands of lifetimes of labour) it's not surprising the Ifugao are pretty handy woodcarvers as well.

The Benguet people of the southwest Cordilleras (Benguet Province in particular) are skilled farmers and miners. Benguet feasts are renowned for their lavishness, particularly the Pesshet, which can last for days on end. Equally spectacular is the Benguet's colourful Bendiyan dance, often involving around 100 dancers.

The Benguet have two major cultural subgroups – the Ibaloy and the Kankana-ey. The Ibaloy hold ancestral domain rights over the southern part of Benguet and share linguistic traits with the tribes of Pangasinan Province to the south. The Kankana-ey, who have linguistic links to the tribes of Bontoc, inhabit the northern and northwestern regions of Benguet Province. Cultural subgroups of the Kankana-ey include the Kalanguya. Despite having separate dialects, the Kankana-ey, Ibaloy and Kalanguya all believe that a spirit or god known as Adikalia created the earth and humankind.

The Bontoc are famed for their rich social traditions and reputation as former 'headhunters'. Inhabiting Mountain Province, the Bontocs are generally divided into the subgroups Aplais (to the west) and I-lagod (to the east). The languages of these groups

Minority Cultures

The Kalipunan ng Katutubong Mamamayan ng Pilipinas (KAMP) is the main mouthpiece of the indigenous peoples of the Philippines. Established as a federation in 1987, KAMP works to unite various indigenous peoples' organisations throughout the Philippines and help articulate their struggles. Professional assistance or help of any kind is always greatly appreciated. Contact **KAMP Secretariat** *(☎/fax 02-921 1058; 70-B Matahimik St, UP Teachers Village, Quezon City, Metro Manila)* for more information.

Mic Looby

differ substantially and each group has its own dance traditions. The I-lagod's most important dance is the Pattong (or Ballangbang), while the wedding dance known as the Takik belongs to the Aplais.

Bontoc groups share a formal system of social division and courtship centred on segregated 'dormitories' known as *ulog* or *egban*. Inhabiting the border of Ilocos Sur and Benguet Provinces, the Bago may be considered a subgroup of the Bontoc by dint of their language, which is similar to that of the Aplai. Religiously, the Bago – or bagong Kristiano (new Christians) – are in a group all of their own.

With the northwestern Luzon province of Abra as their ancestral domain, the Tingguians are Igorots only in that they inhabit the Cordilleras. Collectively, the Tingguians call themselves Itneg. Similarly, the groups inhabiting the Cordillera mountain provinces of Nueva Ecija, Nueva Vizcaya and Quirino call themselves Ikalahan.

The Manobo The term Manobo is used to describe the major indigenous groups of Mindanao. Of these groups, five regard themselves as Muslim – the Badjao, Maguindanao, Maranao (or Maranaw), Tausag (or Tausug) and Samal.

The Badjao are the 'sea gypsies' of the Sulu seas. Regarded as the least-Islamic of the Muslim groups, the animist Badjao are more sedentary than they once were, although their livelihood and traditions remain firmly linked to the sea.

The Maguindanao are famed musicians who inhabit the flood plains of Cotabato

Province. The largest of all Muslim groups, they are known for their brilliant weaving skills.

The Maranao are the traditional owners of Lake Lanao, and are among the Philippines' most ingenious craftspeople. Traditional Maranao homes and ancestral houses *(torogan)* are decorated with detailed carvings, forming large-scale bas-relief sculptures in their own right. The beams of the *torogan* are guarded by swirling *naga* (mythical serpentine figures).

The Tausag were the earliest Philippine Islamic converts back in the 15th century and as such were the ruling class of the ancient Jolo Sultanate.

The Samal are the poorest of the Muslim groups, having long been the loyal subjects of the Tausag dynasties.

Of the non-Muslim indigenous groups of Mindanao, the Bukidnon (of the Bukidnon Province) are well known for their tradition of storytelling, passed down through the ages and performed as epic poetry.

The non-Muslim Bagobo, the Mandaya, and Mansaka are regarded as masters of weaving and dyeing, as well as herbal medicine. Their music, involving great orchestras of percussion players, is often used to accompany the grinding of herbs to be used as dyes or medicines.

EDUCATION

From around 1900 onwards, American colonialists did a thorough job of transplanting the US education system into Philippine society. Starting from age four or five, Filipino children attend classes taught in both the national language Pilipino (Tagalog) and English. Before independence in 1946, classes were taught solely in English, and it wasn't until 1974 that a bilingual Tagalog-English system was put in place. Even so, the former colonial language, Spanish, continued to be a compulsory part of the college curriculum until the 1980s, though by then it was spoken by very few Filipinos, mostly those of Spanish ancestry.

While the Philippines is said to have an adult literacy rate as high as 96%, only 10% of children from families in the low-income bracket complete high school. Schools are either private or public, with the elite going mostly to private institutions (particularly those run by Catholic religious orders) until university age. The government-run University of the Philippines is considered on a par with the leading private universities, such as the University of Santo Tomas (the oldest university in Asia, predating America's Harvard), Ateneo de Manila University and De La Salle University. A handful of schools, which include the International School and Brent School, cater specifically to the foreign community.

ARTS
Dance

Filipinos speak the language of dance fluently and passionately, making dance the most eloquent and far-reaching of Philippine cultural exports. From mainstream, urban society to small town fiestas and remote tribal barangay, dance is as rich and varied as the islands themselves.

Historically, traditional dances began by mimicking the flight of birds, particularly in mountainous regions such as the Cordillera in Luzon. Dance movements in coastal communities often have a strong marine theme. Later, external influences drifted in from China, Indonesia, Spain and the Americas, without ever making the dances any less Filipino.

The Philippines' national folk dance is the *tinikling*, which traditionally involved a boy and a girl hopping between bamboo poles, held just above the ground and struck together in time to music or hand-clapping. Some say this dance was inspired by the flitting of birds between grass stems or a heron hopping through the rice paddies. A version of the *tinikling* is the breathtaking *singkil*, wherein a Muslim princess and her lady-in-waiting weave in and out of four poles struck together at increasing speed.

The mountain people of North Luzon are famed for vigorous hunting dances such as the *tag-gam* and victory dances such as *balangbang*. Down south, an old favourite is the stunningly graceful *pangalay*, a courtship dance from the Sulu islands in which women in flowing robes vie for a man's affection.

One of the best-known and most successful Philippine folk dance troupes is the Bayanihan Dance Company, which first wowed the world in 1958 at the Brussels Universal Exposition. An inspiration for dancers and dance lovers ever since, Bayanihan (from the Tagalog word meaning 'community spirit') is based at the Philippine Women's University in Manila. Bayanihan has served as the model for many folk dance troupes throughout the country, and continues to enthral audiences during its world tours.

Ballet, particularly among the urban sophisticates of Manila, is another passion. Ballet Philippines, the resident dance company of the Cultural Center of the Philippines (CCP), shows a knack for blending modern elements with ancient Philippine folk tales and music.

Many Filipino ballet talents have won international recognition abroad, among them Maniya Barredo, former prima ballerina of the Atlanta Ballet, and Lisa Macuja, who made the role of Giselle her own during her time with the Kirov Ballet in Russia. Macuja now runs her own ballet company, Ballet Manila, and still performs in such classics as *Romeo and Juliet* during the troupe's yearly season.

Music

With its bittersweet themes of love, fate and death, the *kundiman* genre is one of the best-loved modes of musical expression in the Philippines. Modern composers such as Nicanor Abelardo, Francisco Santiago, Levi Celerio and Lucio San Pedro have taken these songs to new heights by combining modern musical forms with traditional folk music.

Traditional musical instruments include the *kudyapi*, a hauntingly melodic lute, and the *kulintang*, a row of small gongs mounted on a *langkungan*, or resonating platform. The *kulintang* has been compared to traditional Indonesian instruments, and is used by Mindanao's Muslim communities, whose dance repertoires effortlessly merge ancient rhythms with their Islamic faith.

Filipino classical performers of note have included composers and conductors such as Rodolfo Cornejo, Antonino Buenaventura, Antonio J Molina and Ryan Cayabyab. Prolific and versatile, Cayabyab composes works ranging from popular songs to full-scale operatic musicals.

The biggest names in the avant-garde crowd have been José Maceda and Lucresia Kasilig, who have both been inspired by indigenous music traditions.

Recent popular music has seen the rise of Filipino adaptations of contemporary Western music. At the other end of the spectrum,

All aboard a bangka, Panagsama Beach, Cebu – the Visayas

Rice terraces, Banaue, Central Cordillera – North Luzon

Durian, Davao – Mindanao

Tarsier *(Tarsius syrichta)*, Bohol – the Visayas

Red-spotted star orchid *(Rananthera mautiana)*

VERONICA GARBUTT

SCOTT D TUASON

JULIAN BENTLEY

Joey Ayala and the group Pinikpikan typify in their own way the recently resurrected interest in ethnic musical instruments and forms.

A Filipino performer who has won acclaim internationally is Lea Salonga, the original *Miss Saigon*. Salonga continues to appear on Broadway, when she is not performing her famously sweet vocals in a play or giving a concert locally or in the region. Cecile Licad has likewise built herself a name globally, principally in Japan, the USA and Europe, as an interpreter of the piano music of Chopin and Schumann.

The father of homegrown popular folk music remains Freddie Aguilar, who shot to fame when his ballad about parent-child relations, Anak, became an international hit in the 1980s.

Aguilar continues to perform in various folk music venues in Manila.

Literature

Philippine 'literature' prior to the Spanish era existed as an oral tradition of folk tales, epic poems or marathon chants. To this day they are passed on from one generation to another in the dialects of indigenous groups.

Like most art under Spanish rule, literature was primarily a religious tool, and it remained so until the introduction of secular European (and later American) novels, short stories and drama. The influences, particularly from England and France, were incorporated in works as those by the novelist, poet and essayist José Rizal, the Tagalog epic poet Francisco Balagtas and the avant-garde English-language poet José Garcia Villa. An enormously influential modern writer has been the journalist, novelist and playwright Nick Joaquin, whose play *Portrait of a Young Artist as a Filipino* has become an icon of Filipino sensibility.

Banned for their biting criticism of colonial rule, José Rizal's ground-breaking novels, *Noli Me Tangere* (Touch Me Not, 1887) and its sequel *El Filibusterismo* (The Reign of Greed, 1891), continue to interest modern readers with their detailed and insightful observations of Filipino society under Spanish rule. Originally written in Spanish, both novels have been translated into English and other languages. Rizal's *Mi Ultimo Adios* (My Last Farewell, 1896) is a masterpiece of verse, and it was penned on the eve of his execution.

Architecture

The simple and utilitarian nipa hut is perhaps the most typical example of Filipino architecture. Made of bamboo poles and dried nipa leaves, its design has remained largely unchanged for thousands of years.

Throughout the Philippines, the nipa hut comes in various guises to suit the peculiarities of the local environment. Among seafaring folk, it rests on stilts to keep the occupants safely above water; among mountain tribes, the nipa roofing is replaced with thicker thatch that provides better insulation against cold winds at high altitude.

Among indigenous communities in Mindanao, the nipa hut is adorned with polychrome ornamentation that reflects the richness of the landscape and the people's cultural heritage.

With the coming of the Spanish, an entirely different form of architecture came into the picture, in the form of the *bahay na bato* (stone house). Fashioned from adobe blocks, it became the basic building material of Intramuros, the fortified city that served as the seat of Spanish colonial rule (for details on Intramuros see its entry under Things to See & Do in the Manila chapter). Beautiful examples of this type of architecture can be seen in the grand (though now decaying) houses that line the streets of Vigan in Ilocos Sur. These ancestral homes were erected by local families who grew rich from a thriving indigo trade in the 19th century.

Western-style architecture in the Philippines reached a golden age in the 1930s, when the country sought to reinvent itself as one of the wealthiest nations in Asia. While Manila's civic centre was being transformed with imposing neoclassical structures, local architects were introducing novel forms of Art Deco to the urban landscape. To the former belong the graceful Old Congress Building and the beautifully symmetrical Manila Central Post Office; among the latter is the highly stylish Metropolitan Theater.

This mixture defined the Manila skyline until WWII when the capital was reduced to rubble, with only San Agustin Church left intact in the whole of Intramuros. Losing no time, the nation launched into another building boom in the postwar era.

The Araneta Coliseum, the world's biggest domed structure at the time, rose in Quezon City, while on Ayala Ave in Makati a whole new mixture of architectural styles emerged, clearly influenced by American models.

The 1970s saw the emergence of the massive ferro-concrete creations of Leandro Locsin. It was Locsin who designed the Cultural Center of the Philippines (CCP) and the Central Bank of the Philippines. There was a time when Locsin's style dominated Philippine architecture, but it has been replaced by the sleek lines of the so-called international style. The contemporary urban landscape is now defined by structures like the twin towers, designed in Fort Bonifacio by American architect Ieoh Ming Pei.

Painting

A unified Philippine art style began to emerge in the late 16th century under the watchful eye of the Spanish, but it was only the artists who depicted Christian themes that flourished. Thus, the earliest extant paintings depict saints and biblical scenes.

It wasn't until the late 18th century that Philippine art began to consider nonreligious themes. Secular art, in the form of well-funded portraiture, became the new dominant style.

One of the first individuals to make an impact on the Philippine art scene in the early 19th century was Damian Domingo, who used single-bristle sable brushes imported from China to produce stunning miniatures. By the latter part of the century, Western-style painting began to come into its own with the emergence of Lorenzo Guerrero and Simon Flores, the former with his sweeping canvases and the latter with his intimate portraits.

While Guerrero and Flores laid the foundations of Philippine realism in painting, the generation that followed produced Juan Luna and Felix Resurreccion Hidalgo, two unchallenged masters of Philippine art. Luna's vast *Spoliarium* and Hidalgo's *Antigone* stunned European art circles when they won Gold and Silver Medals, respectively, at the 1884 Madrid Exposition.

The first half of the 20th century was dominated by Fabian de la Rosa and Fernando Amorsolo, two masters who painted in contrasting styles. Whereas de la Rosa's work is distinguished by disciplined composition and brushwork, Amorsolo's scenes using the chiaroscuro technique are rendered with free-flowing strokes.

After WWII, several well-known artists emerged, such as Victorio Edades, Vicente Manansala, Arturo Luz, Hernando Ocampo, Anita Magsaysay-Ho and Nena Saguil. The vibrant, pioneering work of abstract expressionist José Joya is regarded by many as some of the best in modern Philippine art.

Carlos V Francisco (or Botong Francisco) belongs in a class of his own with his huge canvases, some of which can be seen in the Manila City Hall. He employed highly stylised forms that became the distinguishing mark of his unique idiom.

The brilliant conceptual artist David Cortez Medalla is one the Philippines' best-known international artists. Based in Britain, Medalla has pioneered avant-garde art movements such as minimalism and performance art.

Contemporary Philippine painting continues to be strong and often confronting. Many galleries and museums in Manila and other cities provide Filipino artists with a venue for showing their works as well as a place for lively meetings with fellow artists and art-lovers.

Sculpture

Among the non-Christian minorities, particularly the Muslims of Mindanao and the Ifugao in North Luzon, there is a long tradition of sculpture. Mostly woodcarvings and metalwork with strong religious motifs, such work has influenced contemporary Filipino sculptors including Veloso Abueva and José Alcantara. Contemporary Philippine pottery can also trace its roots back to ancient times; pieces dating from 500 BC to AD 500 were recently excavated in the Ayub Cave in Mindanao.

The *bulol*, the most sacred of figures carved by the Ifugao, are used to guard rice granaries. Some *bulol* are so evocative that they are believed to have killed vermin, thieves and even Japanese soldiers. During fires, some *bulol* are thought to have leapt up and fled to safety.

Traditionally, the names of the sculptors responsible for these powerful creations were rarely recorded (one outstanding exception to the rule was an Ifugao sculptor known as Tagiling, who is thought to have lived and worked in the village of Kababuyan until his death in the 1930s). Such work was never considered art by the ancient Ifugao, but nonetheless it has had an enormous influence on artists of today.

In modern times, classical Philippine sculpture has been epitomised by Guillermo Tolentino's neoclassical masterpiece, the resplendent *Monumento* in Caloocan City, which honours the revolutionary hero Andres Bonifacio. Napoleon Abueva, a Tolentino protégé known for his mixed-media abstract works, has been selected at several Association of Southeast Asian Nations (Asean) sculpture exhibitions.

Cinema

The Philippines has what is easily Southeast Asia's most prolific and diverse film industry, but it's had its ups and downs. Launched by foreigners around the beginning of the 20th century, it attained its 'golden age' during the 1950s, went into a decline in the 1960s, found a powerful social voice in the 1970s (despite repressive censorship under the Marcos regime), and peaked in popularity in the 1980s.

Action movies showing good guy/bad guy chases and stunts remain a firm favourite, as are light romantic comedies featuring matinee idols. Another popular genre is what locals call 'bold' – a euphemism for movies showing steamy and at times semi-explicit sex scenes.

Followers of serious cinema have to turn to the works of Lino Brocka and Ishmael Bernal from the 1970s and 1980s, though a new crop of directors such as Marilou Diaz-Abaya, Mike de Leon, Tikoy Aguiluz and Joel Lamangan offer some interesting contemporary fare.

If you're staying at a hotel with cable TV, the Viva Cinema channel shows nonstop Filipino blockbusters, but there are no English subtitles so you may have to ask a Filipino friend to help you follow the plot.

Theatre

Older, wiser brother to the local movie industry, Philippine theatre has been a powerful artistic and political voice for countless generations. In Manila, the Western theatre tradition is ably represented by Repertory Philippines, the country's oldest English-language theatrical group. Every year Repertory stages a mixed season ranging from Neil Simon comedies to big-scale musicals like *South Pacific* and *Les Miserables*. A sister company specialises in plays for children such as the classic *Peter Pan* and the more recent Disney *Beauty and the Beast*.

Tanghalang Pilipino, the resident theatre company of the Cultural Center of the Philippines, has become a well-rounded and finely tuned troupe under the direction of Nonon Padilla. Another prominent name in local theatre is the late Rolando Tinio, whose Tagalog adaptations of English-language classics such as Shakespeare's tragedies remain unparalleled in their field.

Two sources of consistently fresh material are Bulwagang Gantimpala (Gantimpala Theater Foundation) and PETA (Philippine Educational Theater Association). Founded in 1977, Gantimpala has produced thought-provoking interpretations of the classics and contemporary plays. PETA, which stages its yearly season at the atmospheric Rajah Sulayman Theater in Fort Santiago (the old Spanish fort in Intramuros, Manila), moves with equal ease from something as grand as Bertold Brecht's *Mother Courage* to an intimate one-man show written by a budding Filipino writer.

SOCIETY & CONDUCT

The art of enjoying life despite hardships is a national pastime. A disarming laugh, accompanied by an easy shrug of the shoulders, could almost be classified as an official dance movement. Whether praying, singing, drinking, dancing or talking, the Filipino tends to live for the moment and accept that fate will take its course for better or worse. This notion is best summed up by the much-used everyday term *bahala na*.

In the days before the advent of Christianity, god was called *bathala* by the ancient Filipinos; *bahala na* comes from that and combines faith (God will provide) with fatalism (Come what may). It expresses the idea that all things shall pass and that in the meantime life is to be lived, preferably in the company of one's friends and – most importantly – one's family.

Human Rights

The Marcos regime, and the colonial regimes before that, have had a profound effect on the collective Filipino psyche. By setting appalling precedents in human suffering, they have conditioned the Philippine public to accept the unacceptable.

Although cases of gross human rights violations have tremendously declined since the repressive Marcos era, there are still instances where people have vanished without a trace, yet the lack (or suppression) of evidence has made it impossible to bring the culprits to justice, particularly if they wear a police or military uniform or have powerful connections.

In some places, farmers have been the targets of attack during land disputes, and the culprits are usually unidentified. Suspects tend to include private security guards or figures connected with corrupt local officials, although the victims' families know better than to name names.

Some of the worst victims of human rights abuses are cultural minorities such as the Muslim communities in the south and indigenous tribes in the north. The sense of frustration among these deprived sectors of society partly explains the emergence of such terrorist groups as the Abu Sayyaf (see Troublespots, following, for more details on Abu Sayyaf). For this reason, President Macapagal-Arroyo has made it one of the priorities of her administration to address the needs of these communities.

In the meantime, nonprofit independent groups, such as the **Children's Rehabilitation Center** (CRC; ☎ 02-439 4589; 90J Bugallon St, Project 4, Quezon City, Manila.) are fighting for the most vulnerable members of Filipino society. According to the CRC, the government too often turns a blind eye to human rights abuses against children and/or poor communities by military agencies, police, paramilitary forces, security guards, hired criminals, private individuals and even religious cults.

Prostitution

While prostitution certainly existed before the Spanish and Americans arrived, it wasn't a major social problem. Prostitution became big, illegal business in 1900, when the then US president McKinley effectively condoned 'R&R' under US regulations. From then on, entire towns of girlie-bars grew around US naval and military bases, and the Philippines earned a reputation as one of the cheapest destinations in the world for buying women, men and children.

But a boom of an entirely different kind struck the trade in 1991 when Mt Pinatubo

erupted, forcing the evacuation of prostitution central – Angeles – and, more than a little coincidentally, all US military personnel. The sudden loss of the industry's main client base inspired a wholesale clean-up, spearheaded by the then Manila mayor, Alfredo Lim and local mayor Kate Gordon. Under new laws, the girlie bars and strip joints in Manila's Ermita district were boarded up and thousands of sex-trade workers were forced onto the street, or back to their hometowns.

But poverty, corruption and a tourism-led recovery saw the sex industry revive, and even prosper, by the late 1990s. Sex-seeking males from European countries (and Australia) emerged as a 'new' type of customer. Lim and his band of crusaders proved no match for the crooked police, politicians and bar owners who make a living from exploiting sex workers. The girlie bars and strip joints simply moved to nearby Pasay City, just a kilometre or so south of Ermita.

In 1999 an unofficial estimate put the number of sex workers in the Philippines at 400,000. To put this figure into perspective, this is more than the nation's total manufacturing workforce. It is estimated that up to 25% of these sex workers are minors (see the Child Sexual Exploitation section for details).

The **Coalition Against Trafficking in Women** (CTTW; ⬛ www.catwinternational .org) is an organisation dedicated to fighting trafficking in women and all aspects of prostitution. Its site has information about prostitution in the Philippines and several useful links.

Child Prostitution The Philippines has the fourth-largest number of child prostitutes in the world, with an estimated 75,000 after Thailand (800,000), India (400,000) and the USA (300,000). Driven by poverty, these children are preyed on by men from virtually every nation on earth.

A dreadful culture of silence surrounds child sex abuse in the Philippines. While shame plays a big role in the silence, for the most part this silence is bought. There's big money to be made in paedophilia – not by the children themselves, of course, but by those who arrange meetings between paedophiles and children and by those who threaten to report these paedophiles.

While the number of child sex abuse cases reported to social workers throughout

Child Sexual Exploitation

Child sex tourism is a criminal offence in many countries around the world. Extraterritorial laws in Australia, New Zealand, the USA and many European Union (EU) countries mean that prosecution and punishment can occur in the offender's country of residence, even when the crime took place overseas. In addition to these laws, tougher action (including imprisonment) is now being taken in countries that have been documented as centres for child sexual exploitation.

the Philippines has been rising since 1993, it's likely this indicates an increase in abuse rather than an increase in social responsibility. In the early 1990s, reported cases seemed to have doubled over the course of a year and this figure is estimated to be increasing still. Despite strict laws, the number of foreigners charged and convicted over such sex crimes in the Philippines is so low as to be an encouragement to foreign paedophiles.

Travellers can contact **End Child Prostitution in Asian Tourism** (Ecpat; ☎ 02-925 2803; w www.ecpat.net; 123 V Luna Road Extension, Sikatuna Village, 1101, Quezon City, Manila) a global network of organisations that works to stop child prostitution, child pornography and the traffic of children for sexual purposes.

Treatment of Animals

While not valued in a Western sense except perhaps among the urban upper classes, pets are common in the Philippines. Cats and dogs, many strays, are tolerated in large numbers, although stray dogs are occasionally rounded up, particularly in upper-class gated villages. While many animals eventually end up as dinner – fish, pigs and chickens being the most popular – the rooster, as fighting cock, spends much of its life being pampered like a royal prince. Cockfighting is an extremely popular and lucrative pastime, and woe betide the grumpy traveller who suggests strangling a rooster that crows nonstop on an all-night bus trip! These magnificently groomed and fussed-over birds travel far and wide to cockfights and their owners often buy a separate bus seat for their prize

fighters (see the boxed text 'Fowl Play' in the Facts for the Visitor chapter).

RELIGION

Filipinos are an inherently spiritual people. The Philippines is the only predominantly Christian country in Asia – almost 90% of the population claims to be Christian and over 80% are Roman Catholic. Filipinos account for 60% of Asia's Christians, and their numbers are rising.

In 1986 there were 50 million and by the turn of last century this figure had ballooned to over 65 million.

There are approximately 11 million non-Catholic Christians practising in more than 350 sects, many of which operate under the banner of the National Council of Churches (NCC) in the Philippines. The largest denominations in this group include mainstream Protestant churches such as the Episcopalians, as well as the homegrown Iglesia ni Cristo, a neo-Christian sect which has neo-Gothic churches all over the country.

The largest religious minority group is the Muslims, although Islam is actually an older presence than Christianity. Mindanao Muslims include the Ilanon, Maguindanaw, Maranaw, Tausag and Samal.

Muslims are estimated to account for 5% to 15% of the country's total population of almost 83 million.

The passionate Catholic population has made **Holy Week** the most revered religious festival in the Philippines. Every March or April (it's a movable feast) thousands of devotees take part in pasyon or pabasa (all-night reading or chanting of passages from the Bible) Pilgrims flock to churches as part of the Visita Iglesia (Visit Churches) tradition and Christ's passion and death are observed in stagings of the senakulo (from the Spanish cenaculo meaning 'passion play') or in realistic re-enactments of the Crucifixion (complete with actual nails) – despite the disapproval of the Catholic Church.

Philippine religious faith is found in its rawest form in the ancient animist beliefs of the upland tribes of North Luzon, Palawan, Mindoro and Mindanao. Echoes of these exist even in mainstream religion – often to the horror of institutionalised Filipino faiths.

Examples of the Filipino talent for combining faiths are most notably found on the island of Siquijor (in the Visayas), which is home to healers renowned for their spiritual and medicinal skills. In spite of a stigma created by mainstream Christians, these healers attract big crowds every year at their **Lenten Festival of Herbal Preparation**. Based in the town of San Antonio, the festival kicks off on Black Saturday and centres on a ritual known as Tang-Alap, a gloriously fun-loving gathering of herbs and roots to be used in a pagan form of holy communion and dawn prayers.

Over many years, villagers throughout the Philippines have woven Christian rituals, such as Lent, into coinciding traditional harvest festivals. A well-known example is the spectacular **Moriones Festival** on the island of Marinduque (for details see the Marinduque section in the Southeast Luzon chapter). Wearing huge masks and

dressed like Roman soldiers, the townspeople re-enact the life of Christ with a special focus on the Roman soldier who is believed to have pierced the side of Christ with a lance at the Crucifixion.

Another peculiarly Filipino Catholic practice is the passionate veneration of the Virgin Mary. Every Wednesday in churches throughout the land, particularly at the Redemptorist Church in Baclaran, Manila, prayers are offered to Our Mother of Perpetual Help, a Byzantine-like icon of the Virgin Mary. *Nuestra Señora de La Naval* (Our Lady of La Naval) and *Nuestra Señora de Guia* (Our Lady of Guidance), both in Manila, are just two of the many images of the Virgin Mary that are revered for their miraculous powers.

Facts for the Visitor

BEST & WORST

The siren songs of the Philippines are many and varied, played by an impressive range of people and places. The most familiar with travellers are doubtless Boracay and Banaue but, if you have the time, the country offers visitors a tropical symphony of attractions.

While the larger islands like Luzon, Cebu and Mindanao make the most music, the little islands often have the biggest surprises. Delights in a minor key include Camiguin (Mindoro), for its rainforest and reef; the Visayas' Bantayan beaches and Malapascua Island, 'the thinking person's Boracay'.

Then there are the activities: mountain biking on Guimaras, hiking on Sibuyan Island, and diving and snorkelling off Moalboal, North Pandan Island and southern Leyte.

Other highlights include the sunset over Lake Sebu, in the heartland of Mindanao's T'boli people, and the beautifully preserved historic towns of Silay (on Negros) and Vigan (in North Luzon). The Mt Mayon volcano's perfectly symmetrical cone and the weird lahar (rain-induced landslide of volcanic debris) formations of Mt Pinatubo are just two of the many volcanic sights on the islands.

And the lowlights? An easy inclusion is Angeles, the prostitution and sex-tour capital of the country – at least nearby Mt Pinatubo gives you something else to look at if you have to pass through. Despite efforts to clean up San Fernando (La Union) after the US military left, what remain are a dearth of decent beaches and a swag of tourists in search of prostitutes.

Manila would probably make most travellers' lists of 'Cities You'd Hate to Lose Your Passport In'. It's one of those places resident expats learn to appreciate, if not exactly adore, but first-time visitors often can't wait to escape the grime, crime and eye-popping chasm between rich and poor. Fair enough – though beyond the nightlife, the capital does have enough attractions to keep you entertained for a few lively days.

More than a few towns would charitably fall into the 'Nice Place to Live but I

Top Tips For Travelling in the Philippines

The experienced traveller will probably find the Philippines a relatively easy country in which to travel. Like all countries, however, it does have its own peculiar challenges and frustrations. The following list will (hopefully) help ease you over the rough patches.

- Always carry small denomination bills and coins. You'll be surprised at how many businesses never seem to have change – 'A P100 note?! What are we going to do with that?!'
- When you get off a ferry, hang on tightly to your backpack/luggage and head straight to a café for a cool drink. You'll be spared all the hubbub that greets most passengers and you'll probably get a better taxi fare when you make your move.
- Look out for water refilling stations – you can usually refill a 1L bottle for P3. You'll be doing your wallet and the environment a favour.
- Get plenty of pesos from an ATM or bank before leaving a city. This will save you from having to deal with the Philippines' notoriously crooked moneychangers; and in the sticks, you may not even find one of those. Be warned, though, that ATMs are often 'offline' in the Philippines, so always have a backup and withdraw sufficient cash to carry you through 'lean times.'
- Avoid using credit cards for purchases and accommodation as many businesses charge a hefty surcharge for credit-card transactions.
- If you want to avoid the hassles and crowds of Manila, fly into Cebu. Several airlines service Cebu and it's a more attractive gateway to the Philippines. See the Air section in the Getting There & Away chapter for details.
- Set your inner clock to 'Philippine time'. Learn to relax and understand that not everything works according to a strict timetable here. This, perhaps more than any single thing, will help you enjoy your time in the Philippines.

Wouldn't Want to Visit' category. Danao and Subic Bay and Mactan are particularly devoid of charm; Tagbilaran's air pollution is sobering, and Kalibo saves all its colour for its big festival (see Public Holidays & Special Events later in this chapter for details).

SUGGESTED ITINERARIES

No matter what your itinerary, it will probably take up more time than you might imagine. Whether you're gazing at the surf or groping for a seat on the next bus, plane or boat, you'll be surprised at how quickly time passes. If you plan a long list of sights, it's best to plan carefully but stay loose – your itinerary is also in the hands of the transportation network, and the weather may have plans of its own (for better or worse).

Bahala na, as the Filipinos say. Be realistic and go with the flow – for example, unless you have your own helicopter, you're not going to land in Manila and hike in Banaue on the same day. Consider how you're going to get from A to B, too. A lot of travellers make a beeline for Boracay, but getting there can be less than half the fun – it's often quicker and easier to go by boat to Caticlan on Panay than trying to fly. In fact, if you're doing any serious island-hopping, getting around the Visayas is generally quicker by boat than by plane. If time is limited, one way to conserve energy (yet pack a fair bit in) is to base yourself in a pleasant centre with plenty of nearby attractions for one- or two-day side trips. Sagada on Luzon and Davao on Mindanao suit this purpose well. Alternatively, head for 'do-able' islands such as Samar, Leyte, Camiguin or the Romblon group, where distances are relatively short but there's a great variety of things to see and do. You could also ease into the country (or take a break along the way) on a cosy little island like Biliran, off Leyte.

The following are some suggested itineraries for travel in the Philippines. Keep in mind that these are just the briefest suggestions – use the information in this book to construct a tour that suits your specific interests and comfort levels.

Manila Plus One

Many visitors to the Philippines use Manila simply as a jumping-off point to the more popular tourist destinations like Boracay, Puerto Galera or Palawan, but the capital has plenty to offer and has ample sights to keep you occupied for a day or two. If you have only a week or so to spend in the country, start off your visit with two days in Manila doing a one-day tour of historic sights, such as Intramuros, and another day for modern Manila as embodied by the Ayala Center in Makati City and other centres of contemporary urban development.

Having experienced a little of Philippine life in the big city, you could then head for one of the aforementioned destinations. Boracay is a popular choice and has both the natural attractions and nightlife to keep most visitors entertained. A similar destination is Puerto Galera, with its meandering coastline, innumerable coves and towering cliffs covered in lush vegetation. If you can afford to fly, and have at least 10 days to spare, you might be able to venture as far as Palawan, which is justifiably popular for its stunning scenery and excellent diving.

A Visit to the Cordilleras

Two weeks will give you a better time frame to enjoy the Philippines in its characteristically laid-back mood. Though time seems to come to a standstill here, before you know it a week has gone by. With two weeks, you could do one of the aforementioned Manila and Boracay/Puerto Galera/Palawan itineraries, perhaps adding a day to each of the stops, and then swing up to the north for a look at what has been called 'the eighth wonder of the world': the ancient rice terraces of Banaue. If you've still got time while up in the Cordillera, you could tack on a journey to nearby (as the crow flies, at least) Sagada. With its cool climate and relaxed atmosphere, Sagada is a good place to chill out before returning to 'the real world'.

Island-hopping in the Visayas

If you have a month to spend in the country, then an island-hopping tour of the Visayas is certainly one of the better ways to spend it, particularly if you're a diver or beach-lover. You could start by flying into Cebu, the Philippines' second-largest city. It's possible to fly direct to Cebu from several nearby countries (for details see Air in the Getting There & Away chapter), or you can hop on a flight or ferry down from Manila.

Once in Cebu, the possibilities are nearly endless. Divers and snorkellers might want to check the special section 'Diving in the Philippines' later in this guidebook to pick some of the choicer dive sites in the Visayas.

Of course any island-hopping itinerary is at the mercy of the weather, and you would be well advised to plan this sort of trip between October and March, when the weather is likely to be suitable.

North–South Traverse

From north to south, the Philippines is a country of astonishing diversity in terms of natural scenery, ethnic variety and cultural heritage. With two months to spend here, you could do a grand north-to-south journey starting from the historically rich Ilocos region and Cagayan Valley in North Luzon and ending in the Muslim-influenced provinces of Mindanao. Along the way, you could stop off in the Cordillera to check out Banaue, spend a few nights amid the bright lights of Manila, relax a few days on the white-sand beach of Boracay, hit a few dive sites in the Visayas, and perhaps even make the side trip to Palawan, the Philippines' 'last frontier'.

PLANNING
When to Go

Giving due allowance to island microclimates and the tempestuous twins (El Niño and La Niña), the best time to visit is in the typhoon off-season (September to May). Beware of arriving around Christmas and New Year, though, as this is when legions of overseas Filipino workers return to spend the holidays with their families: accommodation and transport options tend to fill up during this period – book well in advance. Holy Week (around Easter) presents similar problems.

The most lively festivals fall between January and May. The rainy season falls between June and September. The dry season starts when the September rains let up, and from then until early April the weather is at its most travel-friendly (the rice terraces in North Luzon are magnificent during these months). By May, the warm weather turns hot and you'll ache for a sea breeze or the cool shade of the mountains. For further details on weather in the Philippines see Climate in the Facts about the Philippines chapter.

Maps

Unfortunately it's difficult to find accurate maps of the Philippines. For a map of the entire country, the best of the lot is probably Nelles Verlag's 1:1,500,000 scale *Philippines*. For local travel, E-Z Maps (published by United Tourist Promotions) produces a series of maps on several of the country's bigger cities and some islands. The Nelles map is available internationally; the E-Z Maps are best picked up once you arrive. See Maps under Orientation in the Manila chapter for information on maps of the capital.

What to Bring

You can travel light in the Philippines, but among the essential items is a torch (flashlight) – power failures are common, and some parts of the country manage without electricity at all. Instead of a regular torch, you might consider bringing a headlamp, especially if you plan on doing any caving on your trip. A towel or sarong can double as makeshift bedding on the bare boards or plastic sheets that cover the beds on many overnight ferries. You'll also want a range of clothing, from lightweight for tropical beaches to warm (a fleece) for the mountains or volcano summits. A fleece will also stave off pneumonia when the air-conditioning cranks up on newer ferries and buses. A couple of garbage bags will help protect your gear from water and dust. You might want a thicker zip-lock bag for your camera, especially if you plan on taking lots of boat rides.

An almost essential item if you are a light sleeper is a pair or two of good earplugs, which will keep out noise generated by everything from crowing roosters to ship engines or the karaoke machine downstairs. Tampons can be hard to find outside the bigger cities – bring some from home if you use them. Pads are more commonly available, even outside the cities.

Other items you might consider bringing include seasickness medication for those long ferry rides, multivitamins (to supplement the standard travellers' diet), and a lightweight mosquito net for those places that either lack nets or have nets filled with holes.

RESPONSIBLE TOURISM

Being the perfectly responsible tourist is quite a job but there are two main issues to bear in mind: your impact on the people you meet and your impact on the environment.

There are over 100 distinct ethnic minority groups in the Philippines. While it is extremely interesting for travellers to visit these groups, you should consider that your very presence can have a destabilising and corrosive influence on their cultures. Think carefully about your decision to visit, and if you decide to do so, watch your behaviour. Obvious displays of wealth are a no-no, and even the giving of gifts should be carefully considered. Most importantly, keep in mind that your visit may be brief, but the impressions you make might last a lifetime. As with any people anywhere, treat those you meet with respect and apply the rules of politeness that apply in your own country – chances are you won't go far wrong.

Another social issue related to travel in the Philippines is prostitution, and its most insidious form, child prostitution. It is important to understand the social and economic background of prostitution in the Philippines, as well as the effect it has on those involved. Most of the prostitutes in the Philippines are victims of severe poverty and few escape unscathed from the industry. For more on this issue, see Society & Conduct in the Facts about the Philippines chapter.

The environment of the Philippines is under attack every day from a legion of forces. The following is a list of helpful practices that will minimise your impact on the environment as you travel.

- Produce as little garbage as possible by using recyclable containers. Ensure your garbage is disposed of properly, dispose of it properly yourself if necessary.
- If possible, use environmentally friendly methods of transportation or walk from place to place.
- Avoid polluting water sources – use established toilets, or keep at least 100m from rivers or lakes.
- Patronise environmentally friendly tour operators and locally owned businesses, and buy locally produced goods.
- Never buy products made from endangered species.

You'll find heaps of information on the challenges facing the environment of the Philippines, and the various efforts to protect it, set out in the Ecology & Environment and Flora & Fauna sections in the Facts about the Philippines chapter.

Social Graces

The golden rule when travelling in the Philippines is to treat problems with the same graciousness as the average Filipino. A smile and a joke goes a long, long way, and anger or sullenness just makes things worse.

When photographing people, keep in mind that some tribespeople in particular may be superstitious about your camera or suspicious of your motives. Always respect the wishes of the locals. Ask permission to photograph, and don't insist or snap a picture anyway if permission is denied. Do *not* take pictures of soldiers and military installations, unless you enjoy explaining this sort of thing to angry authorities.

TOURIST OFFICES

The Philippine Department of Tourism (DOT) is the official organ of Philippine tourism. The main DOT centre in Manila has helpful staff, but you don't need to load up with brochures and computer printouts – regional outlets stock the same information and it may be more up to date.

You'll find regional DOT offices in many of the more popular destinations throughout the Philippines, although some offices offer more useful services than others.

Tourist Offices Abroad

DOT offices and contacts abroad include:

Australia
 (☎ 02-9283 0711, fax 9283 0755, e cgjones@pdot.com.au) Level 1, Philippine Centre, 27–33 Wentworth Ave, Sydney 2000
China
 (☎ 02-866 7643) c/o Philippines Consulate General, Room 602, United Centre, 95 Queen's Way, Hong Kong
France
 (☎ 01 42 65 02 34, fax 42 65 02 38, e dotpar@club-internet.fr) c/o Philippines Embassy, 3 Faubourg Saint Honoré, 75008 Paris
Germany
 (☎ 069-20893, fax 285127, e phildo-fra@t-online.de) Kaiserhofstrasse 7, 60313 Frankfurt am Main
Japan
 (☎ 03-5562 1583, fax 5562 1593, e dotjapan@gol.com) c/o Philippines Embassy, 5-15-5 Roppongi, Minato-ku, Tokyo 106-8537
Singapore
 (☎ 065-6738 7165, fax 6738 2604, e philtours_sin@pacific.net.sg) 06-24 Orchard Towers, 400 Orchard Rd, Singapore 238875
Taiwan
 (☎ 02-2773 5724, fax 8773 8806) c/o Manila Economic & Cultural Office, 4th floor,

Metrobank Plaza, 107 Chung Hsiao E Rd,
Section 4, Taipei 106
UK
(☎ 207-835 1100, fax 835 1926, e tourism@
pdot.co.uk) c/o Philippines Embassy, 146
Cromwell Rd, London SW7 4EF
USA
New York: (☎ 212-575 7915, fax 302 6759,
e pdotnyc1@aol.com) 556 5th Ave, New
York, NY 10036
Los Angeles: (☎ 213-487 4527, fax 386 4063,
e pdotla@aol.com) Suite 216, 3660 Wilshire
Blvd, Los Angeles, CA 90010
San Francisco: (☎ 415-956 4060, fax 956
2093, e pdotsf@aol.com) Suite 507, 447
Sutter St, San Francisco, CA 94108

VISAS & DOCUMENTS
Visas
Visa regulations in the Philippines are subject to frequent changes: be sure to check
with a Philippine embassy or consulate before making your travel plans. You can also
check the Philippines Department of Foreign Affairs website (w www.dfa.gov.ph)
for more information.

At the time of writing, citizens of nearly all
countries do not need a visa to enter the
Philippines for stays of less than 22 days –
you'll be given a 21-day visa on arrival in the
country. However, you may well be asked for
proof of an onward ticket to enter the country (see Onward Tickets later in this section).

For longer stays, you can apply at a
Philippine embassy or consulate, before you
arrive, for a 59-day single-entry visa. This
usually costs US$35, but it may be more or
less, depending on where you apply. You
can also pay a lot more and apply for
multiple-entry visas (valid for up to a year),
although they're still only good for 59-day
stays.

Most Philippine embassies and consulates
won't issue you a visa without proof of a
ticket for onward travel from the Philippines.
Usually, a photocopy of your itinerary from
your travel agent is enough, but some ask to
see the actual ticket.

Under the Balikbayan Program, former
Filipino citizens and their family members
travelling together can stay visa-free in the
Philippines for up to one year. The 'balikbayan stamp' required is handled by Philippine embassies and consulates and is free
of charge. People over the age of 35 who
wish to stay longer (much longer) can also

apply for a Special Resident Retiree's Visa
(SRRV). This requires the deposit of at least
US$50,000 in a registered Philippine bank,
as well as a processing fee of at least
US$1300. Details are available from any
Philippine embassy, consulate or immigra-
tion office.

Visa Extensions If you want to stay beyond the 21 or 59 days you've been given
on arrival, you'll have to deal with a local
immigration office. Fortunately, you can
now buy your way past a lot of the red tape
with a P500 'express fee', which may be
pricey but it ensures that your application is
processed in only a few hours, rather than
the usual five to seven days.

Currently, 21-day visas can be extended
to 59 days for P2020. Longer extensions
(up to a maximum of six months) are also
possible, with correspondingly higher fees.
You'll need a photocopy of the identity
page and the Philippine entry stamp from
your passport and you may need to show
your onward plane ticket.

Manila's massive **Bureau of Immigration**
(☎ 02-527 3265, Magallanes Dr; open 8am-
noon & 1pm-5pm Mon-Fri) squats between
the Pasig River and the Intramuros city walls.
A visit to this imposing edifice is a formal occasion: casual clothes, such as shorts and sin-
glets, are prohibited – thongs (flip-flops) are
also a bad fashion statement – and you'll
need proof of identity to enter the building.

Visa extensions from 21 to 59 days can
often be handled faster by the regional immigration offices in San Fernando (La Union)
and Cebu City, but remember to dress for
success.

Beware: as many travellers have discovered as they were ready to board the plane
out of the country, there is now an additional
charge, on top of the visa extension fees, if
you stay more than 59 days. This is officially your Emigration Clearance Certificate
(ECC) – which is effectively just another tax
on tourists. In practice, visitors pay a fine
equivalent to the price of the ECC as they
clear emigration at the airport, which saves
the hassle and paperwork of applying for the
certificate itself. The cost is a steep P1000,
plus a P10 processing fee. If you don't have
the money to pay, you will not be allowed
out of the Philippines. This also applies for
travellers departing the Philippines by ship,

although different immigration offices have been known to apply different policies. (To be on the safe side, it's best to inquire at an immigration office prior to departure if you have any doubts.) The only way around this is to go to the Bureau of Immigration in Intramuros and request that you be 'blacklisted for nonpayment', which will get you off the charge but will seriously affect your chances of ever getting back into the country.

The Intramuros office seems to prefer that you just pay your ECC fine at the airport rather than at the office for stays under a year, so make sure you've got the money ready when you leave.

Onward Tickets

Officially, you must have a ticket for onward travel to enter the Philippines. This applies both to those who apply for visas before arriving in the Philippines and those who hope to receive a 21-day visa on arrival. In practice, immigration inspectors at the airport don't always ask to see an onward ticket. But be warned that travelling to the Philippines without an onward ticket is a risky proposition – if you're asked to produce one and don't have one, you'll be boarding the next flight out (and paying accordingly)!

The onward ticket can be for a ship (see the Sea section in the Getting There & Away chapter), though getting the paperwork for one-way boat passage out of the country before you arrive isn't assured. Some travellers hell-bent on leaving by boat from Mindanao for Malaysia or Indonesia get around this by biting the bullet and buying the cheapest return air ticket they can find (say, Hong Kong–Manila–Hong Kong), then not using the return portion of it.

In any case, you won't save money on a return fare by picking up a cheap air ticket in Manila.

Fares from the Philippines are generally expensive, and local travel agents aren't in the business of tracking down bargains for overseas travel (they usually only quote the advertised fares given by the airlines).

Travel Insurance

A travel insurance policy to cover theft, loss and medical problems is a good idea. Some policies offer lower and higher medical-expense options. There is a wide variety of policies available, so check the small print.

Some policies specifically exclude 'dangerous activities', which can include scuba diving, motorcycling and even trekking.

You may prefer a policy that pays doctors or hospitals directly rather than you having to pay on the spot and claim later. If you have to claim later, make sure you keep all documentation. Some policies require that you call back (reverse charges) to a centre in your home country where an immediate assessment of your problem is made.

Check that the policy covers ambulances and an emergency flight home.

Driving Licence & Permits

Your home country's driving licence is legally valid for 90 days in the Philippines. Technically, you are supposed to have an International Driving Permit for any period longer than this.

Hostel Cards

Having a Hostelling International (HI) card will save about P20 per night at a hostel, though there are only a few you are likely to stay at (see Accommodation later in this chapter for details on hostel options).

Student & Youth Cards

An International Student Identity Card (ISIC) is of limited use in the Philippines, although you may be able to get student rates at some museums with them.

Some bus and shipping companies offer 20% to 30% discounts to foreign students.

Seniors Cards

PAL offers a 20% discount on domestic flights for passengers who are least 60 years old. Your passport will suffice as proof of age, though you could also apply for a Golden Years card (P50) from the airline for this purpose.

Vaccination Certificates

You must have proof of vaccination for yellow fever if arriving in the Philippines from an infected area.

Copies

All important documents (passport data page and visa page, credit cards, travel insurance policy, air/bus/train tickets, driving licence etc) should be photocopied before you leave home. Leave one copy with someone at home and keep another with you, separate from the originals. Alternatively, you can securely store details of your vital travel documents in ekno's online travel vault at w www.ekno.lonelyplanet.com.

EMBASSIES & CONSULATES

You should be aware that the embassy of which you are a citizen won't be much help in emergencies if the trouble you're in is remotely your own fault. Your embassy will not be sympathetic if you end up in jail after committing a crime locally, even if such actions are legal in your own country.

In genuine emergencies you might get some assistance, but only if other channels have been exhausted. For example, if you need to get home urgently, a free air ticket is exceedingly unlikely – the embassy would expect you to have insurance. If you have all your money and documents stolen, it will assist with getting a new passport, but a loan for onward travel is out of the question.

Philippine Embassies & Consulates

Countries in which the Philippines has embassies include:

Australia (☎ 02-6273 2535, fax 6273 3984, e cbrpe@philembassy.au.com) 1 Moonah Place, Yarralumla, ACT 2600
Consulate: (☎ 02-9262 7377, fax 9262 7355, e phsydpc@ozemail.com.au) Level 1, Philippine Centre, 27–33 Wentworth Ave, Sydney, NSW 2000
Consulate: (☎ 03-9662 9702, fax 9663 2702, e phconsul@eisa.net.au) Suite 404, 277 Collins St, Melbourne, VIC 3000
Canada (☎ 613-233 1121, fax 233 4165, e ottawape@istar.com) Suite 606, 130 Albert St, Ottawa, ON K1P564
Consulate: (☎ 416-922 7181, fax 922 2638, e torontopc@philcongen-toronto.com) Suite 365, 151 Bloor St West, Toronto, ON M5S1S4
Consulate: (☎ 604-685 1619, fax 685 7645, e VancouverPCG@telus.com) Suite 1405, 700 West Pender, Vancouver, BC V6C1G8
China (☎ 010-6532 2518, fax 6532 3761, e beijingpe@cinet.com.cn) 23 Xiushui Beijie, Jianguomenwai, Beijing 100600
Consulate: (☎ 852-2823 8500, fax 2866 9885, e pcg@philcongen-hk.com) Room 602, United Centre, 95 Queensway, Central, Hong Kong
France (☎ 01 44 14 57 00, fax 46 47 56 00, e AmbaphilParis@wanadoo.fr) 4 Hameau de Boulainvilliers, Paris 75016

Germany (☎ 030-864 9500, fax 873 2551, e Berlinpe@t-online.de) Uhlandstrasse 97, 10715 Berlin
Consulate: (☎ 040-442 952/953, fax 459 987, e hamburgpcg@compuserve.com) Jungfrauental 13, 20149 Hamburg
Indonesia (☎ 021-315 5118, fax 315 1167, e phjkt@indo.net.id) Jalan Imam Bonjol Menteng 6-8, Jakarta Pusat, Jakarta
Consulate: (☎ 0431-861 178, e manadopc@manada.wasantara.net.id) No 12 Jalan Tikala Satu, Tikala Ares Lingkungan I, Manado City
Japan (☎ 03-5562 1600, fax 5562 1603, e phjp@gol.com) 5-15-5 Roppongi, Minato-ku, Tokyo 106-8537
Consulate: (☎ 06-6910 7881, fax 6910 8734, e osakapc@osk.3web.ne.jp) 24th floor, Twin 21 MID Tower, 2-1-61 Shiromi, Chuo-ku, Osaka
Malaysia (☎ 03-2148 4233, fax 2148 3576, e webmaster@philembassykl.org.my) 1 Changkat Kai Peng, 50450, Kuala Lumpur
New Zealand (☎ 04-472 9848, fax 472 5170, e embassy@wellington-pe.co.nz) 50 Hobson St, Thorndon, Wellington
Thailand (☎ 02-259 0139/40, fax 259 2809, e bangkokpe@dfa.gov.ph) 760 Thanon Sukhumvit, opposite Soi 30/31, Bangkok 10110
UK (☎ 020-7937 1600, fax 7937 2925, e embassy@philemb.co.uk) 9a Palace Green, London W8 4QE
USA (☎ 202-467 9300, fax 467 9417, e uswashpe@aol.com) 1600 Massachusetts Ave NW, Washington, DC 20036
Consulate: (☎ 213-639 0980, fax 639 0990, e losangelpc@aol.com) Suite 500, 3600 Wilshire Blvd, Los Angeles, CA 900100
Consulate: (☎ 415-433 6666, fax 421 2641, e SanFranciscoPC@aol.com) 6F, 447 Sutter St, San Francisco, CA 94108
Vietnam (☎ 04-943 7873, fax 943 5760, e phvn@hn.vnn.vn) 27B Tran Hung Dao St, Hanoi

Embassies & Consulates in the Philippines

Manila is a good place to pick up visas for other parts of Asia and countries further afield. The governments of most European and Asian countries are represented; many Latin American nations also maintain a diplomatic presence.

Manila's Makati district is the main area for embassies and foreign consulates.

Embassies in Manila
Australia (☎ 02-757 8100, fax 750 2840) Level 23, Tower 2, RCBC Plaza, 6819 Ayala Ave, Makati

Canada (☎ 02-867 0001, fax 810 4659) 9th floor, Allied Bank Center, 6754 Ayala Ave, Makati

China (☎ 02-844 3148, fax 845 2465) 4896 Pasay Rd, Dasmarine Village, Makata

France (☎ 02-810 1981, fax 817 5047) 16th floor, Pacific Star Bldg, corner Gil Puyat and Makati Aves, Makati

Germany (☎ 02-892 4906, fax 810 4703) 6th floor, Solid Bank Bldg, 777 Paseo de Roxas, Salcedo Village, Makati

Indonesia (☎ 02-892 5061, fax 892 5878) 185 Salcedo St, Legaspi Village, Makati

Japan (☎ 02-551 5710, fax 551 5780) 2627 Roxas Blvd, next to the Hyatt Regency Hotel, Pasay City

Malaysia (☎ 02-817 4581, fax 816 3158)107 Tordesillas St, Salcedo Village, Makati

The Netherlands (☎ 02-812 5981, fax 815 4579) 9th floor, King's Court Bldg, 2129 Don Chico Roces Ave, Makati

New Zealand (☎ 02-891 5358) 23rd floor, Far East Bank Center, Gil Puyat Ave, Salcedo Village, Makati

Singapore (☎ 02-751 2345) 35th floor, Tower 1, Enterprise Center, 6766 Ayala Ave, Makati

Thailand (☎ 02-815 4220, fax 815 4221) 107 Rada St, Legaspi Village, Makati

UK (☎ 02-816 7116, fax 819 7206) 15th floor, LV Locsin Bldg, corner Makati and Ayala Aves, Makati

USA (☎ 02-523 1001, fax 522 4361) 1201 Roxas Blvd, Ermita

Vietnam (☎ 02-524 0364, fax 526 0472) 554 Vito Cruz St, corner of Harrison St, Malate

Consulates in Cebu City
Canada (☎ 032-254 4749) 45-L Andres Abellana St

France (☎ 032-232 0936) 556 Juan Luna St, Mabolo

Japan (☎ 032-255 0287) 12th floor, Metrobank Plaza, Osmena Blvd

Thailand (☎ 032-702 61) Eastern Shipping Lines Bldg, MJ Cuenco St

UK (☎ 032-346 0525) 4 Palmera St, Villa Terrace, Greenhills Rd, Casuntingan, Mandaue City

Consulates in Davao
Indonesia (☎ 082-229 2930) Ecoland Dr, Phase IV

Japan (☎ 082-221 3100) Suite B305, 3rd floor, Plaza de Luisa Complex, 140 R Magsaysay Ave

CUSTOMS
You are permitted to bring in personal effects, and a certain amount of clothing, jewellery and perfume duty free. In addition, 200 cigarettes or two tins of tobacco and 2L of alcohol are allowed duty free.

Illegal drugs, firearms and pornographic material are prohibited. It is forbidden to export coral and mussels, certain types of orchid, and parts of animals such as python skins or turtle shells. There is no longer any restriction on the amount of foreign currency that can be brought in to the country; however, foreign currency taken out must not exceed the amount brought in. Visitors must also declare Philippine currency in excess of P10,000 upon entering or leaving the country.

MONEY
The smartest way to bring cash to the Philippines is in the form of a credit card, cash card or debit card. Provided you bring your PIN, you can use these to get cash or cash advances from thousands of banks and ATMs in the Philippines (but don't expect to find these in rural areas – always stock up on cash before leaving a city). See ATMs, Cash Advances and Credit Cards later for details.

Of course, you'll want to back up your plastic with some cash (US dollars are the most widely accepted) and some travellers cheques. Using plastic with a cash back-up will save you from having to deal with local moneychangers, who seem to have made a science out of ripping off tourists; Lonely Planet receives stacks of letters and emails each year from victims of these schemes – don't say you weren't warned!

Currency
The unit of currency in the Philippines is the peso (P), which is also spelled piso in Tagalog or Pilipino, and is divided into 100 centavos (c). Banknotes come in denominations of 10, 20, 50, 100, 500, 1000 and 2000 pesos. Coins are in 10c and 25c pieces, and P1 and P5.

Exchange Rates
Exchange rates are as follows:

country	unit		peso
Australia	A$1	=	P32
Canada	C$1	=	P36
euro zone	€1	=	P58
Hong Kong	HK$1	=	P7
Indonesia	1000Rp	=	P6
Japan	¥100	=	P45
Malaysia	RM1	=	P14
New Zealand	NZ$1	=	P29
UK	UK£1	=	P89
USA	US$1	=	P54

Exchanging Money

Most major towns have a range of options for changing money, from banks and money-changers to resorts and travel offices. In some cases the exchange rate is quite low, and it's best to arrive with enough pesos for your stay. All in all, it's wise to plan ahead so you don't get caught short of cash – or find yourself pushing around a wheelbarrow full of pesos 'just in case'.

In Manila you should have no trouble changing US dollars, British pounds or euros; Japanese yen is also widely accepted, as are Canadian and Australian dollars, Asean currencies, and some currencies from the Middle East.

Moneychangers are usually easy to find in the commercial centres of most cities; some department stores and shopping malls also have moneychangers on the premises. Moneychangers usually offer the best rates, but they are also notorious for all manner of short-change scams and rip-offs. Because of the risk of rip-offs, it's best to use a money-changer only as a last resort – if possible, change your cash or travellers cheques at a bank, hotel or resort.

In principle, changing travellers cheques is quite simple: you only need to bring along your passport and the original purchase receipts. In practice, banks and moneychangers can be reluctant to accept travellers cheques, so to minimise hassles it's wise to plan your money conversions in towns with a couple of exchange options.

Even in a city such as Manila, only a handful of banks and moneychangers change travellers cheques in currencies other than US dollars. Outside the big cities, US dollars are generally the only currency accepted, either for cash or travellers cheques, though the Japanese yen is gaining greater acceptance as an alternative to the greenback. The rate is generally slightly lower for travellers cheques than for cash.

There are no particular hassles with exchanging pesos when you leave, unless it's some huge amount you're carrying. But even then your only problem might be locating a moneychanger with enough US dollars to change them into.

Cash With the usual precautions, carrying cash (US dollars is the currency of choice) is no particular problem; it's actually a good idea to have a US$50 and/or US$100 note stashed somewhere secure and accessible in case you can't find a bank or an ATM, or you're out of travellers cheques.

As for pesos, 'Sorry, no change' becomes a familiar line – stock up on notes smaller than P100 at every opportunity.

Travellers Cheques US-dollar travellers cheques are the most secure and reliable way to carry funds (see Exchanging Money earlier). American Express (AmEx) is by far the most widely recognised and you may find it difficult to exchange cheques from other companies. An instant replacement policy on lost or stolen cheques is highly desirable, so check that the company will honour this policy in the Philippines before you buy.

Cashing travellers cheques is best done at a bank, although this can be time consuming (HSB bank is reported to be the fastest). Most places charge a small fee to cash travellers cheques – ask about the fee beforehand and decide how many cheques you want to cash at one time.

ATMs Credit, debit and cash cards can be used to get cash or cash advances from thousands of ATMs throughout the country. Check with your bank or credit-card company (or look on the back of your card) to see which ATM network your card is connected to. For getting cash, Cirrus and Plus are the most widely accepted; for cash advances, MasterCard is the most widely accepted, followed by Visa. Cash advances from ATMs are in local currency, and may be subject to a daily withdrawal limit (again, check with your credit-card company or the bank operating the ATM).

Particularly in the big cities, ATMs operate 24 hours daily, and can be found in department stores, supermarkets and shopping malls, in addition to banks. Note that ATMs in the Philippines have a curious system of posting 'online' or 'offline' signs to indicate whether the machine is in operation. Another curious but comforting feature of ATMs in the Philippines is the presence of armed guards – don't be surprised if they ask to check your bags, as this is merely an everyday security procedure.

We have received reports from travellers who have been ripped off by ATMs in Batangas city (accounts were charged without any cash being dispensed). While these reports are difficult to verify, we recommend asking other travellers for advice about reliable ATMs before putting your card into an unknown machine.

Cash Advances You can get cash advances with credit cards from many ATMs and banks in the Philippines. Note that this is different from simply getting cash from your account with a cash or debit card – a cash advance is like a credit-card purchase in that you must pay it back, with interest if you don't pay your account in full each month. Also keep in mind that there may not be any ATMs or banks in smaller towns and rural areas, so, as usual, it pays to cash up (within reasonable limits) before heading into the sticks.

While many ATMs in the Philippines accept cash cards linked to the Cirrus and Plus networks, far fewer are linked to international credit-card networks, such as MasterCard and Visa. If the ATM in question does not accept your credit card, it may still be possible to get an over-the-counter cash advance from the bank. However, this can be a slow and tedious procedure.

Equitable PCI Banks will issue cash advances for most major cards, including MasterCard and Visa, so this is usually a good bet, but be warned that only one branch in any town is likely to offer this service, so you may have to travel to find the correct branch.

Credit Cards Many shops, restaurants, hotels and resorts accept payment by plastic, and credit-card cash advances are possible in larger towns and cities; in small towns and on islands rarely visited there are often no provisions for credit cards (Palawan, in particular, has few places that accept credit cards).

A shop-front sign that reads 'Visa accepted' or 'MasterCard accepted' may well refer only to the Philippines-issued version, so check with the shop personnel by showing them your card. Also note that some establishments will try to add (at times surreptitiously) a surcharge to your bill when you pay with a credit card, on the grounds that they themselves have to pay a surcharge to the credit-card company. It's all up to you whether to accept this rather irritating practice or not. You may be able to avoid this charge by using another card.

If your MasterCard is lost, stolen or eaten by an ungrateful ATM, the toll-free number to call in the Philippines is ☎ 1 800 1111 0061. For Visa card holders, the number is ☎ 1 800 1111 0248. Be forewarned, however, that trying to get through to a ☎ 1 800 number in the Philippines can be as fruitless as trying to reach somebody in the middle of the Sahara!

There are incidents of credit-card fraud in the Philippines, as in many other countries. To prevent this, keep a close eye on your card at all times – never, for example, allow a shop clerk to disappear into a back room with it (where someone would be able to make several imprints with your card). Likewise, keep a careful record of all your credit-card transactions while in the Philippines, save your receipts, and check your credit-card statements.

International Transfers If you are travelling around Asia, places such as Hong Kong and Singapore are more efficient than Manila to have money transferred to you. International transfers to the Philippines can be slow, though the process is much quicker and simpler if you use the right bank connections.

Philippine banks have a working relationship with many overseas institutions, so before you leave ask your home bank for the name of its 'correspondent' bank in the Philippines.

Be sure also to bring your account number, the full address of your bank and any other relevant information. You can then ask your bank to wire funds to you at the Philippine correspondent bank's head office. Your money should arrive in a few days, but don't expect US dollars in cash; local banks normally pay out in pesos.

If you prefer your money to be paid out in US dollars, the way to do it is to open a dollar account at one of the local banks and have your money sent to that account. This will then allow you to withdraw your money in dollars. Many, if not all, of the local banks allow you to keep a dollar account. Your other option is to have your money sent to you via Western Union. This service is quicker than bank transfers, and you can pick up your money in dollars from any of the Western Union outlets that have sprouted all over Manila and in other major cities.

Bank Accounts If you're going to be in the country for a while, you might also consider opening a peso account to ease bill payments, facilitate ATM withdrawals, earn a bit of interest and perhaps pick up a locally issued credit card. To open a peso account, the requirements are similar to those for a US-dollar account: one to three pieces of identification plus a minimum first deposit.

There's a bewildering array of banks operating in the Philippines, so look around before deciding where to put your money. The Philippine National Bank (PNB), Equitable PCI Bank, Metrobank, Rizal Commercial Banking Corporation (RCBC) and Bank of the Philippine Islands (BPI) are some of the big names in local banking; International Exchange Bank (iBank) is one of the smaller but more customer-friendly ones.

Global banks, such as Citibank and HSB (Hong Kong and Shanghai Bank), also provide consumer banking services in the Philippines. If your home bank is Citibank, for instance, it would make a lot of sense to open your account at a local Citibank.

Costs
The Philippines is a bit more expensive than Thailand or Indonesia, but still quite affordable by Western standards. First impressions of prices in Manila or Cebu City aren't necessarily indicative of expenses for the rest of your trip. In particular, Manila's accommodation (especially mid-range) tends to be pricey compared with the provinces.

Heavily developed tourist centres such as Boracay offer few bargains to travellers (though low-season rates in places dependent on the tourist trade are lower). Nonetheless, you can get by even on Boracay for P500 a day. In any case, basic necessities are amazingly cheap year-round. Air fares within the Philippines are also good value.

The following are average prices in Manila for a few sample items:

beer from a store (one bottle)	P13
city Bus (air-con)	P7
city Bus (ordinary)	P4
film (36 exposures)	P180
hotel room (budget)	P350
hotel room (mid-range)	P1000
internet access (per hour)	P40
jeepney	P4
laundry (1kg)	P40
meal (basic)	P100
petrol (1L)	P17.50
shampoo (bottle)	P30

Tipping & Bargaining
Tipping (about 5% to 10%) is expected (though not demanded), especially in restaurants, where it's a component of the staff's wages. Round up taxi fares (eg, from P64 to P70), assuming the meter is correct. Try bargaining in shops and markets, as Filipinos do. After all, foreigners are usually quoted higher prices. In department stores and shopping malls fixed prices are just that.

POST & COMMUNICATIONS
Postal Rates
Domestic mail costs P5 for letters up to 20g (for letters weighing 21g to 40g, add P12 for Metro Manila and P15 for outside the capital) and takes one day to be delivered in Manila and four to five days to more-remote destinations. Express service (P20/P30 for inside/outside Manila) guarantees your letter's on-time delivery.

Rates for international first-class airmail letters of up to 20g are P17 (Asia), P21 (Middle East, Australia and New Zealand), P22 (Europe, Canada and the USA) and P23 (Africa and South America). Aerograms and postcards cost P11 to any country.

Rates for parcels are classified under the same zone system as letters. There are two types of parcel categories – one for printed matter and the other for anything other than printed matter. With either category, keep in mind that the post office needs to look at the contents, so go armed with packing materials but leave everything unsealed.

To give you an idea of parcel rates, the first 20g costs P19 to Australia/New Zealand and P20 to the UK/USA. Double those figures if your parcel weighs over 20g but under 50g. A parcel containing printed matter is restricted to a maximum of 5kg, while non-printed matter can go up to 20kg. These weight restrictions apply to one parcel only – if you need to send more, just split it into two or more parcels. All rates quoted here are for air mail. Sending parcels by sea mail (surface) generally costs less. Ask at a local post office for the latest rates and other details.

Sending Mail
The postal system is generally efficient – even from provincial towns, mail tends to get to where it is intended to go. Just don't tempt fate by enclosing cash (or, if you must send it, sandwich it between two pieces of

carbon paper so it's not visible when the envelope is held against the light). If you're nervous about stamps falling off or being removed, have the items franked instead.

Receiving Mail

Poste restante services are becoming a thing of the past and may be only available at the Manila Central Post Office. If you do need to have some mail sent to you, have it addressed with your name in block letters and/or underlined to help ensure that it gets to you.

Courier Services

LBC is a reliable company that has branches across the Philippines. LBC handles only documents, and you're limited to 500g per package, but it guarantees delivery worldwide within four working days. LBC rates are P600 to Australia/New Zealand, P960 to the UK and P780 to the USA.

Since it elected to make the Philippines the hub of its operations in Asia, FedEx has become a highly visible presence. A network of FedEx outlets (open seven days a week in big shopping malls) now serves customers nationwide. If you want, you may even call to have your parcel picked up. FedEx can deliver to anywhere in the world within two to three working days (provided there are no customs delays).

Telephone

In much of the Philippines, phones are about as common as Velcro dentures – and about as dependable. First you have to find a phone, which in many places will involve a long jeepney ride or a knock on the mayor's door to borrow his mobile phone. Once you've got your hands on a phone, you're often at the mercy of switchboard operators and dodgy lines that make you wish they'd just string together a big network of tin cans and taut wires instead.

OK, we're exaggerating, but not by much. Making telephone calls in the Philippines has gotten much easier with the emergence of other phone companies that have broken the monopoly of the Philippine Long Distance Telephone Company (PLDT), but there are still plenty of bugs in the system. Though International Direct Dial (IDD), Domestic Direct Dial (DDD) and operator-assisted calls are available, placing calls is seldom a simple affair.

In Manila and other big cities PLDT services have vastly improved, thanks to competition from other phone companies. More phone companies mean more available lines for subscribers – whereas it used to take five years or more for a new phone application to get approved, it can now take only months for a line to be installed. The problem is that it's not always easy to get through to a PLDT number from another company's number, and vice versa.

Within Luzon you should now be able to reach most numbers directly, though calls to/from far-flung areas like Samar can often only be placed through the operator, and this depends on you being able to reach the operator in the first place! The number for the PLDT domestic operator is ☎ 109 (☎ 108 for the international operator); for directory assistance in Manila, call ☎ 114 (☎ 112 for area/country code or regional inquiries). Those numbers work only if you're calling from a PLDT phone. You can't access the PLDT operator or directory inquiries from a non-PLDT phone. See the boxed text 'Useful Phone Numbers' for information on international dialling codes.

Mid-range hotels often have IDD/DDD phones in their rooms, but if you're averse to paying the (usually usurious) hotel surcharge, you can make your calls from a payphone in the foyer (lobby) or outside the hotel. In the provinces there are few private or public phones and you can only make or receive calls at your hotel or at the local branch of the main phone companies. At these offices an assistant places your call through the operator and transfers it to a booth when your number has been reached. Calls can literally take hours to get through, however, and it's not uncommon to get cut off or interrupted by the operator mid-call. If you have an important call to make, try and persuade the assistant to let you dial the number yourself so you can keep trying until you get through.

Phone companies have different arrangements for the codes they can access – few places can (or will) call ☎ 1 800 numbers, for example, and some private lines are programmed to receive but not make calls to mobile phones (see Mobile Phones later for details).

Many places (eg, the popular destinations of Puerto Galera and Sagada) are not yet linked by land lines, which means that mobile phones are the only connection to the outside world; if you're in a tourist area, many of the resorts will offer international phone services, but charges tend to be arbitrary and vary from one resort to another, so you'll have to decide whether the amount is reasonable or not.

IDD calls are cheaper than operator-assisted calls, and both PLDT and BayanTel offer a flat rate of US$0.40 per minute to anywhere around the world, regardless of what time you make the call.

At times it may actually be better to call reverse-charges (collect) rather than pay for a call locally. PLDT's Country Direct service puts you through to an operator in the country you are calling, who will then place your call for you. Dial ☎ 105 (☎ 10-10-500 for the USA) to enter the system, followed by the required country code (the most commonly used codes are listed in phone boxes). The service is available to over 40 destinations worldwide.

Many shop owners allow customers to make local calls from their private phone. The price of a call is about P5 for three minutes. These phones, however, are usually programmed not to make long-distance or mobile phone calls.

Throughout this guidebook we refer to telephone numbers with extensions in two distinct formats: where you see a phone number depicted as ☎ 123 4567–70, this indicates the range of the last two digits to be used as extensions, eg, you can dial ☎ 123 4567 or ☎ 123 4568 etc. Alternatively extensions are indicated as ☎ 123 4567/8910. Sometimes Filipinos may refer to extensions as the 'local' number, eg, ☎ 123 4567 local 340.

Phonecards Coin-operated phones are being phased out and have become rare in Manila, but card-operated phones are widely available in hotel foyers, commercial centres and shopping malls. Phonecards can be purchased from vending machines or kiosks in practically any shopping area, and come in various denominations, the most common of which is P100.

PLDT and the other phone companies issue phonecards, but these can be only used in the company's designated phones, so make sure you get the card you want. If only because PLDT phones are more widely available, it's probably best to buy a PLDT Fonkard Plus. PLDT claims you can use the card to call from PLDT payphones nationwide. Phonecards can be used to make IDD and DDD calls from public payphones, but make sure you have the right denomination to save yourself the hassle of getting suddenly cut off.

Another option is getting an international phonecard. Lonely Planet's ekno Communication Card is aimed specifically at travellers and provides cheap international calls, a range of messaging services and free email – for local calls, you're usually better off with a local card. You can join online at W www .ekno.lonelyplanet.com or by phone from the Philippines by dialling ☎ 1 800 1 119 0015. Once you have joined, to use ekno from the Philippines dial ☎ 1 800 1 119 0014.

Mobile Phones Now carried by legions of Filipinos, mobile phones are commonplace in the Philippines. If your phone company offers international roaming for the Philippines, you should be able to use your mobile phone (provided it's a relatively new model) and home SIM card in the Philippines, but check the roaming charges as they may be many times higher than Philippine rates.

In fact, you just might be better off buying a mobile phone locally. In big cities you can pick up a unit with text and other functions for as little as P3000, and that includes a SIM card and a prepaid call card. Globe and Smart are the two front runners in the local mobile phone industry, with Mobiline coming in third. The stiff competition between these service providers works to the advantage of consumers – calls can cost as little as P6.50 a minute. Text messaging costs only P1 to send.

Mobile-phone charges can easily be paid monthly or, as most people do it, with a prepaid card. Like phonecards, these come in various denominations and are readily available at phone kiosks in shopping centres. Locally purchased mobile phones can make IDD/NDD calls as well as receive calls from outside the country. Indeed, international rates for mobile phone calls are so low that mobile phones are usually the cheapest way to make international calls from the Philippines.

Fax
Fax services are offered by telegraph and telephone companies such as PT&T, and are readily available in big towns and cities but not in remote areas. Transmission speed varies widely, ranging from one to three pages per minute.

Email & Internet Access
Email and Internet services have taken off in a big way in the Philippines, and plenty of hotels, resorts and cybercafés will allow you to keep in touch with the virtual outside world. Even many of the smallest towns and islands have email facilities.

Rates for email/Internet access average between P40 and P50 per hour; in Cebu City, where there seems to be a cybercafé at every other street corner, the charge can be as low as P20 per hour. Heavily touristed Boracay, on the other hand, is pricey – P90 to P150 per hour.

If you've got a portable computer for this purpose, note the voltage used (see Electricity later in this chapter for details). US-style RJ-11 telephone adaptors are commonly used in the Philippines, so ensure that you at least have a US RJ-11 adaptor that works with your modem. Check out w www.teleadapt .com or w www.warrior.com for information on travelling with a portable computer.

There are two big Internet Service Providers (ISPs) that currently have dial-in

nodes to the Philippines: America Online (AOL; w www.aol.com) has a node in Manila (US$8 per hour) and another in Cebu (US$6 per hour). CompuServe (w www .compuserve.com) currently has two dial-in nodes in Manila – the World-Connect (INW) line is a steep US$25 per hour, while on Equant (EQT) the rate is US$10 per hour. Whatever ISP you choose, it's probably best to download a list of dial-in numbers before you leave home.

One option for collecting email through cybercafés is to open a free ekno Web-based email account online at w www.ekno.lonely planet.com. You can then access your mail from anywhere in the world from any Net-connected machine running a standard Web browser.

DIGITAL RESOURCES
The Lonely Planet website at w www.lonely planet.com is a good place to start your cyber research. Here you'll find succinct summaries on travelling to most places on earth, postcards from other travellers and the Thorn Tree bulletin board, where you can ask questions before you go, or dispense advice when you get back. You can also find travel news and updates to many of our most popular guidebooks, and the subwwway section links you to the most useful travel resources elsewhere on the Web.

Philippines-related sites pop up and vanish faster than you can say 'Page Not Found', but in addition to the many sites listed throughout this book, here are a few Web resources worth a look.

Dive Buddies Philippines (w www.divephil.com) Offers a lot of general information about diving and dive sites in the Philippines and is a good resource for those planning dive trips to the Philippines.

Lakbay.Net (w www.lakbay.net) The Lakbay site has lots of useful Philippines links, as well as shipping and bus schedules, and an online air-ticket booking service.

Philippines Department of Foreign Affairs (w www .dfa.gov.ph) The DFA's site lists Philippine embassies and consulates abroad, as well as foreign embassies and consulates in the Philippines. It also lists the latest Philippines visa info.

Philippines Department of Tourism (w www .tourism.gov.ph) DOT's site has useful general info about the Philippines, as well as lists of DOT office inside and outside the country.

Tanikalang Ginto (W www.filipinolinks.com) The vast Tanikalang Ginto Web directory is very catholic (with a small 'c') in its orientation – it offers useful links to nearly every topic under the Philippine sun.

US State Department (W www.travel.state.gov /philippines.html) Mildly paranoid but useful travel information and advisories are available from the US State Department.

BOOKS

Most books are published in different editions by different publishers in different countries. As a result, a book might be a hardcover rarity in one country and readily available in paperback in another. Fortunately, bookshops and libraries search by title or author, so your local bookshop or library is best placed to advise you on the availability of the following recommendations.

Lonely Planet

Language is the key to any culture, and those who want to get the most out of their trip to the Philippines would be advised to pick up a copy of Lonely Planet's *Pilipino (Tagalog) phrasebook*, which includes everything from jeepney jargon to gay and lesbian lingo. Likewise, serious divers will find Lonely Planet's new *Diving & Snorkeling Philippines,* a great source of information on the country's myriad dive sites.

Travel

Culture Shock! Philippines by Alfredo & Grace Roces offers some helpful illustrations of Filipino culture, though the points made are often simplistic and too general to take to heart.

Ants for Breakfast – Archaeological Adventures among the Kalinga by James M Skibo is a healthy supplement to the Culture Shock series. The book is a travelogue of asides and insights gleaned from fieldwork among the Kalinga people of the Cordilleras.

History & Politics

In an effort to get to the bottom of a very deep pit of patronage and corruption in the Philippines, James Hamilton-Paterson penned the sordid tale of *America's Boy – A Century of Colonialism in the Philippines*. The conclusion – which is basically, that Philippine politics is a bottomless pit – perhaps says as much about the way new writing on 'the

Third World' has come full circle to old Western notions of 'national character' as it does about the eternal return of patrons and clients in the islands.

A straight-up analysis is Stanley Karnow's *In Our Image – America's Empire in the Philippines*, another in his series of indictments of US foreign policy in Asia.

The Snap Revolution (Granta No 18) by James Fenton is the full-length version of the journalist-poet's entrance into Philippine politics as he rushed to Manila to cover Marcos' 'snap election' – a call that led to the 'people power' movement, or EDSA (Epifanio de los Santos) Revolution, of 1986.

Looking at life after the US military shipped out in the early 1990s, *Looted – The Philippines after the Bases* by journalist Donald Kirk gives another rendition of the familiar refrain, 'the more things change…'.

Brilliantly researched, *Power from the Forest – The Politics of Logging* by Marites Dañguilan-Vitug tells of timber plundered in the fragile archipelago.

Brian McAllister Linn's meticulously researched *The Philippine War 1899–1902* debunks a lot of myths about a conflict that has been the subject of much revisionist history in the past two decades.

Finally, Hiroo Onoda's *No Surrender: My Thirty-Year War* (English translation by Charles Terry) is a fascinating account of a Japanese soldier who remained in the jungles of the Philippines for 30 years, stubbornly refusing to believe that the Japanese had been defeated in WWII. An account of wartime and postwar events from the Japanese perspective, this book is a rarity in the English language.

General

James Hamilton-Paterson's book *Ghosts of Manila* is a chilling yet entertaining 'docufiction' of life, death and the corrupt chains binding Filipinos in the city's slums. He also wrote *Playing with Water – Passion and Solitude on a Philippine Island* while hanging out on an islet near Marinduque.

William Boyd's *The Blue Afternoon* skilfully weaves US–Philippine military relations into a love story/detective drama partly set in Manila in 1902.

Philippine Wildlife by José Ma & Lorenzo P Tan isn't a field guide, but it does provide an overview of the archipelago's nonhuman inhabitants, including those most endangered by humans.

Plundering Paradise: The Struggle for the Environment in the Philippines by Robin Broad et al is an excellent account of the destruction of the flora and fauna of the Philippines, and of some of the efforts to halt the destruction.

Burning Heart – A Portrait of the Philippines, by Jessica Hagedorn with photographs by Marissa Roth, is a coffee-table book with a conscience. A week spent in the country by 35 international photojournalists is recorded in *Philippines – A Journey Through the Archipelago* by James Hamilton-Paterson et al.

FILMS

If you're a fan of seriously B-grade action or horror flicks, you've probably seen a film set in the Philippines. The islands have been the unheralded setting for about 200 internationally released films, nearly all of them belonging to the 'more blood for less' genre. The award for best (or worst) title goes to *Women of Transplant Island* (1973).

Hollywood has also been busy recreating the Vietnam War on Philippine soil. Aside from *Hamburger Hill* (1987) and *Born on the Fourth of July* (1989), the Philippines has famously been host to Francis Ford Coppola's *Apocalypse Now*. The film was shot in Baler and Pagsanjan on Luzon in 1976 and 1977. Surfers might note that there were no waves the day the renowned surf scene was filmed; instead, the crew resorted to detonating explosives in the water. Less than a decade later, *Platoon*, Oliver Stone's passion play on the Vietnam War (the US military called the script 'totally unrealistic' and refused to assist), was filmed in the Philippines while Marcos was being overthrown.

Don't blame Manila, but scenes from *An Officer and a Gentleman* (1982) were shot there. In the same year, the capital became 1965-era Jakarta in Peter Weir's *The Year of Living Dangerously*. The Philippines also did its best to act like Thailand for director Jonathan Kaplan in his teenage fantasy flick, *Brokedown Palace* (1999).

NEWSPAPERS & MAGAZINES

Anyone who misses the hoary old days of a truly free press will feel right at home in the Philippines. After 20 years of severe censorship under Marcos, the EDSA Revolution ushered in a new era for the press as independent national and local newspapers and magazines mushroomed overnight.

A journalistic free-for-all of generally very high standards has resulted, with English-language dailies running the gamut from the conservative *Manila Bulletin* to the critical *Philippine Daily Inquirer*. *Today* is a well-written broadsheet, while the *Philippine Star* is a cheerful feel-good paper. Other papers in the country include Cebu's *Sun Star Daily* and Dumaguete's *Visayan Daily Star*.

Well-stocked newsstands are found in towns and cities all over the country. In addition to the broadsheets, there's a slew of sleazy tabloids that dish up a juicy menu of political and show-biz gossip, but though they're often peppered with recognisable English words, all of these tabloids are in Tagalog or Pilipino.

The *International Herald-Tribune*, a compendium of articles from major world newspapers (plus the *New York Times* crossword puzzle), can be found in the big hotels and in bookshops in larger cities. International magazines on offer include *Time*, *Newsweek* and the *Far Eastern Economic Review*.

Most local magazines are published in English, so you could always turn to them for the latest on the political scene, fashion, eating and drinking etc. *Mega* and *Metro* are fashion/lifestyle glossies, heavily patterned after the American *Vanity Fair*; *Newsbreak* and *Graphic,* that present weekly news summaries along with columns on a variety of topics. *M Zone* caters to the contemporary executive with its mix of hip talk and business, and *Colors* features in-depth and well-written articles on destinations and events in Manila and around the country.

Finally, for scuba divers, *The Philippine Diver* is a glossy magazine that is more environmentally conscious than most. It prints three issues a year and its website (**w** www .diver.com.ph) is worth checking out.

RADIO & TV

There's a lot on offer over the airwaves – Manila alone has nearly 60 radio stations. If your mornings aren't complete without a chatty radio drive show, try RX 93.1 FM Monster Radio, a Manila-based music/variety station. Jazz 83.3 FM and WRR 101.9 FM are also quite popular. Voice of America, Deutsche Welle and the BBC World Service

Singapore (3915.0kHz, 75m band) are all available on shortwave.

Some 22 commercial TV stations vie for your attention, seven of them based in Manila. Manila stations offer both English-language and Tagalog programmes, plus some US camera fodder such as *Saved by the Bell*. Cable TV beams BBC World, Cinemax, CNN, ESPN, Fox News, HBO, Viva Cinema and a whole array of other networks into homes and hotels.

PHOTOGRAPHY & VIDEO
Film & Equipment
It's a good idea to bring your own slide film, as it's probably 'fresher' than the film available in the Philippines. Print film spends less time on shop shelves so it should be more reliable, but it's better to stock up where you can. Kodak Ektachrome 100 ASA costs about P265, 200 ASA around P285 and 400 ASA around P295.

Fast and reliable one-hour film processing is available in Manila and major cities for approximately P5.50 per print plus a P50 developing charge; cheaper processing takes longer. Slide processing is available only at some professional labs.

Airport Security
X-ray equipment is supposed to be safe for film, but it's not worth putting that claim to the test with your precious rolls. You can always ask to have your film inspected separately if you're passing through numerous airports, especially the smaller ones.

TIME
The Philippines is eight hours ahead of Greenwich Mean Time (GMT), also known as Universal Time Coordinated (UTC). Thus, when it's noon in Manila, it's 8pm the previous day in Los Angeles and 11pm the previous evening in New York; 4am the same day in London; 1pm the same day in Tokyo; and 2pm the same day in Sydney.

Official time in Davao, Mindanao's capital, is curiously about 10 minutes ahead of the rest of the country. No-one's quite sure how or why it happened, but no-one seems too troubled about it.

ELECTRICITY
In most places in the Philippines, electricity is 220V, 50Hz to 60Hz; exceptions are Baguio (wired once-upon-a-time by US occupation forces), where voltage is 110V; and some top-end hotels, which have both 220V and 110V outlets. Plugs are of the US-style flat two-pin variety.

Brownouts are common, as are low-power generators in smaller towns – and no electricity at all in others. Power cuts are generally only a minor inconvenience to travellers (unless you're big on sending long emails). Besides, the absence of electricity in far-flung corners offers a rare respite from certain modern conveniences such as 'videoke'.

WEIGHTS & MEASURES
The Philippines uses the metric system. (If *you* don't, see the conversion table on the inside back cover.) Weights are normally quoted in kilograms and distances in kilometres, though feet and yards are still often used to describe short lengths.

LAUNDRY
Coin-operated laundrettes are nonexistent, but your hotel or guesthouse can arrange laundry service, and you'll get clean undies back in one or two days. Laundry charges depend on how many stars your hotel carries next to its name; in star-less hostels or budget establishments a shirt or blouse will probably cost P15 to P20.

In the big cities, you can find fast and efficient laundry services in many neighbourhoods, especially in the vicinity of guest- houses and economical hotels. They may offer a pick-up and delivery service if your laundry meets a certain weight minimum. Charges vary from one place to another, but the average charge is P40 per 1kg of wash and dry (P80 for wash, dry and press). Dry cleaning is also available (a business shirt will cost P80).

TOILETS
A toilet is referred to as a 'comfort room' (or CR). In Tagalog, men are *lalake* and women are *babae*. There are no public toilets, and Filipino men will often avail themselves of the nearest outdoor wall – hence the signs scrawled in many places: 'Bawal Ang Umihi Dito!' ('No Pissing Here!'). If you need a toilet, try the nearest fast-food restaurant.

When camping or hiking in the great outdoors, where there is a toilet you should use it. Where there is none, bury your waste (at least 100m from any watercourse) and cover it with soil and a rock.

HEALTH

Travel health depends on your predeparture preparations, your daily health care while travelling and how you handle any medical problem that does develop. While the potential dangers can seem quite frightening, in reality few travellers experience anything more than an upset stomach.

The information in this section covers the basics of travel health in the Philippines; for more details, see the resources listed under Travel Health Guides later.

Predeparture Planning

Immunisations No vaccinations are legally required for entry into the Philippines unless you are arriving from an area infected with yellow fever. Most travellers from Western countries will have been immunised against various diseases during childhood, but your doctor may still recommend booster shots against measles or polio, diseases still prevalent in many developing countries.

Plan your vaccinations ahead: some of them require more than one injection, and some should not be given together. It is recommended that you seek medical advice at least six weeks before travel. Record all vaccinations on an International Health Certificate, available from your doctor or government health department.

Everyday Health

Normal body temperature is up to 37°C (98.6°F); more than 2°C (4°F) higher indicates a high fever. The normal adult pulse rate is 60 to 100 per minute (children 80 to 100, babies 100 to 140). As a general rule the pulse increases about 20 beats per minute for each 1°C (2°F) rise in fever.

Respiration (breathing) rate is also an indicator of illness. Count the number of breaths per minute: Between 12 and 20 is normal for adults and older children (up to 30 for younger children, 40 for babies). People with a high fever or serious respiratory illness breathe more quickly than normal. More than 40 shallow breaths a minute may indicate pneumonia.

Discuss your requirements with your doctor, but vaccinations you might consider for this trip include diphtheria, tetanus, typhoid, polio, hepatitis A, hepatitis B, tuberculosis, Japanese B encephalitis and rabies.

Malaria Medication Malaria does exist in the Philippines; see Insect-Borne Diseases later in this section for details. Antimalarial drugs do not prevent you from being infected but kill the malaria parasites during a stage in their development and significantly reduce the risk of becoming very ill or dying. Expert advice on medication should be sought, as there are many factors to consider, including the area to be visited, the risk of exposure to malaria-carrying mosquitoes, the side effects of medication, your medical history and whether you are a child or an adult or pregnant. Travellers to isolated areas may like to carry a treatment dose of medication for use if symptoms occur.

Health Insurance Make sure that you have adequate health insurance. See Travel Insurance under Visas & Documents earlier in this chapter for details.

Travel Health Guides Lonely Planet's *Healthy Travel Asia & India* by Dr Isabelle Young is a thorough, user-friendly guide full of valuable tips. *Travel with Children* by Cathy Lanigan also includes advice on travel health for younger children.

There are a number of excellent travel health sites on the Internet. From the Lonely Planet home page there are links at w www .lonelyplanet.com/weblinks/wlheal.htm to the World Health Organization and the US Centers for Disease Control & Prevention.

Other Preparations Make sure you're healthy *before* you start travelling. If you are going on a long trip, make sure your teeth are OK. If you wear glasses, take a spare pair and your prescription (and if you're going to be jungle trekking etc bring some anti-fog solution).

If you require a particular medication, take an adequate supply, as it may not be available locally. Take part of the packaging showing the generic name rather than the brand, which will make getting replacements easier. It's a good idea to have a legible prescription or letter from your doctor to show that you legally use the medication to avoid any problems.

Basic Rules

Care in what you eat and drink is the most important health rule; stomach upsets are the most likely travel problem, but the majority of these upsets will be relatively minor. Don't become paranoid: trying the local food is part of the experience of travel.

Food If you're worried about your stomach, shellfish, such as mussels, oysters and clams, should be avoided, as well as undercooked meat, particularly in the form of mince. (Steaming does not make shellfish safe to eat.) If a place looks clean and well run, and the vendor also looks clean and healthy, then the food is probably safe.

Drinks

The number-one rule is *be careful of the water* and especially ice. Although many people claim that water is safe to drink in Philippine cities, this is not usually the case. Likewise, water in rural areas is not reliable, as it often comes from dodgy wells or unknown sources. Wherever you go, stick to bottled water or drink only water that has been boiled, filtered with a reliable filter or purified with iodine or similar. Only use water from containers with a serrated seal – not tops or corks. Better still, buy or bring one water bottle and have it refilled at 'water stations' in large cities (where many of the locals get their drinking water). These are usually very cheap and the water is trustworthy.

In hot climates you should always make sure you drink enough – don't rely on feeling thirsty to indicate when you should drink. Not needing to urinate, or passing very dark-yellow urine is a danger sign. Excessive sweating is another problem and can lead to loss of salt and muscle cramping.

Medical Problems & Treatment

Self-diagnosis and treatment can be risky, so you should always seek medical help. An embassy, consulate or major hotel can usually recommend a local doctor or clinic. Although we do give drug dosages in this section, they are for emergency use only. Correct diagnosis is vital. We have used the generic names for medications – check with a pharmacist for brands available locally.

Note that antibiotics should ideally be administered only under medical supervision. Take only the recommended dose at the prescribed intervals and use the whole course, even if the illness seems to be cured earlier. Stop immediately if there are any serious reactions and don't use the antibiotic at all if you are unsure that you have the correct one.

Medical Kit Check List

Following is a list of items you should consider including in your medical kit – consult your pharmacist for brands available in your country.

☐ **Aspirin or paracetamol (acetaminophen in the USA)** – for pain or fever
☐ **Antihistamine** – for allergies, eg, hay fever; to ease the itch from insect bites or stings; and to prevent motion sickness
☐ **Cold and flu tablets, throat lozenges and nasal decongestant**
☐ **Multivitamins** – consider for long trips, when dietary vitamin intake may be inadequate
☐ **Antibiotics** – consider including these if you're travelling well off the beaten track; see your doctor, as they must be prescribed, and carry the prescription with you
☐ **Loperamide or diphenoxylate** – 'blockers' for diarrhoea
☐ **Prochlorperazine or metaclopramide** – for nausea and vomiting
☐ **Rehydration mixture** – to prevent dehydration, which may occur, for example, during bouts of diarrhoea; particularly important when travelling with children
☐ **Insect repellent, sunscreen, lip balm and eye drops**
☐ **Calamine lotion, sting relief spray or aloe vera** – to ease irritation from sunburn and insect bites or stings
☐ **Antifungal cream or powder** – for fungal skin infections and thrush
☐ **Antiseptic (such as povidone-iodine)** – for cuts and grazes
☐ **Bandages, Band-Aids (plasters) and other wound dressings**
☐ **Water purification tablets or iodine**
☐ **Scissors, tweezers and a thermometer** – note that mercury thermometers are prohibited by airlines
☐ **Sterile kit** – in case you need injections in a country with medical hygiene problems; discuss with your doctor

Some people are allergic to commonly pre-scribed antibiotics such as penicillin; carry this information (eg, on a bracelet) when travelling.

Hospitals & Clinics

International health organisations are cau-tious by nature (it goes with the territory), and advise travellers to the Philippines to seek medical care for serious problems outside the country where possible. Concerns over blood-supply screening and the availability of single-use, disposable needles and syringes are frequently cited reasons.

Health care is limited in smaller centres, and generally confined to home remedies in remote areas. State-owned hospitals and private practices are often poorly equipped, so in an emergency, try to reach the nearest town and check in to a private hospital.

The local pharmaceutical racket has been under fire in the country for some time: phar-macies dispense brand-name drugs like candy, and at extortionate prices compared to neighbouring countries. Not only does this produce drug-resistant strains of bugs, it's also a strain on the budget of the average Filipino. Note also that doctors often demand cash on the spot for services.

The Americans did leave a number of very good hospitals – Manila's private hospitals are excellent, if expensive, and you'll get treated quickly; see Medical Services under Information in the Manila chapter for more details.

Specialised emergency treatment is in short supply outside Manila: ambulances from the capital regularly attend road wrecks three hours away. In fact, it's fair to say that emergency services are a mess, not least because of the long odds of making good time in traffic anywhere in the event of an emergency.

Dental treatment is adequate, at least in cities and towns.

Environmental Hazards

Air Pollution In Manila, air pollution is an issue. Air pollution can be a health hazard, particularly if you suffer from lung disease such as asthma. It can also aggravate coughs, colds and sinus problems and cause eye irritation. Consider avoiding badly pol-luted areas, especially if you have asthma, or you could invest in a surgical mask.

Prickly Heat Essentially, prickly heat is an itchy rash caused by excessive perspiration trapped under the skin. It usually strikes peo-ple who have just arrived in a hot climate. Keeping cool, bathing often, drying the skin and using a mild talcum or prickly-heat pow-der or resorting to air-conditioning may help.

Heat Exhaustion Dehydration and salt deficiency can cause heat exhaustion. Take time to acclimatise to high temperatures, drink sufficient liquids and do not do any-thing too physically demanding.

Salt deficiency is characterised by fa-tigue, lethargy, headaches, giddiness and muscle cramps; salt tablets may help, but adding extra salt to your food is better.

Anhydrotic heat exhaustion (caused by an inability to sweat) is rare and tends to affect people who have been in a hot climate for some time, rather than newcomers. Treat-ment involves removal to a cooler climate.

Heatstroke This serious, and occasionally fatal, condition can occur if the body's heat-regulating mechanism breaks down and the body temperature rises to dangerous levels. Long, continuous periods of exposure to high temperatures and insufficient fluids can leave you vulnerable to heatstroke.

The symptoms are feeling unwell, not sweating very much (or at all) and a high body temperature (39°C to 41°C, or 102°F to 106°F). Where sweating has ceased, the skin becomes flushed and red. Severe, throbbing headaches and lack of coordination will also occur, and casualties may be confused or ag-gressive. Eventually they will become deliri-ous or convulse.

Hospitalisation is essential, but in the in-terim get casualties out of the sun, remove their clothing, cover them with a wet sheet or towel and then fan continually. Give fluids if they are conscious.

Sunburn In the tropics or at high altitude (on some of the Philippines' volcanos, for ex-ample) you can get sunburnt surprisingly quickly, even through cloud. Use a sunscreen, a hat, and a barrier cream for your nose and lips. Calamine lotion or commercial after-sun preparations are good for mild sunburn.

Protect your eyes with good quality sun-glasses, particularly if you will be near water, sand or snow.

Infectious Diseases

Diarrhoea Simple things like a change of water, food or climate can cause a mild bout of diarrhoea, but a few rushed toilet trips with no other symptoms is not indicative of a major problem. Dehydration is the main danger with diarrhoea, particularly in children or the elderly, as it can occur quite quickly. Under all circumstances, *fluid replacement* is the most important thing to remember. Weak black tea with a little sugar, soda water, or soft drinks allowed to go flat and diluted 50% with clean water are all good.

With severe diarrhoea, a rehydrating solution is preferable to replace minerals and salts lost. Commercially available oral rehydration salts (ORS) are very useful; add them to boiled or bottled water. In an emergency you can make up a solution of six teaspoons of sugar and a half-teaspoon of salt to 1L of boiled or bottled water. You need to drink at least the same volume of fluid that you are losing in bowel movements and vomiting. Urine is the best guide to the adequacy of replacement – if you have small amounts of concentrated urine, you need to drink more. Keep drinking small amounts often. Stick to a bland diet as you recover.

Gut-paralysing drugs such as loperamide or diphenoxylate can be used to bring relief from the symptoms, although they do not actually cure the problem. Only use these drugs if you do not have access to toilets, eg, if you *must* travel. Note that these drugs are not recommended for children aged 12 years and under.

In certain situations antibiotics may be required: any diarrhoea with blood or mucus (dysentery), any diarrhoea with fever, profuse watery diarrhoea, persistent diarrhoea not improving after 48 hours and severe diarrhoea. These suggest a more serious cause of diarrhoea, and in such situations gut-paralysing drugs should be avoided and medical treatment should be sought.

Hepatitis The word hepatitis is a general term for inflammation of the liver. It's a common disease worldwide. Several viruses cause hepatitis and they differ in the way they are transmitted. The symptoms are similar in all forms of the illness, and include fever, chills, headache, fatigue, feelings of weakness and aches and pains, followed by loss of appetite, nausea, vomiting, abdominal pain, dark urine, light-coloured faeces, jaundiced (yellowed) skin and yellowing of the whites of the eyes. People who have had hepatitis should avoid alcohol for some time after the illness, as the liver needs time to recover.

The most common form, hepatitis A, is transmitted by contaminated food and drinking water. You should seek immediate medical advice, but there's not much you can do apart from resting, drinking lots of fluids, eating lightly and avoiding fatty foods. Hepatitis E is transmitted in the same way as hepatitis A; it can be particularly serious in pregnant women.

There are almost 300 million chronic carriers of hepatitis B in the world. It is spread through contact with infected blood, blood products or body fluids, eg, through sexual contact, unsterilised needles and blood transfusions, or contact with blood via small breaks in the skin. Other risk situations include having a shave, tattoo or body piercing with contaminated equipment. The symptoms of hepatitis B may be more severe than type A and the disease can lead to long-term problems such as chronic liver damage, liver cancer or a long-term carrier state. Hepatitis C and D are spread in the same way as hepatitis B and can also lead to long-term complications.

There are vaccines against hepatitis A and B, but there are currently no vaccines against the other types of hepatitis. Following the basic rules about food and water (hepatitis A and E) and avoiding risk situations (hepatitis B, C and D) are important preventative measures.

HIV & AIDS Infection with the human immunodeficiency virus (HIV) may lead to acquired immune deficiency syndrome (AIDS), which is a fatal disease. Any exposure to blood, blood products or body fluids may put the individual at risk. The disease is often transmitted through sexual contact or dirty needles – vaccinations, acupuncture, tattooing and body piercing can potentially be as dangerous as intravenous drug use. HIV/AIDS can also be spread through infected blood transfusions; outside the major hospitals in the Philippines, blood used for transfusions may not have been adequately screened.

If you do need an injection, ask to see the syringe unwrapped in front of you, or take a needle and syringe pack with you. Fear of HIV infection should never preclude treatment for serious medical conditions.

Intestinal Worms These parasites are common in some rural areas of the Philippines. Some worms may be ingested on food such as undercooked meat (eg, tapeworms) and some enter through your skin (eg, hookworms). Infestations may not show up for some time and although they are generally not serious, if left untreated some can cause severe health problems later. Consider having a stool test when you return home to check for these and determine the appropriate treatment.

Rabies This fatal viral infection is found throughout the Philippines. Many animals can be infected (such as dogs, cats, bats and monkeys) and it is their saliva which is infectious. Any bite, scratch or even lick from an animal should be cleaned immediately and thoroughly. Scrub with soap and running water, then apply alcohol or iodine solution. Medical help should be sought promptly to receive a course of injections to prevent the onset of symptoms and death.

Schistosomiasis Also known as bilharzia, this disease is spread by tiny freshwater worms and is present in many parts of the Philippines, particularly on the southern islands (deforestation has made Mindanao a notable risk area). Avoid swimming or bathing in fresh water (ocean water and well-chlorinated swimming pools are OK) – even deep water can be infected. If you do get wet, dry off quickly and dry your clothes as well.

A blood test is the most reliable way to diagnose the disease, but it will not show positive until a number of weeks after exposure.

Typhoid This dangerous gut infection is caused by contaminated water and food. Medical help *must* be sought. In its early stages, sufferers may feel they have a bad cold or flu on the way, as early symptoms are a headache, body aches and a fever that rises a little each day until it is around 40°C (104°F) or more. The victim's pulse is often slow – unlike a normal fever where the pulse increases. There may also be vomiting, abdominal pain, diarrhoea or constipation. In the second week, the high fever and slow

pulse continue and a few pink spots may appear on the body; trembling, delirium, weakness, weight loss and dehydration may occur.

The fever should be treated by keeping the victims cool and giving them fluids, as dehydration should also be watched for.

Insect-Borne Diseases

Malaria This serious, potentially fatal disease is spread by mosquito bites. If you're travelling in rural parts of endemic areas (eg, the southern Philippines), it's important to avoid mosquito bites. Talk to your doctor about antimalarial medication.

Rural areas of many parts of the country, especially those below 600m altitude, are a risk year-round. There's no reported risk in Metro Manila, on the islands of Bohol and Catanduanes or in Cebu Province. Chloroquine-resistant strains have been found on Basilan, Luzon, Mindanao, Mindoro and Palawan, as well as in the Sulu Archipelago.

Malaria symptoms range from fever, chills and sweating, headache, diarrhoea and abdominal pains to a vague feeling of ill-health. Seek medical help immediately if malaria is suspected. Without treatment malaria can rapidly become more serious and can be fatal.

Travellers are advised to prevent mosquito bites at all times. The main messages are:

• Wear light-coloured clothing.
• Wear long trousers and long-sleeved shirts.
• Use mosquito repellents containing the compound DEET on exposed areas (prolonged overuse of DEET may be harmful, especially to children, but its use is considered preferable to being bitten by disease-transmitting mosquitoes).
• Avoid perfumes or aftershave.
• Use a mosquito net impregnated with mosquito repellent (permethrin) – it may be worth taking your own.
• Impregnating clothes with permethrin effectively deters mosquitoes and other insects.

Dengue Fever Dengue is transmitted by mosquitoes and is fast becoming one of the top public-health problems in the tropical world. Unlike the malaria-carrying mosquito, the mosquito that transmits the dengue virus is most active during the day. It's found mainly in urban areas, in and around human dwellings.

Signs and symptoms of dengue fever include a sudden onset of high fever, headache, joint and muscle pains (hence its old name, 'breakbone fever'), nausea and vomiting. A rash of small red spots sometimes appears three to four days after the onset of fever. In the early phase of illness, dengue may be mistaken for other infectious diseases, including malaria and influenza. Recovery even from simple dengue fever may be prolonged, with tiredness lasting for several weeks.

You should seek medical attention as soon as possible if you think you may be infected. Aspirin should be avoided, as it increases the risk of haemorrhaging. The best prevention is to avoid mosquito bites at all times.

Cuts, Bites & Stings

Jellyfish Avoid contact with cone shells, sea snakes or jellyfish – seek local advice. Dousing in vinegar will deactivate any jellyfish stingers that have not 'fired'. Calamine lotion, antihistamines and analgesics may reduce the reaction and relieve the pain.

Leeches You'll find leeches may be present in damp rainforest conditions. Trekkers and hikers often get leeches on their legs or in their boots. Salt or a lit cigarette end will make them fall off. Do not pull them off, as the bite is then more likely to become infected. Clean and apply pressure if the point of attachment is bleeding. An insect repellent may keep them away.

Snakes Cobras, including the king cobra, exist in the Philippines, but you're extremely unlikely to meet one. To minimise your chances of being bitten, always wear boots, socks and long trousers when walking through undergrowth where snakes may be present. Don't put your hands into holes, and be careful when collecting firewood.

Snake bites do not cause instantaneous death and antivenins are usually available. Immediately wrap the bitten limb tightly, as you would for a sprained ankle, and then attach a splint to immobilise it. Keep the victim still and seek medical help, if possible with the dead snake for identification. Don't attempt to catch the snake if there is a possibility of being bitten again. Tourniquets and sucking out the poison are now comprehensively discredited.

Less Common Diseases

The following diseases pose a small risk to travellers, and so are mentioned only in passing. Seek medical advice if you think you may have any of these diseases.

Chikungunya Fever Transmitted by mosquitoes, this viral infection occurs in the Visayas. Sudden pain in one or more joints, fever, headache, nausea and rash are the main symptoms. It is rarely fatal, though stiffness in the joints can last for weeks or months. No vaccine is currently available.

Cholera This is the worst of the watery diarrhoeas, and medical help should be sought. It occurs in many parts of the Philippines, though outbreaks are generally widely reported, so you can avoid such problem areas.

Typhus Mite-borne typhus occurs in deforested areas of the country (eg, on Mindanao). Typhus starts with fever, chills, headache and muscle pains, followed a few days later by a body rash. There is often a large painful sore at the site of the bite and nearby lymph nodes are swollen and painful. Typhus can be treated under medical supervision.

Seek local advice on areas where ticks pose a danger and always check your skin carefully for ticks after walking in a danger area such as a tropical forest. An insect repellent can help, and walkers in tick-infested areas should consider having their boots and trousers impregnated with benzyl benzoate and dibutylphthalate. If a tick is found attached, press down around the tick's head with tweezers, grab the head (and *only* the head) and gently pull upwards.

WOMEN TRAVELLERS

As a rule, Filipino men are unfailing in their efforts to charm women, especially foreign women. Whether chauvinist or chivalrous, the approach taken to women travellers will involve a lot of compliments and attempts to get a conversation going. You may occasionally get the impression that you're being treated to a human version of a rooster ritual, but it's all pretty harmless.

Things get more interesting down south, where young men from conservative Muslim communities in particular have yet to come to grips with your very presence. The novel idea of a woman who may in principle have sexual relations with a man before marriage tends to send some of them into a rather aggressive form of confusion, and you can be subject to unwelcome verbal advances.

It is extremely unlikely to go further than this, however, and one solution is to announce that you are in fact 'a widow' (being 'married' isn't a deterrent).

Women travellers should also be aware that tampons are not widely available in the Philippines (pads are more commonly used and are more commonly available). If you use tampons, be sure to bring an adequate supply from home.

GAY & LESBIAN TRAVELLERS

Homosexuality is generally out in the open, with *bakla* or *bading* (gay men) and *tomboy* (lesbians) generally accepted by society at large.

There are gay cruising places in Manila, such as particular shopping malls and movie houses, but you should be wary of police (or con men masquerading as police) and hustlers. Remedios Circle in Malate is a lively gay area, and lodging in the neighbourhood is usually gay friendly. A gay beauty pageant is held here annually. The Gay Pride March in June also takes place around the Circle.

Online gay and lesbian resources for the Philippines include Dragon Castle (w www.dragoncastle.net/philippines.html) and Utopia Asian Gay & Lesbian Resources (w www.utopia-asia.com).

DISABLED TRAVELLERS

Like most developing countries, the Philippines lacks the convenient infrastructure and services that make getting around easier for the disabled. Very rarely will you find wheelchair-accessible toilets or wheelchair ramps. Moreover, the lack of proper footpaths and the anarchic traffic conditions of cities like Manila make getting around a real problem for the mobility impaired. On the plus side, you will find that Filipinos are quick to offer assistance. Furthermore, prices are cheap enough in the Philippines to make hiring a taxi for the day and/or even a personal assistant a reasonable option.

SENIOR TRAVELLERS

Senior citizens get respect in the family-oriented Philippines and this will be extended to older visitors. The main issue for senior travellers is the tropical heat, which is more quickly enervating than the climate you are probably used to – pace yourself and keep up the fluids.

The local tourism industry has yet to catch on to the concept of independent senior travel, so formal benefits are limited; PAL, Cebu Pacific, Air Philippines and Asian Spirit all offer a 20% discount on the regular fare for people aged 60 years or older, but first check out the two- or three-day advance promotional fares as these may actually be cheaper.

TRAVEL WITH CHILDREN

Filipinos are simply crazy about kids, and rather fond of parents, too – you and your offspring will be the focus of many conversations, and your children won't lack for playful company.

You should supervise your children when swimming or playing on beaches, and make sure they understand not to touch coral. Bring plenty of sunscreen and light clothes for sun protection. It's important to keep small children well hydrated in a hot climate.

You can usually buy disposable nappies (diapers) and infant formula in most towns and all cities, but be sure to stock up on such things before heading off the beaten track.

Lonely Planet's *Travel with Children* by Cathy Lanigan has more useful advice for tropical travel with kids.

DANGERS & ANNOYANCES

There's no glossing over the fact that the Philippines has more than its share of dangers and annoyances. These range from the danger of kidnapping in the south of the country to the wide range of scams and rip-offs that await the unwary traveller in Manila. That said, there is no reason to be overly nervous about visiting the Philippines: most Filipinos are honest folks who will go out of their way to help a traveller. More importantly, most of the dangers in the Philippines are of the opportunistic kind.

Of course, it's not just the outright dangers that can make travel unpleasant in various parts of the Philippines, it's the annoyances. Depending upon your sensibilities and values, you may find the overt prostitution scene quite disturbing, particularly if you are unlucky enough to see evidence of the Philippines' bustling child prostitution industry (in places like Angeles). Fortunately, as you travel away from the

Drug Warning

There has been a wave of drug robberies in the Philippines in recent years. A powerful sedative has been used by thieves to drug their victims before robbing them. Most of these attacks take place in Manila, but there's no reason to suspect that this successful method won't spread to other areas.

The modus operandi is usually the same: two friendly women approach an unsuspecting traveller and offer to show him/her around. After a while, the traveller is invited to a restaurant or home for a drink or a meal. Even though everyone may drink and eat from the same container, at some point, the drug is stealthily placed into the traveller's food or drink. The last thing the traveller remembers is feeling very sleepy. Several hours later, the traveller comes to in an empty lot or an alleyway, minus, needless to say, wallet, passport, watch and jewellery.

We've received several letters from victims of this scheme, most of whom were deeply traumatised by the incident. Thus, we recommend that you treat any overly friendly 'tour guides' with suspicion. More importantly, *do not* accept food and drink from strangers. Naturally, in a friendly country like the Philippines, where 99% of people mean well, this puts the traveller in a dilemma. If you do find yourself in a position of being offered food or drink, think very carefully about the circumstances in which you met your new friends – was it truly accidental or did these people seek you out? The answer could make the difference between a memorable trip and a nightmare.

urban centres and some resorts, you will encounter less and less of this.

It's also worth pointing out that Manila itself can be extremely challenging for some travellers. The poverty, air pollution, crowds and horrendous traffic conditions are enough to make even the most seasoned traveller yearn for escape. Luckily, escape is usually no more than a quick bus or ferry ride away. Moreover, if you just can't face the chaos of Manila, you can avoid it entirely by flying in and out of Cebu, down in the Visayas (see the Getting There & Away chapter for details).

Finally, Filipinos have a unique greeting for male (and sometimes female) Westerners: 'Hey Joe!' ('Hey Kano!' is a less used variation). Both are hangovers from World War II when the country was overrun by GI Joes or American soldiers ('kano' comes from 'Americano') and are used ad nauseam. Of course, if your name's Joe, you'll feel pretty special. If not, you may start to feel like a clown sent especially to give the locals a laugh.

For details on the dangers and scams that exist in the Philippines, and for tips on how to best avoid troubles, see the boxed texts 'Safe Travel in the Philippines' and 'Drug Warning' in this chapter.

LEGAL MATTERS

Like anywhere else, it's best not to have a brush with the law in the Philippines. But should you find yourself in trouble and in need of urgent assistance, your first recourse is your embassy, so make it a point to write down the phone number as a protective measure.

The most common legal problem encountered by travellers in the Philippines is overstaying one's visa. Provided you haven't overstayed by too long, you can usually pay a fine when leaving the country as 'punishment' for overstaying. However, this is very much up to the discretion of the immigration authorities and you could face more severe penalties. All in all, it's best to avoid overstaying (see Visas earlier in this chapter for more details).

Though drug use or smuggling does not automatically carry the death penalty in the Philippines, as it does in some other Southeast Asian countries, it's nonetheless a very serious offence. In fact, depending on the type and amount of drug he/she is carrying, the offender can end up on death row. Another grave offence that tourists would be well-advised to steer clear of is possession of firearms. The Philippines has gained a certain notoriety as a source of illegal firearms; don't be tempted by the availability of these weapons.

If you do get into trouble in the Philippines, after contacting your embassy you may also want to contact a lawyer. Almost all lawyers in the Philippines speak good

Safe Travel in the Philippines

There's no doubt about it: there are some real dangers in the Philippines. That's not to say that travel to the Philippines should be avoided, but it does make sense to arm yourself with knowledge. If you're informed about the dangers and avoid specific trouble spots, you'll almost certainly have no trouble.

Most importantly, you should understand that most crime in the Philippines is of the opportunistic variety. Keep the following things in mind, but remember that this list isn't exhaustive and nothing beats common sense when it comes to safe travel.

- Avoid travelling in dangerous areas of the southern Philippines. At present, this includes many areas of Basilan, Sulu and Mindanao. For more details on this, see the boxed text 'Warning' at the beginning of the Mindanao & Sulu chapter.
- The New People's Army (NPA) is still active in some parts of the Philippines, including rural and mountainous areas of North Luzon, Southeast Luzon and Mindoro. There is always the potential for getting kidnapped or getting caught in the crossfire when travelling in areas where the NPA is active. Check with the locals before heading off the beaten track in these areas.
- Guard your valuables carefully while in transit and beware of pickpockets on board cramped buses and jeepneys, as well as when queuing for transport.
- Do not board ferries that appear overloaded or in bad repair. Do not let your desire to get someplace override your better instincts.
- Take care when riding small bangka (pumpboats or outriggers), particularly in bad weather. The fact that a bangka pilot (or *bancero*) is willing to sail is no guarantee that it's safe to do so. You be the judge.
- Take care when riding in taxis, especially in Manila. There have been incidents of passengers being robbed at gun or knifepoint, sometimes by the driver, sometimes by third parties who jump into the taxi when it's stopped. One way to protect yourself is to take only regulation taxis and to have someone else (a hotel employee, for instance) note down the plate number as you enter the taxi (and be sure the driver sees this). And do not pay until all your bags have been removed from the vehicle.
- There have been incidents of criminals masquerading as police or 'luggage inspectors' at airports and in cities like Manila. Always ask to see a badge and if you have any suspicions, insist that any proceedings take place at the local police station, not on the street.
- We get a seemingly endless stream of letters and emails from people who have been ripped off by moneychangers in the Philippines. Sleight of hand is usually at work here, as well as the victim's desire to get a better-than-average rate. If you must change money or travellers cheques, go to a bank or a moneychanger in a shopping mall, if possible. Better yet, avoid the whole thing completely and use ATMs (remember, of course, that ATMs cannot be found in rural areas and may be out of service when you need money).
- Never accept drinks or food from a stranger – several travellers have been drugged and robbed this way (see the boxed text 'Drug Warning' earlier in this chapter).

Finally, be sure to check the latest travel advisories and warnings issued by your government *before* you visit the Philippines. Most governments post these online, including the US State Department (W www .travel.state.gov/travel_warnings.html), the UK Foreign & Commonwealth Office (W www.fco.gov.uk), and the Australian Department of Foreign Affairs & Trade (W www.dfat.gov.au/consular/advice).

English, so communication should not be an issue. Even in the remotest town, you're bound to find at least one lawyer serving the community. However, to ensure that you get the best possible legal assistance, ask your embassy for a recommendation.

If you find yourself the victim of theft or some other crime you can either seek help at the nearest police station or call the 24-hour service provided by the DOT (☎ 02-524 1660) for Manila visitors. (See also the boxed text 'Useful Phone Numbers' earlier

Ifugao man, Banaue – North Luzon

T'boli woman and child, Cotabato – Mindanao

Vendor at a *sari-sari* store, Mactan Island, Cebu – the Visayas

House decorated for Pahiyas (feast of San Isidro Labrador), Lucban – Quezon

Ati-Atihan Festival reveller, Panay – the Visayas

Pahiyas festival Queen contestant, Lucban

Ati-Atihan Festival procession, Kalibo, Panay – the Visayas

in this chapter.) The mobile patrol can usually be seen around Ermita/Malate, Manila's tourist belt.

BUSINESS HOURS

Banks are usually open from 9am to 3pm Monday to Friday. Public and private offices typically function from 8am or 9am to 5pm, with a lunch break from noon to 1pm on weekdays; a few private companies also work on Saturday morning. Department stores and supermarkets usually stay open until 7pm or 8pm, but at certain times of the year (eg, the Christmas season) some department stores remain open until 8pm or 9pm; some supermarkets in the big cities stay open 24 hours. Boutiques and specialty shops inside malls stay open until around 9pm or 10pm, when most malls close. Market stalls and stores around markets typically close at 6pm to 7pm; convenience stores never close.

Museums are generally open from 8am to noon and 1pm to 5pm on weekdays. Post office hours vary widely across the country, but should usually be open the same hours as museums. Embassies and consulates are open to the public mainly from 9am to 1pm Monday to Friday.

PUBLIC HOLIDAYS & SPECIAL EVENTS
Public Holidays

Many businesses shut for the entire week before Easter (called Holy Week here) and for two weeks (or more) over Christmas and New Year. Expect overseas consulates and many embassies to take some time off during these periods as well.

New Year's Day 1 January
Good Friday 9 April 2004
Araw ng Kagitingan (Bataan Day) 9 April
Labour Day 1 May
Independence Day 12 June
National Heroes Day Last Sunday in August
All Saints' Day 1 November
Bonifacio Day 30 November
Christmas Day 25 December
Rizal Day 30 December
New Year's Eve 31 December

Special Events
Chinese New Year Lunar New Year falls on 22 January in 2004 (Year of the Monkey).

Muslim Holy Days According to Islamic belief, the day actually begins at sunset, so holidays technically begin the evening before the solar-calendar date given here. Dates may also vary a bit from what's written: the Islamic calendar is an approximation – the actual start of Ramadan, for example, is determined by the proper sighting of the moon. The holy day falls 10 to 11 days earlier each year.

Hari Raya Hajj (Feast of Sacrifice) 2 February 2004
Hijra New Year 22 February 2004
Maulod An Nabi (Prophet's Birthday) 2 May 2004
Ramadan 15 October to 14 November 2004
Hari Raya Puasa (Feast of the Breaking of the Fast) Begins on the last evening of Ramadan and may last for three days

Festivals Filipinos certainly have a feel for fiestas. Festivals are plentiful, and range from simple village get-togethers to week-long extravaganzas – such as Kalibo's Ati-Atihan Festival – that rival Rio.

As one would expect in a traditionally agrarian society shepherded by the Catholic church, festival seasons centre on Christmas, the Lunar New Year (January/February), the period of Lent and Easter (March/April), the May harvest and during the rainy season (June to September, though July is strangely quiet). Every town has a patron saint, and every saint has a feast day, which means there's usually a fiesta on somewhere in the country. Whether Catholic priests converted a local ceremony or indigenous traditions used the new-fangled church calendar for their own purposes, the result is essentially the same: a celebration of communal life and its place in the cosmos.

Easter is doubtless the main religious festival, while *pasyon*, the week-long recital of Christ's Passion, exemplifies the common ground between animism and Christianity. For more details, see Religion in the Facts about the Philippines chapter.

Prodigal sons and daughters often return to their villages for festivals – if you're headed to a provincial area during a fiesta, you should arrange transport and accommodation as early as possible (though if you're not fussy, a place to sleep can usually be found). If you're planning to hang out during the huge Ati-Atihan Festival in Kalibo, you'll want to book a hotel at least a month in advance.

The following is a list of noteworthy festivals and special events around the country. For more details, see the relevant destination entry.

January

Three Kings Festival Celebrated in early January, this festival is a handy way to put off the holiday hangover till the New Year; it is the official end of Christmas and is nationally celebrated (especially on the island of Marinduque).

Black Nazarene Procession The Quiapo Church, in Manila's Quiapo district, houses the Black Nazarene, a black wooden cross that is paraded through the streets in a massive procession on 9 January and again during Passion week (the week before Palm Sunday in Easter).

Kabankalan Sinulog Held on the second Sunday of the month in La Carlota on Negros, this is a wild street party in which dancers are daubed in black in honour of the island's Negrito people and a feast is held in honour of Santo Niño (the child Jesus).

Ati-Atihan Festival Peaking on the third Sunday of the month, this week-long mother of all mardi gras rages from sunrise to sunset and is at its most riotous in Kalibo on Panay. Similar festivals are also held in the neighbouring towns of Batan (late January), Ibajay (late January), Makato (15 January) and Altavas (22 January). Cadiz on Negros celebrates its Ati-Atihan Festival in honour of patron saint Santo Niño (residents believe the holy infant protected the settlement from pirate attack) on the weekend nearest 26 January.

Vigan Town Fiesta This is held in the third week of January to commemorate the town's patron saint, St Paul the Apostle, with a parade and musical performances.

Dinagyang Festival Held in the fourth week of January in Iloilo City on Panay, this mardi gras–style festival celebrates Santo Niño with outrageous costumes and dances.

February

Nuestra Señora de la Candelaria On 2 February in Jaro, near Iloilo City on Panay, is the Feast of Our Lady of Candles; it's as much a good old-fashioned street party as it is a religious ritual.

Bamboo Organ Festival In the second week of February, organists from around the world gather in Las Piñas village, near Manila.

Paraw Regatta On the third Sunday of the month is an exciting race from Iloilo City on Panay over to Guimaras Island by traditional sailing outriggers called *paraw*. Dating back to the 16th century, the race is a high-speed version of the trip

supposedly taken by Panay's ancient Malay settlers on their journey to the island from Borneo.

March

Kaamulan Festival For three days in early March, Malaybalay, near Cagayan de Oro on Mindanao, is the setting for this celebration of unity between the tribal people living in the area; activities include dance, song, storytelling, local food, and wine and ritual enactments.

Sinagayan Festival In mid- to late March, Sagay City on Negros holds this festival in honour of St Joseph.

April/May

Lenten Festival of Herbal Preparation During Lent in San Antonio on Siquijor, traditional healers strut their stuff to big crowds. The associated Tang-Alap ritual is a gloriously fun-loving gathering of herbs and roots used in a pagan form of holy communion and dawn prayers.

Crucifixion Re-Enactments Every Easter, morbid fascination drives the flocks to San Fernando (Pampanga) on Luzon to see fanatical Christians offering themselves up for crucifixion. At noon on Good Friday, a number of volunteers are physically nailed to wooden crosses in the barangay of San Pedro Cutud and whipped till they bleed by gangs of flagellants. A more sober affair is Ang Pagtaltal Sa Guimaras in Jordan on Guimaras; this usually features an amateur 'Christ' roped rather than nailed to his cross (and he's often helped up there with a few stiff drinks).

Moriones Festival During Easter's Holy Week, the country's most popular passion plays and processions take place on Marinduque.

Panaad Festival Held in April/May in Bacolod on Negros, this was originally a street festival, but now includes permanent displays of crafts, art and architecture from the various towns and cities in the area. In April you can also join in about a dozen individual minifiestas all going off at once in Bacolod.

May

Pista'y Dayat On 1 May the coastal towns of the Lingayen Gulf on Luzon celebrate the area's foremost fiesta with water-borne parades.

Pasalamat Festival On the Sunday nearest 1 May, La Carlota on Negros holds a fun-filled, three-day thanksgiving ritual to honour the year's harvest and hard labour. A mardi gras atmosphere and homegrown drumbeats build up to a closing ceremony with dazzling ethnic costumes and huge parade floats.

Viva Vigan Biratbatan Festival In the first week of May, Vigan celebrates its heritage with, among other events, a *kalesa* (horse-drawn carriage) festival, *zarzuelas* (operettas) and *abel* (weaving) exhibits.

Kalabaw Races In early May, Pavia, just outside of Iloilo City on Panay, is a good place to watch the water buffalo races.

Balibong Kingking Festival This fiesta, honouring Our Lady of Guadalupe, is held from late May to June in the town of Loboc on Bohol.

Magayon Festival Held in Legaspi throughout May, with sports events, performances and competitions.

June

Araw ng Kutabato Festival In mid-June, the city of Cotabato on Mindanao plays host to mammoth dance parades.

Pintados Held on 29 June, this 'painted festival' in Tacloban on Leyte celebrates the traditional tattooing practiced before the Spanish arrived (though nowadays water-based paints are used for the festival's body decoration).

August

Kadayawan sa Dabaw Festival During the second week of August, Davao on Mindanao showcases its Muslim, Chinese and tribal influences with costumed street parades, dances and performances, along with fantastic displays of fruit and flowers.

Lubi-Lubi Festival On 15 August, the town of Calubian, on Leyte, celebrates the town's namesake, the coconut.

September

Tuna Festival From 1 to 5 September, General Santos on Mindanao celebrates the king of all tinned creatures. Among the highlights is the competition for best-dressed tuna; there's also a parade of fishing floats and a sashimi night.

Peñafrancia Festival Every third week of September thousands of devotees make a pilgrimage to Naga in Southeast Luzon for the celebration of the Virgin of Peñafrancia, the Bicol region's patron saint.

October

Fiesta de Nuestra Senora Virgen del Pilar Held from 10 to 12 October, this is Zamboanga city's main festival. It's a Christian occasion, but also a great opportunity for street parties, parades, dances, markets and food fairs; there's also a big regatta featuring brightly coloured traditional sail boats.

MassKara Festival On the weekend nearest 19 October, Bacolod on Negros goes joyfully crazy with the 'many faces festival', which sees participants wearing elaborate, smiley face masks and dancing in the streets.

November

All Saints Day (Todos los Santos) During the week that leads up to 1 November, Christian cemeteries throughout the archipelago are spruced up and crypts are given a fresh coat of whitewash. On the evening of All Saints Day, families laden with the favourite foods of the deceased loved ones gather at the local cemetery to spend the night snacking and strumming guitars. The atmosphere is surprisingly festive and foreign visitors who stroll through the cemetery will invariably be invited to join in. If you happen to be in Manila during All Saints Day, don't miss the huge party at the Chinese Cemetery.

Pintaflores Festival Held on 3 to 5 November in San Carlos on Negros, this is a famously frenetic street festival that harks back to the days when Filipinos would welcome foreign visitors by dancing en masse.

Lem-Lunay Festival In the second week of November at Lake Sebu on Mindanao is this celebration of T'boli culture, which culminates in horse-fights – the sport of royalty in local culture – when two stallions fight over a mare in heat.

December

Christmas Lantern Festival On the closest Saturday to Christmas, a number of truly gigantic Christmas lanterns are paraded through San Fernando (Pampanga) on Luzon; the lanterns remain on display till January.

Shariff Kabungsuan Festival This December event in Cotabato city on Mindanao commemorates the arrival of Islam in the region and involves river parades of decorated boats.

ACTIVITIES
Canoeing, Kayaking & Rafting

Shooting the rapids on the Pagsanjan River is one of Luzon's major tourist attractions. The town of Pagsanjan has become synonymous with the Magdapio Falls, the starting point for the famous canoe ride through the rapids. Further north, in the Cordillera region of North Luzon, there is good white-water rafting on the Chico and the Pinacanauan Rivers.

The mighty Tibiao River on Panay churns up some healthy white water, and kayaking is popular out of the town of Tibiao. White-water rafting is reportedly good near Cagayan de Oro on Mindanao.

Resorts often rent kayaks and canoes for paddling about, and the natural wonders of places like Apulit Island off Palawan can be appreciated on kayaking tours. If you have your own equipment, sea kayaking is excellent off Naga in Southeast Luzon.

Caving

The Philippines is a spelunker's paradise. The porous limestone that makes up most of the archipelago is riddled with a fantastic variety of caves, many of which are accessible to the average traveller. Luzon, in particular, has many interesting caves to explore. The Callao Caves in Peñablanca, near Tuguegarao, are a major tourist drawcard, and there is also good caving around Sagada and Solano.

Bohol's best caving is near Antequera at the Magaso and Inambacan Falls. Near Surigao on Mindanao is Silop Cave, with its 12 entrances that lead to a big central chamber. Spooky Siquijor is honeycombed with caves that have yielded many surprises, including ancient Chinese pottery. Still more good caving can be found on Panay and Leyte.

Finally, don't miss the Puerto Princesa Subterranean National Park outside Sabang on the island of Palawan. This Unesco World Heritage site is said to the longest underground river-traversed tunnel in the world.

Cycling

The Philippines isn't all beaches and volcanoes, and mountain-biking is taking off as an activity in its own right on a number of islands – see Bicycle in the Getting Around chapter for details.

Diving & Snorkelling

See the special section 'Diving in the Philippines' for the low-down on the top spots to dive in the Philippines, regulations and requirements, rates and other information on diving and snorkelling activities in the Philippines. For even more information, get yourself a copy of Lonely Planet's *Diving & Snorkeling Philippines*.

Hiking & Trekking

Hiking is possible on nearly every island and most famously on Luzon, where a trek through the awesome rice terraces around Banaue and Batad is a highlight of any trip to the country. There are also pleasant hikes around Sagada, and the Batanes offer rugged coastal strolls.

National parks offer networks of trails and plenty of variety. The 40km Leyte Mountain Trail is a treat, taking you past rainforest, lakes and waterfalls as it winds over the central spine of the island to one of two volcanic national parks.

Volcano climbing is a popular pastime, and ranges from short and sweet ascents to long and sweaty treks. Be aware of current conditions – not only are many of these volcanoes active, some (such as the tiny Taal Volcano) are notoriously so. Check with the **Philippines Institute of Volcanology and Seismology** *(Philvolcs; ☎ 02-426 1468; ⓦ www .phivolcs.dost.gov.ph/)* in Manila for the latest conditions.

Hiking around the bizarre lahar formations of Mt Pinatubo rates highly on many visitors' lists, though the dormant volcanoes of Mt Banahaw and Mt Makiling offer fewer crowds and some of the best hiking on Luzon. Lake Taal also has several good hiking options. A two-day hike will get you superb views from Mt San Cristobal.

Hibok-Hibok volcano on Camiguin is a steep, full-day climb. Mt Apo (2954m) on Mindanao is the highest mountain in the Philippines; if you're in good shape, a three-day trek up the mountain is a rewarding adventure.

Sailing

The islands offer year-round sailing, and there are active yacht clubs in Manila and Subic Bay. Lake Taal near Manila is often hyped as a sailing mecca, while Puerto Galera on Mindoro has long been known to yachties as an excellent destination.

The Sail Philippines website (ⓦ www.sail phi.org.ph) has just about everything you need to know before you go, including events, sailing organisations and suppliers.

Surfing

Although Indonesia is the undisputed mecca of Southeast Asian surfing, the Philippines has a good assortment of breaks and some serious local surfers. The main attraction is good breaks at all levels of difficulty, which aren't (yet) crowded with fellow surfers. The main drawback is that waves don't break with the consistency of world-class beaches and you may be gazing at the horizon for a few weeks before tossing your board into the surf (in delight or disgust). Check with locals to find out what you're paddling into – when some of the big sets roll in, reefs and shelfs can make for very challenging, and sometimes dangerous, rides.

Popular destinations on Luzon include San Fernando (La Union) and Bolinao on the Lingayen Gulf, and Daet in Southeast Luzon. Baler, on the eastern coast, is where the famous surfing scene in Francis Ford Coppola's

Apocalypse Now was filmed – from September to February, surfers from around the world stand on the beach munching cigars and yelling 'Charlie don't surf!'. The best waves are actually said to be six hours north of Baler by jeepney.

Off Mindanao's northeastern tip, Siargao Island is famed for Cloud Nine, which is an excellent, if fickle, break. The Siargao Cup surfing competition is held in late September or early October; surfing can be good from April to October and great on the northwestern coast during the northeast monsoon, but be prepared to wait for the right waves to roll in.

Windsurfing

Windsurfing is possible all over the Philippines (Lake Taal on Luzon is an up-and-coming spot), but Boracay is the place to be seen and the island's wilder east coast has the best conditions for surfers of all skill levels. Parasailing is also popular on the island's beaches.

WORK

Nonresident aliens are not permitted to be employed or theoretically look for work, without a valid work permit, while foreign residents require work registration. Contact the **Department of Labor & Employment** *(DOLE;* ☎ *02-527 3585; Palacio del Gobernador, General Luna St, Intramuros, Manila)* to obtain either a work permit or registration.

Volunteer Work

Most NGOs (nongovernmental organisations) in the Philippines work on ecological projects or programmes to aid the poor. Major volunteer organisations active in the Philippines include Australian Volunteers International (ⓦ www.australianvolunteers.com), United Nations Volunteers (ⓦ www.unv.org), the US Peace Corps (ⓦ www.peacecorps.gov) and the UK-based Voluntary Service Overseas (ⓦ www.vso.org.uk).

ACCOMMODATION

There is a wide range of accommodation available in the Philippines, from simple nipa (palm) huts to international-class hotels. Of course, quality varies enormously in any price range, and paying more doesn't always guarantee a better place.

On a few islands, formal lodging doesn't exist; on others it may be full for a festival or other occasion. In the former case, there's usually some resource for pre-arranging a place to sleep; in the latter, a polite visit to the mayor or barangay (neighbourhood or district) captain will almost certainly find you a spot to rest your head for the night.

Advance booking is usually a good idea, especially if you plan your visit to coincide with a festival (in which case a month or two in advance is not out of line). Booking is usually no problem, even in small hotels and guesthouses, and your reservation will usually be honoured on arrival. It's often worth asking for a discount or bargaining a little when you call, as the price might come down.

One final tip: while many hotels in the Philippines are drab and uninspiring, a short trip out of town will usually bring you to a resort where, for a similar price, you can enjoy a festive atmosphere and much more scenic surroundings.

Camping

Formal camp sites are uncommon, though you can camp pretty much anywhere, including the beach – with permission if you are on private land, of course. Camping en route on treks is also common practice. Wherever you set up, be sure to take *all* your rubbish with you when you move on.

Hostels

Having a Hostelling International (HI) card will save about P20 per night at hostels. Manila's youth hostel is pleasant and good value, and there are a few hostels around the capital that make good bases for day trips or hikes. Other than that, hostels around the country aren't generally your best option. Even if you can find one, you'll find that they aren't much cheaper than travellers guesthouses and they tend to be on the noisy side.

Hotels

If your budget only stretches to P100 a night for a hotel, your options will be limited in most parts of the country. A reasonably clean single 'broom closet' can be found in many places for about P120, but you'll probably want to double that price to find anything liveable.

If you're not on a rock-bottom budget, take a look at mid-range hotels. The most expensive rooms in a budget hotel can be very ordinary and P600 or so won't seem worth it;

for the same price, the cheapest rooms in a mid-range place are often far superior.

Hotel maintenance can be rather casual, so check the water and electricity are functioning before agreeing to take a room. Also check that the windows open and fire escapes are accessible – more than a few hotels operate under the assumption that fire laws were made to be broken.

Homestays

There are plenty of homestay arrangements in the Philippines, many of them formal, others ad hoc. You may be invited to stay in someone's home, and be offered the best bed and food in the place, even if it's a financial burden to the owners to do so. If you wish to give money in repayment for the kindness, do it subtly.

FOOD

Filipino cooking is a rich mixture of Malay, Spanish and Chinese influences blended with Filipino creativity and Filipino *joie de vivre*. If well-prepared, Filipino food can be really delicious.

Unfortunately, as is the case with similar food in Malaysia and Indonesia, much of the food on offer is prepared well in advance, and is cold by the time it's eaten, which can detract significantly from its flavour.

Filipinos love to eat – so much so that you could be excused for thinking that that's all Filipinos ever do. Traditionally, a typical Filipino day comprises up to five meals: breakfast, morning *merienda*, lunch, afternoon *merienda* and dinner. Merienda literally means 'snack', but don't let that fool you – the afternoon *merienda* can include something as filling as *bihon* (fried rice sticks) or *goto* (Filipino congee) plus an assortment of rice cakes.

Indigenous (or Pinoy) food is normally laid out on the table like a buffet, allowing the diners to partake of the dishes one at a time or all at the same time. Western palates might find the everyday food a bit too rich and heavy (the Spanish influence), but you can always request something light and healthy like *sinigang na sugpo* (prawns and vegetables cooked in tamarind-flavoured soup).

The basic Filipino eatery is a *turo turo* (which is literally, 'point point'), where – you guessed it – customers can order by pointing at the precooked food on display,

but Filipino restaurants come in a many guises, from small roadside canteens to huge enterprises like the popular Gerry's Grill in Manila. Ordinary restaurants and foodstalls might be all right for a while, but it's definitely worth trying well-prepared, authentic Filipino cuisine in one of the pricier places.

The bad news for lovers of animals and vitamins is that Filipino dishes tend to be long on meat and short on greens. Popular entrees include *kaldereta* (beef stew), *apritada* (pork or chicken in a tomato-based sauce) and *crispy pata* (crackling pork knuckles). *Ihaw ihaw* eateries (which serve the Filipino version of grilled meat and seafood) are everywhere.

One of the few vegetable dishes to make a regular appearance is *pinakbet*, a tasty melange of pumpkin, string beans, eggplant, okra and other vegies seasoned with garlic, onions, ginger, tomatoes, shrimp paste and sometimes coconut milk.

If you find that you aren't getting enough vegetables while travelling in the Philippines, one solution is to buy fruit and vegetables like carrots and cucumber at the many excellent street markets. Self-catering is certainly cheap, and fruit and vegetables come in an astonishing variety, all at very affordable prices. You can also buy fresh fruit and vegetables at the many supermarkets in the cities.

For vegetarians who don't mind eating fish, there's always the option of sticking to a diet of fish and shellfish. The Philippines abounds with all kinds of goodies from the sea – snapper, grouper, tuna, mussels, clams, oysters, crabs etc. Many restaurants specialise in fish and seafood; ask your waiter to have your selection simply grilled and served with dollops of *calamansi* juice (a type of citrus), and you can look forward to a memorable gastronomic treat. If you don't eat fish or meat, however, you'll have a hard time of it in the Philippines and should consider bringing some food products from home.

For dessert (or any time), try *halo halo*, an ever-popular choice. This consists of a tall glass packed with fruit preserves, sweet corn, young coconut and various tropical delights topped with milky crushed ice, a wad of crème caramel and a hearty scoop of ice cream. For hygienic reasons, ice cream from street vendors is probably best avoided, but local brands like Magnolia and Selecta are quite good.

If it's foreign cuisine you're after, you'll find almost everything under the sun in Manila. Other big cities, like Cebu, also have a good smattering of foreign restaurants. Likewise, many resorts usually serve a variety of foreign favourites, with widely varying degrees of success.

American and local fast-food outfits occupy many city street corners, and offer an inexpensive array of Western fast food, from burgers to spaghetti and pizza. If you want to try the local version of all this, stop into Jollibee, a homegrown Filipino fast-food chain.

Local Food

Regional specialities are a real treat, and can be full of surprises. In Manila you can sample practically any type of regional cooking, but there's really nothing like savouring the delicacies in their place of origin. *Tocino* (honey-cured pork) and *longganiza* (sausages), two of Pampanga's specialities, somehow taste better amid the province's cultural heritage. Likewise, Bicolano cuisine, which is distinguished by a spicy creaminess (from a mixture of coconut milk and chillies) tastes especially good in the shadow of elegant Mt Mayon. *Laing* (taro leaves simmered in spiced coconut milk) and *Bicol express* (a fiery pork dish) are two Bicolano dishes that are a feast of flavours.

Main Dishes

Names of dishes are often generic terms: *adobo* means the pork and/or chicken has been stewed in vinegar and garlic; *sinigang* signifies the meat or fish has been boiled in a sour soup; *ginataan* means the meat, fish or vegetables have been cooked in coconut milk; *kinilaw* is fresh seafood marinated in vinegar or *calamansi* juice and spices; and *inihaw* refers to grilled meat or fish. See the Language chapter for more details on food terminology in the Philippines.

DRINKS
Nonalcoholic Drinks

It's not a good idea to drink tap water in the Philippines: stick to bottled, boiled or purified water. The water refilling stations scattered all over the country are safe and are an environmentally friendly alternative to disposing of empty water bottles. Many accommodation options have built-in kitchenettes where you can boil your own water.

Tea is served in Chinese restaurants; elsewhere soft drinks rule.

Buko juice is young coconut juice with bits of translucent coco meat floating in it. It's usually sold in the nut, but you'd best stick to the type that comes in a presealed cup or bottle; *buko* juice is said to be good for staving off dehydration. *Guyanbano* juice is sweet but surprisingly refreshing and is made from the soursop. The popular little citrus known as *calamansi* is used to make a refreshing cordial or added to black tea. Wondrous curative powers are ascribed to it, so take a sip and see what happens.

Alcoholic Drinks

At around P12 to P30 a bottle, San Miguel must be one of the world's cheapest beers – and it's not bad, either. These days, 'San Mig' has stiff competition from other domestic brews and a variety of imports like Carlsberg; in response, San Miguel Light was launched with heavy fanfare in January 2000.

Palatable brandies, whiskies and gins are domestically produced; Tanduay Rum is a perfectly drinkable travelling companion (P20 to P30 for a 375mL bottle) – and a handy antiseptic! Rural concoctions include *basi*, a sweet, port-like wine made from sugarcane juice. *Tuba* is a strong palm wine extracted from coconut flowers; in its roughly distilled form it's called *lambanog*. Local firewater packs quite a punch – your stomach (if not your head) will thank you in the morning if you partake of the *pulutan* (small snacks) always served with alcohol.

ENTERTAINMENT
Bars

Nightlife mostly means bars, which come in two basic types: 'Western' and 'girlie'. These can be further divided into bars run by expats and those owned by locals, but the main issue (aside from the economics and ethics of the sex trade) is cost. An evening's drinking in a Western-style place will cost about P300 to P500 per person; in a girlie bar it will be 10 times that price since (for one thing) you're drinking for two.

In addition to the high prices and the ethical issues involved with patronising such places, girlie bars should be avoided if you don't want to be hassled by prostitutes. Western bars may sometimes have a few prostitutes about, but they will usually leave you alone if it is clear that you are just there for a drink. Naturally, you'll find the biggest selection of Western bars in Manila and Cebu City. In resort areas, you'll also find a variety of beachfront bars, similar to those you'd find in other parts of Southeast Asia.

Karaoke

Many Westerners would sooner have their wisdom teeth removed with pliers than spend an evening listening to inebriated amateurs pay homage to Celine Dion and Julio Iglesias. But when Filipinos want to unwind, they often do it around the karaoke machine. From simple karaoke machines in beer gardens to the latest KTV in nightclubs, Filipinos are unabashed about belting out a tune, whether alone or in company.

Numerous venues offer cheap beer and song menus of Western and Filipino faves. Although most of these places offer 'ladies' drinks', the girls here are usually not required to do anything more than keep the customers drinking and singing.

Karaoke can be good fun, but criticising or making fun of someone's performance is a grave insult, and there have been cases where arguments over karaoke have led to violent exchanges and even murder.

SPECTATOR SPORTS
Basketball

First introduced by the American colonial administration as part of an orchestrated programme to Americanise the locals, basketball has found a place in the national psyche and a home on street courts from Aparri to Sulu.

Teams in the Philippine Basketball Association (PBA) are associated with sponsors rather than towns, with inspiring names like San Miguel Beermen and Santa Lucia Realtors. Professional players in the league are scouted from the amateur teams at universities and colleges, as well as from overseas, mostly the USA.

Basketball is widely perceived as a route out of poverty. In poor areas, teenagers dream of following in the footsteps of Pinoy basketball greats like Robert Jaworski who is now a member of the Philippine Senate. The best way to find out about the many local leagues is to ask the kids on the village basketball court, though you'll probably find yourself talked into joining in the game.

Jai Alai

The fast-paced game of jai alai, or *pelota*, comes from the Basque region of Spain and remains one of the more popular sports. Jai alai is played by groups of six pelotaris in a *fronton*, which is similar to a squash court with wire mesh along one side. Players use a long crescent-shaped wicker basket *(esta)* tied to one hand to launch a small hard ball against the far wall, which returns at a staggering speed (after several returns, the ball can be travelling at nearly 250km/h!). There

Fowl Play

Appealing to the Filipino obsession for gambling, cockfighting is still the No 1 sport in the Philippines. Select birds are raised on special food, treated with special medications and even washed with special shampoos before being taken to the local cockpit for what will almost certainly be the fight of their lives.

Combatants are fitted with a lethal three-inch ankle blade and are allowed to peck each other before a fight, in order to generate fighting spirit. With hundreds of pesos riding on the outcome, the temptation for fight-rigging is high; just before the birds are released, the blades are wiped with alcohol to ensure they are free from poison.

The squabble is usually brutally short. The winner is whisked away to a team of waiting surgeons, who stitch up any gaping wounds and dose the bird with antibiotics. The loser usually makes his way into the cooking pot. Incredibly, it is possible for a cock to have a fighting career; winning birds can be back in the ring in as little as two weeks!

Cockpits are found on the outskirts of most towns and villages in the Philippines, with Sunday being the most popular day for fights. The onlookers often take a gruesome pleasure in explaining the details of the sport to outsiders.

Joe Bindloss

are two pelotaris on court at any one time and if a player fails to catch and return the ball, they cede a point and are replaced by the next player in line, which leaves the spectators on the edge of their seats until the final ball.

SHOPPING

Manila's malls and markets offer a range of authentic items from around the country, and lots of touristy trinkets are available as well. Handicrafts are popular and often of high quality, including ornate wooden salad bowls and utensils, and hanging lamps and chandeliers made of shells.

Items designed for tourists are especially plentiful in Manila's traditional tourist belt – Ermita and Malate – as well as in the huge air-conditioned malls where you can find virtually anything. Many well-known designer brands from the West, such as Polo, Armani and Guess, have shops at these malls. Here you can pick up brand-name clothing at a fraction of its cost in the West. The Barong Tagalog, the traditional embroidered shirt worn by Filipino men, is also a good buy.

Philippine markets are a must-see, if only to experience the amazing riot of colours and

delightful cacophony of sounds. The fruit section will make you want to sample the many types of bananas, mangoes and other tropical fruits on display.

You can find markets of varying sizes in almost all Philippine cities and towns. Some are held only once or twice a week – ask a local for advice.

Traditional items can also be found in cities such as Cebu, Davao and Zamboanga; or, you could go to the source. Towns on tourist routes produce goods for tourists – for example, Banaue is running out of authentic products (and the wood to make them). The pickings are often better off the beaten track: Tacloban on Leyte is famous for the quality of its *abaca* (a native hemp plant) products, Iligan on Mindanao has a good range of Muslim-produced handicrafts, while Lake Sebu is the heartland of the T'boli people and their weaving and betel-nut box-making.

Never buy coral or shell products unless they have a stamp indicating that they come from sustainable resources. If you have any doubts about the source of an item, don't purchase it – there are plenty of legitimate souvenirs to take its place.

Getting There & Away

AIR
Airports & Airlines

Since most people fly to the Philippines and most flights land in Manila, Ninoy Aquino International Airport (NAIA) in Parañaque is likely to be your first taste of the Philippines. Too bad, but don't despair – most of the country is a lot better run than decrepit old NAIA. Doubtless as an incentive to fly with Philippine Airlines (PAL), the national carrier, its passengers get exclusive use of the cushy Centennial Terminal II at NAIA.

Cebu City's Mactan-Cebu International Airport (MCIA) is the country's second-busiest airport and is much better. Depending on your itinerary, Cebu's airport may also be a more practical entry/exit point. The biggest advantage of flying into Cebu is that it saves you having to deal with the chaos of Manila (and its unscrupulous taxi drivers). Cebu has the following international connections: Hong Kong, Kuala Lumpur (via Kota Kinabalu), Tokyo and Seoul with PAL, and Singapore with Silk Air. Since all these cities are well served with international connections, it's easy for the determined traveller to arrive in Cebu rather than Manila.

The only other airport in the Philippines with regular international connections is Davao on Mindanao, which has flights to/from Manado (Indonesia) with Bouraq Airlines, and to/from Singapore with Silk Air.

For more details on NAIA and MCIA, see the Getting There & Away entries in the Manila chapter and in the Cebu City section in the Visayas chapter.

For local contact details of major airlines, see Getting There & Away in the Manila chapter.

Tickets

With a bit of research – ringing travel agents, checking Internet sites, perusing the travel ads in newspapers – you can usually get yourself a good travel deal. Start early, as some of the cheapest tickets need to be bought well in advance and popular flights can sell out.

Full-time students and people under 26 years of age (under 30 in some countries) have access to better deals than other travellers. You have to show a document providing your date of birth or a valid International Student Identity Card (ISIC) when buying your ticket and boarding the plane.

Generally, there is nothing to be gained by buying a ticket directly from the airline (except for tickets purchased on the Web). Discounted tickets are released to selected travel agents and specialist discount agencies and these are usually the cheapest deals going.

Tickets can also be purchased cheaply on the Internet and many airlines offer excellent fares to Web surfers. They may sell seats by auction or simply cut prices to reflect the reduced cost of electronic selling.

Many travel agencies around the world have websites, which can make the Internet a quick and easy way to compare prices. There is also an increasing number of online agents that operate only on the Internet.

Online ticket sales work well if you are doing a simple one-way or return trip on specified dates. However, online fare generators are no substitute for a travel agent who knows all about special deals, has strategies for avoiding layovers and can offer advice on everything from which airline has the best vegetarian food to the best travel insurance to bundle with your ticket.

You may find the cheapest flights are advertised by obscure agencies. Most such firms are honest and solvent, but there are some rogue fly-by-night outfits around. Paying by credit card generally offers protection, as most card issuers provide refunds if you can prove you didn't get what you paid for. Agents who accept only cash should hand over the tickets straight away and not tell you to 'come back tomorrow'. After you've made a booking or paid your deposit, call the airline and confirm that the booking was made.

If you purchase a ticket and later want to make changes to your route or get a refund, you need to contact the original travel agent. Airlines issue refunds only to the purchaser of a ticket – usually the travel agent who bought the ticket on your behalf. Many travellers change their routes halfway through their trips, so think carefully before you buy a ticket that is not easily refunded or changed.

Book well in advance if you plan to arrive in the Philippines during December – expat Filipinos flood the islands to visit their families during Christmas and New Year. If you're flying into Cebu, the lead up to Lunar New Year in late January or early February can also get congested, as the city's sizeable Chinese population prepares to celebrate.

Round-the-World & Circle Pacific Tickets

If you're planning an extended trip with stops in several countries, a round-the-world (RTW) ticket may be your best bet. RTW tickets with a stop in the Philippines start at around US$1600 from the USA, UK£1000 from the UK and A$2300 from Australia. Check with the travel agencies listed in the following sections for the best deals on RTW tickets. Alternatively, check the websites of major international airlines like Qantas, British Airways and American Airlines to see if there are any RTW specials on offer to Web surfers.

Another option from the US west coast is a Circle Pacific ticket, which allows you to hop around the Pacific and Asia. For around US$1500, you can fly from the US west coast to Manila, Hong Kong, Australia, New Zealand and back to the west coast. Another US$100 or so allows a stop on one of the Pacific islands.

Travellers with Specific Needs

If they're warned early enough, airlines can usually make special arrangements for travellers such as wheelchair assistance at airports or for vegetarian meals on the flight.

Children under two travel for 10% of the standard fare (or free on some airlines) as long as they don't occupy a seat. They don't get a baggage allowance. 'Skycots', baby food and nappies should be provided by the airline if requested in advance. Children aged between two and 12 can usually occupy a seat for around two-thirds of the full fare, and get a baggage allowance.

The disability-friendly website ⓦ www .everybody.co.uk has an airline directory that provides information on the facilities offered by various airlines.

Departure Tax

Departure tax for all flights leaving the Philippines is P550, payable in cash only (US dollars or Philippine pesos).

The USA

San Francisco is the discount ticket capital of the USA, although some good deals can be found in Los Angeles, New York and other big cities.

STA Travel (☎ 800-781 4040; ⓦ www.sta travel.com) has offices across the country. There are also plenty of good online airfares on sites like ⓦ www.atevo.com, ⓦ www .cheaptickets.com and ⓦ www.expedia.com. A good source of RTW and Circle Pacific tickets is **Air Brokers International** (☎ 800-883 3273; ⓦ www.airbrokers.com).

PAL offers the only direct flights to the Philippines from mainland USA, with flights from both Los Angeles and San Francisco. Other airlines that serve the Philippines from the USA include Northwest (via Tokyo), Japan Airlines (via Tokyo), All Nippon Airways (via Tokyo), Korean Airlines (via Seoul), and China Airlines (via Taipei).

From the east coast of the USA, return fares to Manila start at around US$1250. From the west coast, return fares to Manila start as low as US$1050. Return fares to Cebu via an Asian city cost about US$100 extra.

Canada

Travel Cuts (☎ 866-246 9762; ⓦ www.travel cuts.com) is Canada's national student travel agency and has offices in all major cities. The websites ⓦ www.expedia.ca and ⓦ www .travelocity.ca also have some good deals.

Return fares from Toronto to Manila with United Airlines or PAL start at around

C$1900. Direct flights to Manila from Vancouver with PAL cost around C$1800 return. Alternatively, it's possible to fly from Vancouver to Manila or Cebu via several Asian cities on a variety of airlines.

Australia

STA Travel (☎ *1300 360 960;* W *www.sta travel.com.au)* has offices in all major cities and on many university campuses. **Flight Centre** (☎ *131 600;* W *www.flightcentre.com .au)* has dozens of offices throughout Australia. Alternatively, you'll find advertisements for many small, independent travel agents in the weekend editions of most major newspapers.

Qantas and PAL offer the only direct flights from Australia to the Philippines (Sydney to Manila); otherwise, it's necessary to fly via cities like Bangkok, Singapore, Kuala Lumpur or Hong Kong.

Return fares from Sydney, Melbourne or Brisbane to Manila start at around A$1125/1450 in the low/high season. Fares to Cebu with Malaysia Airlines or Silk Air are similarly priced.

New Zealand

Flight Centre (☎ *0800 243 544;* W *www.flight centre.co.nz)* has branches throughout the country. **STA Travel** (☎ *0508-782 872;* W *www .statravel.co.nz)* has offices in Auckland, Christchurch, Dunedin, Hamilton, Palmerston North and Wellington.

Currently there are no direct flights between New Zealand and the Philippines; the usual route is to fly to Sydney and pick up a direct flight from there. Alternatively, it's possible to fly direct from New Zealand to an Asian city like Singapore or Hong Kong and fly to the Philippines from there.

Return fares on Singapore Airlines (via Singapore) or Malaysia Airlines (via Kuala Lumpur) start at around NZ$1500/1900 in the low/high season.

The UK

Discount air travel is big business in London. Advertisements for many travel agencies appear in the travel pages of the weekend broadsheet newspapers, in *Time Out,* the *Evening Standard* and in the free magazine *TNT.*

Popular travel agencies in the UK include **STA Travel** (☎ *0870 160 0599;* W *www.sta travel.co.uk);* **Trailfinders** (☎ *020 7938 3939;* W *www.trailfinders.co.uk; 194 Kensington High St, London W8 7RG);* and **Bridge the World** (☎ *0870 444 7474;* W *www.bridgethe world.com; 4 Regent Place, London W1B 5EA).*

The cheapest flights to Manila are with Qatar Airways and cost as little as UK£420 return. Otherwise, return fares on European airlines like Air France, or Asian airlines like Singapore Airlines or Cathay Pacific, start at around UK£520. Malaysia Airlines, Cathay Pacific, and Singapore Airlines offer flights into Cebu for slightly more.

Continental Europe

Recommended travel agencies in continental Europe include: in France **OTU Voyages** (☎ *0 820 817 817;* W *www.otu.fr)* and **Nouvelles Frontières** (☎ *0 825 000 747;* W *www .nouvelles-frontieres.fr);* in Germany **STA Travel** (☎ *01805 456 422;* W *www.statravel .de);* in the Netherlands **NBBS Reizen** (☎ *0900 10 20 300;* W *www.mytravel.nl);* in Italy **CTS Viaggi** (☎ *840 501 150;* W *www.cts.it);* in Spain **Tui Centro de Viajes** (☎ *902 170 979;* W *www.tuiviajes.com);* and in Switzerland **STA Travel** (☎ *1 297 11 11;* W *www.ssr.ch).*

Air France offers direct flights from Paris to Manila; otherwise, you can fly via an Asian or Middle Eastern capital. The cheapest return fares are on the Middle Eastern carriers, with return fares on Kuwait Air available for as little as €680. Return fares on Air France cost slightly more, starting at around €720. As usual, fares to Cebu are slightly more expensive.

Lufthansa offers direct flights from Frankfurt to Manila (stopping in Bangkok). Otherwise, it's necessary to take a connecting flight via an Asian or Middle Eastern capital on Malaysia Airlines, Singapore Airlines or Qatar Airways. Return fares start from €600 (slightly more to Cebu).

There are direct flights from Amsterdam to Manila on KLM, and connecting flights on Cathay Pacific (via Hong Kong), Swiss Air (via Zurich), Singapore Airlines (via Singapore) and Malaysia Airlines (via Kuala Lumpur), among others. Discount return fares can start as low as €700, slightly more to Cebu.

Asia

Most Asian countries offer fairly competitive air fare deals – Bangkok, Singapore and Hong Kong are the best places to shop around for discount tickets.

China Hong Kong has a number of excellent, reliable travel agencies and some not-so-reliable ones. A good way to check on a travel agent is to look it up in the phone book: fly-by-night operators don't usually stay around long enough to get listed. Many travellers use the **Hong Kong Student Travel Bureau** (☎ 02-2730 3269; Room 1021, 10th floor, Star House, Tsimshatsui). You could also try **Phoenix Services** (☎ 02-2722 7378; 7th floor, Milton Mansion, 96 Nathan Rd, Tsimshatsui).

There are flights from Hong Kong to Manila on Cathay Pacific, Cebu Pacific and PAL, and to Cebu on Cathay Pacific and PAL. Return fares to Manila start at around HK$2350, while to Cebu they start at around HK$2650.

It's also possible to fly from Beijing to Manila with China Southern Airways.

Indonesia At the time of writing, Bouraq Airlines had flights between Manado on Sulawesi and Davao on Mindanao for around US$150/260 one way/return. Note that this is an on-again, off-again proposition, so you may wind up having to take the ferry from nearby Bitung (see Sea later in this chapter).

Japan Flights from Japan to the Philippines can be good value, provided you travel outside of the peak travel seasons (Christmas/New Year and Golden Week). Recommended travel agencies include **No 1 Travel** (☎ 03-3205 6073; Shinjuku • ☎ 03-3986 4690; Ikebukuro • ☎ 06-6363 4489; Osaka • ☎ 075-251 6970; Kyoto); **Across Traveller's Bureau** (☎ 03-5467 0077; Shibuya); and **Just Travel** (☎ 03-3362 3441; Takadanobaba). Other listings for travel agencies can be found in the Japan Times or Kansai Time Out.

PAL has direct flights between Manila and Tokyo, Osaka and Fukuoka, as well as direct flights between Cebu and Tokyo. There are connecting flights between Japan and Manila on carriers such as Thai Airways and Northwest Airlines.

Return fares from Tokyo to Manila start at around ¥45,000, while to Cebu they start at around ¥50,000.

Korea In Seoul, **Joy Travel Service** (☎ 02-776 9871; 10th floor, 24-2 Mukyo-dong, Chung-gu),

directly behind City Hall, offers good deals and has English-speaking staff. Cheap deals can also be found at the **Korean International Student Exchange Society** (KISES; ☎ 02-733 9494; 5th floor, YMCA Bldg, Chongno 2-ga).

There are direct flights between Seoul and Manila on Korean Airlines, Asiana Airlines and PAL, and direct flights to Cebu on PAL.

Return fares to the Philippines start at around W700,000.

Malaysia In Kuala Lumpur, try **STA Travel** (☎ 03 2148 9800; 5th floor, Plaza Magnum, 128 Jalan Pudu).

Malaysia Airlines and PAL have direct flights between Kuala Lumpur and Manila, and PAL has direct flights between Kuala Lumpur and Cebu.

Return tickets to the Philippines start at around RM1000.

Singapore Singapore has loads of good travel agents, including **STA Travel** (☎ 065-6737 7188; W www.statravel.com.sg; 33A Cuppage Rd, Cuppage Terrace). Chinatown Point shopping centre on New Bridge Rd is a good place to look for travel agents. Other agents advertise in the Straits Times classified columns.

PAL and Singapore Airlines fly between Singapore and Manila, and Silk Air (a subsidiary of Singapore Airlines), flies to Cebu.

Return fares to Manila start at around S$780, while to Cebu they start at around S$920.

Taiwan A long-running agent is **Jenny Su Travel** (☎ 02-2506 6380; W www.jennysu.com.tw; 4th floor, No 100, Sec 1, Chungshiao W Rd, Taipei); **Wing On Travel** and **South-East Travel** have branches all over the island. All three have good reputations and offer reasonable prices.

There are flights between Taipei and Manila on China Airlines, EVA Air and PAL.

Return fares between Taiwan and Manila start at around NT$9000.

Thailand Khao San Rd in Bangkok is the budget traveller headquarters. Bangkok has a number of excellent travel agents, but there are also some suspect ones; ask the advice of other travellers before handing over your cash. **STA Travel** (☎ 02-236 0262;

W *www.statravel.co.th; 33 Surawong Rd)* is a good and reliable place to start.

Many airlines make the run between Bangkok and Manila, including Thai Airways, PAL, Kuwait Airways, Lufthansa Airlines and EgyptAir.

Fares from Bangkok to Manila cost as little as 11,400B return.

South America

ASATEJ Al Mundo *(☎ 011 4114 7595;* W *www .almundo.com)* is Argentina's agent for STA Travel. The best deals from Buenos Aires to Manila are via Sydney. Expect to pay around US$1500 for a return flight.

In Caracas, **IVI Tours** *(☎ 02-993 6082; Residencia La Hacienda, Piso Bajo, Local 1-4-Y, Final Avenida Principal de las Mercedes)* is the agent for STA Travel in Venezuela and often has a range of good deals. Flights from Venezuela to Manila are via the USA and Japan. Fares start at around US$2000 return.

Student Travel Bureau *(STB; ☎ 011-3038 1555;* W *www.stb.com.br)* does have several branches across Brazil. Flights to the Philippines are via the USA and cost around US$2100 return.

SEA

It's possible to travel by sea between the Philippines and nearby parts of Malaysia

and Indonesia. However, schedules and routes are very liable to change so it's best to be flexible in your plans.

Indonesia

EPA Shipping Line has ferries that sail between General Santos in Mindanao and the deep-water port of Bitung, 55km from Manado (P1800, 36 hours, twice weekly). The office *(☎ 083-380 3591)* is inside the port compound at Makar. This is a cargo boat that takes passengers; officially, there is no problem with foreigners making this trip, but you may want to check with the tourism office in General Santos first. You will need to finalise any Indonesian visa requirements with the consulate in Davao before you leave.

There is also a boat to Bitung from Davao's Sasa Pier (via General Santos) every Friday but details change often so it's best to check with Davao's city tourism officer.

Malaysia

Aleson Lines *(☎ 062-992 4585; PPA Terminal, Port Area, Zamboanga)* leaves Zamboanga for Sandakan in Malaysian Borneo (from P1300/RM130 from Zamboanga/ Sandakan, 17 hours, twice weekly).

Sampaguita Lines *(☎ 062-993 1591)* leaves Zamboanga for Sandakan (P500 to P1500, 17 hours) twice weekly.

Getting Around

AIR
Domestic Air Services
The main domestic carriers are Philippine Airlines (PAL), Cebu Pacific Air and Air Philippines. Smaller carriers include Asian Spirit, SEAIR, Laoag International Airways, and Pacific Air (for Manila contact details, see Getting There & Away in the Manila chapter).

Size is important when it comes to Philippine air travel. Smaller airlines fly smaller planes, and smaller airports have more-basic facilities. You're more likely to get on a flight during popular travel times with a bigger airline; on the other hand, the smaller planes often land (or at least try to) when the big planes turn back or stay on the ground. Generally speaking, PAL flies the largest and newest planes.

Flight routes tend to be skewed towards the major airports, so airlines can fly from busy Airport X to towns A, B and C, but not necessarily *between* A, B and C. Routes in the southern Philippines are particularly hit-and-miss.

Reasonably reliable flight information is available on the Internet from airline websites, and ⓦ www.lakbay.net offers online booking. Cebu Pacific Air, Air Philippines and Asian Spirit have roughly comparable fares, while PAL fares are a little higher. On certain routes you can get promotional (ie, seasonal) discounts of 20% to 30% if you buy your ticket two or three days in advance (check with the airline for exact details). Schedules and prices change, and promotions (as well as airlines) rapidly come and go. Currently, one-way fares from Manila to Cebu vary from P2098 to P3348, depending on which airline you're flying and whether you're paying the promotional or regular fare: a discounted one-way fare to Zamboanga costs P2179 on Cebu Pacific, P2178 on either Air Philippines or Asian Spirit, and P2478 on PAL.

It's best to book in advance, but don't plan too tight a schedule – flight delays are a fact of life in the Philippines. During the wet season, schedules can be erratic due to the weather. If there is a typhoon warning, most flights will be grounded; few ferries will venture out of harbours either, so you may just

have to wait it out. You can bank on the first few flights following a typhoon being massively overbooked. There's also the risk of smaller airlines cancelling flights at the last minute if not enough passengers show up at the airport or airfield.

Christmas, New Year, Holy Week (the week culminating in Easter) and All Saints Day/All Souls Day (1/2 November) are the most heavily booked periods. Wherever you go, be sure to reconfirm your flight, though this isn't always a guarantee against being bumped.

Baggage Allowance
Baggage allowance on small planes is usually limited to 10kg and there's no pay-for-extra policy (if they let extra luggage on, the plane wouldn't be able to take off). Check this when you book your flight, as you may need to leave some of your luggage in storage.

On flights between major cities (eg, Manila to Cebu or Davao), you can pay to have your baggage limit increased from the standard 20kg allowance for economy passengers (30kg for business class). PAL also offers a Mabuhay Miles Sportsplus programme that allows passengers to check in an extra 20kg for their sporting gear (golf set, scuba diving equipment, fishing rods and the like). To take advantage of this offer you need to become a member of PAL's Mabuhay Miles programme (you can apply online at ⓦ www.philippineairlines.com).

Domestic Departure Tax
Domestic departure tax varies from airport to airstrip and even from destination to destination. From Manila it's generally P100. Domestic departure tax at most small airports is P10. Mactan-Cebu International Airport has a curious pricing arrangement: departure tax from Manila to Cebu is P100; *to* Manila and all other domestic destinations it's P53.

BUS
An enormous number of bus services cover the Philippines and generally do it quite cheaply and reliably. Island-hopping on a bus is even an option; in fact, you can travel all the way from the northernmost tip of Luzon

to the southernmost corner of Mindanao without getting your feet wet.

Departures are usually quite frequent, but take care if there's only one bus a day – drivers sometimes decide to leave earlier than scheduled if the bus is full! Many Filipinos like to travel early in the morning or after nightfall, when it's cool, so there are often more buses at this time.

As in most countries, it pays to mind your gear while buses load and unload. Also, mountainous roads such as those in the Cordillera are noted for their hairpin turns and hair-raising, stomach-churning driving. While most drivers on these WWII-era tracks are just as interested in living as you are, some are less adept at driving than others. It may be worth asking locals about the current reputation of bus companies on your route.

Reservations

As noted earlier, drivers get an itchy pedal foot when the bus is full, and clutching a reservation to your chest as the bus zooms away is cold comfort. That said, reservations are useful, especially on popular routes and early morning buses where competition for a seat can be pretty stiff.

In bigger towns, reservations can be made with the bus company by phone or in person; in smaller centres, often a particular shop takes reservations for buses belonging to one or more companies. On some routes you can also ring to request that a bus stop for you at a designated time and place.

Costs

You can roughly calculate the fare and the time a bus journey will take based on distance. Regular buses generally cover a bit under 2km per peso and the average speed is about 50km per hour. *Voilà!* A 100km journey costs P50 or so and takes two hours.

On the other hand, you'd need a slide rule and a crystal ball to factor in chickens crossing the road, the number of flat tyres, heart-stopping spurts of speed and so on, all of which seem to have been magically factored into the actual price you pay. It's a bit easier to take a look at the prices written on chalkboards wherever the buses depart.

Air-con buses are around 15% to 20% more expensive than ordinary buses, and trips on gravel roads are normally pricier than travel on sealed roads.

TRAIN

The route south from Manila to the Bicol region in southeast Luzon is the only railway line in the country. Although it's old and none too speedy, it's a viable option for travel down to Naga and Legaspi and points along the way (see the Southeast Luzon chapter for details).

CAR & MOTORCYCLE

If time is short, driving yourself is a quicker option than relying on jeepneys and other public transport, but it does come with caveats. Philippine driving is possibly at its most manic in and around Manila, and in Luzon's central mountains. It's less life-threatening elsewhere, though, and verges on pleasant in and around cities such as Cebu.

Whatever you do, don't try to emulate the local style – driving in the Philippines is one area of 'cultural difference' where the 'when in Rome' principle doesn't apply.

Road Rules

Driving is on the right-hand side of the road (or at least it's supposed to be). If you do decide to hire a car or motorcycle, defensive driving is definitely the order of the day. Jeepneys and buses will stop at random to drop off and pick up passengers, and you should give way to buses in almost all situations.

In general, the outside lane is the safest place to be, though you can expect people to overtake on both sides if there's a gap in the traffic. On the expressways out of Manila, the hard shoulder is often used as an overtaking lane, so drivers should take extra care when exiting the highway.

Night driving holds its own particular hazards, quite apart from the issue of potential robberies in political trouble-spots (eg, certain parts of Mindanao). It's best to avoid driving at night if you can, but if you find yourself on the road after dark it pays to know that tricycles, motorcycles and even large trucks are often without lights. In small towns you should look out for school zones, which are frequently reduced to one lane, and for people who have put out tables and chairs on the street for an impromptu drinking/eating session.

Also beware of pedestrians suddenly emerging from the dark and darting across the road, or old cans fashioned into crude kerosene lamps, which are sometimes used to mark broken-down vehicles, accidents and roadworks.

With the exception of the expressways out of Manila, most roads in the Philippines are single lane, which can lead to some wild overtaking by local drivers.

Petrol is still cheap by North American or European standards, although prices are higher than in many Southeast Asian nations. One litre of unleaded costs around P17, while diesel is around P14.

Rental

Car Rentals are generally offered on a daily or weekly basis, with or without the added expense of a driver, and terms and conditions can vary widely from one car-hire company to another.

To give you an idea how the system works locally, here's how Budget does it: you must be between 25 and 60 years of age and hold an International Driving Licence. You will also be required to present a valid passport and a valid credit card such as American Express or Visa. You don't have to pay in advance (a requirement with other car hire companies), but a photocopy of your passport and credit card will be made for the company's records. Payment is made when you return the vehicle, at which point you may elect to pay in cash (your credit card imprint will then be destroyed). Both pesos and US dollars are accepted.

The big international car hire companies all have offices in Manila and at NAIA; see Getting There & Away in the Manila chapter for details.

In the Visayas, local car hire companies in Cebu and Iloilo generally charge around P1000 per 12 hours, with special deals for longer periods.

Motorcycle You can rent motorcycles and motor scooters in many tourist spots and shouldn't be too hard to turn. For example, resort-happy Alona Beach on Panglao Island is lined with motorcycles for hire from P600 per day. In towns, popular guesthouses and cafés sometimes have motorcycle rental shops nearby. In more remote areas, just ask around – even if there's no rental shop, you might find somebody willing to rent out their motorcycle for a fee.

As a rule, 125cc Honda or Suzuki cycles cost P500 to P700 per day; smaller cycles are around P350. Finding a helmet can be difficult.

JEEPNEY

A jeepney is what you'd get if you crossed a jeep with a bus. They're used for both long-distance and local transport in the Philippines. When taking long-distance jeepney rides, these are some things to keep in mind:

• Find out what the fare should be before you hop in. You can ask other passengers or passers-by, or, if that fails, try a nearby shop.
• Try not to be the first person to get into an empty jeepney. If the driver suddenly takes off, you may have just bought a ticket on a pricey 'special ride' (which is probably the case if the driver doesn't stop for anyone else). If this happens, ask the driver to stop, and explain that you're only looking for a regular ride.
• Take care if several men suddenly get in and try to sit near you. Chances are you're being set up to be pickpocketed – get off and find another vehicle.
• On long trips it's worth trying to get a seat next to the driver – there's more leg room in the front and the time passes more quickly if you can see where you're going.

Jeepneys are plentiful on most routes, but you may have to wait a while to get your ride: jeepney drivers are not inclined to depart until they've got (at least) a full load. During the rush hours or in the aftermath of a sudden downpour, be prepared to be packed in like sardines, with three or four hardy souls clinging to the roof of the vehicle for dear life. If you don't mind the expense, you can hire a jeepney (plus the jeepney driver, of course) and have it all to yourself for around P1500 a day (sometimes less outside Manila).

For information on local jeepney travel, see the following Local Transport section later in this chapter. For more on jeepneys themselves, see the boxed text 'Jeep Thrills' later.

VAN

Vans (minibuses) have become popular in many parts of the Philippines as rivals to jeepneys and regular buses. Operated privately, these vehicles usually hang around bus depots or busy shopping centres and take passengers (in air-conditioned comfort) to set destinations . The cost of a ride in a van is two or three times more than jeepneys charge (the basic fare in Manila is

P10 per passenger), but the extra comfort is certainly worth the additional cost. Unlike jeepneys and buses, which are often decrepit, without air-conditioning and therefore exposed to exhaust fumes and noise, these vans are generally newer vehicles and are always air-conditioned, sometimes to freezing point. The drawback is that drivers hate to head off with half-empty vehicles, so you may have to wait a while or pay extra to leave straightaway. Conversely, this mode of public transport has become so popular that it may be hard to get a seat (a van accommodates nine passengers plus driver and no 'hangers-on' are allowed).

Many vans, particularly those operating in Manila, are locally assembled Toyota models (Tamaraw) referred to as 'FX'. Like jeepneys, FX vans may be hired privately. The rates are rather arbitrary, so you'll simply have to rely on your common sense to determine whether the driver is asking a reasonable amount.

BICYCLE

Cycling in the Philippines is a seldom-explored option but, away from the treacherous traffic and exhaust fumes, it can be a great way to get around the quieter, less-visited islands such as the Batanes or Guimaras. Locals get around on bikes in many of these places and the promise of peaceful rides along coastal and mountain roads to out-of-the-way villages makes cycling well worth the effort.

You can take bicycles on domestic flights (you may have to partially disassemble the bicycle), but take heed of the baggage allowance on small planes (see Baggage Allowance in the Air section earlier in this chapter). If there's room, you can stow your bike on a bus or jeepney, usually for a small charge.

Rental

As guesthouses and resorts realise the virtues of hiring out bicycles, self-powered transport is getting easier to come by on some islands. Depending on where you are, mountain bikes go for anywhere from P100 to P300 per day.

Purchase

Purchasing a bicycle locally is no better or worse than anywhere else in the world. In the big cities you will most likely find a bicycle

shop or two in major shopping centres, though, unlike in most other Southeast Asian countries, there are very few commuters on bicycles, hence prices tend to be a bit higher.

Repairs

If you do intend to cycle in the Philippines, you'll save yourself a great deal of trouble by carrying a repair kit. It may be possible to obtain some professional repair services from bicycle stores in urban centres, but out in the sticks it's probably best to head for an auto repair shop. These are usually identified by a grease-stained shopfront, adorned by an old tire on which the word 'vulcanizing' has been painted. One or two mechanics in these establishments are bound to know something about bicycles.

HITCHING

Hitching is never entirely safe in any country in the world, and we don't recommend it. Travellers who decide to hitch should understand that they are taking a small but potentially serious risk. People who do choose to hitch will be safer if they travel in pairs and let someone know where they are planning to go. And, needless to say, hitching in the guerrilla territory of Mindanao is positively suicidal.

The cost of transport in the Philippines is generally so low that hitchhiking isn't worth the trouble; you're seldom left stranded without a cheap and willing jeepney in sight. A hitchhiker is such an unusual sight in the Philippines that most regular drivers will probably ignore you if you stand on the roadside with your thumb out; the only ones who might stop are truck or jeepney drivers, who would expect a few pesos if they give you a lift.

BOAT

Spend any length of time in the Philippines and you're bound to find yourself on a boat. Boats range from the high-class multideck WG&A ferries and highly efficient luxury passenger catamarans (known as fastcraft or fast ferries) to the smallest of outriggers (called *bangka* or pumpboats), which shuttle between myriad beaches and piers.

Ferry & Fastcraft

Ferries of all descriptions and levels of seaworthiness ply the waters between islands.

That Sinking Feeling

With 7000-plus islands and a mobile population, the Philippines relies heavily on ships of all descriptions to ferry folks around. Usually this works without a problem and there's no cause for alarm at the prospect of travelling by boat.

Unfortunately, when an accident does happen it can be big, and major accidents receive major coverage. The chances of something going wrong doubles during holiday times, when people desperate to get home roll the dice and hop on ferries in conditions they might otherwise avoid. Shipping companies and port officials don't always mind the extra business, either.

The tales that emerged from a recent ferry sinking are instructive. Whatever the final verdict on what happened, it's worth considering the scenarios before scrambling onto any old boat just to make that ambitious itinerary work.

Two days before the last Christmas of the century, Trans-Asia Shipping's MV *Asia South Korea* was sailing from Cebu City for Iloilo City on Panay when it sank in rough waters near Bantayan Island. Though most of the passengers and crew were rescued from the 27-year-old vessel, at least 54 people died, including several foreign tourists. The accident occurred almost 12 years to the day after the ferry *Doña Paz* collided with a tanker and sank off Mindoro killing 4341 people in history's worst peacetime shipping disaster.

Early evidence suggested that the *Asia South Korea* struck a reef, although it soon became apparent that many more survivors and bodies were recovered than should have been on the ship, at least according to the passenger and crew lists. Questions also arose about the port inspection, when departure was delayed while some 80 people left the boat. Some survivors claimed they'd seen passengers moved to uninspected parts of the ship and more allowed on board before it finally set sail (four hours late) at about 10pm; others also claimed that heavy cargo had been shifted away from the inspected area – which could dangerously unbalance the boat, especially in rough seas. The ship had passed safety inspections a few months earlier and passengers could be forgiven for thinking all was well. Allegations aside, here are three rules of thumb for ferry travel in the Philippines:

- If a boat looks overcrowded, it is.
- If sailing conditions feel wrong, they are.
- If you don't have to get on such a boat, don't.

There are plenty of reasonably safe options for getting from A to B – fastcraft are reliable, and locals can advise you on the better shipping companies on a given route. Remember: you're on holiday. There's always another boat – even if you may be stranded for a few days, there are worse places to be stuck than on a tropical island.

Russ Kerr

They are often overcrowded; cramming every orifice of leaky tubs with passengers doesn't make them watertight, but it does increase the probability of the ship sinking, especially in heavy seas (see the boxed text 'That Sinking Feeling'). You often have options as to which boat to travel on, so ask around about reliable companies and ferries and plan accordingly.

Fastcraft are becoming an increasingly common sight between islands. These are smaller, lighter and newer than the ferries, and well fitted, reliable and safe. They aren't called fastcraft for nothing, as they can cut long rides by half. One modern convenience used to excess on these spiffy ships is air-conditioning, which is permanently set to 'arctic' – take a sweater or fleece.

Three major shipping companies now handle interisland trips from Manila: Negros Navigation, Sulpicio and WG&A. These big players are reasonably reliable and safe. For details on WG&A schedules and routes, try
w www.wgasuperferry.com.

Though service on the main routes is pretty reliable, you'll need to be prepared for changes in the itinerary. Adverse weather conditions (especially during the typhoon season) or renovation of a ferry can totally alter the sailing times and boats used for various trips. As with planes, boats fill to overflowing during Christmas, New Year, Holy Week and All Saints Day/All Souls Day, as well as to the locations of major festivals.

On board, there are several levels of comfort and cost. Bunks on or below deck on 3rd class should be fine, as long as the ship isn't overcrowded.

Ferry prices vary widely but, as a guide, the fare for the 22-hour voyage between Manila and Cebu City costs P1285 to P2100 on Negros Navigation, depending on which class you choose to travel. Before purchasing your ticket, it pays to ask about discounts. Ferries, like airlines, offer promotional discounts (such as 20% off the regular fare if you buy your ticket two days in advance). Also inquire about student discounts: some shipping lines knock 20% to 30% off if you can show a valid student ID.

Small Craft

Ferries may carry more weight, but bangka (pumpboats) are the backbone of interisland travel. In some areas, in addition to single rides, bangka can be hired for day trips at a reasonable cost. Note; you may come across the term 'pax', which refers to the maximum number of passengers allowed on the boat, for example, '4-pax' means a four-person maximum. The cost of the boat trip could be shared between the number of passengers aboard.

Bangka are powered by recycled automotive engines, so it's best to plant yourself near the bow. They are often on regular schedules, but won't hit the surf if seas are rough; bangka pilots aren't always crazy about night trips either.

Be wary of crossing fast-flowing rivers, especially when swollen by floods. Jury-rigged and overloaded 'ferries' – often just several bangka tied beneath a wooden platform – are particularly prone to capsizing.

WALKING

The myriad paths and trails criss-crossing nearly every island make walking an easy way to meet people, find hidden spots and generally discover the joys of nature. In fact, the hardest thing about walking is convincing solicitous tricycle and minivan drivers that you really are doing it by choice.

Pedestrians should note that zebra crossings are for decoration – never assume that cars will stop for you; also, drivers tend to regard traffic lights as negotiable requests.

LOCAL TRANSPORT
Light Rail

Some parts of Manila are served by an elevated railway system (for details see Getting Around in the Manila chapter).

Jeepney

Jeepneys are the main mode of public transportation in most towns. They can be flagged down anywhere, but usually prefer to stop where there is a crowd of potential customers. The Tagalog phrase *bayad ko* (buy-yad-ko) translates as 'here is my fare' and will get the driver's attention.

Jeepneys follow a set route (though this can suddenly change due to traffic conditions) and stop on demand, but it can be hard to see where you are from inside the vehicle – the best seats are up the front next to the driver. In big cities like Manila, jeepneys are festooned with signboards indicating where the vehicle goes; in other places, there's one sign in the front. Occasionally they are unmarked and you'll have to ask the driver where it's going.

Paying for a jeepney ride is straightforward – there's a price (ask other passengers if you're unsure) and you pay it, usually under the watchful eye of fellow travellers, who will help with translations if need be.

The average price for a short trip in Manila is P4 and you can pay anywhere along the way. The driver usually has change, at least for smaller bills. If you are too far from the driver, simply hand your money to a passenger near the driver – not only will they pass on your money to the driver but will hand you back your change as well.

When you want to get off, you can rap on the roof, hiss (you'll be joined by a chorus of 'Psst!' from the other passengers) or use the correct term, *pára* (**pa**-ra), which is Tagalog for 'stop'.

Taxi

Manila is reputed to have Southeast Asia's cheapest taxi fares. However, since most Manila taxi drivers refuse to use their meters this is something of a moot point. Officially, flag fall is P25, after which the rate

Jeep Thrills

The traditional recipe for the jeepney, a uniquely Philippine concoction, is as follows: take one ex-US Army jeep, put two benches in the back with enough room for about 12 people, paint it every colour of the rainbow, add badges, horns, aerials, air fresheners, icons, lots of mirrors, a tape deck that plays only Philippine pop, a chrome horse (or a whole herd of them) and anything else you can think of. Then stuff 20 passengers on those benches, add four in front, hang a few more off the roof and drive like a maniac.

Alas, the old jeepneys are rapidly disappearing victims of rust, wear and tear and the desire to put a 'Made in the Philippines' stamp on this national institution. Products of a kinder, gentler international economy, blander vehicles are now being mass-produced from globalised automotive parts in Cebu and near Manila.

These roll off assembly lines pre-'jeepney-fied', leaving little room for the personal touches dear to purists.

This 'add chrome and stir' formula might sound like the automotive equivalent of the instant microwaved adobo, but remember the basic ingredient of the original – it's unlikely we've seen the last incarnation of the tried-and-true jeepney.

Mic Looby & Russ Kerr

is P2 for every 300m or every two minutes of waiting time.

Thousands of taxis ply the streets of Manila, but when you're desperately in need of their services there's suddenly not a single one available. The few that will stop are wont to 'interview' you regarding your destination and will drive off if they're not satisfied with your answers. Even locals are subjected to this irritating practice, a fact that might provide some paranoid travellers with a little comfort.

Thanks to a government drive to punish rude and dishonest drivers, many taxis now use meters. Some will still try to strike up a deal with you (foreigners are often subjected to this), but most will comply if you insist on the use of the meter (this may, of course, put you on the most roundabout course to your destination). On the other hand, you might want to privately hire a taxi, in which case the normal practice is to hire it by the hour (P200) or the day (P1500). As with everything else in the Philippines, the arrangement will depend on what (and how well) you negotiate with the driver.

Though it's become less common recently, there have been cases of taxi passengers

being robbed at gun or knife point, sometimes with the driver in cahoots with the culprits or the driver himself holding up the passengers. Nowadays, the drivers seem to be preferred prey of the criminals, perhaps because they're more likely to be carrying cash than the passengers!

The chances of getting robbed in a taxi are pretty slim during daylight hours, although it's wise to stay alert when travelling in deserted areas. Keep your pack or bag beside you or on your lap at all times and get out straight away (in a populated area, of course, not in the middle of nowhere) if you suspect you're being taken for a ride in more ways than one.

Tricycle

The tricycle is basically the Philippine rickshaw: a little, roofed sidecar bolted to a motorbike or, less often, a bicycle. Tricycles are found in their various forms nearly everywhere and are useful – essential even – for short trips. In many areas, they can also be rented by the hour for around P100.

The flat fare around town is often officially the same for tricycles and jeepneys (usually P4 per passenger; for longer trips, add 50% to 100%, depending on the driver's mood). You may get away with the locals' rate in some towns; in most touristy areas your chances of getting such a rate range from slim to nonexistent.

In these areas, drivers of motorised tricycles will routinely quote P150 – especially if night is fast approaching and/or the trip involves unsealed roads. Locals would pay a fraction of this price, so feel free to haggle.

Though often garishly done-up in the mode of a jeepney, you'll likely hear a tricycle before you see one – if the smoke-belching two-stroke engine doesn't get your attention, the persistent call of 'Hey Joe!' definitely will.

Tricycles in Manila (where they're also called pedicabs or sidecars) are normally confined to residential villages or subdivisions and will seldom venture away from their regular beat.

Kalesa

Horse-drawn carriages, generally known by the Castilian/Tagalog word *kalesa* (in Cebu City they're called *tartanillas*), are still the main form of transport in a few rural areas. Some of these two-wheeled remnants of Spanish days are quite ornate. They can be seen in such places as the historic town of Vigan in northern Luzon. In Manila, *kalesa* are mainly used to take tourists for a ride (sometimes, unfortunately, not just in the literal sense), particularly around Intramuros and Chinatown in Binondo. Set the price beforehand, without hesitating to haggle, to save yourself an unpleasant surprise later.

ORGANISED TOURS

For reliable local agencies offering a variety of tours, see Travel Agencies under Information in the Manila chapter. Live-aboard dive tours are plentiful – see the special section 'Diving in the Philippines' for more details.

Manila

☎ 02 • pop 10 million

HISTORY

Under Spanish rule, Manila was known as 'The Pearl of the Orient', the jewel of Spain's empire in the Pacific. Early tourists, like the 19th-century traveller Fedor Jagor, described it as a splendid, fortified city of wide, cobbled streets and regal townhouses. Sadly, little remains of that splendid city today. Ravaged during WWII, Manila has grown into a modern metropolis with few vestiges of its Spanish colonial past.

History records that Manila was founded in 1571 by the Spaniard Miguel Lopez de Legazpi although, in fact, a Muslim settlement had already existed on the site for centuries. King Philip II of Spain conferred on the city the illustrious title *Isigne y Siempre Leal Ciudad* (Distinguished and Ever Loyal City), but the city continued to be called by its pre-Hispanic name of Maynilad (presumed to be from *may*, meaning 'there is', and *nilad*, a mangrove plant that grew in abundance on the banks of the Pasig River), which was later corrupted to Manila.

Present-day Metro Manila is actually a conglomeration of 17 cities and municipalities unified by presidential decree in 1976. At the core of this vast urban sprawl is the City of Manila, which is formed by the districts of Intramuros, Ermita, Malate, Paco, San Miguel, Quiapo, Santa Cruz, Binondo, San Nicolas and Tondo, spread around the mouth of the Pasig River as it spills into Manila Bay. Intramuros, Ermita and Malate (the main area for budget accommodation) are important for tourists, and to a lesser degree Binondo and Quiapo (for Chinatown and the area around Quiapo Church).

Around this core are the other cities and municipalities. In the north, Caloocan (also spelled Kalookan) and the Cubao district of Quezon City are important departure points for north-bound buses, while the terminals for many south-bound buses are south of the centre in Baclaran, Pasay. The Manila Domestic Airport is in Pasay, but the Ninoy Aquino International Airport (NAIA) and Centennial Terminal (NAIA II) are located further south in Parañaque (pa-ran-**ya**-ke). East of Pasay lie other centres such as Makati

Highlights

- Walk on the walls of Intramuros in late afternoon, then watch the legendary sunset over Manila Bay
- Stroll through the weird and wonderful markets and side streets of Quiapo, Santa Cruz and Binondo
- Get into the action of a cockfight, after which take in the sights of Baclaran Market
- Pay your respects at the bizarre Chinese Cemetery with its air-conditioned houses for the dead
- Explore the other face of the city with a tour of bustling Ayala Center and Ortigas Center
- Check out the trendy eateries and nightspots on J Nakpil St and surroundings
- See the treasures at the National Museum and Manila's other museums and art galleries

Metro Manila pp90-1
Intramuros p96
Binondo, Santa Cruz & Quiapo p99
Rizal Park, Ermita, Malate & Paco pp102-3
Parañaque & Pasay p110
Makati p114
Quezon City & Cubao p109
Makati Avenue & P Burgos Street p107
M Adriatico & A Mabini Streets p104
Bus Destinations from Manila p128

✪ MANILA

(the main business district), Pasig, Mandaluyong and the municipality of San Juan.

While remnants of the Spanish colonial era, including historic structures like San Agustin Church, are still seen in the old walled city of Intramuros, few of the highrises in Makati's Ayala Center are more than 30 years old. Fringing the centre are exclusive neighbourhoods like Forbes Park and Bel-Air, where Manila's wealthy citizens

The *nilad* – a mangrove plant used to make soap; also part of the name given to Manila

live in secluded luxury, guarded by their own security forces.

In stark contrast, the coastline north of the Pasig River is home to sprawling shantytowns, the most infamous being Tondo, where some 200,000 people are crammed into an area of only 1.5 sq km. Successive governments have tried to improve living conditions and demolish the shantytowns, but the population of slum-dwellers continues to hover at around 1.5 million.

Most tourists only use Manila as a base for a couple of days before heading north to the cooler highlands, or south to the beaches of Mindoro and other islands. However, there's plenty to see and do in the capital if you're prepared to give it the time, from excellent museums to lively markets and cultural oddities such as cockfighting and the Chinese Cemetery.

ORIENTATION

The 'tourist belt' formed by Ermita and Malate is probably the best place to be based in Manila. Most of the budget and mid-range accommodation is found here, as well as many good restaurants and nightspots. The area of greatest interest to tourists is bound by Roxas Blvd, P Ocampo Sr St (Vito Cruz St), Taft Ave and the Pasig River.

Rizal Park, Intramuros, the Manila Central Post Office and the Immigration Office are all just north of the tourist belt, while long-distance ferries leave from the far side of the Pasig River at North Harbor. Nearby

Divisoria Market (see the Binondo, Santa Cruz & Quiapo map) is a major centre for cheap clothing. In the same area are colourful Chinatown (Binondo) and Quiapo, where you'll find a fascinating maze of markets and crowded side streets.

All these destinations can be reached by jeepney from A Mabini St in Ermita or Malate. The business centre of Makati is accessible by air-con FX van from M H del Pilar St, and by bus from Quiapo and the western end of Sen Gil Puyat Ave (Buendia Ave) or Epifanio de los Santos Ave (EDSA) in Pasay.

The Light Rail Transit (LRT) runs from Baclaran in Pasay to Monumento in Caloocan, but it isn't convenient for Makati or Quezon City, and it only runs along the eastern fringes of the tourist belt. You can, however, take the LRT to EDSA and then change to the Metro Rail Transit (MRT), which makes stops in Makati, Mandaluyong and Quezon City. For more details on transport options in Manila see Getting Around at the end of this chapter.

With all the heat, noise, traffic and smog, getting around Manila can be quite an ordeal. To add to the general confusion, many streets are known by two, or even three, names. Rizal Ave, the main road from Santa Cruz to Monumento, is usually referred to as Avenida; A Arnaiz Ave in Makati is also called Pasay Rd, its former name; P Ocampo Sr St is alternately known as Vito Cruz St; and Sen Gil Puyat Ave is often referred to as Buendia Ave or simply Buendia. To make matters worse, street numbers are often unmarked. Instead, an address is usually specified as an intersection, eg, corner Pedro Gil and A Mabini Sts.

Maps

The E-Z Maps, published by United Tourist Promotions, cover Manila, Makati and Quezon City in fine detail, though they lack a scale (P90). The Philippine Motor Association issues a very detailed 1:20,000 scale map of Metro Manila (P185), but it's not suitable for carrying around. Nelles Verlag publishes a Manila map (1:17,500) and a combined Philippines and Manila map (1:1,500,000), both of which show important buildings in the metropolitan area. However, the best all-round map of Manila is the portable CitiAtlas Metro Manila guide (P330), available at major bookstores around Manila.

INFORMATION
Tourist Offices

DOT Information Center (☎ 524 2384, hotlines 525 2000, 526 2257; Room 106, DOT Bldg, Rizal Park; open 7am-6pm daily) offers helpful information and friendly advice on anything related to travel in the Philippines. The staff will readily answer inquiries, in person or over the phone. It's best to enter the building from T M Kalaw St. There's a satellite DOT kiosk in the arrival lounge at NAIA and another at NAIA II.

Corregidor Foundation (☎ 525 3429, 525 3420; Room 212, DOT Bldg, Rizal Park; open 8am-6pm Mon-Fri) handles general inquiries about the historic island of Corregidor, a popular day-tour destination from Manila. (For details on Corregidor island and how to get there see that entry in the Around Manila chapter.)

Corregidor Visitors Center (☎ 834 5048, 550 1347; CCP Complex, Roxas Blvd; open 7.30am-5pm daily) accepts tour/hotel reservations for the former island fortress.

Intramuros Administration (☎ 527 3138; 5th floor, Palacio del Gobernador, General Luna St, Intramuros; open 8am-5pm Mon-Fri) provides general information on Intramuros as well as details of activities such as Intramuros Evenings, a series of cultural shows inside the walled city.

Intramuros Visitors Center (☎ 527 2961; Fort Santiago, Santa Clara St, Intramuros; open 8am-noon & 1pm-6pm daily) hands out information on the walled city and also arranges guided tours of the historic site.

Money

For general information on changing money in the Philippines, see Money in the Facts for the Visitor chapter.

It is easy to change money in Manila, but you will need your passport and the original receipts to change travellers cheques. Also note that only a handful of banks and moneychangers accept travellers cheques in currencies other than US dollars.

The whole of Malate and Ermita is peppered with moneychangers, and there are places all over the city where you can change foreign currency into Philippine pesos (but beware of rip-offs; see Exchanging Money

under Money in the Facts for the Visitor chapter for advice on avoiding scams etc). Some department stores also have foreign-exchange sections.

Most banks in Manila have ATMs and these are usually your safest and most hassle-free way to get local currency. You can also change foreign cash and travellers cheques at most banks in Manila.

American Express (AmEx) and Thomas Cook maintain offices in Manila and can be contacted to issue replacements if your travellers cheques are lost or stolen.

American Express (Malate ☎ 524 8681, 524 8682; 1810 A Mabini St; open 8.30am-4pm Mon-Fri, 9am-noon Sat • Makati ☎ 867 4888; ACE Bldg, cnr Rada & De la Rosa Sts; open 9am-4pm Mon-Fri, 9am-noon Sat • Mandaluyong ☎ 689 1052; SM Megamall, Epifanio de los Santos Ave; open 10am-5.30pm Mon-Fri, 10am-1pm Sat) for cash and AmEx travellers cheques.

Thomas Cook (Makati ☎ 816 3701; Skyland Bldg, cnr Sen Gil Puyat Ave & Tindaloo St; open 8.30pm-4pm Mon-Fri • Pasig ☎ 638 5309; Metrobank Bldg, cnr Julia Vargas & San Miguel Aves, Ortigas Center; open 8.30am-4pm Mon-Fri) for cash and Thomas Cook travellers cheques.

Post & Communications

Post The **Manila Central Post Office** (☎ 527 8561; between Jones & MacArthur Bridges, open 8am-noon & 1pm-5pm Mon-Fri, 8am-noon Sat) handles all kinds of postal transactions. The imposing building is a magnificent example of neoclassical architecture, one of a few survivors of an early 1900s plan to convert Manila's civic centre into a complex of Greco-Roman structures. It's worth visiting the building even if only to admire the architecture.

If you're just buying stamps, you might be better off going to the tiny **Rizal Park Post Office** (Katigbak Drive, Rizal Park; open 8am-noon & 1pm-5pm Mon-Fri), opposite the Manila Hotel. There are also post offices throughout the city, such as the **Makati Central Post Office** (☎ 844 0150; Sen Gil Puyat Ave near cnr of Ayala Extension; open 8am-5pm Mon-Fri) and the **Domestic Road Postal Center** (☎ 831 0509; Domestic Rd near Manila Domestic Airport; open 7am-5pm Mon-Fri). Satellite post offices operate at both the domestic and international airports.

METRO MANILA

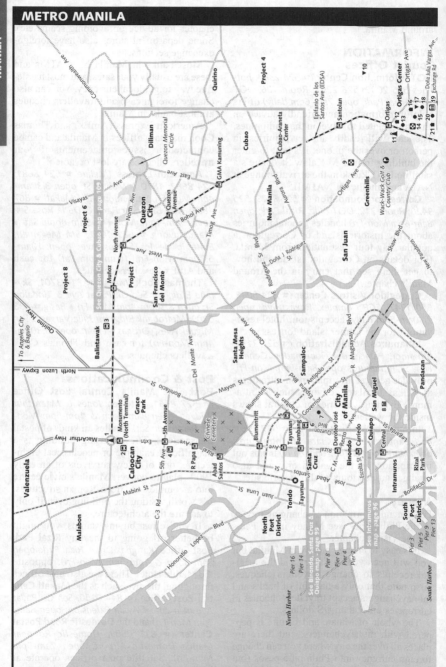

See Quezon City & Cubao map - page 109

See Binondo, Santa Cruz & Quiapo map - page 99

See Intramuros map - page 96

MANILA

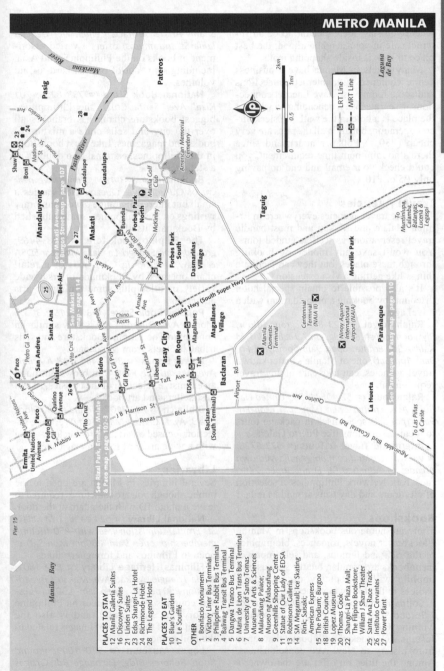

METRO MANILA

LRT Line

MRT Line

PLACES TO STAY
12 Manila Galleria Suites
16 Discovery Suites
21 Linden Suites
23 Edsa Shangri-La Hotel
24 Richmonde Hotel
28 The Legend Hotel

PLACES TO EAT
10 Blue's Garden
17 Le Soufflé

OTHER
1 Bonifacio Monument
2 Victory Liner Bus Terminal
3 Philippine Rabbit Bus Terminal
4 Baliwag Transit Bus Terminal
5 Dangwa Tranco Bus Terminal
6 Maria de Leon Trans Bus Terminal
7 University of Santo Tomas
   Museum of Arts & Sciences
8 Malacañang Palace;
   Museo ng Malacañang
9 Greenhills Shopping Center
11 Statue of Our Lady of EDSA
13 Robinsons Galleria
14 SM Megamall; Ice Skating
   Rink; Saisaki;
   American Express
15 The Podium; Burgoo
18 British Council
19 Lopez Museum
20 Thomas Cook
22 Shangri-La Plaza Mall;
   The Filipino Bookstore;
   William J Shaw Theater
25 Santa Ana Race Track
26 Instituto Cervantes
27 Power Plant

Email & Internet Access No matter where you stay, there's bound to be an Internet café in your neighbourhood; the best place to look is inside shopping malls.

Many hotels in Manila have a business centre equipped with Internet connections and some rooms also have Internet connections. User rates vary, depending on whether the place is a hole in the wall or a sleek aircon operation, but all in all the rates are very cheap (P30 to P60 per hour); and since there's no minimum time requirement, you could check your email and end up paying only P5 or P10.

Travel Agencies

There are travel agencies everywhere in Ermita, Malate and Makati and most handle travel reservations as well as guided tours. You won't save any money by booking through these places, but they can facilitate things like getting a visa extension.

It's also possible to obtain special hotel discounts by booking a prepaid room with a travel agent.

Rajah Travel (☎ 523 8801; ground floor, Plywood Industries Bldg, cnr A Mabini & T M Kalaw Sts, Ermita; open 9am-5pm Mon-Fri, 9am-1pm Sat), one of Manila's better known travel agencies, can take care of any travel requirement.

Rajah Tours (☎ 522 0541; 533 United Nations Ave, Ermita; open 9am-5pm Mon-Fri, 9am-1pm Sat) specialises in package tours to local destinations like Puerto Galera.

Interisland Travel & Tours (☎ 523 8720; W www.interisland.com.ph; Manila Midtown Arcade, M Adriatico St, Ermita; open 24hr) runs Tour Network Philippines, a selection of city tours and day trips around Manila.

Bookshops

There are numerous bookshops in Manila. Blockbuster novels, romances, biographies of the rich and famous, and self-improvement books are popular, but the serious bibliophile will find plenty of alternative choices in the following places.

Solidaridad Bookshop (P Faura St near cnr J Bocobo St, Ermita), owned by the award-winning Filipino author Francisco Sionil Jose, is well stocked with books that range from history to New Age consciousness. Among the titles on offer are the owner's own collections of short stories and essays.

Tradewinds Books (☎ 527 2111; 3rd floor, Silahis Arts & Artifacts Center, 744 General Luna St, Intramuros) offers a varied assortment of books on the Philippines and Asia, including some out-of-print or hard-to-find volumes.

National Book Store (☎ 733 8256; 701 Rizal Ave, Santa Cruz), the Philippines' biggest bookstore chain, has branches all over the city and sells quite a mixture of books and magazines. Like most bookshops in the Philippines, National also doubles as a stationers.

Bookmark (☎ 373 1811; Timog Ave near cnr of Quezon Ave, Quezon City) carries a small but interesting range of contemporary writings on the Philippines, some published by Bookmark itself.

The Filipino Bookstore (☎ 638 4469; ground floor, Shangri-La Plaza Mall, cnr EDSA & Shaw Blvd, Pasig City), part of a retail chain operated by Bookmark, offers a wide variety of titles plus some Philippine arts and crafts.

Popular Book Store (☎ 372 2162; 305 T Morato Ave, Quezon City) is very similar in concept to The Filipino Bookstore and sells tribal artefacts from Mindanao.

Power Books (☎ 844 4455; 918 A Arnaiz Ave, Makati City) lets you browse through an extensive selection of the classics, recent best-sellers and art books.

Bibliarch (☎ 752 7107; ground floor, Glorietta 3, Ayala Center, Makati City) carries a selection focused on art and architecture, along with a wide array of foreign magazines.

Libraries

Several libraries in Manila are open to the public, though you are sometimes required to leave a photo ID with the guard at the door.

National Library (☎ 524 0498; T M Kalaw St, Ermita; admission free with P50 lifetime membership; open 9am-4.30pm Mon-Sat) is open to Filipinos and foreigners alike.

Filipinas Heritage Library (☎ 892 1801; Ayala Triangle, Makati Ave, Makati City; admission P50 per day; open 9am-4.30pm Tues-Sat) contains good resources on Philippine history, art and culture, and is also the repository of thousands of images related to the Philippines.

Lopez Museum (☎ 910 1009; ground floor, Benpres Bldg, Exchange Rd, Ortigas Center, Pasig City; admission P70; open

8.30am-5pm Mon-Fri, 8am-4pm Sat) owns an impressive collection of 13,000 books.

Photographic Services

One-hour film processing is offered by Kameraworld, Island Photo and Kodak Express, all of which have outlets throughout the city.

Expect to pay about P50 per roll for processing, plus P5.50 per print.

Cultural Centres

Several countries have cultural centres in Manila. Most have their own libraries and stage regular cultural events, such as film screenings.

Alliance Française (☎ 895 7585) 209 Nicanor Garcia St, Bel-Air II, Makati City
Australia Centre (☎ 754 6135) Ground floor, 104 Paseo de Roxas, Makati City
British Council (☎ 914 1011–14) 10th floor, Taipan Place, Emerald Ave, Ortigas Center, Pasig City
Goethe Institut Manila (☎ 722 4671) 687 Aurora Blvd, Quezon City
Information Resource Center (☎ 523 1001, 897 1994) US Embassy, Roxas Blvd, Ermita
Instituto Cervantes (☎ 526 1482–85) 2515 Leon Guinto St, Malate

Laundry

Though do-it-yourself laundromats are quite a rarity, there are plenty of places offering cheap laundry services throughout Manila. Walk around the area where you're staying and soon you will find a glass-fronted shop with rows of washing machines inside.

It usually costs P30 to P50 per 1kg of washing. One such place is the **Sea Breeze Laundry** *(☎ 525 4971; 1317 M Adriatico St, Malate; open 8am-8pm Mon-Sat, 8am-5pm Sun)*; another is the musically named **Laba Laba Doo** *(☎ 522 8438; 1647-D M Adriatico St, Malate; open 7am-9pm Mon-Sat, 9am-5pm Sun)*.

Medical Services

Reliable private medical services are provided by the following centres:

Makati Medical Center (☎ 815 9911) 2 Amorsolo St, Makati City
Manila Doctors Hospital (☎ 524 3011) 667 United Nations Ave, Ermita
Manila Medical Center (☎ 523 8131) 1122 General Luna St, Ermita

A charity hospital, the government-funded **Philippine General Hospital** *(☎ 521 8450; Taft Ave, Ermita)* tends to be overcrowded, while the **Philippine Heart Center** *(☎ 925 2401; East Ave, Quezon City)* specialises in ailments of the heart.

For some alternative therapy or just plain good massage, try the **Balikatan Therapeutic Massage Clinic of the Blind** *(☎ 843 1081; A Arnaiz Ave, Makati City; open 11am-8pm Mon-Sat)*. An hour-long massage by one of the blind masseurs costs P250.

Emergency

As in any big city, crime is a part of life in Manila, with foreigners seen as easy prey by pickpockets and petty criminals. As much as possible, avoid walking around on your own, particularly at night and in deserted places. Public parks are best visited during the day; venture into them at night only in the company of Filipino friends or fellow tourists.

If the worst happens, call ☎ 117, the police patrol number, or contact the **Tourist Police Assistance Unit** *(☎ 524 1660, 524 1728; DOT Bldg, T M Kalaw St, Rizal Park)*.

The **Western District Police Station** *(☎ 523 8391, 521 9695; United Nations Ave, Ermita)* and **Rizal Park Police Detail** *(☎ 527 1808; Katigbak Dr, Rizal Park)* are both within easy reach if you're in the tourist belt.

Dangers & Annoyances

With a total population of close to 10 million people, Manila has earned a reputation for being overcrowded. Traffic, noise, crime and air pollution are also major annoyances, though the latter plays an important part in producing Manila Bay's legendary sunsets.

THINGS TO SEE & DO

Perhaps because Manila is such an overwhelming place, most foreign visitors can't wait to leave the capital. However, there are plenty of attractions for those prepared to overlook Manila's flaws – from vibrant markets and historic buildings to museums celebrating every aspect of the Philippines' unique cultural mix.

Rizal Park

Still widely known as Luneta (its name until it was officially changed in the 1950s), Rizal Park is spread out over some 60 hectares of open lawns, ornamental gardens, paved walks and wooded areas, dotted with monuments to almost every Filipino hero you care to mention.

Every day hundreds of Filipinos come here to stroll, jog, picnic, sing and play music, or just relax away from the swarming traffic. At dawn, various groups gather to practise t'ai chi or the local martial art of *arnis*, or *arnis de mano*, a pre-Hispanic style of stick-fighting. There are formalised displays of martial arts on Sunday afternoon. The long-running *Concert at the Park* also takes place at the **Open Air Auditorium** *(admission free; starts around 6pm Sun)*.

The park is dedicated to the Philippine national hero, Dr José Rizal, who was executed here by the Spanish colonial authorities on 30 December 1896 for inciting revolution. The **Rizal Monument**, guarded by sentries in full regalia, contains the hero's mortal remains and stands as a symbol of Filipino nationhood (visiting heads of state customarily lay a wreath here). Across the boulevard, directly in front of the Rizal Monument, the **0km Post** marks the spot from where distances in the Philippines are measured.

To one side of the monument you will find the **Site of Rizal's Execution** *(admission P10; open 8am-5pm)*; at the entrance is a black granite wall inscribed with Rizal's *Mi Ultimo Adios* (My Last Farewell). Eight tableaux of life-size bronze statues recreate the dramatic last moments of the hero's life; at night these statues become part of a light-and-sound presentation entitled **The Martyrdom of Dr José Rizal** *(admission P50; staged in Pilipino 7pm & in English 8pm Wed-Sun)*.

At the western end of the park stands the **Quirino Grandstand** where Philippine Presidents take their oath of office and deliver their first address to the nation. At the opposite end you will find the **Relief Map of the Philippines**, which shows the entire Philippine archipelago in miniature. The centre is dominated by the **Central Lagoon and Fountains**.

Along one side are three ornamental gardens – the whimsical **Chinese Garden** *(admission P5)*, the austere **Japanese Garden** *(admission P5)* and the tropical **Manila Orchidarium** *(admission P100)*. The **Chess Plaza** is a shady spot where aspiring grandmasters test their skills against each other and the clock.

Designed to complement each other, the neoclassical Department of Tourism (DOT) Building and National Museum (for details see Museums later in this chapter) face each other across the **Teodoro Valencia Circle** (formerly Agrifina Circle). On the northwestern edge of the park, the **Planetarium** *(☎ 527 7889; P Burgos St; adult/child P50/30; open 8am-4.30pm Tues-Sat)* stages projections of the stars.

Beautifully illuminated at night, the clock tower of the **Manila City Hall** is visible above the treetops as you face northeast. Further north, fronting the Manila Central Post Office, stands the **Metropolitan Theater**, now in a state of disrepair but still a stunning piece of Art Deco architecture. To one side of the theatre lies one of Manila's best-kept secrets – the **Arroceros Forest Park** *(admission free; open 8am-5pm daily)*, an unexpected pocket of untamed nature in the middle of the concrete jungle.

Intramuros

When Miguel Lopez de Legazpi wrested control of Manila, he chose to erect his fortress on the remnants of the Muslim settlement by the mouth of the Pasig River. Intramuros, as Legazpi's walled city came to be called, was invaded by Chinese pirates, threatened by Dutch forces, and held by the British, Americans and Japanese at various times, yet it survived until the closing days of WWII, when it was finally destroyed by US bombing during the Battle of Manila.

From its founding in 1571, Intramuros was the exclusive preserve of the Spanish ruling classes. Within its massive walls were imposing government buildings, stately homes, numerous churches, convents, monasteries, schools, hospitals and cobbled plazas.

The native populace was settled in surrounding areas such as Paco and Binondo, while the 'troublesome' Chinese were kept under permanent supervision in a ghetto called the Parian.

Fortified with bastions (baluarte), the wall enclosed an area of some 64 hectares. Gates (puerta) with drawbridges provided access to and from the outside world.

At its height, Intramuros instilled fear in Spain's enemies as a mighty European city, the only one of its kind in Asia. By the end of WWII, the walls here were almost all that remained of the once proud city, and nearly 100,000 Filipino civilians had perished in the crossfire.

Despite the devastation, one can still feel a strong sense of history on a visit to Intramuros. Most of the walls, gates and bulwarks have been restored, and it is possible to walk on the 4.5km-long rampart. Start your walking tour by dropping into the Intramuros Visitors Center at the entrance to Fort Santiago for information (for details see Fort Santiago later). The tour is best done during the day as some sections of the walls are closed or inadequately lit at night.

Just outside the walls, on what used to be the moat surrounding the city, is the manicured golf course of Club Intramuros (☎ 527 6612; Bonifacio Dr).

San Agustin Church & San Agustin Museum

San Agustin Church (☎ 527 4060; General Luna St, Intramuros; open 6.30am-8.30am & 4.30pm-7.30pm Mon-Sat, 8am-11am & 6pm-8pm Sun) was the only building left intact after the destruction of Intramuros. Built between 1587 and 1606, it is the oldest church in the Philippines. The present structure is actually the third to stand on the site, and has weathered seven major earthquakes, as well as the Battle of Manila.

The massive facade conceals an ornate interior filled with objects of great historical and cultural merit. Note the intricate trompe l'oeil frescoes on the vaulted ceiling. In the chapel to the left of the main altar is a crypt containing the mortal remains of Miguel Lopez de Legazpi.

Spread over two floors of the adjacent Augustinian monastery, the San Agustin Museum (☎ 527 4060; adult/child P45/20; open 9am-noon & 1pm-5pm daily) is a treasure house of antiquities that give the visitor tantalising glimpses of the fabled riches of old Manila.

Manila Cathedral

The Manila Cathedral (☎ 527 5836; cnr Postigo & General Luna Sts, Intramuros; open 8am-noon & 3pm-6pm daily) was destroyed in WWII, but the present edifice, erected in 1951, looks suitably ancient with its weathered Romanesque facade and graceful cupola. This is actually the sixth church on the site. Inside are a gilded altar, a 4500-pipe organ and rosette windows with beautiful stained glass.

The cathedral fronts Plaza de Roma, which was a bloody bullring until it was converted into a plaza. To one side lie the forlorn ruins of the Ayuntamiento, once the grandest building in all of Intramuros. Palacio del Gobernador, on the other side of the square, is a modern structure that houses the Intramuros Administration, custodians of the historic site.

Casa Manila & Bahay Tsinoy

Casa Manila (☎ 527 4084; Plaza Luis Complex, General Luna St, Intramuros; adult/student P40/15; open 9am-noon & 1pm-6pm Tues-Sun) is a faithfully restored Spanish colonial home that offers a window into the opulent lifestyle of the gentry in the 19th century. The three-storey house is furnished with antiques from the period.

Bahay Tsinoy (☎ 527 6083; Kaisa Angelo Heritage Center, cnr Anda & Cabildo Sts, Intramuros; adult/student P100/60; open 1pm-5pm Tues-Fri, 9am-5pm Sat & Sun) features three-dimensional dioramas and a vast collection of photos that shows the role played by the Chinese in the growth of Manila. Present-day Chinese-Filipinos call themselves Chinoys or Tsinoys, hence the museum's name. For details on other museums around Manila see Museums later in this chapter.

Fort Santiago

Guarding the vital entrance to the Pasig River, Fort Santiago (☎ 527 2961; Santa Clara St, Intramuros; admission P40; open 8am-6pm daily) was once the seat of Spanish military power. Designated a Shrine of Freedom in 1950, today it is a memorial to José Rizal, who was imprisoned here in the final days before his execution, and to all Filipinos who fought or died for the cause of freedom.

The Rizal Shrine (admission free; open 8am-4pm daily), in the building where Rizal was incarcerated, contains various displays of Rizal memorabilia, including a reliquary containing one of his vertebrae, the first draft of his novel Noli Me Tangere (Touch Me Not) and the original copy of Mi Ultimo Adios (My Last Farewell) which was smuggled out of his cell inside an oil lamp.

At the far end of the fort you will find the infamous dungeon where prisoners were drowned in water seeping through the walls.

INTRAMUROS

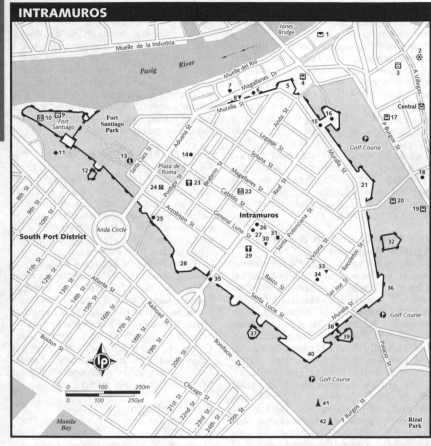

The dungeon remains closed to visitors, though it has been restored after being ripped apart in 1988 by government-sanctioned treasure hunters looking for the legendary treasure of General Tomoyuki Yamashita (for more information see the boxed text 'Gold-Diggers' in the Facts About the Philippines chapter).

Nearby, the shell of a Spanish military barracks has been turned into an open-air theatre called **Dulaang Rajah Sulayman**. Rizal spent his last night in a cellblock at one end of these barracks. Brass footprints set into the pavement mark his final steps to the execution spot in Rizal Park. For more information on Rizal see 'The Spanish Era' under History in the Facts about the Philippines chapter.

Cultural Center of the Philippines

The Cultural Center of the Philippines (☎ 551 3725; Roxas Blvd, Malate; free admission to building, varied admission charges to performances; building open 9am-5pm Mon-Fri, 10am-6pm Sat & Sun), usually referred to as CCP, was conceived to be a celebration of Filipino culture during the early years of the Marcos regime. Costing some P40 million of people's money to build (a great sum of money at the time), it was opened with great aplomb in September 1969.

The CCP never quite lived up to its promise of being a centre of culture for the masses, but the building has a grand design by noted Filipino architect Leandro Locsin. Inside are an art gallery, a museum of musical instruments and three theatres that

INTRAMUROS

PLACES TO STAY & EAT
8 Starbucks
30 Barbara's
31 Hotel Intramuros de Manila
33 Ilustrado

OTHER
1 Manila Central Post Office
2 Arroceros Forest Park
3 Metropolitan Theater
4 Saulog Transit & St Anthony Transit Bus Terminal
5 Baluarte de San Gabriel
6 Puerta Isabel II
7 Immigration Office
9 Dulaang Rajah Sulayman
10 Rizal Shrine
11 Club Intramuros

12 Reducto de San Francisco
13 Intramuros Visitors Center
14 Ayuntamiento
15 Puerta del Parian
16 Revellin del Parian
17 Jeepneys & FX to Quiapo & Santa Cruz
18 Manila City Hall
19 Buses, Jeepneys & FX to Makati & Pasay City
20 Alps Transit Bus Terminal
21 Baluarte de San Francisco de Dilao
22 Bahay Tsinoy
23 Manila Cathedral
24 Intramuros Administration; Palacio del Gobernador

25 Puerta del Postigo
26 Casa Manila
27 Galeria Andrea
28 Baluarte de Santa Lucia
29 San Agustin Church; San Agustin Museum
32 Revellin de Recoletos
34 Silahis Arts & Artifacts Center; Tradewinds Books
35 Puerta de Santa Lucia
36 Baluarte de San Andres
37 Reducto de San Pedro
38 Puerta Real
39 Puerta Real Gardens; Acuario de Manila
40 Baluarte de San Diego
41 Legazpi Statue
42 Ninoy Aquino Statue

regularly present performances by local artists such as the Philippine Philharmonic Orchestra and Ballet Philippines and foreign artists.

Dotted around the complex are the **Folk Arts Theater** (Tanghalang Balagtas), the **Philippine International Convention Center**, the **Westin Philippine Plaza** and the haunted-looking Former Manila Film Center, which is now being put to good use by **Amazing Philippines Theatre** (☎ 833 5785; admission P1100 including unlimited drinks; performances staged 7.30pm & 9pm daily), a transvestite revue of lovely 'ladies' in their feathers and sequins. (For information on Theatres in Manila see Entertainment later.)

Nearby, the **GSIS Museo ng Sining** (☎ 551 1301; GSIS Bldg; admission free; open 9am-11am & 1pm-4pm Tues-Sat) houses an extensive collection of contemporary Filipino art. On display are paintings, sculptures and tapestries by such famous Filipino artists as Fernando Amorsolo and Hernando Ocampo.

To get to the CCP from Malate or Ermita, take any Baclaran-bound jeepney on M H del Pilar St and get off at Harrison Plaza. You can then either walk to the CCP or look around P Ocampo Sr St (Vito Cruz St) for one of the jeepneys that ply a circular route around the complex.

Another way is to head south on Roxas Blvd on foot or by private car. As you approach the complex, to your left is the **Bangko Sentral ng Pilipinas** which oversees the country's monetary affairs, and to

your right is the **Manila Yacht Club** where the moneyed few keep their pleasure craft.

Museums

Whether you are interested in archaeology, tribal art or contemporary sculpture and painting, you're likely to find something to satisfy your curiosity in this city's many museums.

The **National Museum** (☎ 527 1209; Former Finance Bldg, T Valencia Circle, Rizal Park; admission P100, free Thur; open 9am-5pm Tues-Sun), also known as the Museum of the Filipino People, houses the best of the museum's vast collection, including the skullcap of the Philippines' earliest known inhabitant, Tabon Man (said by some to actually be a woman), who lived around 24,000 BC (for more information see Way, Way Back under History in the Facts about the Philippines chapter). A large section of the museum is devoted to porcelain plates, coins, jewellery etc recovered from the wreck of the *San Diego*, a Spanish galleon that sank off the coast of Luzon in 1600. Other treasures include a large collection of pre-Hispanic artefacts and musical instruments.

With most of its treasures now in the building across the road, the **Old Congress Building** (☎ 527 0306; P Burgos St; admission free, ID required; open 9am-5pm Tues-Sun) has only a few rooms currently open to the public while the building is renovated. Most of what is on display are natural science exhibits, such as fossils and stuffed animals, but in the central hall you will find the stunning

MANILA

Spoliarium, painted by Filipino master Juan Luna, which won the Gold Medal at the 1884 Madrid Exposition.

The **Metropolitan Museum of Manila** (☎ 521 1517; BSP Complex, Roxas Blvd; adult/student P50/30; open 10am-6pm Mon-Sat) showcases a collection of gold ornaments and ancient pottery (owned by the Bangko Sentral ng Pilipinas) plus changing exhibits of contemporary art.

The **University of Santo Tomas Museum of Arts & Sciences** (☎ 781 1815; University of Santo Tomas, España Blvd; adult/child P30/20; open 10am-4pm Tues-Fri) was formally founded in 1870, but some natural history items date back to as early as 1682. Rare antiques and relics are also on display.

The **Ayala Museum** (☎ 812 1191; Makati Ave, Makati City; adult/child P55/30, guided tour P100; open 10am-6pm Tues-Sun) is best known for a series of miniature dioramas depicting key events in Philippine history. There are also changing exhibits by contemporary artists.

The **Museo Pambata** (☎ 523 1797; cnr Roxas & South Blvds; adult/child P60/40; open 9am-5pm Tues-Sat, 1pm-5pm Sun) uses interactive displays to entertain and instruct children, though adults can easily spend hours with the fascinating hands-on exhibits.

Malacañang Palace

The official residence of the President of the Philippines (J P Laurel Sr St, San Miguel) was originally a Spanish grandee's summer house. It used to be possible to go on a tour of the palace but tours are no longer offered. Likewise, the **Museo ng Malacañang** (☎ 735 6201), which displayed memorabilia related to the Philippines' past 13 presidents, along with old photos of Manila, is now temporarily closed. Check with the museum or the DOT Information Center for the latest update. For details on other museums around town see Museums earlier.

Quiapo

Quiapo Church (☎ 736 2854; Quezon Blvd; open 6am-noon & 2pm-8pm daily) is a 1933 replacement of an older structure destroyed by fire. Its cream-coloured edifice is designed along Baroque lines and the church is one of Manila's best-known landmarks. A Catholic parish since 1586, Quiapo is the home of the **Black Nazarene**, an image of

Christ believed to be miraculous. The life-size statue, carved from ebony, was first brought to Quiapo in 1767. Every year, on the second Tuesday of January, the greatly revered image is borne on the shoulders of thousands of frenzied devotees in one of Manila's biggest religious festivals, the **Black Nazarene Procession** (for more details on this festival see its entry under Special Events in the Facts for the Visitor chapter).

In front of the church lies **Plaza Miranda**, where the common folk came to watch beauty contests, political rallies and various events and festivities, until it was destroyed by a bloody bombing that preceded Marcos' imposition of martial law. After many years of neglect, Plaza Miranda has been recently renovated into a Roman-like square with pillars, arches and decorative urns.

Also recently renovated, the **Arsenio Lacson Underpass**, named in honour of one of Manila's most colourful mayors, is next to the plaza, allowing pedestrians to cross over to the other side of Quezon Blvd.

On a crowded side street on the other side, you will find **Bahay Nakpil-Bautista** (☎ 734 9341; 452 A Bautista St; adult/student P20/10; open 9am-noon & 1pm-5pm Tues-Sun), where the widow of Andres Bonifacio, father of the Philippine Revolution, lived after his death. An historic landmark in itself, the house is used for historical and cultural exhibits.

At the top of R Hidalgo St, your attention will be caught by the soaring spires of **San Sebastian Church** (☎ 734 8908; R Hidalgo St; open 6.30am-8.30am & 5pm-6pm Mon-Sat, 7.30am-7pm Sun), a Gothic structure that is actually constructed of prefabricated steel. The jewel-like interior is accentuated with lovely stained-glass windows.

The **Golden Mosque** (☎ 734 1508; Globo de Oro St), erected on a site where a hotel named Globo de Oro used to stand, serves the Muslim community that has settled in the vicinity.

Chinatown

After centuries of suppression by the Spanish, Manila's Chinese population quickly rose on the economic and social ladder under more liberal administrations. Today the centre of the vibrant Chinese community is Chinatown in Binondo.

Chinatown is demarcated by a **Goodwill Arch** in the east (at the corner of Ongpin and

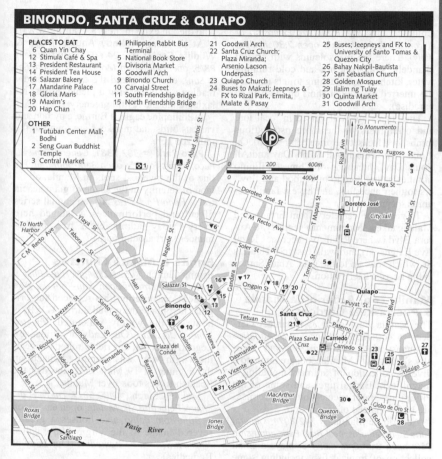

BINONDO, SANTA CRUZ & QUIAPO

PLACES TO EAT
6 Quan Yin Chay
12 Stimula Café & Spa
13 President Restaurant
14 President Tea House
16 Salazar Bakery
17 Mandarine Palace
18 Gloria Maris
19 Maxim's
20 Hap Chan

OTHER
1 Tutuban Center Mall;
  Bodhi
2 Seng Guan Buddhist
  Temple
3 Central Market

4 Philippine Rabbit Bus
  Terminal
5 National Book Store
7 Divisoria Market
8 Goodwill Arch
9 Binondo Church
10 Carvajal Street
11 South Friendship Bridge
15 North Friendship Bridge

21 Goodwill Arch
22 Santa Cruz Church;
  Plaza Miranda;
  Arsenio Lacson
  Underpass
23 Quiapo Church
24 Buses to Makati; Jeepneys &
  FX to Rizal Park, Ermita,
  Malate & Pasay

25 Buses; Jeepneys and FX to
  University of Santo Tomas &
  Quezon City
26 Bahay Nakpil-Bautista
27 San Sebastian Church
28 Golden Mosque
29 Ilalim ng Tulay
30 Quinta Market
31 Goodwill Arch

Dasmariñas Sts), another in the west (corner Juan Luna and San Fernando Sts), and a third at the southern tip of Quintin Paredes St, a few metres north of **Jones Bridge**.

As in any other Chinese enclave around the world, here you'll find dozens of goldsmiths, herbalists, teahouses and shops selling mooncakes, incense, paper money to burn for ancestors, trinkets and all kinds of curios.

Off Quintin Paredes St is a small alley – **Carvajal St** – lined on both sides with stalls piled with fruits, sweets and freshly roasted chestnuts. At the northern end of Paredes St stands the bell tower of **Binondo Church** (cnr Quintin Paredes & Ongpin Sts; open 6am-7pm daily), which is an unusual octagonal structure dating back to 1596.

There aren't a great many sights in Chinatown, but there is a lively atmosphere of industry and tradition and numerous Chinese eateries can be found along Ongpin St (see Chinese under Places to Eat later).

As you emerge from the southeastern end of Ongpin St, you will see a classic European-style fountain, behind which stands **Santa Cruz Church** (☎ 733 0246; open 6am-10pm daily). A church was first erected here in 1608 to minister to the swelling ranks of Chinese Christian converts, but the present edifice only dates back to 1957, after its predecessor was destroyed in WWII.

Chinese Cemetery

As in life, so it is in death for Manila's wealthy Chinese citizens, who are buried with every modern convenience in the huge Chinese Cemetery (*Rizal Ave Extension or Aurora Blvd; South Gate open 7.30am-7pm daily*). There are mausoleums with crystal chandeliers, air-con, hot and cold running water, kitchens and flushing toilets (in case the interred are caught short on the way to paradise).

The guards are well versed in local lore and offer tours of the more ostentatious tombs for a fee (set the price beforehand). On 1 and 2 November (All Saints Day and All Souls Day), hundreds of Chinese-Filipino families gather here to offer food and flowers to their ancestors, and have a family reunion themselves.

To get to the cemetery from Ermita and Malate, take a 'Monumento' jeepney to Aurora Blvd (where Rizal Ave becomes Rizal Ave Extension), and walk east to F Heurtes St, which runs up to the gate. Abad Santos is the nearest LRT station.

Manila Zoo, Acuario de Manila & Puerta Real Gardens

The Manila Zoological & Botanical Gardens (☎ 400 1885; *entrance on M Adriatico St; admission P6; open 6am-7pm daily*), usually shortened to Manila Zoo, are home to a diverse collection of animals including a magnificent Bengal tiger and some of the Philippines' rarer species, but the premises are badly in need of renovation.

Acuario de Manila (☎ 742 8074; *General Luna St, Intramuros, near Rizal Park; admission P50; open 8am-6pm daily*) displays a small collection of tropical fish, including some tiny sharks, inside glass tanks set against the walls of one of Intramuros' fortifications.

Puerta Real Gardens (*General Luna St, Intramuros, near Rizal Park; open 7am-6pm daily; admission free*) are sometimes used as a venue for cultural shows in the evening, with **Puerta Real**, the gate once reserved for the Spanish governor-general, as an impressive backdrop.

Other Parks

Quezon Memorial Circle (*open 6am-10pm daily; admission free*) is to Quezon City what Rizal Park is to Manila. Particularly on Sunday, people come here to stroll, jog, cycle, fly a kite, or practise some ballroom dancing. In the centre stands a towering monument honouring Manuel L Quezon,

President of the Philippine Commonwealth who died in exile in the USA during WWII.

At the nearby **Ninoy Aquino Parks & Wildlife Center** (☎ 924 6031; *adult/student P8/5; open 9am-4pm Mon-Fri, 9am-5pm Sat & Sun*), one can spend the day contentedly reading a book, having a picnic, or just relaxing amid the restful greenery.

A Philippine eagle, a Burmese python and various birds and monkeys are found in the mini zoo here.

Paco Park (☎ 302 7381; *General Luna St, Paco; admission P5; open 8am-5pm daily*) is one of the loveliest spots in Manila, an island of serenity in the shade of giant acacia trees. *Paco Park Presents*, an annual series of cultural performances, is staged here every Friday (admission is free; performances start around 6pm).

Ermita & Malate Churches

Ermita Church (☎ 523 2754; *M H del Pilar & A Flores Sts, Ermita; open 6am-7pm daily*), a modern construction that replaced the original hermitage destroyed during WWII, is home to the widely venerated *Nuestra Señora de Guia* (Our Lady of Guidance). Legend has it that this richly robed image of the Virgin Mary was found by Legazpi on the evening of 19 May 1571, the day the Spanish forces took over Manila.

Malate Church (☎ 400 5877; *cnr M H del Pilar & Remedios Sts, Malate; open 6am-noon & 3pm-8pm daily*) also houses a greatly revered image of the Virgin Mary, called *Nuestra Señora de Remedios* (Our Lady of Remedies).

ACTIVITIES
Swimming

Most of the bigger hotels have their own pools, but if you are billeted at a budget accommodation without one, you can (for a fee) use the facilities at the following places.

Century Park Hotel (☎ 528 8888) 599 P Ocampo Sr St, Malate. Admission P275; open 7am to 8pm daily.

Manila Midtown Hotel (☎ 526 7001) corner Pedro Gil & M Adriatico Sts, Ermita. Admission P150; open 8am to 9pm daily.

Ninoy Aquino Memorial Stadium (☎ 525 2408) F B Harrison St, Malate. Admission P30; open 8am to 11.30am and 1pm to 5pm Tuesday to Sunday.

Ice Skating

If you're looking for some wholesome entertainment, you could join the skaters at **SM Megamall Ice Skating Rink** (☎ 633 5007; Bldg A, SM Megamall, EDSA, Mandaluyong City; open 10am-8pm daily; admission P125 for 2hrs). Skates are available for rent (P35), and for a small fee (P100 for 30 minutes) an instructor will guide you through your paces.

PLACES TO STAY

Manila has accommodation to suit all price ranges, from spartan P300 box-like rooms to luxurious US$1000 penthouse suites comprising several rooms, a private swimming pool and a butler. Accommodation in Manila tends to be more expensive than in some Southeast Asian countries, but hotel rooms are usually air-conditioned and fitted with modern conveniences, such as cable TV and minibar.

Places to Stay – Budget

Most budget accommodation is found in Malate and Ermita, particularly along M Adriatico, A Mabini and M H del Pilar Sts. The cheapest rooms are fan-cooled and share a common bathroom, but air-con rooms with private bathroom are available at higher rates.

Malate The **Malate Pensionne** (☎ 523 8304–06; 1771 M Adriatico St; dorm beds with fan/air-con P200/300, doubles & twins with fan P500, doubles with air-con & shower P1050) is the longest-standing travellers' centre in Malate. Set back from the road in a pleasant courtyard, it is something of an oasis for global travellers. The lounge is cosy and comfortable, and there's a booth by the front desk where you can check your email or surf the Net.

Pension Natividad (☎ 521 0524; 1690 M H del Pilar St; dorm beds P200, singles/doubles with fan P300/550, doubles with/without air-con P900/650) is another friendly guesthouse set around its own courtyard, with an inexpensive coffee shop that does good breakfasts. There's a loud karaoke bar at the back, but soundproof windows in most of the rooms keep some of the noise out.

Victoria Mansions (☎ 525 9444; 600 J Nakpil St; twins with air-con P600) offers rooms fitted with kitchenette, TV, fridge and bathroom.

Joward's Pension House (☎ 338 3191–93; 1730 M Adriatico St; singles/doubles with fan P220/308, air-con doubles with/without bathroom P550/440) is well located, but the rates at this very rudimentary lodging house do not include blanket, towel or soap.

Ermita Tucked away in a tiny street between A Flores and Arquiza Sts, **Richmond Pension** (☎ 525 3864; 1165 Grey St; singles/doubles with fan P225/390, doubles with air-con P650) is a family-run place with simple rooms, sharing a common bathroom.

Pension Filipina (☎ 521 1488; 572 Engracia Reyes St; singles/doubles with fan P400/500, with air-con P600/700) near Richmond Pension, offers similar rooms, all sharing a bathroom.

New Casa Pensionne (☎ 522 1740; cnr Pedro Gil & Leon Guinto Sts; singles/doubles with fan P350/460, with air-con P520/590; double with air-con & bathroom P750) offers very clean rooms and good security. All rooms except the air-con double share a bathroom.

Mabini Pension (☎ 523 3930; 1337 A Mabini St; fan room without/with bathroom P400/550, air-con doubles/twins with bathroom P850/900), in one of the gracious residences that used to line A Mabini St, is a long-running pension that remains popular despite its somewhat run-down look.

Ermita Tourist Inn (☎ 521 8770; 1549 A Mabini St; singles/doubles with air-con & bathroom P720/800) offers clean accommodation and the added advantage of helpful staff. The rates include breakfast.

Midtown Inn (☎ 525 1403; 551 P Faura St; singles/doubles with fan P500/600, single with air-con & bathroom P750) has passable though somewhat overpriced rooms. It is, however, centrally located within the tourist belt.

Parañaque Their proximity to the airport makes these two inexpensive lodgings especially handy if you're catching an early morning flight.

Manila International Youth Hostel (☎ 832 0680; 4227-9 Tomas Claudio St; member/nonmember dorm beds with fan P150/180, with air-con P210/250) is pleasant, with friendly staff and clean linen. This is where you can meet fellow backpackers and young travellers.

MANILA

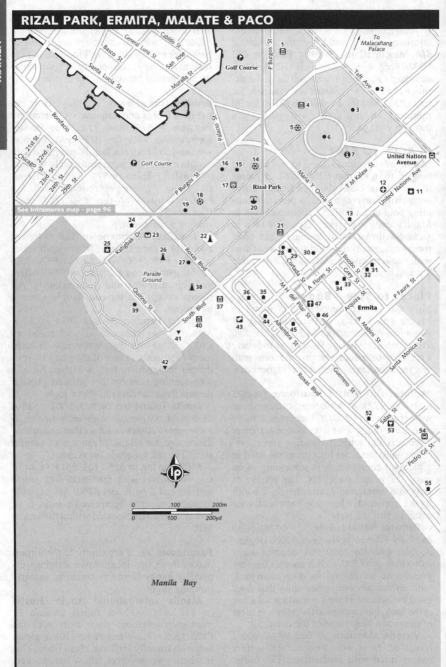

RIZAL PARK, ERMITA, MALATE & PACO

See Intramuros map - page 96

Manila Bay

0   100   200m
0   100   200yd

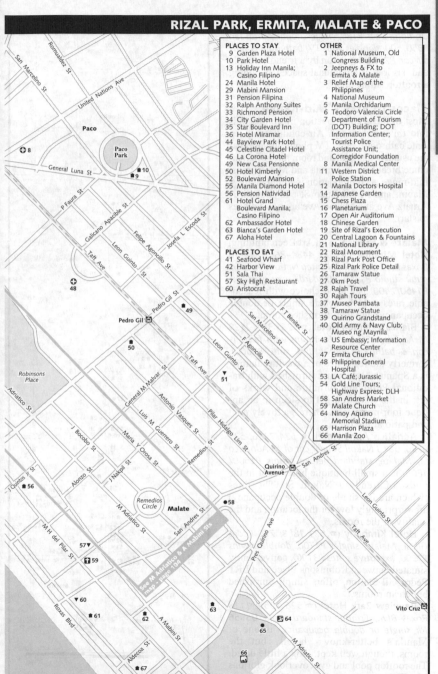

RIZAL PARK, ERMITA, MALATE & PACO

PLACES TO STAY
9 Garden Plaza Hotel
10 Park Hotel
13 Holiday Inn Manila;
   Casino Filipino
24 Manila Hotel
29 Mabini Mansion
31 Pension Filipina
32 Ralph Anthony Suites
33 Richmond Pension
34 City Garden Hotel
35 Star Boulevard Inn
36 Hotel Miramar
44 Bayview Park Hotel
45 Celestine Citadel Hotel
46 La Corona Hotel
49 New Casa Pensionne
50 Hotel Kimberly
52 Boulevard Mansion
55 Manila Diamond Hotel
56 Pension Natividad
61 Hotel Grand
   Boulevard Manila;
   Casino Filipino
62 Ambassador Hotel
63 Bianca's Garden Hotel
67 Aloha Hotel

PLACES TO EAT
41 Seafood Wharf
42 Harbor View
51 Sala Thai
57 Sky High Restaurant
60 Aristocrat

OTHER
1 National Museum, Old
   Congress Building
2 Jeepneys & FX to
   Ermita & Malate
3 Relief Map of the
   Philippines
4 National Museum
5 Manila Orchidarium
6 Teodoro Valencia Circle
7 Department of Tourism
   (DOT) Building; DOT
   Information Center;
   Tourist Police
   Assistance Unit;
   Corregidor Foundation
8 Manila Medical Center
11 Western District
   Police Station
12 Manila Doctors Hospital
14 Japanese Garden
15 Chess Plaza
16 Planetarium
17 Open Air Auditorium
18 Chinese Garden
19 Site of Rizal's Execution
20 Central Lagoon & Fountains
21 National Library
22 Rizal Monument
23 Rizal Park Post Office
25 Rizal Park Police Detail
26 Tamaraw Statue
27 0km Post
28 Rajah Travel
30 Rajah Tours
37 Museo Pambata
38 Tamaraw Statue
39 Quirino Grandstand
40 Old Army & Navy Club;
   Museo ng Maynila
43 US Embassy; Information
   Resource Center
47 Ermita Church
48 Philippine General
   Hospital
53 LA Café; Jurassic
54 Gold Line Tours;
   Highway Express; DLH
58 San Andres Market
59 Malate Church
64 Ninoy Aquino
   Memorial Stadium
65 Harrison Plaza
66 Manila Zoo

The **Townhouse** (☎ 833 1939; 31 Bayview Dr; dorm beds P180, singles/doubles with fan P350/500, doubles with TV, bathroom & fan/air-con P700/950) is run by a friendly couple and has lots of communal spaces, including a rooftop sitting area.

Places to Stay – Mid-Range
Most of the accommodation in Manila falls into this price range. Air-conditioning, en suite bathroom, cable TV, phone and minibar are usually standard; and room rates often include breakfast. In Ermita and Malate, most mid-range accommodation is found along A Mabini and M Adriatico Sts. In Makati, A Arnaiz Ave and Makati Ave are good places to start.

Malate & Ermita In an Art Deco building, **Hotel Miramar** (☎ 523 4484–86; 1034-36 Roxas Blvd near cnr of United Nations Ave, Ermita; studio P1250, standard/superior rooms P1450/2400) is a good choice with reasonable rates (which include single or double occupancy) and well furnished rooms.

Bianca's Garden Hotel (☎ 526 0351; 2139 M Adriatico St, Malate; rooms with fan/air-con & bathroom P800/1800, suite P2000), formerly the residence of a wealthy family, is a Spanish-style house furnished with traditional Philippine furniture and works of art; in the suite you get to sleep in an antique four-poster bed. There's a lovely pool and patio at the back.

Adriatico Arms Hotel (☎ 524 7426, 521 0736; 561 J Nakpil St near cnr of M Adriatico St, Malate; standard/deluxe rooms P1500/1800) is a small boutique hotel right in the midst of trendy J Nakpil St. The rates (which are for single or double occupancy) are surprisingly low for the location and the quality of the rooms.

Hotel Kimberly (☎ 521 1888; 770 Pedro Gil St, Malate; singles P1700, doubles/twins P1900, executive suites P3100), conveniently situated between Robinsons Place and LRT Pedro Gil Station, offers simply furnished but clean rooms.

Bayview Park Hotel (☎ 526 1555; 1118 Roxas Blvd, Ermita; standard room US$55 for single or double occupancy) is one of Manila's better-known hotels, but the rooms, though well kept, look a little dated. The rooftop pool and gym overlook glorious Manila Bay.

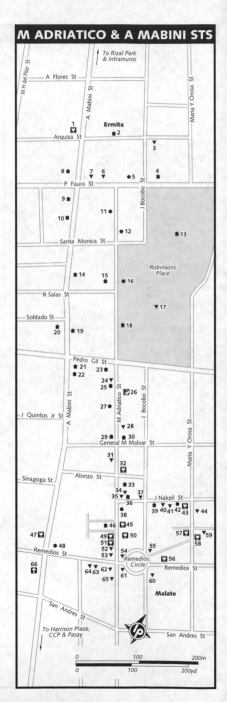

M ADRIATICO & A MABINI STS

M ADRIATICO & A MABINI STS

PLACES TO STAY		PLACES TO EAT		OTHER	
2	Pacific Place Apartelle	3	Sea Food Market	1	Cowboy Grill
	Suites	6	Kashmir	5	Solidaridad
4	Midtown Inn	7	Kamayan		Bookshop
8	Lotus Garden Hotel	18	Figaro	11	Sea Breeze Laundry
9	Mabini Pension	28	Donau	12	JB Rent-a-Car
10	Citystate Tower Hotel	24	Zamboanga Restaurant	16	Interisland Travel &
13	Cherry Blossoms Hotel	31	Rickshaw Bar & Resto		Tours
14	Centrepoint Hotel	34	Steak Town	26	Kim Luan Taoist Temple
15	Casa Blanca I	35	Bravo!	27	Laba Laba Doo
17	Manila Midtown Hotel; China	37	Casa Armas	32	Suburbia
	Air Lines; Northwest Airlines	40	Sala	38	The Source Asia
19	Hotel Frendy	41	People's Palace		Philippines
20	Ermita Tourist Inn	44	Café Breton	42	Firma
21	Riviera Mansion	52	Korean Village	43	Bargo
22	Las Palmas Hotel	53	Korean Palace	45	Padi's Point
23	Palm Plaza Hotel; KEI	54	Cafe Adriatico Premiere	47	The Hobbit House
	Transport	55	Patio Guernica	48	American Express
25	Rothman Hotel	59	Raj	49	The Library
29	Pan Pacific Hotel	60	Ciboney	50	Anthology
30	Dakota Mansion	61	Mil Novecientos	51	Mr Piggy
33	Joward's Pension House	62	Cafe Havana	56	Café Penguin
36	Adriatico Arms Hotel	63	Old Manila Coffee House	57	Sonata
39	Victoria Mansions	64	The Red Crab	58	Acquario
46	Malate Pensionne	65	Bistro Remedios	66	Malate Church

Rothman Hotel (☎ 523 4501–10; 1633 M Adriatico St, Malate; doubles P1700, suites with kitchen P3200) features double and twin rooms, and apartment-style suites. Rates are discounted if you pay cash in advance (a standard double drops to P1275).

Palm Plaza Hotel (☎ 522 1000; cnr Pedro Gil & M Adriatico Sts, Malate; singles from US$72, doubles/twins from US$78) is a modern 10-storey hotel with business facilities in the lobby and an outdoor pool. Weekly and monthly rates are available.

Las Palmas Hotel (☎ 524 5602; 1616 A Mabini St, Malate; singles from US$55, twins & doubles from US$60), around the corner from Palm Plaza Hotel, is an average hotel that also offers weekly and monthly rates.

City Garden Hotel (☎ 536 1451; 1158 A Mabini St, Ermita; singles/doubles from US$45/50) is a modern business hotel with well-maintained rooms. Promotional discounts are available, as are weekly and monthly rates.

Citystate Tower Hotel (☎ 400 7351; 1315 A Mabini St, Ermita; superior/deluxe rooms P1700/1850), in a modern tower block, features rooms fitted with all mod cons. The rates are for single or double occupancy and include breakfast. The tourist bus that connects with the Si-Kat ferry to Puerto Galera

leaves from here. For details see the Malate entry under Bus in Getting There & Away later in this chapter.

Lotus Garden Hotel (☎ 522 1515; 1227 A Mabini St, Ermita; rooms P1200, deluxe singles/doubles & twins P1800/2000), formerly Royal Palm Hotel, offers clean, comfortable rooms at low rates inclusive of Filipino or American breakfast. A bus for transfer to MV Island Cruiser for Puerto Galera departs from here. For details see the entry for Malate under Bus in Getting There & Away later in this chapter.

Centrepoint Hotel (☎ 521 2751–61; 1430 A Mabini St, Ermita; doubles/twins P1150/1600) has rooms that are a little run-down compared to the lobby, but are passable for the price.

Hotel Frendy (☎ 526 4211–14; 1548 A Mabini St, Ermita; standard/superior/deluxe rooms P1400/1600/2000, suites P2500) does not have a very inviting entrance (the pavement is unkempt) but it's sufficiently clean and quiet inside. The rates here include breakfast.

The rates at **Riviera Mansion** (☎ 523 4511–25; 1638 A Mabini St, Ermita; doubles with/without kitchenette from P2200/1800) apply for single or double occupancy and are discounted if you pay cash in advance.

MANILA

La Corona Hotel (☎ 524 2631–38; 1166 M H del Pilar St, Ermita; singles or doubles P1450), operated by the American chain Best Western, features simple, comfortable rooms. Rates include buffet breakfast and discounts are available for longer stays.

Celestine Citadel Hotel (☎ 525 3347; 430 Nuestra Señora de Guia St, Ermita; doubles/triples P1320/1440) is a quiet, modern place with slightly futuristic rooms. The rates are affordable and breakfast is included.

Star Boulevard Inn (☎ 536 1775; 415 United Nations Ave, Ermita; singles/twins/suites P1200/1250/1500) has a central location and tastefully furnished rooms with wooden floors.

Cherry Blossoms Hotel (☎ 524 7631; 550 J Bocobo Extension, Ermita; premium/deluxe P1250/1815) has clean, though somewhat cramped, rooms. Rates (for single or double occupancy) include an American, Filipino or continental breakfast.

Ambassador Hotel (☎ 524 7756; 2021 A Mabini St, Malate; singles/doubles P2178/2541), at the southern end of the tourist belt, is a long-established place that is somewhat in need of renovation.

Aloha Hotel (☎ 526 8088; 2150 Roxas Blvd, Malate; room with/without bay view P1875/1650) has seen too many heavy smokers. Ask for a renovated room to minimise the stale air. Rates are for single or double occupancy.

Orchid Garden Suites (☎ 523 9870, 523 9860; 620 P Ocampo Sr St, Malate; superior singles/doubles US$55/60, deluxe singles/doubles US$65/75, suites from US$100) is an excellent choice. Guests stay in a modern tower block behind a beautifully restored old house containing the reception hall, bar and restaurant. One of the highlights of staying here is breakfast on the terrace as a breeze is blowing in from Manila Bay.

Intramuros Located in a reconstructed 18th-century house, **Hotel Intramuros de Manila** (☎ 524 6730–32; Plaza San Luis, cnr Cabildo & Santa Potenciana Sts; standard singles/doubles US$40/50, deluxe singles/doubles US$50/60) features a period-style lobby but the rooms are fitted with mod cons.

Paco Both of these inexpensive hotels are located in the relaxingly quiet neighbourhood around historic Paco Park.

Malate and Ermita are within walking distance from Paco.

Garden Plaza Hotel (☎ 522 4835, 1030 Belen St; standard/deluxe P1800/2500) is a well-kept property with modest but comfortable rooms. Rates are for single or double occupancy, and include an American or Filipino breakfast.

Park Hotel (☎ 521 2371; 1032 Belen St; standard/superior rooms P1200/2000, suites P3000) features rooms laid out around a lovely secluded pool and sports bar.

Makati Cheap accommodation is pretty thin on the ground in Makati, but you can find a number of mid-range hotels around Makati Ave and P Burgos St.

Robelle House (☎ 899 8209; 4402 B Valdez St; singles/doubles with fan from P650/750, with air-con from P1078/1225) is one of the better inexpensive hotels in the area. The hallways look rather dusty, but the rooms are well kept and the pool is clean.

Jupiter Arms Hotel (☎ 890 5050; 102 Jupiter St; singles/doubles from P1600/1800) is a compact business hotel with spacious rooms fitted with the usual mod cons. Rates include an American, Filipino or continental breakfast.

Millennium Plaza Hotel (☎ 899 4718; cnr Makati Ave & Eduque St; rooms from P2000, 1-bedroom suites from P3622) is a well-maintained hotel condominium with a good restaurant. Rates include use of sauna, jacuzzi and pool.

Primetown Century Tower (☎ 750 3010; Kalayaan Ave; studios/1-bedroom suites from P1950/2350) follows the usual Century standards. Room rates include a buffet breakfast and use of the indoor pool.

Century Citadel Inn (☎ 897 2370; 5007 P Burgos St; studio/1-bedroom suites from P1950/2350) is another Century-owned property with well-furnished rooms and a pool. Rates include a continental breakfast.

Sunette Tower (☎ 897 1804; Durban St off Makati Ave; studio US$75, 1-bedroom suites US$100) is a condominium with a variety of studios and suites, all with kitchenette. The rates are a bit high for what you get.

City Garden Hotel (☎ 899 1111; 870 Makati Ave; singles/doubles from P1900/2100) provides outstanding value with spotlessly clean rooms and a roof-deck pool offering superb views of Makati. Rates give guests free access to the heated pool and to the health spa.

Great Eastern Hotel *(☎ 898 2888; 7842 Makati Ave; singles/doubles/twins from P1399/ 1599/1699)* encompasses three floors of guest rooms plus a swimming pool and gym.

Fersal Tourist Inn *(☎ 897 9123; 107 Neptune St; rooms P1500)* is a small, popular inn with inexpensive rates but you must pay in advance by cash or credit card.

Herald Suites *(☎ 759 6270; 2168 Chino Roces Ave; singles/doubles from US$60/70)* mixes modern convenience with old-world charm. Every room in this boutique hotel is artfully furnished. The foyer's decor is classic European.

El Cielito Inn *(☎ 815 8951; 804 A Arnaiz Ave; standard singles/doubles P1238/1500,* *deluxe singles/doubles P1750/2000)* has clean rooms and a quiet coffee shop that serves full meals. Rates for deluxe rooms include breakfast.

Charter House *(☎ 817 6001; 114 Legaspi St; deluxe rooms/suites P1700/2500)* offers clean, comfortable rooms, and rates (which are for single or double occupancy) include an American or Filipino breakfast. There is a rooftop pool.

Ortigas Center With its dense concentration of shopping malls and high rises, Ortigas Center (which sits on the border of Quezon City, Mandaluyong and Pasig) has become Manila's second-biggest business/commercial hub. Hotels here tend to be pricey, but here's one that's surprisingly affordable.

MAKATI AVENUE & P BURGOS STREET

PLACES TO STAY
1 Robelle House
3 Great Eastern Hotel
4 Fersal Tourist Inn
5 Regine's Hotel
6 Millennium Plaza Hotel
8 City Garden Hotel
9 Sunette Tower; Hertz
10 Primetown Century Tower
11 Travelers Inn
14 Century Citadel Inn
18 Jupiter Arms Hotel

PLACES TO EAT
2 Barrio Fiesta
7 North Park Noodle House
12 Shinjuku Ramen House
13 Jerusalem
15 Hossein's Persian Kebab
16 Korea Garden
17 Mann Hann
19 Baan Thai
20 Nanbantei of Tokyo

The Legend Hotel *(☎ 633 1501; cnr Pioneer & Madison Sts, Mandaluyong City; standard singles/doubles P2275/2625; deluxe singles/doubles P2975/3325)* offers spacious, comfortable rooms in a complex of three-storey buildings. Next to the reception area is a compact pool surrounded by tropical plants. Rates are inclusive of buffet breakfast. There are jacuzzi baths in the deluxe rooms.

Quezon City The area around Timog Ave and Tomas Morato St is the most desirable address if you're looking for a hotel in Quezon City. Many of the upmarket restaurant chains have branches here and it's also convenient for the big 'disco-theatre' nightclubs.

Rembrandt Hotel *(☎ 373 3333; 26 T Morato Ave; standard/deluxe rooms P2700/3000)* is popular with businessmen, with spacious air-con rooms fitted with bathroom, cable TV and telephone.

Century Imperial Palace Suites *(☎ 411 0116–35; cnr Timog Ave & T Morato Ave; studios US$70, 1-bedroom/2-bedroom suites US$80/100)* offers studios and suites with kitchenette. There is a gym and rooftop pool as well as a bar and restaurant.

Villa Estela Hometel *(☎ 371 2278–80; 33 Scout Santiago St; old/new rooms P1050/1150)*, on a quiet residential street, has a homy feel to it, with a relaxing pool located next to a bar and a couple of billiard tables. The rooms in the newer wing of the Villa are better-looking. There are discounted rates for weekly and monthly stays.

Camelot Hotel *(☎ 373 2101–10; 35 Mother Ignacia Ave; doubles/twins from P1200/1775)* is housed in a rather bizarre mock castle, decorated inside with numerous suits of armour and medieval weapons, also fake.

Sulo Hotel *(☎ 924 5051–71; Matalino St near cnr of East Ave; singles/doubles from P2310/2590)* is a business hotel of long standing. Though somewhat in need of renovation, the rooms are comfortable. There are discounts for long stays.

Places to Stay – Top End

As in other Southeast Asian countries, Manila's top-end hotels are on par with luxury hotels elsewhere in the world. Rates are usually quoted in US dollars, but outside the high season (November to March), reductions of 25% to 50% are available. You may also obtain a discount by booking a prepaid room with a travel agent.

Malate & Ermita In a sleek steel-and-glass tower, **Pan Pacific Hotel** *(☎ 536 0788; ⓦ www.panpacific.com; cnr M Adriatico & General M Malvar Sts, Malate; singles/doubles from US$190/210, suites from US$280)* features all the usual luxuries plus a computer in each room and British-trained butler service. Room rates include full buffet breakfast, cocktails and laundry service.

Manila Diamond Hotel *(☎ 526 2211; cnr Roxas Blvd & J Quintos Jr St, Malate; singles/doubles US$240/260, deluxe/executive suites US$270/400)*, Japanese-owned and much patronised by Japanese tourists, boasts an excellent pool and a top-floor lounge that offers great views of the city. Rates (which are for single or double occupancy) include one meal daily (breakfast, lunch or dinner) plus one-way airport transfer and free use of gym, pool and outdoor jacuzzi.

Hotel Grand Boulevard Manila *(☎ 526 8588; 1990 Roxas Blvd, Malate; singles/doubles from US$180/200, deluxe singles/doubles US$200/230, executive suites US$400)* is a bit expensive, considering that there are no 'freebies', such as a complimentary breakfast or airport transfer, but the hotel continues to draw its own share of customers, perhaps because of the popular Casino Filipino here.

Manila Midtown Hotel *(☎ 526 7001; ⓦ www.manilamidtown.com; cnr Pedro Gil & M Adriatico Sts, Ermita; singles/doubles from US$150/160, suites from US$210)* is a huge property (582 rooms and suites) located right next door to Robinsons Place. Among the comprehensive list of facilities are an outdoor pool and an indoor sports centre.

Holiday Inn Manila *(☎ 526 1212; cnr United Nations Ave & Maria Y Orosa St, Ermita; standard singles/doubles US$140/150, deluxe singles/doubles US$160/170)* offers the same standard of accommodation as any Holiday Inn around the world, except that there's a Casino Filipino on the premises. Rates do not include breakfast or airport transfer.

Manila Hotel *(☎ 527 0011; Rizal Park; singles/doubles from US$200/250, Presidential Suite US$2500)*, one of Asia's historic grand hotels, encompasses a modern tower constructed behind the original 1912 structure. This hotel was once the most prestigious

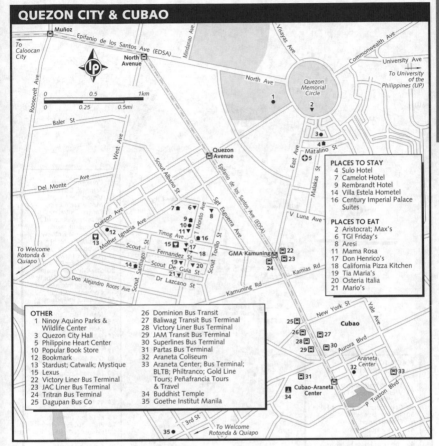

QUEZON CITY & CUBAO

PLACES TO STAY
4 Sulo Hotel
7 Camelot Hotel
9 Rembrandt Hotel
14 Villa Estela Hometel
16 Century Imperial Palace Suites

PLACES TO EAT
2 Aristocrat; Max's
6 TGI Friday's
8 Aresi
11 Mama Rosa
17 Don Henrico's
18 California Pizza Kitchen
19 Tia Maria's
20 Osteria Italia
21 Mario's

OTHER
1 Ninoy Aquino Parks & Wildlife Center
3 Quezon City Hall
5 Philippine Heart Center
10 Popular Book Store
12 Bookmark
13 Stardust; Catwalk; Mystique
15 Lexus
22 Victory Liner Bus Terminal
23 JAC Liner Bus Terminal
24 Tritran Bus Terminal
25 Dagupan Bus Co
26 Dominion Bus Transit
27 Baliwag Transit Bus Terminal
28 Victory Liner Bus Terminal
29 JAM Transit Bus Terminal
30 Superlines Bus Terminal
31 Partas Bus Terminal
32 Araneta Coliseum
33 Araneta Center; Bus Terminal; BLTB; Philtranco; Gold Line Tours; Peñafrancia Tours & Travel
34 Buddhist Temple
35 Goethe Institut Manila

place to stay in Manila; the lobby still impresses with its stately pillars, marble floors and huge chandeliers.

Traders Hotel Manila (☎ 523 7011; 3001 Roxas Blvd, Malate; standard/deluxe/Traders Club US$140/160/200, suites from US$220), run by Shangri-La Hotels, is a large property catering to business executives. Rates (for single or double occupancy) include breakfast, two-way airport transfers, laundry service and free local calls.

Century Park Hotel (☎ 528 8888; W www.centurypark.com; 599 P Ocampo Sr St; singles/doubles & twins US$200/210, deluxe singles/doubles & twins US$220/230, suites from US$400) is an ANA (All Nippon Airways) hotel with well-maintained rooms, courteous service and a full range of amenities. The piano bar on the 19th floor offers stunning views of Manila Bay.

Pasay Located right beside Manila Bay, **Westin Philippine Plaza** (☎ 551 5555; W www.westin.com/manila; CCP Complex, Roxas Blvd, Pasay City; singles/doubles & twins US$225/245, deluxe singles/doubles & twins US$245/265, suites from US$375) offers a great vantage point for enjoying Manila's legendary sunsets. A lagoon-shaped swimming pool, an 18-hole putting green and tennis courts heighten the feeling of being in a resort.

The Heritage Hotel (☎ 854 8888; W www .heritagehotelmanila.com; cnr EDSA & Roxas Blvd; singles or doubles US$240, Millennium Club rooms US$350), located near but not

MANILA

PARAÑAQUE & PASAY

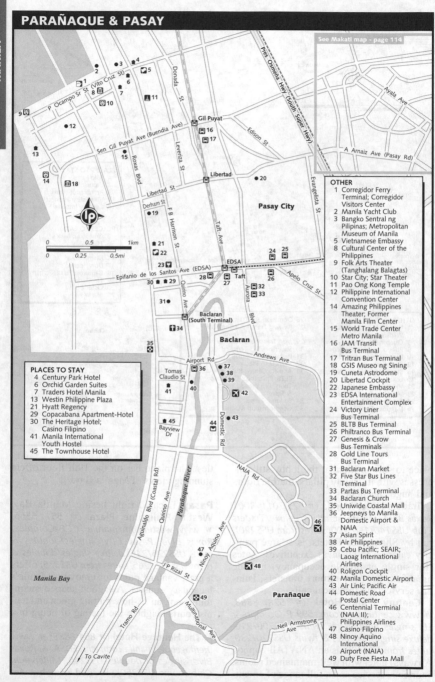

See Makati map - page 114

PLACES TO STAY
4 Century Park Hotel
6 Orchid Garden Suites
7 Traders Hotel Manila
13 Westin Philippine Plaza
21 Hyatt Regency
29 Copacabana Apartment-Hotel
30 The Heritage Hotel;
Casino Filipino
41 Manila International
Youth Hostel
45 The Townhouse Hotel

OTHER
1 Corregidor Ferry
Terminal; Corregidor
Visitors Center
2 Manila Yacht Club
3 Bangko Sentral ng
Pilipinas; Metropolitan
Museum of Manila
5 Vietnamese Embassy
8 Cultural Center of the
Philippines
9 Folk Arts Theater
(Tanghalang Balagtas)
10 Star City; Star Theater
11 Pao Ong Kong Temple
12 Philippine International
Convention Center
14 Amazing Philippines
Theater; Former
Manila Film Center
15 World Trade Center
Metro Manila
16 JAM Transit
Bus Terminal
17 Tritran Bus Terminal
18 GSIS Museo ng Sining
19 Cuneta Astrodome
20 Libertad Cockpit
22 Japanese Embassy
23 EDSA International
Entertainment Complex
24 Victory Liner
Bus Terminal
25 BLTB Bus Terminal
26 Philtranco Bus Terminal
27 Genesis & Crow
Bus Terminals
28 Gold Line Tours
Bus Terminal
31 Baclaran Market
32 Five Star Bus Lines
Terminal
33 Partas Bus Terminal
34 Baclaran Church
35 Uniwide Coastal Mall
36 Jeepneys to Manila
Domestic Airport &
NAIA
37 Asian Spirit
38 Air Philippines
39 Cebu Pacific; SEAIR;
Laoag International
Airlines
40 Roligon Cockpit
42 Manila Domestic Airport
43 Air Link; Pacific Air
44 Domestic Road
Postal Center
46 Centennial Terminal
(NAIA II);
Philippines Airlines
47 Casino Filipino
48 Ninoy Aquino
International
Airport (NAIA)
49 Duty Free Fiesta Mall

fronting Manila Bay, sometimes offers up to 50% discount but check before making your booking. Millennium Club guests have their own check-in/check-out, a bar-restaurant and business facilities on the 9th floor.

Hyatt Regency (☎ 833 1234; 2702 Roxas Blvd; deluxe rooms US$88, Regency Club rooms from US$118) offers the kind of services and amenities that Hyatt is known for around the world. Regency Club rooms are located higher up (8th floor upward) and command a better view of the bay; rates include complimentary continental breakfast and evening cocktails.

Makati Probably the best traditional luxury hotel in Manila, **Makati Shangri-La** (☎ 813 8888; W www.shangri-la.com; cnr Ayala & Makati Aves; superior/deluxe rooms US$260/280, premier/deluxe suites US$340/400) is a grand hotel with all the modern amenities and then some. Rates include complimentary breakfast, laundry service and airport transfer.

The Peninsula Manila (☎ 810 3456; cnr Ayala Ave & Makati Ave; deluxe/superior rooms US$280/290, junior suites with city view US$400) boasts 500 rooms, but the service is efficient. Rates include a buffet breakfast. If you want to be whisked from the airport to your room, the helicopter service costs US$304 per person.

Mandarin Oriental Manila (☎ 750 8888; W www.mandarinoriental.com/manila/; cnr Makati Ave & Paseo de Roxas; singles/doubles US$260/280, premier singles or doubles US$310, suites from US$460) features rooms furnished in traditional Western style, and has an understated elegance.

Dusit Hotel Nikko (☎ 867 3333; cnr EDSA & A Arnaiz Ave, Ayala Center; deluxe/Landmark Club rooms US$138/165) offers well-appointed rooms, good service and room rates (single or double occupancy) inclusive of complimentary buffet breakfast and one-way airport transfer.

New World Renaissance Hotel (☎ 811 6888; cnr Esperanza St & Makati Ave, Ayala Center; deluxe/superior rooms US$250/270, suites from US$370) has expensive published rates but offers promotional discounts of up to 50% with breakfast included. Check with the hotel on the current deal.

One of Manila's oldest luxury hotels is the **Hotel Inter-Continental Manila** (☎ 815 9711; 1 Ayala Ave, Ayala Center; executive/club rooms US$129/149), but it has maintained its standard of quality. Rates include breakfast and use of gym and pool. The lobby, with its well-known coffee shop, is a popular meeting place for executives working in the nearby offices.

Ortigas Center Following the same high standards of quality as other Shangri-La establishments, **Edsa Shangri-La Hotel** (☎ 633 8888; W www.shangri-la.com; Gardenway, Mandaluyong City; standard/superior/deluxe rooms with city view US$195/210/240) offers room rates that include buffet breakfast and free use of gym and pool.

Linden Suites (☎ 638 7878; W www.lindensuites.com; 37 San Miguel Ave, Pasig City; executive rooms/studios US$160/170) is an efficient Swiss-run place. Each room is practically a fully furnished flat, complete with fax machine and stereo system. There is an indoor pool and gym on the 9th floor. Rates include breakfast.

Manila Galleria Suites (☎ 633 7111; W www.galleriasuites.com; ADB Ave, Pasig City; singles & doubles US$180, studios US$210, 1-bedroom suites US$240), towering above Robinsons Galleria, offers very spacious rooms furnished in traditional European style. Rates include an excellent buffet breakfast, airport transfer, laundry service and massage.

Discovery Suites (☎ 635 2222; W www.discoverysuites.com; 25 ADB Ave, Pasig City; junior/1-bedroom/2-bedroom suites US$160/180/270) is in a sleek modern tower and features various fully furnished suites.

Two-bedroom suites can sleep up to four people while three-bedroom units can accommodate a party of six. Buffet continental breakfast is included and the rates apply regardless of occupancy.

Richmonde Hotel (☎ 638 7777; 21 San Miguel Ave, Pasig City; standard/premium rooms US$140/150), frequented by global business travellers, rates include a buffet breakfast.

Places to Stay – Apartments

Malate & Ermita For longer stays, it may be worth renting an apartment. Several places offer fully furnished suites for not much more than the cost of a hotel room.

Dakota Mansion (☎ 521 0701; 555 General M Malvar St, Malate; standard 1-bedroom daily/monthly P1500/25,000, superior 1-bedroom P1800/37,500) is one of five apartment hotels belonging to the Mansion chain which follows generally high standards. Daily rates are inclusive of breakfast. Electricity charges are added to the monthly rates.

Casa Blanca I (☎ 523 8251; 1447 M Adriatico St, Ermita; 1-bedroom daily/monthly P990/14,300, doubles room daily/monthly P1650/22,000) offers passable fully furnished apartments. A one-bedroom unit sleeps two people, a doubles room can accommodate up to four. Casa Blanca's monthly rates come with a 10% discount.

Pacific Place Apartelle Suites (☎ 521 2279; 539 Arquiza St, Ermita; standard/deluxe/superior daily P1708/2074/2318, monthly P30,500/35,380/37,820) offers a variety of clean, modern apartments and is one of the better choices in this price range. Standard and superior units are designed for one to two people, deluxe suites for two to three people. Electricity and water charges are added to the monthly rates.

Mabini Mansion (☎ 521 4776–89; 1011 A Mabini St, Ermita; standard rooms/superior rooms/suites daily P1500/2300/3500, monthly P24,500/36,800/44,000) is another hotel belonging to the Mansion chain. All units hold one or two people.

Boulevard Mansion (☎ 521 8888; 1440 Roxas Blvd, Ermita; studios/1-bedroom suites/deluxe suites daily P1386/1650/2040, monthly P24,500/26,500/37,500), another Mansion property, offers various suites for single or double occupancy. Deluxe corner suites offer a view of Manila Bay.

Ralph Anthony Suites (☎ 521 1107, 521 5590; Maria Y Orosa St, Ermita; studios/1-bedroom suites daily US$26/35, monthly US$635/1030) offers upmarket accommodation secluded from the busy part of Ermita. One-bedroom suites are equipped with kitchenette. No extra charges are added to monthly rates.

Makati The **Oakwood Premier** (☎ 729 8888; Glorietta 4, Ayala Center; studios US$200, 1-bedroom/2-bedroom/3-bedroom US$250/310/$415, all daily rates) is very expensive but many expats use it as a temporary home away from home. The full-service apartments come with 24-hour concierge,

daily maid service, health club, swimming pool, tennis courts and business centre.

Amorsolo Mansion (☎ 818 6811; 130 Amorsolo St, studios/1-bedroom daily P1200/1500, monthly P29,200/31,600 plus electricity charges) is another good Mansion-chain hotel, conveniently located near eateries, bars and entertainment centres.

Travelers Inn (☎ 895 7061; 7880 Makati Ave; standard rooms with kitchenette daily P1350, monthly P25,000 plus P5000 deposit) offers large rooms and the usual travelles' conveniences.

Regine's Hotel (☎ 897 3888; 8429 Kalayaan Ave; studios daily/monthly P2300/50,000, 1-bedroom P3500/70,000) has studios plus as one- and two-bedroom apartments.

Pasay Convenient for the airports and EDSA, **Copacabana Apartment-Hotel** (☎ 831 8711; 264 EDSA Extension; studios daily/monthly P1650/30,800, 1-bedroom P1870/35,200) has good apartments varying from studios to three-bedroom units. Copacabana's studios here at look like regular hotel rooms, but the apartments are equipped with kitchenettes.

PLACES TO EAT

A huge range of cuisine is on offer in Manila, from Chinese, Korean and Filipino to European specialities like pizza, pasta and paella. Meals are generally of high quality, and prices are moderate compared to Europe or the USA, although slightly higher than in other Southeast Asian countries.

Many of the restaurants listed in this section have several branches across the city; the prices listed here are for mid-range dishes at these places. See also Eating Cheaply later.

Filipino

Zamboanga Restaurant (☎ 525 8828, 525 7638; 1619 M Adriatico St, Malate; open 10am-11pm daily; most dishes P200-400) prepares a variety of Zamboangan dishes – plus it offers the added attraction of a dinner show of traditional Filipino dance at 8.30pm nightly.

Bistro Remedios (☎ 523 9153; M Adriatico St near Remedios Circle, Malate; open 11am-11pm Sun-Thur, until midnight Fri & Sat) serves specialities from Pampanga province, which is renowned for its cuisine. If you like it rich, try some *bulalo*, chunks

Catamarans on Manila Bay

A busy market street, Chinatown – Manila

Market near Quiapo Church, Carriedo St – Manila

Paintings for sale, Ermita – Manila

of tender beef shank and marrow in a steaming hot broth.

Kamayan (☎ 518 1725; P Faura St, Ermita; open 11am-10.30pm daily) allows you the unique experience of eating with your hands in traditional Filipino style. The restaurant is best known for its seafood platter (a hearty assortment that includes crabs and king prawns) and its lunch buffet (P275; 11am to 2pm daily).

Aristocrat (Malate ☎ 524 7671; cnr Roxas Blvd & San Andres St; open 24hr • Quezon City ☎ 924 3411; Quezon Memorial Circle; open 11am-10pm daily) first opened in 1936 and has served Filipino food at reasonable prices to several generations of customers. House specialities, such as the crispy pata (deep-fried pork knuckles) start at around P300.

Barrio Fiesta (☎ 899 4020; Makati Ave, Makati City; dishes around P200, open 9am-10.30pm daily) belongs to a large chain that was once very popular but is now showing its age. Dishes include kare-kare (tripe and vegetables in peanut sauce) and inihaw na baboy (char-grilled pork).

Gerry's Grill (☎ 897 9862; 20 Jupiter St, Bel-Air, Makati City; open 11am-midnight Sun-Thur, until 1am Fri) represents a new crop of Filipino restaurants that are redefining favourites like sisig (chopped pork on a hot plate, P110). Part of the restaurant's success is in its casual decor, which includes a stylised ethnic motif with lots of plants.

Mama Rosa (☎ 372 6591; Timog Ave near cnr of T Morato Ave, Quezon City; open 11am-11pm daily) is known for lighter, leaner and tastier renditions of traditional Filipino dishes. On the menu are some regional vegetable dishes, such as Pinakbet Tagalog (okra, eggplant, squash etc cooked in shrimp paste sauce, P180), which is suitable for nonmeat eaters.

Cabalen (☎ 893 4396; ground floor, Glorietta 3, Ayala Center, Makati City; buffet P242; open 11am-11pm daily) has a buffet table (open until 10pm daily) laden with Pampanga specialities ranging from honey-cured pork to desserts enriched with coconut cream.

Harbor View (☎ 524 1532; South Boulevard near Quirino Grandstand, Rizal Park; open 11am-midnight daily) is hard to beat for its combination of hearty Filipino fare and laid-back ambience. The restaurant is actually on a jetty, but you're under the illusion

you're out cruising on the bay. The nilasang na hipon (drunken shrimp, which is shrimp soused in a marinade containing rum or palm wine, P180) is great with ice-cold beer.

Max's (☎ 924 3392; Quezon Memorial Circle, Quezon City; open 7am-10pm daily) has been around so long, it's become an institution. A budget meal of the house speciality (fried chicken) costs only P120 and comes with noodles, rice and iced tea.

Filipino & European

Many restaurants in Manila combine traditional Filipino cooking with European cuisine. There's a pronounced Spanish influence in the dishes, but there are also French, Italian, and even nouvelle cuisine touches.

Ilustrado (☎ 527 3674; 744 General Luna St behind Silahis Arts & Artifacts Center, Intramuros; coffee shop, open 8am-10pm daily, restaurant 10am-2pm & 6pm-10pm daily), set in a reconstructed Spanish-era house, serves both Filipino and European dishes, including some exotic mains like adobong usa (venison stewed in vinegar and garlic, P280).

Mario's (☎ 372 0360; T Morato Ave, Quezon City; open 7am-2.30pm & 5.30pm-11pm Mon-Sat, until 10pm Sun) features a varied menu that includes Spanish-based dishes like lengua estofada (ox tongue in mushroom sauce), as well as pasta, steak, salads and a very good version of Oysters Rockefeller (P220). The Sunday brunch buffet is good value at P350/180 per adult/child.

Cafe Adriatico Premiere (☎ 525 2509; 1790 M Adriatico St, Malate; open 7am-6am Mon-Sat, until 5am Sun) serves a wide array of Filipino and European dishes in a converted old house done up in traditional Filipino style. Many of the dishes, such as callos (tripe and chickpeas in tomato sauce), bear strong Spanish influences.

Barbara's (☎ 527 3893; Plaza San Luis Complex, General Luna St, Intramuros; open 11am-2pm & 6pm-10pm Mon-Sat; lunch buffet 11am-2pm Mon-Fri) also offers a mixture of Filipino and European dishes, but here diners sit under a huge, crystal chandelier in a room that looks like a 19th-century European salon. The lunch buffet (P285) changes daily.

Blue's Garden (☎ 021-439 5759; St Ignatius Village, Quezon City; open by appointment only) serves gourmet meals in an English-style tropical garden setting. Both the food and the garden are the creations of

MANILA

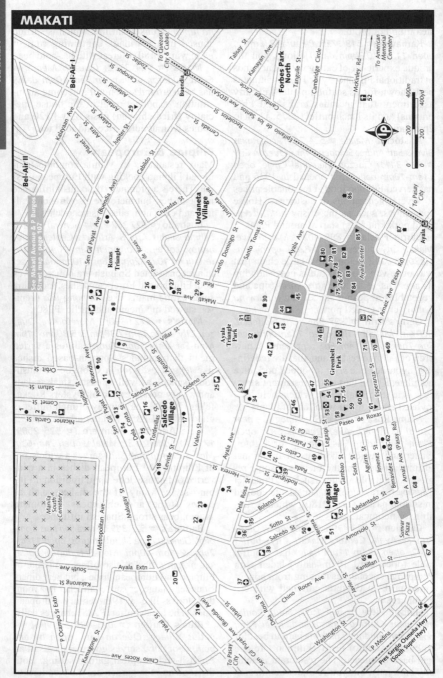

MAKATI

MAKATI

PLACES TO STAY			OTHER		35	British Airways; Qantas Airways
26	Mandarin Oriental Manila	84	Kimpura		36	Asiana Airlines
30	The Peninsula Manila; Budget	85	Outback Steakhouse		37	Makati Medical Center
45	Makati Shangri-La				38	Indonesian Embassy
47	Charter House	1	Alliance Française		39	Thai Embassy
51	Amorsolo Mansion	3	Pravda Wine Bar		40	American Express
65	Herald Suites	4	New Zealand Embassy		41	Korean Air
68	El Cielito Inn	5	Emirates		42	Canadian Embassy
70	New World Renaissance Hotel	6	Royal Brunei		43	UK Embassy
82	Oakwood Premier	7	French Embassy		44	Conway's Bar
86	Hotel Inter-Continental Manila	8	Cathay Pacific Airways		34	United Airlines
87	Dusit Hotel Nikko	9	KLM-Royal Dutch Airlines		46	Australian Embassy; Australia Centre
		10	Air France		48	Qatar Airways
		11	Thai Airways International		49	Lufthansa Airlines
PLACES TO EAT		12	Spanish Embassy		50	Northwest Airlines
2	Le Coude Rouge	13	Saudi Arabian Airlines		52	Singapore Embassy
27	Schwarzwälder German Restaurant	14	Malaysia Airlines		53	Greenbelt Mall
29	Gerry's Grill	15	Singapore Airlines		57	The Prince
54	Luk Yuen Noodle House	16	Malaysian Embassy		60	Greenbelt II
55	Flavours & Spices	17	Korean Air		62	El Al Airlines
56	Banana Leaf Curry House	18	Gulf Air		63	American Express
58	Italianni's	19	Swiss International Airlines		64	Vietnam Airlines
59	Segafredo	20	Makati Central Post Office		66	EVA Air
61	L'Opera	21	Thomas Cook		67	Balikatan Therapeutic Massage Clinic of the Blind
71	Bookmark	22	Egypt Air		69	Power Books
75	Haagen-Dazs Café	23	Continental Micronesia		72	Ayala Center Bus Terminal
76	Cabalen	24	Japan Airlines		73	Greenbelt III
78	Furusato	25	German Embassy		74	Ayala Museum
79	Zen	28	Czech Airlines		77	Bibliarch
81	Tony Roma's	29	American Airlines		80	Hard Rock Café
		31	Filipinas Heritage Library		83	Glorietta
		32	Philippine Stock Exchange Plaza			
		33	Ninoy Aquino Statue			

an 'itinerant chef' whose culinary skills are legendary. Dinner is by appointment only – call a day in advance.

Spanish

Patio Guernica (☎ 521 4415; cnr J Bocobo St & Remedios Circle, Malate; open 11.30am-2pm & 5.30pm-11pm Mon-Sat, 6pm-11pm Sun) is a long-established Spanish eatery that specialises in Iberian dishes such as the classic paella. The set menu (P960) includes soup, salad, paella, steak, dessert and coffee.

Casa Armas (☎ 523 0189; J Nakpil St, Malate; open 11am-2am Mon-Sat, 6pm-midnight Sun) has built a dedicated following since it opened not too long ago. Many people come here just for the Paella Negra (paella blackened with squid ink, P450 for two to three people), though there's quite a variety of dishes to choose from.

Mil Novecientos (☎ 521 6682; Remedios Circle, Malate; open 11am-3pm & 6pm-midnight Mon-Thur, until 2am Fri & Sat, lunch

buffet 11am-2pm Mon-Fri) features an extensive menu of Spanish and Mediterranean dishes but is best known for its lunch buffet, which changes daily.

Italian

Italianni's (☎ 728 0283; ground floor, Greenbelt 2, Greenbelt Park, Makati City; open 10am-midnight daily) serves New York–style Italian food, which means thick tomato sauce and big portions. In addition to the usual pizza and pasta (from around P200), main courses include such dishes as chicken parmagiana (P295). There are some vegetarian items on the menu.

Bravo! (☎ 303 3508; cnr J Nakpil & M Adriatico Sts, Malate; open noon-midnight Sun-Thur, until 2.30am Fri & Sat) is a stylish new breed of Italian restaurant, with the emphasis on authentic, yet contemporary, Italian food. The thin-crust pizza comes in several variations, all very tastily garnished with herbs and spices.

MANILA

Osteria Italia (☎ 929 2357; 186 T Morato Ave, Quezon City; open 11am-2pm & 6pm-10.30pm daily) is a proper *ristorante* offering such specialities as tagliatelle all' Ara Mina (P290), which is pasta and seafood in saffron sauce, named after the Filipina movie star Ara Mina (the restaurant's owner).

L'Opera (☎ 844 3283; cnr Paseo de Roxas & Esperanza St, Makati City; open 11.30am-2.30pm & 6.30pm-10.30pm daily) started off as purveyor of Tuscan specialities but has since become known for its seafood dishes, including whole lobster, simply grilled and served with lemon wedges. The *pasta pescatora* (P297) is a favourite with both lunch and dinner crowds.

California Pizza Kitchen (☎ 372 7370; 243 T Morato Ave, Quezon City; open 11am-midnight Sun-Thur, until 1am Fri & Sat) dishes up pasta and pizza with touches of Californian cuisine. The Original BBQ Chicken Pizza, introduced in the chain's first restaurant in 1985, costs P295. There is a selection of great salads for vegetarians.

Don Henrico's (☎ 448 5564; T Morato Ave, Quezon City; open 11am-11pm Sun-Thur, until midnight Fri & Sat), a homegrown chain, does its own pizza and pasta concoctions, served by friendly staff. Small/medium/large pizzas cost P163/300/389. Some Mexican items are also on the menu.

Other European

Schwarzwälder German Restaurant (☎ 893 5179; ground floor, The Atrium, Makati Ave, Makati City; open 7am-10pm daily) is a long-standing restaurant offering German cuisine, with mains such as schnitzel (around P500) and German sausages (around P300). The salad bar (P225) is a satisfying option for both vegetarians and nonvegetarians. See also this entry under Breakfast later.

Le Soufflé (☎ 887 5108; Ruby Rd near cnr of J Vargas Ave, Ortigas Center, Pasig City; open 11am-midnight daily) is an excellent French restaurant with a very good wine list. Naturally, soufflé is the speciality here. The dinner set menu (P850) changes daily.

Le Coude Rouge (☎ 895 7585; 209 Nicanor Garcia St, Bel-Air II, Makati City; open 8am-6pm Mon, Tues, Thur & Fri, 8am-9pm Wed, 8am-5pm Sat) offers authentic yet affordable French cuisine.

The set menu (P360) includes a starter, salad, main, dessert, coffee and drink – all served in a convivial atmosphere of French art and culture.

Aresi (☎ 312 6234; cnr T Morato Ave & Scout Albano St, Quezon City; open 11am-2am Sun-Tues, until 3am Fri & Sat) serves contemporary fusion cuisine that local gourmets cross town for. The meat lover's pasta (P195) and fish trio (three types of fish, panfried or poached, P265) are favourites.

Sala (☎ 524 6770; 610 J Nakpil St, Malate; open noon-2.30pm Mon-Fri & 7pm-11pm Mon-Sat, 6pm-10.30pm Sun) serves what the owner calls 'modern European cuisine'. It's a tasty mixture of such things as slow-cooked Australian lamb shank with parmesan cheese and potato puree (P540).

Donau (☎ 521 0701; cnr General M Malvar & M Adriatico Sts, Malate; open 9am-1am daily) is a German bistro offering excellent food at very affordable prices. The lunch/dinner set menu (from 11am) is priced at only P190, yet it includes generous portions of soup, entree, dessert and coffee. The restaurant also sells a selection of deli items that you can take away and make into sandwiches.

Steak & Ribs

Manila abounds in good steak restaurants. The meat is usually Black Angus beef airfreighted from the USA, though Australian beef is served in some places. Expect to pay at least P400 to P500 for a 300g steak.

Steak Town (☎ 522 2632; 1738 M Adriatico St, Malate; open 11am-11pm Sun-Thur, until midnight Fri & Sat) is one of the oldest steakhouses in Manila. With any entree, you get soup, garlic bread, unlimited helpings from a salad bar and free tea or coffee. A 200g steak costs P360.

Tony Roma's (☎ 757 1926; ground floor, Glorietta 4, Ayala Center, Makati City; open 11am-11pm Sun-Thur, until midnight Fri & Sat), an American import, serves steaks, burgers and the house speciality – ribs in smoked, pepper or chilli-flavoured sauce. The executive lunch (P300, 11am to 4pm Monday to Friday) offers good value for money.

Outback Steakhouse (☎ 729 8459; ground floor, Glorietta 4, Ayala Center, Makati City; open 11am-11pm Sun-Fri, noon-2am Fri & Sat) serves Australian steaks in an Australian-inspired ambience (boomerangs, stuffed koala bears etc). Be prepared to pay about P700 for a meal here.

American

TGI Friday's (☎ 372 8497; Hotel Rembrandt, T Morato Ave, Quezon City; open 11am-11pm Sun-Thur, until midnight Fri & Sat) features bottle-juggling bartenders and scraps of 1950s Americana plastered over the walls; burgers, fried chicken, ribs and the like are standard fodder for the rowdy crowd. A basic Friday's burger with a platter of fries will set you back about P250.

Burgoo (☎ 687 5254; The Podium, ADB Ave near cnr of J Vargas Ave, Pasig City; open 10am-11pm daily) features a very eclectic menu, with appetisers like *quesadilla* and *chimichanga* (two popular Mexican dishes) and chicken, steak and ribs as main courses. A 'Hamburgoo' costs P175, a T-bone steak P425.

Chinese

Chinatown The **Mandarine Palace** (☎ 736 5767; 789-793 Ongpin St, Santa Cruz; open 6am-11pm daily), one of the big restaurants in Chinatown, specialises in seafood dinners, with sets ranging in price from P4000 to P8800. Good for 12 people, the P4000 menu includes prawns, clams, fish lips and king fish in various preparations.

President Restaurant (☎ 244 7235; 746-750 Ongpin St, Santa Cruz; open 10am-11pm daily) holds the distinction of being the oldest restaurant in Chinatown. Gather a group of 12 people and come here for a *lauriat* (banquet). At P4980, the cheapest set menu would come to P415 per person, and it's a nine-course feast that includes Peking duck and steamed crab.

Two final Chinatown choices are **Stimula Café & Spa** (☎ 242 7295; Ongpin St, Santa Cruz; open 8am-9pm daily), which serves reasonably priced Western-style meals and excellent Italian coffee; and the nearby **Salazar Bakery** (☎ 733 1392; Ongpin St, Santa Cruz; open 5am-10pm daily), which first opened for business in 1947 and is a reliable source of mooncakes.

Seafood Throughout Manila you will see huge Chinese restaurants with an astonishing variety of live seafood displayed in aquariums in the window. Mud crabs, prawns, lobster and *lapu-lapu* (a delicately flavoured fish) are standard items, though flashier places may also have terrapin, sea cucumber and giant eel.

Sea Food Market (☎ 521 6766; 1190 J Bocobo St, Ermita; open 11am-midnight daily) is probably the best-known seafood place in town. You select the raw ingredients from a refrigerated counter, after which a team of chefs will cook your meal in a glass-fronted booth. Expect to pay from P500 per person for a meal here.

Sky High Restaurant (☎ 524 1726; 463 Remedios St, Malate; open 11am-2pm & 5.30pm-11.30pm daily) offers the full Chinese seafood experience – from conch shells to terrapins and poisonous rock-fish. A seafood dish with vegetables and rice will set you back around P400. A 10-course set menu for 12 people costs P3800, which comes out at just over P300 per person.

Seafood Wharf (☎ 400 5066; South Blvd, Rizal Park; open 7am-11pm daily) is one of the better seafood places that have exploited the natural backdrop of Manila Bay. As at Sea Food Market, the restaurant cooks whatever selection you make from the fresh seafood and vegetables on display; 200g of prawns with vegetables and rice costs about P400. See also this entry under Breakfast later.

The Red Crab (☎ 400 9979; 536 Remedios St, Malate; open 11am-11pm Sun-Thur, 11am-midnight Fri & Sat) can prepare crab in 12 different ways, each one as tasty as the next. The live crabs are weighed to determine the price – it costs P95/85 per 100g for female/male.

Mann Hann (☎ 895 3966; 108 Jupiter St, Bel-Air, Makati City; open 10am-11.30pm daily) stands apart from other Chinese restaurants with dishes that mix Sichuan cooking with local ingredients like salted shrimp paste. The flavoursome meat and seafood *chami* (thick noodles) costs P110.

Teahouses The **Gloria Maris** (☎ 734 0540; 913 Ongpin St, Santa Cruz; open 10am-11pm Mon-Fri, 6pm-11pm Sat & Sun) lets you feast on tasty Chinese food at very reasonable prices. On the menu are rice dishes (P90 to P130), noodles (P85 to P160) and various á la carte choices.

Hap Chan (☎ 733 3710; 649 T Mapua St, Santa Cruz; open 6am-2am daily), one of the more popular teahouses, specialises in hot-pot dishes (around P180) but also serves dim sum, noodles and rice dishes.

Maxim's (☎ 734 4193; 965 Ongpin St, Binondo; open 6am-10pm daily) offers *mami* (noodles in soup), *siopao* (steamed dumpling with meat filling) and various dim sum from P60 to P80.

President Tea House (☎ 243 9079; 809-813 Salazar St, Santa Cruz; open 6.30am-11pm daily), no relation to President Restaurant, isn't as famous as its bigger namesake, but the food has its own character. Try the *congee* (rice porridge) for breakfast.

Rickshaw Bar & Resto (☎ 521 6129; 1723 M Adriatico St, Malate; open 10am-1am daily) is clean, well lit with some semblance of style, and very cheap. The dim sum start at P35, the noodles at P60. A rice topping set, served with soup and iced tea, costs only P80.

North Park Noodle House (☎ 896 3475; 1200 Makati Ave, Makati City; open 11am-midnight Sun-Thur, 24hr Fri & Sat) serves what some consider to be the best bowl of Chinese noodles in town. A basic order of noodles costs P95.

Luk Yuen Noodle House (☎ 892 5889; ground floor, Greenbelt 1, Greenbelt Park, Makati City; open 8am-10pm daily) offers tasty noodles and dim sum at cheap prices. Beef brisket with noodles in soup costs P85; shrimp dim sum and chicken feet cost P40 each.

Japanese

Furusato (☎ 892 5115; ground level, Glorietta 3, Ayala Center, Makati City; open 11am-10pm daily) is easily the classiest Japanese restaurant in Manila. The sushi and sashimi are excellent but expensive (around P1000 per person). It's best to come for lunch when you can have sushi or teppanyaki for only P350.

Zen (☎ 892 6851; ground level, Glorietta 3, Ayala Center, Makati City; open 11am-11pm daily) features a more modern and streamlined decor, attracts a generally younger clientele, and charges slightly lower prices than its sister restaurant next door, Furusato.

Kimpura (☎ 892 8274; 2nd level, Glorietta 2, Ayala Center, Makati City; open 11.30am-2.30pm & 6pm-10.30pm daily) is another popular Japanese choice. Dishes include tempura (P150 to P300) and sushi sets (P250 to P400).

Saisaki (☎ 633 1758; SM Megamall, EDSA, Mandaluyong City; open 11am-9.30pm daily) offers a good-value Japanese buffet (P450; 11am to 2.30pm and 6pm to 9.30pm daily), with a sushi/sashimi bar and a generous se-

lection of other dishes, such as tempura and teppanyaki.

Nanbantei of Tokyo (☎ 757 4130; 47 Polaris St, Bel-Air, Makati City; open 11am-2pm & 6pm-midnight daily) has become the regular hangout of fanciers of the restaurant's speciality – the simple *yakitori* (Japanese barbecue) elevated to near art. An order of 21 sticks costs P750.

Shinjuku Ramen House (☎ 890 6105; cnr Makati Ave & Hercules St, Makati City; open 10am-1am Sun-Thur, until 2am Fri & Sat) serves fairly authentic ramen (Japanese noodles), along with various Japanese specialities, such as *gyoza* (pan-fried dumplings). A small bowl of miso ramen costs P135, a regular serving costs P190.

Korean

Korean Palace (☎ 521 6695; cnr M Adriatico & Remedios Sts, Malate; open 10am-2am daily) is probably the best Korean restaurant in town, with a tasteful meal of marinated meat or seafood, side dishes and rice costing about P300.

Korean Village (☎ 524 4958; 1783 M Adriatico St, Malate; open 11.30am-2.30pm & 5.30pm-1.30am Mon-Sat, 5.30pm-1.30am Sun) is huge, but the service is friendly, the beer is cheap, and a meal of beef barbecue with rice and side dishes costs only about P200.

Korea Garden (☎ 895 5443; 128 Jupiter St, Makati City; open 11.30am-2.30pm & 5.30pm-10.30pm daily) is an unpretentious place and the food is as good as any. Barbecue choices start from around P175.

Thai & Malaysian

Flavours & Spices (☎ 894 5624; ground floor, Garden Square, Greenbelt Park, Makati City; open 11am-2.30pm & 6.30pm-10.30pm daily) is perhaps the best-known Thai restaurant in town. Curries with rice cost P350 to P500. Though the food is tasty, the spiciness has been toned down to better suit local palates; tell the waiter if you'd like it hotter.

Baan Thai (☎ 895 1769; cnr Makati Ave & Jupiter St, Makati City; lunch buffet P297; open 11.30am-2.30pm & 6.30pm-10.30pm daily) serves authentic Thai food in a laid-back atmosphere. The curries start from around P230, and are good for two.

Sala Thai (☎ 522 4694; J Nakpil St, Malate; open 10am-2.30pm & 6pm-10pm Mon-Sat) is one of the oldest Thai restaurants in Manila. The dishes are authentic and the prices are reasonable (P100 to P150 for a meat or seafood curry with steamed rice).

People's Palace (☎ 523 4561; 612 J Nakpil St, Malate; open noon-2pm & 6pm-11pm Mon-Sat, 6pm-10pm Sun) serves very refined (almost nouvelle) renditions of classic Thai dishes; it's expensive but the food is delicious.

Banana Leaf Curry House (☎ 812 8618; ground floor, The Plaza Bldg, Greenbelt Park, Makati City; open 11am-3pm & 6pm-10pm daily) offers different varieties of curry, including its own fish-head version (P368).

Indian & Middle Eastern

Kashmir (☎ 523 1521; P Faura St, Ermita; open 11.30am-11pm daily) serves north Indian curries that are good but perhaps a bit heavy for some people's taste. Prices, too, tend to be expensive, particularly when you add the 30% tax and service charge.

Raj (☎ 525 4858; 1820 Maria Y Orosa St, Malate; open 6.30pm-midnight Sun-Thur, until 1am Fri & Sat), in a secluded courtyard, has an earthy yet elegant ambience. The raan (roast leg of lamb; P3500) is a real feast but has to be ordered a day in advance. The cost may seem extravagant, but this meal is good for six to eight people.

Jerusalem (☎ 899 6505; Makati Ave, Makati City; open 7am-3am daily) offers shwarma (kebab in rolled pitta bread) and a good range of main courses such as salona (spicy stew). Hummus costs P140/90 with/ without meat. A vegetarian/meat biryani costs P120/220. See also this entry under Breakfast later in this section.

Hossein's Persian Kebab (Makati Ave, Makati City; open 11am-1am daily) is a place that also offers a good range of kebabs, plus north Indian curries, including some vegetarian dishes.

Latin American

Cafe Havana (☎ 521 8097; cnr M Adriatico & Remedios Sts, Malate; open 11.30am-2am Mon-Thur, 11.30am-4am Fri & Sat, 5pm-midnight Sun) conjures the illusion that you're in Havana just before the city's fall to Castro. The menu is extensive, but you could opt to have an all-Cuban evening starting with Cuba Libre (P125) and ending with a Cuban Cohiba Esplendido cigar (P2530), with some

Arroz a la Cubana (P275) or Cuban chili con carne (P258) in between.

Ciboney (Remedios Circle, Malate), named in honour of Cuba's Ciboney tribe, features colourful cocktails, danceable live music and an exotic menu that requires some clever deciphering.

The house speciality is a thing called senina (P250), which turns out to be sizzling spiced goat meat. Infectiously happy, it has Caribbean ambience and tables on a veranda overlooking Remedios Circle.

Tia Maria's (☎ 371 1473; cnr T Morato Ave & Scout de Guia St, Quezon City; open 11am-midnight Sun, 11am-2am Mon-Thur, 11am-3am Fri & Sat) is a popular bar and restaurant offering live music and a selection of Mexican dishes. Tacos and enchiladas cost around P120 each.

Vegetarian

Vegetarian options are somewhat limited in Manila, but most restaurants feature some vegetarian dishes on their menu. Korean restaurants can replace meat with bean curd in their dishes. Most Italian places offer vegetarian pizza and pasta options. All-you-can-eat salad bars are available in many restaurants, even in the larger fast-food chains.

Vegetarian-friendly local foods include lumpiang sariwa (fresh spring rolls), tortang talong (eggplant omelet, sometimes with ground beef or pork) and atsara (pickled unripe papaya). For dedicated vegetarians, a few restaurants in Binondo cater to the Chinese Buddhist community, with lots of tofu and soybean-based dishes.

Quan Yin Chay (Soler St, Chinatown; meals P80-100; open 7am-9pm daily) is a tiny vegetarian canteen with a selection of Chinese dishes.

Bodhi (Tutuban Center Mall, C M Recto Ave; open 10am-8pm daily) offers vegetarian health food with soya in place of meat. Bodhi has outlets at shopping mall food courts all over the city.

Breakfast

Between 6am and 10am, all major hotels serve a buffet breakfast at an average price of P400 to P500 per person. Here are three options outside the hotel circuit.

Seafood Wharf (☎ 400 5066; South Blvd, Rizal Park; regular breakfast from 7am daily, *buffet breakfast P190, 7am-10.30am Sun)* provides a Filipino, American or continental breakfast, while you enjoy a view of the bay. On Sunday you can fill up at the hearty buffet breakfast.

Schwarzwälder German Restaurant *(☎ 893 5179; ground floor, The Atrium, Makati Ave, Makati City; buffet breakfast P275, 7am-10am Mon-Sat)* also serves a generous spread that ranges from cereals and fruits to German sausages and Filipino specialities.

Jerusalem *(☎ 899 6505; Makati Ave, Makati City; breakfast P150, from 7am-3am daily)* welcomes early diners with an Arabic breakfast.

For a really fast and cheap breakfast, both **Mister Donut** and **Dunkin' Donuts** offer two donuts and hot coffee for just P30. A rank higher, **Delifrance** and **Le Ceour de France** serve an altogether better brew combined with croissant or other French pastry. You'll find these places in practically any mall.

Cafés

Starbucks *(☎ 527 4282; Muralla St, Intramuros; open 8am-9pm daily)* has become extremely popular and is now found all over the city. A no-frills order of coffee costs around P70.

Figaro *(☎ 536 7890; ground floor, Robinsons Place, entrance from Pedro Gil St, Ermita; open 10am-11pm daily)* is a homegrown (or should we say 'homebrewed'?) Viennese-inspired coffee chain that has effectively promoted the underrated local bean *barako*. A cup costs about P40.

Segafredo *(☎ 757 4058; ground floor, Greenbelt 2, Greenbelt Park, Makati City; open 10am-11pm daily)* serves what is probably the best coffee in Manila – real Italian brew that packs a punch. A single espresso (P70) should wake up even the sleepiest heads!

Old Manila Coffee House *(☎ 400 6415; 548 Remedios St, Malate; open 11am-midnight Mon-Thur, until 2am Fri & Sat)* is a quiet retreat amid Malate's flashier joints. Here you can read the morning papers while sipping a cup of freshly brewed coffee (P50).

Café Breton *(☎ 536 0953; 1810 Maria Y Orosa St, Malate; open 5pm-12.30am Mon-Thur, 5pm-2.30am Fri & Sat; 3pm-11pm Sun)* is a pretty little café were crepes are cooked and served by ladies wearing nifty berets. A cup of frothy cappuccino (P45) goes well with the crepes (from around P70).

Haagen-Dazs Café *(☎ 892 2873; ground level, Glorietta 2, Ayala Center, Makati City; open 10am-10pm daily)* is a good spot for those with a sweet tooth. Ice cream costs P99 per scoop and you can indulge in some good people-watching while enjoying it.

Eating Cheaply

Food stalls commonly found in some Southeast Asian countries are conspicuously absent from the streets of Manila, but there are roadside *carinderia*, or canteens. These basic eateries, often family owned, display a selection of pre-cooked dishes on a counter or in a glass case, usually including *adobo* (pork and/or chicken cooked in vinegar, soy sauce and garlic), *sinigang* (pork, fish or prawns in sour soup) and various preparations of *bangus* (milkfish, native to the Philippines). These places are called *turo-turo* (literally point-point) as ordering is a simple case of pointing at whatever takes your fancy.

The food courts in the big shopping malls such as Robinsons Place in Ermita/Malate offer another way of eating cheaply. The variety at these places may seem bewildering, but the food is conveniently on display, the prices are clearly marked (a standard meal costs around P150 or less) and you can take your time making your selection in air-conditioned comfort. The general cleanliness is another plus.

The usual global fast-food players are all here, but local competitors like **Jollibee** (hamburgers), **Chowking** (Chinese) and **Greenwich** (pizza) are equally visible throughout town.

ENTERTAINMENT

Thanks to the country's free-wheeling brand of democracy and to the Filipinos' essentially easygoing nature, Manila's nightlife is probably the most diverse in Southeast Asia.

Bars

Malate The area around J Nakpil St is the centre of Manila's new young bar scene. Due to the fickleness of fashion, many of these bars disappear after just one season. Here are some of the current crop.

Acquario *(☎ 522 7066; 1820 Maria Y Orosa St, open 9pm-2am Tues-Thur, until 3am Fri & Sat)* has the sophistication that one expects to find in London and New York, with glass tables that look like melting ice and a shimmering light projection above the bar.

Just the sort of place to enjoy one of the bar's Martini concoctions (P180).

Bargo (☎ 404 2482; cnr J Nakpil & Maria Y Orosa Sts; open 11am-4am daily) typifies the new breed of Manila nightspot with its chrome decor, young crowd, inexpensive beer (P40 per bottle) and eclectic bar food. There is KTV and billiards upstairs.

Sonata (☎ 523 9680; Maria Y Orosa St, Malate; open 5pm-1am Mon-Thur, until 4am Fri & Sat) offers pasta and the like (set menu P295) plus acoustic live music from 9pm Thursday to Saturday.

Suburbia (☎ 450 1685; 1718 M Adriatico St, Malate; open 7.30pm-1am Mon-Thur, until 2.30am Fri & Sat; minimum charge P200 or P400, depending on band playing), easily identifiable by the marquee above its entrance, is a live-music venue that often features well-known local artists.

The following selection includes some well-established venues in Malate.

Café Penguin (☎ 303 7355; Remedios St near Remedios Circle; open 6pm-2am Tues-Sat) is a bar-cum-gallery that has been the hangout of artists and bohemians for nearly two decades.

The Hobbit House (☎ 521 7604; A Mabini St; open 5pm-3am daily), which opened for business long before the current revival of The Lord of the Rings, is a folk music club run by – you guessed it – little people.

Padi's Point (☎ 400 3993; M Adriatico St; open 11am-4am daily) is another hangout for young people where pitchers of beer and sizzling snacks are the main attraction.

Anthology (☎ 523 4975; M Adriatico St; open 5pm-2am or later Mon-Sat), formerly Ten Years After, is known for what looks like an old seaplane sticking through its upper-storey windows. There's live music from Monday to Saturday.

The Library (☎ 522 2484; 1179-A M Adriatico St; open 7pm-2am Mon-Thur, until 4am Fri & Sat), across the road from Anthology, is a tiny stand-up comedy and karaoke bar that draws in a mixed crowd.

Mr Piggy (☎ 523 8776; 1179 M Adriatico St; open 7pm-2am Mon-Thur, until 4am Fri & Sat), next door to The Library, is one of Manila's few openly gay bars. This place stages weekend parties.

Ermita In addition to the latest flavours, you'll also find some old favourites going strong in Manila, including the following.

Cowboy Grill (☎ 525 1474; cnr A Mabini & Arquiza Sts; open 6pm-4am daily) draws its own regular crowd with pitchers of beer, sizzling snacks and at least three live bands nightly.

L A Café (M H del Pilar St; open 24hr) has it all – live music, billiards, cheap food and drinks, rowdy crowd, raunchy atmosphere – and, best of all, it never sleeps.

Jurassic (M H del Pilar St; open 10am-3am daily), next door to L A Café, has a long happy hour lasting from 10am to 11pm, during which you get one free drink for each one you buy.

Makati There are some good nightspots in Makati, specifically at Ayala Center and the corner of Makati Ave and Jupiter St.

Hard Rock Café (☎ 893 4661; Glorietta 3, Ayala Center; open 11am-3am daily) is Manila's own contribution to the global chain, except that here live music is played, including some mainstream jazz, instead of the usual canned rock.

The Prince (☎ 815 4274; Greenbelt Mall, Greenbelt Park; open 11am-midnight Sat-Thur, until 1am Fri), formerly Prince of Wales, is a long-standing British-style pub that's popular with locals and expats alike.

Conway's Bar (☎ 813 8888; 2nd floor, Makati Shangri-La, cnr Ayala Ave & Makati Ave; open 5pm-midnight Mon-Thur, until 1am Fri & Sat) gets packed with yuppies, expats and all sorts of characters out to have a good time; Friday is particularly active.

Pravda Wine Bar (☎ 890 1287; 225 Nicanor Garcia St; open 1pm-5am daily) is anything but proletarian, what with caviar on offer to go with your vodka. Dinner is served until 10pm, which is followed by merrymaking until daybreak.

Karaoke

The old-fashioned nightclub is a disappearing species in Manila and has been replaced by huge karaoke palaces. For the full 'KTV experience', there are dozens of disco-theatres around Quezon Ave and Timog Ave in Quezon City, including **Stardust**, **Catwalk**, **Mystique** and **Lexus**.

The **EDSA International Entertainment Complex** (EDSA; Pasay City) also offers a variety of KTV choices, as do hundreds of other places all over the city.

Casinos

Operated by a government agency in charge of legalised gambling, **Casino Filipino** (☎ 854 1605–09; Ninoy Aquino Ave, Parañaque City; admission P100; open 24hr) is located in front of NAIA, and (if one were to believe the advertising hype) is 'Asia's friendliest casino'. At this huge gambling palace, players try their luck at craps, blackjack, roulette, stud poker, bingo etc. This is one way to kill time if you want to stay up all night to catch a very early morning flight. There's also a Casino Filipino at **The Heri-tage Hotel** (☎ 854 8888; W www.her-itagehotelmanila.com; cnr EDSA & Roxas Blvd; admission P100; open 24hr), **Holiday Inn Manila** (☎ 526 1212; cnr United Nations Ave & Maria Y Orosa St, Ermita; admission P100; open 24hr) and **Hotel Grand Boulevard Manila** (☎ 526 8588/7324; 1990 Roxas Blvd, Malate; admission P100; open 24hr).

Cinemas

Manila boasts hundreds of movie houses. Many feature state-of-the-art facilities, particularly those in the upmarket malls, and Hollywood blockbusters are often shown simultaneously with their US release, yet it costs only P50 to P100 to watch a movie here. All of the local newspapers have extensive film listings. English movies are screened with their original English dialogue.

If you're feeling more adventurous, the Philippines has the world's third most prolific film industry, though most of the films are formulaic action movies and sentimental romantic comedies. All of the mall theatres show some local movies.

Be warned that the cinemas in Quiapo and Santa Cruz, specifically along Rizal Ave and C M Recto Ave, should be avoided at all costs – unless you want to rub elbows with pickpockets and other criminals.

Theatres

Manila has an active theatrical tradition. Theatre groups mount a season every year, such as 'Tanghalang Pilipino' at the Cultural Center and 'Repertory Philippines' at the William J Shaw Theater. Plays are staged in both English and Pilipino, ranging from Broadway musicals to Filipino originals.

There are also yearly seasons for ballet and classical music. Rock/pop concerts, by both local and foreign performers, are held throughout the year in venues like the Araneta Coliseum.

Call the **DOT Information Center** (☎ 524 2384) or the theatres to find out the current programmes. Listings are also published in some newspapers and magazines.

Araneta Coliseum (☎ 911 3101) Araneta Center, corner EDSA and Aurora Blvd, Cubao, Quezon City
Cultural Center of the Philippines (CCP; ☎ 832 3678) Roxas Blvd, Malate
Dulaang Rajah Sulayman (☎ 722 6911) Fort Santiago, Santa Clara St, Intramuros
Folk Arts Theater (Tanghalang Balagtas; ☎ 832 1120) CCP Complex, Roxas Blvd, Malate
Star Theater (☎ 512 5031) Star City, CCP Complex, Roxas Blvd, Malate
William J Shaw Theater (☎ 633 4821) 6th level, Shangri-La Plaza Mall, corner EDSA and Shaw Blvd, Mandaluyong City

SPECTATOR SPORTS
Cockfighting

Bloody cockfights take place at several venues around Manila and the atmosphere is always highly charged (for more information on this sport see the boxed text 'Fowl Play' in the Facts for the Visitor chapter). The huge **Libertad Cockpit** (Dolores St, Pasay City) is close to the tourist belt, and there is action every afternoon except Thursday and Saturday; Sunday is the best day to visit. To get there, take a jeepney or the LRT to Libertad station and change to an eastbound Evangelista–Libertad jeepney.

No less impressive, the **Roligon Cockpit** (☎ 833 1638; 505 Quirino Ave, Tambo, Parañaque; admission P150-300; open around 11am-6pm) sees action from Thursday to Sunday, with derby events held regularly throughout the year. To get there, take a jeepney or the LRT to Baclaran and change to a jeepney bound for Sucat Hwy. Tell the driver to drop you off at Roligon Cockpit.

Basketball

The **Araneta Coliseum** (☎ 911 3101; Araneta Center, cnr EDSA & Aurora Blvd, Cubao, Quezon City) and **Cuneta Astrodome** (☎ 832 7000; Derham St, Pasay City) are popular venues for professional basketball games managed by PBA (Philippine Basketball

Association), the Philippines' equivalent to America's NBA. Like football in other countries, basketball is a national passion in the Philippines. The professional league follows a yearly season – check with either the Araneta Coliseum or the Cuneta Astrodome for the current schedule of games.

Horse Racing
Like cockfighting and basketball, a day at the races is a popular pastime among Filipino males. The **Santa Ana Race Track** (☎ 890 4015; A P Reyes Ave, Makati City; admission P5) stages afternoon and evening races on Wednesday, Thursday, Saturday and Sunday.

SHOPPING
Manila is a bargain-hunter's paradise, with everything ranging from simple street markets to ritzy boutiques. The largest variety of stores can be found in Manila's many shopping malls, which also have the advantage of being air conditioned.

But for a real taste of Filipino life, be sure to check out one of Manila's many excellent markets.

Markets
The lively stalls around **Carriedo St** near Quiapo Church (in Quiapo) sell clothes, alarm clocks, karaoke CDs and just about anything else under the sun. Nearby, under Quezon Bridge, otherwise known as **Ilalim ng Tulay** (literally 'under the bridge'), you can find good basketware, shell work and a variety of handicrafts. Across the road, at **Quinta Market**, you'll find vendors boisterously peddling fish, meat, vegetables, fruits and other foodstuff.

Around Quiapo Church there are dozens of dubious apothecary stalls selling all manner of herbal and folk medicines, as well as amulets (carved stones and medallions believed to have magical powers). Don't even think of trying any of this stuff, though you may want to buy yourself a garland of *sampaguita*, a delicately scented local variety of jasmine, from one of the young vendors.

Further north of Quiapo Church, along Andalucia St, the dingy **Central Market**, by the **Manila City Jail**, sells clothes, military uniforms, knives and hardware.

On C M Recto Ave, in the direction of the harbour, are hundreds of stalls selling household goods and bale clothing and the **Tutuban**

Center Mall, a former train station is converted into a shopping arcade.

Also in the area, **Divisoria Market** is a major centre for bale clothing and textiles, with cheap fakes of practically every brand name on the market.

At **Baclaran Market** in Pasay, you can pick up all kinds of bargains – food, clothes, household goods and even electronics at prices lower than elsewhere in town.

In Malate, **San Andres Market** (open 24hr) looks like one big cornucopia of fruits including exotic *guyabano* (soursop) and durian.

Handicrafts & Souvenirs
Manila has a reputation as an arts and crafts centre. You can find some very attractive examples of Filipino craftsmanship such as countless varieties of basketry, lamps and chandeliers made of translucent Capiz shell, and the colourful *parol* (lanterns) that Filipinos traditionally hang outside their houses at Christmas.

Along M H del Pilar St in Ermita there are dozens of shops selling paintings by local artists. The standard is often quite high and the subject matter varies, even though the artists turn these things out at an alarming rate.

Shells, too, are a popular purchase, but environmentalists have serious concerns about the impact of uncontrolled shell harvesting. In particular, trident shells and certain giant clams are protected under international laws governing trade in endangered species.

You should also be aware that the Batangas or Laguna *balisong* (fan or butterfly knife), a popular handmade souvenir sold at numerous stalls in Central Market, are banned in many countries.

Silahis Arts & Artifacts Center (☎ 527 2111; 744 General Luna St, Intramuros; 10am-7pm daily) carries a wide variety of good quality native handicrafts.

Galeria Andrea (☎ 527 4089; Plaza San Luis Complex, General Luna St, Intramuros) is small but filled with all kinds of antique wood carvings, porcelain pieces and jewellery.

Lastly, Malate's J Nakpil St has some trendy shops worth a look, including **The Source Asia Philippines** (☎ 521 8308; 562 J Nakpil St, Malate), which displays lamps and artefacts from all over Asia, and **Firma** (☎ 525 4990; 616 J Nakpil St, Malate), which

MANILA

looks more like an art gallery than a store with its artful arrangements of Oriental and Indian pieces.

Clothing

You can buy authentic brand-name clothes in Manila for a fraction of the prices charged in Europe, Australia, Japan or the USA. Many of these brand names operate a counter in department stores; some have stores or boutiques of their own.

If you're after authenticity, the latter are the most reliable source, but if you don't care about authenticity, you can pick up cheap copies in practically any market, such as the bale-clothing markets in Divisoria and Baclaran.

The Barong Tagalog, the traditional dress-shirt (which usually includes an embroidered front) worn by Filipino men, is a popular purchase among tourists. The best *barong* are made from *pinya* (**peen**-ya), a fabric woven from pineapple fibres. *Jusi* (**hoo**-see), from ramie fibres, is more common and less expensive.

The long-sleeved *pinya* or *jusi barong* is usually worn at formal occasions, while the cotton version, in either long or short sleeves (the latter is called *polo barong*), is suitable for everyday use.

Ready-to-wear *barong* are available at most handicraft shops and department stores, and most tailors will gladly sew one to your specifications. Most shops also carry ladies' wear made from the finely embroidered material.

A cheaper form of *jusi* is made into elegant tablecloths and napkins.

Shopping Centres

Manila is a city of shopping malls. **Ayala Center** *(Makati City)* revolves around **Glorietta** *(open 10am-9pm daily)*, which is actually four malls (Glorietta 1 to Glorietta 4) under one big roof.

Nearby, in **Greenbelt Park**, you will find the newly expanded **Greenbelt Mall** *(open 10am-8pm daily)* along with the newly built **Greenbelt II** and **Greenbelt III**. The **Power Plant** *(open 10am-8pm daily)* is in the Rockwell Center near the northern tip of Makati Ave.

Ortigas Center has no less than four malls, including the biggest one of all: **SM Megamall** *(open 10am-9pm daily)*. Stretch-

ing over a kilometre, SM Megamall sprawls between two other malls, **Shangri-La Plaza Mall** *(open 10am-9pm daily)* and **Robinsons Galleria** *(open 10am-9pm daily)*. Just behind Megamall is **The Podium** *(open 10am-11pm daily)*.

Greenhills Shopping Center *(Ortigas Ave, Greenhills, San Juan; open 9am-10pm daily)*, not far from Robinsons Galleria, is somewhat like a flea market, with stall after stall selling everything from mobile (cell) phones to antiques.

Further northeast along EDSA lies **Araneta Center**, the main commercial hub of Quezon City. Renovation work is under way to turn the centre into what will become the world's biggest commercial space.

Ermita and Malate are served by **Robinsons Place** *(open 10am-9pm daily)* and **Harrison Plaza** *(open 9am-9pm daily)*.

On the way to or from the airport, at the top of Roxas Blvd, you'll notice the **Uniwide Coastal Mall** *(open 10am-8pm daily)*, which opened big but has somehow failed to join the major league.

South of NAIA is the **Duty Free Fiesta Mall** *(open 9am-8pm daily)* where newly arrived passengers can pick up cigarettes, chocolates, liquor, cosmetics, electronic goods, household appliances etc at duty-free prices. Grab a taxi, private car, bus, or jeepney to get there.

GETTING THERE & AWAY
Air

With the exception of Philippine Airlines (PAL), international flights to/from Manila use the Ninoy Aquino International Airport (NAIA) in Parañaque. International and domestic PAL passengers use the Centennial Terminal (NAIA II). See Getting Around later for details of transport options to/from NAIA and NAIA II.

A P550 departure tax is payable for international departures. Call **NAIA** (☎ 877 1109) for information regarding arrivals and departures.

The offices of nearly all international airlines are in Makati, although a few have branches in Ermita and Malate. Opening times vary slightly, but all offices can be contacted from 9am to 5pm Monday to Friday; some are also open 9am to noon on Saturday.

Air France (☎ 887 7581) Trident Tower Bldg, 312 Sen Gil Puyat Ave, Makati City

Air Macau (☎ 243 3111) 508 Plaza del Conde (near corner Santo Cristo and San Fernando Sts), Binondo

American Airlines (☎ 817 8645) Olympia Condominium, Makati Ave, Makati City

Asiana Airlines (☎ 892 5681, 892 5688) I-Care Bldg, Dela Rosa St, Legaspi Village, Makati City

British Airways (☎ 817 0361, 815 6556) Filipino Merchants Bldg, corner Dela Rosa and Legaspi Sts, Legaspi Village, Makati City

Cathay Pacific Airways (☎ 849 2747) Trafalgar Plaza Bldg, 105 Dela Costa St, Salcedo Village, Makati City

China Air Lines (☎ 526 3738) Manila Midtown Hotel Arcade, corner Pedro Gil and M Adriatico Sts, Ermita

China South Airlines (☎ 551 3333) Almeda Bldg, 300 Roxas Blvd, Pasay City

Continental Micronesia (☎ 818 8701) SGV Bldg I, Ayala Ave, Makati City

Czech Airlines (☎ 892 6006) Peninsula Court, 8735 Paseo de Roxas, Makati City

Egypt Air (☎ 843 5901) RCBC Plaza, Ayala Ave, Makati City

El Al Airlines (☎ 816 2387, 816 4121) Rajah Sulayman Bldg, Benavidez St, Legaspi Village, Makati City

Emirates (☎ 811 5278) Pacific Star Bldg, corner Sen Gil Puyat Ave and Makati Ave, Makati City

EVA Air (☎ 894 5671–76) Don Tim Bldg, Osmeña Hwy (South Super Hwy) near Magallanes Bridge, Makati City

Gulf Air (☎ 817 8383) 100 Alfaro St, Salcedo Village, Makati City

Japan Airlines (☎ 886 6868) Standard Chartered Bank Bldg, 6788 Ayala Ave, Makati City

KLM-Royal Dutch Airlines (☎ 815 4790) The Athaeneum, 160 Leviste St, Salcedo Village, Makati City

Korean Air (☎ 893 4909) LPL Plaza Bldg, Alfaro St, Salcedo Village, Makati City • (☎ 893 0463) SGV Bldg, Ayala Ave, Makati City

Lufthansa Airlines (☎ 810 4596) Legaspi Parkview Condominium, corner Legaspi and C Palanca Sts, Legaspi Village, Makati City

Malaysia Airlines (☎ 525 9404) Legaspi Towers, 300 P Ocampo Sr St, Malate • (☎ 867 8767) World Centre, Sen Gil Puyat Ave, Makati City

Northwest Airlines (☎ 810 4716) La Paz Center, corner Salcedo and Herrera Sts, Legaspi Village, Makati City • (☎ 521 1928) Manila Midtown Hotel, corner Pedro Gil and M Adriatico Sts, Ermita

Qantas Airways (☎ 812 0607) Filipino Bldg, corner Dela Rosa and Legaspi Sts, Legaspi Village, Makati City

Qatar Airways (☎ 812 1888) The Colonnade Residences, corner Legaspi and C Palanca Sts, Legaspi Village, Makati City

Royal Brunei (☎ 897 3309) Saville Bldg, corner Sen Gil Puyat Ave and Paseo de Roxas, Makati City

Saudi Arabian Airlines (☎ 896 4046) Metro House Bldg, Sen Gil Puyat Ave near Reposo St, Makati City

Singapore Airlines (☎ 810 4951–59) 138 Dela Costa St, Salcedo Village, Makati City

Swiss International Airlines (☎ 818 8351) Zuellig Bldg, Malugay St, Makati City

Thai Airways International (☎ 812 4744) Country Space I Bldg, Dela Costa St, Salcedo Village, Makati City

United Airlines (☎ 884 8272) The Enterprise Center, Tower II, corner Ayala Ave and Paseo de Roxas, Makati City

Vietnam Airlines (☎ 812 7794) 152 Xanland Corporate Bldg, Amorsolo St, Legaspi Village, Makati City

Domestic PAL flights leave from NAIA II, while Cebu Pacific, Asian Spirit, Air Philippines, SEAIR and Laoag International Airlines operate from the Manila Domestic Airport, just north of NAIA. (**Note**: In early 2003, Laoag International Airlines suspended all services; it is uncertain when it will resume operations.) All of these companies have express ticket offices at the terminals where you can buy tickets for same-day travel. The ticketing offices of Cebu Pacific, Asian Spirit, Air Philippines, SEAIR and Laoag International Airlines are lined up along Domestic Rd, next to Manila Domestic Airport; the PAL office is located between the two wings of NAIA II. At either terminal, a P100 terminal fee is charged for domestic departures.

Throughout the city, all of the domestic airlines have offices that can be identified by the airline logo and corporate colours. Travel agents or authorised ticket agents can also handle reservation and ticketing procedures in lieu of airline offices. If you're staying in a four- or five-star hotel, you can entrust the task to the butler, concierge or front desk.

Airline offices are usually very crowded – get a number as you come in and wait for your turn, which can take a couple of hours. You can save yourself the trouble by making your reservation over the phone and picking up your ticket at the airline office near the airport (the airport express ticket offices are considerably less crowded than the town offices). The following is a list of 24-hour reservation hotlines.

Air Philippines (☎ 855 9000)
Asian Spirit (☎ 851 8888)
Cebu Pacific Air (☎ 636 4938)
Philippine Airlines (☎ 855 8888)

One important thing about domestic air travel in the Philippines is that there are often promotional deals available. A very common way to obtain a discount is to purchase your ticket two or three days before your flight. Check with the airlines or look for related advertisements or announcements in the newspapers to find out what the current deal is.

Air Philippines (☎ 551 7505) Manila Domestic Airport Passenger Terminal, Domestic Rd, Pasay City. Open 2am to 8pm daily.
Asian Spirit (☎ 853 1957, 8514 4310) corner Domestic Rd and Andrews Ave, Pasay City. Open 3am to 6pm daily.
Cebu Pacific Air (☎ 852 1318) Manila Domestic Airport Passenger Terminal, Domestic Rd, Pasay City. Open 1am to 8pm daily.
Laoag International Airlines (☎ 551 9729) Manila Domestic Airport Passenger Terminal, Domestic Rd, Pasay City. Open 7am to 6pm daily.
Pacific Air (☎ 851 1501, 851 1509) 3110 Domestic Rd, near Manila Domestic Airport, Pasay City. Open 7am to 5.30pm daily.
Philippine Airlines (☎ 879 5601, 879 6037) Centennial Terminal (NAIA II), NAIA Rd, Parañaque. Open 3am to 8pm daily.
SEAIR (☎ 851 5555) Manila Domestic Airport Passenger Terminal, Domestic Rd, Pasay City. Open 7am to 5.30pm daily.

Luzon PAL flies to Naga (once daily except Tuesday and Friday), to Legaspi (at least once daily) and to Tuguegarao (once daily Monday, Wednesday and Saturday).

Air Philippines flies to Laoag (once daily Tuesday, Friday and Sunday) and to Subic (one on Sunday).

Laoag International Airlines did have a flight to Laoag (once daily Monday, Wednesday and Friday). The Monday and Friday flights continued to Basco and Tuguegarao, before returning to Manila. The Wednesday flight went on to Basco only, before returning to Manila.

Asian Spirit flies between Manila and Baguio City once daily (P1800).

SEAIR flies to Cauayan (once daily Tuesday, Thursday and Sunday) and to Clark (once daily except Tuesday and Saturday).

Batanes Laoag International Airlines flew to Basco (once daily Monday, Wednesday and Friday) via Laoag.

Catanduanes Asian Spirit flies to Virac (once daily except Tuesday and Thursday).

Marinduque Asian Spirit has flights to Santa Cruz (once daily Monday, Thursday and Saturday) and to San José (once daily). Air Philippines also flies to San José (once daily Tuesday, Friday and Sunday).

Bohol Asian Spirit flies to Tagbilaran (at least once daily; with two flights on Monday, Friday and Sunday), while Laoag International Airlines also had services (once daily Monday, Wednesday, Friday and Sunday).

Cebu PAL offers frequent daily flights to Cebu City. There are also Air Philippines flights (four daily) and Cebu Pacific services (eight daily).

Leyte PAL flies to Tacloban (twice daily), while Cebu Pacific also has services (three daily).

Masbate Asian Spirit flies to Masbate (once daily) and Laoag International Airlines also had a flight (once daily Tuesday, Thursday, Friday and Sunday.

Negros PAL flies to Bacolod (four daily). Air Philippines also flies to Bacolod (two daily) and to Dumaguete (two daily). Cebu Pacific has flights to Bacolod (three daily) and to Dumaguete (once daily).

Panay PAL flies to Iloilo City (four daily), to Kalibo (at least twice daily) and to Roxas City (once daily).

Air Philippines flies to Iloilo (three daily) and to Kalibo (once daily).

Cebu Pacific flies to Roxas (once daily), to Iloilo (three daily) and to Kalibo (once daily).

Asian Spirit has flights to Caticlan (seven daily) for Boracay.

Pacific Air has scheduled flights to Caticlan (three daily), but the airline follows the schedule only if there are enough ticketed passengers.

SEAIR also has regular flights to Caticlan (three daily).

Romblon Laoag International Airlines had a flight to Tablas (once daily Tuesday, Thursday and Saturday).

Samar Asian Spirit flies to Calbayog (once daily Tuesday, Thursday and Sunday) and to Catarman (once daily Monday, Wednesday and Friday).

Palawan PAL flies to Puerto Princesa (once daily), while Air Philippines also has a flight (once daily).

SEAIR flies to Sandoval (once daily) and to El Nido (once daily Monday and Friday).

For the diving resort of Coron, Asian Spirit has a flight to Busuanga (once daily Tuesday, Wednesday, Friday and Sunday). There are also SEAIR services (at least once daily) and Pacific Air flights (once daily).

Mindanao PAL flies to Cagayan de Oro (three daily), to Davao City (three daily), to General Santos City (once daily), Butuan City (once daily), to Zamboanga (twice daily), to Cotabato (once daily) and to Dipolog (once daily except Sunday).

Air Philippines has flights to Zamboanga (once daily), to Cagayan de Oro (once daily), to General Santos (once daily) and to Davao (twice daily).

Cebu Pacific flies to Davao (four daily), to Cagayan de Oro (twice daily), to Zamboanga (once daily) and to Butuan (once daily).

Bus

Getting out of Manila by bus is harder than you might expect as there is no central bus terminal. The dozens of private operators have their own terminals scattered around the city. Most are close to EDSA (Manila's ring road), which connects the highways going north and south of the capital. All the terminals are accessible by public transport; the suggested routes (jeepney or LRT/MRT) to the terminals are from Ermita and Malate. It should be noted that Filipino bus drivers are among the most maniacal on the face of the earth, although the number of ac-

cidents is surprisingly low. If you're not used to travelling at breakneck speed, you may well be in for a white-knuckle ride.

Note the information here refers to the suburb from which your journey originates.

Malate A couple of bus companies operate services to Legaspi, via Naga; the buses leave from the **DHL office** *(cnr Pedro Gil & M H del Pilar Sts)*. **Gold Line Tours** and **Highway Express** next door each have one evening service.

There are also buses that connect with the boats for Puerto Galera (Mindoro). A daily bus leaves the **Citystate Tower Hotel** *(A Mabini St)* to connect with a boat to Puerto Galera (P350 for bus and ferry). Alternatively, an earlier daily bus leaves the **Lotus Garden Hotel** *(A Mabini St)* to connect with another boat to Puerto Galera (P360/695 one way/return). Both buses can be booked at representative counters in the hotels.

Intramuros & Santa Cruz Close to the tourist belt, there are bus terminals offering services to destinations such as Batangas City pier (for ferries to Puerto Galera), Cavite, Ternate, Angeles and the Bataan peninsula. To get to the terminals, catch a jeepney from Taft Ave or A Mabini St.

No 1 Alps Transit, Concepcion St near Baluarte de San Francisco de Dilao, Intramuros, across from Manila City Hall. Alps Transit has buses to Batangas City pier every 20 minutes. To get to the terminal, take a Monumento or Divisoria jeepney and get off by the Manila City Hall.

No 2 Saulog Transit and **St Anthony Transit**, Anda St near Baluarte de San Gabriel, Intramuros. These companies have buses to Cavite and Ternate every seven minutes. To get to the terminal, take a Divisoria jeepney and get off just before Jones bridge.

No 3 Philippine Rabbit (☎ 734 9836) corner Oroquieta St and Rizal Ave, Santa Cruz. Philippine Rabbit has buses every 20 minutes to Angeles in Pampanga province, and Balanga and Mariveles in Bataan province. All buses go via San Fernando (Pampanga). To get to the terminal, take a Monumento jeepney or the LRT to Doroteo José station.

Sampaloc Northeast of the tourist belt are a number of bus companies serving northern destinations such as Bangued in Abra province, Vigan in Ilocos Sur, Laoag in Ilocos Norte, Tuguegarao in Cagayan, Banaue

MANILA

BUS DESTINATIONS FROM MANILA

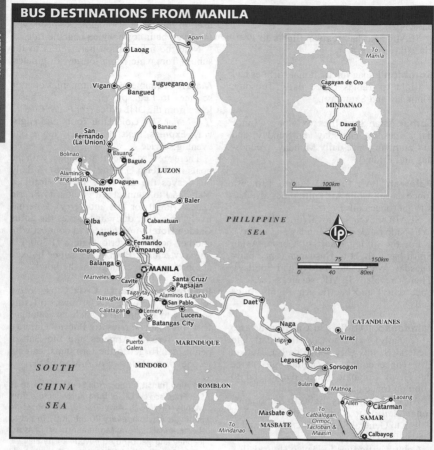

in Ifugao and Baguio in Benguet. To get to the terminals, catch a jeepney from Taft Ave or A Mabini St.

No 4 Autobus Transport Systems (☎ 743 2227) corner Dimasalang and Laong Laan Sts. Autobus has a daily bus to Banaue and regular buses to Tuguegarao, Vigan and Laoag. To get to the terminal, take a Blumentritt via Dimasalang jeepney.

No 5 Dangwa Tranco (☎ 731 2859) 1600 Dimasalang St. Dangwa has buses to Baguio every few hours. To get to the terminal, take a Blumentritt via Dimasalang jeepney.

No 6 Dominion Transit (☎ 743 3612) corner Blumentritt and Laong Laan Sts. Dominion has evening buses to Vigan via San Fernando (La Union). To get to the terminal, take a Dapitan jeepney.

No 7 Fariñas Trans (☎ 743 8580–82) 1238 DH Lacson St. Fariñas Trans has half-hourly buses to

Laoag via Vigan. To get to the terminal, take a Blumentritt via Dimasalang jeepney.

No 8 Maria de Leon Trans (☎ 731 4907) corner Geliños and Dapitan Sts. Maria de Leon Trans has hourly buses to Laoag via San Fernando (La Union) and Vigan. Dapitan jeepneys pass close to the terminal.

Caloocan Caloocan is an important departure point for north-bound buses. Destinations include Olongapo in Zambales province, San José del Monte and Baliwag in Bulucan province, Cabanatuan in Nueva Ecija province, as well as Vigan, Laoag and Baguio.

No 9 Baliwag Transit (☎ 364 0778) 199 Rizal Ave Extension. Baliwag Transit has buses every 40 minutes to Cabanatuan (a jumping-off point for

Bus Destinations from Manila

destination	km	duration (hrs)	bus company number
Alaminos (Laguna)	78	1½	20, 21, 22, 27, 33
Alaminos (Pangasinan)	254	6	13, 17, 25
Angeles	83	1½	3
Aparri	596	13	12, 18
Baguio	246	6	5, 10, 11, 13, 17, 26
Balanga	123	2½	3, 29
Baler	—	7	29
Banaue	348	9	4
Bangued	400	8	6, 10, 15, 16
Batangas City	111	3	1, 20, 21, 22, 27, 35
Bolinao	283	6	25
Cabanatuan	115	2½	9, 12, 18, 25
Cagayan de Oro	—	72	23, 34
Calatagan	—	4	27
Calbayog	—	12	27, 30, 34
Catarman	—	20	34
Catbalogan	—	16	19, 27, 30, 34
Cavite	—	1	2
Daet	350	7	23, 24, 30, 34
Davao	—	72	23, 34
Iba	210	5	11
Laoag	487	10	4, 7, 8, 10, 16, 32
Legaspi	550	12	23, 24, 27, 30, 34
Lemery	—	3½	21, 27
Lingayen	227	5½	13, 17
Lucena	136	3	20, 21, 22, 24, 27, 30, 33, 34, 35
Maasin	—	28	27, 30, 34
Mariveles	—	3½	3, 29
Matnog	670	17	27, 30, 34
Naga	449	9	23, 24, 27, 30, 34
Nasugbu	102	2½	27, 28
Olongapo	126	3½	11, 26
Ormoc	—	26	19, 23, 27
San Fernando (La Union)	269	7	6, 8, 15, 16, 32
San Fernando (Pampanga)	66	1	3, 26, 29
San Pablo	87	2	21, 22, 27, 34, 35
Santa Cruz/Pagsanjan	101	2½	21, 27, 33
Sorsogon	604	14	19, 27, 30, 34
Tacloban	—	24	19, 23, 27, 30, 34
Tagaytay	56	1½	28
Tuguegarao	483	10	4, 12, 13, 18
Vigan	407	9	4, 6, 7, 8, 10, 15, 16, 32

the surfing beaches of Baler), as well as regular services to Baliwag and San José del Monte. Take a Monumento jeepney to the corner of 2nd Ave; the terminal is about midway between R Papa and 5th Ave stations of the LRT.

No 10 Philippine Rabbit (☎ 364 3477) EDSA, Balintawak. Philippine Rabbit has hourly buses to Baguio and Bangued, and buses every few hours to Laoag and Vigan. Take a jeepney or the LRT to Monumento, then a south-bound bus for Cubao.

No 11 Victory Liner (☎ 361 1506) 713 Rizal Ave Extension. Victory Liner has four daily buses to Baguio. There are half-hourly buses to Olongapo, Iba and Santa Cruz in Zambales. Take a jeepney or the LRT to Monumento; the terminal is just before the Monumento roundabout.

Cubao (North-Bound) Most buses from Cubao head north to Cabanatuan, San Fernando (La Union), Baguio, Tuguegarao, Vigan, Laoag or even Aparri, at the top of Cagayan province. The bus terminals are clustered near **Araneta Center** *(cnr EDSA & Aurora Blvd)*; there's one terminal in the centre itself. Take a Cubao jeepney or FX van to Araneta Center or, alternatively, take the LRT to EDSA station, then change to the north-bound MRT and get off at Cubao-Araneta Center station.

No 12 Baliwag Transit (☎ 912 3343) EDSA, near the corner of Aurora Blvd. Baliwag Transit has buses leaving for Cabanatuan via Baliway every 20 to 30 minutes. A few doors away is another Baliway terminal from where buses bound for Tuguegarao (via Cauayan) depart every two hours and buses leave for Aparri (twice daily).

No 13 Dagupan Bus Co (☎ 727 2330) corner EDSA and New York St. Dagupan Bus Co has buses every hour to Dagupan, Alaminos and Lingayen in Pangasinan province. There are also hourly buses to Tuguegarao and Baguio.

No 15 Dominion Transit (☎ 727 2334) EDSA. Dominion has hourly buses to San Fernando (La Union), Bangued and Vigan.

No 16 Partas (☎ 725 7303, 725 1740) Aurora Blvd. Partas has hourly buses to Bangued, Vigan and Laoag. Most Buses stop in San Fernando (La Union).

No 17 Victory Liner (☎ 727 4688) EDSA. Victory has buses to Alaminos and Lingayen in Pangasinan province every 40 minutes. There are also hourly buses to Baguio.

No 18 Victory Liner (☎ 921 3296) corner EDSA and East Ave. Victory has eight buses to Tuguega- rao and two to Aparri daily. All buses stop in Cabanatuan on the way to Cagayan.

Cubao (South-Bound) Services also run south from Cubao, including buses to Batangas, Lucena in Quezon province, Daet in Camarines Norte, Naga in Camarines Sur, Legaspi in Albay, Tacloban and Ormoc in Leyte, and Davao in Mindanao. From the **Araneta Center Bus Terminal**, in addition to BLTB and Philtranco, several smaller operators run buses to Bicol, Visayas and Mindanao. The smaller operators include **Gold Line Tours** (☎ 743 3389) and **Peñafrancia Tours & Travel** (☎ 366 6717). Take a Cubao jeepney or FX van to Araneta Center or, alternatively, take the LRT to EDSA station, then change to the north-bound MRT and get off at Cubao-Araneta Center station.

No 19 BLTB (☎ 913 1526) Araneta Center Bus Terminal, behind Ali Mall. BLTB has buses to Sorsogon (Bicol) and Catbalogan (Visayas).

No 20 JAC Liner (☎ 928 6140, 929 6943) corner EDSA and East Ave. JAC has buses to Bantagas City and Lucena every 20 to 30 minutes from 2am to 9pm daily.

No 21 JAM Transit (☎ 414 9925) corner EDSA and Monte de Piedad St. JAM has buses every 30 minutes to Batangas City, Lucena and Santa Cruz (Laguna).

No 22 Tritran (☎ 925 1759) corner EDSA and East Ave. Tritran has half-hourly buses to Lucena and Dalahican, and buses to Batangas City every 20 minutes.

No 23 Philtranco (☎ 913 3602) Araneta Center Bus Terminal, behind Ali Mall. Philtranco has daily buses from 7am until 9pm to Legaspi and Naga (Bicol), Tacloban and Ormoc (Visayas), and Davao and Cagayan de Oro (Mindanao).

No 24 Superlines (☎ 414 3319) 670 EDSA. Superlines has at least 16 buses daily to Daet via Lucena, and less frequent buses continuing to Naga and Legaspi.

Pasay (North-Bound) A couple of bus companies head north from Pasay for destinations like Baguio, Cabanatuan and Olongapo. To find your way to these terminals, take a Baclaran jeepney from M H del Pilar St or the LRT to EDSA station and change to a north-bound bus for Makati and Quezon City.

No 25 Five Star Bus Lines (☎ 833 4772) Aurora Blvd. Five Star has regular buses to Cabanatuan. There are also buses to Bolinao in Pangasinan every half-hour.

No 26 Victory Liner (☎ 833 5019) EDSA. Victory has at least hourly services to Baguio. Buses to Olongapo leave every half-hour.

No 32 Partas (☎ 851 4025) Aurora Blvd. Partas has a bus to Vigan and Laoag (four daily).

Pasay (South-Bound) Most buses out of Pasay head south, with some connecting by ferry to other islands. Destinations include Batangas, Lucena, Nasugbu and Santa Cruz. A few buses go further afield to Daet, Naga, Legaspi, the islands of Samar and Leyte, and on to Mindanao.

No 27 BLTB (☎ 833 5501) EDSA. BLTB has buses every 15 minutes to Batangas City, Nasugbu and Lucena. There are also hourly buses to Dalahican Port, Calatagan (near Matabung- kay beach) and Santa Cruz, as well as long-haul trips to Bicol, Samar and Leyte. For Leyte, there's a service to Ormoc, two buses to Maasin, and a service to Tacloban. To get to the terminal, take a Baclaran jeepney from M H del Pilar St or the LRT to EDSA station and change to a north-bound bus for Makati and Quezon City.

No 28 Crow Transit (☎ 551 1566, 804 0616) corner Taft Ave and EDSA. Crow has buses to Nasugbu every 30 minutes and buses to Tagaytay (for Lake Taal) every 15 minutes. To get to the terminal, take a Baclaran jeepney from M H del Pilar St or the LRT to EDSA station.

No 29 Genesis (☎ 551 0842) corner Taft Ave and EDSA. Genesis has buses to Mariveles in the Bataan peninsula via San Fernando (Pampanga) and Balanga, leaving every 15 minutes. There is also an early morning bus to the surfing beaches of Baler in Aurora province. To get to the terminal, take a Baclaran jeepney from M H del Pilar St or the LRT to EDSA station.

No 30 Gold Line Tours (☎ 831 9737) corner Taft Ave and EDSA. Gold Line has a daily bus to Samar and Leyte. Stops include Calbayog, Catbalogan, Tacloban and Maasin. To get to the terminal, take a Baclaran jeepney from M H del Pilar St or the LRT to EDSA station.

No 33 JAM Transit (☎ 831 4390) corner Taft Ave and Sen Gil Puyat Ave. JAM has buses every 15 minutes to Lucena and Santa Cruz in Laguna. To get to the terminal, take the LRT to Gil Puyat station or a Baclaran jeepney to the corner of Taft Ave and Sen Gil Puyat Ave.

No 34 Philtranco (☎ 833 5061, 832 2456) EDSA. Philtranco has daily buses to Davao and Cagayan de Oro, both in Mindanao. There are services to Tacloban (four daily) in Leyte, stopping at Calbayog and Catbalogan in Samar. There is also a bus to Catarman (three daily) in Northern Samar. Buses stop in Daet, Naga, Legaspi and Sorsogon. To get to the terminal, take a Baclaran jeepney from M H del Pilar St or the LRT to EDSA station and change to a north-bound bus for Makati and Quezon City.

No 35 Tritran (☎ 831 4700) 2124 Taft Ave. Tritran has buses every 30 minutes to Batangas and Lucena (via San Pablo). To get to the terminal, take the LRT to Gil Puyat station or a Baclaran jeepney to the corner of Taft Ave and Sen Gil Puyat Ave.

Boat

The port of Manila is divided into two sections, South Harbor and North Harbor. Unfortunately for the traveller, all passenger ferries departing from Manila use the hard-to-reach North Harbor.

It's best to take a taxi, as the port area isn't a place for a foreigner to be wandering around with luggage. On the taxi meter from Malate or Ermita, the fare should cost around P70. In the opposite direction, ie, from the North Harbor port to Malate or Ermita, you'll have to be a very good bargainer to get the driver down to P100.

There are three major shipping lines handling interisland boat trips from Manila:

Negros Navigation (☎ 245 5588) Pier 2, North Harbor. This company sails to Panay, Negros, Palawan, Bohol and Mindanao.

Sulpicio Lines (☎ 245 0616) Pier 12, North Harbor. Sulpicio goes to Cebu, Leyte, Masbate, Negros and Mindanao.

WG&A (☎ 528 7000, SuperTours hotline 528 7100, ✉ reservations@wgasuperferry.com) Pier 4 and Pier 14, North Harbor. WG&A has services to Cebu, Negros, Panay, Bohol, Leyte, Masbate, Palawan and Mindanao.

All three shipping companies have ticket offices at North Harbor and in town, although nowadays you needn't go to the shipping offices to make a reservation or buy a ticket. Independent travel/ticket agents (the same ones that handle airline reservations and ticketing) can make bookings and issue tickets.

There are several of these agents in Ermita and Malate (they're easy to identify as they carry the logos of the airlines and shipping companies on their front signage).

You can even purchase tickets online (try 🌐 www.wgasuperferry.com or 🌐 www.lakbay.net .ph). Note, however, that shipping schedules are prone to change; adverse weather conditions or renovation work on one ferry can totally disrupt or alter the sailing times and boats specified for the scheduled trips.

Cebu, Negros, Panay & Bohol Destinations and travel times include: Cebu City (18 to 22 hours); Bacolod and Dumaguete on the island of Negros (19 to 22 hours); Iloilo, Roxas City and Dumaguit on Panay (18 to 25 hours); and Tagbilaran on Bohol (28 to 31 hours).

Departing Pier 2, Negros Navigation sails to Bacolod (once daily except Wednesday and Friday), Iloilo (once daily except Thursday), Roxas City (once daily Sunday and Tuesday), Estancia (one on Friday) and Tagbilaran (one on Friday), which continues to Dumaguete.

Departing Pier 12, Sulpicio Lines sails to Cebu City (once daily Tuesday, Wednesday,

Thursday and Sunday), Iloilo (one on Tuesday) and Dumaguete (one on Wednesday).

Departing Piers 4 and 14, WG&A sails to Cebu City (once daily Monday, Tuesday, Thursday and Sunday), Iloilo (once daily Monday, Thursday and Saturday), Dumaguit (once daily Monday, Wednesday and Saturday) and continues to Roxas City, Bacolod (once daily Thursday and Sunday), Dumaguete (once daily Wednesday and Monday), and Tagilaran (once daily Monday and Friday).

Leyte Departing Pier 12, Sulpicio Lines sails to Ormoc (one on Friday) and Maasin (one on Wednesday) via Calubian and Baybay.

Masbate Departing Pier 12, Sulpicio Lines sails to Masbate (once daily Wednesday and Friday).

Departing Pier 14, WG&A also sails to Masbate (one on Monday), continuing to Palompon on Leyte.

Mindanao Destinations and travel times: Cagayan de Oro (29 to 48 hours); Cotabato (45 to 57 hours); Davao (52 to 74 hours); Dipolog (42 hours); Iligan (46 to 53 hours); Nasipit (31 to 40 hours); Ozamis (40 hours); Surigao (32 to 53 hours); General Santos (48 to 70 hours); and Zamboanga (43 hours).

Departing Pier 2, Negros Navigation sails to Cagayan de Oro (once daily Monday and Friday, with stopovers in Bacolod and Iloilo respectively), Iligan via Ozamis (one on Sunday), Zamboanga (one on Tuesday, with a stopover in Iloilo) and General Santos (one on Monday).

From Ozamis, Negros Navigation runs a service for Manila via Iloilo, Panay, once a week (43 hours).

From Butuan, the Negros Navigation boat runs once a week to Manila.

Departing Pier 12, Sulpicio Lines sails to Zamboanga (one on Tuesday, via Iloilo), Cagayan de Oro (once daily Saturday and Wednesday, the latter sailing via Cebu and Nasipit), Surigao (once daily Wednesday via Masbate and Leyte and Sunday via Cebu and continuing to Davao), Davao (one on Thursday via Cebu and continuing to Dadiangas), Ozamis (one on Wednesday via Dumaguete), Cotabato (one on Saturday via Estancia, Iloilo and Zamboanga) and

Dipolog (one on Wednesday via Tagbilaran and continuing to Iligan).

Departing Piers 4 and 14, WG&A sails to Surigao (once daily Monday and Thursday, continuing to Nasipit), Cotabato (one on Saturday via Zamboanga), Davao (one on Saturday with stopovers in Iloilo and General Santos and one on Monday via Zamboanga and General Santos) and Cagayan de Oro (once daily Monday and Thursday).

Mindoro Boats to/from Mindoro use the port at Batangas (see that entry in the Around Manila chapter).

Palawan & Busuanga Departing Pier 2, Negros Navigation sails to Puerto Princesa (one on Thursday). Departing Pier 4, WG&A sails to Coron and Puerto Princesa (one on Friday).

Car Rental

The big international car hire companies, including **Budget** (☎ 818 7363; The Peninsula Manila, cnr Ayala Ave & Makati Ave, Makati City • NAIA) and **Hertz** (☎ 897 5151; Sunette Tower, Durban St, Makati City • NAIA), have offices in town and at NAIA.

There are also several good independent car rental operators, such as **JB Rent-a-Car** (☎ 526 6288; ground floor, Midland Plaza Hotel, M Adriatico St, Ermita; open 8am-9pm daily), near the corner of Pedro Gil St, where you can hire a Toyota Corolla/Toyota Corona for P1200/2500 per day (P8400/15,400 weekly, with one day free), and **KEI Transport** (☎ 524 6834; Ground Floor, Palm Plaza Hotel, cnr Pedro Gil & M Adriatico Sts; open 8am-10pm Mon-Sat, 8am-5pm Sun), which hires out a Toyota Corolla for P1400/9000 per day/week.

GETTING AROUND
To/From the Airport

For most visitors, the first point of contact with the Philippines is Ninoy Aquino International Airport (NAIA), some 10km south of central Manila. Though immigration and customs procedures are fairly quick and easy (provided there are no long lines), getting from here to town can be quite a challenge.

Collect your luggage at the carousel specified for your flight (luggage trolleys

A tricycle (or pedicab) driver weaves in and out of Manila's confronting street mayhem

RICHARD I'ANSON

all the way. A line of booths in the arrivals lounge offer coupons for airport taxis, which charge more or less the same flat rates – for example, P375 to Makati, P345 to Ermita/Malate and P420 to Mandaluyong. Before you get into a taxi, it's best to establish with the staff issuing the coupon where you want to go and how much it will cost you to get there.

It may be possible to go upstairs to the departures concourse and wait for a metered taxi that's dropping off passengers, but sometimes the interconnecting stairs are closed. Also, the driver will likely make a big fuss of offering you a special deal and charge you P200 to P300 anyway. You could always walk down to Ninoy Aquino Ave and flag a taxi there, but the fare is unlikely to be much cheaper and travellers have been robbed (and even murdered) on the way from the airport in unlicensed taxis.

Bear in mind that licensed airport taxi rates are for a vehicle and not per person, so three or four passengers could share one taxi, making the fare very cheap by any standard.

If you're headed for Makati, Quezon City or other destinations along EDSA, you could pick up a local bus on the road immediately outside the terminal building. Upon leaving the building, turn right and walk past the car park – soon you'll see a bus stop across the road. However, this can be done only if you have little luggage and it exposes you to the dangers mentioned earlier.

If the dangers and annoyances of arranging your own taxi into town put you off, do what many sensible travellers do: arrange to be picked up by a car from the hotel in which you're staying. Many hotels in Manila offer a pick-up service at the airport, which usually costs around P400. While it may cost a bit more than independent taxis, there are few things more welcome after a long flight than a driver patiently waiting for you with a sign bearing your name. Pop your bags in the boot (trunk) and off you go!

Coming to the airport, you should be able to get a taxi to use its meter. Otherwise, the flat fee charged by some drivers for the trip from Ermita/Malate to NAIA is only slightly elevated at P150 to P200.

are free of charge), then proceed to the arrivals area where you will find hotel and airport taxi counters. You might also find some free telephones in the baggage-claim area that allow you to call ahead to make or confirm accommodation arrangements. Otherwise, you can make your hotel booking at the arrivals area.

Beyond customs, there are some banks and moneychangers offering different exchange rates (for details on moneychangers see Money in the Facts for the Visitor chapter). If you need to change some money, shop around for the best deal, and change only what you need. You'll get much better rates from the moneychangers or banks in town. If you change money, ask for a few small bills, as you may need them for the taxi or for public transport. A better alternative to changing money is to withdraw money from an ATM linked to international cash networks; there are ATMs that service MasterCard, Cirrus and AmEx cards in the arrivals area. You'll also find a small DOT counter here.

Getting through NAIA is the easy part. From the airport to central Manila, it's uphill

MANILA

'Baclaran–Domestic–MIA' jeepneys run from the corner of Airport Rd and Quirino Ave (across the road from a McDonald's) in Baclaran to Centennial Terminal (NAIA II), NAIA and Manila Domestic Airport, finishing back in Baclaran. The fare for a journey is only P4. If you have a bit of luggage, however, take note that the jeepneys do not take you to the door of the airport terminal buildings.

From the same Airport Rd and Quirino Ave intersection, it's a 400m walk north to the LRT Baclaran station (South Terminal) on Quirino Ave, or you can take a tricycle (pedicab) for P15 to P20. The LRT fare is P12 to Pedro Gil station in Malate or United Nations Ave station in Ermita.

Jeepneys to Malate and Ermita leave from opposite the modernist Iglesia ni Cristo church, which is just around 100m south of the LRT Baclaran station. Jeepneys with a 'Mabini' signboard run right through the middle of Malate and Ermita, passing close to most of the accommodation in the area.

If you're transferring from NAIA to NAIA II, the Sunshine Shuttle Service (which charges P30/20 per passenger/luggage) runs from outside Exit 2 of the arrivals lobby every 15 minutes. The shuttle service operates between NAIA and NAIA II and from either of those terminals to the Manila Domestic Airport, but it does not run *from* Manila Domestic Airport. Alternatively you can pick up a 'Baclaran–Domestic–MIA' jeepney in front of the domestic airport (they pass the domestic airport and Baclaran before looping back to NAIA II and NAIA), or join the line for a metered taxi outside the passenger terminal building.

Bus

Local buses are only really useful to get to places on the main roads such as Taft Ave, Espana Blvd or Epifanio de los Santos Ave (EDSA), as they are prohibited from most streets in the centre of town. Depending on the journey, ordinary buses cost from P4 to P10; air-con buses cost from P7 to P14.

Like jeepneys, buses have their destinations written on signboards placed against the front windshield, for example 'Ayala' (for Ayala Center) and 'Monumento' (for Caloocan). Probably the most useful local bus is the air-con PVP Express bus from Quezon Blvd by Quiapo Church to Ayala

Center. A 'Quiapo' jeepney will take you from Ermita/Malate to Quiapo.

Car & Motorcycle

Your first experience of Manila traffic may put you off the idea of renting a car permanently, but if you don't mind the traffic jams and unorthodox local driving habits, a rented car is probably the best way to visit the attractions around Metro Manila. Remember, though, that you are prohibited from driving your car in the capital on certain weekdays: number-plates ending in 1 and 2 are banned on Monday, 3 and 4 on Tuesday etc.

Taxi

Manila is rumoured to have the cheapest taxi fares in Asia, but since many drivers refuse to use their meters with foreign travellers, you may wind up paying more than the rock-bottom fares that locals enjoy. It's a matter of personal choice whether you want to insist that the driver uses the meter (in which case you may end up taking the most circuitous route to your destination) or just pay up. The official flag-fall rate is P25 plus P2 for every 300 metres or two minutes of waiting time. For more on taking taxis in the Philippines, see Taxi under Local Transport in the Getting Around chapter.

Jeepney

For the uninitiated, Manila jeepneys can be a challenging experience. The long wheelbase jeeps offer a bewildering array of destinations and, though these destinations are written on signboards stuck in the window, few people arrive exactly where they intend to on their first jeepney ride. However, if you stick to the more common routes, some of which are listed here, you shouldn't go too far astray.

Heading south from Ermita/Malate along M H del Pilar St, jeepneys to 'Baclaran' pass close to Harrison Plaza and the CCP. They also provide access to the southern end of EDSA, where you can pick up buses to Makati and Quezon City.

Heading north from Baclaran, jeepneys pass along A Mabini St or Taft Ave, heading off in various directions from Rizal Park. 'Divisoria' jeepneys take Jones Bridge, passing close to the Immigration Office; 'Santa Cruz' and 'Monumento' jeepneys take MacArthur Bridge, passing Manila's Central Post Office;

and 'Quiapo' and 'Cubao' jeepneys take Quezon Bridge, passing Quiapo Church.

Useful final destinations include: 'Divisoria' for Divisoria Market; 'Monumento' for Santa Cruz, the Chinese Cemetery or the bus terminals in Caloocan; and 'Cubao' via 'España' for the bus terminals in Cubao.

For more on riding jeepneys in the Philippines, see Jeepney under Local Transport in the Getting Around chapter.

FX

Manila has numerous air-con Toyota Tamaraw FX vans, sometimes bearing a Mega-Taxi sign, which follow similar routes to the jeepneys, picking up and setting down passengers en route.

The fare is P20 for long rides and P10 for shorter hops. They can also be hired as taxis, at pre-arranged flat rates, to places like the airport or tourist destinations outside the metropolitan area.

LRT & MRT

The LRT (Light Rail Transit) is an elevated railway line that runs from Baclaran in Pasay to Monumento in Caloocan, following Taft Ave and Rizal Ave.

Electronic cards are issued for single/multiple rides and cost P12/120 (multiple cards are for 10 rides). Not all trains are air-conditioned – ask the staff if you particularly want one. Avoid peak times (7am to 10am and 4pm to 6pm), as trains are packed to capacity.

Monumento (North Terminal) For Philippine Rabbit and Victory Liner terminals.
5th Avenue For Baliwag Transit terminal.
R Papa For Baliwag Transit terminal.
Abad Santos For Chinese Cemetery.
Blumentritt For Chinese Cemetery.
Tayuman For Sampaloc bus terminals.
Bambang For University of Santo Tomas and Sampaloc bus terminals.
Doroteo José For Philippine Rabbit terminal in Santa Cruz.
Carriedo For Santa Cruz Church, Chinatown, Quiapo Church and surrounding markets.
Central For Manila City Hall, National Museum, Manila Central Post Office, Metropolitan Theater, Arroceros Forest Park, Rizal Park and Intramuros.
United Nations Ave For Rizal Park, DOT Information Center, hospitals and Paco Park.
Pedro Gil For Robinsons Place, J Nakpil St, hotels and restaurants.

Quirino Ave For San Andres Market, Manila Zoo and Remedios Circle.
Vito Cruz For CCP Complex, Harrison Plaza, and Ninoy Aquino Memorial Stadium.
Gil Puyat For south-bound bus terminals and buses to Makati and Cubao.
Libertad For Libertad Cockpit and Cuneta Astrodome.
EDSA For south-bound bus terminals and buses to Makati and Cubao. Change here to MRT for northbound trains to Makati and Quezon City.
Baclaran (South Terminal) For Baclaran Market, Baclaran Church and jeepneys to airport.

The MRT (Metro Rail Transit) travels a south–north route along EDSA. Inaugurated in 1999, the MRT features modern trains with arctic air-conditioning and its stations are equipped with escalators and lifts (elevators).

Though newer and better than the LRT, the MRT actually charges less. The cheapest fare is P9.50. As with the LRT, electronic cards are issued for single or multiple journeys.

Taft Board North Avenue–bound train to go to Makati and Quezon City. Coming from opposite direction, change here to LRT.
Magallanes For some bus terminals along EDSA.
Ayala For Ayala Center (Glorietta, Ayala Museum etc), Greenbelt Park, the eastern end of A Arnaiz Ave (Pasay Rd) and the southern end of Makati Ave.
Buendia For Jupiter St, Makati Ave/P Burgos St intersection and Rockwell Center (Power Plant).
Guadalupe For Pasig River.
Boni For jeepneys to Mandaluyong.
Shaw For Shangri-La Plaza Mall, SM Megamall, Edsa Shangri-La Hotel, hotels and eateries at the southern end of Ortigas Center.
Ortigas For SM Megamall, The Podium, Robinsons Galleria, Manila Galleria Suites, hotel and eateries at the middle/northern portion of Ortigas Center.
Santolan For Camp Aguinaldo and the north-western part of Greenhills.
Cubao-Araneta Center For Araneta Center (Araneta Coliseum etc) and bus terminals in Cubao.
GMA Kamuning For hotels and eateries along Timog Ave and T Morato Ave and some bus terminals on EDSA.
Quezon Avenue For Quezon Memorial Circle and Ninoy Aquino Parks & Wildlife Center.
North Avenue For SM City North.

Kalesa

Horse-drawn carriages known as *kalesa* are still a form of public transport in some rural areas, but in Manila they're confined to Chinatown and Intramuros, where they're mainly used to take tourists for a ride (sometimes in the figurative sense). If you wish to use one of these carriages, agree on the price before you board. The pricing is totally arbitrary so you'll have to rely on your own judgement. As a rule of thumb,

you can bring down the driver's asking price to half and haggle from there.

Tricycle

Tricycles (also known as pedicabs) are bicycles or motorbikes with sidecars, which are useful for short hops around town, though they aren't the cheapest way to get around. Short journeys can cost anywhere from P15 to P50, depending on how well you bargain.

Around Manila

The regular transport links to/from Metro Manila allow a huge range of day or overnight trips to the surrounding area. Whether you're interested in beaches, scuba diving, historic churches or volcanoes, there should be something here that appeals.

The principal tourist attractions in the area are Lake Taal and the Taal Volcano; the rapids on the Pagsanjan River; historic Corregidor island in Manila Bay; the hot springs at Los Baños; hiking around the Mt Pinatubo volcano, near Angeles; and scuba diving off the coast near Nasugbu and Anilao. All of these places see large numbers of tourists, particularly in the high season.

As an alternative, the dormant volcanoes of Mt Banahaw and Mt Makiling and the historic Bataan Peninsula offer the chance to get away from the crowds and do a little exploring on your own.

Most of these attractions can be visited in a day, but others, particularly the hikes around the many volcanoes in the area, really deserve an overnight trip. Transport is frequent and there are several places that can be visited as half-day trips from Manila, or combined to make a whole day trip.

Be warned, however, that travel times out of Manila can increase dramatically depending upon traffic – avoid peak hour for the swiftest departures and arrivals into the big smoke.

LAS PIÑAS
☎ 02
The tiny village of Las Piñas, 20km south of Manila, has long been swallowed up by Metro Manila, but it still has a pleasant village atmosphere and many of its buildings have been restored using traditional methods.

The principal attraction here is the **bamboo organ** (☎ 825 7190, 826 7718; admission adult/child P20/10; open 9am-noon & 2pm-5pm Mon-Sat) in the **San José Church** (Quirino Ave). The famous organ was built in 1821, during a lean period, by the Spanish priest Padre Diego Cera, who instructed bamboo to be used instead of the more expensive metal for the majority of the organ pipes. The custodians will play the organ for you, demonstrating its unique sound, when you visit.

Highlights

- Hike through the impressive landscape created by the Taal and Mt Pinatubo Volcanoes
- Shoot the rapids on the Pagsanjan River
- Tour the WWII relics on the historic Corregidor
- Scuba dive on the coral reefs off Anilao and wreck dive in Subic Bay

Subic Bay p153

◆MANILA

In the second week of February, organists from around the world gather here for the **Bamboo Organ Festival**.

Minibuses and buses travelling from Manila to Cavite stop in Las Piñas (see Getting There & Away under Cavite later).

CAVITE
☎ 02 • pop 99,400
The protected harbour of Cavite, 35km southwest of Manila, was the site of the destruction of the Spanish fleet during the US invasion of Luzon in 1898.

The city is now the home of the Philippine Navy and has a few resorts strung along the unimpressive beaches on the west side of the peninsula.

The main reason for coming here is to visit the **Aguinaldo House** (admission free; open 8am-noon & 1pm-5pm Tues-Sun), where the revolutionary army of General Aguinaldo proclaimed the Independence of the

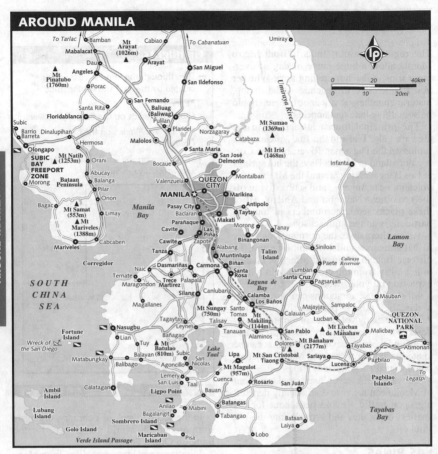

AROUND MANILA

Philippines on 12 June 1898 – a short-lived triumph soon quashed by the Americans. The house is now a shrine and you can tour Aguinaldo's private rooms and visit his mausoleum in the gardens.

Places to Stay

Cavite isn't really worth an overnight stay, but there are a couple of luxury resorts about 40km south of here, in Ternate, that are far enough away from Manila to have clear water and clean beaches.

Caylabne Bay Resort (☎ 841 1318, 841 1324–6; W www.caylabne.com.ph; rooms with air-con & bathroom from P3013) is a luxurious property with good beaches, tennis courts, a swimming pool and water sports.

Puerto Azul Resort (☎ 522 9382/5; W www.puertoazulgolfcc.net; native-style cottages with air-con & bathroom P2300) is an established place with similar facilities to Caylabne Bay Resort.

Getting There & Away

Saulog, Tamaraw FX and St Anthony have air-con buses leaving every few minutes from Lawton Plaza and Baclaran to Cavite and Ternate, via Las Piñas (P30 to P35, 1½ hours).

CALAMBA
☎ 049 • pop 28,100

Calamba, southeast of Manila on the shores of the Laguna de Bay, was the birthplace of the Philippine national hero José Rizal, and the Spanish-colonial house where Rizal was born is now venerated as the **Rizal Shrine** (*admission free; open 8am-noon & 1pm-5pm Tues-Sun*). On display are numerous items of Rizal memorabilia. Calamba also has spa resorts with natural **hot springs** and swimming pools open to day-trippers, for a fee.

Near the Santa Rosa exit from the South Luzon Expressway, **Enchanted Kingdom** (☎ 02-830 2111-16; W *www.enchantedking dom.com.ph; tickets P100-320; open 10am-10pm Sat, Sun & holidays, variable opening hours Wed-Fri*) is Luzon's most popular theme park, with a good selection of roller coasters and other thrill rides.

Places to Stay
The main spa resorts are all along the highway towards Los Baños.

Batu-Bato Mountain Resort (☎ 545 1777, 545 5084, 02-721 8008; e *kuwintas@pa cific.net.au; rooms with fan/air-con P850/1000, with 20 beds & minipool P7000; open 24hr*) is a 5-hectare resort with six pools, putting green and restaurant.

Monte Vista Hot Springs Resort (☎ 545 1259, 545 2109; e *monte_vista@netasia.net; rooms with air-con & bathroom weekdays/weekends P1500/1900, with private pool P2000/2500; open 24hr*), halfway between Calamba and Los Baños, is a huge place with numerous pools, spas and water slides. Day admission is P95 from Monday to Thursday, and P125 from Friday to Sunday.

Crystal Springs Waterworld (☎ 545 2496, 842 3597; *doubles P1600*), just past Monte Vista towards Los Baños, is an impressive property that boasts eight swimming pools, open to the public from 7am to 5pm. Day admission per adult/child is P240/150. The double rooms have air-con, bathroom and private spa pool.

Getting There & Away
From Pasay City, Buendia and Quezon City there are BLTB, JAM and Tritran buses to Santa Cruz that stop in Calamba (regular/air-con P70/90, one hour). Get out at the Calamba bus terminal only if you want to visit the Rizal Shrine, as the resorts are along the highway, towards Los Baños. Batangas buses also stop here.

For information on transport to Los Baños, see Getting There & Away under Los Baños later.

LOS BAÑOS
☎ 049 • pop 82,0...
A few kilometres s... Baños trades heav... springs, with numerou... slides, Olympic-sized ... hotel rooms with their ov...

If you get tired of the wa... of the Philippines Los Bañ... pus is the starting point for ... top of 1144m Mt Makiling, a... with some impressive forest ... slopes.

It takes about two hours to wa... from the UPLB campus to the sum... neys to the College of Forestry co... the start of the trail.

The UPLB College of Forestry has a ... **natural history museum** (*admission ...; open 8am-5pm Mon-Sat*) and the **Makili... Botanic Gardens** (*admission P10, swimming P15; open 8am-4.30pm Mon-Sat*), which has a captive breeding programme for the endangered Philippine eagle, and a peaceful swimming pool in the middle of the forest.

Places to Stay
There are a string of resorts on the highway towards Calamba (also see Places to Stay under Calamba, earlier), but the cheaper ones are all in 'Bayan', the city proper. The main road through Bayan branches off the highway as it turns inland just outside of town; look out for the green Region Bank sign.

City of Springs (☎ 536 0731; W *www.city ofsprings.com; 147 Villegas St, Bayan; dorm beds P275, rooms with fan/air-con from P660/1313*) has a good main pool and restaurant and a wide variety of rooms. Some of the air-con rooms have a private pool, spa, or a view of the lake.

Splash Mountain Resort (☎ 536 0731, 536 6400, fax 536 1001; W *www.cityofsprings .com; National Hwy; rooms with air-con & with/without pool P1774/1358*), owned by the same people as City of Springs, has numerous waterslides and some of the best pools (day/night admission P70/80; open 24 hours) in Los Baños.

Getting There & Around
From Pasay City, Buendia and Quezon City there are BLTB, JAM and Tritran buses to Santa Cruz that stop in Los Baños (regular/air-con P70/90, 1½ hours).

Jeepne... (P7.50, 1... pus 24 h... of Fores... Jollibee... last tri...

PAG... ☎ 0... The ... 100... no... m... p... r...

AROUND MANILA

...ys run from Calamba to Los Baños (...5 minutes) and up to the UPLB cam-...ours. Jeepneys up to the UP College ...try (for Mt Makiling) leave from the ...restaurant on the National Hwy. The ...downhill leaves at about 5pm.

SANJAN
...9 • pop 32,600

...town of Pagsanjan (**pag-san-han**), ...km southeast of Manila and 20km ...theast of Lucban, has become synony-...us with the **Magdapio Falls**, the starting ...int for the famous canoe ride through the ...apids of the Pagsanjan River. This is one of ...uzon's major tourist attractions and boat ...trips along the river form a huge part of the town's income.

Some of the final scenes of Francis Ford Coppola's epic Vietnam War movie *Apocalypse Now* were filmed along this stretch of river and a few relics from the movie can still be seen along the banks.

Several years ago tourist numbers declined as a result of *banceros* (boatmen) demanding astronomical rates and tips, prompting the government to issue official rates. These are displayed outside the church on General Taiño St and at some resorts – at time of writing, the rates were P580 per person, or P1080 for a solo passenger, plus P50 for a life jacket (mandatory) and P30 for a cushion. On top of this, the *banceros* may still request a tip, and for all their hard work, you'll probably feel they deserve it. Despite the price regulating, booking a trip through your accommodation is still the best way to ensure a hassle-free journey; most resorts have their own *banceros*.

For the ride up to the falls, two *banceros* paddle each canoe for 1½ hours, against the fearsome flow of the river, through an awesome gorge hemmed by towering cliffs and vegetation. At the top, the *banceros* will take you under the 10m-high falls on a bamboo raft for an additional P50. From here, you let the water do the work. The trip downstream is fast and exhilarating.

The height of the wet season (August to September) is the best time to ride the rapids. At any time of year it's best to avoid weekends, as half of Manila seems to descend on Pagsanjan. You should bring a plastic bag for your camera, and prepare to get very wet.

Places to Stay
There are three budget lodging houses in town, all within short-walking distance of one another.

Camino Real Lodging House (*☎/fax 808 3217; 39 Rizal St; rooms with fan P300-400, with air-con P600-800*) has large rooms and flexible prices – approach with a smile. There is an 'annex' hotel on Garcia St.

Willy Flores Guesthouse (*☎ 500 8203; 821 Garcia St; rooms with fan P300*), behind the municipal hall, is a spotless and friendly family-run place that has its own boat.

Riverside Bungalow (*☎ 828 4039; 792 Garcia St; rooms with fan & bathroom P400*) has two clean rooms.

Pagsanjan Rapids Hotel (*☎ 02-834 0403, 808 4258, fax 808 4258; General Taiño St; singles P960-1440, doubles P1200-1920*), west of the town plaza, has good facilities, including a pool and a bar overlooking the river; however, the view is not as green as from the resorts along the highway.

On the highway towards Lucban, there are several well-positioned resorts with great views overlooking the river.

La Corona de Pagsanjan Resort (*☎ 02-524 2631; rooms with air-con, TV, hot-water bathroom & breakfast P1500*) is a large well-maintained place that has three pools, a restaurant and tasteful rooms.

Pagsanjan Garden Resort (*☎ 02-808 4451; dorm beds P300, triples with air-con & bathroom P700; air-con cottage for 8 P1650*), nearby, is a popular place owned by the Department of Tourism (DOT).

Places to Eat
Dura-Fe (*General Taiño St; meals P25-100; open 7am-8pm daily*) has good Filipino food at low prices.

83 Gallery Cafe & Restaurant (*☎ 808 4967; 83 Rizal St; meals around P170; open 9am-9pm daily*), a few minutes' walk from the plaza, is a colourful Mexican-style restaurant with tasty Filipino-influenced meals.

Exotik Restaurant (*☎ 820 0086, fax 557 1009; Hi-way Longos, Kalayaan; most meals P180-280; open 7am-9pm daily*), 10km along the highway towards Paete, serves good Filipino food in a native-style restaurant overlooking Laguna Bay. The speciality is the 'exotik' food – depending upon availability, you can sample wildlife such as monitor lizard (P290), boa constrictor (P290) and wild boar (P320).

Getting There & Away

There are no direct buses to Pagsanjan, but there are regular services from Manila to nearby Santa Cruz. The bus terminal is on the highway, about halfway between the two towns; from Pagsanjan, take one of the many jeepneys towards Santa Cruz and ask for the JAM terminal (P5).

BLTB, JAM Transit and Tritran have buses at least once an hour to Cubao, Buendia and Pasay City (regular/air-con P76/100, 2½ hours). There are also minivans that leave when full from the FX terminal next to the Shell service station on Rizal St, in Pagsanjan, and from Metropolis in Alabang in Manila (P50). Vans also leave from the JAM terminal in Buendia, Manila (P90). From Pagsanjan, there are also minivans to Lucena (P50, three hours).

For San Pablo and Los Baños, jeepneys leave from the plaza in front of Santa Cruz's city hall. For Calamba, you can pick up a jeepney from next to the unappealing modern Church of Santa Cruz.

From Pagsanjan you can take a jeepney to the pretty mountain town of Lucban (P20, 45 minutes), and connect from there to Lucena. Jeepneys also head north along General Taiño St to the craft villages of Lumban and Paete.

AROUND PAGSANJAN

There are a few interesting spots in the immediate vicinity of Pagsanjan. **Lumban** is a small village on the edge of the Laguna that is famous for its Barong Tagalog shirts and embroidery.

A little further around the lake, **Paete** is known for its papier-mâché sculptures and woodcarving.

ALAMINOS AREA

Just outside Alaminos, **Hidden Valley Springs Resort** (☎ 02-818 4034; overnight single/ double package P5356/8225) is a jungle resort with lush tropical flora, hot springs and numerous natural pools for swimming. The price tag for this 'back to nature' experience is P1600 per head for day-trippers, including a buffet lunch of native Filipino food. Overnight packages include all meals and admission to the springs. Rooms have varnished

wood furnishings, windows overlooking forest or garden, air-con and bathroom.

As well as swimming in the springs, guests can hike through the forests, visit 'hidden' falls or enjoy a poolside massage (P500) and other treats. Visit during the week to avoid the crowds.

JAM (Taft Ave, near the Buendia LRT station), BLTB and Tritran have buses for Lucena that pass through Alaminos (P55, two hours). Jump off at the Caltex service station and ask for the Hidden Valley tricycles (P100, 10 minutes). From Los Baños or Santa Cruz, it's best to take a jeepney to San Pablo and change to a Manila-bound bus or a jeepney.

SAN PABLO

☎ 049 • pop 207,900

San Pablo, 15km east of Alaminos, is known for its seven **volcanic lakes**, which offer some pleasant walks. Closest to the centre is the appealing Sampaloc Lake on Schetelig Ave. You can walk around the lake and there are several restaurants on stilts which sell the tasty *tilapia* (carp) that are raised here. Across the road is the small Bunot Lake, and further north are the lakes of Calibato, Palacpaquen, Mohicap, Yambo and Pandin. The town is also the jumping-off point for hikes up the sacred slopes of Mt Banahaw (see Mt Banahaw & Mt San Cristobal later).

About 10km south of San Pablo, on the outskirts of Tiaong, is the **Villa Escudero**, an exclusive resort with an artificial lake, a lovely swimming pool and a native restaurant with tables on the water. Day admission Monday to Thursday is P636, Friday to Sunday, P728. The estate doubles as a coconut plantation and houses an eclectic museum of handicrafts and curios. You can get here by Tiaong jeepney from San Pablo.

In the second week of January, San Pablo celebrates **coconut festival** – one week of street dancing and show-casing the many coconut-based products for which the area is famous. For more information on this and other local activities, contact the **information and tourist office** (☎ 562 5743; City Government Bldg, San Pablo; open 8am-noon & 1pm-5pm Mon-Fri).

Places to Stay

Sampaloc Lake Youth Hostel (☎ 562 3376; Doña St, Efarca Village; rooms with fan & with/ without view P200/150) overlooks peaceful

Lake Sampaloc and has steps down to the road around the lake. To get here, follow Schetelig Ave, the main road to the lakes (P5 by tricycle).

Platinum Lodge (*☎ 562 4279; Maharlika Hwy; rooms with air-con, TV & bathroom P600*) and **Pine Hotel** (*☎ 562 7521; Maharlika Hwy; fan/air-con rooms with bathroom P350/ 500, with TV P750*) both have decent rooms on the highway that runs between Manila and Lucena. Platinum Lodge is closer to the Manila end of town; Pine Hotel is closer to Lucena.

Villa Escudero (*☎ 02-523 2944; day admission Mon-Thur P636, Fri-Sun P728; singles/ doubles from P2720/4130*), in Tiaong, offers cottages with fan and bathroom. The tariff includes admission and all meals.

Getting There & Around
Numerous buses from Manila pass through San Pablo (P55, two hours) on the way to places like Lucena, Daet, Naga and Legaspi. Most buses stop on Schetelig Ave, close to the San Pablo church. BLTB has a terminal just outside of town on the road to Alaminos and Manila.

Jeepneys run from San Pablo up to Santa Cruz (P20, 45 minutes) and Los Baños (P12, 30 minutes). You can wave one down anywhere along the highway. Tiaong jeepneys (P12, 30 minutes) leave from the bus stop by the San Pablo church.

The lakes are all within 5km of the city and can be reached by jeepney (P5) from Schetelig Ave. Jeepneys to Dolores (for Kinabuhayan and Mt Banahaw) leave from the public market (P10, 20 minutes).

MT BANAHAW & MT SAN CRISTOBAL
The vast dormant volcanic cone of Mt Banahaw, 15km east of San Pablo, is almost always accompanied by the term 'mystic'. The Rizalistas, a religious sect, gather in the Banahaw crater to wash in the 'River Jordan' and pray for the rebirth of José Rizal, and every Easter, up to 30,000 devotees begin the ascent of the holy mountain.

Mt Banahaw offers some of the most impressive hiking in southern Luzon. The weather is an important consideration, however, as the awe-inspiring views from the rim, down into the 600m-deep crater, can vanish entirely in low cloud. Even in the dry season

cloud can suddenly rise up from the crater bottom, adding to the spooky atmosphere.

The trek up to the crater rim (2177m) and then down into the crater, returning via the canyon on the western side of the volcano, takes two to three days, but the crater rim can be visited as an overnight trek. The more popular entry point is from the eastern (Dolores) side, up either Via Christalino, the short but steep path with great waterfalls; or Via Tatlongtang, the longer but easier path. Consult weather forecasts before the treacherous climb and don't camp in the crater as flash flooding can occur. The path is well worn, but branching trails make guides necessary. The starting point is Kinabuhayan, near Dolores, although supplies are best bought in San Pablo. You will need to bring your own camping gear, but water is in good supply on the mountain. Guides can be hard to find in the area – the best option is to contact **Real Outdoor Adventures** (*☎ 02-932 7273; e powerup@mindgate.net; Power Up Center for Climbing and Fitness, 690 T Sora Ave, Old Balara, Quezon City*), Luzon's most experienced mountaineering group, who arrange guides (P2000 per day, good for six people) and camping gear rental, as well as food and transport (cost extra). Two weeks' notice is required for organising packages.

A more challenging trek up the mountain can be started from Tayabas, on the western side (see Tayabas later). The starting point for treks up to Mt San Cristobal is 4km from Dolores. You can either walk or hire a jeepney to the mountain, which has the reputation of being haunted. The only problem you're likely to encounter is a scarcity of drinking water, so it's best to carry your own. The walk to the summit takes six hours, with good views over the Visayan Sea. Guides can be hired through Real Outdoor Adventures.

Getting There & Away
Jeepneys to Dolores leave from the public market in San Pablo every few minutes during daylight hours. From Dolores you can pick up another jeepney to Kinabuhayan. It's best to get an early start so you can reach the crater rim in daylight.

LUCENA
☎ 042 • pop 196,100
Most people only pass through Lucena, 120km southeast of Manila, on the way to

the lively fishing port of Dalahican, which is the departure point for passenger boats to Marinduque. The capital of Quezon, Lucena province is a pleasant enough place to overnight before catching a boat in the morning.

Quezon Ave is the main shopping street in Lucena, where you'll find numerous banks and restaurants and the **San Ferdinand Cathedral**. There are several **Internet cafés** (P30 per hour) near the corner of Gomez and Granja Sts, most open until at least 10pm.

Next to the Provincial Governors Office, **Museo ng Quezon** (*Provincial Health Bldg, Quezon Capitol compound, Quezon Ave; admission free; open 9am-noon & 1pm-4.30pm Mon-Fri*) houses numerous items of memorabilia from Manuel L Quezon, the dapper first president of the Philippines.

North of town, Quezon Ave forms the road to Tayabas and Lucban. Follow P Gomez St for the highway which leads to Atimonan and Dalahican port.

Places to Stay
Halini Hotel is the best option among a handful of indistinguishable lodging houses in Lucena city proper (Bayan). The other hotels are a jeepney ride from town; two of them are on Diversion Rd, which leads to Bicol.

House of Halina Hotel (*☎ 710 2902, fax 660 3667; 104 Gomez St; singles/doubles with fan & bathroom P225/295, with air-con from P538/638*) has a variety of reasonably priced rooms, a restaurant, coffee shop, disco and function hall.

Fresh Air Hotel & Resort (*☎ 710 2424; singles/doubles with fan P195/250, with bathroom from P275/330, with air-con from P500/585*), on the road to Manila, is a clean conference hotel and resort with a swimming pool and restaurant.

Ouan's Worth Farm (*☎ 373 4728, 710 4552; Km 133 Diversion Rd; rooms with air-con, cable TV & hot-water bathroom P1100-2500*) is a lush 70-hectare fruit farm that has developed a slice of its grounds for accommodation, including a good restaurant, swimming pool and tennis, basketball and volleyball courts. To get here from the Grand Central bus terminal, take a Calauag jeepney to Ouan's (P5); from the port, take a tricycle (P80).

Queen Margarette Hotel (*☎ 373 7171–3, fax 373 6218; e queen@quezon.net; Diver-*

sion Rd, Domoit; singles P700-2800, doubles P1650-3000*) is Lucena's ritziest hotel and has a swimming pool, spa, business centre, bar and restaurant, convention centre and limousine service. A Domoit jeepney will bring you here from Bayan (P5).

Getting There & Away
Bus BLTB, JAM Transit and Tritran buses run every 15 minutes between Cubao, Buendia or Pasay City and Lucena Grand Central terminal or the port of Dalahican (regular/ air-con P130/150, four hours). From the far side of Grand Central, there are air-con buses to Legaspi (P300, eight to nine hours) running three times daily. Regular jeepneys connect Grand Central with Bayan (city proper) and Dalahican port (both P4). There are plenty of fast-food outlets at Grand Central.

Out of town on the road to Manila (near the Fresh Air Hotel), Supreme Lines has buses to Batangas City (P37, 3½ hours) and Santa Cruz (three hours). To get here, take an Iyam jeepney from Bayan (P4).

Train Lucena is connected by rail to both Manila and Legaspi; unfortunately, the Manila trains run in the middle of the night. There are two trains to Manila (regular/air-con P79/218, three hours) and two evening trains to Naga, Bicol (P144/265, eight hours) and Legaspi (P204/335, 13 hours). The **station** (*☎ 710 4831*) is next to the Quezon Capitol compound (P5 by tricycle from Bayan).

Boat Several shipping lines have offices at Dalahican port (*☎ 373 3992*). **Blue Magic Ferries** (*☎ 710 4168*) runs the fastest service to Balanacan, in Marinduque (P120, 1½ hours, twice daily). **Montenegro Shipping Lines** (*☎ 373 7084*) services the same route (P75, 2½ hours, four times daily) and **Santa Cruz Shipping Services** (*☎ 321 1742*) goes to Buyabod (P141, 2½ hours, twice daily).

Blue Magic Ferries also plies the route to Masbate on Masbate Island (P300, 12 hours, three times a week).

Phil-Nippon Kyoci Corp (*☎ 373 2458*) goes to Cawit, Cavite (south of Manila; P85, three hours, twice daily).

TAYABAS
☎ 042 • pop 71,000
Approximately halfway from Lucena to Lucban, Tayabas is another typical mountain

town. It is the site of the delightful St Michael Archangel Basilica, which was built in 1856 over the ruins of a 1585 church. About 4km from Tayabas, on the dirt road to Mauban, the stone **Malagunlong Bridge** was built by the Spanish in the 16th century and is a popular picnic spot. You can get here by tricycle.

Tayabas is also the eastern entry point for the climb up Mt Banahaw, a much tougher trek than the more popular western climb, requiring a lot of bushwalking. At least three days are required and a guide is necessary. For information and guides, contact **Real Outdoor Adventures** (☎ 02-932 7273).

On the highway to Lucban, **Nawawalang Paraiso Resort & Hotel** (☎/fax 373 6575; e nawawala@quezon.net; cottages with fan from P800, rooms with air-con from P1000) is a pleasant resort with the usual array of swimming pools (day admission P50) and picnic huts.

Further towards Lucban, **Kamayan Sa Palaisdaan** (☎ 793 3654; meals P110-200; open 10am-10pm daily) is a well-known seafood restaurant. Tables are within private bamboo shelters, some built into the landscape, some on bamboo rafts floating on a fish pond. If you bring your own rod, you can throw in a line from your table and pay for what you catch.

Tayabas is connected by jeepney to Lucena (P10, 25 minutes) and Lucban (P15, 25 minutes).

LUCBAN
☎ 042 • pop 38,800

Hidden away in the foothills of Mt Banahaw, the quiet mountain town of Lucban comes alive on 15 May for **Pahiyas**, the annual harvest festival and feast of San Isidro Labrador. All the houses in town are adorned with multicoloured rice-starch decorations called *kiping* and giant papier-mâché effigies are marched through the streets up to the town church.

The air here is pleasantly cool and the narrow streets are full of atmosphere. There are a number of old Spanish townhouses. **The Church of St Louis of Toulouse** dates from 1738, though it sits atop the ruins of several far older churches.

Among other things, Lucban is known for its *longanisa* (Chinese-style pork sausages) and *pansit* (fried noodles). There are also a few little handicraft shops around the plaza.

Banahaw Lodge (rooms with air-con & bathroom P530-610, with spa P750), a part of 'Jeffrey's Super Station' – a service station-restaurant on the road to Tayabas – is the only accommodation in town.

There are regular jeepneys from Tayabas (P15, 25 minutes) that originate from Lucena. In the reverse direction, jeepneys leave from the Lucban Academy near the Rizal Monument, but you can pick up minibuses and jeepneys on Quezon Ave. Heading on to Pagsanjan, jeepneys run along Rizal St.

LAKE TAAL & TAAL VOLCANO

One of the world's smallest and deadliest volcanoes, Taal boasts over 47 craters and 35 volcanic cones. In 1977, the calm of this peaceful spot was shattered by explosive eruptions as subterranean magma flows tried to escape to the surface.

Every few years there are rumbles from the crater, and a team of vulcanologists keeps a 24-hour vigil from the village of Talisay on the lake shore.

The picturesque volcanic island sits in a lake in the middle of a vast crater. There are splendid views over the volcano from Tagaytay and other towns that follow the ridge.

The bulk of the island emerged from the lake during the savage eruption of 1911, which claimed hundreds of lives in the area. Over the next 66 years, eruptions sculpted and resculpted the island's appearance.

The main Taal crater is in the middle of the island (the obvious cone visible from the ridge is Binitiang Malaki, which last erupted in 1715). Within the Taal crater is a yellow sulphurous lake (itself containing a small island), which is about an hour's hike from the island's shore.

The most active crater is Mt Tabaro on the west side of the island, which saw some dramatic lava flows in the late '60s and mid '70s. Since then, Taal Volcano tours have become a popular activity, with several villages on the lake's shore offering motorised bangka (pumpboats) across to the island, and horses up to the main crater and lava flows.

TAGAYTAY
☎ 046 • pop 45,300

Sprawling along the crater rim north of the volcano, picturesque Tagaytay offers the classic view of Lake Taal. November to March is the best time to visit, as Tagaytay

Bus driver's seat, Subic Bay – Olongapo

Taal Volcano – Luzon

Pacific War Memorial – Corregidor

Magdapio Falls, Pagsanjan River – Luzon

Villa Escudero, San Pablo – Luzon

is often covered by low cloud during the wet season.

The **viewing gallery** (admission P20) at the Taal Vista Hotel on the main highway offers the best view of Taal. Next best is the view from the DOT-owned **Tagaytay Picnic Grove** (*admission P20; open 6am-midnight daily*), which also has a skating rink and horse riding. It's 8km from Tagaytay on the road to Mt Sungay (jeepney from Olivarez mall near Silang rotunda, P4.50).

For great views over the whole area, the **Peoples Park in the Sky** is perched on top of 750m Mt Sungay and includes a shrine, a restaurant and a walking trail. To get here, take a jeepney marked 'Peoples Park' from the Olivarez mall (P7, 15 minutes).

With an elevation of 600m, Tagaytay is pleasantly cool after the heat of Manila, and exclusive country clubs are springing up all along the ridge. The climate allows for plant nurseries, which sell many flowering pot-plants and bonsai along the road. Other street stalls sell bananas, pineapples and coconuts.

There is a **tourist information centre** (*☎ 860 1600; open 8am-noon & 1pm-5pm Mon-Sat*) at Mahogany market. **PNB**, **BPI** and **Allied Bank** all have branches in town.

Places to Stay

Most of the accommodation is on the Aguinaldo Hwy, and some is out of town.

Taal Vista Hotel (*☎ 413 1223–4; rooms with air-con, cable TV & hot-water bathroom P2700-3700*) could do with a fresh coat of paint; however, the garden is well tended and the views magnificent. Also here is the **Casino Filipino** (*consumable nonguest admission P100*).

Days Hotel (*☎ 843 6813, fax 413 2410; W www.dayshotel.ph; singles/doubles from P5200/5400*), near Silang rotunda, caters to the top dollar.

MC Mountain Home Apartelle (*☎ 413 2232, 02-850 5438 in Manila, 0917 794 7500; W mcmountaintagaytay.com; rooms P1700-1900*), 8km west of town, is a spotless, friendly family-run resort and has excellent views. Guests are authorised to visit and dine at the nearby exclusive Tagaytay Country Club, and also attain discounts at other clubs in the area.

From Tagaytay, take a jeepney towards Nasugbu (P15) and get out just after the Country Club.

Tagaytay Picnic Grove (*☎ 860 0216/7; camping P100-200, singles/doubles with breakfast P1300/2200*), at the eastern end of the highway, has cottages with good views, but is often booked out. Horse riding, roller-skating and games are offered.

There are also some reasonably priced places on the eastern side of the Silang rotunda that are convenient for the jeepneys to Talisay.

Fortune Duck Residence Inn (*☎ 860 0166, 413 4231; rooms with air-con, cable TV & hot-water bathroom P1300*), opposite the Talisay turn-off, has clean, spacious rooms.

Nearby, **Keni Po** (*☎ 860 1035; singles/doubles with air-con, TV & bathroom P1000/1200*) and **5R** (*☎ 413 4249; rooms with fan, TV & bathroom P800, with air-con P1200*) have decent budget rooms.

Places to Eat

There are many popular *bulaluhan* (restaurants serving bone-marrow stew) along the roadside, as well as canteens serving *buko* (coconut) pie.

Josephine (*☎ 413 1801; meals around P250; open 7.30am-10.30pm daily*), is between the Taal Vista Hotel and the Silang rotunda. It has a view of the volcano and is a local restaurant institution. Meat and seafood are cooked in a variety of traditional styles, including *inihaw* (grilled), *halabos* (steamed) and *sinigang* (in sour soup). Breakfast (P220) and lunch (P385) buffets are available on weekends.

Sonya's Garden Restaurant (*☎ 0917 532 9097, 0917 531 4550; Buck Estate Rd; set meal P500-600*), 2km west of town, is part of the 1.5-hectare dream garden of Sonya Garcia. There is no menu, but she offers a three-course gourmet vegetarian feast, mostly using the organic produce from her 16 greenhouses. Bookings are necessary.

Getting There & Around

BLTB and Crow Transit have buses from EDSA in Pasay City, to Nasugbu that pass through Tagaytay (regular/air-con P39/55, two hours).

Jeepneys leave, when full, from the Lemery and Taal villages (P40, 45 minutes), junction of the Diokno and Aguinaldo Hwys, about 10km west of Tagaytay near the 'Nasugbu' sign – get here on a Nasugbu-bound bus.

Buses to Nasugbu (P30, 45 minutes) leave from the rotunda, and jeepneys to Talisay (P20, 30 minutes) leave from the road opposite Fortune Duck Residence Inn .

TALISAY
☎ 043 • pop 32,500

The small town of Talisay on the edge of Lake Taal is the start of a string of small barangay (villages or neighbourhoods) that offer bangka trips out to Taal Volcano. There are dozens of operators vying for the attention of arriving tourists. Depending on where you hire them, motorised bangka to the island cost P800 to P1400 for the whole boat (life jackets are P15 to P30 extra).

The volcanic island offers several hikes. Easily the most popular is the trip to the main crater with its evil-looking yellow pool and island. The walk takes about an hour (or you can hire a tired old horse for P300-350), and although most boat trips come with a guide, you don't really need one. Other options include the neat cone of Binitiang Malaki and the longer hike to the active cone of Mt Tabaro, which is probably the most impressive part of the island.

For all the walks it's wise to bring plenty of drinking water and a hat, as the craters are hot and dusty and there's little shelter on the island.

You can take a dip anywhere along the lake, and most of the resorts are on the water. In barangay Santa Maria, the **Taal Lake Yacht Club** (☎ 773 0192; W www.sailing.org.ph/tlyc; admission P100; open 8am-5pm daily) has a good selection of water-sport equipment that you can hire.

If you want to find out more about the volcano, the **Philippine Institute of Volcanology & Seismology** (Philvolcs; open 8am-5pm), in barangay Buco, houses the monitoring station, an interesting museum and seismographs.

Places to Stay & Eat
Gloria de Castro's (☎ 773 0138; triples with fan & bathroom P400, with air-con & TV P1000), at the far western end of Talisay, has one of the cheapest boats to Taal (P800 with guide). The rooms are comfortable and one has a view. The simple seafood dishes (P60) are great and the ambience friendly.

Natalia's Guest House (☎ 0918 873 7217; rooms with fan/air-con P700/1500), on the

water opposite Gloria's, is OK if Gloria de Castro's is full.

San Roque Beach Resort (☎ 773 0271, 0919 310 7976; huts with fan & bathroom P800, 3-bedroom house with air-con & kitchen P4000) is a clean and relaxed place. Taal boats are P1000 and the friendly family management will happily organise out-of-town trips.

Talisay Green Lake Resort (☎ 773 0247; rooms with air-con, TV & bathroom P1500), close to the Taal Lake Yacht Club, has good overnight rooms and pleasant facilities for day-trippers (admission P70), including swimming pool and picnic huts. Boats are P1200.

Rosalina's Place (☎ 0918 538 0411, 0916 374 1116; doubles/triples with fan P200/300) in Banga, close to the main road to Tagaytay, is across the road from the beach and it has a good restaurant with a daily midday buffet (P100) and cheap boats to Taal (P800).

Getting There & Away
There are regular jeepneys to Talisay from Tanauan (P15, 30 minutes), on the main bus route between Manila and Batangas. BLTB and JAM Transit both pass through here on their way from Pasay City to Batangas (P50, 1½ hours). The last jeepney trip to Tanauan from Talisay leaves at 6pm. There are also jeepneys to Tagaytay (P20, 30 minutes).

NASUGBU
☎ 043 • pop 96,100

About 50km west of Tagaytay is Nasugbu, which has some of the most popular **beaches** close to Manila. The sand on the main beach in Nasugbu is dark brown; however, a few kilometres north there are some small white-sand coves and good beaches at Natipuan, Munting Buhangin. A bangka to the beaches from the Wawa pier in Nasugbu will cost about P500. Wawa is also the departure point for the exclusive Fortune Island Resort on nearby Fortune Island.

You don't need any help to find the resorts in town; they're all on the Boulevard, two streets down from the highway (P5 by tricycle).

Places to Stay
Maya-Maya Reef Resort (☎ 0918 909 7170, 0918 909 7167, fax 0918 932 0483; W www .mayamaya.com; cottages P2500-3000, public

holidays P3750-4500), a large, shady resort in Natipuan, is a popular destination for yachties. It has a private marina, water sports, a dive school and smart air-con cottages arranged around a lovely pool.

Fishing, boating and other activities are available.

Fortune Island Resort *(☎ 02-818 3458;* w *www.dive-info.com/pdc/fortune_island .htm; singles/doubles US$33.60/66)* is a plush place with a swimming pool, good beaches and a dive school (one dive US$18 to US$21, equipment rental US$7, openwater diving certificate US$330). Transfers from Wawa pier are US$16.10.

Maryland Beach Resort *(☎ 216 2277; day admission P50; nipa huts with fan P1200, rooms with air-con P2800-4000)*, in Nasugbu proper, has a good pool and a restaurant with a variety of set meals (P100 to P200).

Vitug Beach Resort *(☎ 0919 557 0919; doubles from P1500)*, a large place close to Maryland Beach Resort, is a well-run family resort with nice lawns, a pool, spa and a variety of rooms with fan and air-con. Day admission costs P100.

Places to Eat
Many **eateries** along the boulevard serve sizzling Filipino meals, grills and cold beers. Most are open from 7am to midnight and some are open 24 hours.

Kainan sa Dalampasigan *(☎ 931 1134, 216 2590; Ruiz Martinez St; meals P60-180; open 7am-9pm daily)* is regarded as the best restaurant in town. It offers excellent, reasonably priced seafood and other dishes in a peaceful pavilion and garden setting, set back from the seafront on the southern end of the boulevard.

Getting There & Around
BLTB and Crow Transit have regular buses from Pasay City to Nasugbu (regular/aircon P80/100, two hours). The BLTB terminal is by the park in the middle of Nasugbu; Crow has a terminal on the highway, north of town. Crow also has buses to the pier in Batangas every 45 minutes (P70, two hours).

For Matabungkay, take a jeepney to Lian and change at the Shell petrol station to a bus or jeepney bound for Calatagan. There are also jeepneys for Tagaytay (P30, 45 minutes).

MATABUNGKAY
Matabungkay is touted as the finest beach around Manila, but most visitors agree Nasugbu is better and less crowded. The water is clean though, and it's possible to hire floating bamboo picnic huts (P800 to P1500) anchored out over the reef, which are good bases for snorkelling and generally kicking back.

Most of the resorts are close together on the beach (P10 tricycle from the Matabungkay junction).

Places to Stay
Matabungkay Beach Resort & Hotel *(☎ 02-752 5252, 819 3080, fax 02-817 1176;* e *in quiry@matabungkay.net; doubles P2500-3000, 6-person rooms P3500-3950)* is on large grounds and has all the amenities you'd expect from a fine hotel, plus a good pool, a restaurant, well-maintained grounds and a tidy strip of beach out front. Diving is available via the dive centre at Coral Beach Club. The resort is about 500m south of the pier.

Greendoors Cottages *(☎ 046-540 3130, 0917 619 9796; rooms with fan from P1000, with air-con P2500)*, nearby, is a humble, inexpensive option that is clean and quiet, with leafy grounds and large rooms. There is no restaurant but guests can cook at the communal kitchen.

Coral Beach Club *(☎ 0917 901 4635, fax 0919 430 0084;* w *www.coralbeach.ph; rooms with air-con, TV & hot-water bathroom P1075-1625)*, north of the pier, is popular with older holiday-makers and has a secluded pool, restaurant, bar and a new dive centre (one dive P1100 to P1450, equipment rental P200 to P300, open-water diving certificate P17,000). The resort has a pick-up service for guests leaving from Lian.

Punta Baluarte Resort *(☎ 02-892 4202–5, in Manila 02-899 4546;* w *www.puntabaluarte .com; rooms from P3600)* is an exclusive hilltop resort in Calatagan, 10km south of Matabungkay. The extensive, secluded grounds house fresh-water and saltwater pools, tennis courts, water sports and horse riding. The rooms are well appointed and have good views.

Getting There & Away
BLTB buses leave Manila for Calatagan every few hours, passing the junction to Matabungkay (P107, three hours), but you

can also take a bus to Nasugbu and change to a Calatagan-bound jeepney at Lian. From Batangas pier, Crow buses to Nasugbu pass through Lian.

TAAL

Taal is an appealing old town with a number of old Spanish colonial buildings, but the atmosphere is marred slightly by Lemery, the modern township across the river. Taal is famous for its embroidery and *Balisong* (fanknives), and the truly massive **Basilica ng Taal church** (built 1849–65). JAM Transit and JAC Liner buses to Cubao, and Crow buses travelling from Batangas to Nasugbu, leave Lemery every few minutes.

There are occasional jeepneys up to the junction of the Diokno and Aguinaldo Hwys, where you can pick up a bus into Tagaytay. Most services leave from near the McDonald's on the main road through Lemery.

ANILAO

Anilao, 20km south of Taal on a small peninsula, is a popular diving centre and has a good reputation. It has somehow avoided the top-dollar development that has transformed other resort areas, maintaining a quiet seaside charm. There are dozens of dive resorts strung out along the coastal road south of the village; most of the dive sites are coral gardens, making it perfect for beginners, though there are some walls with strong currents further from the shore.

There are 36 dive sites accessible from Anilao, in Balayan Bay and around the Sombrero and Maricaban islands. In general, the further you go from shore, the more chance you have of getting a dive site to yourself. Diving rates include boat hire and a dive guide, and individual prices drop significantly if you dive in a group.

The attractions here are all below the water. There isn't much of a nightlife in Anilao and the beaches are rocky and poorly maintained.

Places to Stay

The best dive resorts are outside of Anilao in the small barangay along the edge of the peninsula. Resorts are listed in order of proximity to Anilao.

Anilao Seasports Center, just outside Anilao town, was closed for renovation when we last visited, and accommodation details were not available. It is a well-designed resort with a large *nipa*-roofed restaurant-bar.

Vistamar Beach Resort (☎ *0917 504 4831;* Ⓦ *home1.pacific.net.ph/~vistamar; rooms with fan/air-con & bathroom P1600/2000, with TV & hot-water bathroom P2400*) is a large, clean and friendly resort (day admission to beach and pool is P50/100) with spacious double rooms. The resort has a nice pool, a dive shop (one dive P2585, daily equipment hire P1000), restaurant and disco. A tricycle from Anilao costs P30.

Dive Ocean Corp Beach Resort (☎ *0912 883 6368; doubles/quads with air-con & bathroom P1500/2000*) is a small rustic resort run by a friendly Korean team. There is no real beach but there's a great sundeck, picnic huts and lots of diving on offer (one dive US$20, daily equipment hire US$20, open-water diving certificate US$350). Meals are P200 each and a tricycle from town is P50.

Aqua Tropical Sports (☎ *02-523 2126, 523 1989; rooms with air-con, bathroom & 3 meals P2000*), in barangay Ligaya, is a large, leafy dive resort (one dive P1850, daily equipment hire P1000, open-water diving certificate P10,500). A tricycle here costs P70.

Getting There & Away

Regular jeepneys leave from P Burgos St in Batangas for the tiny cocoa-producing town of Mabini, where you may have to change jeepneys to continue to Anilao (P13, 20 minutes).

BATANGAS

☎ 043 • pop 247,600

The capital of Batangas province boasts a busy port and numerous chemical plants and oil refineries, but the town itself isn't particularly attractive. Most people only come here to pick up a boat to Puerto Galera on the beach island of Mindoro or further afield to Romblon Island in the Visayas.

Places to Stay

Travellers Inn (☎ *723 6021; JP Rizal Ave Extension; singles/twins with air-con, TV & bathroom from P500/625*), the best of the cheap hotels, has clean, comfortable rooms, and is on the way to the ferry terminal.

Avenue Pension House I (☎ *300 1964, 150 JP Rizal Ave; rooms with fan & bathroom P300, with air-con P400*), on the other side of Padre Burgos St, is a short-stay place that has passable rooms. There is a second Avenue Pension House at 163 MH del Pilar St.

Alpa Hotel (*☎ 723 1025, fax 723 0340; rooms with air-con & bathroom P880-2200*), at Kumintang Ibaba on the outskirts of town in the direction of Manila, has a quiet location near the Provincial Capitol building. Rooms from P1700 also have hot water, bath tub, fridge, cable TV and phone, and there's a swimming pool. To get here, turn off the highway near the Mabini monument. Jeepneys to the suburb of Balaytas pass nearby.

Days Hotel (*☎ 02-747 1270, 635 5099, fax 02-635 6699; ⓦ www.dayshotel.ph; singles/ doubles P4900/5100*) has the best rooms in town and prices to match. It's 10 minutes from the town centre (P20 by tricycle).

Getting There & Away

Bus BLTB, Tritran and JAM Transit have buses every 15 minutes from Batangas to Cubao, Buendia, Lawton and Pasay City (regular/air-con P90/116, three hours). There is also a bus terminal on the road to Bauan – you can get here by 'Bauan' jeepney from the McDonald's on Padre Burgos St in Batangas.

Near the out-of-town bus terminal, there are minivans for Nasugbu (P75, 1½ hours).

Boat Batangas is the main jumping-off point for the extremely popular resort town of Puerto Galera on Mindoro, and there are also boats to White Beach, Sabang, Calapan, Abra de Ilog and San José (also on Mindoro), and to Romblon, Tablas and Sibuyan Islands. Batangas pier is at the end of Rizal Ave, P4 by Batangas pier jeepney.

All of the boat companies operating out of Batangas have desks in the terminal building and the competition is quite fierce. Although tourists are now less likely to be harangued, it's advisable to deal only with ticket-sellers behind company desks. The terminal fee is P10, payable at the terminal counter.

Mindoro Ferries and outriggers operate until about 6pm between Batangas and Puerto Galera (or Sabang and White Beach). **Super Diamond Shipping Lines** (*☎ 0917 350 8121*) goes to Puerta Galera (P140, 70 minutes, four to five times daily); **Si-Kat Ferry** (*☎ 02-521 3344*) goes to Puerta Galera (P140, 1½ hours, once daily); **Datinguinoo Shipping Lines** goes to Sabang (P100, 80 minutes, six times daily); **Brian Shipping Lines** (*☎ 0919 696*

6506, 0916 440 7450*) goes to White Beach (P120, one hour, twice daily); **Golden Falcon Shipping** (*☎ 0918 518 2683*) goes to White Beach (P120, 45 minutes, four times daily); **Montenegro Shipping Lines** (*☎ 723 8294, 723 7598*) goes to Abra de Ilog (P85, 2½ hours, four times daily), San José (P260, 12 hours, every day except Sunday) and Calapan (P82, two hours, eight times daily); **SuperCat** (*☎ 723 8227*) goes to Calapan (P230, 45 minutes, four times daily); **Manila Ace Shipping** goes to Calapan (P82, two hours, once daily); **Viva Fast Craft** (*☎ 723 1422*) goes to Calapan (P165, 70 minutes, once daily).

There is also a combined bus-boat trip from Manila to Puerto Galera, leaving **Citystate Tower Hotel** (*☎ 02-521 3344, 526 2733; Mabini St*) at 8am daily, connecting with the Si-Kat ferry to Puerto Galera (one way/return P400/700, four hours). Book through Si-Kat or the hotel.

Romblon MV *Princess Camille,* operated by **Shipshape Shipping** (*☎ 02-723 7615*), departs Batangas once a week for San Agustin (Tablas Island; P310, 10 hours), then goes on to Romblon town (P313, or P60 from San Agustin, one hour) and Magdiwang (Sibuyan Island; P325 or P160 from Romblon, two hours) and returns along the same route. MV *Princess Colleen* departs Batangas three times a week for Odiongan (P250, eight hours), then goes on to Romblon town (P170, two hours), returning via the same route.

Viva Shipping Lines' (*☎ 723 2986*) MV *Penafrancia III* services the same route as MV *Princess Camille* (but without stopping in San Agustin) three times a week. It also has a boat from Batangas to Odiongan (P260, eight hours) three times a week.

Montenegro Shipping Lines has boats plying the route between Batangas and Odiongan (P250, 10 hours) three times a week.

CORREGIDOR

Corregidor (Corrector) island, 48km west of Manila, was exploited by the Spanish as the ideal first line of defence against trespassers. It was the scene of fierce fighting during WWII and became the last bastion of resistance by American forces during the Japanese invasion of Luzon in 1941. It was also the place from which General Douglas MacArthur masterminded his operations until March 1942, when he left to spearhead

'I Shall Return'

As the USA's most famous soldier, General Douglas MacArthur is also credited with one of the most famous war-time quotes: 'I Shall Return.' Contrary to popular opinion, 'Dugout Doug' – as he was christened by the embittered troops on the Bataan Peninsula – didn't come up with these words himself. Nor did he say them until he was safely docked in Australia and facing an adoring throng of reporters. Reading from a prepared statement, the general said:

'The President of the United States ordered me to break through the Japanese lines for the purpose, as I understand it, of organising the American offensive against Japan, a primary object of which is the relief of the Philippines. I came through and I shall return.'

Long before this, MacArthur's chief of staff had proposed the slogan 'We Shall Return' – 'we' being the USA. This was then modified at the urging of the Philippine diplomat and writer Carlos P Romulo, who felt that his people wanted an assurance from MacArthur himself, not from a faceless country that had betrayed them so badly. The famously egocentric general happily obliged and the rest is history.

Mic Looby

the defence of Australia. His successor, General Jonathan Wainwright, finally surrendered to the Japanese in May 1942. Huge numbers of American and Filipino prisoners of war died on the Death March from Mariveles to the concentration camp in Tarlac.

Corregidor was occupied by the Japanese until January 1945, when MacArthur returned to liberate the island, honouring his promise (see the boxed text 'I Shall Return'). The second battle for the island was no less bloody than the first, and as American forces gained a foothold on the island, the Japanese detonated an underground arsenal, killing 2000 of their own troops and countless American soldiers.

At the island's highest point is the American-built **Pacific War Memorial**, a shrine to the thousands from both sides who died in the conflict. There's a symbolic metal flame and an open-topped dome that catches the sun on 6 May, the day on which the island fell.

Things to See & Do

The Corregidor Foundation has opened the island as a tourist attraction to anyone interested in the battles of WWII. The admission fee of P125 includes a guided jeepney tour of the devastated military buildings and rusting heavy armaments, as well as the numerous war monuments on the island. Significant sights include **General MacArthur's HQ**, the mile-long **barracks**, the **gun batteries** and the **Spanish lighthouse**, which offers good views over Manila Bay. There is also a small **museum**.

Another attraction is the sound-and-light show in the **Malinta Tunnel** (admission P100), a bomb-proof bunker that was used as a hospital during the conflict.

Places to Stay

Most visitors organise accommodation on the island as part of package tours, which include several meals, tours and boat transfers from Manila. **Corregidor Visitors Information Centre** (☎ 02-550 1347, 834 5048; ⓦ www.skybusiness.com/corregidor; CCP Complex, Roxas Blvd, Manila) and **Sun Cruises** (☎ 02-831 8140, 834 6857/8; ⓦ www.corregidorphilippines.com) offer similar packages – you can book through them directly or through most Manila travel agents.

There is a **camp site** (per person P30) on the South Beach area, if you have your own tent. There are shower facilities and a grill for cooking.

Lodging Row House (4-person room with fan & bathroom P500) has the cheapest rooms on the island.

Corregidor Hotel (1st night per person P1500, extra night P950) is an attractive, but slightly overpriced, place. Rooms are fitted with traditional rattan furniture and have air-con and bathroom, and they have a swimming pool.

Buffet lunches at the hotel are P300, plated meals are P195.

MacArthur's Café (☎ 02-911 4997; meals P100; open all day if booked in advance), beside MacArthur's Monument, serves Filipino food.

Getting There & Away

Day tours from Manila start at P500 and include boat transfers, an island tour, admission and terminal fee. There are optional extras including a buffet lunch at Corregidor Hotel (see Places to Stay earlier). The cruises often run on the weekends only and depart from the jetty in the CCP complex on Roxas Blvd in Manila between 7.30am and 8am. You can book at the jetty, through the tour operator, or with any of the travel agents in town. If you stay for a night, you must pay the day-trip boat fare as well as a P200 return boat fare the following day.

You can also get to Corregidor by bangka (P1500 return for the whole boat) from Cabcaben, near Mariveles on the Bataan Peninsula. Buses run from Mariveles to Balanga and Olongapo every few minutes, stopping in Cabcaben. You can pick them up near the Jet Ferries terminal in Mariveles and the Mt Samat Ferry Express terminal in Orion.

BATAAN PENINSULA

For WWII veterans, few places have such bitter associations as the Bataan Peninsula. Both sides saw some of their darkest moments in the jungles around Mt Mariveles. The Dambana ng Kagitingan (Shrine of Valor) atop nearby Mt Samat is a monument to the grim battles that were fought here before the US finally surrendered to the Japanese on Corregidor Island in 1942.

Since the war the majority of tourists to the area have been returning servicemen. There are opportunities for hiking on the upper slopes of **Mt Natib** (1253m) – for information and guides contact the Balanga City **DENR** (☎ 047-237 3550; Poblasyon; open 8am-noon & 1pm-5pm Mon-Fri) – and some sites, like the shrine on Mt Samat, can easily be visited on a day trip from Manila.

Balanga

☎ 047 • pop 71,100

The capital of Bataan province is a friendly little place with a few hotels, a cathedral, a busy town market and a couple of good restaurants. It's a good base for hikes up to the summit of nearby Mt Natib or the WWII shrine at Mt Samat and there are a few interesting churches in the area, most notably in Orion and Abucay (the church here dates to at least 1610 and housed the first printing press in the Philippines). The trail to Mt Natib starts from the village of Abucay, just north of Balanga; it's a long day or an easier overnight climb to the summit.

There is a very helpful **Provincial Tourism Office** (☎ 791 4785; W www.bataan.gov.ph; open 8am-noon & 1pm-5pm Mon-Fri) inside the Provincial Capitol building.

Places to Stay & Eat On the expressway heading north, **Hillside Garden Mansions** (☎ 237 1771; Roman Hwy; rooms with air-con, cable TV & hot-water bathroom P1500, with private spa P2160) is a large place with elegant rooms and good business and travel services. Breakfast is included.

Elison Hotel (☎ 971 1187, fax 237 2942; Lerma St; singles/doubles with air-con, TV & bathroom P650/800) is the better of the two budget hotels in town. It's near the cathedral and city hall.

D'Samat Hotel (☎ 791 1606; 32 Camacho St; rooms with bathroom & fan P400, singles/ doubles/triples with air-con P550/600/650), close to the terminal for Mariveles minibuses, has OK rooms.

Radio City Bar & Restaurant (☎ 237 5277; St Joseph's St; meals P100-200; open 6pm-3am daily), behind the mall, has live music and lots of 'sizzling' dishes. It draws a young crowd.

Joyous Restaurant & Resort (☎ 237 2849; Doña Francisca Subdivision; meals P100-150; open 9am-1pm & 6pm-1am daily), five minutes from town (P10 by tricycle), is a peaceful open restaurant that looks out over a fish pond. There are good Chinese and Filipino dishes with a few extras (like tuna sashimi, P105), a well-stocked bar, and live music from 7pm. It attracts an older crowd than Radio City.

Getting There & Away Ferries from Manila's CCP complex (Roxas Blvd) to the Bataan village of Orion are run by **Mt Samat Ferry Express** (☎ 237 3295 in Balanga • ☎ 02-551 5290 in Manila), three times a day in each direction (P195, one hour). In Balanga, you can inquire about trips at Jollibee. To get from Balanga to Orion port, take a Limay jeepney from the Bataan transport mall and ask to be let out at the port (P8, 30 minutes). Jeepneys leave Balanga only when full, so allow extra time. It's a five-minute walk or short tricycle ride (P10) to the port from the jeepney.

From the Bataan transport mall, Victory Liner has buses to Olongapo (P45, two hours) hourly from 3am to 6pm. There are also jeepneys to Bagac (P18, 45 minutes), Orion (P6, 20 minutes), Abucay (P4.50, 15 minutes) and Orani (P9, 30 minutes), and minibuses for Mariveles (P50, 1½ hours).

Out of town on Capitol Rd, Philippine Rabbit has air-con buses to Rizal Ave in Manila every hour from 2.30am to 4.20pm (P110, four hours). Viva Aladdin, Genesis Transport and Panther Express also have terminals around town – just ask a tricycle driver to take you to 'the bus to Manila'. There are also buses to San Fernando (La Union) and Baguio (both P270, seven hours).

Mt Samat

Every 9 April, American and Japanese veterans gather at the **Dambana ng Kagitingan** (Shrine of Valor; ☎ 02-911 4296; admission P40; open 8am-noon & 1pm-5pm daily), on top of Mt Samat, and pay tribute to the thousands of their comrades who fell in the surrounding jungles. The centrepiece of the shrine is a 90m-high **crucifix** with battle scenes carved around its base. There is also a memorial wall, an open-air chapel and a small **museum** of weapons captured from the Japanese.

If it's working, you can take the lift up to the crossbar of the massive crucifix, where there is a long **viewing gallery** with great views out over Mt Mariveles, Manila Bay and the South China Sea.

Unless you hire a car, the only way to get here is to take a jeepney from Balanga or Orion towards Bagac, get out at the foot of Mt Samat in barangay Diwa, then walk 7km to the shrine. From Balanga, jeepneys leave from the Bataan transport mall (P5, 12km). A tricycle from Balanga or Orion will do the trip for around P50.

OLONGAPO & THE SUBIC BAY FREEPORT ZONE

☎ 047 • pop 211, 000

Until 1992, the natural deep-water harbour of Subic Bay was the base for the huge 7th Fleet of the US Navy. Olongapo and the other communities along the coast were entirely dependent on the naval base, generating much of their revenue from the sex industry. The area has now been rechristened the Subic Bay Freeport Zone (SBFZ) and is run by the Subic Bay Metropolitan Authority (SBMA).

America's last possession in the Philippines was returned to the country after 12 Filipino senators made the bold decision to reject the extension of America's lease of the facility. A monument on the wharf here displays the prints of the 12 hands that 'freed the nation'.

The former naval base is evolving into a busy industrial zone and resort area, with numerous luxury hotels and casinos, and charter flights bringing in gamblers from across Asia. The sex industry was already in decline when Kate Gordon, the mayor of Olongapo, closed down all the girlie bars several years ago. Today, most tourists come here to scuba-dive on one of the 27 shipwrecks that lie on the bottom of Subic Bay, or to tour the Jungle Environment Survival Training (JEST) Camp. With a hire car, Olongapo is also a good base from which to explore Bataan, the area around Mt Pinatubo and the Zambales coastline.

Information

The **SBMA Tourism Department** (☎ 252 4123; w www.sbma.com; 2nd floor, Bldg 662, Taft St, SBMA; open 8am-5pm daily) has a lot of information on activities, accommodation and restaurants. Olongapo's **City Tourism Office** (☎ 222-8492; City Hall; open 8am-noon & 1pm-5pm Mon-Fri) is also helpful.

Internet cafés that charge P25 per hour are concentrated along Rizal Ave.

Baryo Barretto & Subic Village

During the lifetime of the naval base, the whole strip of coast from Olongapo to Subic village was 'Sin-upon-Sea', with dozens of seedy restaurants, nightclubs and girlie bars. Today, the bubble has definitely burst and fishing is once again becoming the main industry in the villages, though there is still enough action here to attract the Angeles crowd at weekends.

Baloy Long Beach, at the north end of baryo Barretto, is probably the best beach for a day trip. You can get here by blue jeepney from the Victory Liner terminal (P5).

Diving & Other Activities

Of the seven **wrecks** commonly visited by divers, the USS *New York* (27m) is probably the most impressive. The battle cruiser was built in 1891 and was scuttled by American troops in 1941 to keep it out of Japanese

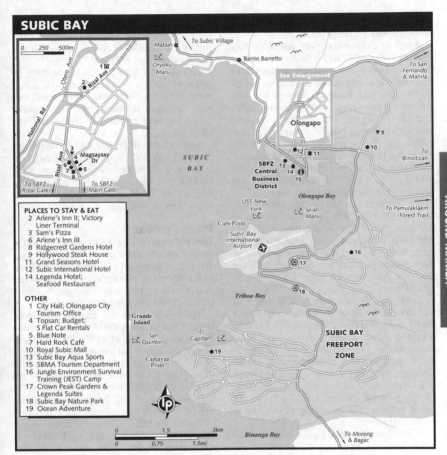

SUBIC BAY

0   250   500m

Otero Ave

Rizal Ave

National Rd

Matain

To Subic Village

Oryoku
Maru

Barrio Barretto

Rizal Ave

1

2

See Enlargement

Olongapo

To San
Fernando
& Manila

9

3
Magsaysay
Dr
4
5
7 6
8

10

To
Biinictican

To SBFZ
(Rizal Gate)

To SBFZ
(Main Gate)

S U B I C
B A Y

SBFZ
Central
Business
District

13
14
15

12   11

Olongapo Bay

USS New
York

Seian
Maru

To Pamulaklakin
Forest Trail

PLACES TO STAY & EAT
2 Arlene's Inn II; Victory
   Liner Terminal
3 Sam's Pizza
6 Arlene's Inn III
8 Ridgecrest Gardens Hotel
9 Hollywood Steak House
11 Grand Seasons Hotel
12 Subic International Hotel
14 Legenda Hotel;
   Seafood Restaurant

OTHER
1 City Hall; Olongapo City
   Tourism Office
4 Topsan; Budget;
   S Flat Car Rentals
5 Blue Note
7 Hard Rock Café
10 Royal Subic Mall
13 Subic Bay Aqua Sports
15 SBMA Tourism Department
16 Jungle Environment Survival
   Training (JEST) Camp
17 Crown Peak Gardens &
   Legenda Suites
18 Subic Bay Nature Park
19 Ocean Adventure

Cubi Point

Subic Bay
International
Airport

Triboa Bay

Grande
Island

San
Quintin

El
Capitan

Camayan
Point

16

17

18

19

SUBIC BAY
FREEPORT
ZONE

0   1.5   3km
0   0.75   1.5mi

Binanga Bay

To Morong
& Bagac

hands. Other wrecks include the *Oryoku Maru* (20m), the *Seian Maru* (27m), *El Capitan* (20m), the 1898 wreck of the *San Quintin* (16m) and several small patrol boats and landing craft.

Subic Bay Aqua Sports (☎ 252 3005, 252 3343; Waterfront Dr; open 8am-5pm daily) charges US$15 a dive. It also offers one-hour bay cruises (an 11-person boat is P2500) and parasailing (P1000 for 12 minutes) and rents out two-person jet skis (P2000 per hour) and two-person kayaks (P250 per hour). Seaplane tours over Mt Pinatubo lahar (volcanic mud) flows can also be booked here (US$150, maximum of three passengers).

The beaches here are fairly undesirable; probably the best are those on **Grande Island** (day-tripper admission P15) in the bay. Mo-

torised bangka (P120) leave every hour from the SBMA Telecommunications Department on Waterfront Rd. There are also beaches in the red-light districts of baryo Barretto and Subic if you don't mind the seedy company.

The other highlight in the SBFZ is the **Jungle Environment Survival Training (JEST) Camp** (☎ 252 9072, 252 2319; admission P40; open 8am-5pm daily), where the indigenous Aeta people of the area were employed to teach US servicemen how to survive in the jungle. Today the facility offers demonstrations of survival techniques from producing fire to making soap from jungle plants, and there's a **minizoo** and **museum**. For P250/125 (adult/child), you'll get a two-hour hike, survival-skills demonstration and tour of the jungle, museum and minizoo. You can get here by Winstar bus from the SBFZ gate (P10).

South of the Subic airport, the **Subic Bay Nature Park** *(☎ 252 4123, 252 4242; admission P15)* is one of the SBFZ's initiatives to recreate Subic Bay as an ecotourism destination. The park has trails through bamboo forests and mangroves, and interesting sights include the 50-year-old US Navy bunkers and the 'driftwood garden' – mangroves petrified by the sulphuric ashes from Mt Pinatubo. In the same area is **Bat Kingdom** – the biggest known roosting site of the world's largest bats: the Philippine fruit bat and the golden-crowned flying fox.

On the next headland south, **Ocean Adventure** *(☎ 252 9000; W www.oceanadventure.com.ph; Camayan Wharf, West Ilanin Forest Area; admission adult/child P400/320; open 9am-6pm daily)* is an open-water marine park where you can see dolphins and sea lions, and swim with false killer whales (P2200).

Subic Bay Nature Park and Ocean Adventure can be reached only by private vehicle (see car-rental companies in Getting There & Around later). If you have your own transport, the SBMA Tourism Department can organise a guided **bay tour** (P150 per person) taking you on a flexible itinerary around the area.

Admission prices are not included in the price, but you can stay as long as you like at each destination.

If you feel like testing your luck, the **casinos** *(nonguest admission P100; open 24 hr)* at the Legenda and Grand Seasons Hotels in the SBFZ will gladly take your money.

Places to Stay

The top hotels are all within the SBFZ.

The Legenda group (☎ 02-732 9888, fax 02-712 8575; W www.subiclegend.com) owns the luxurious **Legenda Hotel** *(☎ 252 1888; Waterfront Rd; rooms from US$95)* and **Grand Seasons Hotel** *(☎ 252 2888; Canal Rd; rooms from US$95)*, both of which have smart, comfortable rooms.

Subic International Hotel *(☎ 252 2222, 02-843 7794/7, fax 02-894 5579; Santa Rita Rd; singles/doubles from US$75/85)*, also within the SBFZ, has well-appointed executive rooms.

Ridgecrest Gardens Hotel *(☎ 222 2006, fax 223 7380; 15 Magsaysay Dr; rooms with air-con & hot-water bathroom from P600)*, in Olongapo, is newly renovated and has comfortable rooms. Some rooms have cable TV (P700) and fridge (P1000).

Arlene's Inn II *(☎ 222 2629; 18/18th St; singles/doubles with air-con, cable TV & hot-water bathroom P700/1000)*, above the Chowking fast-food restaurant near the Victory Liner bus terminal, has friendly staff and clean rooms.

Arlene's Inn III *(☎ 222 8877; cnr Fendler St & Magsaysay Dr; singles/doubles with air-con, cable TV & hot-water bathroom from P800/1000)*, opposite Sam's Pizza on busy Magsaysay, is closer to the restaurants and clubs than its sister inn.

Places to Eat

Sam's Pizza *(☎ 222 3686; Magsaysay Dr; burgers P50-70, other meals from P120; open 10am-2am daily)* is probably the friendliest of the dozens of pizza places in town. It has live music in the evenings, good square pizzas (P150-200) and free delivery.

The big disco-theatres like the **Blue Note** *(Magsaysay Dr; admission Fri & Sat P50; open 7pm-3am daily)* and **Hard Rock Café** *(Magsaysay Dr; admission Fri & Sat including 1 drink P70; open 6pm-2am daily)* all offer live music, GROs ('Guest Relation Officers' are officially glorified waitresses; unofficially they are sex workers), happy hours and bar meals.

Within the SBFZ are several hotel-owned restaurants, including the slick **Seafront Restaurant** *(☎ 252 2222; meals P180-350; open 11am-2pm & 6pm-11pm daily)*, which has good seafood meals and a wide window's view across the bay. It's opposite the Legenda Hotel.

The **Hollywood Steak House** *(☎ 252 5111; George Dewey complex; meals P200-300; open 11am-10.30pm Mon-Fri, 8am-10.30pm Sat, 6am-10.30pm Sun)*, near the Royal Subic Mall, is a local 'fine dining' experience with burgers, steaks and a well-stocked bar. During the day, a Winstar bus (P7) will bring you to the Hollywood from the SBFZ gate; at night, call the restaurant to organise a taxi from the gate (P60).

Getting There & Around

The only flights into **Subic Bay international airport** *(☎ 252 9360)* are charter flights from overseas.

Victory Liner (☎ 222 2241, 222 4719) and **Saulog Transit** (☎ 02-825 2926–30) both have buses at least once an hour between Manila and Olongapo (three to four hours). Saulog buses (P139) leave from Quirino Ave, Parañaque in Manila. Victory Liner buses (regular/air-con P94/121) leave from EDSA Pasay. Victory Liner also has buses from its Olongapo terminal behind Rizal Ave to Baguio (P278, seven hours), San Fernando (P70, two hours), Caloocan City (P130, three hours), Sampoloc (P135, three hours) and Balanga (P27, one hour).

Jeepneys in Olongapo are colour-coded. Yellow jeepneys run along Rizal Ave to the SBFZ main gate (P4). Blue jeepneys leave for Subic village (P5) from the street behind the Victory Liner terminal.

Budget (☎ 223 2609), **Topsan** (☎ 224 9016, 224 4828) and **S Flat** (☎ 223 2444) all have offices on Magsaysay Dr. They all charge around P2300/1500 a day (with/without driver) for an air-con car.

SBFZ shuttle buses depart from the Park-n-Shop car park next to the main gate for the waterfront (P5), the Royal Subic Mall (P5), the airport (P10) and Upper Cubi (for Crown Peak Gardens, returning via the JEST camp; P10). There are buses every few minutes from 8am to 6pm, then hourly till midnight.

SAN FERNANDO (PAMPANGA)
☎ 045 • pop 221,900

The busy industrial town of San Fernando – not to be confused with San Fernando (La Union) northwest of Baguio – is the capital of Pampanga province and was right in the line of fire when the liquid mud from Mt Pinatubo came sliding down, entirely swallowing the suburb of Bacolor, in 1996. You can still see a few old rooftops sticking out of the reeds on the road to Olongapo.

One of the main reasons people come here is to see fanatical Christians taking part in a **crucifixion ceremony** every Easter. At noon on Good Friday, in barangay San Pedro Cutud, volunteers are physically nailed to wooden crosses and whipped till they bleed.

The other big event in San Fernando is the annual **Christmas Lantern Festival**. At about 8pm on the closest Saturday to Christmas, a number of gigantic Christmas lanterns are paraded through the town and up to the Paskuhan Village park, accompanied by the

usual fiesta shenanigans. The lanterns remain on display till January.

The **DOT office** (☎ 961 2665, 961 2612; e dot3@mozcom.com; open 8am-noon & 1pm-5pm Mon-Fri) is in the **Paskuhan Village**, as is the **Pinatubo House** (built from the material that rained down on the town) and a public **swimming pool** (admission P20). The complex is shaped like a Christmas star, and houses numerous stalls selling lanterns and other souvenirs.

Places to Stay
Boliseum Motel (☎ 961 2040; rooms with air-con, TV & bathroom P575), in the Juliana subdivision on the outskirts of San Fernando, is a passable short-stay place with quiet rooms.

Hotel Grace Lane (☎ 860 1234, 860 6060, fax 961 5358; e hglane@mail.irnet.net.ph; rooms with air-con, cable TV & hot-water bathroom P1250-3250) is a new place just off the MacArthur Hwy on the way into town. Breakfast is included in the rates.

Days Hotel (☎ 963 5440, 843 6478, fax 02-843 6478; w www.dayshotel.ph; Paskuhan Village; singles/doubles from P2000/2200), just off the northern expressway, behind the tourist office, offers its usual top-dollar rooms.

Getting There & Away
Buses from Manila to Olongapo pass through San Fernando (see Getting There & Away under Olongapo & the Subic Bay Freeport Zone earlier); it's two hours and P70 to P75 from either end. There are also buses north to San Fernando (La Union; P187, six hours), Baguio (P275, six hours) and Balanga (P50, 1½ hours).

A jeepney ride north to Angeles (P10, 30 minutes) and a second trip on to Dau (P4) will get you to the Mabalacat terminal, which is a stop for buses on most of the main routes north.

ANGELES
☎ 045 • pop 264,000

If it wasn't for the destruction caused by the eruption of Mt Pinatubo, there would be little reason to visit the strip of girlie bars and cheap hotels known as Angeles. The dusty highway outside the perimeter fence of the former Clark Airbase has seen nearly a century as the centre of the sex industry in the Philippines.

AROUND MANILA

The sex industry first took hold here when US servicemen began taking R&R in the villages surrounding the US military base. Today, the young girls who work the bars along Fields Ave cater mainly to middle-aged Australian, American and European men who are ferried in from Manila, baryo Barretto and Subic by highly profitable international sex-tourism cartels. Angeles is a one-trick town and there's not much here to delay the traveller.

Pinatubo can easily be visited as a day trip from Manila, particularly if you have your own transport, or you can stay in nearby San Fernando or Clark Special Economic Zone, so there isn't really any need to contribute your tourist dollars to this place.

Orientation & Information

Balibago (the downtown red-light district – Angeles is actually a small village 2km further south) doesn't consist of much more than Fields Ave and its extension, Don Juico Ave. Philippine Rabbit buses stop on Henson St, which meets the MacArthur Hwy near Balibago. Dau is 2km north along the highway.

Places to Stay & Eat

There are dozens of cheap hotels along Fields Ave and Don Juico Ave, but unless you're here for the 'entertainment', it's a fairly dispiriting place to stay.

If you do stop over, the business hotels at the far end of Fields Ave from MacArthur Hwy are probably the most discreet.

Oasis Resort Complex (☎ 322 3301–5, fax 322 3164; w www.oasishotel.com.ph; rooms with air-con, cable TV & bathroom P1950-2700) seems to be the only hotel where conferences actually take place.

Clarkton Hotel (☎ 322 3424, fax 322 2267, 625 6887; e clarkton@checkmark.net; rooms with air-con, cable TV & hot-water bathroom P890-2090), nearby, is one of several generic mid-range hotels on Don Juico Ave with pool, bar and restaurant.

Vistillana Hotel (☎ 892 5004; cnr Charlotte St & Arayat Ave; rooms with fan & bathroom P300, with air-con, TV & bathroom P400), on a side street off MacArthur Hwy, is clean and sees less action than the Fields Ave hotels.

It can be hard to find a meal in Angeles without receiving unwelcome attention; fast-food places are often a good bet.

Pearl of India Restaurant (☎ 0919 595 5700; Friendship Hwy; meals P75-150; open 11am-midnight), the one stand-out eatery, was about to move premises from Fields Ave to Friendship Hwy when we last visited. This friendly Indian family-run place serves up excellent fresh and spicy (or less spicy) meals, including a large array of vegetarian dishes. It will deliver meals to locations within the Balibago area.

Getting There & Around

Philippine Rabbit has air-con buses every 30 minutes from Rizal Ave (Avenida) in Manila, to its terminal on Henson St in Angeles village (P72, 1½ hours). Victory Liner buses leave EDSA, Pasay City, every hour and travel via Angeles to the Mabalacat bus terminal in Dau (regular/air-con P60/80), a few kilometres north of Angeles. Yellow jeepneys run between Dau and Angeles village (P4) 24 hours a day.

CLARK SPECIAL ECONOMIC ZONE

After the 1991 eruption of Mt Pinatubo, the USA finally ceded to the Philippine government's demands and vacated the Clark Airbase. Like Subic Naval Base, Clark, on the edge of Angeles, has now been given special economic status in an attempt to encourage industrial development, but this has been far from a resounding success.

Every February Clark holds a large **Balloon Festival** with lots of colourful hot-air balloons and a race over the volcano. Regular air-con buses and jeepneys leave from the main gate and do a circuit around the Special Economic Zone.

If you need to stay in the area, Clark is a less seedy option than Angeles. **Blu Bianco Suites** (☎/fax 045 599 3956; rooms with air-con, cable TV & hot-water bathroom P900-2200) is a low-key, friendly place with a restaurant. Jeepneys from the Clark main gate will take you to any of the hotels (P4).

MT PINATUBO

For centuries the residents of Angeles took the nearby volcanoes of Mt Pinatubo and Mt Arayat for granted. That changed suddenly on 15 June 1991, when Pinatubo, the larger of the two volcanoes, literally blew itself apart, sending a column of ash and rock 40km into the air. The mountain lost 300m in height and fine dust and fist-sized fragments of rock rained down on nearby Angeles, Clark Airbase and Subic Bay.

The eruption was caused by magma superheating pockets of water within the rock, creating an explosive force akin to a nuclear detonation. Earthquakes shook the ground, lightning and thunder boiled in the sky and everywhere ash fell in unbelievable quantities. The main centres of the sex industry were right in the path of the destruction, prompting many church groups to draw biblical conclusions. As if to support this, a savage typhoon chose this moment to lash northern Luzon, turning the ash into lethal lahar (mobile volcanic mud), which flooded downhill from the volcano, burying 1000 hectares of prime farmland and claiming over 1000 lives.

Pinatubo is unlikely to erupt again in the near future, but the lahar deposits are prone to remobilisation by the annual rains and continue to cause fresh devastation every year. In September 1995 the suburb of Bacolor in San Fernando was entirely swallowed up by new lahar flows.

The sex industry quickly bounced back in Angeles, and Pinatubo tours were conceived as a way to revive the fortunes of some of the worst-affected areas. But a lot of the money has ended up in the pockets of Angeles businessmen.

Touring Pinatubo

The easily eroded lahar flows have created a stunning landscape around the volcano. The Abacan and Pasig-Potrero Rivers continually cut new channels through the sediment, leaving towering pinnacles of lahar, hanging valleys and steep-sided **canyons**. In the dry season it's possible to wander for hours through the canyons or even trek all the way up to the volcano itself.

Many people book guided tours through travel agents in Angeles, but it's easy to arrange the trip yourself, bypassing the Angeles tourist machine and ensuring that the money goes directly where it's needed. You can also arrange guides and camping gear through **Real Outdoor Adventures** in Manila (☎ 02-932 7273; ⓔ powerup@mindgate.net).

The starting point for the trip is at Santa Juliana, about 40km from Angeles. You can get here on a north-bound jeepney or bus from San Fernando or Angeles: ask the driver to let you out at the intersection for Santa Juliana. Then take a tricycle (P40) to the visitor assistance centre near the barangay hall, receive a briefing, register and pay for a Pinatubo permit (P20). Mountain guides are mandatory, and DOT-accredited ones can be arranged here (P500 for up to five people). Tips or donations are gratefully received and go into a communal pot to pay for road repairs and loans to farmers in the village.

You can hike all the way to the summit (1760m) in the dry season, but it will be a very long day. An overnight trip is more advisable, but visitors will need to bring their own food and camping equipment. Hiking through the lahar is hot and dusty work, so bring plenty of water. It's best not to attempt the hike if there's a chance of rain.

An easier option is to hire a 4WD jeep to take you most of the way, shortening the hike to the summit to three hours. Jeeps can be hired from **Edwin Manalang** (☎ 0919 208 1534). Another option would be to contact the San Fernando **DOT** (☎ 045-961 2665, 961 2612; ⓔ dot3@mozcom.com) or Leonida Reyla at the **Santa Juliana Tourism Council** (☎ 0973 538 475). Leonida can also organise a **homestay** (per person P150), including breakfast, in Santa Juliana.

After you return from your trip, log out at the visitor assistance centre so they know you are safely off the mountain.

Road Tours & Scenic Flights With a hire vehicle you can easily do a circuit from Angeles to Porac and on to the vanished suburb of Balocor, returning via San Fernando. The route crosses the Mega Dike project outside Porac, where you can still see the ruins of buildings sticking out of the lahar. You can also do the first part of the trip by public transport. Jeepneys leave for Porac from Rizal Ave Extension near the Angeles public market.

Scenic flights over Pinatubo (three-person seaplane US$150) are run by **Michelo Farrell** (☎ 047-252 2230, 0919 325 1106) and **Subic Bay Aqua Sports** (☎ 047-252 3005, 252 7343) in Subic Bay.

MT ARAYAT

Many people arriving in Angeles mistake the towering volcanic cone of 1026m Mt Arayat for Pinatubo, as it dominates the skyline. The volcano affords several half-day hikes to peaks on the crater rim, from where there are stunning views over Pampanga province. Also here are a network of swimming **pools** fed by a **natural spring** which, legend has it, produces the purest water on earth.

Guides are presently being trained in Arayat town for tours up the mountain. You could try contacting the Arayat **tourist office** (☎ 045-885 1791), but you are probably better off organising a guide through **Real**

Outdoor Adventures (☎ 02-932 7273; ℮ powerup@mindgate.net) in Manila, whose members have been climbing the mountain for around 10 years.

Getting There & Away

Arayat is about 25km east of Angeles. Jeepneys to Arayat leave from Plaridel St near the Angeles public market. The last trip back to Angeles leaves at about 6pm. A tricycle from Arayat market to the national park costs about P20.

North Luzon

The Zambales Coast runs north of Subic up to Santa Cruz and is dotted with beach resorts. This stretch of coastline deserves a brief stop if you're heading into the Cordilleras and want to spend a couple of days on the beach along the way. The coast surrounding the Lingayen Gulf and its two provinces (Pangasinan and La Union) is home to many of North Luzon's most well-known beach resorts. You can find your own small private beach in Hundred Islands and while San Fernando is very popular, the beaches here don't compare with Luzon's southern neighbours.

The Cordillera region is the Philippines' largest mountainous area, spilling over into five provinces. The rice terraces around Banaue and Batad are a most impressive and sight and deservedly famous.

More remote regions in Kalinga, Abra, Kabayan and Ifugao offer tremendous opportunities for trekking. Pristine and laid-back Sagada is the place to see hanging coffins and caves.

Ilocos province is home to the charming city of Vigan, the oldest surviving Spanish colonial city in the Philippines. On the north coast of Luzon, Pagudpud is the nicest beach in this part of the country.

The Northern Sierra Madre National Park in Isabela province is the largest remaining rainforest in the Philippines and is largely untouched. Not far from the commercial town of Tuguegarao in Cagayan province are an extensive series of cave systems and the bats of the Pinacanauan River.

Batanes is a mini-archipelago 280km north of Luzon and 190km south of Taiwan, where the Pacific Ocean meets the South China Sea. There are only three inhabited islands – Batan, Sabtang and Itbayat – but each has unique, striking scenery and a slow and pleasant pace of life. Batan is excellent for hiking, Sabtang has timeless stone villages and Itbayat is the most remote.

Zambales Coast

The beaches along this stretch of coast, west of Mt Pinatubo, are better than those further north in San Fabian and San Fernando (La Union) and quieter and less de-

Highlights

- Feast your eyes on the awesome rice terraces around Batad and Banaue
- Hike around Sagada's tranquil mountain-top setting
- Take a carriage ride through Vigan's cobblestone streets and view the beautiful baroque churches of the Ilocos region
- Enjoy the slow pace, striking coastline and beautiful hills of Batanes

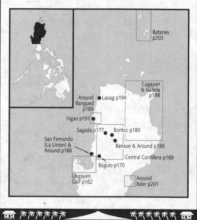

Batanes p203

Cagayan & Isabela p198

Around Bangued p189

Laoag p194

Vigan p191

Sagada p177

Bontoc p180

San Fernando (La Union) & Around p166

Banaue & Around p185

Central Cordillera p169

Baguio p170

Lingayen Gulf p162

Around Baler p201

veloped than the area around Subic Bay. The swimming is good in parts and small resorts are sprinkled along the shoreline from Pundaquit to Pangasinan province.

The major bus companies, including Victory Liner, offer frequent trips to Olangapo, from where it's easy to transfer to another bus or jeepney heading north. Coming from Iba or beyond, you won't have to wait long on the National Rd for a bus south.

PUNDAQUIT
pop 1800

Just 5km southwest of San Antonio is baryo Pundaquit, where you can hire a pumpboat for P350 a day to take you to the beautiful white-sand beach on the nearby island of **Capones**.

Closer to San Antonio is baryo San Miguel, with a wider though busier beach, where you can also arrange a trip to Capones.

NORTH LUZON

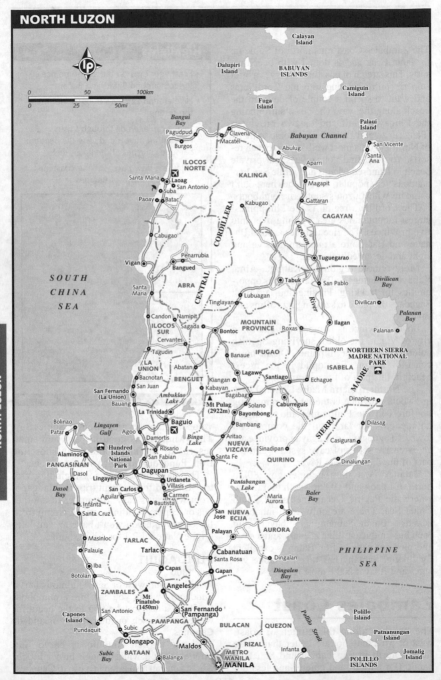

Places to Stay

Capones Beach Resort *(☎ 918-902 7845; rooms with bathroom & fan/air-con P950/ 1500)* is friendly and is on a quiet, fairly out-of-the-way part of the beach, though to use the beach you do have to pay P50 to the 'resort' (palm-covered shelters) that is right in front of Capones. The building itself is not so attractive but the rooms are clean.

Nora's Beach Resort *(rooms with bathroom & fan/air-con P1000/2500)*, next to Capones Beach Resort, is basic but does have beach access.

San Miguel Beach Garden Resort *(☎ 0919 333 7134; rooms with fan & bathroom P275)* right before the beach in baryo San Miguel has a couple of very attractive brick-walled rooms on the ground floor. There are small balconies in the 2nd-floor rooms and a pool table in the bar.

BOTOLAN
pop 46,000

A few more beach resorts dot the coast south of the small town of Botolan. The beaches here are more isolated and the waves somewhat larger than at Iba to the north.

Places to Stay

West Coast Beach Resort *(☎ 0917 732 0716; rooms with bathroom & fan/air-con P800/ 1100)* is almost halfway between Botolan proper and San Antonio (Pundaquit). The beach here is wider and more private than in Iba. There is a pool on the grounds and the large air-con rooms have a small sitting area. **Rama Beach Resort** *(☎ 0918 910 1280; e ramabeach@eudoramail.com; nipa hut P550, rooms with fan/air-con & bathroom P695/ 995)* is nearby. The rooms are not as nice but it's friendly and the grounds, which include a pool, are more attractive.

IBA
☎ 047 • pop 34,500

Only 30 minutes up the coast from Botolan, is Iba, the province's capital. The largest concentration of resorts along the Zambales Coast is a couple of kilometres north of town, where the beach is long but fairly narrow. The tourism office in the capitol building and locals in Palauig, the next town north of Iba, can provide information about hikes in the area. **Santa Barbara Falls** is an easy two-hour hike from barangay Santa Barbara

and you can climb **Mt Tapulao** in the Zambales mountain range.

In Masinloc, to the north, you'll find **Stingray Diving Resort** *(☎ 821 1624; w www .baysideresort.com)* the area's only diving facility.

Places to Stay

Palmera Garden Beach Resort *(☎ 811 2109; e palmera@mozcom.com; rooms with bathroom & fan/air-con & TV P850/980)* is the most well established and service oriented of any of the resorts in Iba. There is a large, open-air restaurant with an eclectic menu and tasty food. Other amenities include a pool, pool table and Internet access. The modern rooms are small but well kept.

La Playa Del Norte *(☎ 311 2363; cabana with bathroom & fan P970)* is a complex of attractive white cottages, however the rooms themselves are nothing special. Give the ocean view cottages a miss if you really do want to see the ocean. It does have a large, cheerful outdoor restaurant.

Lingayen Gulf

With the exception of Hundred Islands, the water along the Lingayen Gulf is often murky and the beaches are generally narrow. The beach resorts still manage to draw tourists hoping to escape Manila's smog-choked streets, those keeping the sex trade alive and surfers. Like the Zambales Coast, resorts are scattered along the coastline from Lucap to San Fernando (La Union), the majority north of San Fabian.

HUNDRED ISLANDS NATIONAL PARK & LUCAP
☎ 075

West of the Lingayen Gulf, just off the coast of Lucap, this small national park (18.4 sq km) contains 123 separate islets, although some are just large rocks. Numbers aside, the water is clear and shallow and it's possible to have a small, pristine white-sand beach all to yourself. The further north you go, the better the quality of the water, although much of the coral reef has been destroyed by dynamite and cyanide fishing. Nature has also played a part in this; both El Niño and the typhoons that hit the area in 1998 have taken their toll. In an effort to try

NORTH LUZON

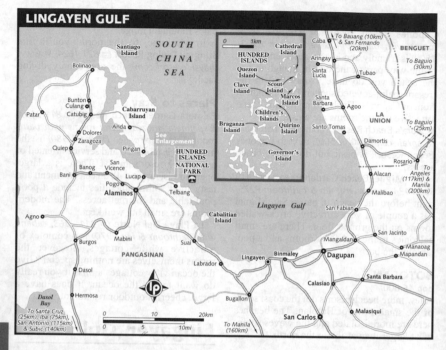

LINGAYEN GULF

NORTH LUZON

to regrow the coral, the Philippines Tourism Authority (PTA) and the University of the Philippines Marine Science Institute are placing giant clams, some over 1m long, in strategic locations around the islands.

Lucap is the jumping-off point for the Hundred Islands National Park, and where most of the accommodation is found. The town itself has no beach and is primarily a single row of small hotels along the shoreline.

Information

The friendly and informative **Philippines Tourism Authority** (PTA; ☎ 551 2505; ⓔ pta hinp@usatv1.net; open 8am-5pm daily) is to the left at the end of the Lucap wharf. You can pay the park entrance fee (P15 per day, P30 per night) here or at the small, round information office in the parking lot. PTA plans to offer guided kayak tours in the near future.

Equitable PCI, BPI and **Metrobank** all have ATMs in Alaminos. On your right, coming from Lucap, just before reaching the major intersection in Alaminos, is **Cyberkadahan** (open 6am-9pm Mon-Fri), where you can access the Internet for P50 per hour.

Things to See & Do

The three most popular islands are **Quezon Island, Governor's Island** and **Children's Island**. On the weekends especially, families crowd the picnic areas and a spot of sand is hard to come by. An easy climb to the top of Governor's Island will reward you with a pretty view of the whole park. Tandem **kayaks** (P150 per hour), which can be rented on Quezon Island, are a fun way to explore some interesting spots like **Marcos Island** and **Scout Island**, which has a nice beach and a cave. You can paddle through a water-filled cave on **Quirino Island**, while bats swarm overhead. If you don't mind falling guano (bat waste), you can sit and eat on the 'picnic rock' at low tide.

There are some areas with good **snorkelling** but it's best to get exact locations from the PTA in Lucap. The area around Clave Island has some coral, mostly of the cabbage and staghorn variety. Gear can be rented at the PTA office or the information centre (P175) and some hotels in Lucap as well. If you want to snorkel around one of the giant clam sites, you must ask for permission from the PTA in advance.

There is no dive shop in Lucap, but there are a few scattered **dive sites**. Areas surrounding **Braganza Island**, **Kagaw Island** and **Cathedral Island** are the best, however coral has been damaged by destructive fishing methods even 15m down. The closest place to rent equipment is in San Fernando (La Union).

Places to Stay & Eat

If you decide to stay in the park, be sure to bring your own food and supplies. You can **camp** anywhere for P100 to P300 depending on the tent's size. Children's Island has a **cottage** *(P560)* and a couple of **nipa huts** *(P559)* and Governor's Island has a **guesthouse** *(P1900)* that sleeps six people. For reservations, contact Manila's **PTA office** (☎ 632-524 2502; e *sales@philtourism.com)* or the office in Lucap.

The following places are all located in Lucap.

Hundred Islands Resort Hotel *(☎ 551 5753; doubles with bathroom, air-con & TV P1200)* is a nice place with good service, and it has hot water. The rooms are very large and you might have to ask the staff to remove few beds.

PTA Hostel *(☎ 551 2505; rooms with fan/air-con P500/800),* conveniently located on the wharf, just above the information office, has seven clean, light-filled rooms.

Barny's Lodge & Restaurant *(☎ 551 6148;* e *chrisb@digitelone.com; doubles with bathroom, air-con & TV P1500)* is a friendly place right on the water. It has five nice rooms with rattan furniture.

Seaside Heaven *(☎ 551 2711; doubles with air-con & bathroom P800, cottages P1000)* has two rooms upstairs, but the small, white clapboard cottages over the river are especially cosy.

Villa Milagros Pension House *(☎ 551 3040; rooms with bathroom & fan/air-con P500/750),* next to the petrol station, has fine, clean rooms but no hot water. There is a two-bedroom penthouse with a large rooftop balcony for P4500.

Vista Del Mar *(☎ 551 4455; rooms with air-con & bathroom P1500)* has basic, not-so-attractive rooms. It is the most hotel-like of all the options and has a coffee shop and restaurant that serves good Chinese food.

Maxine By The Sea Lodge & Restaurant *(☎ 551 2537; rooms with bathroom & air-con*

P700) is the best place to eat in town, however its rooms are only adequate. The restaurant juts out over the water and is a relaxing place to watch the sunset, have a drink and snack on tasty fried calamari.

Getting There & Away

Victory Liner and Dagupan Bus both have hourly services from Manila to Alaminos (P200, six hours), departing from Cubao. From Manila you can also take a Dagupan-bound bus and change at Tarlac for one heading to Alaminos.

It's a 10-minute tricycle ride from Alaminos to Lucap (P30, 5km). You will likely be charged more at night.

To reach the park from Lucap, it's about a 20-minute ride in a motorised bangka. You can hire a boat that holds four people from the wharf or from Maxine's By the Sea for P400 per day or P800 if you stay overnight on an island. Beware. If you want to return after 6pm, you will be charged the overnight rate. The tourist office regulates boat rental rates, so you can check with them for current prices.

Jeepneys and buses (P30, 45 minutes) leave frequently for Bolinao. You can wait at one of the terminals or along the road heading west.

Byron Express and Philippine Rabbit run between Alaminos and Baguio (P130, three hours).

BOLINAO & PATAR BEACH
☎ 075 • pop 61,000

Even though it is a buzzing, provincial fishing town on the extreme northwestern tip of the Lingayen Gulf, Bolinao is not visited by many tourists. It was once a prosperous trade centre, attested to by the sunken Chinese junks and Mexican galleons said to be lying just offshore. A Japanese munitions ship is sunken off nearby Santiago Island, however underwater visibility is usually poor, so the area hasn't been developed as a diving destination. But if you come out this way, Patar Beach, 12km away, is more likely to be your destination. It's a long stretch of narrow sand on one side and forests of coconut palms on the other. Low tide makes swimming virtually impossible unless you want to venture out over the reef. At night, locals search the shallow waters with flashlights looking for shellfish.

NORTH LUZON

Things to See

Built by the Augustinians in 1609, the **Church of St James** in the town plaza is a rarity because of its Mexican influence. On its antique altar are two tongue-protruding, Aztec-like statues said to have been brought to Bolinao by early traders. Also rare are the wooden *santos* (religious statues) on the church's facade, which, unlike many churches in the Philippines, have not been pilfered by collectors.

Across from the high school on the main road into town is the **Bolinao Museum** *(admission free; open 8am-noon & 1pm-5pm Tues-Sat)*. There are a few unimpressive exhibits on general geography and local churches. Out the back are two Philippine monkeys and a palm civet caged in less than ideal conditions.

Visitors are welcome to view the laboratory at the **University of the Philippines Marine Service Institute** *(☎ 554 2755; open 8am-5pm Mon-Fri)*, across the street from the lighthouse. Researchers here cultivate near-extinct indigenous species with the aim of transplanting them into their natural environment; the lab also aims to transfer the technology to other parts of the Philippines. The coral-producing giant clams in the Hundred Islands National Park are grown here.

Places to Stay & Eat

Aside from El Piscador, all of the region's accommodation is in Patar.

El Piscador *(☎ 554 2559; rooms with bathroom & fan/air-con P500/1200)* is the only real option in town. To get here, follow the main road to the right after it passes the church and then turn left down one of the side streets. The hotel is near the water in a large, crumbling compound. There is no hot water and even though the place feels closed, the rooms are OK.

Garden Paradise Resort *(☎ 969 9360; nipa huts with fan P800, doubles with bathroom & air-con P2000)* is the most modern and attractive of the Patar places. The grounds are dotted with picnic sheds and coconut trees and there is a roof-deck piazza overlooking the reef. The nipa huts have good ventilation and a nice little porch.

Bing's Beach Resort *(☎ 0912 856 1585; nipa huts P800, rooms with air-con & bathroom P1500)* is one of the last places along the road from Bolinao. The nipa huts are only average

but it has a friendly feel and there is a large, two-storey annex going up across the road.

Dutch Beach Resort *(☎ 0920 786 9037; rooms with fan/air-con & bathroom P700/1600)*, also known as the White Beach Resort, is situated on a nice part of the beach and has large, clean bungalows.

Short Time Restaurant, behind the Bayanihan Hall, across from the Municipal Library, has air-con and serves basic Filipino dishes.

Tummy Teasers *(A Celino St)*, not far from town on the road to Patar, has pizza, spaghetti and even tacos.

Getting There & Away

To get from Manila to Bolinao, you have to first pass through Alaminos – see Hundred Islands National Park & Lucap Getting There & Away earlier. Five Star has buses from Manila to Bolinao (P195, six hours) every half-hour from Pasay city.

To get to Patar from Bolinao, take A Celino St, which is about halfway between the church and the museum – the street eventually turns into a bumpy all-dirt road. There are no buses; there are some jeepneys that go most of the way to Patar but some only go part of the way because of the bad road. The most common way to get there is to take some form of tricycle. If you take a tricycle (P300 return, 45 minutes), try to arrange the return trip, as their numbers wane the further down the beach you go.

Five Star makes frequent trips to Alaminos (P30, 45 minutes), the last leaving around 10.30pm. Other bus companies and jeepneys also serve this route.

Byron Express and Philippine Rabbit run a few times a day from Bolinao to Baguio (P150, 3½ hours).

LINGAYEN

☎ 075 • pop 89,000

Although it is the provincial capital of Pangasinan, Lingayen is less hectic than neighbouring Dagupan. The commercial centre and its central plaza was built by the Spanish while the Capitol Building area 1km away was built by the Americans. Here you'll find the small open-air **Lingayen Gulf War Memorial Museum**, which has interesting photos of the US beach landing in January 1945, as well as pictures of the Japanese military, Filipino guerrillas and an American fighter plane.

The beach here is not as nice as San Fabian or the Zambales coast and there's nothing particularly remarkable about the town. Every 1 May the coastline comes alive with a raucous water-borne parade in celebration of **Pista'y Dayat**, the province's foremost fiesta.

Places to Stay & Eat

Hotel Consuelo (☎ *542 8933; cnr Avlear St & Maramba Blvd; singles/doubles P650/750*), across from the Capitol Building, is a modern, well-run hotel. It has a restaurant that serves Chinese cuisine and fresh seafood.

Lingayen Gulf Resort Hotel (☎ *542 5871; e tourism@pangasinan.com; dorm beds P150, doubles with bathroom, air-con & TV P780*), now under the management of the provincial government, has a swimming pool (P50) on nice grounds and a restaurant that serves Chinese food and sushi.

Getting There & Away

Victory Liner and Dagupan Bus have hourly services to/from Cubao in Manila (P210, 5½ hours).

From Dagupan, any Alaminos-bound bus passes through Lingayen and there are frequent jeepneys (P15, 50 minutes) leaving from AB Fernandez Ave, opposite the CSI shopping centre.

SAN FABIAN

☎ 075 • pop 66,000

Beaches here are far more inviting than those around Dagupan and Lingayen. Next to the town proper is baryo Nibaliw, where there is a cluster of beach resorts along a pleasant residential road. Four kilometres north is baryo Bolasi and another 4km along is baryo Alacan.

Places to Stay & Eat

Except for the San Fabian PTA Beach Resort, all of the following accommodation is in baryo Nibaliw.

Sierra Vista Beach Resort (☎ *075-511 2023; cottages with bathroom, air-con & TV P1500*) is at the end of the road and has rooms far superior to the others nearby. There's a nice pool and a pleasant open-air restaurant that serves elaborate tropical fruit cocktails.

Lazy 'A' Beach Resort (☎ *075-511 5014; rooms with bathroom & fan/air-con P950/1300*) has large, ordinary bungalows and a

restaurant that serves Mexican dishes and Filipino food. The beach here is wide and brown and there are no waves.

Riverside Resort (☎ *0917 245 9149; rooms with fan/air-con P1000/1500*) does not front the beach but is nevertheless on a lovely site over the river. However, it's a motel-like building with large but unappealing rooms.

San Fabian PTA Beach Resort (☎ *075-523 6502; e sales@philtourism.com; beds in dorm with fan P250, rooms with air-con & bathroom P1250*) in baryo Bolasi, a 15-minute tricycle ride north of baryo Nibaliw, is a large compound with pool, restaurant and private beach access. It has spacious, exceptional rooms with thick carpeting.

San Fabian Yacht Club is near the resorts in baryo Nibaliw and specialises in American-style meals.

Getting There & Away

From Manila, any bus bound for San Fernando (La Union) from Sampaloc or Cubao passes through here.

From Baguio, get on a bus heading to Dagupan or Alaminos. To leave San Fabian, just wait on the side of the highway for a bus or jeepney heading in your direction.

You'll have to get a tricycle (P20) to take you from the highway to the resorts.

SAN FERNANDO (LA UNION) & AROUND

☎ 072 • pop 102,000

The provincial capital of La Union, San Fernando is surrounded by dozens of beach resorts dotting the coastline both north and south of the city. This stretch of brown sand beach is narrow in most parts and lined with fishing boats. **Bauang** (ba-**wahng**), which encompasses the stretch of coastline south of the city, sprung up around Poro Point, which until 1991 was the sight of the US military's Wallace Air Station. Like Angeles and other former US military bases, prostitution here is rampant – as are tourists in search of it.

Information

The best place to ask for information is at the **mayor's office**, which is located in the Town Hall.

Things to See & Do

The striking Taoist and Catholic Chinese **Ma-Cho Temple** sits atop a hill just north of San

SAN FERNANDO (LA UNION) & AROUND

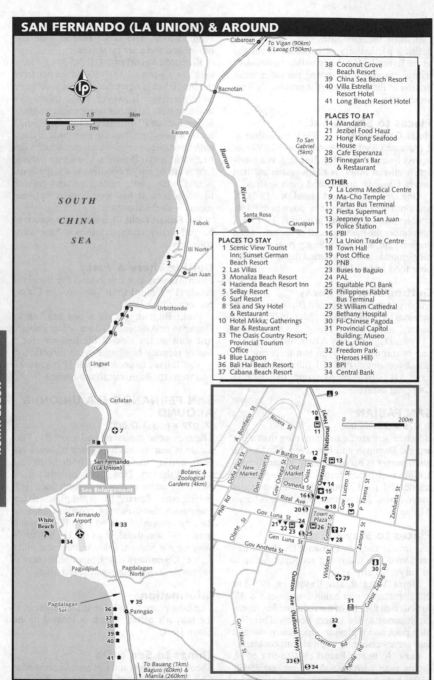

PLACES TO STAY
1   Scenic View Tourist Inn; Sunset German Beach Resort
2   Las Villas
3   Monaliza Beach Resort
4   Hacienda Beach Resort Inn
5   SeBay Resort
6   Surf Resort
8   Sea and Sky Hotel & Restaurant
10 Hotel Mikka; Gatherings Bar & Restaurant
33 The Oasis Country Resort; Provincial Tourism Office
34 Blue Lagoon
36 Bali Hai Beach Resort;
37 Cabana Beach Resort
38 Coconut Grove Beach Resort
39 China Sea Beach Resort
40 Villa Estrella Resort Hotel
41 Long Beach Resort Hotel

PLACES TO EAT
14 Mandarin
21 Jezibel Food Hauz
22 Hong Kong Seafood House
28 Cafe Esperanza
35 Finnegan's Bar & Restaurant

OTHER
7   La Lorma Medical Centre
9   Ma-Cho Temple
11 Partas Bus Terminal
12 Fiesta Supermart
13 Jeepneys to San Juan
15 Police Station
16 PBI
17 La Union Trade Centre
18 Town Hall
19 Post Office
20 PNB
23 Buses to Baguio
24 PAL
25 Equitable PCI Bank
26 Philippines Rabbit Bus Terminal
27 St William Cathedral
29 Bethany Hospital
30 Fil-Chinese Pagoda
31 Provincial Capitol Building; Museo de La Union
32 Freedom Park (Heroes Hill)
33 BPI
34 Central Bank

Fernando. The original image of the Virgin of Caysasay, the patroness of San Fernando's Filipino-Chinese community, is brought here in the second week of September as part of the week-long activities in celebration of the Feast of the Virgin (a replica is on display for the rest of the year).

The **Museo de La Union** *(open 8am-5pm Mon-Fri, Sat by appointment)* displays archaeological finds from the area. In front of the museum is **Freedom Park**, where statues of Philippine national heroes and presidents line the steps leading to the park.

The large grounds of the **Botanic & Zoological Garden**, 6.5km east of the city, has a variety of life and pavilions. Before visiting, especially in large groups, you should pay a courtesy call at the mayor's office.

The **Ocean Deep Diver Training Center** (☎ 888 4440; e *oceandp@sflu.com)*, at Km 263 along the national highway between Bauang and San Fernando can arrange scuba trips.

Places to Stay

San Fernando itself has some accommodation although Bauang, 6km south, has the largest concentration of resorts. San Juan, 8km north of San Fernando, is also dotted with places to stay.

San Fernando With no real competition in the city itself, **Sea and Sky Hotel & Restaurant** (☎ 242 5579; Quezon Ave; singles P400, basement doubles with bathroom P700) has spectacular ocean views and balconies. The basement rooms are unexpectedly comfortable. There is a full-service restaurant and a friendly, helpful staff.

Hotel Mikka (☎ 242 5737; Quezon Ave; singles/doubles with bathroom P625/750), just above the Partas bus terminal has clean modern rooms, an efficient staff, a rooftop sports bar, and **Gatherings Bar & Restaurant**, which has live music from the karaoke hit list.

Bauang Away from the beach, **Oasis Country Resort** (☎ 242 5621; singles/doubles with bathroom P1750/2250) is a convention-style place on the highway. It has a bowling alley, pool table and an inexpensive 24-hour roadside restaurant. Inside is **The Oasis Sushi Bar** which has all-you-can eat buffets from 6pm Wednesday to Saturday. Friday night is a Mongolian buffet (P295).

Blue Lagoon (☎ 888 2531; doubles with bathroom P850) is isolated and quieter than the rest, away from the strip, near the airport. The doubles are large and clean and even have their own spacious sitting rooms.

China Sea Beach Resort (☎ 705 0833; e *chinasea@sflu.com; doubles with air-con & TV P1375)* has thatched-roof bungalows surrounding a nice little pool. The **restaurant** *(dishes P200)* serves sandwiches, seafood and Filipino cuisine.

Coconut Grove Beach Resort (☎ 888 4276; e *resort@coco.com.ph; rooms with fan & bathroom P1100)* is another bungalow-style place but it's probably the only resort with lawn bowling. It has a pool and a pleasant restaurant with a Thai menu.

Long Beach Resort Hotel (☎ 242 0609; e *lbrh@lu.csi.com.ph; rooms with fan/air-con P525/600)* is unique, since it seems to cater exclusively to families and large groups. The rooms are poor but the common areas are often lively and full of activities. There is live entertainment from Monday to Saturday nights and the **restaurant** is worth trying for Tuesday pasta nights (P150) and the all-you-can-eat breakfast buffet (P200).

Bali Hai Beach Resort (☎ 242 5679; e *bali hai@net.com.ph; rooms with bathroom & fan/air-con P975/1250)* has bungalows set in a lush garden. Rates include breakfast. The **restaurant** serves Indonesian, Filipino and Western-style food and is good but somewhat more expensive than the others.

Villa Estrella Resort Hotel (☎ 242 5643; w *www.sflu.com/villa_estrella; rooms with bathroom, air-con & cable TV P1600)* has large, once-elegant rooms in a two-storey concrete building. The **restaurant** overlooking the water is popular.

Cabana Beach Resort (☎ 242 5585; e *ca bana@sflu.com)* is like the others: small cottages around an equally small pool. Rooms are fine and include bathroom.

San Juan The lush grounds of **Sunset German Beach Resort** (☎ 888 4719; rooms with bathroom & fan/air-con P450/650) have a few extremely cosy and attractive rooms with exposed brick. Potted plants are everywhere and you can rent a surfboard for P40.

Las Villas (☎ 242 3770; doubles with bathroom P650) is a classy, Mediterranean style resort with good-quality rooms (but no hot water).

NORTH LUZON

SeBay Resort (☎ 242 5484; rooms with fan/air-con P450/700) is right on the surfing point break and a popular place to hang out; the A-frame-style huts, however, are grubby.

Scenic View Tourist Inn (☎ 242 2906; doubles with bathroom & air-con P700) is at the opposite end of the road to Sunset German Beach Resort. The standard rooms include a free breakfast.

Hacienda Beach Resort Inn (☎ 242 1109; rooms with bathroom & fan/air-con P500/1000) is run down but nevertheless seems to retain its popularity. There is no hot water.

Surf Resort (☎ 720 0340; [e] landrigan@sflu.com; rooms with bathroom & fan/air-con P600/750) has average rooms but rents surfboards and sells any other surfing supplies you may need.

Places to Eat

San Fernando For good Chinese food, head to **Mandarin** (Quezon Ave), which also serves tasty Filipino dishes.

Cafe Esperanza (Gomez St) overlooking the town plaza, serves pastries and coffee in a nice relaxed atmosphere.

Jezibel Food Hauz (Gov Luna St) is open 24 hours and has all you can eat lunch/dinner buffets for P45/95. There is indoor and outdoor seating.

Hong Kong Seafood House (Gov Luna St) has appetising fish and shrimp dishes.

Bauang Most of the resorts also have restaurants that serve both Filipino and international fare.

Finnegan's Bar & Restaurant, along the highway, across from the Bali Hai Beach Resort, serves European and Filipino dishes in a comparably sophisticated and elegant setting.

Getting There & Away

There are frequent buses from Manila to San Fernando (seven hours), departing from Sampaloc and Cubao. Partas has air-con morning buses (P265).

Buses to Baguio (P50, 1½ hours) leave from Gov Luna St every 15 minutes until 6.30pm. Philippine Rabbit has hourly buses to Baguio from the south of San Fernando, the last leaving around 11.30pm.

Partas and Philippine Rabbit travel to Vigan (P139, four hours) regularly until midnight. Or you can get on any Laoag-bound bus (P219, 5½ hours).

Central Cordillera

BAGUIO
☎ 074 • pop 252,300 • elevation 1450m

Originally constructed as a mountain retreat by US military forces in the early 1900s, Baguio's (**ba**-gee-oh) relatively cool temperatures still draw Manila's wealthy when the lowlands are sweltering. But the city's character is shaped by the throngs of young college students. The area's original inhabitants, the Ibaloi and Kankana-ey, have assimilated into present-day society and much of the Igorot ancestral lands have been developed. Filipinos make this a vacation destination, while most foreign travellers stop here to break up the long trip to Sagada or Banaue.

It's no idyllic mountain getaway. However, if you're returning from the mountains, the small-scale urban mayhem, nightlife and youthful population can be refreshing for a day or two. The city has been rebuilt twice since the mid-20th century, first after it was flattened by US bombs dropped to drive out the Japanese, who had already left, and second, after a massive earthquake in 1990. Severe traffic congestion – and this is minus tricycles, since they can't make it up the hills – makes getting around the city centre by vehicle frustratingly slow. The easiest way to get around and to reach all of these destinations is by regular taxi (though they're not as cheap as the tricycles).

Orientation

Baguio was modelled after Washington, DC. The rectangular Burnham Park functions as the geographical centre, and the primary commercial hub, Session Rd, runs roughly parallel to its northeastern side. You'll also find many restaurants, hotels and bars slightly northwest of the park. Centre Mall is located on Magsaysay Ave, which runs north from Session Rd in the direction of La Trinidad. South and east of the city is where many of the lavish summer homes of Manila's elite are located, as well as the Botanic Gardens, Wright Park, Baguio Country Club and Mines View Park.

Information

The best source for city and regional info is Tam-awan Village, northwest of the city centre.

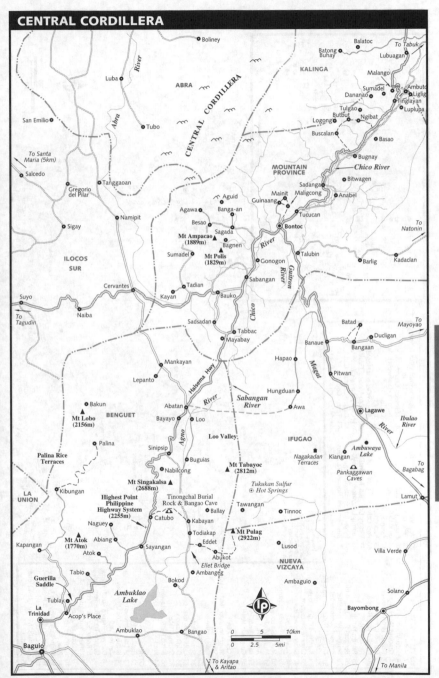

CENTRAL CORDILLERA

BAGUIO

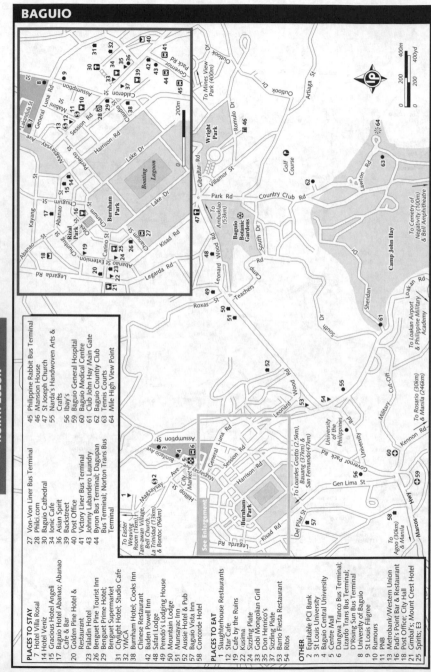

PLACES TO STAY
7 Hotel Villa Rosal
14 Hotel Veniz
15 Gracous Hotel Angeli
17 Baguio Hotel Abanao; Abanao Cafe & Bar
20 Golden Pine Hotel & Restaurant
23 Paladin Hotel
26 Benguet Pine Tourist Inn
29 Benguet Prime Hotel; Benguet Supermarket
31 Citylight Hotel; Studio Cafe
32 YMCA
38 Burnham Hotel; Cooks Inn Chinese Restaurant
42 Baden Powell Inn
48 Safari Lodge
49 Peredo's Lodging House
50 Mountain Lodge
51 Munsayac Inn
52 Aussie Hotel & Pub
57 Baguio Vista Inn
58 Concorde Hotel

27 Von-Von Liner Bus Terminal
28 Philci.com
30 Baguio Cathedral
34 Ionic Cafe
36 Asian Spirit
39 Backstreet
40 Post Office
41 Victory Liner Bus Terminal
43 Johnny Labandero Laundry
44 Byron Bus Terminal; Dagupan Bus Terminal; Norton Trans Bus Terminal

45 Philippine Rabbit Bus Terminal
46 Mansion House
47 St Joseph Church
55 Narda's Handwoven Arts & Crafts
56 Ibay's
59 Baguio General Hospital
60 Baguio Medical Centre
61 Club John Hay Main Gate
62 Baguio Country Club
63 Tennis Courts
64 Mile High View Point

PLACES TO EAT
1 Slaughterhouse Restaurants
12 Star Cafe
19 Cafe by the Ruins
22 Kusima
24 Sizzling Plate
33 Gobi Mongolian Grill
35 Don Henrico's
37 Sizzling Plate
53 Barrio Fiesta Restaurant
54 Ritos

OTHER
2 Equitable PCI Bank
3 St Louis University
4 Baguio Central University
5 Centre Mall
6 Dangwa Tranco Bus Terminal; Lizardo Trans Bus Terminal; D'Rising Sun Bus Terminal
8 University of Baguio
9 St Louis Filigree
10 St Louis University
11 PNB
13 Metrobank/Western Union
16 Padi's Point Bar & Restaurant
21 Gimbal's; Mount Crest Hotel
25 Spirits; E3

There are several **banks** on Session Rd that have ATMs accepting MasterCard and Cirrus but Philippine National Bank (PNB) seems to be the only one that changes travellers cheques.

Session Rd and its arteries are now flooded with Internet cafés. **Philci.com** (2nd fl, Doña Anita Bldg, 62 Session Rd; open 24 hrs) charges P40 per hour.

There are a few drop-off laundry kiosks, including **Johnny Labandero Laundry** (Governor Pack Rd), next to the Baden Powell Inn.

Burnham Park

The city radiates in all directions from this park, named after the American architect who planned the city. If you're in the mood you can rent a swan-rowboat to explore the artificial lake around which the park is centred. It's a pleasant place to stroll, even in the afternoon mist but it's probably best to avoid it at night.

City Market

Just north of Burnham Park, City Market is a maze covering 3 sq km. Vendors sell everything: fruit, vegetables, meat, dozens of varieties of rice, clothes, shoes, used books etc. You can also pick up mass-produced weavings and carvings. It's a good place to wander and inevitably get lost in.

Baguio Cathedral

Set on a hill overlooking Session Rd, the twin-spire cathedral served as a refuge for 5000 locals during heavy bombing in WWII. Some victims of the bombing are buried on its grounds. You can reach the cathedral from the stairway off Session Rd.

Lourdes Grotto

Established by the Spanish Jesuits in 1907, the small grotto sits at the top of 252 steps. From the top, there's a nice view of the city's rooftops.

Tam-awan Village

Eight traditional Ifugao homes were taken apart piece by piece and then reassembled here at the Tam-awan Village (☎ 446 2949; e tamawan@skyinet.net; Long-Long Rd, Pinsao), 15 minutes northwest of the city. On a clear day you can see the South China Sea, hence the name Tam-awan, which literally means 'Vantage Point'.

The Chanum Foundation, which developed the project, is dedicated to the preservation and teaching of the art and culture of the Cordillera people. It's probably the only place where you can learn papermaking and indigenous music and dance or see a demonstration of arnis, a form of martial arts that uses rattan sticks and the curiously named empty hand technique – look: nothing there! Workshops and demonstrations should be arranged in advance (P350 per session). There are three artists in residence and others that are just hanging out.

Chit Asignacion, the vice president of the foundation, is a great source of historical and practical information about the area. See Places to Stay later for information on sleeping in one of the native huts.

To get here, take a taxi or a Quezon Hill–Tam-awan or Tam-awan–Long-long jeepney from the city market.

Camp John Hay

Formerly a US military rest-and-recreation facility, Camp John Hay is being renovated into an upmarket vacation resort. Although the US lease on the land expired in 1991, the US ambassador to the Philippines still has a summer home on the grounds. WWII in the Philippines began here when the first bomb was dropped by the Japanese in 1941 and ended here when General Yamashita signed the official surrender documents four years later. Worth a look is the attractively landscaped **Bell amphitheatre**, just across from the **Cemetery of Negativity**, where strange epitaphs are engraved on mock headstones (eg, Knot A Teemplayer, Born a Star, Lived a Meteor, Died in Flames). There's a nice panorama from the **Mile High viewpoint** and you don't have to wade through a cluster of souvenir stalls.

Baguio Botanic Gardens

North of Camp John Hay, off Leonard Wood Rd, is the Botanic Gardens, where you'll find souvenir stalls, some Igorot houses and a few Igorot people in tribal costume, who, for a few pesos, will pose for a photo.

Wright Park & Mansion House

Parents bring their kids to Wright Park, east of the Botanic Gardens, to ride ponies around a track. Across the street is the president's luxurious summer home, known as

Mansion House. The hills in the neighbourhood are dotted with the holiday residences of the wealthy, but the ostentatious front gate, modelled on that of Buckingham Palace, stands out.

Mines View Park

Baguio's most well-known viewpoint, Mine's View Park, is basically a small viewing platform at the end of a row of souvenir stalls. There is an interesting view of the mines (no longer in operation) carved into the Benguet mountain range. Within walking distance is the **Good Shepherd Convent** where the sisters sell first-rate strawberry jam and peanut brittle. Proceeds go towards advocacy programmes for single mothers.

To get here from Baguio, take the Kias to PMA (Philippine Military Academy) jeepney.

Philippine Military Academy

Referred to as the 'West Point of the Philippines', this is a popular tourist destination for Filipinos. The visitor centre houses a small **museum** with an eclectic collection of military memorabilia. There are also nice views of the Benguet mountain range from here.

From Baguio, it's about a 30-minute ride in the Plaza–Kias–PMA jeepney.

Bell Church

You can get your fortune told at one of the ornate, pagoda-roofed temples clustered on a hill near La Trinidad. Though originally a Buddhist temple, the priests practice a mixture of Buddhism, Taoism, Confucianism and Christianity.

La Trinidad

It's hard to tell where Baguio ends and La Trinidad begins. There aren't really any interesting sights here but it is the capital of Benguet province and so you'll have to visit if you have any government-related business to conduct.

Places to Stay – Budget

Citylight Hotel (☎ 444 7544; 245 Upper General Luna Rd; singles P450) is just down the hill on the other side of the Baguio Cathedral. While the building is modern looking, the rooms are very small. The **Studio Cafe** gets busy on Saturday and Sunday nights.

Baden Powell Inn (☎ 442 5836; 26 Governor Pack Rd; dorm beds P400, with air-con & bathroom P850), just around the corner from busy Session Rd, has rooms that are clean, but without much charm. Downstairs is a bar and restaurant with an outdoor deck.

Benguet Pine Tourist Inn (☎ 442 7325; 82 Chanum St; dorm beds/doubles with bathroom P300/500) is a family-run place on a quiet, isolated corner at the northwestern edge of the park. The satisfactory rooms include a curious circular one, and breakfast is included.

Peredo's Lodging House (☎ 442 5091; 5 CM Recto St; doubles P495) is out of town, off Leonard Wood Rd. It's a two-storey pink clapboard house with warm and cheerful rooms and an inviting front porch. Meals can be prepared or you can cook your own food.

Baguio Hotel Abanao (☎ 304 4794; 90 Abanao St; singles with/without bathroom P800/390), in front of the Shell petrol station, has simple rooms, on the verge of crumbling.

Tam-Awan Village (☎ 446 2949; e tamawan@skyinet.net; Long-long Rd, Pinsao; huts P500) has seven nipa huts, which were meticulously transported from their original locations in the mountain province and then rebuilt on the side of a hill outside the centre of Baguio. Everything is authentic, except for the electricity and lights, which are available; there are shared bathroom facilities.

YMCA (☎ 443-4766; Post Office Loop, Session Rd; rooms with bathroom P885) is near the Baguio Cathedral and has two rooms that can hold up to five people each. Discounts are given to members.

Places to Stay – Mid-Range

Burnham Hotel (☎ 442 2331; 20 Calderon St; doubles with bathroom, air-con & TV P1100) is a good choice, only two blocks from Session Rd. The small, warm hotel is decorated with native handicrafts and the cosy rooms are very attractively decorated.

Munsayac Inn (☎ 442 2451; 21 Leonard Wood Rd; doubles with bathroom, fan & TV P950) is in a really quiet part of the city. Native carvings and baskets are everywhere and there is a quaint balcony where you can sip the free coffee. Rooms are cosy but the furniture has seen better days.

Safari Lodge (☎ 442 2419; 191 Leonard Wood Rd; family rooms with bathroom P2000) has a trophy room hung with elephant, rhino, and lion heads and a few other horned creatures. The big-game theme is reinforced by the size of the rooms – enough space to skin a cat – and leopard-skin bed sheets.

Mountain Lodge (☎ 442 4544; 27 Leonard Wood Rd; doubles with bathroom P1200) is out of town, just past the Munsayac Inn. It has large yet cosy rooms and the hallway is decorated with photographs of 19th-century Baguio.

Gracious Hotel Angelì (☎ 442 5078; 25 Abano St; doubles with bathroom & TV P900), formerly the Baguio Hotel Ambassador, has clean, cosy rooms, near where the city market spills over.

Aussie Hotel and Pub (☎ 442 5139; 92 Upper General Luna St; doubles with bathroom, air-con & TV P800), a little out of town, is where a good number of veteran expats hang out. It has good-sized rooms and a rooftop terrace. Every Wednesday, the restaurant serves an all-you-can eat Thai buffet (P175).

Baguio Vista Inn (☎ 443 5208; 18 MH del Pilar St; rooms with air-con, bathroom & TV P1000) is on a quiet street, a short walk from Burnham Park and has good, spotless rooms.

Places to Stay – Top End

Hotel Veníz (☎ 446 0700; 1 Abanao St; doubles with bathroom & air-con P1500) is hard to miss at the northeast corner of the park. It recently opened and has all the perks and luxury of an international quality hotel. **Cafe Veníz** (open 7am-10pm daily), on the 2nd floor, has a wiener-schnitzel lunch special for P99.

Hotel Villa Rosal (☎ 444 8523; General Luna Rd; singles with bathroom & fan P1500) has a pleasant lobby and nice rooms but many don't have windows, and for the money, it's not in the same league as the others.

Paladin Hotel (☎ 442 2644; 136 Abanao St Extension; doubles with common bathroom P600) is immaculate but there isn't much space for anything besides the bed in the tiny standard rooms.

Golden Pine Hotel & Restaurant (☎ 444 9965; e goldenpinehotel@skyinet.net; Legarda Rd; doubles with bathroom P1800) has the standard luxuries and amenities of a high-class place.

Concorde Hotel (☎ 443 2058; e con corde@mozcom.com; Europa Centre, Legarda Rd; doubles with bathroom, air-con & TV P1782) has very nice, cosy rooms, especially the brick-walled ones. It's a large complex

with several buildings, two restaurants, two bars and a 24-hour coffee shop.

Benguet Prime Hotel (☎ 442 7066; Session Rd; doubles with bathroom & TV P1500) is in a prime spot and the staff is professional but it's fading and not good value.

Places to Eat

Barrio Fiesta Restaurant (☎ 442 6049; Session Rd Extension) seems more like the latest Disney theme park than a place to eat. It's a complex of three separate restaurants connected by a stairway lined with larger-than-life painted wood statues. There's an Ifugao lady, a head-hunter and even a smaller version of a two dogs humping. By far the most popular of the three restaurants is the Barrio Fiesta (dishes P250). Seafood and meat is cooked in a hotpot at your table at Pinoy Hotpot. The third, Bakahann at Manukan was closed for renovation at the time of writing.

Cafe by the Ruins (☎ 442 7128; Abano St Extension; open 7am-9pm daily) is in the remains of the former residence of the governor of Benguet, near Rizal Park. Although the service is not so attentive, it's an especially nice place for breakfast. Try the *chocolate-eh at suman* (hot chocolate and sticky rice cake).

Kusima ni Ima Restaurant (Legarda Rd; set dinner meals from P150; open 8am-10.30pm daily) serves exotic kapangpangan specialties like escargot, frogs stuffed with chicken and pork, frog *adobo* (salty stewed frog) and *camaru* (crickets made into adobo and deep-fried with garlic).

Star Cafe (Session Rd) has good Chinatown-style Chinese food.

Gobi Mongolian Grill (93 Session Rd; all-you-can eat lunch & dinner P145; open 11am-10pm daily) puts out a buffet, but there are more condiments than food. The à la carte dishes are a better alternative.

Sizzling Plate (☎ 442 4219; 86 Session Rd) has a few branches in town, where you can get filet mignon (P140) or BBQ chicken (P70) in a Western-style setting.

Don Henrico's (☎ 442 8802) is a popular place for pizza.

Entertainment

Baguio is a college town so there's no shortage of nightlife.

Padi's Point Bar & Restaurant (admission free; open 9.30pm-2am daily) draws a young crowd interested in music. Professional-sounding R&B, jazz, and hip-hop groups play every night.

Gimbal's, in the Mount Crest Hotel, has live rock music from Tuesday to Sunday nights.

Abanao Cafe & Bar in the Baguio Hotel Abanao, has live folk and country music every night from 5pm to 1am, but it's not unusual for there to be an audience of one.

Spirits *(Otek St; admission P150)* is an up-market disco with all the red-velvet furniture you could want. On the 3rd floor is **E3** *(admission free)* where you can surf the Internet for P120 per hour, which includes one drink.

Rumours *(Session Rd)* is a nice, sophisticated place to down a beer or glass of wine.

Backstreet, off the main road, is a pleasant place to relax and have a drink.

Ionic Cafe *(Session Rd)* is a smoky, dimly lit place where you can drink a beer in peace.

There are also several **pool halls** and **discos** in the neighbourhood of Rizal Park.

Shopping

Baguio is a good place to buy local handicrafts, including weavings, wood-carvings, baskets and reasonably priced silver jewellery. The city market sells mostly low-quality stuff, while **Easter Weaving Room** *(☎ 442 4972; ℮ estrwvng@skyinet.net; Easter Rd)* and **Narda's Handwoven Arts & Crafts** *(☎ 442 2992; 151 Upper Session Rd)* sell high-quality items at higher prices.

Easter Weaving Room sells everything from hand-woven bookmarks to *tapis* (traditional wrap skirts). It's well organised and an easy place to shop, since prices are clearly marked.

Good places to buy silver are **St Louis Mission Center Inc** *(☎ 442 2139; Assumption Rd; open 8am-12noon & 1pm-5pm Mon-Sat)* and **Ibays Silver Shop** *(☎ 442 7082; Governor Pack Rd)*. St Louis sells silverware sets, jewellery, picture frames and even intricate silver nativity scenes. You can witness artists at work next door. Ibay's has a wider and more modern selection and you can also watch pieces being made.

Munsayac Inn has a large shop in which you can buy just about any wood-carved item imaginable.

For antiques, try **Teresita's** *(Upper General Luna St)*, **Christine's Gallery** *(Chanum St)* or **Sabado's** *(Outlook Drive)*.

Getting There & Away

Air Air Philippines and PAL have discontinued service to Baguio. **Asian Spirit** *(☎ 304 2813, 02-840 3811 in Manila; 2nd floor, Philippine Treasures Bldg, Session Rd)* flies between Baguio and Manila (P1800, four weekly).

Bus There are three main roads to Baguio: Kennon Rd (aka Zigzag Rd), which is only open to light vehicles; the Marcos Hwy, connecting Baguio and Manila; and Naguilian Rd to San Fernando (La Union).

Philippine Rabbit, Victory Liner, Dagupan Bus, Amiana Trans and Dangwa Tranco make the trip to/from Manila via Angeles (P285, six hours). In Manila, the buses depart from Sampaloc, Caloocan City, Cubao and Pasay City. In Baguio, these companies can be found on Governor Pack Rd.

Philippine Rabbit, Victory Liner and Byron Bus travel to Alaminos and Bolinao.

San Fernando (La Union)–bound buses (P50, 1½ hours) leave every 15 minutes or so from Governor Pack Rd.

Lizardo Trans and D'Rising Sun buses leave hourly to Sagada (P190, seven hours, seven daily) each morning, up the winding, perilous Halsema Hwy – don't look down! It's not a bad idea to lean into the mountain when going around a curve.

Dangwa and D'Rising Sun leave every hour or so for Bontoc (P186, seven hours); the last Dangwa trip is around 10am and the last D'Rising Sun around 3pm.

Dangwa Tranco buses travel to Banaue (P240, nine hours, two daily) along the southern route (via Bayombong). Von-von Liner also makes regular trips to Banaue, leaving from the terminal on Chanum St, across from Burnham Park.

Norton Trans runs a few morning buses to/from Kabayan (P107, 82km, seven hours). Be prepared for a bumpy, dusty and sometimes frightening ride.

Kiangan Motor Service runs an evening trip (around 8pm daily) from Baguio to Kiangan from the western end of Burnham Park.

MT PULAG

Mt Pulag (2922m) is the second-highest peak in the Philippines, after Mt Apo in Mindanao. Climbers have a few options as to route, depending on their time and strength. The **Akiki Trail** (25km) is by far the steepest and most demanding hike, an ascent that begins in Du-acan, a barangay of **Todiakap**, which is on the Halsema Hwy just south of Kabayan. An easier hike is the **Grassland Trail** (16km), which begins around 12km from **Ambangeg**, where the **Protected Areas Office** *(PAO;* ☎ *0919 631 5402)* and **visitors centre** *(*☎ *0918 916 0369)* are located. For a longer hike to the summit, considered sacred ground by the Ibaloi and Kalanguya, you can go via **Ballay** and **Tawangan**. Once at the grassy top, you can of course return the way you came or descend down the back side to **Lusod**, home of the Kalanguya and then to Tawangan, where you'll cross the Ba-ay river and a lush valley.

You must register at the PAO in Ambangeg to secure an entrance fee (P750) and hire a guide (around P1500 for two days and one night – cost depends on trail). There is an additional camping fee (P50) and a local permit (P25).

If you want more information before taking the intimidating Halsema Hwy north, contact the Baguio **Protected Areas and Wildlife Division** *(PAWD;* ☎ *074-443 4909)* or the Department of Environment and Natural Resources (DENR) in Baguio. Visibility is best in March and April and the area sees regular, heavy downpours in July and August.

Getting There & Away

Norton Trans (which leaves from the terminal on Magsaysay Avenue) runs three morning buses from Baguio to Kabayan (P107). To reach Ambangeg and the Grassland Trail from Baguio it's a 3½-hour bus ride. The Akiki Trail junction is another 1½ hours north at Todiakap; from the junction you can take a jeepney on a less accessible road to the park and trail heads. To return to Baguio, there's a morning bus from Ambangeg and a few other Norton Trans buses that leave in the morning from Kabayan.

KABAYAN

pop 10,500 • elevation 1500m
Ever since the 1970s, mummies have catapulted Kabayan to international fame. The centuries-old procedure used in Kabayan is unique from the nine other cultures that have practiced mummification worldwide because the internal organs are not touched. The corpses were dried using the heat and smoke of a small fire and then the skin peeled back

after a month or so. Kabayan mummification was ended by the Spanish.

Mummies have a history of disappearing from their burial places and turning up in museums around the world and so some of the caves are now under lock and key and guarded diligently. If you visit the caves, consider whether you're willing to disturb the burial place: locals customarily make offerings of gin and *pinikpikan* (a special chicken dish) before entering.

If mummies aren't your thing, Kabayan is a nice place to hike and breathe in fresh, tricycle-free air. Night-time is remarkably quiet and the sky is full of stars. Kabayan is believed to be the site of the first Ibaloi settlement, and Ibaloi is the principal dialect spoken here. The area is also known for strong Arabica coffee and tasty red *Kinto-man* rice.

Things to See

You get a good overview of the history and culture of the region at the **Kabayan National Museum** *(open 8am-noon & 1pm-5pm Mon-Fri)*, in a small house just beyond the bridge leading west from town. A few mummies are on display, one in a *kalabaw*-shaped (water buffalo–shaped) wooden coffin and another with its tattooed skin still intact. Ritual artefacts of the Ibaloi, Kankanai and Ikalahan are also on display. Ask the friendly curator to take you to some of the surrounding caves.

Behind the building next to Kabayan Farm Supply is the **Opdas Mass Burial Cave** *(admission P20)* containing hundreds of skulls and bones between 500 and 1000 years old. You can get the gate key at the homestay/*sari-sari* (small neighbourhood stall) close by.

A footpath next to the museum leads to the **Tinongchal Burial Rock** 3km away, where several coffins are stored.

A longer hike past beautiful vistas of vegetable fields (three hours one way, 6km) takes you to the town of Bangao. From here it's a steep climb up to the **Bangao Cave** where you'll find five coffins.

Places to Stay & Eat

There are really only two options in Kabayan: a **guesthouse** *(dorm beds P100)* that can hold 12 and has cooking facilities (get keys at municipal hall), and a friendly **homestay** *(rooms P200)*, next to Opdas Mass Burial Cave, with

Mummy's Home

On the night of the new moon, 20 May 1999, all those gathered at the National Museum in Manila drank a glass of wine in Apo Anno's honour. After nearly 80 years away, he was finally going home. Apo Anno (*apo* is similar to 'sir' and denotes respect for an elder) was among 80 mummies missing, all presumed stolen, from burial sites all over the Benguet region (in Benguet itself, only the Ibaloy practise mummification).

He is particularly important because it's believed he was not only an accomplished hunter who lived for 250 years but also had a mother who was a goddess. She was forced to give up custody to her mortal lover because the other divine spirits wouldn't accept a child of a mixed union.

His tattooed remains are believed to have been taken in 1918 or 1920, depending on whose story you believe, from under a boulder outcropping in Nabilcong. Some people point to an Englishman, some blame a local Ilocano, while others accuse a Christian pastor who thought the corpse had become a pagan symbol. Regardless of the culprit, the severe storms and landslides that struck soon after were seen by locals as retribution for the local's carelessness. The details of Apo Anno's odyssey are still being discovered. It's rumoured that he was exhibited at the 1922 Manila Carnival and at a museum in Seattle, Washington but what is known is that in 1984 he was finally rescued from an antique shop by Dr Jaime C Laya, the Philippine secretary of education at the time. Dr Laya convinced the owner of the antique shop, who himself had paid P20,000 for the mummy in 1973, to donate the mummy to the National Museum in Manila. But even then, the magnitude of the find was unknown until some Kankanay elders were informed that their revered ancestor was only 325km away.

To mark his homecoming, dogs (believed to bark and run after evil spirits), pigs and *kalabaw* were slaughtered. The corpse was placed on a *sawadil* (death chair) and those keeping vigil introduced themselves to Apo Anno by chanting their family tree.

good rooms. Meals can be arranged if you order in advance.

Getting There & Away

Norton Trans runs a few morning buses to/from Baguio and Kabayan (P107). Be prepared for a bumpy, dusty and sometimes frightening ride.

There are also many points along the Halsema Hwy from which you can hike in: Km 57 and Km 61 (kilometre markers on the side of the road) both lead to Timbac Cave (four hours); Km 63, from barangay Natubleng, is an easy, four-hour hike or if you have a private vehicle, a rough drive over a very bad road (two hours, 12km); and Km 73, from where you can see Kabayan, is the easiest and shortest route.

Travelling north, it is possible to go from Kabayan to Abatan, and then meet one of the many buses or jeepneys travelling from Baguio to Sagada or Bontoc.

To do this, you need to hire an early-morning private jeep to first take you to Soysoyesen (P200, 40 minutes) and from there catch a bus to Abatan (P50, two hours) at around 6.30am.

SAGADA
pop 10,500 • elevation 1477m

The absence of noise and pollution are probably the first things you'll appreciate about Sagada, a tranquil mountaintop town, where you can walk down the middle of the road and only occasionally be disturbed by a passing vehicle. Sagada's hanging coffins are popular but the region's true appeal lies in its easy-going nature, cool climate and pleasurable hikes.

Despite its popularity, Sagada manages to stave off changes that would detract from its appeal as an 'ecotourism' destination – there are no massive hotels or blaring discos and karaoke is conspicuously in short supply. For many Sagadans, the traditional way of life remains intact. During harvest celebrations, women wear *tapis* (a wrap-around skirt, woven with traditional patterns) and older men thongs (not the Western style thong but a type of loincloth, originally made from beaten bark, which is now made from woven fabric) and gather in their *dap-ays;* chickens are sacrificed, gongs are played and general eating and drinking goes on. Sagadans are of Kankanay ancestry and their native language is Kankanay, although as in the rest of the Cordilleras, Ilocano and English are widely spoken.

Sagada gets chilly at night, especially from December to February, when temperatures can drop as low as 4°C (39°F). From March to May temperatures rise as high as 30°C (86°F) during the day. The rest of the year is the rainy season, when the normal pattern is a sunny, pleasant morning followed by a heavy, long afternoon shower. And of course, the Halsema Hwy, the road between Baguio and Sagada, becomes difficult to negotiate.

Information

The **tourist information centre** in the municipal building is more interested in providing a guide than it is in providing information, although a good tourist-friendly map is sold here for P10. Sometimes when nobody is in the booth there are some guides hanging out in the bus shelter overlooking the street. Official guide (P300 caving, P500 Big Waterfalls, P700 Mt Polis) and jeepney (P250 caves, P200 Kiltepan tower, P450 Big Waterfalls) rates are posted here. A P10 fee goes towards environmental protection and the restoration of regional landmarks.

In the lower level of the building is the **Sagada Rural Bank** *(open 8am-11.45am & 1.15pm-4.30pm Tues-Sat)*, which will change cash and travellers cheques – at a poor exchange rate. The **post office** is also in this building.

Across from the bank is a small **store** that sells domestic newspapers, including the

SAGADA

To Lake Danom (6km) & Besao (12km)

To Banga-an (5km) & Bomod-ok Falls (12km)

Bokong Waterfalls

Matangkib Burial Cave (closed)

Latang Cave (Underground River)

Bridge

Cemetery

Demang

Lookout

Kiltepan Peak (1636m)

Kiltepan Tower

Echo Valley

To Mt Ampacao (10km), Bagen (21km) & Mt Polis (24km)

Ambasing

Sugong Coffins

To Bontoc (18km)

To Sumaging Cave (800m), Lolo-ong Cave & Suyo (6km)

Lumiang Burial Cave

◆ Coffins
◇ Hanging Coffins

PLACES TO STAY
2 Sagada Guesthouse & Cafe
4 Alfredo's B&B
11 Greenhouse
12 Igorot Inn
13 Olahbinan Resthouse
17 St Joseph's Resthouse
21 Mapiya-aw Pensione

PLACES TO EAT
1 Log Cabin
9 Shamrock
10 Masferre Country Inn & Restaurant
14 Yoghurt House
22 Right Turn Cafe

OTHER
3 Radio Communications Incorporated
5 Buses to Baguio
6 Jeepneys to Bontoc
7 Tourist Information; Rural Bank; Town Hall; Police Station; Post Office
8 Market
15 St Mary's School
16 St Mary's Episcopal Church
18 St Theodore's Hospital
19 Sagada Weaving
20 Masferre Photographs

NORTH LUZON

Inquirer, which arrives every day in the afternoon. This store and the Yoghurt House lend books; most are in English.

Radio Communications Philippines Incorporated *(RCPI; open 8am-9pm daily)* has Internet access for P95 per hour but the connection is often down. You can also make overseas telephone calls here for P75 for the first minute and P19.50 for each additional minute; apparently the rates will be cheaper in the future.

Hiking

A popular one-hour hike is through **Echo Valley**, a sacred burial area where you'll see many **hanging coffins** high on the surrounding limestone cliffs. There are many intersecting paths through the valley and it's tricky to figure out which way to go. Many people head out for a stroll and return hours later covered in mud, picking leaves and thorns out of their hair. Unless you have a compass or are with a guide, you'll probably have to come back the way you came. The following is one route which takes you past some interesting scenery:

Walk past St Mary's Episcopal Church, then up the steps to the left. Don't enter the gate at the top, but follow the path to the left to the cemetery. Walk all the way through the cemetery to the large cross at the top of the hill. Facing the cross, take the path on the right that leads downhill. Keep going right when other paths intersect. When you come to the lone pine tree on the edge of the rockface, take the path going down. From here you should be able to see hanging coffins across the valley both in front of you and on your right side. Go through the broken wooden gate and at the next fork go left. Go right at the following fork, then follow the path uphill, which will give you a close-up view of some hanging coffins.

From the hanging coffins take the path on your left downhill. At the fork go left, and at the next fork take the path leading downhill. There are more hanging coffins on the cliff face here; it's a mystery as to how they were placed so high. When you come to the clearing, go left. Cross the riverbed (there will be a small cave on your left) and continue following the path along the riverbed; at times you'll be walking in the riverbed itself. After a short while you'll come to some big rocks; cross over these and the

river, then follow the river upstream along the path.

Soon you'll come to the **Latang** (Underground River Cave). In theory it's possible (if you have a strong torch or flashlight) to walk through the cave (about 250m, or 20 minutes) and emerge behind the Rocky Valley Inn and Cafe. This is easier said than done. The same goes for returning to the road without backtracking. The surest way of leaving the valley is to make an about-turn and retrace your steps.

There are superb panoramic views of the rice terraces and surrounding mountains from the **Kiltepan tower**, which is about a 40-minute hike from town. Take the road heading east out of town and then the driveway leading up to the Mapiya-aw Pensione. Before you reach the *pensione* take the stone path on your right going uphill (don't go through the gate). At the top of the ridge the path forks – go left. When you see the fence on your left, walk right along the better-marked grass path to a dirt road and follow this uphill.

If you don't want to take the same route back, follow the dirt road down to the main road; from there it's a longer walk back to town (although you may get lucky and be able to hitch a ride).

About a half-hour walk east of town are the small **Bokong Waterfalls**, where you can take a refreshing dip. To get here, follow the road east out of town and take the steps just after Sagada Weaving on the left. Follow the path through the rice fields down to a small river. Cross the river and continue upriver to the falls and then eventually to the road leading to the town of **Banga-an**, about another 40 minutes away. Forty minutes beyond Banga-an is the picturesque village of **Aguid** (take the right fork after the school in Banga-an).

Access to the larger **Bomod-ok Falls** (Big Waterfalls), a two-hour walk from town, is often restricted because of traditional ceremonies and an ongoing land dispute between two neighbouring villages. Check with the tourist information centre before going; a guide is recommended.

Caving

On the road to Ambasing, just before the Right Turn Cafe, you can see the **Sugong coffins** suspended from the cliff face. A short distance past the Right Turn Cafe is a paved road going off to your left. Follow the paved road and you'll see a path to your left that leads down to the **Lumiang Burial Cave**. Over 100 coffins are stacked in the entrance, the oldest believed to be about 500 years old. There are some more recent, longer coffins as well.

Eight-hundred metres further down the road is the path leading to exhilarating **Sumaging** (Big Cave). The further into the cave you go, the more wet you get and the more invigorating and thrilling the cave becomes. For a full tour of the cave you'll need a guide (they provide a gas lantern). Muddy and slippery rocks make the initial descent tricky but you should take your shoes off when you reach the smooth limestone and calcium formations. It looks slick, but bare feet have remarkably good grip. Freezing, crystal-clear water cascades over spots like 'Kings Curtain' and the 'Rice Terraces' and there are ropes to assist at a few awkward points.

Lolo-ong (Crystal Cave) and **Matangkib Burial Cave** are still closed; the former because of the looting of stalactites, the latter due to safety concerns after a tourist fell 53m to his death while exploring the cave on his own.

Other Attractions

On the outskirts of town is **St Mary's Episcopal Church**, first established in 1905 by an American priest. The church is a stone building with stained-glass windows and the grounds include a basketball court, store, hospital, high school and cemetery. Most Sagadans are now buried here and not in hanging coffins.

Masferré Photographs, just outside of town, displays the work of Sagada-born photographer Eduardo Masferré. His excellent photos of Cordillera people have been exhibited around the world, including the Smithsonian Institute in Washington, DC. Unfortunately, it's rarely open but you can see prints in the Masferré Country Inn and other places around town.

Weavers are at work at **Sagada Weaving** producing backpacks, money belts and other practical items, all done in the traditional patterns of the region. You could probably accessorise in stripes from head to toe. Prices are competitive but you probably won't find the more elaborate and intricate designs available in Baguio.

Places to Stay

Olahbinan Resthouse (*doubles with/without bathroom P800/300*) is at the bottom of a stairway, next to the Sagada Igorot Inn. Everything is wood inside this immaculately kept home, and while the rooms are sparse, they have an immensely warm feel about them.

Sagada Guesthouse (*doubles with/without bathroom P600/100*) can be a bit noisy in the morning, but the rooms are clean and cheerful.

St Joseph's Resthouse (*dorm beds P100, rooms with bathroom P500; cottages with small kitchen & bathroom P1500*) is set amid a garden overlooking the town. It's a nice spot and the cottages are cosy but the quality of the rooms is hit and miss.

Green House (*doubles P150*) has a few pleasant, small rooms in a private home.

Alfredo's B&B (*doubles P300*) is just up the stairs from the tourist office below and has basic rooms with hot water.

Sagada Igorot Inn (*doubles with/without bathroom P1500/800*), formerly the Prime Hotel, is in a large, plain concrete building. It's not good value and the front desk attendant is often missing.

Mapiya-aw Pensione (*doubles P450*) is a 20-minute walk from town and is attractively set in what resembles a Chinese rock garden. Rooms with balconies have a fine view of the mountains.

Places to Eat

Log Cabin (*meals from P300; open dinner*) is a surprise and a pleasure. The Western-style food is hearty and elegantly prepared by a French chef. A number of delicious fresh baked breads are available, including tasty mint-frosted rolls. Good wine and a cosy wood-panelled room with a fireplace make this an excellent place to spend an evening. However, it can get busy in the high season and it's always best to place your order a few hours in advance. Just above and behind the restaurant there's one large, all wood, beautifully decorated **room** (*P1500*) with two beds and a marble bathroom.

Yoghurt House (*mains P200; open breakfast-dinner*), formerly Shamrock II, is probably the next best place for a full meal,

NORTH LUZON

especially breakfast, when you can get fruit cups and muesli with yoghurt. Dinner specials must be ordered in advance.

Shamrock *(banana pancakes & coffee P80; open breakfast-dinner)*, next to the Municipal Building, serves filling pancakes and other standbys. It is a good place to drink coffee and just pass the time.

Masferré Country Inn & Restaurant *(lunch around P150)* has a friendly and cosy restaurant in a large wood-panelled room.

Getting There & Away

From Manila, the quickest way to get to Sagada is via Banaue and then Bontoc. See the Getting There & Away sections of both later for details.

From Sagada, Lizardo Trans and D'Rising Sun depart for Baguio (P190, seven hours, seven daily) each morning. The Halsema Hwy cuts through terrific mountain scenery, but 'highway' is certainly a misnomer. Construction crews seem to be in a perpetual battle with nature and altitude (the highway is 2255m at its highest).

Whizzing around hairpin turns with barely an arm's length to spare produces either amazement in the driver's skill, or terrible anxiety.

Jeepneys to Bontoc (P25, one hour) leave as soon as they are full from 6am to noon.

To get to Banaue, you first have to go to Bontoc and then transfer to a jeepney or bus there. See Bontoc Getting There & Away later for details.

BONTOC

☎ 074 • pop 22,000 • elevation 900m

Compared to serene Sagada, Bontoc is a bustling metropolis. It deserves a visit not because it's the capital of Mountain Province and the prime commercial centre in the area, but because it's the gateway to Mainit, Maligcong and Kalinga.

Information

Kinad (Raynoldo Waytan) acts as a de facto tourist information centre. Not only is he very knowledgeable and speaks several languages, but he has years of experience as a guide. He tailors trips to Maligcong, Mainit and further afield for around P700 per day for groups of one to four (you must supply your own food).

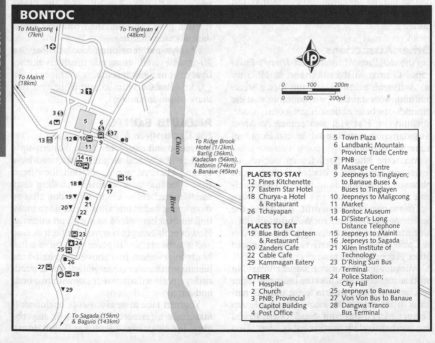

BONTOC

To Maligcong (7km)
To Tinglayan (48km)
To Mainit (18km)
To Ridge Brook Hotel (1/2km), Barlig (36km), Kadaclan (56km), Natonin (74km) & Banaue (45km)
To Sagada (15km) & Baguio (143km)

Chico River

0   100   200m
0   100   200yd

PLACES TO STAY
12 Pines Kitchenette
17 Eastern Star Hotel
18 Churya-a Hotel & Restaurant
26 Tchayapan

PLACES TO EAT
19 Blue Birds Canteen & Restaurant
20 Zanders Cafe
22 Cable Cafe
29 Kammagan Eatery

OTHER
1 Hospital
2 Church
3 PNB; Provincial Capitol Building
4 Post Office
5 Town Plaza
6 Landbank; Mountain Province Trade Centre
7 PNB
8 Massage Centre
9 Jeepneys to Tinglayen; to Banaue Buses & Buses to Tinglayan
10 Jeepneys to Maligcong
11 Market
13 Bontoc Museum
14 Di'Sister's Long Distance Telephone
15 Jeepneys to Mainit
16 Jeepneys to Sagada
21 XiJen Institute of Technology
23 D'Rising Sun Bus Terminal
24 Police Station; City Hall
25 Jeepneys to Banaue
27 Von Von Bus to Banaue
28 Dangwa Tranco Bus Terminal

NORTH LUZON

Just ask for Kinad at City Hall or Pines Kitchenette. Plans are in progress to form a guide association with an office on the main street.

Landbank and **PNB** have branches in Bontoc that will change cash and travellers cheques. Landbank gives slightly better exchange rates.

Internet access is available at **XiJen Institute of Technology** (*2nd floor, Fagsao Bldg*) for P50 per hour.

Bontoc Museum
Worth a look, is the Bontoc Museum (*admission P40; open 8am-noon & 1pm-5pm daily*), just up the hill and behind the market square. Outside the main building are replicas of traditional Ifugao, Sagada and Bontoc dwellings. Inside is an array of Igorot artefacts, including Ibaloi, Kalinga and Ifugao baskets, brass gongs with human jawbones as handles (proof the owner has taken a head) and traditional woven clothing. There are also photos of head-hunters and their booty.

Places to Stay & Eat
Ridge Brook Hotel & Restaurant (*doubles with bathroom P600*), away from the bustle on the eastern side of the Chico River, is easily the best place in town. It has large, basic clean rooms. The newer annex just up the road is noisier.

Pines Kitchenette (*doubles with bathroom P500*) is right in the middle of things, but it's a dilapidated place and the rooms without bathroom are barely acceptable. Larger doubles are better but still grungy.

Churya-a Hotel & Restaurant (*doubles with bathroom P300*) is on the 2nd floor and although the roadside rooms can be loud, rooms at the back are recommended.

Eastern Star Hotel (*doubles with/without bathroom P300/100*) is a no-frills place, suitable for a night.

Tchayapan (*doubles with/without bathroom P400/100*) is quite nice and has a popular restaurant with balcony seating.

Cable Cafe (*lunch P90*) has no real competition. There's live music every night – OK it's mostly '80s pop but it's something. No other place stays open past the informal 10pm curfew and you can snack on nachos and drink beer until who knows, maybe even 11pm. Chicken and pork standbys are served in a modern and clean setting.

Shopping
Woven goods made in nearby Samoki are sold in the Bontoc **market** on Sunday. The **Mountain Province Trade Centre** in the Multipurpose Centre on the plaza has handicrafts and woven materials at very good prices. The Bontoc Museum **gift shop** also sells quality items.

Getting There & Away
Dangwa Tranco and D'Rising Sun make the trip to Baguio (P186, seven hours); the first bus leaves at 6am and the last D'Rising Sun bus leaves at 4pm.

Jeepneys and buses to Banaue (P80, two hours) start leaving at 7.30am and the last bus heads up the snaking, high-wire road at 4pm. It certainly shouldn't prevent you from making the trip, but there have been a few recent violent robberies of private vehicles along this route.

Frequent jeepneys to Sagada (P25, one hour) leave from 8.30am to 5.30pm from near the Eastern Star Hotel.

The fact that there is only one jeepney a day to and from Mainit means you should be prepared to spend the night.

There are four jeepneys that go to Maligcong (P20, 40 minutes) between 7.30am and 4.30pm. You can also go by private vehicle with a guide. Kinad, Juliet Soria and Francis Pa-in are all recommended. All three also lead treks to Kalinga; ask for them at City Hall or Pines Kitchenette.

For details on services to Tinglayen see that section later.

AROUND BONTOC
Maligcong & Mainit
The rice terraces of Maligcong, although not built as high into the mountains as those around Banaue, are special in their own right. The best time to visit is between June and September, when the terraces change from green to gold. Maligcong is on the way to the hot springs at Mainit, so you might as well combine the two into a single trip.

From where the Bontoc jeepney stops in Maligcong (17km, two hours), it's a half-hour hike to spectacular stone-walled rice terraces and a small village with some traditional houses.

You can take a steady two-hour downhill hike back to Bontoc from here or stay the night in Maligcong at **Padukar Guest House** (rooms P70) or in Mainit at **Odyssey Guest House** (rooms P150).

See the Bontoc Getting There & Away section earlier for transport information.

Barlig, Kadaclan & Natonin

East of Bontoc, the villages of Barlig, Kada-clan and Natonin have magnificent rice terraces. In Kadaclan you can stay at the **Kadaclan Tourist's Homestay** (ask for Grace Chungalan).

Jeepneys from Bontoc leave for Barlig (1½ hours, 7am & 1.30pm) and for Natonin (six hours, three daily) via Kadaclan (four hours). Be prepared for dust and bone-shaking bumps.

KALINGA PROVINCE

Kalinga is the most pristine and rugged of all the Cordillera provinces, consequently hiking is the main draw. Not only is the landscape unique from Banaue and Sagada – though it does have hanging bridges, water-falls and rice terraces – but ongoing tribal conflicts demand sensitivity and knowledge of the current state of affairs. At the time of writing, the villages of Butbut and Bitwa-gen were off-limits due to sporadic violence and tension over a long-standing boundary dispute. Check the conditions before going.

Despite all of this, the consensus is that it's safe to travel in Kalinga, provided you have a guide, not only to find your way geo-graphically, but to offer advice on behav-iour and suggestions for appropriate gifts; matches are popular, so stock up. In Bontoc you can contact Kinad or Francis-Pa, who is from Kalinga, or else try to find a guide in Tinglayen. Hiking in this region is challeng-ing and made even more difficult in the rain. A sleeping bag is handy if you are planning a long trip. Ask Kinad for information on **white-water rafting** trips on the Chico River.

Tinglayen

A good starting point for treks in Kalinga is Tinglayen (2½ hours from Bontoc, 48km). If you don't come with a guide, you'll need one for hikes in the area. Victor Baculi, the barangay captain of Luplupa, just across the hanging bridge from Tinglayen, is an excel-lent source of information. There's a 30m **waterfall** in the village of Tulgao.

Trekking A good two-hour walk in the im-mediate vicinity is Tinglayen–Ambuto–Liglig–Tinglayen, which takes you through some small rice terraces and villages where a few native houses remain. You may also come across some village elders with tattooed arms, possibly an indication that they were once head-hunters. More commonly you'll see decorative tattoos on women.

An excellent one-day hike is Tinglayen–Ngibat–Butbut–Buscalan–Bugnay–Tinglayen. You have to be in reasonably good shape and

---

The Kalinga & the Outside

The Kalinga have a fierce sense of culture and community, and while they have been successful in shunning outsiders intent upon exploiting the province's natural resources, ongoing boundary dis-putes between villages sometimes erupt into violence. In the past, the area was considered risky for travellers, chiefly due to plans by the national government to construct the Chico Valley dam, which would have completely flooded the Kalinga valley, destroying centuries-old villages and forcing the resettlement of tens of thousands of Kalinga.

The New People's Army (NPA), together with the Kalinga, who were uninterested in communist ideology, joined forces to stop the dam, resulting in often violent fighting against the Philippine mili-tary. Although the project has been stopped, the Kalinga are understandably wary of outsiders, es-pecially as rumours of plans to mine the area continue to circulate.

With the dam project scrapped, travellers need to be more aware of tribal tensions over agricul-tural lands. Over a period of five bloody months in 2001, eight people were killed and many oth-ers wounded in fighting between the Bitwagan and Bugnay (Butbut). And while headhunting is mostly a thing of the past, it's not unheard of for enemy heads or other body parts to be taken as booty. A truce was signed in May 2001 but formal peace talks scheduled to begin in June 2002 have been postponed after the natural death of a young Butbut villager. Considered a bad omen by the Butbut, the death and the ngilin (mourning period) have left the future of the negotiations in doubt.

prepared to negotiate a few precarious sections with steep drop-offs on one side. Take the 7am jeepney from Tinglayen to Bontoc, and get off a few kilometres south of Tinglayen, in the vicinity of Basao, from where the path starts. If you miss the jeepney, it's a one-hour walk to the path. From here it's a steep one-hour climb to Butbut.

From Butbut it's an easy 40-minute walk to the beautiful village of Buscalan, which is surrounded by pretty stone-walled rice terraces and many traditional houses. From Buscalan to Bugnay is the most striking section – it's mostly flat – taking you past some rolling, grassy mountain terrain, and if you're lucky, you'll get a good view of the Sleeping Beauty mountain chain, said to resemble, what else, but a sleeping woman. You should be in Bugnay by 3.30pm to catch the jeepney back to Tinglayen.

Otherwise, it's a long 14km walk back; hiring your own ride back will cost you around P400.

Places to Stay & Eat
You can stay at the **Good Samaritan Guesthouse** (*rooms P150*) or the **Sleeping Beauty Resthouse** (*rooms P150*) in Tinglayen. The **Luplupa Riverside Inn & Restaurant** in Luplupa, can also help you find a guide. Victor Baculi, the barangay captain mentioned previously, will also put you up in his **home**. There is no set fee but you should offer some money upon departure (P100 per person per night). It's also good to bring some gifts, maybe a bottle of gin, fruit or even a chicken.

Be prepared to sleep on the floor and as there are no toilets in the village, a small shovel would be handy. Take all of your rubbish with you when you leave.

There's a **restaurant** across the street from Sleeping Beauty Resthouse but you may want to stock up on food before coming. Tinglayen also has a small **store** that sells water, rice, instant noodles and canned goods.

Getting There & Away
There are four early morning buses and jeepneys from Bontoc that pass through Tinglayen (P55, three hours) on their way to Tabuk. The first leaves from the rotunda at 7am. From Tinglayen to Bontoc, a jeepney leaves at 7am and there are others that pass through, coming from Tabuk.

SOLANO, KIANGAN & LAGAWE
☎ 078
In Ifugao province, Banaue receives all the accolades and attention, but this part of the Cordilleras, usually bypassed by travellers on their way further north, holds some appeal.

Solano (pop 52,000) is a fairly typical commercial centre but it does make a convenient stop for those who want to break up their journey from Manila or from Isabela and Cagayan to the north. The **Alayan Caves**, purported to be the second-largest cave system in the Philippines, is outside the village of Kasibu, 40km (three hours) east of Solano. A guide is always around in Kasibu, where you can also eat.

Kiangan (pop 14,000), believed to be the first human settlement in Ifugao, was the site of some of the fiercest fighting in the Philippines during WWII. A pyramid-shaped **War Memorial Shrine** is dedicated to the Ifugao and American troops who helped force General Yamashita, the 'Tiger of Malaya', to make his informal surrender here in 1945. Nearby is **Million Dollar Hill**, so named because it's believed that's how much it cost the Americans to bomb the Japanese forces. Across the lawn from the shrine is the **Ifugao Museum**, which houses a small collection of Ifugao artefacts. Worried that traditional forms of singing, dancing and chanting will vanish with the next generation, the 1 May **Gotad Ad Kiangan Festival** celebrates Ifugao performing arts. Kiangan is a good place anytime of the year to try the locally manufactured **rice wine**.

Lagawe (pop 15,000), just north across the Ibulao River from Kiangan, is a small bustling provincial capital.

Hiking
All of the following hikes are around Kiangan. **Ambuwaya Lake**, 4km east of town, is a good spot for a swim.

You can hike up into the dramatic **Nagakadan Terraces** and then descend to Maggok village; to really extend your hike you can carry on north, cross three rivers and finally arrive at **Hungduan**.

Kiangan to **Tinoc** is a strenuous full-day hike and nearby are the **Tukukan Sulfur Hot Springs**.

A three-hour hike from Kiangan is **Pankaggawan Cave**; there are other caves in the vicinity.

The Decline of a Wonder

Often (justly) called the eighth wonder of the world, North Luzon's renowned rice terraces are in danger of going the way of the other seven; they once stretched northeast to Cagayan and as far south as Quezon. Especially in the immediate area of Banaue, the terraces are being abandoned and are showing signs of deterioration. No doubt there have been boom and bust cycles over their 2000 year history, but it is only recently that a whole host of environmental and social factors have combined to put their long-term survival in jeopardy.

A severe 1990 earthquake that damaged irrigation systems, El Niño–triggered droughts, and giant earthworms that erode the soil are a few of the natural culprits. Furthermore, the rice variety most suited to the area's cool climate is simply not a high-yield crop (it can sustain a household for only four months) and because it takes so long to mature some Ifugao families sell their rights in the rice terraces and buy property in Nueva Vizcaya and Cagayan, where they can have as many as three plantings a year.

Tourism is regarded by some as the most serious threat. It has encouraged the commercial production of woodcarvings, resulting in the depletion of local forest resources and a dwindling water supply. The water used by tourist services contributes further to this water scarcity.

In addition, lodging facilities are built on property that otherwise would be part of the terraces. But even more importantly, the Ifugao culture that is so closely interwoven with the terraces is eroded as young people especially opt out of the backbreaking field work in favour of more lucrative jobs elsewhere.

The Ifugao Terraces Commission created by President Ramos in 1994 got axed by his successor, President Estrada, who then established the Banaue Rice Terraces Task Force. This agency was abolished in early 2002 by current president, Gloria Macapagal Arroyo. Scientists and local activists left out of the loop rely on the terrace's designation by Unesco as a World Heritage site to bolster their campaign for more and immediate attention.

Places to Stay & Eat

L&M Travellers Inn (☎ 326 7295; 2nd floor SSS Bldg, JP Rizal St, Solano; rooms with fan/air-con & TV P500/600) has clean, well-kept rooms. Try to get a room away from the street or else you'll be bothered by the noise.

Governor's Garden Hotel (☎ 326 6033; J Manzano St, Solano; rooms with air-con & TV P870) is more upmarket but the rooms have seen better days. There's a pool and outdoor garden area.

In Kiangan, **homestays** (beds around P100) are offered; Manuel Dulawan's house is one option. There is also the **Kiangan Youth Hostel** (dorm beds around P100); for more information, visit the Kiangan Municipal Hall or Remi Allaga, next to the youth hostel.

Dutch Pancake House (☎ 326 7981; General Santos St, Solano) has plans to open another branch in Lagawe. The owners Kurt and Dixie are extremely friendly and infor-

mative. They can help arrange accommodation or trips in the area. They serve 50 types of pancakes, and filling European and Filipino dishes.

Getting There & Away

Autobus (which leaves from Sampaloc), Pasay Royal Eagle, Victory Liner and Baliwag make night trips from Manila to Solano around 9pm and arriving in Solano at around 5am. From Solano to Banaue (P58, three hours), the last jeepney leaves at around 5pm.

There are frequent jeepney connections between Solano, Kiangan and Lagawe (P17, one hour) and from Kiangan to Banaue (one hour).

The Kiangan Motor Service runs a midafternoon service (one daily) from Kiangan to Baguio. In Baguio there is one evening trip daily to Kiangan, which leaves from the western end of Burnham Park.

MARTIN HARRIS

NORTH LUZON

BANAUE

☎ 074 • pop 20,500 • elevation 1200m

Hemmed in and dwarfed by the surrounding scenery, Banaue, though far from pristine, sits at the foot of a spectacular display. When the sun sets, the colours emerge and it appears as if the rice terraces' neatly arranged square plots have domesticated the mountains. It's North Luzon's most famous site, touted as the 'Eighth Wonder of the World', and while some travellers coming from the more charming Sagada may be disappointed by the tin, dilapidated buildings, it's difficult not to be moved by the confrontation between man and nature taking place on the mountainside.

They are impressive not only for their symmetry and order but because they were carved over 2000 years ago by the Ifugao, using simple wooden tools. This highly sophisticated irrigation system was a remarkable innovation, utilising bamboo tubes and elaborate mud channels to bring water to the terraces.

April and May are the best times to visit, since this is just prior to harvest, when the sun reflects the bright green colour of the rice shoots. Only one crop of rice per year is planted which means rather unbelievably, rather than exporting rice, Banaue must import rice to survive.

Information

There is a small, often unstaffed, **tourist information centre** in the town hall, where you'll also find the **post office**, but you're

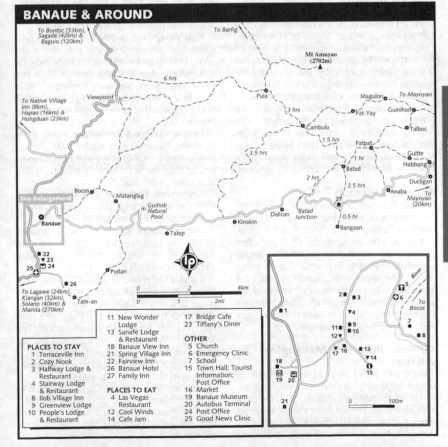

BANAUE & AROUND

To Bontoc (33km),
Sagada (42km) &
Baguio (120km)

To Barlig

Mt Amuyao
(2702m)

6 hrs

To Native Village
Inn (8km),
Hapao (16km) &
Hungduan (23km)

Viewpoint

Pula

Magulon   To Mayoyao

3 hrs   Pat-Yay   Guinihon

Cambulo   Talboc

1.5 hrs   Patpat

3.5 hrs   1 hr   Guitte
Batad   Habbang

2 hrs   2.5 hrs   Duclig-an
Anaba   To
Mayoyao
(20km)

Bocos   Matanglag   27

See Enlargement   Guihob
Natural   Batad
Banaue   Pool   Dalican   Junction   0.5 hr
Kinakin   Bangaan

Talop

22
23
25   24

26

Poitan

To Lagawe (24km),
Kiangan (32km),
Solano (40km) &
Manila (270km)   Tam-an

0   2   4km
0   1   2mi

River

5
2   3   6
1   To
Bocos

11   9
12   10

18   17   16   13
14
1   15
19   20

21   0   100m

NORTH LUZON

PLACES TO STAY	11 New Wonder Lodge	17 Bridge Cafe	5 Church
1 Terraceville Inn	13 Sanafe Lodge & Restaurant	23 Tiffany's Diner	6 Emergency Clinic
2 Cozy Nook	18 Banaue View Inn	**OTHER**	7 School
3 Halfway Lodge & Restaurant	21 Spring Village Inn		15 Town Hall; Tourist Information; Post Office
4 Stairway Lodge & Restaurant	22 Fairview Inn		16 Market
8 Ilob Village Inn	26 Banaue Hotel		19 Banaue Museum
9 Greenview Lodge	27 Family Inn		20 Autobus Terminal
10 People's Lodge & Restaurant	**PLACES TO EAT**		24 Post Office
	4 Las Vegas Restaurant		25 Good News Clinic
	12 Cool Winds		
	14 Cafe Jam		

better off getting information at your hotel. A good, detailed map of the surrounding area is P10. Fixed rates for jeepneys and tricycles are posted around town.

It's a good idea to have all the pesos you'll need before coming to Banaue, as the exchange rates are a little low. Many hotels will change cash and the Banaue Hotel will change travellers cheques (bring the original purchase receipt and your passport).

Guides aren't necessary for hikes to Batad, Bangaan, Cambulo and even Pula, but they will make it easier and probably more interesting. The paths are usually clear but anytime you're hiking on the rice terraces, it's not difficult to find yourself one level off and then be forced to backtrack a long way.

The Viewpoint

It's only a 10-minute ride (P100 return by tricycle) northeast, on the road to Bontoc, to the viewpoint, where a cluster of souvenir shops conceal a small platform. The view of the surrounding terraces is magnificent, but it's somewhat marred by the unsightly tin roofs of the town below. You can hike back to Banaue from the viewpoint (three hours) but it requires steady balance to navigate your way along the edge of the terraces. The path is clear most of the way if you head straight back to the road from Bocos, skipping Matanglag. The trail on the detour from Bocos to Matanglag is a little less obvious.

Banaue Museum

Banaue Museum (*admission P30; open 8am-5pm daily*), next to the Banaue View Inn, contains an interesting collection of Ifugao, Kalinga and Bontoc artefacts. There are a few photos of the 'death chair', in which a corpse was placed for up to two weeks before being buried. The bodies of the murdered didn't get the chair. They were instead propped up against the house in uncomfortable positions and neglected in order to make the soul angry and inspire it to seek vengeance.

Tam-an, Poitan & Matanglag Villages

Tourist brochures still advertise these as artist's villages, but you're not likely to see a whole lot of creating going on. Still, the two-hour hike from Tam-an (down some concrete steps a short distance behind the Banaue Hotel) through Poitan and back to Banaue

will take you past some traditional Ifugao houses and pretty views of small rice terraces. Much of the path follows a century-old irrigation canal. On reaching the road from Poitan, it's another 30 minutes to Matanglag, starting from the steps on the opposite side, a little towards Banaue. There are a couple of bronzesmiths at work in Matanglag and a small waterfall where you can wash.

Places to Stay

Banaue View Inn (☎ 386 4078; *dorm beds P150, doubles with bathroom P600*) is at the top of a hill overlooking the town. Rooms are pleasant and clean but it's a good idea to have mosquito repellent since the windows are not airtight. Karen, the owners' daughter, is a great source of information. The owners will store your bags if you travel elsewhere in the area. If the connection is up, you can access the Internet for P120 per hour.

Ilob Village Inn (☎ 386 4052; *cottage with common bathroom P500*) is just across the river. It intends to offer dorm beds as well.

Sanafe Lodge & Restaurant (☎ 0919 891 6366; *singles/doubles with bathroom P400/700*) is a wood-panelled lodge with small, homey rooms that get really good light in the afternoon.

People's Lodge & Restaurant (☎ 386 4014; e *jerwin_T@yahoo.com; rooms P100, doubles with bathroom P400*) is popular but its rooms are nothing special. There's a balcony with a nice view to the rear.

Greenview Lodge (☎ 386 4021; *doubles P100*) has well-kept, basic rooms and a good restaurant down below.

Spring Village Inn (☎ 386 4037; *doubles P600*) is just south of town. The rooms have wooden floors and are cheerful and clean; some have verandas.

Banaue Hotel (☎ 386 4087, 02-524 2502 in Manila; *doubles with bathroom P1200*) is the large, low-slung white building a few minutes from town. Unless it's busy, you may feel inspired to act out scenes from 'The Shining' – depressing long hallways leading to rooms with water-stained carpets. But it does have a restaurant, gift shop and swimming pool (P50 for non-guests).

Fairview Inn (☎ 386 4002; *singles/doubles with bathroom P300/600*) is south of town, near the Banaue Hotel, and has bright rooms that get good afternoon light. Some have balconies.

Native Village Inn *(houses with bathroom P400)* is about 45 minutes from Banaue on the way to Hapao. It's in a rather striking location, perched atop a cliff with views of the surrounding terraces. Set in a pretty and well-kept garden are seven traditional Ifugao houses with immaculate bathrooms and hot water. A large pit fireplace warms up the restaurant when it's cold.

Places to Eat
Restaurants in town close when all the lights in town go off (around 9pm).

Cafe Jam *(meals P110)* is the nicest looking restaurant in town. The food is good but it doesn't seem to stick to regular hours.

People's Lodge & Restaurant *(dinner P150)* is a popular place to eat or hang-out and serves Filipino classics.

Las Vegas Canteen & Restaurant is clean and the food is good.

Bridge Cafe & Restaurant *(meals P50)*, up a steep flight of stairs, serves inexpensive chicken and pork dishes.

Tiffany's Diner serves similar quality food as the rest but it's best to avoid the pizza, which is made with tomato paste and cheese that looks like it came from a can.

Entertainment
Banaue shuts down pretty early. Most of the restaurants close at 9pm and there are no bars or late-night hang-outs. Whenever there's a large group staying at the **Banaue Hotel**, it's likely the owners will put on a performance of traditional Ifugao dancing.

Getting There & Away
From Manila, Dangwa Tranco and Autobus have direct buses to Banaue (nine hours) from Sampaloc. From Banaue to Manila, a Dangwa Tranco bus leaves in the early morning and an Autobus in the afternoon. It's a good idea to reserve your ticket the day before: Dangwa Tranco tickets can be reserved at Niclyn's store, near the town hall, and Autobus tickets at Esther's, near the market. You can also take a jeepney to Solano (P58, three hours), from where buses leave frequently for Manila.

Two buses on their way to Bontoc pass through Banaue in the morning (P80, two hours). There are no direct buses or jeepneys to Sagada so you can either first travel to Bontoc or hire a private jeepney (P2500).

You can catch a tricycle t (P400 round trip same day, P7... up on another day or from Banga... Hapao (P400 round-trip, one hour one way).

See Mayoyao Getting There & Away later for details on services to Mayoyao.

Dangwa Tranco and Autobus travel between Banaue and Baguio (P220, nine hours) via the less scenic southern route through San Jose and Bayombong. Dangwa leaves at 7am and Autobus leaves at 6pm from the top of the steps at the foot of the driveway leading to the museum in Banaue.

Be early, though, since they leave when full. From Baguio, Dangwa departs at around 7am and 7pm and Autobus leaves at 7:30pm. The other climbs up along the spectacular Halsema Hwy from Baguio to Bontoc and then to Banaue.

There are frequent jeepneys that connect Solano and Banaue (P58, three hours), the last leaving both places around 5pm. It's an hour to Kiangan (P40), a little less to Lagawe (P45); both are serviced by frequent jeepneys.

AROUND BANAUE
Besides Banaue, four other Ifugao rice terraces are included on the Unesco World Heritage list: Batad, Mayoyao, Hapao and Kiangan (see earlier). With the exception of Batad, these terraces can all be seen from the road.

Batad & Around
pop 1100 • elevation 902m
Adjectives fall short of accurately describing the amphitheatre-shaped rice terraces of Batad. The village itself sits in the middle, rather incongruously, since it's strange to think that people actually live and work in such a tremendously beautiful place.

It's a 40-minute hike to the 30m-high **Tappia Waterfall**, where you can sunbathe on the rocks or swim in the chilly water. To get here, walk down to the village and then up to the promontory, just to the left of the Waterfall Side Lodge. The path down the other side is quite steep and taxing and should be avoided in the rain.

You can reach the top of **Mt Amuyao** (2702m), which looms in the distance, in a day and you can sleep at the radar station on the top. You'll need a guide (P800 per day) for the arduous hike.

The recommended hike out of Batad ends up by the road a short distance from **Bangaan** where you can take walks to appreciate the beauty of the surrounding rice terraces. You can be dropped here by a jeepney or tricycle.

If you feel like a longer hike to/from Batad, try one of the following routes:

Batad–Cambulo–Kinakin The hike from Batad to Cambulo is around two hours and from Cambulo to Kinakin (13km) it's 3½ hours. There are some steep sections and the hike is demanding in parts, but you're rewarded by the thrill and beauty of edging along the terraces.

The path from Cambulo to Kinakin is still being made into a road. There is accommodation in remote Cambulo (see Places to Stay & Eat later), but the town is nowhere near as beautiful as Batad.

Batad–Cambulo–Pula–Banaue Road The hike from Batad to Cambulo is around two hours, from Cambulo to Pula is about three hours and from Pula to the road, it's about six hours.

If you take this route, you might plan on spending a night in Pula, although as there's no official accommodation here it's best to try to arrange a place to stay before leaving Banaue; otherwise, ask Pula's barangay captain for assistance.

Much of the hike is through rice terraces. The section from Cambulo to Pula follows a winding river, with terraces carved high into the mountains on either side. About halfway between Cambulo and Pula you'll cross over a small **hanging bridge**. Pula is a tiny collection of Ifugao houses on a hilly outcrop.

Just outside of Pula on the way back to Banaue, there's a **waterfall** and a deep **swimming pool** under a bridge. The path from Pula to the road is through lush forest, a nice change after so many rice terraces.

Places to Stay & Eat Accommodation in Batad is primarily found on a spectacular cliff overlooking the village. **Rita's**, **Hillside** and **Simon's** all have restaurants and similar quality, exceptionally clean rooms for P50. Simon's has the most extensive menu (including *malawech* – Yemeni flatbread) and a large terrace. The very friendly Rita's has solar-powered electricity for a room where

you can eat and read and also makes fresh-brewed coffee.

Waterfall Side Lodge *(rooms P50)*, is perched atop a cliff on the opposite side of the valley. You pass by here on the way to the Tappia Waterfall.

In Bangaan, **Family Inn** *(rooms P150, nipa huts or bungalows P400)* is a nice, relaxing place with a small restaurant.

In Cambulo, **Cambulo Friends Inn** and **Cambulo Riverside** have basic rooms for P50. Both places can provide meals.

Getting There & Away There are three ways to hike into Batad (all of which can be walked in reverse). The first involves a strenuous two-hour hike from Batad junction, most of the way uphill, except for the final 40-minute downhill section from the small kiosk. You can get to the Batad junction by tricycle (P400 round trip same day, P700 to be picked up on another day from junction or Bangaan) or jeepney from Banaue.

For the second option you can be dropped off at the kiosk by motorcycle (P350 one way, 1½ hours) and then just do the downhill part by foot. Many tricycle drivers are willing to unhook their sidecars, but this should be arranged in advance. Taking motorised transport is not a bad idea if you want to avoid hiking the section of the road that's being carved out of the mountainside and paved, or if you plan to hike into and out of Batad on the same day.

The third option is a marvellous two-hour hike beginning near the junction to Bangaan. (Ask at the Family Inn for directions to the trailhead.) The path is very clearly marked most of the way but as you near Batad it can be slightly confusing because you can't really see the village until you reach Rita's.

It's easier to explain if you are leaving Batad for Bangaan: take the path behind Rita's down to the small river at the bottom. Cross to the other side and then cross the small concrete bridge to the left.

Follow the clearly marked path up to the top of the hill. When you come to a few houses, take any path that leads you down and slightly to the right and then you should be able to pick up the main path again. Do not keep walking past the homes (you will have gone too far). The rest of the way, the path is very narrow in some parts but always offers fantastic views.

Mayoyao
pop 14,000 • elevation 1157m
Some 40km and four hours east of Banaue are the stone-walled Mayoyao rice terraces. Home to the Itananga and Ayyangan, Mayoyao also saw some of the last fighting in the Philippines during WWII. From the **Akakoy Viewpoint**, 600m from the town hall, you can see all of central Mayoyao and the Isabela plateau. Local legend has it that a beautiful woman named Mahencha jumped into the water at the **O'phaw Mahencha Falls**, 6km from town, to retrieve a necklace lost while she was bathing. You can bathe in a pool here, hopefully without losing any jewellery, or at **Tenogtog Falls**, 5km from town. There are a few **burial caves** in the vicinity and you can reach **Mt Amuyao** (2628m) from here, although you'll need a guide.

Popular Lodge (dorm beds P50) has a room that can sleep three and meals can be arranged. It's also easy to find a local family to put you up.

Getting There & Away Jeepneys leave from Banaue in the morning for the three- to four-hour trip to Mayoyao. A motorcycle can make the journey in about 1½ hours but the road is extremely bumpy, or you can rent a private jeepney (P2100 return the same day).

Hapao
pop 2000 • elevation 1000m
Spread out over the valley floor, the rice terraces in Hapao, 15km northwest of Banaue (P400 by tricycle round-trip, one hour one way), are dazzling. The ride itself offers spectacular scenery that warrants the trip.

To walk to a small **pool** beside a river, take the concrete steps behind the viewpoint and turn left at the bottom. Follow the paved irrigation canal for about 10 minutes until you reach a small group of houses. It's about another 15 minutes to the river, where you'll probably need to cool off in the refreshing water. Though it's a short, easy walk, there is no shade and the sun can be relentless. To return a different way, you can follow the pathway back to the houses and then uphill to the Hapao Elementary School, further up the road from where you began. You can get water and sodas from a *sari-sari* but there is no lodging in Hapao.

BANGUED
☎ 074 • pop 39,000
Bangued is the commercial centre of Abra, one of Luzon's least travelled and most economically depressed provinces. The town itself has little appeal, but is the jumping-off point for treks to remote highland towns populated by the Itneg (also known as the Tingguian). Bangued is in a valley so it

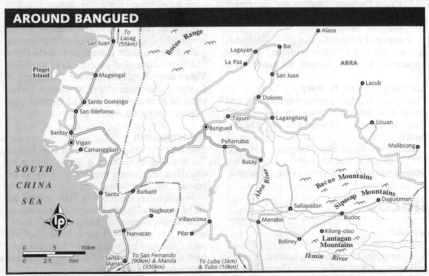

AROUND BANGUED

SOUTH
CHINA
SEA

NORTH LUZON

doesn't enjoy the cooler climates of Abra's high-altitude towns.

Simple joys are available in Bangued: watching the sun rise over the Cordilleras from the banks of the Abra river in Callaba or taking a stroll up to **Victoria Park**, from where you can get a view of the famous Sleeping Beauty mountain range and the town below.

You can also walk across a precarious **hanging bridge** to the Itneg village of **Peñarrubia**, a 10-minute tricycle ride from town. The village is trying to revive the indigenous art of **natural dyeing**. Mang Luis is one of the few Itneg artists still versed in this dying art. The Luis family embroidery is known as *kinamayan,* with designs representing rice, hands, caterpillars, horses and other traditional symbols. Their weavings and other handicrafts from the region are sold in the trade centre across from the capitol building in Bangued.

From Bangued, jeepneys make daily trips to the highland villages of **Sallapadan** (three hours), **Bucloc** (six hours), **Daguioman** (seven hours) and **Boliney** (seven hours), all southeast of Bangued, from where it's possible to trek to Itneg villages.

Places to Stay & Eat
King David Palace Hotel (☎ 752 8404; *doubles with air-con P650)* is a standard, modern hotel that has seen better days.

Marysol Pension *(doubles with air-con & with/without bathroom P400/250)* has small, dark ordinary rooms.

Diocesan Pastoral Centre *(rooms with air-con & bathroom P350)* is affiliated with the church on the plaza. Rooms are acceptable.

Getting There & Away
Philippine Rabbit, Dominion Transit and Partas Bus have services to/from Caloocan City and Cubao in Manila (P21, eight hours, hourly).

Partas has buses from Bangued to Baguio (P150, five hours, three daily) and there are frequent minibuses to Vigan (P40, 1½ hours).

Ilocos

VIGAN
☎ 077 ● pop 45,000
The antiquated Spanish-era mansions, cobblestone streets and *kalesa* (horse-drawn carriages) found in Vigan give the city a touch of character.

Located near where the Govantes River meets the South China Sea, Vigan became a convenient stop on the Silk Route linking Asia, the Middle East and Europe, and a thriving trading post where gold, logs and beeswax were bartered for goods from around the world.

In 1572 Spanish conquistador Juan de Salcedo (grandson of Legazpi) took possession of the bustling international port. Salcedo became the lieutenant governor of the Ilocos region, and Vigan became the centre of the political, religious and commercial activities of the north. It became a hotbed of social dissent against the Spanish when, in 1762, Diego Silang captured Vigan and named it the capital of Free Ilocos. He was eventually assassinated (the Spanish paid a close friend of Silang to shoot him in the back), and his wife, Gabriela Silang, took over. The first woman to lead a revolt in the Philippines, she was eventually captured and publicly hanged in the town square.

The city is struggling to maintain its colonial era buildings, which did well just to survive WWII. In December of 2000, Vigan was designated a Unesco World Heritage site, however it's not clear how the dual demands of preservation and development will play out.

A good time to visit is during the first week of May, when the city throws the **Viva Vigan Binatbatan Festival**, based around the removal of the cotton seeds in preparing yarn. There is street dancing, a fashion show, a *kalesa* parade and of course lots of food. The **Vigan town fiesta**, held in the third week of January, commemorates the town's patron saint, St Paul the Apostle, with a parade and musical performances.

Information
You can get information from **city hall** or the new **Vigan Culture & Trade Center** located in the former home of poet Leona Florentino, on Florentino St.

Just off Plaza Burgos is **PNB**, where the ATM accepts Cirrus, Plus, MasterCard and Visa cards. Nearby is **Equitable PCI Bank**, which has an ATM accepting MasterCard and Cirrus. There are also a number of **banks** on Quezon Ave, the city's modern commercial thoroughfare.

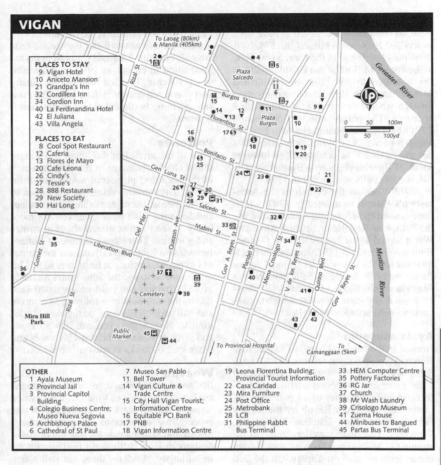

VIGAN

To Laoag (80km)
& Manila (405km)

Plaza
Salcedo

Plaza
Burgos

0   50   100m
0   50   100yd

Govantes River

Mestizo River

Mira Hill
Park

Public
Market

To Provincial Hospital

To
Camanggaan (5km)

PLACES TO STAY
9 Vigan Hotel
10 Aniceto Mansion
21 Grandpa's Inn
32 Cordillera Inn
34 Gordion Inn
40 La Ferdinandina Hotel
42 El Juliana
43 Villa Angela

PLACES TO EAT
8 Cool Spot Restaurant
12 Caferia
13 Flores de Mayo
20 Cafe Leona
26 Cindy's
27 Tessie's
28 888 Restaurant
29 New Society
30 Hai Long

OTHER
1 Ayala Museum
2 Provincial Jail
3 Provincial Capitol
   Building
4 Colegio Business Centre;
   Museo Nueva Segovia
5 Archbishop's Palace
6 Cathedral of St Paul

7 Museo San Pablo
11 Bell Tower
14 Vigan Culture &
    Trade Centre
15 City Hall Vigan Tourist;
    Information Centre
16 Equitable PCI Bank
17 PNB
18 Vigan Information Centre

19 Leona Florentina Building;
    Provincial Tourist Information
22 Casa Caridad
23 Mira Furniture
24 Post Office
25 Metrobank
28 LCB
31 Philippine Rabbit
    Bus Terminal

33 HEM Computer Centre
35 Pottery Factories
36 RG Jar
37 Church
38 Mr Wash Laundry
39 Crisologo Museum
41 Zuema House
44 Minibuses to Bangued
45 Partas Bus Terminal

NORTH LUZON

HEM computer centre *(32 Gov A Reyes St; open 8am-8.30pm daily)* offers Internet access for P60 per hour.

Mestizo District

Vigan's old town, popularly known in the past as 'Kasanglayan' (Where the Chinese Live), contains the largest concentration of ancestral homes and other colonial-era architecture. The area is bounded roughly by Plaza Burgos, Gov A Reyes St, Quirino Blvd and Abaya St. It is centred around Plaridel St and Crisologo St, where most of the tourist shops are located.

The colonial mansions here were built by Chinese merchants who settled, intermarried and, by the 19th century, had become the city's elite. Although generally considered Spanish, the architecture is actually a combination of Mexican, Chinese and Filipino styles (eg, the sliding *capiz* shell windows are of Filipino design). Several homes are open to the public, including **Casa Caridad** and **Nolasco House**. Knock on the door and ask the owners' permission or coordinate a visit through city hall.

Plaza Salcedo & Plaza Burgos

Vigan has two main squares: Plaza Salcedo, dominated on one end by the Cathedral of St Paul; and the more lively Plaza Burgos, where locals stroll and hang out.

The interesting **Cathedral of St Paul** is built in 'earthquake baroque' style (ie, thick walled and massive), after an earlier incarnation was damaged by two quakes in 1619 and

1627. The construction of the original church of wood and thatch is believed to have been supervised by Salcedo himself in 1574.

At the eastern end of the church complex, at the corner of Burgos and Crisologo Sts, is the entrance to the recently established **Museo San Pablo**, dedicated to conservation through what it describes as a faith-culture approach. The photo collection (admission P10) of a German pharmacist who lived in Vigan for a number of years in the late 1800s deserves a look. The octagonal **bell tower** is south of the church, across Burgos St. The oldest of its bells was forged in 1776.

Slightly behind the church is the **Archbishop's Palace**, completed in 1783, which once housed the ecclesiastical court. During the Philippine Revolution/Spanish American War it served as the headquarters of General Emilio Aguinaldo in 1898, and then as headquarters for US forces under Colonel James Parker in 1899. Inside is the **Museo Nueva Segovia** (admission P10; open 8.30am-11.30am & 2pm-5pm Mon-Fri), which houses ecclesiastical artefacts and relics.

Ayala Museum
Housed in the ancestral home of Father José Burgos, Ayala Museum (admission P10; open 8.30am-11.30am & 1.30pm-4.30pm Tues-Sat) is an extensive collection of Ilocano artefacts, including a series of 14 paintings depicting the 1807 Basi Revolt by the locally famed painter Don Esteban Villanueva. Weavings, Tingguian jewellery, musical instruments, pottery, and farming and fishing implements are also on display. On the 2nd floor is the Ilocano Hall of Fame, with photos and captions describing the achievements of famous Ilocano.

Next door to the Ayala Museum is the **provincial jail**, built in 1657. Several leaders of dissent against the US forces in 1899 were detained in this jail and former president Quirino was also born here in 1890, while his father was the jail's warden.

Crisologo Museum
The Crisologo family, one of Vigan's most prominent, has converted their home (open 8.30am-11.30am & 1.30pm-4.30pm Sun-Fri) into a strange but interesting shrine to former governor and congressman Floro Crisologo. In addition to the usual fare of books, photos and other personal items, is the 1940 Chevy

the governor was driving when he was ambushed in 1961. He survived this attempt on his life but was not so lucky the second time around. The blood-stained pants from his assassination in church in 1970 are preserved in a glass case. The 2nd floor is kept mostly as it was when occupied. Check out the massive perfume bottle collection in the master bedroom.

Potteries
Prior to the arrival of the Spanish, Chinese settlers took advantage of the abundant clay in the area and pioneered a still-active industry. The *burnay* earthen jars are used in the fermentation of *basi* (sugarcane wine) and *bagoong* (fish paste), but you are more likely to see them scattered about in homes and gardens. There are a couple of pottery factories on Liberation Blvd, near the corner of Gomez St, or you can head over to RG Jar on Gomez St to see the 50m-long kiln made in 1823, which can hold nearly 1000 jars. Kevin the *kalabaw* is employed as a mixer and will periodically walk on the clay. In addition to *burnay* jars, you can buy all types and sizes of beautiful brown-clay vases and other knick-knacks at reasonable prices.

Weaving
In Camanggaan village, just a 10-minute tricycle ride southeast of Vigan, you can watch weavers hard at work at their looms. It's an especially good place to purchase blankets, towels and placemats at unbeatable prices in designs that are difficult to find elsewhere. In barangay Mindoro, there are still a few weavers making *binakol* weavings that incorporate a traditional psychedelic-looking design.

Places to Stay
The relatively attractive exteriors of some of the hotels belie rooms that are of less than comparable quality. The following hotels are all in and around Vigan's Mestizo District.

El Juliana (☎ 722 2994; Liberation Blvd; doubles with bathroom, air-con & TV P700) has large, basic rooms. Access to the pool costs P40, even for hotel guests.

Aniceto Mansion (☎ 722 2383; 1 Mena Crisologo St; rooms with bathroom, air-con & TV P1200) has an immaculately restored interior and features large family portraits in the stairwell and an eating area that resembles a series of medieval chambers. There is also a small plant-filled garden out the back. Unfortunately, the quality of the rooms is average.

Villa Angela *(☎ 722 2914; 26 Quirino Blvd; rooms with fan P715, with air-con & bathroom P1320)* is also well preserved and its majestic hallway and living room retain an old-world charm and authenticity. The rooms have high ceilings and old-fashioned beds. Breakfast is included.

Grandpa's Inn *(☎ 722 2118; 1 Bonifacio St; rooms with/without bathroom & fan P500/ 300; rooms with air-con & bathroom P800)* is the place to stay if you want to sleep in a *kalesa*. Only two rooms have these very charming carriages-cum-beds.

Exposed brick, old sewing machines and other antiques lend the Inn character and clutter. There is a nice, modern café open until midnight where you can get coffee, beer and wine.

Gordion Inn *(☎ 722 2526; V de los Reyes St; rooms with bathroom, air-con & TV P1200)* is easy to spot with its newly painted blue and yellow facade. The rooms are clean but basic and there is a small outdoor restaurant that serves vegetarian food. Breakfast is included.

Cordillera Inn *(☎ 722 2727; Mena Crisologo; rooms with bathroom & fan/air-con P850/1300)* is located in the heart of the Mestizo district, but its rooms are old and crumbling.

Places to Eat
Cafe Leona *(Mena Crisologo St; dishes P120-300)*, just off Plaza Burgos, serves excellent Japanese and Ilocano specials. It's a deservedly popular place and stays open late.

Flores de Mayo *(Florentino St)*, next to the Vigan Culture & Trade Center, serves Filipino and Ilocano meals like *longanisa* (sausage) and tiger prawns.

Cool Spot Restaurant *(Burgos St; dishes P120-200)*, located in a large open-air pavilion behind the Vigan Hotel, focuses on pork, with at least 16 varieties, but still finds space on the menu for seafood and vegetable dishes.

Tessie's, New Society and **Hai Long**, located next to each other on Gen Luna St, all serve similar quality Filipino and Chinese dishes.

Caferia *(Plaza Maestro)* is an American-style coffee shop with frosticcinos and other

cold coffee-based drinks and a selection of pastries and cakes.

Evening **street stalls** *(Plaza Burgos)* serve cheap, tasty snacks such as *empenadas* (deep-fried flour tortillas filled with shrimp, cabbage and egg) and *okoy* (deep-fried shrimp omelettes).

There are several air-con fast-food joints on Quezon Ave, including **Cindy's,** which serves decent Filipino-style dishes.

Shopping
There are several antique shops in the Mestizo District, which are fun to browse in but mostly carry reproductions. Ornate wooden furniture is produced in Vigan, and shops such as **Mira Furniture** *(cnr Bonifacio & Plaridel Sts)* take orders for custom-made furniture. *Abel* (a type of weaving) can be found in the **public market**, at **Rowildas** *(Mena Crisologo St; Camanggaan)* and **Hi-Q** *(Salcedo St)*. Try **RG Jar** *(Gomez St)* for clay jars.

Getting There & Away
There are many bus services to/from Manila; try Philippine Rabbit to/from Caloocan City (P312 air-con, nine hours, hourly) or Partas Bus from Cubao. Both companies also have hourly buses from Vigan to Baguio (P180, five hours) that pass through San Fernando (La Union; P139).

Philippine Rabbit and Partas make frequent morning trips to Laoag (P80, 1½ hours), less often in the afternoon. You can also go to Bantay (just north on the National Hwy), and wait for a Laoag-bound minibus at the Caltex petrol station.

Frequent minibuses to Bangued (P40, 1½ hours) leave from next to the public market.

Getting Around
Vigan is one of the few remaining towns in the Philippines where *kalesa* are still in use. If you stay in the city centre, the cost of a *kalesa* ride is the same as a tricycle ride (P5). If you go out of the city centre, negotiate a price beforehand.

AROUND VIGAN
Worth the one-hour trip south is the **Santa Maria Church**. Designated a World Heritage site by Unesco in 1990, this massive baroque structure, built in 1769, sits atop a hill overlooking the town of Santa Maria. The church was used as a fortress during the

Philippine Revolution in 1896. Stairs on one side lead down an overgrown path into an old walled cemetery with a crumbling altar.

Also worth a visit is the architecturally interesting, primitive baroque-style **Church of San Vincente**, south of Vigan and not far from Santa Maria. Chinese and Japanese missionaries were once housed here. Inside the church the holy-water pits are Qing dynasty blue-and-white ware.

There is a branch of the **National Museum** *(open 8.30am-11.30am & 1.30pm-4.30pm Mon-Fri)* in Magsingal, 11km north of Vigan, where Ilocano relics are on display. The two-storey museum houses pottery, porcelain, baskets, farming equipment and a wooden sugarcane crusher used for making sugarcane wine. Next door is the **Magsingal**

Church (1827), which houses two rather interesting sculptures of pregnant-looking angel mermaids.

LAOAG
☎ 077 • pop 95,000

Long before Laoag (la-**wahg**) was established in 1580 with St William the Hermit as its Patron Saint, Chinese and Japanese merchants visited the area, renowned for its gold mines. Laoag eventually became the capital of Ilocos Norte and loyal Marcos country. Imee Marcos, daughter of Ferdinand and Imelda, is a congresswoman here, and her brother Ferdinand R (Bong Bong) Marcos is the current governor.

There's not a whole lot to do in Laoag itself, although it attracts a fair number of

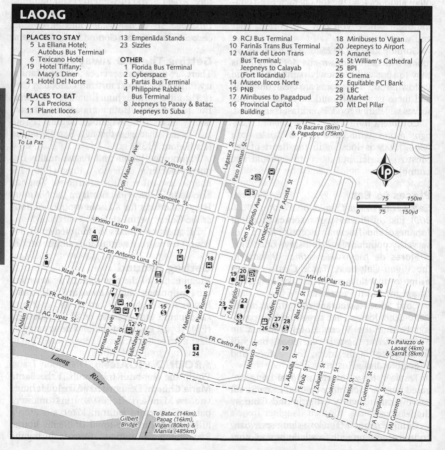

LAOAG

PLACES TO STAY	13 Empenāda Stands	9 RCJ Bus Terminal	18 Minibuses to Vigan
5 La Elliana Hotel;	23 Sizzles	10 Farinās Trans Bus Terminal	20 Jeepneys to Airport
Autobus Bus Terminal		12 Maria del Leon Trans	21 Amanet
6 Texicano Hotel	**OTHER**	Bus Terminal;	24 St William's Cathedral
19 Hotel Tiffany;	1 Florida Bus Terminal	Jeepneys to Calayab	25 BPI
Macy's Diner	2 Cyberspace	(Fort Ilocandia)	26 Cinema
21 Hotel Del Norte	3 Partas Bus Terminal	14 Museo Ilocos Norte	27 Equitable PCI Bank
	4 Philippine Rabbit	15 PNB	28 LBC
PLACES TO EAT	Bus Terminal	17 Minibuses to Pagadpud	29 Market
7 La Preciosa	8 Jeepneys to Paoay & Batac;	16 Provincial Capitol	30 Mt Del Pillar
11 Planet Ilocos	Jeepneys to Suba	Building	

tourists from Taiwan. It's a logical stop if you are heading farther north and there are some interesting places to visit around town.

Laoag's main commercial thoroughfare is Rizal Ave. Here **Bank of the Philippine Islands** (BPI) has an ATM that accepts AmEx, MasterCard and Cirrus. The **PNB** branch near the capitol building is a hassle-free place to exchange travellers cheques at good rates.

You can check the Internet at **Amanet** (MH del Pilar St) for P50 per hour.

The new **Museo Ilocos Norte** (☎ 770 4587; Gen Luna St; admission P20; open 9am-5pm Tues-Sat), housed in the historic Tabacalera warehouse, has an excellent collection of Ilocano, Igorot and Itneg cultural artefacts. Lectures and performances can be arranged for groups.

Places to Stay
La Elliana Hotel (☎ 771 4876; Rizal Ave; rooms with bathroom, air-con & TV P650), only a few minutes away from the bustle and smog, is in a modern multi-storey building that's in better condition than the other options around the city centre. Rooms are clean and the staff competent.

Hotel Tiffany (☎ 770 3550; Gen Segundo Ave; doubles with bathroom, air-con & TV P730), above Macy's Diner, seems to have been designed with similar aesthetic principles in mind – Hollywood Art Deco. Pink and blue walls are complemented by silver stars. Basic rooms, however, are less than stellar.

Hotel Del Norte (☎ 772 0209; 26 Fonacier St; singles with fan P225, doubles with air-con & TV P750) is not so inviting, even though it has large, clean rooms with bathroom.

Palazzo De Laoag Hotel (☎ 773 1842; e palazzo@iln.csi.com.ph; 27 P Paterni St; rooms with bathroom, air-con & TV P1080) is a step up in quality and value from the other hotels in the city centre and is only a short tricycle ride to the east. The rooms are small but clean with nice bathrooms. It has a pool, gym and business centre. Its homey **Café Theresa Coffee Shop** serves good omelettes for breakfast.

Fort Ilocandia Resort (☎ 772 1166; w www .fortilocandiaresortcasino.com; Barangay Calayab; rooms with bathroom P4600), 9km south of town on the beach, was originally built by the Marcos family for their daughter Irene's wedding reception. The low-slung sprawling complex now provides a whole host of non-

matrimonial-related facilities like a shooting range, paint ball and archery. Marketed primarily at tourists who fly in directly from Taiwan and Hong Kong, it has the works, including an attractive pool and beach access. Rooms are of the standard you would expect for the price.

Places to Eat
La Preciosa (Rizal Ave; mains P120) is highly recommended for its large portions of delicious Ilocano specialties. The soups are enough for four.

Planet Ilocos (Balintawak St) is what it sounds like – a place to try the full spectrum of local cuisine. There is a set menu with seafood, steaks and hotpot.

Macy's Diner (Gen Segundo Ave; full meals P180), under Hotel Tiffany, plays the 1950s American-style diner to the hilt, replete with large photos of Marilyn Monroe, James Dean and Elvis, not to mention hamburgers, hot dogs and refreshing shakes. Filipino dishes are available as well.

Sizzles (Gen Segundo Ave) is not easy to spot, on the 2nd floor of a building just around the corner from Rizal Ave. It's also not easy to get service but if you do, you can enjoy a steak at a reasonable price.

A number of **empanada stands** along Rizal Ave, are a good place to pick up a snack on your way to one of the nearby bus terminals.

Getting There & Away
Laoag International Airlines (☎ 772 1793, 02-551 9729 in Manila) flies to/from Manila (P2000, three weekly) and to/from Basco (three weekly). **Philippine Airlines** (☎ 772 1166, 02-400 0723 in Manila), whose office is in the Fort Ilocandia Resort, also flies to/from Manila (P2200, three weekly). Cathay Pacific has direct flights to/from Hong Kong and Taiwan.

Jeepneys to the airport (P15, 10 minutes) leave from Fonacier St. If you have an early flight, take a tricycle, as jeepneys don't start filling up until mid-morning.

Fariñas Trans, Autobus, Dominion Trans, Philippine Rabbit, RCJ, Partas, Franco and Maria de Leon Trans all have frequent buses to/from Manila (P435, 10 hours) from Sampaloc, Caloocan City and Cubao.

Minibuses to Pagudpud (P40, 1½ hours) leave every 30 minutes or so from behind the Provincial Capitol Building. You can also take any Tuguegarao-bound bus and get off on the highway at Pagudpud, although you'll have to take a tricycle into town. Florida, Autobus and RCJ have frequent buses to Tuguegarao.

Frequent minibuses leave from behind the Capitol Building for Vigan (1½ hours). Philippine Rabbit and Partas also have services to Vigan (P80) and to Baguio (P240).

Philippine Rabbit has hourly buses to Baguio (6½ hours) and Batac (P5).

Jeepneys to Batac and Paoay leave from Hernando Ave. Calayab-bound jeepneys go to Fort Ilocandia Resort.

AROUND LAOAG
Batac

The **Marcos Museum & Mausoleum** (Barangay Lacub; admission free; open 9am-noon & 1pm-4pm daily) should be visited, if only to contemplate the strange anonymity of Ferdinand Marcos' (1917–89) final resting place. It's a sign of the family's continued political influence and lingering ambivalence as to his legacy, most especially for Ilocano, some of whom benefited from Marcos' largesse, that the body was allowed to be returned to his boyhood home. All the same, the Bureau of Internal Revenue constantly threatens to 'evict' the late dictator to help pay off his P23.5 billion tax debt. Of course, it's this same legacy that prompts many Filipinos to suspect the body is a fake, simply a wax figure, one last-ditch con put. Whatever it is, it's laid out on a mattress and lit by floodlights in an otherwise dark room. Full creepiness is achieved by eerie choral music played on a continuous loop.

To reach Batac (P5, 15km), get on any south-bound bus from Laoag.

Paoay

About 4km west of Batac, a P30 tricycle trip off the main highway, is Paoay (pow-**why**). The town's massive, fortress-like **Paoay Church** – built in 'earthquake baroque' style (with Gothic elements, as well as Chinese and Japanese influences) – is included on Unesco's World Heritage list. The church is built of thick coral blocks and stucco-plastered bricks, sealed with limestone mortar mixed with sugar-cane juice; with its 26 external buttresses, it has the appearance of a fort. Construction began in 1804 and was finished

90 years later. A few metres away is a three-storey coral stone belltower, dating from 1793. There's nothing much else around here so ask your tricycle driver to wait.

Overlooking Paoay Lake, on the border of Laoag City, is the **Malacañang of the North** (admission P20; open 9am-noon & 1pm-4pm Tues-Sun). Legend has it that the lake was once the site of a town, submerged as divine condemnation of the inhabitants' extreme materialism. Now it's known for the opulent former residence of the Marcoses, and opened to the public in 1986. A guide will show you around the place, which is replete with an emergency medical clinic in one of the master bedrooms. To get here from Laoag, take a Suba-bound jeepney. If coming from the Paoay Church, it's a 30-minute tricycle ride (P100). Again, be sure to ask the driver to wait.

Nearby is the road to a long, desolate stretch of brown sand, known as Suba Beach. It's surrounded by sand dunes and there are no real facilities or places to get out of the way of the intense sun. But this also means you will probably have the place to yourself and the isolation is a refreshing respite from the urban chaos. You can get drinks and even meals from a family who live here. If you return to Laoag by tricycle from Paoay or Suba Beach (P60, 30 minutes), your driver will likely have to drop you just before the bridge over the Laoag River because he's not licensed for the city. You can catch a tricycle from Laoag to either destination (P150).

PAGUDPUD
☎ 077 • pop 19,300

Palm trees, white sand and isolation make Pagudpud the most attractive and pleasant beach in this part of the country. The quiet and calm come at a price though, as there's no real budget accommodation.

A 45-minute tricycle ride north (P300 return), the last part over a rough and bumpy road, is **Dos Hermanos** (Blue Lagoon), a beautiful beach hemmed in by small cliffs, with very clear and shallow water perfect for swimming. Once here, you might as well stop at **Agua Grande** (P10), a nice spot only 10 more minutes north from the highway. It can get crowded on weekends, when locals come here to picnic and take a dip in the freshwater pools created by a small waterfall.

Places to Stay

Terra Rika Beach Resort *(☎ 764 1047; rooms with bathroom & fan/air-con P1000/1500, camping per adult P50)* consists of a few separate buildings with different names but all owned by members of the same extended family. The nicest is probably Apo Idon, four very appealing rooms with stone walls and good lighting. Rates are higher than listed but negotiable. A small pool is free for guests but P50 for everyone else. Some rooms in other buildings have TVs. Tent and mattress hire for camping is P400. Order your meals in advance at the **Terra Rika** restaurant, which serves excellent fresh seafood.

Klasik Beach Resort *(☎ 722 2917; rooms with bathroom & fan/air-con P800/2500)* and **Northridge Resort** *(☎ 764 1057; rooms with bathroom & fan/air-con P1000/1500)*, both with similar acceptable rooms, are next to the Terra Rika complex.

Saud Beach Resort *(☎ 764 1005; doubles P2384, A-frame houses P4000)* is the most upmarket choice, with wooden floors and bamboo furniture; rooms include bathroom. There is a nice restaurant here as well. Enter from the beach or else a guard will likely charge you P50.

Arinaya White Beach Resort *(☎ 764 1079; rooms with fan P1100, with air-con & bathroom P1650)* fronts the beach but the rooms are sparse and the bathroom primitive.

Villa Del Mar Ivory Beach Resort *(☎ 764 1080; rooms with bathroom & fan/air-con P1400/1700, camping per person P250)* does have a swimming pool but its rooms are only basic.

Getting There & Away

For details on travel to/from Laoag, see that section earlier.

For Claveria (P40, 1½ hours), wait along the highway for any east-bound bus.

Cagayan, Isabela & Aurora

TUGUEGARAO

☎ 078 • pop 12,000

Tuguegarao is the political and commercial capital of Cagayan province, a fertile agricultural region, criss-crossed by the Cagayan River, the longest and widest in the country.

Travelling south from Magapit, the road runs through the lush Cagayan Valley bordered on the west by the Cordilleras and on the east by the Sierra Madre and Philippine Sea. The 14,000 licensed tricycles in Tuguegarao are a rude interruption to the otherwise bucolic surroundings but the small city centre is manageable on foot and serves as a convenient base for short hikes and longer trips in the region.

Information

Tuguegarao's main thoroughfare is Bonifacio St, where most of the **banks**, the **mall** and **market** are located. The centre of town is essentially bounded by City Hall and St Peter's Cathedral on opposite ends of Luna St. The **Department of Tourism & Sierra Madre Outdoor Club** *(☎ 844 1621; e dotr02@yahoo .com; 2nd floor, Supermarket Bldg, Bonifacio St)* has information about activities in the area, including the club's periodic long treks.

BPI *(cnr Bonifacio & Gonzaga Sts)* has ATM facilities.

You can connect to the Internet at **ZOOP Computer Center** *(☎ 846 2031; Bonifacio St; open 9am-9pm daily)* for P50 per hour.

Things to See & Do

Over 300 caves have been discovered in the municipality of Peñablanca, about 40 minutes east of town. The seven-chambered **Callao Cave** is reached by walking up a 187-step flight of stairs. A little chapel with pews and an altar is set up in the first chamber. To get here catch a jeepney from in front of the market on Bonifacio St. Many make the trip between 6am and 3.30pm while the last one returns around 4pm.

Further afield, **Odessa Cave** – estimated to be the longest cave system in the country at 12.5km – and **Sierra Cave** are more challenging and call for a guide and a torch (flashlight) or headlamp. A change of clothes may be helpful, since you'll get extremely muddy crawling through narrow passageways.

Adventure & Expeditions Philippines *(☎ 844 1298; e aepi@cag.pworld.net.ph; 29 Burgos St)* organises white-water rafting and kayaking trips down the Pinacanauan River (a freshwater tributary of the Cagayan River) whose clean, green water cuts through the limestone cliffs. The water is refreshing and there is a pebble beach with a picnic shed a short way upstream from the Odessa and

CAGAYAN & ISABELA

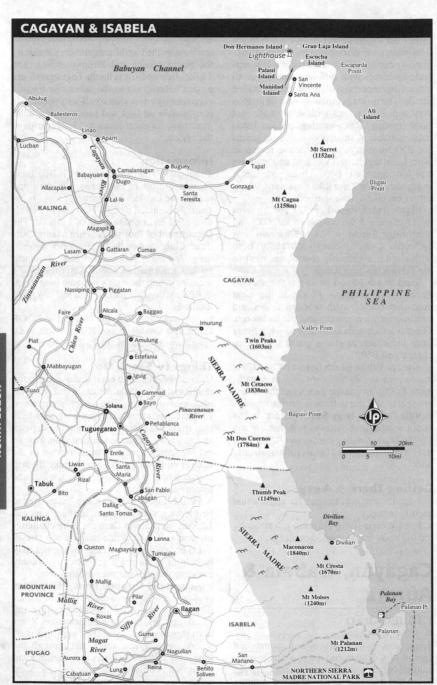

Babuyan Channel

Don Hermanos Island
Lighthouse
Gran Laja Island
Escucha Island
Escaparda Point
Palaui Island
San Vincente
Manidad Island
Santa Ana
Ati Island

Abulug
Ballesteros
Linao
Lucban
Aparri
Cagayan River
Babayuan
Camalaniugan
Buguey
Dugo
Allacapan
Santa Teresita
Lal-lo
KALINGA
Magapit
Tapal
Gonzaga
Mt Sarret (1152m)
Illigau Point
Mt Cagua (1158m)
Lasam
Gattaran
Cumao
River
Zinundangan
Nassiping
Piggatan
Faire
Alcala
Baggao
Imurung
CAGAYAN
PHILIPPINE SEA
Piat
Amulung
Valley Point
Twin Peaks (1603m)
Chico River
Estefania
SIERRA MADRE
Mabbayugan
Iguig
Mt Cetaceo (1838m)
Tuao
Gammad
Bayo
Solana
Pinacanauan River
Peñablanca
Baguio Point
Tuguegarao
Abaca
Mt Dos Cuernos (1784m)
Enrile
Liwan
Santa Maria
Rizal
Cagayan River
Tabuk
Bito
San Pablo
Thumb Peak (1149m)
Dallag
Cabagan
Santo Tomas
KALINGA
Divilian Bay
Lanna
Divilian
Quezon
Magsaysay
Tumauini
Maconacon (1840m)
SIERRA MADRE
Mallig
Mt Cresta (1670m)
MOUNTAIN PROVINCE
Pilar
Mallig River
Palanan Bay
Ilagan
Mt Moises (1240m)
Palanan Pt
Roxas
Siffu River
Guma
ISABELA
Palanan
IFUGAO
Aurora
Naguilian
Magat River
Lung
Cabatuan
Reina
Benito Soliven
San Mariano
Mt Palanan (1212m)
NORTHERN SIERRA MADRE NATIONAL PARK

0   10   20km
0   5   10mi

Underground Money

Treasure hunting has always been both the most adventurous and tedious of pursuits. After all, once you find the proverbial 'x' on the map, hours of digging await. Of course, backbreaking labour is not enough to deter true believers (especially when other people can be hired to do the hard work) and the prospect of billions of dollars of buried gold has drawn a fair share of dreamers to the Philippines.

Sunken Spanish and Chinese trading galleons have taken a backseat to the loot supposedly buried by the retreating Imperial Army of Japan. During the Japanese occupation, the Philippines became the safe-deposit box for riches plundered from all over Southeast Asia; there are supposedly 172 'documented' burial sites, the majority in North Luzon. The story goes that the speedy American advance prevented the Japanese from withdrawing their treasure, estimated by the hopeful to be the equivalent of US$100 billion today.

As if the public coffers were not enough, some even say that ex-president Marcos supplemented his fortune by locating many of the sites. Even recently, a Japanese delegation allegedly searching for the bones of relatives in Isabela, were discovered by the government to actually be on a treasure hunt. No doubt there are many amateurs, hucksters and con-artists, but there are 'professionals' as well, and enough validity to some of the claims to keep them coming. The Philippine government is not likely to discourage them either, since the law stipulates that it's entitled to a hefty chunk of any findings.

Sierra Caves. If you can, stick around until dusk when tens of thousands of bats pour out of the caves for a flight over the river. Stretch canoes transporting residents and all manner of household belongings (even a horse or two) are for hire. One hour upstream is the village of **Tunggi** while **Baclay** is another 1½ days by foot from here. Aeta (Negrito) settlements are further on from Baclay.

Places to Stay & Eat

Hotel Candice (☎ 844 2001; e hotel_can dice@hotmail.com; Blumentritt St; doubles with bathroom, air-con & TV P600) has very nice, modern, comfortable rooms with an attentive staff.

Hotel Lorita (☎ 846 2565; 67 Rizal St; doubles with bathroom, air-con & TV P615) also has good-quality rooms in a more homey atmosphere. **Ristorante Lorita** serves Chinese meals and seafood.

Hotel Delfino (☎ 844 1953; Gonzaga St; singles/doubles with bathroom, air-con & TV P400/500) has tidy rooms but they are vulnerable to street noise.

Ybang Cottage (rooms with bathroom & air-con P1500), **La-Cagayana** (3-room cottage with bathroom P1200), **Romero Cottage** (rooms with bathroom & fan P800) and **JPC Building** (dorm beds P100) are all next to each other on the bank of the Pinacanauan River, opposite Callao Cave. La-Cagayana is the nicest of the group.

Pampenguana (Bonifacio St) is a bakery that's been serving a wide variety of cakes since 1956.

Getting There & Away

PAL flies to/from Manila (P2388, three weekly); From Laoag, a Laoag International Airlines flight proceeds to Basco and Tuguegarao (twice, weekly), before returning to Manila. **Chemtrad Airlines** (☎ 078-844 3113) flies to Palanan (45 minutes) in the Northern Sierra Madre National Park. Flights are out of Cauayan Airport, along the National Hwy, 2km south of the city centre.

EMC, Victory Liner, Delta, Baliwag Transit and Florida Liner all run regular buses between Tuguegarao and Manila (nine hours) from Sampaloc and Cubao. To get to Solano (P160, two hours), take any Manila-bound bus. For Banaue (five hours), you can transfer in Solano or nearby Bagabag.

Florida, Autobus and RCJ have frequent buses to Laoag.

CLAVERIA
☎ 078

In the northwest of Cagayan province, the small coastal town of Claveria has a long, pretty and clean beach, nicely framed by a couple of small mountains on one side and hills on the other. It's four hours by bus from Santa Ana, and three hours from Laoag. There are a few small, beachside resorts and

NORTH LUZON

if you have the time **Macatel** and **Portabaga Falls** are both around two hours away.

Places to Stay

Bayview Inn and Restaurant (☎ 098-199 3683; rooms with bathroom & fan/air-con & TV P400/700) is a family-run place. The rooms surrounding the dining area are fine but can be quite noisy if there is a large group around. It can cook up whatever you like, but the blue marlin sinigang is delicious.

Cabicungan Inn, Beach Resort & Restaurant (☎ 078-866 1011; rooms with bathroom & fan/air-con & TV P350/1000), further down the beach, in a less-congested spot, is more attractive and slightly better kept. Rooms are small and simple.

Jay & Joy Guesthouse (cottages P800) has small stand-alone cottages that can sleep up to five people and **Lakay Lakay** (rooms with fan/air-con P400/900) is acceptsable if nothing else is available.

Getting There & Away

There are regular buses from Claveria to Manila. There are frequent direct buses from Claveria to Laoag and Vigan that leave from the town centre via Pagudpud (P40, 1½ hours). There are also buses to Tuguegarao.

To go to/from Santa Ana, you have to change bus in Magapit.

NORTHERN SIERRA MADRE NATIONAL PARK

Formerly known as the Palanan Wilderness Area, this 3590 sq km of protected area is the largest rainforest in the Philippines. Its rugged terrain is inhabited by 29 endangered bird species and over 60% of the plant species found in the country. Because of the area's inaccessibility, the Dumagat, a semi-nomadic Aeta group who inhabit the park's coastline, live a lifestyle relatively unchanged for generations. The region was also a refuge for the last holdouts during the Philippine Revolution – American-led forces finally captured General Emilio Aguinaldo in the area on 23 March 1901.

You basically have two options if you want to trek in the area: you can enter from the settlement of **Palanan**, near the Pacific coast; or inland from the town of San Mariano, the last stop before the road disappears. You can find accommodation at the DENR **guesthouse** in Palanan, but you will need to bring all of your own cooking equipment and supplies from outside.

In **San Mariano**, you can find a guide at the local government unit (LGU) who can help plan your itinerary and routes through the rough and difficult terrain. If you want to make your way further into the interior before starting your hike, it's possible to hire a logging truck in San Mariano to take you further east to **San Jose**. From San Jose, it's a few hours hike to **Deviakden**, another small settlement. It's conceivable that you can arrange a guide in San Jose for the trip to Deviakden or in Deviakden to venture further afield. San Mariano is also the only place in the Philippines where you can see the **Philippine crocodile**, the most endangered crocodile in the world, in its natural habitat. If you want to sort things out before committing to the rough journey from San Mariano, you can speak to the Protected Areas Superintendent in Tuguegarao or visit the Environment Information Center (EIC) of the Isabela State University in **Cabagan**, not far south of Tuguegarao. Cabagan has a **hostel**.

Getting There & Away

Chemtrad Airlines (☎ 078-844 3113) flies to Palanan (45 minutes) from Tuguegarao.

Cargo ships to Palanan leave Cemento wharf in Baler on an irregular schedule (sometimes weekly, sometimes monthly). The trip is about 14 hours, with a stop in Casiguran. Be warned that you might have to wait a month for the next boat to bring you back.

You can catch a jeepney or bus to San Mariano and the park from Ilagan.

BALER & AROUND

☎ 042 • pop 30,000

Situated between the formidable Sierra Madre mountains and the Philippine Sea, Baler feels cut off from the outside, which makes it a nice place to relax. Surfers from around the world come here from September to February to take advantage of the ocean swell from the seasonal monsoon winds.

Information

The staff at the **Provincial Tourism Office** (☎ 209 4373; Provincial Capitol Compound) is friendly and helpful.

For high-speed Internet access, try the **Aurora State College of Technology** (ASCOT;

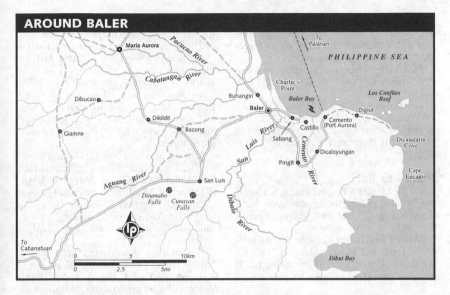

AROUND BALER

Maria Aurora

Pacucao River

Cabatangan River

To Palanan

PHILIPPINE SEA

Dibucao

Dikildit

Bacong

Buhangin

Charlie's Point

Baler Bay

Baler

Los Confites Reef

Digisit

Castillo

Cemento (Port Aurora)

Giamne

Sabang

Cemento River

Dicasalarin Cove

San Luis River

Dicaloyungan

Pingit

Cape Encanto

Aguang River

San Luis

Ditumabo Falls

Cunayan Falls

Dibalo River

To Cabanatuan

0   5   10km
0   2.5   5mi

Dibut Bay

open 8am-5pm daily), 4km southeast from
town, which charges P40 per hour.

There are no ATMs and **banks** do not
change cash.

Things to See & Do

The best surf breaks, up to 4m high, are
around **Cemento Wharf** (P60, 30 minutes),
but are for the more experienced because
of the potentially dangerous reef. **Sabang
Beach**, where almost all of the accommodation is concentrated, provides gentler waves
and is good for swimming. **Charlie's Point**,
where Francis Ford Coppola shot the famous
surfing scene in *Apocalypse Now*, is nearby at
the point where the river flows into the ocean.

If you continue on the road past Cemento,
you'll come to **Digisit**, where you can
snorkel off the reef. Another 45 minutes in
the same direction over a rough but passable
road, is **Dicasalarin Cove**, where there is a
nice white-sand beach. You can also hike
here or hire a fishing boat from the bridge
just outside Baler on the road to Sabang.
Further south is **Dibut Bay**, about a two-hour
boat ride from the bridge. The beach is similar to Sabang's and the town is mostly populated with Aeta descendants.

Inland from Baler is San Luis, from
where you can reach **Cunayan Falls** and **Ditumabo Falls**. Vehicles can almost drive
right up to Cunayan but Ditumabo is larger

and more impressive, dropping over 40m.
There is a sign for the turnoff (unfortunately,
if coming from Baler you only see the back
of the sign) just before a small bridge. A tricycle *(P200 return; ask the driver to pick you
up later)* from Baler can take you almost all
the way to the trailhead or at least to the fork
in the road (go right), from where it is only
another 1.7km. When you cross the small
dam, follow the path on the left or if you like
to get wet you can try to hike through the
river. There are a series of small pools along
the way and the water at the falls itself is
cold and invigorating.

In Baler, **Pasalubong Centre**, between the
bus terminals and market, sells locally made
crafts and hand-woven hats at good prices.

Places to Stay

With the exception of Amihan Hotel, all of
the following accommodation is in Sabang.

Angara Beach Resort *(☎ 209 4352; rooms
with fan/air-con & TV P350/550)* is a friendly
family-run place with basic rooms (with
bathroom) surrounding a nice garden. Noise
from the disco next door is unfortunate.
Bring earplugs if you're a light sleeper.

Bay's Inn *(☎ 209 4312; rooms with bathroom & fan/air-con & TV P350/650)* is also
within earshot of the disco. Rooms are OK
and it has a popular outdoor restaurant along
the beach. Laundry service is available.

Amco Beach Resort (☎ 209 4209; rooms with bathroom & fan/air-con P350/550), further down the road, is a large, clean three-storey place with pleasant rooms.

MM Lodge (rooms with bathroom & fan P300) has a few plain rooms attached to a house.

Amihan Hotel (☎ 209 4352; rooms with fan P100, with air-con & bathroom P100/500) is in Baler. Rooms are decaying but you could stay here if there were no vacancies elsewhere.

Places to Eat

Bahia Restaurant & Bar, in Sabang, is a large, sterile place, striving for sophistication, but it does have air-con and good seafood. There's live music on some nights.

Melly's Restaurant (Quezon St) has self-serve food, and roasts chicken (P180 for whole chicken) in front of the restaurant. It also has a good selection of ice cream.

Getting There & Away

Genesis and ABC both have bus services to/from Pasay City in Manila (P219, 230km, seven hours, three daily); ABC makes a few more trips later in the day or when the bus fills up. Genesis has air-con and is much more comfortable. Be prepared for a very bumpy and dusty ride through the southern Sierra Madres.

All other buses and jeepneys go via Cabanatuan (P105, four hours) from where you can catch buses to Baler; the last ABC bus leaves Cabanatuan for Baler around 4pm. It may be possible to get a jeepney leaving later but probably isn't such a good idea because of the condition of the road.

Cargo ships leave from Cemento wharf on an irregular schedule (sometimes weekly, sometimes monthly) bound for Palanan, in Isabela province. The trip is about 14 hours, with a stop in Casiguran, but as boat trips are infrequent, you may have to wait a month for the next one to bring you back.

SAN VINCENTE & PALAUI ISLAND

On the northeastern tip of Luzon, the road ends at the barangay of San Vincente. Deep-sea fishers from around the world, especially Manila, flock here from March to July for the annual **fishing tournament** in pursuit of blue marlin, swordfish and bar-racuda. It's best to avoid visiting here during the July to February rainy season.

There's not much in San Vincente itself or in the neighbouring town of **Santa Ana**, but there are some beautiful spots to visit nearby. A 30-minute pumpboat ride (P200) from San Vincente takes you to **Angib Beach**, a thin, meandering stretch of sand and crushed corals. It's a very serene spot and a few rocky outcroppings dot the clear, green water.

You can also hike here (1½ hours) from a trailhead in a nearby barangay. Visible from **San Vincente's pier** is **Manidad Island** (P150 return, 15 minutes), essentially a large rock which locals say looks like a crocodile with a fin. You can camp overnight on the sand and the shallow water is excellent for swimming.

For an even slower pace, head over to Palaui Island (P150 return, 20 minutes). Aeta people live in the village of **Punte Verde** and there are no roads, motorised vehicles or electricity. A three-hour hike across the island takes you to **Cape Engano** and **Siwangag Cove**, where there is an old lighthouse, originally built by the Spanish, and a gorgeous white-sand beach. You can stay at the DENR, where there are a few **beds** or at Terry Callado's **guesthouse**. Ask the barangay captain for any information and also to negotiate if you think you are being overcharged for a boat ride.

Next to the Petron petrol station in San Vincente is **Mell & Eddie Lodging Inn** (rooms with fan P300). There's no sign but just ask for Mell or Eddie at the store. Rooms are basic but make sure the shower and taps work (no hot water).

You can eat instant pansit (a thick- or thin-noodle dish) at **Valderama Eatery** near the pier. The **Franciscan Mission House** and **Benz Guesthouse** in Santa Ana offer a couple of rooms each.

Getting There & Away

Florida Liner and Cal Trans make frequent early-morning trips to Tuguegarao (P80, 3½ hours). They depart less frequently in the afternoon and the last leaves around 3pm.

Both jeepneys and vans leave throughout the day to Magapit (P60, 85km), from where it's easy to catch another ride further west to Claveria and Pagudpud or south to Tuguegarao.

Batanes

Located over 860km from Manila, this group of 10 islands, three inhabited, seems displaced in time and space. From Y'ami, the northernmost island of the Batanes, you can see Taiwan on a clear day. Efforts are underway to promote tourism, however the area's sheer isolation and the fact that it sits in a typhoon alley will probably ensure that the number of visitors are kept low. After all, there are only two flights a week here and these are sometimes in doubt because of threatening weather. You can really appreciate its remoteness if you happen to be lucky enough to be in Basco when one of the biannual Navy cargo ships arrive. Everywhere but the port is deserted, where people flock to claim their share of the goods.

Geographically, the islands seem less tropical and more like the Scottish Highlands, but the pace is slow and the residents friendly to visitors. Doors and windows are kept unlocked and open, as theft seems to be unheard of.

The Spanish didn't set foot in the islands until 1686 and forced the Ivatan (literally, 'Place Where Boats are Cast Ashore'), to settle in the lowlands where they could be administered more easily. Today, many are subsistence farmers – rice, corn and garlic are common – and while the average income remains among the lowest in the country, people barter to meet their needs. Homes are built to be typhoon tough and have metre-thick limestone walls. Of course, the sea is vital to the Ivatan way of life, and if the weather is right, you'll eat well in Batanes.

If it looks like a plant is growing from the heads of some Ivatan women, you are partially correct. *Vakuls*, the name for the headgear, is made from the abaca fibre of the vuyavuy palm, found only in Batanes. Each item takes three weeks to make but should last a lifetime, protecting the wearer from the sun and rain. When not being worn, they are usually being combed or stored in the house.

Typhoon season is from July to December, and it's not uncommon for six typhoons to hit the archipelago in one year alone. The best time to visit is from March to May, when the weather is relatively hot and dry, but the weather is unpredictable so you may need reserves of patience and flexibility.

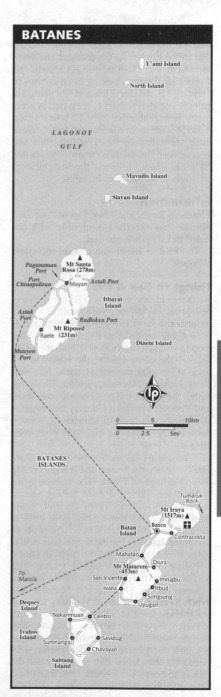

BATANES

Y'ami Island

North Island

LAGONOY GULF

Mavudis Island

Siayan Island

Paganaman Port
Port Chinapoliran
Mayan
Mt Santa Rosa (278m)
Axtak Port
Itbayat Island

Axtak Port

Rudloken Port
Mt Riposed (231m)
Raele

Dinem Island

Mauyen Port

BATANES ISLANDS

Tumaruk Rock

Mt Iraya (1517m)
Basco
Batan Island
Contracosta

Mahatao
Diura

Mt Matarem (453m)
San Vicente
Imnajbu
Itbud
Ivana
Songsong
Uyugan

To Manila

Dequey Island

Nakanmuan
Centro

Ivahos Island
Sumnanga
Savidug
Chavayan

Sabtang Island

0   5   10km
0   2.5   5mi

BATAN ISLAND

Basco is the largest town in Batanes and the seat of the provincial government and commercial centre. Most people get around this thoroughly modern-looking town on foot or bicycle, but motorcycles and tricycles are gaining popularity. Nights are quiet, as electricity is available for only 12 hours a day. Abad St is the main commercial street, where there are a few *sari-sari* selling fruit and vegetables. The islands' main road, called National Hwy, follows the magnificent coastline from Basco to Imnajbu.

Information

Elizabeth Reyes and Lory Tan put out *Trek Batanes*, an excellent miniguide with detailed trekking information.

The **PNB** in Basco can change travellers cheques.

Things to See & Do

As there are few motorised vehicles, an excellent way to explore the island is to rent a **mountain bike** (P150 per day) from one of the lodging houses. You'll generally have the road to yourself. From Basco, National Hwy follows the coast around the island to the town of Imnajbu, passing Mahatao, San Vincente, Ivana and Uyugan en route. From Imnajbu, the gravel and grass inland road takes you through Marlboro Country and eventually brings you back to Mahatao. It's not a particularly strenuous ride but does take around six hours.

A couple of kilometres before Mahatao, you'll see a paved road and a sign for the fishing village of **Diura**. The village is inhabited only during dorado fishing season from March to June. From the end of the road in Diura, it's about a half-hour walk to the dark, narrow Crystal Cave. Inquire about **accommodation** at the municipal hall in Mahatao if you want to spend a night in Diura.

Batanes beaches are mostly strewn with pebbles or boulders and the surf can be dangerously strong. The **beach** in Mahatao and **White Beach**, just south of Mahatao, are generally considered safe for swimming. North of Basco, the boulder beach at **Songsong Bay** is quite beautiful. Not to be confused with the bay, the ghost barangay of **Songsong**, only ruins now, abandoned after a tidal wave in the '50s is an hour's drive south from Basco and has a good beach for swimming.

Mt Iraya (1517m), a dormant volcano that last erupted in 505 AD, can be climbed in about five hours and descended in three, though the summit is usually obscured by clouds. A climb to the top of the abandoned US weather station, **Radar Tukon** (which is on a hilltop almost 3km from Basco), offers magnificent 360-degree views. It's 30 minutes from the wharf at Kanyuyan Beach Port in Basco to the turnoff, and then around another 40 minutes uphill.

Places to Stay & Eat

The following places are all in Basco.

Mama Lily's Inn *(rooms with bathroom per person P150, with meals P500)*, next to the Provincial Capitol Building on the plaza, is very pleasant and comfortable, although there are only nine beds. Hefty seafood meals are served here. Loudspeakers hooked up to the nearby church blast prayers around 5am every morning.

Mataw Inn *(rooms with fan P150, with meals P450)* makes you feel at home and the owners also serve up large portions of food.

Batanes Resort has a few comfortable cottages with bathroom by the ocean.

Iraya Lodge *(rooms with fan P150)* can accommodate up to 30 guests and has a roof deck. It's only a few minutes from the plaza.

St Dominic's College provides cheap dorm beds.

The aptly named **Honesty Cafe** is a coffee shop/*sari sari,* where you are trusted to leave what you owe in a cup.

Getting There & Away

Laoag International Airlines *(☎ 02-551 4813 in Manila, ☎ 077-772 1793 in Laoag)* has flights from Manila to Basco (P4800, three weekly). The airport is a 10-minute walk north of the Basco plaza or you can take a tricycle (P10, plus P10 per bag).

Two cargo ships owned by the Batanes Multi-Purpose Cooperative regularly ply the Manila–Basco route bringing in food and supplies. Both the MV *Queen of Fatima* and the MV *Don Rudito* accept passengers, although there is no reliable schedule.

For details on transport to Itbayat, see the Itbayat Getting There & Away section later.

Getting Around

Jeepneys regularly ply the road between Basco and Imnajbu from around 4am to 4pm.

In Basco, wait for jeepneys in front of Builder's Bank near the wharf. A few tricycles are usually parked on Abad St and can be hired for special trips.

Ask your hosts to arrange hiring a vehicle for the day so that you're not stranded far away in the afternoon. There are also a number of bicycles for rent.

SABTANG ISLAND
pop 6200

It's hard to believe, but travelling to Sabtang from Basco increases the feeling that you have somehow left the rest of the world behind.

The lifestyle here is more traditional and less influenced by the outside. The small limestone-house villages, the steep mountains and deep canyons of the interior, and the rocky coastline, punctuated by small beaches, make it ideal for **hiking** and even more stunning than Batan. Migratory **birds** from China flock here in October.

You can do a round-trip hike around the island. From Centro, where the ferry docks, hike south on the road to **Savidug** for about an hour (6km). Outside of town is an *idjang* (large rocky hill), where in pre-Hispanic times Ivatan villages were built and more easily defended by throwing rocks at their attackers.

It's another 2km hike from Savidug to picturesque **Chavayan**, where there's an eye-catching pastel-painted church right next to the beach. Hand-woven *vakul* can be picked up for P150. From here, it's a two-hour hike through the interior to **Sumnanga**, nicknamed 'Little Hong Kong', because the houses are crammed up to the shoreline. Follow the road north to **Nakanmuan** and back to Centro. If you can find someone with a boat, you can visit **Ivahos Island**, a small, uninhabited island west of Sabtang, which locals say has the best beaches and snorkelling.

To do all of this, you will likely need the entire day and so miss the last boat back to Basco, which leaves at 3pm. If you need to stay the night, the School of Fisheries in Centro has a nice **dormitory** *(dorm beds P50)* with a canteen downstairs. It's also not unlikely that a friendly Ivatan family would open their home to you. Small gifts, such as books on fishing, or hooks and lines would be a nice way of showing your appreciation

for their hospitality. There are also a few **sari-sari** in Centro.

Getting There & Around
It's possible to hire a jeepney (P1500 per day) in Centro (ask the mayor), to get to Savidug and Chavayan.

Ferries and *falowa* (round-bottom boats) to Centro leave Batan from Ivana. Two ferries leave early in the morning and return from Centro the following morning. There is also one afternoon ferry from Centro to Ivana. If you hire a *falowa,* be sure to arrange your return trip before you leave.

ITBAYAT ISLAND
pop 3000

Although only 40km north of Batan, the only way to get to Itbayat, is a rough four-hour boat ride. The Philippines ends here, at least as far as inhabited land is concerned, and electricity was not introduced here until 1997. There are no beaches and no piers, which make disembarking from boats a test of athleticism and timing. You must time your jump for when the wave is at an equal height to one of the narrow, concrete ledges carved into the cliffs.

Itbayat's 'ports' are connected by gravel roads – except for the 3km Chinapuliran–Mayan road which is paved – to the main town of **Mayan**, at the bottom of the bowl-shaped island. There is no coastal road.

The area around **Raele**, 9km south of Mayan, is rolling grass hills, with the odd palm tree as a tropical reminder. Trails crisscross the centre of the island, making it a great place for trekking in good weather. There are nice views from **Mt Riposed** (231m), east of Raele.

It's a beautiful half-hour walk from Mayan to **Paganaman port**, where at dusk you'll see farmers returning from the fields and fishermen with their day's catch. If you arrive at low tide, you can soak in a little natural swimming pool in the rocks next to the port.

The mayor, who can be found at the municipal building, will let you stay in a **guesthouse** *(beds P100)* with access to a kitchen. It's recommended that you bring some food and water, since the water here must be boiled before drinking. Keep an eye out for delicious coconut crabs caught on the island's cliffs.

Getting There & Around

Chemtrek Airlines flies a 10-seater twin engine plane from Basco to Itbayat (P750 one way, 12 minutes, two daily). The landing strip is in Raele, in the middle of a livestock farm but jeeps are there to transport you to town. Be sure to book the return flight before leaving Basco.

It's a taxing ferry trip from Basco to Port Chinapoliran (four hours). Motion sickness is pretty common due to strong currents and large waves. The boat will also probably be packed with goods and livestock.

Be prepared to stay longer than anticipated, since during typhoon season it's not unheard of for a month to pass before the journey back can be safely ventured. The boat leaves Itbayat for Basco shortly after it arrives.

There's no public transport on the island but there are some residents with motorbikes.

Southeast Luzon

Outdoors-lovers will find plenty to do on the rarely-visited southern Luzon peninsula known as Bicol. It's home to delectable, fiery food, laden with hot peppers and coconut; and the famously volatile Mt Mayon volcano, which is a popular hiking destination when it's not spilling lava down its slopes. Other good climbs are Mt Isarog, near Naga, and Mt Bulusan, in Sorsogon.

The largely undeveloped island of Catanduanes offers peace, quiet and the erratic waves at Puraran, which attract surfers from around the world. Other major attractions for visitors are island-hopping, swimming (with friends, loved ones or the world's largest fish) and doing your bit for the environment by soaking up those harmful UV rays on gorgeous beaches.

The island province of Marinduque, also unspoiled, lies between Bicol and Mindoro. Here you can join a Passion play during the island's popular Moriones Festival, hang out with the bats in caves near Santa Cruz or (should you feel the urge) repent your sins in Boac's lovely church.

Highlights

- Swim with the glorious whale sharks at Donsol
- Climb to the knife edge of Mt Mayon
- Relax and wait for the surf to kick in at wide and wild Puraran, in Catanduanes
- Explore the limestone cliffs and pristine beaches of the beautiful Caramoan Peninsula
- Soak in the hot springs near Buenavista on Marinduque

Bicol

Bicol technically includes Luzon's southeastern peninsula and the islands of Catanduanes and Masbate, but this section of the chapter covers peninsular Bicol only. (Catanduanes is covered in a separate section later in this chapter, and Masbate is included in the Visayas chapter).

Getting There & Away

Boat Many people travel overland from Manila to Matnog, at the southern tip of Luzon, and take a boat from here to Samar in the Visayas (see Matnog in this section later for details). Ferries bound for Masbate depart from Bulan, also in Sorsogon.

Bus A number of bus companies have frequent services throughout the region, including BLTB, Philtranco, Peñafrancia Transit and Gold Lines.

Train It's possible to take a train from Manila to Naga and Legaspi and points along the

way. Call **Philippine National Railways** (☎ 02-254 9772) for information and see Naga and Legaspi later in this section for fares and times.

DAET

☎ 054 • pop 80,632

The capital of Camarines Norte, Daet (Daeet) is a busy commercial centre. Its main attraction is the big waves at **Bagasbas Beach**, 4km north of town (P15 by tricycle). The narrow, brown-sand beach at Bagasbas is popular for swimming, but if you do decide to go in, be careful: the current is very strong and up to 40 people get stuck in the rip each year.

Mercedes, 6.5km east of town (P20 by tricycle), is a ragtag but charming little fishing village from where you can hire a boat to explore the islands in **San Miguel Bay**.

SOUTHEAST LUZON

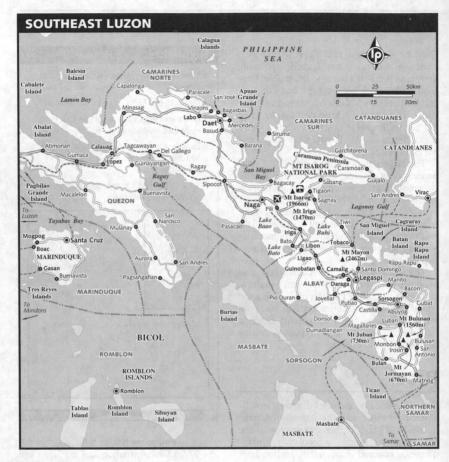

Information

You can change American Express (AmEx) travellers cheques at the **Metrobank** *(Vinzons Ave)* and it has an ATM that accepts MasterCard and Cirrus.

You can access the Internet at a few places in town; the most central is **Joycom** *(Vinzons Ave; open 9am-9pm daily)*, which charges P35 per hour.

Surfing

The best time for surfing is July to October. Alvin Obusan, of Alvino's Pizza House in Bagasbas (see Places to Stay & Eat), is the president of the Bagasbas Wave Riders Club, and is a good source of information about surfing in the area. He can also set you up with a surf guide (P150 per day), who can

take you to the best waves further afield, such as at Mercedes, San José and some offshore islands.

Places to Stay & Eat

Dolor Hotel *(☎ 721 2167, fax 511260; Vinzons Ave; singles/doubles with fan & bathroom P220/400, with air-con P450/650)* is good value and is the cleanest place to stay. Rooms are spacious and there's a café and restaurant. The hotel is on the 3rd floor.

Kariligan Hotel *(☎ 721 2236; Moreno St; singles/doubles with fan & bathroom P150/200, with air-con & hot shower P400/550)*, nearby, has run-down and tacky rooms but there's a warm family atmosphere.

Sampaguita Tourist Inn *(☎ 571 2646; Pimentel Ave; singles/doubles with shared bath-*

room P100/150, with fan & private bathroom P175/225, with air-con P350/400) has basic, fairly clean rooms and a café.

Travellers Hotel *(☎ 440 1521; rooms with fan/air-con P250/500, cottages P150)*, off Bagasbas Beach, has simple but clean and well-kept rooms. The air-con rooms have hot showers. It also has some cute but very basic cottages.

Alvino's Pizza House *(☎ 440 1085; dorm beds P150)*, at Bagasbas, across the street from the beach, has some cramped bunk beds where surfers crash. The restaurant is open from 7am to 11pm daily. It offers great pizza (P185) and sizzling dishes (around P90), and catches refreshing sea breezes.

TS Resorts *(☎ 0916 540 9461; 440 2123 for reservations; cottages with fan & bathroom from P660)*, on Apuao Grande Island, was once a grand resort, but it's seen better days. The resort has tennis courts, a golf course and swimming pool in various states of upkeep. The reservation office is on Salcedo St, Daet, and can arrange transport.

Kusina ni Angel *(open 8am-11pm daily)*, behind Alvino's, serves modern Filipino food. Run by the charming Angel de la Cruz, it has a creative menu and specialises in seafood (around P150), as well as exotic shakes such as avocado, mango, apple or peach brandy (P20 to P28).

Jhoy & Mike's Beach Resort *(☎ mgam brill@hotmail.com; nipa huts P200-500)* was just about to open when we visited, 3km north of San José. Jhoy and Mike plan to rent equipment, such as surfboards, bodyboards and snorkel gear, and offer surfing and kiteboarding lessons.

Getting There & Away
Philtranco *(☎ 571 2718)* has buses between Daet and Manila (P239/355 ordinary/air-con, six daily, eight hours) operating from the terminal on Martinez St, south of the town centre. Buses to Naga (P65, 2½ hours) and Legaspi (P150, five hours) leave from the Central Terminal. Air-con vans to Naga (P70, 1½ hours) also leave from here.

NAGA
☎ 054 • pop 141,300
Naga, in Camarines Sur, is one of Luzon's more cosmopolitan commercial centres. At its core are two pleasant plazas, both surrounded by shops and restaurants. Naga's prosperity is evident in its large number of banks, shops and restaurants. It's also a college town, with a student body active in the area's outdoors scene.

In September thousands of devotees make a pilgrimage to Naga for the **Peñafrancia Festival**, in celebration of the Virgin of Peñafrancia, Bicol's patron saint. The town's population swells at this time and you need to book accommodation at least two months in advance.

Information
The friendly **Naga City Visitors Center** *(☎/fax 472 2136; ⓔ info@naga.gov.ph)* is in the city hall compound, a P10 tricycle trip from the plazas. At the time of writing, it was developing guided trips to Mt Isarog and the Caramoan Peninsula.

The **main post office** *(open 8am-noon & 2pm-5pm Mon-Fri)* is next door to city hall, and there's a branch at the University of Nueva Caceres.

The **Metrobank** *(Peñafrancia Ave)* has an ATM that accepts MasterCard and Cirrus. On the other side of the town centre, **Equitable PCI** *(Carceres St)* has an ATM that accepts Visa and MasterCard. These banks will also change AmEx travellers cheques.

There are a couple of places to check email in Naga: **Mindoro Central Computers** *(Traders Square; open 8.30am-7pm daily)*, behind Chow King, charges P30 per hour and **Pearltech Cyber Cafe** *(Elias Angeles St; open 9am-9pm daily)* charges P25 per hour.

Hiking & Diving
The range of outdoor activities in the Naga region is one of Luzon's best-kept secrets. The beautiful Caramoan Peninsula offers secluded camping spots and gorgeous beaches far from the tourist hype, while local dive sites are relatively unexplored by divers. These isolated places are easily accessed with the support of two professional outfits in town.

Kadlagan Outdoor Shop *(☎ 472 3305; ⓔ kadlagan@hotmail.com; 17 Dimasalang St; open 9am-noon & 1.30pm-8pm daily)* leads guided trips to Mt Isarog and Caramoan Peninsula. It also rents tents and other camping gear. The manager, Jojo Villareal, is an excellent source of information about mountaineering and other outdoor activities in the area, and is usually here in the evenings. The

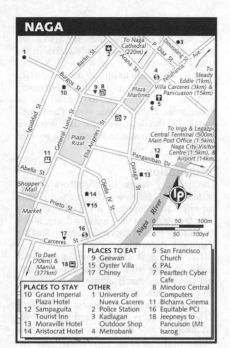

NAGA

PLACES TO EAT		5 San Francisco
9 Geewan		Church
15 Oyster Villa		6 PAL
17 Chinoy		7 Pearltech Cyber
		Cafe
PLACES TO STAY	OTHER	8 Mindoro Central
10 Grand Imperial	1 University of	Computers
Plaza Hotel	Nueva Caceres	11 Bicharra Cinema
12 Sampaguita	2 Police Station	16 Equitable PCI
Tourist Inn	3 Kadlagan	18 Jeepneys to
13 Moraville Hotel	Outdoor Shop	Pancuison (Mt
14 Aristocrat Hotel	4 Metrobank	Isarog

shop sells a wide range of outdoor gear, jewellery and bags.

Steady Eddie (☎ 811 7333; AMS Press Compound, Peñafrancia Ave; open 8am-7pm daily) is the only dive centre in the area. You can hire diving gear here, or join one of the dive expeditions that run most weekends to local sites such as Pasacao, Sabang, Burias Island and Catanduanes (bookings essential).

Places to Stay

Most of the hotels offer a free shuttle service to and from the airport.

Moraville Hotel (☎ 473 1247, fax 811 1685; Dinaga St; doubles with fan, cable TV & hot shower from P310, with air-con from P460) is a friendly place, a short distance from Plaza Rizal. Rooms are clean but worn and some have no windows.

Sampaguita Tourist Inn (☎ 473 8896; singles with shared bathroom P100, singles/doubles with air-con & private bathroom P350/450) has grotty basic rooms and better (but still mediocre) air-con rooms.

Aristocrat Hotel (☎ 473 8832, fax 811 6605; singles/doubles with fan & shared bathroom P295/344, with air-con & hot shower

P669/731) has a complicated collection of rooms, ranging from cheap, dank and small to more expensive and reasonable.

Grand Imperial Plaza Hotel (☎ 473 6535, fax 811 6886; e gip@techasia.com.ph; doubles with hot shower, cable TV & air-con from P1380) is very overpriced – although staff quickly offer a 25% discount. It offers basic and slightly run-down rooms.

Villa Caceres (☎ 811 6083, fax 473 9327; e villa-cc@mozcom.com; Magsaysay Ave; singles/doubles with hot shower, cable TV & air-con from P950/1400), a 10-minute ride north- east of town is Naga's most upmarket lodging. It has a 24-hour restaurant, a swimming pool, gym, sauna, reflexologist and spacious, but surprisingly tatty, rooms.

Places to Eat

There are plenty of good eateries in Naga.

Oyster Villa (☎ 473 7971; dishes around P150; open 9am-10pm daily) is popular with locals and has a large array of Chinese dishes in four different sizes. A medium stir-fried crab with straw mushrooms is P200.

Chinoy (dishes P140; open 10am-10pm daily) is modern and stylishly decorated. It specialises in seafood, as well as sizzling plates and snacks such as fresh lumpia (vegetable or meat spring rolls).

Geewan is one of several fast-food joints around the plaza. It serves local food in cafeteria style. There's a 20% discount if you arrive after 8.30pm.

Getting There & Away

Air The airport is 14km from Naga. **Philippine Airlines** (PAL; ☎ 473 2277) has flights between Manila and Naga (P2028, 45 minutes five weekly). The ticket office is in the plaza above Greenwich.

Bus All bus, jeepney and air-con van services use Naga's central terminal. Philtranco, Gold Lines and Peñafrancia have buses that go to Manila (air-con from P388, eight hours). There are also bus services to Legaspi (P75/92 ordinary/air-con, 2½ hours) and Daet (P65, 2½ hours).

Train There are daily trains between Manila and Naga. The air-con train (P265) leaves Manila's Pasay station at 5.11pm and arrives in Naga at 5am; in the other direction it leaves Naga at 5pm. The ordinary train

(P223) leaves Pasay at 7.14pm and arrives in Naga at 8am; it leaves Naga at 7.30pm. It's also possible to catch the train to Legaspi (P60/90 ordinary/air-con, two/three hours).

CARAMOAN PENINSULA

A four-hour journey from Naga brings you to the beautiful and isolated Caramoan Peninsula, where you can kick back on the unspoiled, gorgeous white-sand beaches. A short way offshore there are several limestone islets with small beaches.

The limpid, turquoise water is great for swimming, and it's possible to rent a *sibid-sibid* (small fishing boat) and paddle from island to island.

About 4km from Caramoan town is **Gota Beach**, a pretty white-sand beach that's excellent for swimming. There are fishing boats at one end; ask a local if you can hire one. The mountainous interior of the Caramoan Peninsula still sees some New People's Army (NPA) insurgency, so check at the Caramoan municipal hall for the latest news if you plan to head into the interior.

There are small eateries where you can buy meals, but only one hotel on the peninsula – the small **Rex Inn** *(Caramoan town)*, which has basic rooms with fan. But the peninsula is best enjoyed outdoors and you're better off bringing your own camping equipment (or arranging this with Kadlagan; see under Naga earlier) and camping on Gota Beach.

Getting There & Away

Most people visit the Caramoan Peninsula on a guided trip. These can be done through Kadlagan Outdoor Shop (from P1500 per person for groups of 10 to 20) or the Visitors Centre in Naga.

Alternatively, you can take a bus or jeep from the central terminal in Naga to Sabang (P42, two hours). From Sabang, there are boats to Guijalo (P80, two hours) around 9am, 10am and noon, leaving as they fill up. You can also hire your own boat for P2000. From Guijalo, it's a 10-minute jeepney or tricycle ride to Caramoan town.

There are intermittent jeepney services from Naga to Caramoan but the boat journey from Sabang to Guijalo is a highlight of a visit to the peninsula, offering beautiful views of the coastline.

Philtranco buses go direct from Manila to Sabang daily.

MT ISAROG NATIONAL PARK

Dominating Camarines Sur's landscape is Mt Isarog (1966m), Bicol's second-highest volcano, now dormant. From Panicuason (pan-ee-**kwa**-sone) a steep, half-hour walk along a dirt track leads to the entrance of the national park *(foreigner/citizen US$1/P10; open 8am-5pm daily)*. Admission for foreigners is calculated based on the US dollar exchange rate, but you can pay pesos. From the entrance, a path to the left leads to **Nabuntolan Falls**, about 1km away. To the right, a short walk leads down some very steep stone steps to **Malabsay Falls**, where you can swim. On clear days there are beautiful views of Mt Isarog rising up behind the falls.

If you plan to hike any further, you must get a permit from the Department of Environment & Natural Resources (DENR) on Panganiban Drive, Naga, near the city hall. Guides are available at the Kadlagan Outdoor Shop in Naga (around P350 per day, plus food, equipment, transport and permit) or at the Naga City Visitors Center. You can reach Mt Isarog's summit in one day and descend the next. Trails are well maintained and there are camps with water sources along the way. Hiking fees are US$10/P100 for foreigners/citizens for three days and camping fees are P25 per day, in addition to the entrance fee.

At Panicuason, **Mt Isarog Hot Springs** *(admission P50; open 7am-6pm daily)* has five natural pools (two hot and three cold) and these are a good way to relax after a trek in the park. The springs are 1.3km off the main road, just before the road to the national park.

From Naga, take a jeepney to Panicuason (P11, 30 minutes). From here it's an easy half-hour walk to the entrance of the park. The last jeepney back to Naga leaves Panicuason around 5pm.

LEGASPI

☎ 052 • pop 157,010

The capital of Albay Province, Legaspi is a friendly town situated at the foot of the striking Mt Mayon (2462m) volcano. The town celebrates the **Magayon Festival** throughout the month of May, with sports events, performances and competitions.

Information

The friendly and informative **Department of Tourism** *(DOT; ☎ 482 0712, 214 3215, fax*

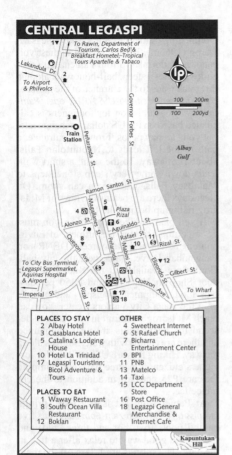

CENTRAL LEGASPI

PLACES TO STAY	OTHER
2 Albay Hotel	4 Sweetheart Internet
3 Casablanca Hotel	6 St Rafael Church
5 Catalina's Lodging House	7 Bicharra Entertainment Center
10 Hotel La Trinidad	8 BPI
17 Legaspi TouristInn; Bicol Adventure & Tours	11 PNB
	13 Matelco
	14 Taxi
PLACES TO EAT	15 LCC Department Store
1 Waway Restaurant	16 Post Office
8 South Ocean Villa Restaurant	18 Legazpi General Merchandise & Internet Cafe
12 Boklan	

820 5066; Regional Center Site), on the out-skirts of town is worth visiting. From Peña-randa St (Legaspi's main commercial street) take a Rawis-bound jeepney (P4), and get off just after the bridge, about a 10-minute ride from town.

There are a couple of places to check your email in Legaspi: **Sweetheart Internet** (open 8.30am-7pm Mon-Sat, 1.30pm-7pm Sun), which charges P40 per hour, and the **Legazpi General Merchandise and Internet Cafe** (open 9am-8.30pm daily), which charges P30 per hour.

You can make long-distance calls at **Matelco** (Mabini St; open 6am-10pm daily). The **Bank of the Philippine Islands** (BPI; Quezon Ave) has ATMs that accept Cirrus, MasterCard and AmEx cards.

The Philippine Institute of Volcanology & Seismology (Philvolcs), where Mt Mayon is monitored, is near the airport. (See the Mt Mayon section under Around Legaspi later.)

Organised Tours

Bicol Adventure and Tours (☎ 480 2266, fax 820 1483; e bicoladventure@digitelone.com; Suite 20, V&O Bldg) organises a wide range of outdoor activities, including spelunking, scuba diving, kayaking and island hopping. A three-day Mayon hike costs US$50 per person per day, including transportation, guide, equipment, fees, food and porter. A trip to see the whale sharks at Donsol (ex Legaspi) costs P3450 per person, including guide, transport, boat and fees.

The **DOT** also offers package climbs of Mt Mayon (US$100 per person for two days, for up to two climbers). The package includes a guide, porter, food and camping equipment. Additional people are an extra P1500 each.

You can rent a car at **Tropical Tours** (☎/fax 482 0463; e benjysantiago@hotmail.com; Pag-asa, Rawis), for P1750 plus petrol for 12 hours (includes driver). The company also offers package tours to sights around the area. Al-ternatively, there's a taxi stand in front of the Legazpi Tourist Inn, where you can negotiate sightseeing trips with the drivers.

Places to Stay

Catalina's Lodging House (☎ 480 7841; 96 Peñaranda St; singles/doubles with shared bathroom P130/170, singles/doubles/triples with private bathroom P180/200/380, with private bathroom & air-con P360/500/600), near the cathedral, has clean, cheap, very basic rooms. The hotel has no sign – access is through the After Six eatery.

Legazpi Tourist Inn (☎ 480 6147, fax 820 4880; V&O Bldg, 3rd floor; singles/doubles with bathroom & fan P450/510, with air-con P700/800) offers the best moderately priced accommodation in town. This modern place has clean and well-kept rooms, lots of mir-rors, and a small café.

Carlos Bed & Breakfast Hometel (☎ 482 0738; singles/doubles with air-con P660/770), in Rawis, has nicely decorated and very clean rooms, some with cable TV and hot shower. 'Hometel' aptly describes this B&B – although larger than a regular house, its com-mon areas include a living room with TV and dining room. Roosters being raised nearby for cockfighting are sure to rouse you early in the morning.

Tropical Tours Apartelle *(☎/fax 482 0463; e benjysantiago@hotmail.com; Pag-asa, Rawis; rooms with cable TV, hot shower & air-con P850)* has comfortable apartment-style accommodation and a restaurant in a tranquil garden.Not easy to find; it's signposted down a side street on the western edge of Rawis.

Hotel La Trinidad *(☎ 480 7469, fax 214 3148; singles/doubles with air-con, cable TV & hot shower from P870/970)* is a quiet and dark place, with rooms preserved intact from the 1970s.

Casablanca Hotel *(☎ 480 8334, fax 480 8338; e lee@globalink.net.ph; doubles with air-con, cable TV & hot shower from P1070)* is a good option in this price range. It has modern, well-kept and clean rooms.

Albay Hotel *(☎/fax 480 8660; 88 Peñaranda St; doubles from P2020)*, a bit further down the road from Casablanca Hotel, is another motel-style place with similar (and therefore overpriced) rooms.

Places to Eat

Boklan *(Elizondo St)*, in a bit of a dodgy neighbourhood, is a simple Chinese restaurant that serves good cheap food.

South Ocean Villa Restaurant *(Quezon Ave; dishes around P200)*, on the 2nd floor of the Bicol Wei-One Fraternity Building, has a wide range of Chinese dishes, such as sizzling spiced bean curd (P105).

Waway Restaurant *(Peñaranda St; dishes around P90; open 8am-9.30pm Mon-Sat)*, on the northern side of town, has an excellent buffet and is well known for its local dishes.

Getting There & Away

Air There are daily **PAL** *(☎ 481 0780)* flights to/from Manila (P2738, 40 minutes); PAL's office is at Legaspi airport.

Bus There's a daily **Gold Line** *(☎ 214 3734)* service to Manila (P480 air-con, 10 hours). **Philtranco** *(☎ 820 1889)* also travels this route (from P200/495 ordinary/air-con). There are buses to Naga (P75/92 ordinary/air-con, 2½ hours), Tabaco (P25 ordinary, 45 minutes) and Sorsogon (P25 ordinary, one hour).

There are direct buses to Donsol (P45, two hours), with the first exiting the bus terminal at 4.20am and the last at 3.30pm.

Train There are two daily trains from Manila to Legaspi: an air-con service departing Manila's Pasay station at 5.11pm (P335, 14 hours) and an ordinary service departing at 7.14pm (P283). In the other direction, the air-con service departs Legaspi at 2pm and the ordinary service departs at 4.30pm. You can also catch the train to Naga (P60/70 ordinary/air-con, three hours) at these times.

AROUND LEGASPI
Daraga Church

Set on a hill overlooking Daraga is the interesting Baroque-style Daraga church, constructed completely of volcanic rocks. From Legaspi take any Daraga-bound jeepney (P4).

Cagsawa Ruins

A few kilometres north of Daraga, the remains (basically the belfry) of the sunken Cagsawa Church *(adult/child P5/2.50, after 6pm P10/5; open 6am-10pm daily)*, are a popular tourist attraction, and the site offers a terrific view of Mayon. In 1814, the 1200 people who took refuge in the church during Mayon's violent eruption were buried alive here. However, this is no peaceful memorial – the site is bustling with ice-cream stands, souvenir hawkers and restaurants.

Also at the site, the interesting **National Museum of the Philippines** *(admission free; open 8am-noon & 1pm-4.30pm Tues-Sat)* will tell you everything you ever wanted to know about volcanos, from harnessing their thermal energy to watching them evolve over the millennia.

To get from Legaspi to Cagsawa, take any jeepney headed to Camalig, Guinobatan or Ligao. Ask the driver to drop you off at the ruins, which are about 500m from the road. If you hire a car for the visit, there's a P10 parking charge.

Hoyop-Hoyopan Caves

A popular tourist destination for locals, this series of caves near Camalig, 8km from Legaspi, includes the easy-to-traverse Hoyop-Hoyopan Caves, where 2000-year-old artefacts have been found. The name means 'blow-blow', a reference to the eerie wind in the cave. To explore the caves you must have a guide; Frederic Atun speaks good English and charges P100 for up to seven people for a 30-minute tour of Hoyop-Hoyopan. He also runs tours to the more challenging **Calabidongan Cave** (literally, 'Cave of the Bats'), about 2.5km away.

To reach Hoyop-Hoyopan from Legaspi, take any jeepney heading towards to Camalig, Polangui, Guinobatan or Ligao. Get off at Camalig (P10, 30 minutes) and take another jeepney to Cotman (P8, 30 minutes). Vehicle entry costs P10/20 for motorcycles/cars.

Santo Domingo

About 30 minutes north of Legaspi is a stretch of black-sand beach with a few beach resorts, the nicest of which is the **Mayon Spring Resort** (☎ 0917 469 2940; doubles with air-con P750). It's prettily laid out, with orchids planted everywhere, and the grounds include a swimming pool and restaurant. You can use the resort's facilities for the day for P50. Much more basic is the **Reyes Beach Resort** (doubles with bathroom & fan/air-con P230/550). To reach Santo Domingo, take any jeepney from the Legaspi market (P8, 30 minutes).

Mt Mayon

One of the Philippines' most photographed sights, Mt Mayon (2462m) rises dramatically from the flat Albay terrain, and can be seen from as far away as Naga. It is truly a mesmerising sight; in fact, the volcano's name derives from the Bicolano word *magayon*, meaning 'beauty'.

Legend has it that Mayon was an ancient king. His beautiful niece ran away with a young warrior and he never got over it – his anger is still bubbling beneath the surface, ready to erupt at any time.

Mayon is considered one of the most dangerous volcanoes in the world, due to its relatively frequent eruptions. Its most recent blast was in June 2001, when the lava flow miraculously formed the shape of the Virgin Mary and the volcano's once perfectly symmetrical cone was cracked near the top. There were also eruptions in February and June 2000 but the last fatalities were in February 1993, when the eruptions continued for two months. A team of American volcanologists who were doing research on its slopes were among the 77 people killed. At the time, equipment monitoring Mt Mayon had been temporarily moved to Mt Pinatubo, which had recently erupted.

Mayon is carefully monitored by Philvolcs, which closes off an area of up to 8km around the volcano when there is danger of an eruption. People are evacuated and flights to Legaspi are cancelled. In quiet times, however, Mayon is a popular place to visit.

You can drive to the Mayon Skyline Hotel, halfway up the northwestern side of Mt Mayon, at an altitude of 810m. At the time of writing, the hotel was closed and undergoing a leisurely refurbishment, but there are picnic facilities here and the view over the Pacific coast is spectacular. Portions of the road can be rough and there is no public transport, so you must hire your own car to get here; it is one hour from Legaspi.

It's also possible to climb Mt Mayon. You don't need to be an experienced mountain climber to ascend the volcano, although you should be in good shape. Guides can be arranged through the DOT in Legaspi (☎ 482 0712, 214 3215, fax 820 5066), as well as through Bicol Adventure and Tours (☎ 480 2266, fax 820 1483; ℮ bicoladventure@digitelone.com), and your agency should register you with the relevant authorities.

There are three ways to reach Mayon's crater: two routes ascend the southeastern slope via Buyuan or Lidong, while the third starts from the Mayon Skyline Hotel on the northwestern side. Local guides and the tourist office advise climbing the southeastern side because it's safer than the other two routes.

Plan on two days to climb Mayon's southeastern slope. Both routes lead to Camp One, where there is a fresh-water source, in about three hours. The climb to Camp Two, where you'll spend the night, is about another three hours. There is no fresh water source here, but there is usually rainwater that you can purify. The path from Camp One to the summit is a hardened lava gulch, basically increasingly steep black rock and boulders with no shade. From Camp Two to the knife edge, where you can look down into the crater, it's about 2½ hours. Flash floods often occur near the summit, which turn the lava gulch (ie, the path you're hiking on) into a waterfall.

The best time to climb is in March or April, after which the weather gets unbearably hot and wet.

TABACO
☎ 052

Tabaco, in the shadow of Mt Mayon, is the departure point for boats to Catanduanes.

Carolyna Hotel (*☎ 830 0169; P1 San Roque; doubles with bathroom & air-con from P650*) has clean and comfortable rooms with fussy decorations.

Casa Eugenia Hotel (*☎ 830 0425, fax 830 1948; doubles with air-con, hot shower & cable TV from P1300*) is a well run and comfortable hotel. There's a good restaurant here, with live entertainment in the evenings.

You can take a bus to Tabaco from Naga (P90, three hours) or Legaspi (P25, 40 minutes). For information on boats to Catanduanes, see Getting There & Away at the start of that section later in this chapter.

DONSOL

Until the recent 'discovery' of **whale sharks** off the coast here, Donsol, about 25km south of Legaspi, was an obscure, sleepy fishing village in one of Sorsogon's more remote areas. In 1998 a local diver shot a video of the whale sharks and a newspaper carried a story about Donsol's *butanding* (the local word for whale shark). Days after the story was published, poachers from other provinces arrived in the area.

The local and central governments quickly drafted a municipal ordinance together, prohibiting the catching of whale sharks and the poachers were arrested (although illegal poaching still occurs). Since then

Donsol has quickly become one of Bicol's most well-known locations, with travellers and media from around the world descending on the town to see the famous creatures.

It's truly an exhilarating experience swimming along with these huge blue-grey, silver-spotted creatures. You need to be a decent swimmer and in relatively good shape to keep up with the sharks, although if you're lucky your crew will be able to position your boat close to a shark so you don't have to swim far to see one.

Only snorkelling equipment is allowed; scuba diving is prohibited. There is a limited supply of snorkelling equipment available for rent (P200 per day) at the visitor centre, so it's safer to bring your own.

It's difficult to predict your chances of seeing a whale shark. The peak months are February to May, although in some years sharks migrate here as early as October and November and stay as late as June.

Upon arrival in Donsol, stop in at the **visitor centre** (*open 7.30am-5pm daily Jan-June, 7.30am-5pm Mon-Fri July-Dec*) next to the municipal hall. It will arrange a boat, spotter and a Butanding Interaction Officer (BIO) for you. The cost is P2500 per day, including boat, spotter and BIO, plus a P300/100 foreigner/citizen registration fee for the season. A boat can accommodate up to seven people. It's possible to make a reservation by calling Donsol's only phone line, (*☎ 056-411 1109*), and leaving a message for Ronald Malilim from the visitors centre.

Whale Sharks

Known as the largest fish in the world, the whale shark can grow up to 18m long, although it's more common to see them about half that size. The gentle creatures are considered harmless and friendly, and don't seem to mind humans swimming alongside them. No-one knows why the sharks gather in such large numbers near the shore of Donsol; the only other places in the world where they're found in similar numbers are off the shores of Ningaloo (Australia) and the Galapagos Islands.

In association with the World Wide Fund for Nature (WWF), local authorities have established the following code of conduct for interacting with whale sharks:

• Don't touch or ride the sharks
• Don't restrict their movement or impede their path
• Stay at least 3m from their body and 4m from their tail
• Don't use flash photography
• Don't scuba dive or use water scooters, jet skis or other vehicles with motorised underwater propulsion
• Restrict numbers to one boat and a maximum of six swimmers per whale shark

Places to Stay & Eat

Santiago Lodging House *(triples with shared bathroom P300)*, next to the visitors centre, has a few good, clean rooms. The 'lodging house' is basically a homestay and you have use of the kitchen. The friendly owner, Iderlina Santiago, used to be a schoolteacher in Donsol.

Amor Farm Beach Resort *(doubles with/ without bathroom P450/350)* is another option, although it's about 4km west of town. This peaceful resort has nice, well-kept cottages on the black-sand beach. A tricycle from Donsol costs P10, but during the wet season the road is washed out and you must hire a boat to get here.

Woodland Farm Beach Resort *(triples with fan & bathroom P600)*, near Amor Farm and similarly cut off in the wet season, is a stylish place with well-kept, comfortable cottages and a restaurant.

Getting There & Away

There are direct buses from Legaspi to Donsol (P45, two hours), between 4.20am and the last at 3.30pm. Air-con minivans also ply the route (P50).

You can't get a direct bus from Sorsogon. Take a bus to Putiao (P25, 30 minutes) and from there catch a bus or jeepney bound for Donsol (P20, one hour).

Philtranco has direct buses travelling to/from Manila (P250/400 ordinary/air-con, 11 hours).

SORSOGON

☎ 056 • pop 92,512

The capital city of the province of the same name, Sorsogon is in a beautiful area of fertile farmland, thick forest and natural springs. Note that the NPA is still sometimes active in the region, so check on the latest conditions before setting out into Sorsogon's more remote areas. For background on the NPA, see The Marcos Era section in Facts about the Philippines.

Information

You can contact the **Sorsogon Tourism Council** through the energetic Cecilia Duran at Fernandos Hotel (☎ 211 1357). She can help you to hire a car (P1500 to P2000 per day) and organise a guide for climbing Mt Bulusan, or trips to see the whale sharks at Donsol.

There is an **Equitable PCI Bank** *(Rizal St)* with an ATM that accepts MasterCard and Visa. You can check your email at a few places, including **FE Internet Cafe** *(Rizal St; open 8.30am-11pm daily)*, which charges P30 per hour.

Places to Stay

Mercedes Country Lodge *(☎ 211 4261; Peralta St; doubles with shared bathroom P200, with private bathroom & fan/air-con P350/ 700)* is a very simple but clean and cheap place on the 3rd floor.

Fernandos Hotel *(☎ 211 1357, fax 211 1573; e fernandohotel@hotmail.com; N Pareja St; budget room P400, singles/doubles with air-con P950/1120)* has good, well-decorated rooms and a pleasant garden restaurant.

Villa Kasanggayahan *(☎/fax 211 1275; doubles with air-con from P850)* has modern, nicely decorated rooms in a quiet garden. It can arrange mountain-biking tours and whale-watching tours in Donsol.

Getting There & Away

Philtranco *(☎ 211 1359)* has bus services to/from Manila (P350/549 ordinary/air-con, 14 hours), as does BLTB and AMA. There are regular buses to Legaspi (P25, one hour).

For Donsol, you have to take a bus to Putiao (P25, 30 minutes) and switch to a bus or jeepney (P20, one hour).

MT BULUSAN AREA
Bulusan Volcano National Park

This national park *(adult/child P8/5; open 7am-5.30pm daily)*, 8km west of the town of Bulusan, is dominated by an active volcano. Just inside the park **Bulusan Lake**, overlooked by Sharp Peak, is a popular picnic spot, and there's a **walking trail** around the lake that takes about one hour. Mt Bulusan (1560m), which last erupted in 1983, is well known among local climbers and is appreciated for its interesting and varied terrain. The majority of the climb is through forest but eventually you'll arrive at an open field where there are excellent views of the Bicol Peninsula and out to the sparkling blue sea.

The path up the mountain begins at Lake Bulusan. From here, you can climb to the summit and descend the same day, although most people take two days. A hiking guide can be hired through the Sorsogon Tourism Council, or in **San Roque**, a village on the road between Irosin and Bulusan. In San Roque the guided tour will cost around P700 for two days (for a maximum of three people), plus equipment, which you can hire in town – ask for the Barangay Captain, who can help you organise a trip. Bring gloves and wear long sleeves to protect yourself from leeches that drop down on you after it's rained.

From Sorsogon, you can take a jeepney to the town of Bulusan (P25) and from there you can hire a tricycle (P50, 1 hour) to get to the national park.

Mineral Springs

Around 15km from Bulusan, the **Palogtoc Falls** *(admission P 10; open 5am-6pm daily)* are highly recommended for a soak. This idyllic grotto is accessible by a 500m walk along beautiful village tracks and features a cold-water pool beside a shady river. Nearby, but not as good, is the **Masacrot Springs** *(P15/18 per day/night)*. This is a very popular, more developed pool with a 'videoke' setup.

A tricycle from Bulusan will cost around P100. Arrange a time for the driver to meet you when you want to return.

Barcelona

You can climb the belfry of the Spanish-built **Barcelona Church** (1874) for a great view over the ocean. The **Barcelona Multi-purpose Cooperative** *(Poblacion Norte; open 8am-5pm Mon-Sat)* is also well worth a visit. This cooperative of 300 **weavers** sells a wide range of very reasonably priced products made of natural fibres, such as boxes of all shapes and sizes, pencil cases (P7), Christmas decorations (P10) and sunhats. This is a fair-trade group linked to the International Federation for Alternative Trade (IFAT; [W] www.ifat.org) and a couple of its customers have included Oxfam and the Body Shop.

Places to Stay

Villa Luisa Celeste *(doubles with bathroom & fan/air-con P500/700)* is a good-value place located 2.5km from the town of Bulusan (P12 by tricycle). It has well-kept, tastefully decorated rooms, a small pool and a noisy collection of fighting cocks. The surrounding scenery – rice fields and lush coconut trees – is gorgeous.

Mateo Hot & Cold Springs Resort *(camping P25, dorm beds P150, doubles with bath P350)*, just outside of Irosin at the foot of Mt Bulusan, has pretty and well-maintained grounds that include natural hot, warm and cool pools.

You can camp here or spend the night in a dorm or a run-down cottage.

RIZAL BEACH
☎ 056

About 45 minutes from Sorsogon, 4km outside of the town of Gubat, is a nice stretch of brown-sand beach with a few small resorts. The **Rizal Beach Resort** *(☎ 311 1829, fax 211 1056; doubles with bathroom & fan/air-con P780/960)* has basic but clean rooms, as well as a restaurant and pool. Next door there's a better option that's slightly less expensive: **Veramaris Resort** *(☎ 311 1824, fax 311 182; [e] veramaris@yahoo.com; doubles with fan/air-con P700/900)* is a pleasant and well-kept villa-style resort with a small swimming pool. Ask for a room with a view of the beach; they're the same price as the rooms that overlook the road.

From Sorsogon, you can take a jeepney to Gubat (P10) and then catch a tricycle to Rizal (P25).

MATNOG

At the southernmost tip of Luzon is Matnog, a one-road town leading to the pier from where you can catch a ferry bound for Samar. If you miss the last ferry, you can stay at the **AG Primo Lodging House** *(doubles P200)*, a dilapidated place around the corner from the pier. You're much better off taking a tricycle (P50) to **New Port Beach Resort** *(doubles with bathroom & fan/air-con P650/850)* in Santa Magdalena, about 9km from Matnog. It's located on a gorgeous beach and has simple, clean cottages where water is available by the bucket.

Direct bus services from Manila to Matnog are offered by Philtranco (P350/603 ordinary/air-con, 14 hours) and BLTB (P333 ordinary). Jeepneys make the run to Sorsogon for P38.

Ferries depart from Matnog for Samar, going to Allen (P60, 1½ hours) and San Isidro (P60, two hours).

SOUTHEAST LUZON

Catanduanes

A rugged and rural island with its east coast open to the Pacific Ocean, Catanduanes has a narrow coastal strip rising abruptly to a range of mountains running north to south. Beyond the capital (Virac) the island is little developed. Buffalo sleds are a common mode of transportation in the smaller villages, and stands of native forest remain in the centre of the island.

Catanduanes is the wettest place in the Philippines; its exposed position makes it prone to *bagyo* (typhoons), and the big wind of 22 October 1998 flattened all the coastal communities and many people died. The least amount of rain falls between the months of April and June.

Getting There & Away

Air The **Asian Spirit** (*052-811 1056, San Juan St*) makes daily flights to Virac from Manila (P1923, 1¼ hours). The airport is 5km from town; a tricycle ride will cost P20.

Boat Bicolandia Lines has two daily boats from Tabaco, on Luzon, to Virac (P70/100 ordinary/air-con, three hours), as does Star Ferry (P73/106). Montenegro operates three daily fast-craft services from Tabaco to San Andres (P15, 1¼ hours). Jeepneys meet all arriving boats – the trip between San Andres and Virac costs P12 and takes 30 minutes.

VIRAC
☎ 052 • pop 57,067

This is a compact town and everything is within easy walking distance. It's a good base for day trips around the island. **Maribina Falls** is a popular spot, 5km east of town and a 200m walk off the road. There are a few souvenir shops near the roundabout selling woven baskets, shoes and bags.

Information

The **Tourism Unit** (*☎ 811 1141; 2nd floor, Provincial Capitol Bldg, Rizal St*), at the Governor's Office, is helpful.

You can only change US dollars at the **Philippine National Bank (PNB)** and there's an ATM at **Equitable PCI** that accepts Master-Card and Cirrus. **Sophia Internet Cafe** (*San José St; open 8am-8pm Mon-Sat*) offers Internet access for P55 per hour.

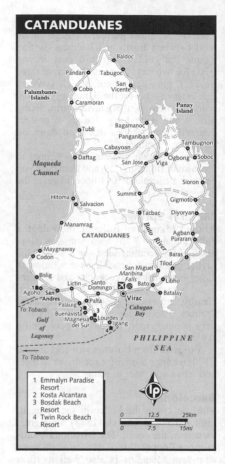

CATANDUANES

1 Emmalyn Paradise Resort
2 Kosta Alcantara
3 Bosdak Beach Resort
4 Twin Rock Beach Resort

Places to Stay & Eat

Marem Pension House (*☎ 811 1821; e marem_ph@hotmail.com; Rafael St; singles/doubles with fan & shared bathroom P100/150, with air-con & private bathroom P650/775*) offers the best value and variety. It's an easy-going place with a bar, a restaurant and helpful staff.

Catanduanes Midtown Inn (*☎ 811 0527, fax 811 1526; San José St; singles/doubles with air-con, cable TV & hot shower from P900/1200*) is a new and popular place with a pleasant coffee shop. You can rent a car from here.

Solybel Lodge (*☎ 811 1194; singles/doubles with fan & shared bathroom P135/200*) offers budget lodging in dark, basic rooms, but there is a pleasant communal veranda.

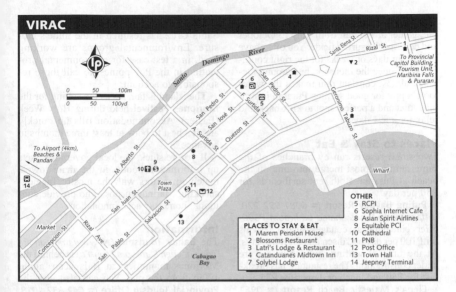

VIRAC

PLACES TO STAY & EAT
1 Marem Pension House
2 Blossoms Restaurant
3 Latri's Lodge & Restaurant
4 Catanduanes Midtown Inn
7 Solybel Lodge

OTHER
5 RCPI
6 Sophia Internet Cafe
8 Asian Spirit Airlines
9 Equitable PCI
10 Cathedral
11 PNB
12 Post Office
13 Town Hall
14 Jeepney Terminal

Latri's Lodge & Restaurant (☎ *811 1499; Geronimo Tabuzo St; singles/doubles with fan & shared bathroom P130/230, doubles with air-con & private bathroom P650*) has tiny plywood rooms.

Blossoms Restaurant (*open 8.30am-9pm daily; dishes P100*), at the roundabout, is a stylish place with a nice terrace for alfresco dining and good Western and Filipino food.

SOUTH COAST
☎ 052

The beach resorts on the south coast are all very isolated, but offer gorgeous views across to Mt Mayon in Luzon. The best of these and the closest to Virac is **Twin Rock Beach Resort** (☎ *0918 736 1168; doubles with fan & hot shower P1200*), with a lovely garden, a beautiful twin-rocks formation in the bay and coral just offshore.

Bosdak Beach Resort (☎ *811 1753; doubles with fan P800*), near Magnesia del Sur, was under renovation at the time of writing. It has pretty grounds on a white-sand beach and offers free pick-up from Virac, San Andres or the airport.

Kosta Alcantara (☎ *811 1459; doubles with/without bathroom P1800/1600*), in the village of Marilima near Buenavista, is a classy but overpriced place on a white-sand beach. You have to bring your own food, which the kitchen will prepare for you.

Emmalyn Paradise Resort (☎ *0917 344 6667; doubles with air-con & hot shower from P1400*), 7km west of San Andres, has a gorgeous view over San Andres, and a swimming pool. It has newly built and comfortable concrete cottages, as well as a dive centre (P2000 per dive, including equipment).

WEST COAST

The road from Virac to **Pandan** is bumpy, beautiful and sometimes hair-raising as it follows the rocky coastline. It's a good way to see rural island life, with great views across Maqueda Channel. There is no commercial lodging in Pandan.

A possible day trip from Virac is to arrive on the early bus (four hours), ask the driver to drop you at Pandan's pretty little beach for a few hours, and walk the few hundred metres back into town to pick up the later bus back to Virac.

EAST COAST
Puraran

The stunning wide bay of **Puraran** is about 30km north of Virac on the east coast, along an extremely bumpy and beautiful road; look out for the monumental ruins of the **Spanish church** at Bato on the way. There is coral reef just offshore with good **snorkelling** and safe swimming inside the reef, but beware of dangerously strong currents beyond the reef.

Surfers, particularly Australians and Japanese, gather at Puraran from May to October and describe the surf as fickle. You often have to wait for days or weeks for the right conditions and once the monsoon hits around October, almost constant rain makes the water too choppy for good surfing. Puraran is simple, quiet and a perfect spot to kick back and relax for a few days.

Places to Stay & Eat
Two small resorts run by branches of the same family almost merge into one on the beach at Puraran. Both rent surfboards for P50 per day.

Puting Baybay Resort (☎ 0981 992 220; *cottages with fan & shared bathroom P300*) offers cute but basic cottages, surfing lessons for P100 per day and discounts for long stays. At the time of writing, hotel rooms were under construction. The restaurant has breakfast for P50 and lunch or dinner for P75.

Elena's Majestic Beach Resort (☎ 0981 991 109; *cottages with bathroom P300 per person*) has name that describes the scenery rather than its simple and pretty bamboo cottages. The restaurant offers three meals a day for P200.

Getting There & Away
Getting to Puraran can be a hassle. If you're with a group and you're staying at Puting Baybay for at least a week, the resort will pick you up for free from Virac or the airport. There is a jeepney from Virac to Gigmoto via Puraran at around 10am (P25, 2½ hours) and a jeepney to Virac from Puraran at around 3am (going to the early market).

There may be other services; ask at the terminal in Virac. Otherwise, get a more regular jeepney from Virac to Baras (P20, one hour) and hire a tricycle (P50, one hour) to Puraran.

You can charter a tricycle from Virac for P300 to P400 one way (two hours) or P500 for a one-day return.

Marinduque

Marinduque is a gem of an island province, its 120km coastal strip rising to a ridge of hills. Its economy is based on copra production, while many people fish for a living or are subsistence farmers.

Toxic seepage from a copper mine near Santa Cruz has resulted in the mine's closure. Environmental groups are working hard, in a test case for environmental protection in the Philippines, to call those responsible to account.

The island is famous as the setting for the **Moriones Festival** held during Holy Week (Easter). Accommodation fills up quickly and it's best to book at least three months in advance.

If you're stuck, the local government sets up information booths in the main towns, matching visitors with the mostly Tagalog-speaking Marinduqueños, who provide additional homestay accommodation.

Information
The **Bahay Tourismo** (Ⓦ *www.marinduque .gov.ph; open 8am-5pm Mon-Fri*) is behind the Moriones monument at Balanacan, about 100m from the pier. You can also visit the **Provincial Tourism Office** (☎ *042-332 1018; open 8am-5pm Mon-Fri*) in the Capitol Compound, 2km west of Boac town centre.

Getting There & Away
Air Asian Spirit flies between Manila and Marinduque's airport in Gazal (P1400, 45 minutes, four weekly). Gazal is a 12km (15 minute) trip from Boac that you can do by jeepney (P20) or tricycle (P60). The Asian Spirit booking office is in the Boac Hotel (☎ 042-332 1121).

Boat Several vessels go from Balanacan to Lucena's Dalahican Port (until 3.30pm), from where there are regular buses to Manila. **Montenegros Shipping Lines** (☎ *042-373 7084*) has four daily services between Balanacan and Lucena (P75/90 ordinary/air-con, 2½ hours).

Phil-Nippon (☎ *042-373 7652*) has two daily services (P85/100 ordinary/air-con, three hours) between Dalahican and Cawit, which is around 8km (P20/100 by jeepney/tricycle) south of Boac.

From Santa Cruz's port at Buyabod the fast boat MV *Santa Cruz* leaves for Dalahican (P160, three hours) at 5am daily and returns to Buyabod at 9am. Slower boats take four hours.

A boat leaves Gasan at 8.30am daily for Pinamalayan on Mindoro (P80, 2½ hours). Schedules can change without notice.

MARINDUQUE

1 A & A Beach Resort
2 Villa Carlos Highway Grill
3 Castaway Beach Resort
4 Blue Sea Resort
5 Sunset Garden Resort
6 Katala Beach Resort & Restaurant
7 Malbog Sulphur Hot Springs
8 Susanna Hot Spring Resort
9 Torrijos Loomweavers

Getting Around

Car-hire is available through Mr Adollo M Lazares (☎ 042-332 1302) for P1500 to P1700 per day (including driver) for an air-con car. Jeepneys run frequently over the island in all directions.

Tricycles usually make local runs but can be chartered for half a day for P350. Air-con minivans connect with boats to/from Balanacan; it costs P60 to Boac and P100 to Santa Cruz.

BOAC

☎ 042 • pop 48,504

Boac is Marinduque's capital. It is a pretty town, with pot plants everywhere and many attractive, dilapidated **Spanish-era wooden houses**. The beautiful **cathedral**, built in

1792 on the hill in the centre of town, and its attached convent are the focal points. In one building on the grounds, a **carved Black Christ** lies under a glass dome on a massive wooden carriage that is pulled through the streets during Moriones.

The dusty **museum** (admission free; open 8am-noon & 1pm-5pm Mon-Fri) on the Plaza houses a good collection on Marinduque's history and an extraordinary selection of Moriones masks and costumes. Also worth a look is the **Marinduque Butterfly Park** (admission free; open 8am-5pm Mon-Fri), next to the Capitol Complex, which houses a breeding programme for tropical butterflies in a pleasant garden.

The **PNB**, near the market, changes US dollars and travellers cheques. **Nets Cafe**

Moriones Madness

During this fabulous Easter festival, combining folk mysticism with Catholic pageantry, the streets of Marinduque's towns are incongruously overrun with *moriones* – Roman soldiers.

Moriones began in 1807, when Padre Dionsio Santiago, a Mogpog parish priest, organised a group of players to tell the story of Christ's crucifixion. He based it on Longinus, the Roman centurion assigned to execute Christ.

Today the play has evolved into a colourful festival with around 100 *moriones*. They don wonderful costumes decorated with feathers, woven vines and shells, and arm themselves with wooden swords, spears and shields.

Moriones is most famous for the fierce and sometimes gruesome masks that hide the faces of the players. Masks are made of hand-carved and painted wood or papier-mâché and are adorned with paper flowers, coloured foil, golden helmets and magnificent beards. Traditionally, they take months to prepare and are kept secret from even close friends and family so that the *moriones'* true identity is never known.

On each day of Holy Week a different part of the story is told. There are stage performances at the Boac stadium on Wednesday and Thursday but on Good Friday the celebrations spill onto the streets. The *morions* run amok, engaging in sword fights, dances and sneaky pranks on by-standers. You have been warned!

(open 8.30am-7pm), behind the Boac Hotel, charges P60 per hour for Internet access.

Places to Stay & Eat

Tahanan sa Isok *(☎ 332 1231, fax 311 1402; Canovas St; doubles with bathroom, cable TV & fan/air-con P400/800)* is easily the best value in town. There is a gorgeous garden restaurant here, with books and newspapers supplied.

Boac Hotel *(☎ 332 1121; Nepomuceno St; singles with bath & fan P250; singles/doubles with bath & air-con P600/700)*, opposite the cathedral, has run-down but reasonably clean rooms. It also has a restaurant and a good bakery.

Lucky 7 Pension House *(☎ 332 2777, fax 332 2003; Mercado St; singles/doubles with bathroom, cable TV & air-con from P700/900)* offers clean and modern motel-style accommodation, and a great view over the town from the roof.

Cely's Kitchenette & Lodging House *(☎ 332 1519; 10 de Octobre St; singles/doubles with fan P150/200)* has an attached restaurant and recently renovated rooms.

ALB Foodworld *(open 7am-9pm daily; buffet dishes around P30)*, next to the Boac Hotel, has a good Filipino buffet for lunch and dinner, as well an American breakfast for P65.

Kusina sa Plaza *(open 5.30am-7pm daily; dishes P20)*, opposite the museum, is clean and bright and serves pasta dishes and coleslaw, as well as Filipino food.

AROUND BOAC
☎ 042

There is a selection of **beach resorts** south of Boac along the pebbly beach. Take your own snorkelling equipment.

A & A Beach Resort *(☎ 332 2817; doubles with bathroom & fan/air-con P100/500)*, 2km from Boac, has basic cottages and small, run-down air-con rooms with TV.

Villa Carlos Highway Grill *(☎ 332 1882; doubles with bathroom & air-con P1300)*, 4km from Boac over the bridge, is right on the water and rather overpriced. There's an outdoor restaurant open 6am to midnight.

Castaway Beach Resort *(doubles with fan P400)*, 5km from Boac, has seen better days, but its simple, stylish rooms are good value at this price. There are live bands in the restaurant on Friday and Saturday nights.

The **Blue Sea Resort** *(☎ 332 1334; doubles with bathroom & fan/air-con P380/550)*, 8km south of Boac, has pleasant landscaped gardens leading to the beach.

GASAN
☎ 042

Gasan, 17km south of Boac, thrives on its **Three Kings Festival** and **Moriones Festival**. There are many souvenir shops in town, especially along Rizal St, selling wooden masks and basketry. There are also some lodging houses in town, but these are closed except during Moriones.

Sunset Garden Resort (☎ 342 1004; Ⓔ sun setgarden@vasia.com; cottages with bathroom & fan/air-con P530/730), 3km north of town, has a great beach setting. Diving with qualified dive instructors can be arranged and equipment can be hired. There is a comfortable restaurant and bar offering Filipino and Western food.

Katala Beach Resort & Restaurant (☎/fax 333 7117; Ⓔ katalaresort@gmx.net; rooms with fan/air-con from P500/700), 3km south of Gasan, is good value, with spotless, balconied rooms in a great location overlooking the Tres Reyes Islands. It has a pleasant bar, lapped by waves, and diving can be arranged.

There are regular jeepneys between Gasan and Buenavista (P10) and Boac (P16). Boats run at 8.30am daily between Gasan and Pinamalayan on Mindoro (P80, 2½ hours).

BUENAVISTA

This town in the south of the island is about 15km south of Gasan. The nearby **Tres Reyes Islands**, with the wonderful names of Gaspar, Melchor and Baltazar, can be visited by bangka from Pingan Beach, weather permitting. It takes 40 minutes to reach Gaspar and costs P500 return, to see all three islands costs P1500.

There's at least waiting time thrown in for free. Gaspar Island is a marine reserve and there is good snorkelling just off the northern beach. An old Chinese **shipwreck** lies offshore and some of its ceramics, dating from the late 16th century, can be seen in the museum in Boac. There are no facilities on any of the islands.

The **Malbog sulphur hot springs** (admission P10; open 7am-sunset daily) are a pretty 2km walk or jeepney ride out of town, but are cut off by the river in the wet season.

Susanna Hot Spring Resort (☎ 042-332 1997; singles with shared bathroom P250, doubles with private bathroom & fan P400), 2km out of Buenavista at Malbog, is a friendly resort with three small hot pools and a pleasant garden. You can use the pools for P30/50 per day/night.

Jeepneys (P20) are infrequent from Torrijos. There is a more regular daily service from Boac (P20). From Buenavista to Malbog costs P5 per person by tricycle.

MOGPOG

Mogpog is a pretty hillside town in the north of the island, at the junction of the roads to Balanacan, Boac and Santa Cruz. The town's only hotel is the **Hill Top Lodge** (☎ 042-332 3074; rooms with shared bathroom & fan/air-con P350/400, doubles with air-con & private bathroom from P500), which has reasonable but scruffy rooms and balconies with beautiful views across the hills. This is the nearest hotel to Balanacan if you arrive late at night by boat.

BALANACAN

This is the small port area in the northwest of the island servicing Luzon. Jeepneys meet all boats and go directly to all parts of Marinduque. The **tourist office** (Ⓦ www.marinduque.gov.ph; open 8am-5pm Mon-Fri), is behind the Moriones monument at Balanacan.

SANTA CRUZ

Santa Cruz is set on a ridge. It holds a **Three Kings Festival** in January and a **Moriones Festival**. The quiet **Holy Cross Parish Church** was completed in 1760. Inside there are hundreds of bats hanging from the walls and rafters.

Places to Stay & Eat

Rico's Inn Lodging House (☎ 042-321 1085; rooms with shared bathroom & fan P150), opposite the PNB, serves decent Filipino and Western food. You can ask for a room in the family house of the owner, Miss Norma, around the corner. It's a noisy and friendly homestay.

Santa Cruz Hotel (Tavera St; doubles with bathroom & air-con P1200-1400) is a bland place aimed at business travellers. Meals are available.

Laica's Restaurant (Palomares St; dishes P60) has a garden setting but dull food and a 'videoke'.

Tita Digs (Claudio St; dishes around P45) is a tatty restaurant, with an absurdly low ceiling, that serves a small number of cheap and tasty dishes of the day. The elderly Tita Amie, who cooks, is a delight.

Getting There & Away

There's a regular jeepney service from Boac (P20). There's a boat that runs twice daily between Santa Cruz's port at Buyabod and Lucena, on Luzon.

AROUND SANTA CRUZ

The privately owned **Bathala Caves** *(admission P40; open sunrise-sunset daily)*, beyond Ipil, are terrific. If you're prepared to clamber a bit, you can explore two or three of the eight main caves in a couple of hours.

With luck, you'll see rock formations of the faces of the Holy Spirit and the Virgin Mary. There are thousands of bats and swifts, and several enormous rock pythons. Cool off afterwards in the natural **pool** behind the caretaker's house.

A guided tour costs P150. Take a torch (flashlight) and charter a tricycle for the bumpy 10km trip from Santa Cruz. Half-day charter costs P300.

About 15km south of Santa Cruz is the **Torrijos Loomweavers** *(open 7am-5pm daily)*, a cooperative of 60 weavers who use *buri*, a stiff local fibre which is bleached, dyed and woven, to prepare placemats (P40), table runners (P150) and coasters (P12 to P15) in many designs.

You can watch the weavers at work; their products are light and make good gifts. A jeepney to the co-op, close to the turn-off to Suha, costs P10 from Torrijos or Santa Cruz.

POCTOY

Visit **White Beach** *(admission P3)* in Poctoy, the longest stretch of sandy beach on the island. From here there are wide views of **Mt Malindig**, a dormant volcano and the highest point on Marinduque. You can rent a shade hut for P100.

Rendezvous Cottages *(singles/doubles with bathroom & fan P200/300)*, on White Beach itself, has rickety cottages. Water is by the bucket and costs P5. Motorboats can be hired and meals are available.

Quiet **Jovita's Paradise Resort** *(rooms with bath fan/air-con P700/1200)*, just to the north of White Beach, is a peaceful spot with tidy rooms and a beautiful private stretch of sand and a garden along the shore. Bangka can be hired for P200 per hour and there's a restaurant. The irregular jeepney service from Santa Cruz to Torrijos costs P18 per person. It runs more frequently at the weekend. A tricycle from Torrijos to White Beach costs P5.

Cathedral of St Paul and bell tower, Vigan, Ilocos – North Luzon

Kalesa on Crisologo St, Vigan – North Luzon

Cagsawa Church ruins, Bicol – Southeast Luzon

Mt Mayon, coconut groves and rice paddies, Bicol – Southeast Luzon

Hundred Islands National Park, Lingayen Gulf – North Luzon

Mindoro

A great mountainous chunk of an island just south of Luzon, Mindoro is packed with resorts along its north coast. Its premier spots are Puerto Galera and Sabang, though some of the country's most idyllic offshore islands, brilliant diving, excellent hiking and mountain climbing can be found beyond these places.

Even in the touristy northern areas, Mindoro's roads are stunningly bad, especially in the wet season. Roads connecting quite large towns are often no more than vague scratches on a flood plain. In any other country, you would pay a lot of money for this sort of cross-country 4WD adventure. Here, you get it for less than P100!

Getting There & Away

Air Mindoro's two commercial airports are at Pinamalayan and San José, servicing the provinces of Mindoro Oriental and Mindoro Occidental, respectively.

If you're headed for the resorts on the north coast, bear in mind that Pinamalayan is a rough four-hour overland journey from Puerto Galera, so most people prefer to travel by bus and boat. See the Pinamalyan and San José sections for details on flights from Manila.

The Mindoro Oriental airport is 12km south of Pinamalayan, 4km off the main road to Roxas. At the time of writing there were **SEAIR** (☎ 02-843 7308) flights to/from Manila on Monday and Thursday (P1290, 40 minutes), although there was speculation that flights may be discontinued. Tricycles wait at the airport to take passengers to Pinamalayan (P100), or you can take an air-con minivan to Calapan (P65).

Boat Most visitors end up coming to Mindoro by boat.

Luzon The typical route is from Manila to Batangas (on Luzon) by bus and from there to Puerto Galera or Sabang by boat.

One popular and convenient way to transfer from Manila is on the combined bus and boat trip offered by the swish Si-Kat ferry. An air-con bus leaves Manila's Citystate Tower Hotel daily at 9am, connecting with the Si-Kat ferry at 11.45am and arriving in Puerto

Highlights

- Submerge yourself and partake in superb diving and snorkelling
- Revel in Puerto Galera's coast and its *après*-dive attractions
- Hide from the world on North Pandan Island
- Trek to the top of Mt Halcon or Mt Iglit

Galera at 1pm. The trip costs P400/700 one way/return. There's a **booking desk** (☎ 02-521 3344) at the Citystate Tower Hotel in Manila, and another at Muelle Pier in Puerto Galera (☎ 0918 332 8933).

In future the Si-Kat may move from Muelle pier to the Balatero pier, which is 3km to the west.

A cheaper option is to take a bus from Manila to the Batangas pier (around two hours; for details see Getting There & Away under Batangas in the Around Manila chapter) and then a boat to Puerto Galera, Sabang, Balatero or White Beach.

Boats leave regularly during the day until around 4pm and you will find offices for all the main shipping lines at the pier. These lines include **Super Diamond Shipping Lines** (☎ 0917 350 8121), with four to five daily fast-craft services to Puerto Galera (P140, one hour); **Datinguinoo Shipping Lines** (☎ 0917 361 0772), with six daily outrigger services to Sabang (P100, one hour); and

MINDORO

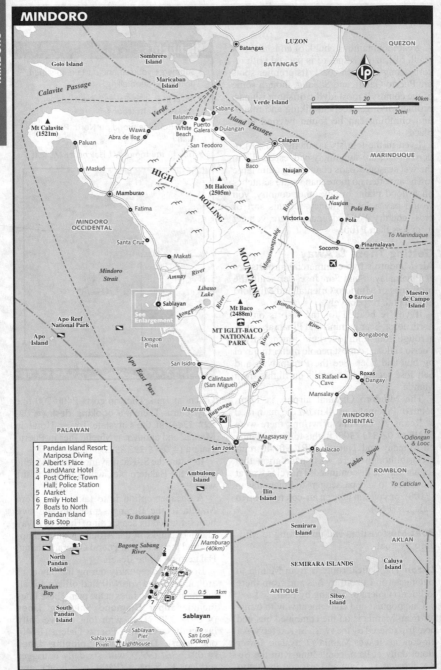

MINDORO

Key (Sablayan enlargement):
1 Pandan Island Resort; Mariposa Diving
2 Albert's Place
3 LandManz Hotel
4 Post Office; Town Hall; Police Station
5 Market
6 Emily Hotel
7 Boats to North Pandan Island
8 Bus Stop

The Mangyan

The indigenous people of Mindoro are collectively known as the Mangyan. They comprise at least seven different tribes, including the Batangan (population 36,000) from the central highlands, the Iraya (35,000) from the Mt Halcon region, and the Hanunoo (18,500) from southeastern Mindoro.

The Mangyan are slash-and-burn farmers who have lived on Mindoro for 600 to 700 years. They were originally a coastal people, but with the arrival of new settlers were forced to relocate to the rugged interior of Mindoro. They have preserved their traditional culture to a much greater extent than many other Philippine indigenous groups, and have long viewed outsiders with suspicion – to the point where the Hanunoo warn young children to stop crying or the *damu-ong* (non-Mangyan) will get them! Their attitude is not surprising, given the history of their contact with outsiders.

The Spanish invaded in the 16th century, angered by the fact that over the centuries some of the Mangyan tribes had converted to Islam. The Mangyan fought the invaders but were defeated by the superior force and were massacred or sold as slaves by the Spanish.

With the arrival of the Americans at the beginning of the 20th century, Mangyan people were put to work on sugar estates or forced into reservations, much like those created for Native Americans. Even today, many Mangyan people feel that the lowlanders are swindlers who cheat them in business deals.

The Mangyan are famous for their woven baskets, traditionally created by the women. Iraya designs include small, hexagonal household baskets, while the Hanunoo make baskets with a square base and a round mouth.

Tourists from Puerto Galera and Sabang often visit Mangyan communities on Mindoro's nearby north coast.

ERIC L WHEATER

Brian Shipping Lines (☎ 0917 273 5070), with six to eight daily outrigger services to White Beach (P120, 1¼ hours).

Be careful when you get off the bus at the Batangas pier, as some travellers have been scammed by boat operators and touts: they'll claim that the last boat to Mindoro has just left, hoping that you'll pay for a special trip (costing an outrageous P2000) in their small and rickety outriggers. Even if it's late in the day, check with the ticket offices in the terminal building before resorting to a special trip, as there are often late departures of passenger boats. Alternatively, you can take one of the frequent services to Calapan, which run later, and which travel overland to Puerto Galera the next day.

There's a P10 terminal fee for all passengers leaving Batangas; pay at a booth in the terminal. For details on boats to Calapan, San

José and Abra de Ilog from Luzon, see those entries later in this chapter.

Palawan A pumpboat, the MB *Socorro 2*, sails from San José to Concepcion, on Busuanga Island, at 5am on Monday (P200, nine hours). This can be a rough voyage.

Panay There are pumpboats from Roxas to Caticlan on Panay four times weekly (P220 to P280, four to five hours); see under Roxas for more details. Caticlan is an entry point for Boracay.

Larger pumpboats operate about twice a week between San José and Libertad (east of Caticlan), going via the Semirara Islands.

Romblon Large ferry-type pumpboats operate between Roxas and Odiongan (P100, three hours), as well as between Roxas and Looc (P100, three hours). See under Roxas for details.

Marinduque There's a boat to Gasan (P80, 2½ hours), in Marinduque, from Pinamalayan pier at around 8.30am daily.

Mindoro Oriental

Mindoro's High Rolling Mountains slice the island into two provinces. The eastern province is known as Mindoro Oriental, with the northeastern city of Calapan as its capital. Of main interest to visitors is the northern area around Puerto Galera, where there is good diving and gorgeous secluded resorts to get away from it all.

PUERTO GALERA
☎ 043 • pop 21,925
Puerto Galera (**pwair**-toe gal-**air**-ah) is the main gateway to Mindoro, but most people simply pass through on their way to the more exciting locales of Sabang and White Beach, or to a secluded beach in one of the isolated coves nearby.

Today Puerto Galera is something of a haven for foreign, alcoholic retirees. With no nightlife beyond sinking a few beers and watching a wall-mounted TV, this place is often fast asleep by 9pm.

There's talk of making Balatero pier – roughly halfway between Puerto Galera and White Beach – the main point of entry to the

area by sea. The new facilities at Balatero's port are much better than those at Puerto, but local protests have so far kept most services at Puerto Galera's Muelle pier.

Information
From the tourist office and other tourist haunts, you can pick up the free *Puerto Galera Today* newspaper, which is published every three months and includes local news, tourist information and an events calendar. There's a website on the Puerto Galera area at ⓦ www.travelpuertogalera.com.

Tourist Offices The **tourist office** *(☎ 281 4051; Muelle pier; open 8am-5pm Mon-Sat, 8am-noon Sun)* can help with organising vehicle hire (from P1000/2000 per day for a tricycle/jeepney) and a local guide (P500 per day). Outside, there's a board on pumpboat fares.

Money Make sure you bring enough money with you, as many travellers are caught short of cash and the closest ATM is in Calapan. The **Rural Bank** *(open 8am-noon & 1pm-3pm Mon-Fri)* and the **Allied Bank** *(open 9am-4pm Mon-Fri)* change US dollars in cash. There are also a few moneychangers in town that change US dollars, but it's generally easier to change money in Sabang.

Post & Communications The **post office** *(E Brucal St; open 8am-noon & 1pm-5pm Mon-Fri)* is next to the Hotel California.

Puerto Galera's phone services are unreliable at best – the region relies heavily on mobile and satellite phones. There are international phones on the Puerto Galera pier, as well as at a few call offices in town, including **Bayan Tel** *(open 7am-8pm Mon-Fri, 7am-6pm Sat & Sun)*, opposite CJ Trading, which charges P65 per minute to Australia and the USA and P70 per minute to Europe and the Middle East.

There are a couple of Internet cafés in town. **CJ Trading** *(open 8am-8pm Mon-Sat, 9am-8pm Sun)* is the most reliable; it has a satellite connection and charges P150 per hour.

Medical Services The **Palm Medical Clinic** *(☎ 442 0250)* is just out of Puerto Galera proper, on the road to Sabang. The **Holy Family Medical Clinic** *(☎ 281 4017; P Concepcion St)* has its own pharmacy.

PUERTO GALERA

To Balatero Pier (3km);
White Beach (6km) &
Talipanan Beach (10km)

Muelle Bay

Muelle Pier

To Sabang (6km)

Varadero Bay

Balete
Beach

PLACES TO STAY
6   Won Dive Resort
11 Coco Point
22 Melxa's Beach House
     Annexe
23 Melxa's Greenhills
     Nipa Hut
27 Hotel California
32 Dog & Duck Pub;
     Jeepneys to Calapan
33 Bahay-Pilipino Pension
     House & Restaurant

PLACES TO EAT
4   Pier Pub Pizza
5   Harbour Point
     Restaurant
31 Fely's Carinderia

H Axalan St

R Garcia St

E Brucal St

L Axalan Sr St

OTHER
1   Puerto Galera Yacht
     Club
2   Si-Kat Ticket Office
3   Boats to Batangas;
     Boats to Puerto Galera
     Yacht Club
7   Margarita Shopping
     Center
8   Jeepneys to Aninuan
     & Talipanan
9   Tourist Office
10 Pumpboats to Other
     Beaches
12 Badladz Adventures
13 Bayan Tel
14 CJ Trading
15 Allied Bank
16 Immaculate
     Conception Church
17 Excavation Museum
18 Rural Bank
19 Police Station;
     Municipal Building;
     Basketball Court
20 Jeepneys to Sabang
21 Palm Medical Clinic
24 Puerto Galera Central
     School
25 Souvenir Shops
26 Butiki Souvenir Shop
28 Post Office
29 Holy Family Medical
     Clinic
30 First People's Bank

0   50   100m
0   50   100yd

To Python Cave (2km),
Dulangan (7km),
Tamaraw Falls (10km)
& Calapan (48km)

*Hondura
Beach*

Emergency The **police station** (☎ 281 4043;
H Axalan St) is in the Municipal Building.

Things to See & Do
The small **Excavation Museum** (admission by
donation; open 8am–noon & 1pm–5pm Wed–
Sun) has ancient Chinese and Thai burial jars
on display, as well as Filipino pottery dating
back more than 2000 years. The donation box
always appreciates P10 or so. The museum is
inside the grounds of the Immaculate Conception Church. Enter the church grounds
through the gate in front of the bell tower then
turn right.

Badladz Adventures (☎ 0919 577 2823)
rents out snorkel sets for P300 per day,
mountain bikes for P300 per day and motorbikes for P200/800/5000 per hour/day/week.

It also offers **paintball** on a secluded beach
for P1200 per player, including transport,
paint guns, protective gear, 80 paintballs,
food and drinks.

There are a couple of **Mangyan tribal villages** near Puerto Galera, where you can see
these expert basket weavers at work. You'll
need a guide and vehicle to visit these villages (see Information earlier in this section
and Sabang Beach later in this chapter), and
remember that you're entering a private
community.

Off the road to Calapan, a 2km unsealed
road snakes its way up to **Python Cave**. This
really is home to a 2m-long python, along
with a colony of bats. A tricycle from town
will cost around P300 return, including a
half-hour wait.

The most popular day trip from Puerto Galera is to mighty **Tamaraw Falls** *(adult/ child P10/5; open 7am-5pm Mon-Fri, 7am-4pm Sat & Sun)*. Cool mountain water plummets into a natural pool from high above the road, gushing down to two man-made swimming pools and disappearing into a deep valley below. Several swimmers have slipped while climbing the rocks around the top pool, hence the 'no trespassing' sign in this section.

The Tamaraw Falls are popular on the weekend, but during the week you can just about have this brilliant place to yourself. Small shelters, perched on the edge of the pools, are available for picnicking (P50 per day). There's a small kiosk selling snacks, soft drinks and beer.

To get here from Puerto Galera, catch a Calapan-bound jeepney from next to the Dog & Duck Pub (P25, 30 minutes). Puerto Galera tricycle riders tend to demand hundreds of pesos for the trip – expect to pay up to P400 for the 45-minute journey. Sure, the road is bad but it's not *that* bad. If you have your own motorcycle, this trip is a must.

Places to Stay

Rooms in Puerto Galera are generally cheap.

Bahay-Pilipino Pension House & Restaurant *(☎ 442 0266; singles/doubles P180/280)* has basic rooms with fan and shared bathroom, as well as a restaurant (for more information see Places to Eat). There's a common balcony that overlooks the busy street.

Dog & Duck Pub *(☎ 0918 235 1400; P Concepcion St; doubles with/without private bathroom from P400/200)*, not far from the market, has basic rooms above the bar (see Places to Eat for details).

Melxa's Greenhills Nipa Hut *(☎ 0919 569 2972; doubles with/without private bathroom from P350/250)*, up the hill, is a modest place with small, very basic rooms with fan. Rooms in the beachside annexe are rough, but the bay view is good.

Hotel California *(☎ 442 0256; E Brucal St; doubles from P300)* has simple, good-value rooms with fan and private bathroom.

Coco Point *(☎ 442 0109; 4-bed rooms P500, doubles with view P700)*, right at the pier, is another good option, with rattan-lined rooms with fan and bathroom. Breezy room No 7 looks straight out over the water.

Won Dive Resort *(☎/fax 442 0264; triples with hot shower & fan/air-con from P1000/ 1500)*, prominently placed above the pier, has motel-style rooms. There is also a swimming pool and a restaurant, with live bands Tuesday to Sunday.

Diving trips can be organised here. There's another branch of this hotel on the road to Balatero.

Places to Eat

The restaurants along the pier, interspersed with souvenir shops, offer relaxed dining with great views of the boats bobbing on the harbour.

Harbour Point Restaurant *(open 7am-9.30pm daily; dishes P140)* is a cosy spot, with Western and Filipino options.

Pier Pub Pizza, at the end of the pier, is going for a trattoria feel, with painted wooden beams and checked tablecloths. It has thick, fruity pancakes for P65 to P75 and tasty pizzas for P195 to P245. *Calamares* (squid) with fries and salad is P220.

Puerto Galera Yacht Club *(☎ 442 0136)* is something a little different. It has a café and bar, with happy hour from 4pm to 6pm daily. A free shuttle service ships you there and back from the pier (a few minutes each way), and operates from 8am to 9pm daily.

Dog & Duck Pub, down the southern end of town, is an English-style pub that cooks up beef and chicken curries for around P140. Steak is P180 to P290 – good with the crusty French rolls and imported beer.

Bahay-Pilipino Pension House & Restaurant *(dishes P140)*, near Dog & Duck Pub, specialises in Swiss, German, Austrian and Filipino food.

Fely's Carinderia *(dishes P40)*, opposite the Dog & Duck, is a humble place serving a wide range of fine Filipino dishes.

Getting There & Away

Jeepney & Tricycle Jeepneys (P10) leave when full for Sabang from the northeastern end of town, and tricycles can also be hired for the ride (around P150).

Jeepneys en route to Aninuan and Talipanan beaches leave from just above the pier and cost P15 (20 minutes). Tricycle riders will ask P150 for a special trip to Talipanan, or P100 to White Beach. Jeepneys to Calapan cost P30 (two hours) and leave from outside the Dog & Duck Pub.

Boat There are many services between Puerto Galera and Batangas on Luzon. See Getting There & Away at the beginning of this chapter.

At the time of writing, only two boat services ran between Balatero, about 3km west of Puerto Galera, and Batangas: the outrigger *Blue Penguin* (P120) and the car ferry *Starlite* (P95). Other services may move to Balatero from Puerto Galera in the future. A jeepney/tricycle between Puerto Galera and Balatero will cost around P5/10.

Pumpboats can be hired for the trip to/from Sabang (P230) or any other beach you fancy. From Puerto Galera to Small La Laguna Beach it's P200, to Big La Laguna Beach P180, to White Beach P438 and to Talipanan P500.

If you want to head west to Abra de Ilog from Puerto Galera, there's no road between these two towns. A rented pumpboat to Abra's pier at Wawa will cost you P1500 (two hours). A cheaper, less-direct option is to go to Batangas and catch a passenger boat to Wawa.

NORTH COAST RESORTS
Around Puerto Galera
About 1km from Puerto Galera, on the road to Sabang, is a choice bunch of tranquil and secluded resorts where you can hide away from the bright lights

Franklyn Highland Beach Resort (☎ 0917 449 8085; doubles with fan & bathroom from P1000) is a friendly place on the high ridge above the main road. You can negotiate discounts on longer stays here. The restaurant and pool have great views over the water to the south.

Tanawin Bay Resort (☎ 0916 455 1857, fax 043-442 0112; e flyphil@flyphilippines .com.ph; rooms US$28-73), near the Franklyn, is a luxurious resort on a vast plot of prime land. The stylish and creative design includes such weird architectural delights as the Snail House and the Circle House, both with great views over the water. Tanawin has a beautiful pool and low-season discounts of up to 25%.

Kalaw Place (☎ 0917 532 2617, fax 043-442 0209; e kalaw@kalawplace.com.ph; rooms with fan & hot shower P980-3400) is easy to miss – it's just to the north of Tanawin Bay, on a point overlooking Port Galera. As unique for its low-key approach to tourism as it is for its stunning position and accommodation, it has several cottages and one vast, timber, traditional-style villa.

Pirate Cove Beach Resort (☎ 0919 729 5275; e pirate_betty@yahoo.com; cottages with bathroom from P600), next door to Kalaw Place, is good value, with spacious nipa huts. Ring ahead for a free pick-up from any beach in the area.

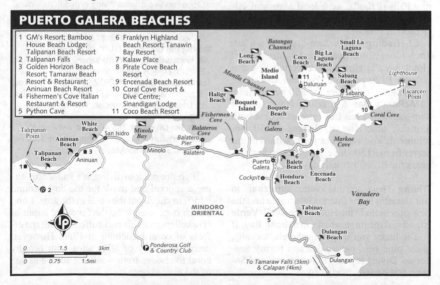

PUERTO GALERA BEACHES

1 GM's Resort; Bamboo House Beach Lodge; Talipanan Beach Resort
2 Talipanan Falls
3 Golden Horizon Beach Resort; Tamaraw Beach Resort & Restaurant; Aninuan Beach Resort
4 Fishermen's Cove Italian Restaurant & Resort
5 Python Cave
6 Franklyn Highland Beach Resort; Tanawin Bay Resort
7 Kalaw Place
8 Pirate Cove Beach Resort
9 Encenada Beach Resort
10 Coral Cove Resort & Dive Centre; Sinandigan Lodge
11 Coco Beach Resort

Encenada Beach Resort (☎ 043-281 4082; e sunlink@mozcom.com; doubles with fan/ air-con from P800/1000), on a beach of the same name, is 3km from Puerto Galera (P50 by tricycle). It's in a lovely spot and most people find it has a laid-back and pleasant atmosphere.

Fishermen's Cove Italian Restaurant & Resort (☎ 0917 533 2985; cottages with fan & hot shower US$20), west of Puerto Galera, comes with a secluded beach and pretty nipa huts. The restaurant serves handmade pasta (P190 to P240).

Sabang Beach

Sabang's beachfront is jammed with hotels, restaurants and dive shops. Rowdier than anywhere else on the island, Sabang still has one or two quiet patches of paradise if you look hard enough.

Information Cash advances are available on credit cards from **Filipino Travel Center** (☎ 281 4108) and **Going Places into the Land of Paradise** (☎ 0919 473 9040; open 8am-9.30pm daily); both charge 7.5% commission. The Filipino Travel Center will also change travellers cheques.

Tarzan Trek Tours (☎ 0919 410 1020; open 7am-10pm daily) and Going Places into the Land of Paradise offer day trips, including food and transport, to places such as Tamaraw Falls (P1000), some local Mangyan villages (P1000) and a nearby river for kayaking (P1800 to P2000).

CJ Trading (open 8am-10pm Mon-Sat, 1pm-10pm Sun), near the Atlantis Resort Hotel, has a satellite Internet connection and charges P120 per hour. You can also make international calls here for P50 per minute.

McRom's Bar & Sizzling House (open 6am-2am daily) has free Internet access with a meal; otherwise it charges P1.50 per minute. It also rents out jeeps with/without driver from P1500 for eight hours and speedboats for P1200 per half-day.

Diving There are underwater attractions to suit all tastes in the Puerto Galera area and the best sites include the **Hole in the Wall**, **Verde Island** and the three wrecks in **Sabang Bay**. If you're lucky you'll spot mackerels, trevally, ghost pipe fish, barracudas and pigmy seahorses. Diving is possible year-round and Sabang is the main diving centre.

The quoted price for a single dive with all equipment included is around US$20 to US$25 but you can find cheaper deals, especially if you have your own equipment or if you book a number of dives. Most of the dive centres offer PADI-approved courses – an open-water course will set you back US$250 to US$300, including all equipment and three days of tuition. A range of courses for more experienced divers is also available.

Following are some of the dive centres in and around Sabang which are accredited by the Puerto Galera Dive Association.

Action Divers (Sabang ☎ 0917 795 9062, in Small La Laguna ☎ 0973 751968, e info@ actiondiversvip.com) English, German, French, Italian, Tagalog and Spanish spoken.

Asia Divers (☎ 0917 814 5170, fax 0973 782094, e admin@asiadivers.com) El Galleon Beach Resort, Small La Laguna

Big Apple Dive Resort (☎ 0912 308 1120, w www.dive-bigapple.com) Sabang

Capt'n Greggs (☎ 0917 540 4570, e captngreggs@gmx.net) Sabang

Cocktail Divers (☎ 0917 812 6625, e info@ wetexpedition.com) Sabang

Frontier Scuba (☎ 0917 540 8410, e fdivers@ mozcom.com) Sabang. Specialises in naturalist and eco-tours; Japanese, Spanish, English and Tagalog spoken.

Octopus Divers (☎ 0917 562 0160, w www .octopusdivers.org) Villa Sabang, Sabang. Organises live-aboard diving expeditions around March to June.

Rudy's Dive Center (☎ 0919 391 6399, e dive@ rudysdivecenter.com) Small La Laguna.

Sabang Inn Beach Resort (☎ 0973 490101, w www.sabang-inn.com) Sabang. German, English, Danish and Swedish spoken.

Scandinavian Divers (☎ 0917 903 7582, w www .scandinaviandivers.com) Queen Mary's Inn, Big La Laguna. Danish, Swedish, Norwegian and English spoken.

South Sea Divers (☎ 281 4052, w www.south seadivers.com) Sabang. English, French, Japanese and Spanish spoken.

If you're not into diving, it's still worth hiring a snorkel and mask for the day (around P150) to check out the coral in the area. Long Beach once used to be the favoured haunt of snorkellers, but this reef suffered from the effects of coral bleaching in 1988. However, there are plenty of other sites with healthy coral to choose from – ask for advice at one of the dive shops.

SABANG BEACH

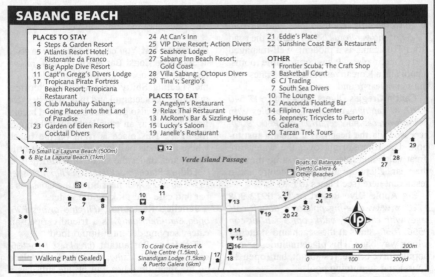

PLACES TO STAY
4 Steps & Garden Resort
5 Atlantis Resort Hotel;
   Ristorante da Franco
8 Big Apple Dive Resort
11 Capt'n Gregg's Divers Lodge
17 Tropicana Pirate Fortress
   Beach Resort; Tropicana
   Restaurant
18 Club Mabuhay Sabang;
   Going Places into the Land
   of Paradise
23 Garden of Eden Resort;
   Cocktail Divers

24 At Can's Inn
25 VIP Dive Resort; Action Divers
26 Seashore Lodge
27 Sabang Inn Beach Resort;
   Gold Coast
28 Villa Sabang; Octopus Divers
29 Tina's; Sergio's

PLACES TO EAT
2 Angelyn's Restaurant
9 Relax Thai Restaurant
13 McRom's Bar & Sizzling House
15 Lucky's Saloon
19 Janelle's Restaurant

21 Eddie's Place
22 Sunshine Coast Bar & Restaurant

OTHER
1 Frontier Scuba; The Craft Shop
3 Basketball Court
6 CJ Trading
7 South Sea Divers
10 The Lounge
12 Anaconda Floating Bar
14 Filipino Travel Center
16 Jeepneys; Tricycles to Puerto
   Galera
20 Tarzan Trek Tours

Places to Stay Unless otherwise indicated, the prices quoted here are for the high season. Rates drop dramatically in the low season (April to September); expect discounts of 50% to 70%. You can also negotiate a discount on longer stays.

Tina's and **Sergio's** (☎ 0910 456 1032; doubles with fan/air-con from P800/1000) are linked guesthouses at the eastern end of Sabang Beach. They have no-frills cottages, and some have good views of the beach. You can also arrange treks, tours and island-hopping trips here.

Villa Sabang (☎ 0917 562 0214; e vsabang@vasia.com; doubles with fan/air-con P700/1400), next to Tina's, is a popular place, with powder-blue air-con rooms and cottages (fan only) with kitchenette. Octopus Divers is based here and the Villa also has a restaurant, pool tables, bar and swimming pool.

Gold Coast (☎ 0919 810 4009; cottages P500-700) has two rows of solid, brightly painted cottages overlooking a garden. All have balcony, bathroom and fan. The pricier cottages have a kitchen and TV.

Sabang Inn Beach Resort (☎ 0973 490101; w www.sabang-inn.com; doubles with fan/air-con from P350/700), next door to Gold Coast, offers tidy rooms with bathroom. Rates stay the same year-round. There's a popular dive centre here and package deals can be booked over the Internet, including an open-water

course, four nights of air-con accommodation and breakfast for US$303 per person.

Seashore Lodge (☎ 043-281 4021; rooms with cable TV & fan/air-con from P600/1200) has a leafy compound with modern, balconied huts. The better rooms have a bathtub and fridge.

VIP Dive Resort (☎ 0917 795 9062; doubles with bathroom & fan from P250, 2-bedroom air-con apartment P1200) has rooms above Action Divers with good views. Rates stay the same year-round and dive and accommodation packages are available.

At Cans Inn (☎ 0917 463 8233; doubles with TV & fan/air-con 700/1000) is big, plain and reasonable value, with clean, balconied rooms right on the water.

Garden of Eden Resort (☎ 0917 812 6625; e info@wetexpedition.com; doubles with bathroom & fan/air-con P1000/1800) has pleasant, modern cottages in a garden setting with a pool and restaurant.

Tropicana Pirate Fortress Beach Resort (☎ 0919 387 3827; e paultropicana@yahoo.com; doubles with air-con, minibar, hot shower & cable TV from P1500), on Sabang's main street and towering over the Tropicana Restaurant, is a bizarre, over-the-top artificial castle. It has several levels of outrageously plush rooms with four-poster beds and marble bathrooms. There's a newly opened dive centre here.

Club Mabuhay Sabang (☎ 281 4097; e gojwp@hotmail.com; doubles with air-con, TV & hot shower from US$30), across the road from Tropicana, is a modern, well-managed and peaceful place. It has comfortable rooms, a pool and a Korean restaurant. The rates stay the same year-round.

Capt'n Gregg's Divers Lodge (☎ 0917 540 4570; e captngreggs@gmx.net; doubles with hot shower, cable TV & fan/air-con P600/900), accessed via the beach, is a Sabang institution. The rooms, right over the water, are great value and rates stay the same most of the year. There are also a dive centre and a restaurant here (see Places to Eat).

Big Apple Dive Resort (☎/fax 0912 308 1120; w www.dive-bigapple.com; double cottages with cable TV, bathroom & fan/air-con P550/1050) starts at the beach and stretches a long way back. This place includes a very popular dive centre, restaurant, bar (open 24 hours) and swimming pool.

Atlantis Resort Hotel (☎ 0917 562 0294; w www.atlantishotel.com; singles/doubles with air-con, minibar, cable TV & hot shower from US$45/55, single/double suites from US$65/75) is the area's most upmarket place to stay. With barely a right angle in sight, this terraced building looks almost organic, with rooms set into a lush, green hill. The Ristorante da Franco is open to nonguests (see Places to Eat later), as is the swimming pool (P100/70 per adult/child). There's also a pricey dive centre here.

Steps & Garden Resort (☎ 0919 861 4363; e tamarind86@hotmail.com; doubles with bathroom & fan/air-con P750/1350) is Sabang's best-kept secret. Cute cottages with thatched roofs and stone floors are set among beautiful, sloping gardens. To get here, take the narrow well-signposted path off the western end of the main path.

Coral Cove Resort & Dive Centre (☎ 0920 229 1815, Manila booking office ☎ 02-845 0674, fax 02-753 3316; e coral-cove@asia gate.net; triples with hot shower & fan/air-con P850/1500), to the southeast of Sabang, has cute, well-kept rooms. This sleepy, secluded place has a restaurant with great views and a pool table. Dive trips are a speciality, and staff will pick you up for free from Sabang or Puerto Galera.

Sinandigan Lodge (☎ 0919 607 0345; triples with fan/air-con P650/850), nearby to Coral Cove, is not as well-placed as Coral

Cove but the rooms are spacious and clean. The rates stay the same all year.

Places to Eat You can start the day in style at **Sunshine Coast Bar & Restaurant** (breakfast P50-175; open 7am-midnight daily) with the 'Feeling Shitty Breakfast' (one coffee, one coke, paracetamol and two cigarettes) for P50. You can also get more substantial breakfasts, as well as an excellent Indian banquet for P225. This place is right on the beach where the boats pull in, and has a great little eating area under the shade of a talisay tree.

Eddie's Place (breakfast P75, Filipino dishes P150; open 24 hrs), near Sunshine Coast, is a bar and café overlooking the water.

Janelle's Restaurant (Filipino dishes P95; open 6am-3am daily) is a friendly, open-air eatery serving decent Filipino food.

Tropicana Restaurant (breakfast P95-165; open 7am-11pm daily), the big, timber place on the main drag heading up the hill, has a giant international menu. Mains include fresh seafood and Italian dishes, with imported wines. Miso soup is P70, spaghetti carbonara P145 and tofu with ginger and leek P130. The food is great, but the restaurant's proximity to the main road can make it noisy.

Lucky's Saloon (dishes P160; open 10.45am-1am daily) is a popular little upstairs bar and steakhouse, with comics in its menus.

McRom's Bar & Sizzling House (dishes P100-235; open 6am-2am daily) specialises in sizzling dishes and offers 30 minutes of free Internet access with a meal.

Relax Thai Restaurant (veg dishes P75-165; open 10.30am-10pm daily) is trapped down Sabang's narrow central footpath. If you can do without a view, you'll enjoy excellent, authentic Thai food. There's a whole page of vegetarian dishes, but a word of warning when ordering: 'spicy' here means gum-achingly spicy.

Ristorante da Franco (breakfast P95-295; open 7am-11pm daily), at the Atlantis Resort Hotel, is a classy place with authentic Italian dishes that aren't cheap but are worth every peso. Other fine foods include sweet-and-sour lapu-lapu (grouper) fillet (P345) and good create-your-own pizza. Imported wines are around P650.

Capt'n Gregg's Divers Lodge has a 2nd-floor, open-air restaurant right on the water. The American breakfast (P100) is good value and there's a nightly barbecue. Big eaters might like to take up the 'Pizza Challenge': you have one hour to eat a 50cm pizza. The kitchen needs four-hours' notice for this.

Angelyn's Restaurant (*dishes P150; open 6am-9.30pm daily*), also by the water, has Filipino and international dishes. The vegetable omelette with toast (P75) makes for a filling, meat-free breakfast.

Entertainment Sabang's reputation as a seedy, girlie-bar sort of place has faded as more straightforward, diver-oriented drinking holes have gained ground. The surviving 'exotic-dancer' venues tend to pass themselves off as discos. Huddled around the beach end of the main street, these places certainly don't dominate Sabang's nightlife like they once did.

The Lounge, opposite the Relax Thai Restaurant, is an indoor bar with frozen cocktails and a sporty theme. Happy hour is from 5pm to 6pm.

Anaconda Floating Bar (*open 9am-6pm daily*) is one of two floating bars moored off Sabang's central shore. If you really want to drink like a fish, this is the place to go. Take plenty of protection against the sun – you can almost smell the foreign flesh roasting. A free shuttle boat will take you there and back from Capt'n Gregg's Divers Lodge.

Getting There & Away Pumpboats chug between Batangas, on Luzon, and Sabang (P100, one hour, daily), or you can take one of the many passenger services to Puerto Galera and a jeepney (P10) or tricycle to Sabang from there.

A bangka from Puerto Galera costs P230; during peak wet season (July to August) this is the only way to reach Sabang, as the road becomes impassable.

Small La Laguna Beach

An easy stroll from Sabang is Small La Laguna Beach, where the beach is better and the atmosphere a little more relaxed.

El Galleon Beach Resort (*☎ 0917 814 5170, fax 0973 782094; ℮ tommy@asiadivers .com; rooms with hot shower, cable TV & fan/ air-con P1550/2550*) has spacious poolside hut-style rooms. The stylish open-air restaurant has excellent simple treats – such as Cornish pasties (P65) – right up to Thai green curry with chicken (P150) and even cheese fondue (P600).

El Galleon's **The Point** (*open 10am-midnight daily*) is a beautifully breezy bar. It does bar snacks and has a big, eclectic CD collection and cocktail list. Happy hour is from 5.30pm to 6.30pm.

Sunsplash Restaurant, next door to El Galleon, beside the Scuba Plus Dive Center, does European specials such as goulash for P165. Behind the restaurant, **Sunsplash Cottages** (*☎ 0917 459 8639; doubles with hot shower, TV & fan/air-con P1000/1200*) are in a pretty, quiet garden setting.

Full Moon Restaurant specialises in Aussie food such as rump steaks for P325. Videos are screened most nights.

Mabuhay Resort (*☎ 043-281 4110; ℮ dive mabuhay@hotmail.com; rooms with air-con & cable TV from US$30*) is a new resort and dive centre with Korean and European management. At the time of writing it was about to open with spacious suites, a pool and spa.

Nick & Sonia's Cottages (*☎ 0917 456 7824; cottages with hot shower, kitchen & fan/ air-con P1000/1500*), behind Action Divers, offers simple cottages.

Portofino (*☎/fax 0973 776704; ℮ resort@ portofino.com.ph; doubles with air-con, hot shower, kitchen & cable TV US$45*) is Small La

BIG LA LAGUNA & SMALL LA LAGUNA

To Batangas, Puerto Galera & Other Beaches

Verde Island Passage

Big La Laguna Beach

Small La Laguna Beach

Sabang Beach

See Sabang Beach map - p233

0   250   500m
0   250   500yd

PLACES TO STAY & EAT
1 Scandinavian Divers; Queen Mary's Inn
3 La Laguna Beach Club; Villa Estelita Bar & Restaurant
5 Deep Blue Sea Inn; Portofino
6 Rudy's Dive Center; Action Divers; Nick & Sonia's Cottages

7 Sunsplash Restaurant & Cottages; Scuba Plus Dive Center; Full Moon Restaurant; Mabuhay Resort

OTHER
2 Pumpboat Fares Board
4 Penman's Pass
8 Asia Divers
9 El Galleon Beach Resort; The Point

MINDORO

Laguna's answer to Sabang's stylish Atlantis. Less organised, this comfortable villa doesn't accept guests for less than two nights.

Deep Blue Sea Inn (☎ 0917 562 0209; e dbs@batangas.i-next.net; doubles with hot shower, cable TV & fan/air-con P900/1200), next door to Portofino, has good rooms stacked all the way up the steep hill, ensuring great views and firm calf muscles.

A pumpboat that can take you between Puerto Galera and Small La Laguna Beach costs P200 (20 minutes).

If you're feeling really lazy, you can even get a pumpboat between Small La Laguna and Sabang (P50, five minutes).

Big La Laguna Beach

Next to Small La Laguna, Big La Laguna also has some accommodation options.

La Laguna Beach Club (☎ 0973 855545, fax 0973 878409; e lalaguna@llbc.com.ph; doubles with fan/air-con US$35/50) has a swimming pool and comfortable cottages. You can rent a kayak for P300 per hour.

Villa Estelita Bar & Restaurant (☎ 0917 459 5485; doubles with fan/air-con P600/1500) has simple nipa huts with screened verandas in a peaceful garden. There's also a breezy restaurant offering Filipino dishes for around P95.

Coco Beach Resort (☎ 0973 772115, fax 0919 547 0347; e resort@cocobeach.com; huts per person for 2 days & 1 night from US$38, for 3 days & 2 nights US$48), west of Big La Laguna, is an exclusive 10-hectare resort, with about 90 meticulously finished nipa huts hidden among the palms of a big, beautiful beach. Prices include round-trip transport (Manila–Coco Beach–Manila) and buffet breakfast.

A pumpboat between Puerto Galera and Big La Laguna Beach is P180 (10 minutes). A pumpboat should cost about P100 (less than 10 minutes) between Big La Laguna and Sabang.

White Beach

A cheaper, simpler alternative to Sabang (see earlier), White Beach offers more sand and more interaction with locals. There are no girlie bars here, and you don't need a diving licence just to hold a conversation. The beach's dazzling expanse of sand, which hosts regular games of volleyball, can make it extremely hot compared with Sabang or

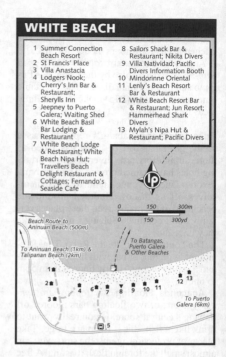

WHITE BEACH

1 Summer Connection Beach Resort
2 St Francis' Place
3 Villa Anastacia
4 Lodgers Nook; Cherry's Inn Bar & Restaurant; Sherylls Inn
5 Jeepney to Puerto Galera; Waiting Shed
6 White Beach Basil Bar Lodging & Restaurant
7 White Beach Lodge & Restaurant; White Beach Nipa Hut; Travellers Beach Delight Restaurant & Cottages; Fernando's Seaside Cafe
8 Sailors Shack Bar & Restaurant; Nikita Divers
9 Villa Natividad; Pacific Divers Information Booth
10 Mindorinne Oriental
11 Lenly's Beach Resort Bar & Restaurant
12 White Beach Resort Bar & Restaurant; Jun Resort; Hammerhead Shark Divers
13 Mylah's Nipa Hut & Restaurant; Pacific Divers

Puerto Galera. The best swimming area is at the eastern end of the beach.

Diving There are a few dive shops at White Beach offering equipment hire and dive courses for the same prices charged in Sabang. The most professional is **Pacific Divers** (☎ 0920 606 2212, fax 0912 283 9418; e paci ficdivers@yahoo.com), which also runs a helpful information booth, next to Villa Natividad, where you can rent snorkel sets for P150 per day and jet skis for P2500 per hour. There's also **Hammerhead Shark Divers**, catering mostly to Korean clients, and **Nikita** (☎ 0920 233 8835; e sweetlipscave@yahoo .com), at the Sailor Shack Bar & Restaurant.

Places to Stay While there are plenty of places to stay at White Beach, prices and standards are very similar: there's one long, sandy row of resorts offering cheap rooms and cottages. Unless otherwise stated, prices listed here are for the high season. In the low season (April to September) you can negotiate discounts of 50% to 75%.

Summer Connection Beach Resort and **St Francis' Place** (☎ 0912 3165910; cottages with *bathroom P500-1500)* are two resorts run by the same management. They're at the western end of White Beach, away from the squeeze at the centre. Some of the cottages are nicely placed on the hill overlooking the beach.

Villa Anastacia *(cottages P700)*, nearby, is set back from the beach in a secluded compound. It's good value with solid, brightly painted cottages with kitchen facilities. There's a dirt road leading to Villa Anastacia from the main road.

Lodgers Nook *(☎ 0917 837 7478; Mon-Fri doubles with bathroom & fan P600-800, Sat & Sun P800-1000, high season up to P2500)* is by the beach and can be reached from the dirt road leading from the main road. It has some of the only cottages that actually face the water, as well as an open-air billiard hall, table tennis facilities and volleyball courts.

Next to the Lodgers Nook, **Cherry's Inn Bar & Restaurant** *(☎ 0917 788 8239; doubles P1000)* and **Sherylls Inn** *(☎ 0917 203 5284; doubles P1000)* offer your bog-standard beach cottages.

White Beach Basil Bar Lodging & Restaurant and **White Beach Lodge & Restaurant** *(☎ 0917 732 7674; cottages with fan/air-con on Mon-Fri from P800/1500, Sat & Sun P1000/2500)* are two popular resorts run by the same management. They have a larger-than-usual, open layout on opposite sides of the wide walkway to the road.

White Beach Nipa Hut *(☎/fax 0912 270 7371; doubles with fan/air-con Mon-Fri P800/1200, Sat & Sun P1000/1500)* has no nipa huts, but two cramped rows of clean, solid rooms with verandas.

Travellers Beach Delight Restaurant & Cottages *(☎ 0912 312 6826; quad rooms with bathroom & air-con P2000)* has clean, tiled rooms, some with fridge and TV.

Villa Natividad *(☎ 0917 482 0505; doubles with fan/air-con P1000/1800)* is a large, two-storey resort that has beachy, basic rooms.

Lenly's Beach Resort Bar & Restaurant *(☎ 0917 466 2546)*, **White Beach Resort Bar & Restaurant**, and **Mylah's Nipa Hut & Restaurant** offer OK cottages with bathroom and fan/air-con from around P1500/2500.

Jun Resort *(☎/fax 0912 283 9418; quad rooms with fan/air-con 1500/2500)* caters mainly to Korean guests. It has rooms and nipa huts, all with bathroom, and a restaurant.

Mindorinne Oriental *(☎ 0917 442 6929, Manila booking office ☎ 02-531 9980, fax 02-*

532 5661; doubles with fridge, air-con & hot shower P2000), newly opened, is the most upmarket place to stay at White Beach. It has modern, comfortable, motel-style rooms and rates are the same year-round.

Places to Eat Just as there are few exceptional places to stay here, there are no really outstanding restaurants. There are, however, heaps of good, honest eateries, often attached to the hotels. In the evenings, the restaurants set up outdoor grills all along the beach, covering the sunset strollers in thick clouds of smoke. Most places open around 7am and close about midnight.

Fernando's Seaside Cafe *(breakfast P85, Filipino dishes P70)*, right on the beach in front of Travellers Beach Delight, has excellent sizzling dishes for around P120.

Travellers Beach Delight Restaurant is noted for its big, cheap breakfasts (P30 to P80), pancakes (P30 to P60) and pizzas (P120 to P160), including vegetarian options. Nice touches are the ginger tea (P20 a cup) and the fresh orange juice (P60).

Sailors Shack Bar & Restaurant *(dishes P50-100)* does a good vegie curry (P50), as well as spaghetti bolognese (P75) and *calamares adobo* (squid marinated in vinegar and garlic, P80). The whole-fish dishes are also well worth trying.

Getting There & Away While it's an easy enough 15- to 20-minute jeepney ride from Puerto Galera (P10), White Beach is at its most attractive when approached by boat. Official one-way rates (posted outside Villa Natividad) include P400 to Puerto Galera, P500 to Sabang and P500 to Big La Laguna. You can also travel directly to Batangas by bangka (P120, 1¼ hours) – the last boat leaves around 3.30pm.

Aninuan Beach
White Beach's western neighbour is a much more peaceful place to base yourself. It's close to White Beach and offers a wider, cleaner beach, better swimming and a more chilled-out atmosphere. Around October you'll share the beach with **fireflies**. As with White Beach, big discounts are available in the low season.

Aninuan is a 15-minute walk from White Beach, along the main road, or a five-minute scramble around the rocky point. Jeepneys

MINDORO

run fairly regularly between Aninuan and Puerto Galera (P12), or else you can take a tricycle (P60).

Places to Stay & Eat Accommodation choices are concentrated along the eastern end (ie, the end closest to White Beach).

Golden Horizon Beach Resort (☎ 0912 304 8769; doubles with bathroom & fan/air-con P650/1300), just around the rocks from White Beach, is a family-run place, with a loud, aqua-coloured main building. It has spotless, tiled rooms and there's a shared balcony overlooking the water. Out the front, a café offers sandwiches (P30 to P65) and meals (around P80).

Tamaraw Beach Resort & Restaurant (☎ 0916 427 4715; doubles with bathroom & fan P1300), next door to Golden Horizon and stretched out along the beach, offers a great location and good value nipa huts with balcony. Excellent, small Filipino dishes (around P100 per dish) and brewed coffee (P75 a pot) can be served to you under thatched-roof shelters right on the sand.

Aninuan Beach Resort (☎ 0912 287 1868; e aninuanbeachresort@yahoo.com; double cottages with fan P600, quads with fan/air-con P700/1500), a little further along from Tamaraw, has comfortable rooms, each with a small balcony, and a small gym. The food here is very good and can be served at tables on the sand, next to the bar. Big breakfasts cost P85 to P150 and fine seafood dishes cost P120 to P300.

Talipanan Beach

Taking tropical seclusion one big step west, Talipanan Beach is another great choice. A few kilometres inland, **Talipanan Falls** are a popular place for a swim. You can take a tricycle (P150) to the access track, from where it is a 30-minute walk.

GM's Resort (☎ 0912 882 2756; doubles with fan P600, quads with air-con & hot shower P2000) is a friendly place in a bright and breezy spot. The tidy rooms have attached bathroom and one even has a water bed. There's a 2nd-floor, open-air eating area with wonderful ocean views; breakfasts are P60 to P75, vegie curry P50 and Filipino dishes P85 to P100.

Bamboo House Beach Lodge (doubles with fan in low season P500), next door to GM's, lives up to its name with simple but pleasant rooms in a building made of bamboo. There are also rooms in an ordinary building out the back.

Talipanan Beach Resort (☎ 0916 850 5574; quads with fan/air-con P700/1200) has good-value, spotless rooms in one long block, but is a little low on atmosphere.

To get to Talipanan Beach from White Beach, wait for one of the irregular jeepneys (P10), take a tricycle (P50) or simply walk via Aninuan Beach along the sand, following the trails up and over the rocky outcrops. It takes about half an hour. GM's resort also has a bangka for hire (P500 to Puerto Galera or P1200 for a day of island hopping).

CALAPAN

☎ 043 • pop 105,910

Calapan (**kal**-ah-pan), the busy capital of Mindoro Oriental, is 48km from Puerto Galera via a rough, winding road with spectacular views across Verde Island Passage. The city hosts the annual **Sanduguan Festival** and is a good base for hiking to Mt Halcon.

JP Rizal St is the main drag of Calapan, and it's this street that jeepneys and buses crawl along, before terminating at the market, just off JP Rizal St on Juan Luna St.

Information

There's a **tourist assistance desk** (☎ 288 5622; open 9am-4pm daily) at the pier, about 4km from the town centre, that sells a useful map of Calapan (P60).

You can change US dollars at the **Equitable PCI Bank** and **Metrobank**; the latter also has an ATM that accepts MasterCard. Both can be found around the intersection of Juan Luna and JP Rizal Sts.

You can check your email at **Arki Net** (Leuterio St; open 7am-10pm daily), a block south of Juan Luna St, for P40 per hour.

Hiking

While there's not a lot to see in Calapan, there's plenty of adventure nearby – and that's where **Calapan's Base Camp Outdoor Shop** (☎ 288 3391; Quezon Drive, Salong) comes in. As the headquarters of the Halcon Mountaineers, the shop has the unmistakable stench of well-worn hikers' shoes – and you can buy them here (P250/350 for sturdy flip-flops/sandals, soled with tyre rubber). Just as strong is its reputation for hard-core hiking and climbing trips on **Mt Halcon**, about 30km southwest of Calapan. At 2505m, Halcon is the country's fourth-highest mountain, but according to the mountaineering lads it's the toughest to climb.

The standard trip is two days up, two days down, taking in the perilous **Monkey Bridge** (a tangle of tree trunks spanning the Dulangan River), the breathtaking **Knife Edge** ridge walk and, finally, the peak itself, which often juts well above the clouds.

The mountaineers have an arrangement with the local Mangyan tribespeople, who are employed as porters on request (a few days notice is appreciated). It costs around P1000 per person per day, including a porter, equipment and guide, but you have to pay extra for food (yours and the porter's), jeep hire (about P1000 return per jeep) and hiking registration (P40). The maximum number of people per guide is five.

There's also an annual climb held over four days during Holy Week, with around 200 people taking part. The climb costs P400 per person, including transport, T-shirt, food and guide. For more information, contact Vic or Richard at the Base Camp Outdoor Shop, which is between the town centre and the pier.

It's P5 by tricycle. Ask the driver to let you out at the Land Transportation Office (LTO); the shop is directly across the road.

Places to Stay & Eat
Riceland 1 Inn (☎ 288 4253; JP Rizal St; singles/doubles with fan & shared bathroom P150/180, doubles with air-con & private bathroom from P650), around the corner from the market and public transport terminal, is a multistorey property. Rooms here are tiled and tidy. There's a P150 key deposit on all rooms.

Hotel Mayi (☎ 288 4437; JP Rizal St; doubles with shared bathroom & fan P300, singles/doubles with private bathroom & fan P400/500), diagonally opposite Riceland 1 Inn and slightly taller, is an impersonal establishment with rather grotty rooms. Air-con doubles are also available (P800).

Riceland 2 Inn (☎ 288 5590; twins with bathroom & fan P280-450, with bathroom & air-con P500-750, doubles with fan/air-con P300/500) is the best bet in town. From JP Rizal St, wander down nearby MH del Pilar St, over the bridge, to this single-storey, grey complex, which has quiet lodgings and a con-

crete sculpture of a man and his buffalo in the car park.

There are a few resorts on the black-sand beach 3km east of town (P10 by tricycle) that offer far more relaxed accommodation:

Anahaw Island View Resort (☎ 288 4024; doubles with fan, bathroom & cable TV P600) is a good choice, with simple, peaceful nipa huts. It has a speedboat for hire (P3000 for half a day) that can take you to the islands off the coast.

Panang Beach Resort (☎ 288 6120, fax 441 0014; doubles with air-con, bathroom & cable TV from P1500) has comfortable and well-maintained nipa huts, and a reasonably priced restaurant. The restaurant speciality is sizzling chicken barbecue (P75).

Hong Kong Restaurant (MH del Pilar St), diagonally opposite the Riceland 2 Inn, is a cute little place specialising in combo meals, such as spaghetti with french fries and soft drink (P35).

La Paulina (Leuterio St; pizza P33-198) is a popular air-con restaurant with treats such as asparagus tips in oyster sauce (P135). It's one block south of Juan Luna St.

Getting There & Away
Bus & Jeepney From Puerto Galera jeepneys to Calapan leave hourly from around 6am to 2pm daily (P45, two hours). These jeepneys can be found on P Concepcion St, outside the Dog & Duck Pub in Puerto Galera. Jeepneys run from Calapan to Puerto Galera, about every hour until 4.30pm. They wait at the market on Juan Luna St. Buses don't operate between Calapan and Puerto Galera. Small buses leave from the market on Juan Luna St, and depart regularly until about 3pm for Roxas (P125, three hours, daily) and Pinamalayan (P60, 1½ hours).

Large buses operate from the Calapan pier to Roxas (P120, three hours) via Pinamalayan (P60, 1½ hours). These buses run from around 5am to around 4pm daily. Air-con minibuses compete with the large buses for passengers, operating throughout the day but only heading off when full. To Roxas it's about three hours and costs P120.

Boat A tricycle between JP Rizal St and the pier should cost P10 to P15. From here, it's a quick and easy boat ride between Calapan and Batangas (Luzon) on the daily **SuperCat** (☎ 288 3179, in Batangas ☎ 043-723 8227) fast-craft service (P230, 45 minutes). From Calapan to Batangas, boats leave every two hours between 5am and 5.30pm. From Batangas to Calapan there are departures from 6am until 6.30pm. Viva Shipping Lines also has fast-craft services (P160, two daily).

Montenegro Shipping Lines (☎ *723 8294*) runs bigger, slower boats between Calapan and Batangas from 1.30am to 9.30pm (P82, two hours).

ROXAS
☎ 043 • pop 41,265

If you happen to be in urgent need of medical advice, Roxas (**raw**-hahs) will suit you nicely. This dusty little town is packed with pharmacies, dentists and medical clinics. If you're fit and healthy, you'll probably be keen to hop on one of the regular boats to Panay or Romblon and get out of here as soon as possible. On Morente Ave, the main drag, the town's **market** is centrally placed and full of life, especially on Wednesday and Sunday, when Mangyan people and other local villagers come into town to sell their wares. You can take a day trip from Roxas to visit local **Mangyan villages** and **Saint Rafael Cave**. The cave features stalagmites and stalactites and is located about 12km from Roxas, with a 1.2km walk off the highway. A guide and transport will cost around P900 for up to six people – for more information see the Roxas Villa Hotel entry.

Information

Engineer 'Bhoy' Villaluna is vice-president of the **Roxas Tourism Council** and is a good source of information. You'll find him at the Roxas Villa Hotel. The **PLDT Roxas Calling Office**, which has an international telephone service, is also at Roxas Villa. You can change US dollars at the **Land Bank** (*Administration St*), which is opposite the hotels.

Places to Stay & Eat

The town's three central hotels stand shoulder to shoulder on Administration St, facing the market.

Hotel Danna Rose (☎ *289 2346; doubles with/without bathroom P350/150*) is a creaky, timber establishment, with narrow corridors and grubby rooms with fan. The front rooms can be noisy, but the shared terrace is a good place for you to watch the activity at the market across the street.

Santo Niño Hotel (☎ *289 2422; doubles with/without bathroom P200/150*) is big, old and dark, with polished floorboards and box-like rooms with fan. The friendly restaurant on the ground floor has good Filipino food for around P35 per dish.

Roxas Villa Hotel & Restaurant (☎ *289 2026, fax 289 2283;* e *roxasvillahotel@yahoo .com; doubles with fan/air-con from P250/ 500*), with its reception desk hidden down the covered drive, is the best option. This place has clean, simple rooms with good showers, though some rooms are windowless/airless. The hotel's restaurant menu includes a decent chop suey with beef (P85) and *pansit bihon* (thick- or thin-noodle dish; P50).

Getting There & Away

Bus & Jeepney Large buses operate between Calapan and Roxas (P120, three hours) via Pinamalayan (P50, 1½ hours). They run daily from around 6am to around 2pm from the Roxas terminal on the corner of Morente and Magsaysay Aves. Air-con minivans to Calapan pier (P120, three hours) can also be found here. In the dry season you can take a jeepney to San José (P190, seven to eight hours) from outside the Caltex petrol station on Magsaysay Ave at 9am daily. In the wet season the rough road between Bulalacao and San José becomes impassable and you have to take a boat for this leg of the journey. Jeepneys from Roxas to Bulalacao leave from 5am to around 3pm daily (P45, two hours), but you need to catch one before 7am to make the pumpboat to San José, which departs Bulalacao at 10am. From Bulalacao, a Roxas-bound jeepney waits for passengers arriving by pumpboat from San José at around 1pm. The road between Roxas and Bulalacao can be extremely dusty, but if you're tackling it by jeepney all the passengers piled on top of you will probably shield you from the dust.

Boat Roxas' small Dangay pier is a P10 tricycle ride from the centre of town. For those headed to Panay or Boracay, outrigger pumpboats run from Roxas to Caticlan (P300 to P350, four to five hours, three weekly). From Caticlan to Roxas, you'll find boats thats run twice weekly. Note that schedules change frequently, so it's best to check at the Roxas pier (☎ *289 2356*) for the latest details.

(Continued on page 251)

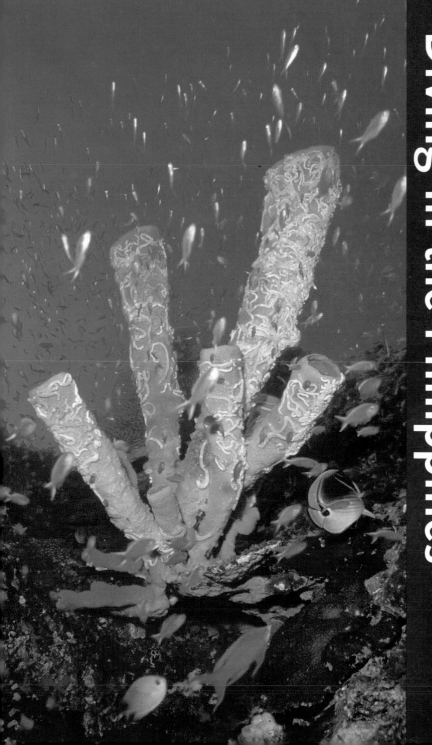

Diving in the Philippines

One of the seven marine lakes of Coron, Busuanga Island – Palawan

Sea fan, Sulu Sea – Mindanao

Wreck diving – Mindoro Occidental

T he Philippines archipelago forms a natural barrier between the basin of the South China Sea and the vast expanse of the Pacific Ocean. The islands split these bodies of water into the Philippine, Sibuyan, Visayan, Sulu, Mindanao, Bohol and Celebes Seas. Each of these seas has its own characteristics and marine life, which makes for an extraordinary range of dive sites.

With 7107 islands spread across a broad swath of tropical sea, it's hardly surprising that the Philippines is a diver's paradise. From coral gardens to caves, deeply plunging undersea walls and isolated coral seamounts, the natural diversity of the Philippines archipelago makes it Asia's premier dive destination. And while it's true that dynamite fishing and pollution have taken a toll on some of the undersea environment here, it's still possible to see pristine coral and sea life, provided you're willing to venture off the beaten track.

COSTS & SERVICES

Divers were quick to recognise the potential of the Philippines: the first dive centre opened its doors here in 1966 – practically prehistory as far as diving goes – and now there are hundreds of dive centres spread across the length of the archipelago. Much of the diving is resort based, but there are also plenty of independent dive shops, and serious divers can visit some of the more remote dive sites on live-aboard dive boats.

In general, you'll pay around US$60 for a one-day boat trip with two dives. Some resorts charge extra for boats (P500 to P1000); others charge an extra P500 for a dive master to accompany you. You can also do single dives for anything from US$15 to US$40, depending on the location, but you'll often pay as much for a few hours' use of a boat as you would for a whole day.

Safety Guidelines for Diving

Before embarking on a diving or snorkelling trip, carefully consider the following points to ensure a safe and enjoyable experience:

- Possess a current diving certification card from a recognised scuba-diving instructional agency.
- Be sure you are healthy and feel comfortable diving.
- Be aware of local laws, regulations and etiquette regarding marine life and the environment.
- Dive only at sites within your realm of experience; if possible, engage the services of a competent professionally trained dive instructor or dive master.
- Obtain reliable information about physical and environmental conditions at the dive site (eg, from a reputable local dive operation).
- Be aware that underwater conditions vary significantly from one region, or even site, to another. Seasonal changes can significantly alter any site and dive conditions. These differences influence the way divers suit up for a dive and what diving techniques they use.
- Ask about the environmental characteristics that can affect your diving and how locally trained divers deal with these considerations.

Many resorts offer good-value dive and accommodation packages, which are probably the best way to dive in the Philippines. Packages often include transport between the resort and the nearest major town. For an overnight stay with all meals and two dives, expect to pay from P3000. These packages can usually be booked at travel agencies and dive shops in Manila and other major cities.

In some marine sanctuaries, divers and snorkellers must pay a fee which goes towards programmes to protect and rehabilitate reefs. This varies from place to place, and in some locations permission must be obtained from the village head before diving or snorkelling. In these cases the fee is usually P50. For more on this, see the boxed text 'From Dynamite to Diving Fees' in the Panglao Island section of the Visayas chapter.

Certification

The only thing you need to dive in the Philippines is a valid open-water diving certification from a recognised diving instructional agency. As in the rest of Asia, the PADI certification is the most widely recognised, although most dive centres will allow you to dive with certifications from other authorities. If you have any doubts about your certification, contact the dive centre you intend to dive with before setting out, ideally before you arrive in the Philippines.

Courses The Philippines is a good place to learn how to dive, with warm, clear water and plenty of shallow reefs and bays. There are hundreds of dive centres, mostly PADI affiliated, and the quality of instruction is generally quite high. Technical diving courses are available for more advanced divers, and there are plenty of wreck and cave dives for you to practise your skills.

VERONICA GARBUTT

Left: Scuba diving instruction, Zamboanga del Norte – Mindanao

Emergency

There are five recompression chambers in the Philippines, but air evacuation options are limited and transport times can be lengthy. For this reason it pays to dive conservatively in the Philippines.

Your dive operator should be able to make the necessary arrangements in an emergency. If this is not the case, the following information may be useful in arranging evacuation and medical treatment.

Recompression Chambers

Never arrive at a recompression chamber without calling first. You can save valuable time if the chamber staff can assist with transportation or refer you to another facility when their chamber is in use.

Batangas (Luzon; ☎ 043-723 7098) Batangas Hyperbaric Medicine and Wound Healing Center, St Patrick's Hospital Medical Center, Lopez Jaena St, Batangas City
Contact: Michael Perez, MD
Cavite (Luzon; ☎ 046-524 2061 – ask for the Sangley operator and request local 4490, 4191 or 4193) Sangley Recompression Chamber, Philippine Fleet, Naval Base Cavite, Sangley Point, Cavite City
Contact: Capt Pablo Acacio
Cebu City (Cebu; ☎ 032-232 2464–8, local 3369) VISCOM Station Hospital, Camp Lapu Lapu, Lahug, Cebu City
Contact: Mamerto Ortega or Macario Mercado
Manila (Luzon; ☎ 02-920 7183, 921 1801, local 8991 or 6445) Armed Forces of the Philippines Medical Center, V Luna Rd, Quezon City
Contact: Jojo Bernado, MD, or Fred C Martinez
Subic (Luzon; ☎ 047-252 7052, 252 7566) Subic Bay Freeport Zone, SBMA, Olongapo City, Zimbales
Contact: Lito Roque

Evacuation Services

Both the Philippine Air Force and private operators such as Subic Seaplanes can assist with evacuations. However, their range is limited and you can't expect them to miraculously appear in the middle of places like the Sulu Sea.

Philippines Air Force Search & Rescue (☎ 02-854 6701, 853 5013, 853 5008) Villamor Air Base, Pasay City, Metro Manila
Subic Seaplanes (☎ 047-252 2230, 0919 325 1106)

Because of the low cost of living in the Philippines, it's a cheap place to get your certification, and it rivals Thailand and Bali as the cheapest place in Southeast Asia to get certified. PADI open-water courses generally run about US$250 to US$300, while dive master courses start at around US$500. Many dive centres also offer underwater photography courses and have equipment available for rent.

Equipment

Rental equipment is widely available at dive centres, dive shops and resorts in the Philippines. Most live-aboard operators also offer their clients equipment rental. In many places, the gear on offer is fairly new and of a high standard, although you'll occasionally run into antique or otherwise questionable gear – if you're not completely confident, ask for something newer or head to another dive centre.

Full equipment rental rates in the Philippines average US$10 per day, but can be two or even three times this amount at popular resort areas and during the high season. Snorkelling equipment can usually be rented for P250 to P300 per day, but it's often in poor condition. If you plan to do a lot of snorkelling, it may be a good idea to bring your own equipment, both to save money and to ensure good quality. Likewise, if you're a serious diver and picky about your gear, you may want to bring your own BCD, mask, snorkel and fins.

Although you can usually dive in the Philippines wearing nothing more than a bathing suit, most divers prefer to dive in a 3mm wetsuit or Lycra dive skin, both for sun protection and to protect against contact with the reef and marine organisms. Most dive centres have wetsuits available for rent.

You can buy diving and snorkelling equipment in big cities such as Manila and Cebu, but you'll find very little on offer away from these city centres. If you do plan on making some gear purchases, be sure to do so before you head out to the more remote islands.

SEASONS & CONDITIONS

Dive seasons vary across the islands, although many sites are accessible year-round. The dry season from late November to early June generally brings the best and most reliable weather conditions for diving.

Typhoons can strike the Philippines – mainly Luzon and the northern Visayas – at any time, but usually hit between June and September. Water temperatures in the Philippines range from 25°C to 28°C (77°F to 82°F), with the warmest temperatures coming between March and June. Some areas have swift, unpredictable currents, while other areas have hardly any. Tidal ranges are generally less than 1m and tides are usually a factor only in terms of visibility and current.

TOP DIVING AREAS

With such an abundance of sites, it's difficult to pick the real highlights. The coral gardens off El Nido, in northern Palawan, are justifiably popular. The Visayas are packed with good dives, and you can island-hop by ferry from one to the next, or explore the whole region by liveaboard boats. For those with time and money to spare, it's hard to beat the Philippines' two famous open-water reefs: Apo and Tubbutaha. And if you're a fan of wreck dives, you'll already know about the incredible underwater graveyard of Coron, where nine Japanese ships lie rusting on the ocean floor.

In this section we introduce some of the most popular and interesting dive sites in the Philippines. Keep in mind that this list is *not* in order of preference and is not exhaustive.

For more details on the areas listed here, see the destination chapters in this book. For a more complete overview, check out Lonely Planet's *Diving & Snorkeling Philippines*.

Luzon & Around The main diving regions of Luzon are Anilao, which boasts easy access from Manila and at least 36 dive sites on coral gardens and walls; San Fernanda (La Union), which has eight main reefs and a few good drop-offs; Matabungkay and Nasugbu, with coral gardens similar to Anilao; and Subic Bay, one of the Philippines' most famous wreck-diving sites.

Donsol, near Sorsogon in Southeast Luzon, is the only place in the world apart from Ningaloo Reef in Western Australia where you can rely on seeing whale sharks. Large numbers of these huge, harmless plankton-feeders gather in the waters off Donsol from February to May. There are plenty of opportunities for snorkellers to see them.

Mindoro Puerto Galera and Sabang both offer excellent year-round diving and snorkelling, within easy reach of Manila (it's just a short hop across the Verde Island Passage from the port of Batangas on Luzon). There are more than 30 dive sites in the bays and coves east of Puerto Galera and several more around Escarceo Point, near Sabang.

Because the waters off Puerto Galera have been declared a marine sanctuary, the reefs are generally in quite good shape, with species such as Spanish mackerel, tuna, yellowtail, and black-tip reef sharks often visible. As it's close to Manila, the diving infrastructure is excellent. This is one of the best options for divers who want to escape the crowds of Luzon but can't make the trip to some of the more exotic dive locales.

About 30km west of Mindoro, within reach of dive trips from North Pandan Island, San José and Puerto Galera, Apo Reef is one of the Philippines' most famous dive sites. Long popular with live-aboards, the reef is one of the best places in the Philippines to see sharks, mantas, stingrays, jacks, tuna and a host of smaller fish. The deeper coral is particularly impressive, and includes some lovely gorgonian sea fans. There are also three wrecks on the reef, which is best visited between January and June. Outside this season, rough seas make the trip from Mindoro both difficult and dangerous.

Cebu & Around In the middle of the Visayas, Cebu is the jumping-off point for many of the Philippines best and most popular dive sites – there are literally hundreds to choose from.

Right: Dive boat off Moalboal, Cebu – the Visayas

PAUL DYMOND

The closest diving to Cebu is off Mactan Island, including such sites as Kon Tiki House Reef and the popular Marigondon Cave. Unfortunately, Mactan Island sites can be overcrowded and have been damaged by pollution and dynamite fishing.

Many divers prefer to head to the Moalboal region, on the western side of Cebu Island, where there are many pristine sites. Moalboal's Panagsama Beach has decent snorkelling and excellent diving, and tiny Pescador island, off Moalboal, offers some of the region's most spectacular diving.

Another up-and-coming dive centre is Malapascua Island, north of Cebu, which boasts excellent white-sand beaches and fine dive sites nearby, including Gato Island, Monad Shoal, and the Manocmanoc Islands. This is a good choice for those who want to escape the crowds further south.

Bohol The island of Bohol is blessed with numerous smaller offshore islands. Some of the best sites are off of Panglao Island, which lies just off the southwest coast, and Cabilao Island, which is just off the west coast.

Panglao's Alona Beach is a busy diving centre, with several accommodation options and plenty of dive shops. Some of the best dives in this region are around Balicasag Island, where the stunning corals and

STEVE ROSENBERG

Left: School of bigeye jacks off Balicasag Island, Bohol – the Visayas

Responsible Diving

The reefs of the Philippines are under tremendous pressure from dynamite fishing, pollution and global warming. Follow these tips to avoid causing further damage.

- Don't touch living marine organisms with your body or drag anything across the reef. Polyps can be damaged by even the gentlest contact. Never stand on corals, even if they look robust. If you must secure yourself to the reef, only hold fast to exposed rock or dead coral.
- Be conscious of your flippers (fins). Even without contact, the surge from heavy flipper strokes near the reef can damage delicate organisms. When treading water in shallow reef areas, take care not to kick up clouds of sand. Settling sand can easily smother the delicate organisms of the reef.
- Practise and maintain proper buoyancy control. Major damage can be done by divers descending too fast and colliding with the reef. Make sure you are correctly weighted and that your weight belt is positioned so that you stay horizontal. If you have not dived for a while, have a practice dive in a pool before taking to the reef. Be aware that buoyancy can change over the period of an extended trip: initially you may breathe harder and need more weighting; a few dives later you may breathe more easily and need less weight.
- Take great care in underwater caves. Spend as little time within them as possible, as your air bubbles may be caught within the roof and thereby leave previously submerged organisms high and dry. Taking turns to inspect the interior of a small cave will lessen the chances of damaging contact.
- Resist the temptation to collect or buy corals or shells. Aside from the ecological damage, taking home marine souvenirs depletes the beauty of a site and spoils the enjoyment of others. The same goes for marine archaeological sites (mainly shipwrecks). Respect their integrity.
- Ensure that you take home all your rubbish, and any litter you may find as well. Plastics in particular are a serious threat to marine life. Turtles will mistake plastic for jellyfish and eat it.
- Resist the temptation to feed fish. You may disturb their normal eating habits, encourage aggressive behaviour or give them something that is detrimental to their health.

fish life are protected as part of a marine sanctuary. Other good sites include Tangan Wall, which has beautiful gorgonian fans, and Napaling, which has some impressive walls and overhangs.

Cabilao Island is famous for its hammerhead sharks, but many of these have been caught by local fisherman or driven away by divers. Fortunately, there's still some great diving around the island, particularly in the deeper portions of the reef, which have escaped damage from typhoons and fisherman.

Negros Diving is a year-round activity on Negros. Most diving is centred on the university town of Dumaguete, on the southeast coast of the island. The most popular site in this region is Apo Island (not to be confused with Apo Reef, west of Mindoro). The reef around Apo is protected as part of a marine sanctuary and the results are impressive – it's festooned with large corals that are home to a fantastic variety of colourful fish. The diving is best here from December to May.

Other dives in this region include Sumilon Island, which is a marine sanctuary; the Tacot Seamount, which attracts large pelagic fish; and Calong Calong, a shallow reef that offers good snorkelling and easy diving.

Siquijor Diving is popular here year-round. Favourite spots include Paliton Beach, Salagdoong Beach, and Sandugan and Tongo. Larena is the main port of entry to the island, and there are a couple of pleasant beach resorts at nearby Sandugan Beach that offer snorkelling and diving.

Boracay Although the diving is better in other parts of the Philippines, the combination of a fabulous white-sand beach, plenty of nightlife and lots of dive centres makes Boracay a popular choice for many divers, especially those with nondivers in tow.

There are several sheltered dive sites so you can dive here year-round, but conditions are usually best from January through June. Dive sites off Boracay include Cathedral Cave, a large hollow in an undersea wall that can be visited by intermediate divers, and the much more challenging dive at Yapak, a deep wall that is home to large fish and strong currents.

Left: Nudibranches (or sea slugs) off Boracay island– the Visayas

Leyte Easily accessible by ferry from Cebu City, Southern Leyte may be the next big thing in Philippines diving, with some pristine diving in relatively uncrowded conditions. Enterprising local divers have documented at least 20 dive sites in the area and there are several dive centres servicing them.

Some of the best diving is around Padre Burgos: Panaon Island, where Rio's Wall (also known as Toshi's Wall) has some lovely coral and a thriving population of colourful fish; and sites around Tangkaan Point, which offers diverse underwater topography and the chance to see whales, dolphins, manta rays and whale sharks.

Mindanao & Camiguin If you're not put off by the danger of travelling in the southern Philippines, there's plenty of good diving around Mindanao and off the island of Camiguin. Much of the diving around these islands is accessible year-round, which makes it a good choice when dive sites to the north are off-limits due to weather conditions.

Easily accessible from Cagayan de Oro, Camiguin is perhaps the most popular dive region in this area, and there are occasionally dive safaris here from the Visayas. There are several dive resorts on the island servicing popular dive sites like Agutaya Reef, Jigdup Reef and Cauan Point. All three of these are an underwater photographer's delight, with good coral and a variety of fish. Another interesting site in this area is Medina Underwater Springs, a series of fresh-water springs bubbling out of the sea floor.

There is good, year-round diving near Davao, including two good wreck dives and a cave dive, as well as some of the country's best wall dives. Likewise, there are some excellent wall dives off of General Santos, on the south coast of Mindanao.

Palawan The northern end of Palawan has some great diving and unmatched topside scenery. The fantasy-land of limestone karsts rising steeply out of aquamarine waters draws crowds of snorkellers and divers to the islands off of El Nido. The coral here has been damaged by dynamite fishing and typhoons, which means that novice divers and snorkellers will probably enjoy it more than experienced divers will.

Experienced divers, or those who've never tried wreck diving, will probably be happier heading north to Coron, on Busuanga Island in the Calamian group. Here, on the bottom of Coron Bay, nine ships from a Japanese WWII naval fleet lie rusting on the sea floor, luring wreck divers from all over the world. Watching one of these giant ships coalesce out of the murky darkness as you descend is one of diving's most memorable experiences. There are plenty of dive centres in the area that run trips out to the wrecks.

Although they're not as popular as El Nido and Coron, Port Barton and Puerto Princessa also have some good dive sites. Puerto Princessa is also the jumping-off point for dive trips to the Sulu Sea.

Sulu Sea About 180km from Puerto Princessa, in the middle of the Sulu Sea, Tubbutaha Reefs (a Unesco World Heritage site) and other nearby reefs offer some of the best diving in the Philippines. With awesome walls, flourishing reefs, big pelagics and a couple of wrecks, the diving here is well worth the long journey from the mainland.

Tubbutaha North and South, the two main dive sites here, are rivalled in beauty by the nearby Jessie Beazley seamount. Named for a ship that sank after hitting it, this isolated seamount has all the ingredients of a classic dive site: walls that plunge away into abysmal depths, gorgeous coral and large pelagic fish.

Yet another Sulu Sea dive site is Basterra Reef, southwest of Tubbutaha Reef. Here you'll find large fish and two wrecks, the *Tristar B* and the *Oceanic II*. Because most of the action starts at a depth of around 30m, this site is best visited by intermediate and advanced divers.

The dive sites of the Sulu Sea are accessed by live-aboard dive boats, usually sailing from Puerto Princessa on Palawan, or occasionally from dive centres in the Visayas (a longer and more difficult trip). The dive season is short here: from February to mid-June – try to book a place on a live-aboard early so as not to miss out on this superb destination.

(Continued from page 240)

For Romblon, big pumpboats operate between Roxas and Odiongan (P100 to P150, five hours, three weekly), as well as between Roxas and Looc. Two of these services go on to Looc. From Odiongan to Roxas, boats run three times weekly, coming from Looc twice weekly.

BULALACAO TO SAN JOSÉ

If you want to round the rugged southern coast of Mindoro, you may find yourself in the remote fishing town of Bulalacao (bull-**ah**-la-cow). The trip can be done by road or by sea.

The track between Bulalacao and San José is steep and treacherous, traversed by ridiculously overcrowded, top-heavy jeepneys that struggle over the mountain separating the two towns. If you value your peace of mind, or behind, opt for the boat instead. When the wet season arrives around July, even Mindoro's go-anywhere jeepneys won't tackle this road and the only way to San José is by boat.

The pumpboat which travels to/from San José must moor in Bulalacao's deeper waters outside a breakwater. Small boats shuttle passengers back and forth from the shore (P5 one way).

One pumpboat leaves Bulalacao around 10am daily (P150, three hours), and another leaves San José around 11am daily.

When the road is passable, there are around four jeepneys that come from Roxas daily, and stop in Bulalacao on their way through to San José. The jeepney stop is under a large tree about 500m from town on the Roxas road. From Bulalacao the trip costs P150 (3½ hours).

If you're travelling in the other direction, a jeepney waits for passengers on the boat from San José, and heads for Roxas when it's very, very full (P45, two to three hours).

Mindoro Occidental

The province of Mindoro Occidental is well off the tourist trail, but rewards visitors with beautiful beaches, stretches of wilderness where wild *tamaraw* (small native buffalo) still roam and the exquisite Apo Reef, one of the best diving sites in the country.

ABRA DE ILOG

Remote Abra de Ilog (**ah**-bra de **ill**-og), a nondescript little town 7km inland, is the northern gateway to Mindoro's west coast.

Little more than a bundle of small buildings, Abra's port of Wawa (**wah**-wah) is well served by boats from Batangas. If you arrive by boat you'll see why there's no useable road west of Puerto Galera: a cloud-scraping wall of jagged mountains runs right to the shore.

Most people move straight on to more inviting Mamburao after arriving in Abra, but it's possible to stay overnight.

L & P Lodging House *(rooms around P150)* is the closest accommodation to the pier – about 1km away (P5 by tricycle) – with no-frills, fan-cooled rooms. A couple of small eateries by the pier should help get you through the night.

Getting There & Away

Montenegro Shipping Lines operates four daily car-and-passenger ferries between Batangas and Abra (P85/105 ordinary/aircon, 2½ hours) from 3am to midnight. The MV *Lady of Manaoag II* makes the trip twice daily for the same fares.

A pumpboat between Wawa (for Abra de Ilog) and Puerto Galera should cost around P1500; alternatively, you can go to Batangas and take a passenger service from there.

Jeepneys connect with the boats to take passengers south to Mamburao (P35, one hour), but the trip is smoother by air-con minivan (P70, one hour).

MAMBURAO

☎ 043 • pop 30,378

Mamburao (mam-bor-**ow**) is a quiet, relatively undeveloped town. Fishing and boat building are the main industries, and there's a good beach just north of town.

You can check your email at **X-Files Computers** *(National Rd; open 7.30am-9pm daily)*, just south of La Gensol Plaza Hotel. It charges P70 per hour.

Places to Stay & Eat

La Gensol Plaza Hotel *(☎/fax 711 1072; National Rd; doubles with fan & bathroom P250, doubles with air-con P850)* is on the road that runs through the centre of town. This place is pretty fancy by Mamburao standards, but the service is still sloppy. There's a fast-food restaurant here, with meals for around P50.

Travellers Hotel & Restaurant *(☎ 711 1136; National Rd; singles/doubles with fan & bathroom from P150/180, singles/doubles with air-con P500/700)* is near the Iglesia Ni Cristo Church, with its three-pronged facade. It's a rambling, two-storey place with bucket showers. The floral-wallpapered, air-con rooms are a little cramped. The restaurant serves Filipino favourites such as *pansit Canton* for P50.

Tayamaan Palm Beach Club Resort *(☎ 711 1657; e bambanegra@yahoo.com; 1-room/2-room cottages P500/900)* is the best place to stay. It's a quiet resort about 4km north of town (P30 by tricycle) on the edge of a pretty beach cove. Concrete cottages are nicely laid out among rows of palm trees on a large lawn. The cottages are complete with bath, murals, fan and balcony. Arjan Boer, the Dutch owner, can help organise trips to the natural pool at nearby **Calawagan Falls** (around P350 by tricycle, including waiting time). A simple continental breakfast here is P70, Filipino dishes are around P110.

Getting There & Away
There are no commercial flights to Mamburao's airport. Buses between Mamburao and Sablayan take about three hours (P77), leaving from the bus stand on the northern side of town.

Jeepneys between Abra de Ilog and Mamburao run all day, departing from near the bridge on the northern edge of town, in synch with boats to/from Wawa pier. On the pot-holed old road, the 32km trip takes at least one hour (P35). Air-con minivans (P70, 45 minutes) also connect with the boat to/from Wawa. They leave from their terminal near the bus stand.

SABLAYAN
A welcome sight after a long road journey from either the north or the south, Sablayan (sab-**lay**-an) sits astride the Bagong Sabang River. It has a lively market, and boats of all shapes and sizes are strung out along its river-mouth port. For most travellers, Sablayan's beauty lies in its proximity to North Pandan Island, but there are other attractions in the area. At **Libauo Lake**, famed for its white lotuses, there is good fishing and (for something a bit different) you can visit nearby

Sablayan Prison Farm, where the inmates farm, fish and make handicrafts that are for sale. See the Eco-Tourism Office for further details. You could also walk out to the **lighthouse** on Sablayan Point.

Information
The friendly **Eco-Tourism Office** *(open 7am-5pm daily)* is on the pier near the Emily Hotel. It can assist you with vehicle and guide hire; a jeepney will cost around P1500 per day for local sightseeing.

Places to Stay & Eat
Emily Hotel *(115 Gozar St; singles with fan & shared bathroom P100, doubles with fan & private bathroom P250)*, next to the market, the river and boats to North Pandan Island, is a well-run, single-storey place with small, basic rooms. The restaurant does budget meals for P40.

LandManz Hotel *(☎ 198 1661; Arellano St; doubles with shared bathroom & fan P150, with private bathroom & fan/air-con P250/600)* has neat but tiny rooms, some with no windows. You'll also find a restaurant and 'videoke' here.

Albert's Place *(singles/doubles with fan & bathroom P650/1300)* is over the river. It costs P50/100 by bangka at low/high tide, but at low tide you can walk here. This resort has a pleasant beachfront location overlooking North Pandan Island. The two-storey cottages are in spacious grounds and there's a restaurant and bar here. Guided trekking trips are a speciality and can include Libauo Lake (P1400 per person) or Mt Iglit-Baco National Park (P4900). You can also hire kayaks and speedboats.

Getting There & Away
Boats to North Pandan Island wait for customers near the market. The standard one-way fare is P100 per boat (20 minutes).

Buses and large jeepneys go via Sablayan on their way north to Mamburao (P77, three hours) or south to San José (P77, three to 3½ hours). Most can simply be flagged on National Rd, which runs along the town's eastern edge.

NORTH PANDAN ISLAND
This slice of paradise is as close to tropical perfection as you can get without buying your own island. It has a curvaceous, white sand

beach in the south and untamed forest stretching across to its northern shore. All around the island are prime **dive spots**, and there are at least two enchanting, easy hiking trails across the island to the gloriously named **Spaniard's Nose Point** and to **White Lagoon**.

North Pandan Island is the ideal base from which to explore nearby Apo Island, part of the exceptional divers' sanctuary of the **Apo Reef National Park** (not to be confused with the Apo Island Marine Reserve and Fish Sanctuary of *another* Apo Island, off the south coast of Negros). It features 533 species of fish and 190 species of coral. Here, divers have a good chance of seeing large marine animals such as hammerhead sharks, turtles and manta rays, as well as 47 species of birds, including the endangered Nicobar pigeon.

Mariposa Diving (e *info@pandan.com*), which can be contacted through the Pandan Island Resort (for details see Places to Stay & Eat later), charges US$25/19 for 'fun dives' with/without equipment. A range of dive courses is offered from October to June, including open-water courses (US$290).

Apart from dives around the island, the dive shop offers package **boat trips** to Apo Island (from US$75 for two; full day with picnic), or overnight live-aboard trips to Apo Island (from US$150 for two; with meals and park entry fee) and Busuanga (US$389 for two; three nights and four days). The best time for diving is October to May.

The resort's minimal lighting makes the beach an ideal place for **star-gazing**. Other pursuits include **snorkelling** (gear hire P125 per day), **water-skiing**, **wakeboarding** and **monoskiing** (P600 per half-hour, including instructor) and **ocean kayaking** (P500 per day for two).

Places to Stay & Eat

Pandan Island Resort (☎ *0982 810050; or book through Asiaventure Services in Manila,* ☎ *02-526 6929, fax 525 1811,* W *www.pandan .com; budget singles/doubles US$10/12, standard double bungalows US$20, deluxe cottages US$32*), an idyllic combination of simple living and pure, tropical decadence, is the sole occupant of the island. This laid-back, smoothly run place has budget rooms with shared bathroom, standard bungalows, and deluxe cottages for one to four people. All have balconies and sliding bamboo doors, and the showers are salt water (fresh water is provided in buckets). Security is low here – there are no locks or room keys. The nightly buffet dinner is a feast that would outdo any five-star restaurant. Breakfast is a flat US$3, and main meals are US$7. It costs P50 for a day visit.

Getting There & Away

Pumpboats will ferry you back and forth between Sablayan and North Pandan Island (P100/120 for one/two people, 20 minutes).

The Tamaraw

The *tamaraw (Bubalus mindorensis)*, one of the world's most endangered land mammals, is found only on Mindoro. The stout little native buffalo has fallen victim to hunting, disease and, most recently, large-scale deforestation. In 1975 its numbers had dropped to an estimated 200 from 10,000 in 1900.

The animal's horns grow straight upward in a distinctive 'V' formation and scientists believe it is descended from three species: the cow, the deer and the *kalabaw*. Although it has been a protected species since 1936, it was not until 1979 that the Tamaraw Conservation Program was established and the breeding programme, known as the Gene Pool, was set up the following year at Mt Iglit-Baco National Park. Over the next 13 years, 20 *tamaraw* were captured and the once-solitary cud-chewer was subjected to a flurry of scientific scrutiny that included carefully monitoring how often it urinated and defecated each day (an average of 10.15 and 6.28 times). Unfortunately, most of the captured animals did not survive, and today there are only four animals remaining at the Gene Pool. One of these individuals is the programme team's pride and joy: the first ever *tamaraw* born in captivity, Kalibasib arrived in 1999. The programme has also seen an increase in the *tamaraw* population at the national park, from 154 in 2000 to 187 in 2001, and there are an estimated 356 *tamaraw* across the island.

There is now a movement to make the *tamaraw* the national animal of the Philippines, to increase public awareness of its plight. It has already been given the dubious honour of lending its name to a Toyota 4WD.

MINDORO

They can be hired from in front of the Emily Hotel in Sablayan. The resort can arrange your trip back to Sablayan.

MT IGLIT-BACO NATIONAL PARK

Intrepid travellers who trek to the top of these remote mountains may be rewarded with a sighting of the elusive wild *tamaraw* (native buffalo). However, this is really a trip for hard-core bovid enthusiasts – there are rumours of NPA (New People's Army) activity in the area, and recent reports suggest that deforestation has taken its toll on all but the upper-most reaches of the park. It's a nine-hour climb to the top of Mt Iglit, where you can camp overnight. Inside the park, the **Tamaraw Conservation Program** has a breeding station known as the Gene Pool that you can visit. The first and only *tamaraw* bred in captivity lives here.

Albert's Place, in Sablayan (see earlier in this chapter), organises trips; alternatively the Tourism Council in San José (see later) can arrange a local guide with a week's notice. It's very difficult to make the climb in the wet season – October to May is the best time. Coming from Sablayan, there's a signposted road to the sanctuary 6km north of Calintaan.

SAN JOSÉ

☎ 043 • pop 111,009

On Mindoro's southwest coast, San José (san ho-**say**) is notable for taking its 'videoke' sessions very seriously.

You can hire a bangka from the pier (around P1000) to visit **Ambulong Reef**. There's good diving here, but you must bring your own gear. Locals head out to the beaches to the north of town to relax by the water with a few drinks.

Information

Gilbert P Yulo (☎ 0918 354 0996) is the president of the local Tourism Council and is a great source of information on the region. Gilbert works at the Air Philippines office on Rizal St and can help you with hiring transport and a guide to visit the nearby Mangyan villages or Mt Iglit-Baco National Park.

The **Metrobank** has an ATM that accepts MasterCard and Cirrus cards. Both Metrobank and the **PNB** (Philippines National Bank) will change travellers cheques.

On the corner of C Liboro and Rizal Sts you'll find an **RCPI International Telephone Office** (open 7am-10pm Mon-Fri, 8am-5pm Sat & Sun). The **21st Century Business Center** (C Liboro; open 7.30am-10pm daily), opposite the Mercury Drug Store, also has an international phone service.

Millennium One Computer Center (C Liboro St; open 8am-6.30pm daily), is actually called Mindoro One Computer Centre, but at the time of writing it hadn't got round to changing its sign. It charges P75 per hour for Internet access.

Places to Stay

There's not much accommodation to get too excited about in San José proper, but what's here is cheap. Just north of town, a couple of beachside hotels cater to all budgets and make for more peaceful holidaying.

Sikatuna Town Hotel (☎ 491 1274; Sikatuna St; P140, doubles with bathroom & fan P190, with air-con P595), a friendly place in San José proper, has small rooms that could be cleaner and a bunker-like canteen that does big Filipino breakfasts for around P45. A word of warning: every night, this hotel's front rooms cop the full force of the Kusina Folkhouse Videoke over the road (next door to the Kusina Restaurant). This place shatters the nation's reputation for producing good singers.

Plaza Hotel (☎ 491 4661; Zamora St; singles with fan & shared/private bathroom P200/300, doubles with bathroom & fan/air-con from P400/700) is the best option in town. It is a large but rather soulless place, with clean, tiled rooms above an enormous lobby.

A P5 tricycle ride north of town will bring you to two beachside hotels that are better options and well out of earshot of San José's 'videoke' bars. The hotels are next door to each other, facing the brown-sand beach.

Sikatuna Beach Hotel (☎ 491 2182; singles/doubles with shared bathroom P150/175, doubles with private bathroom & fan/air-con from P270/670) is the budget choice. In an annexe building, it has drab but spacious rooms. In the main building, the restaurant does half a fried chicken for P150, which you can eat in the shade cottages overlooking the water.

White House Safari Beach Hotel (☎ 491 1656; e edithpark@yahoo.com; doubles with air-con & hot shower P2200, 4-bed suites P3300) is friendly. There are luxurious standard rooms with balcony, private bathroom, fridge, TV and generous furnishings. The

SAN JOSÉ

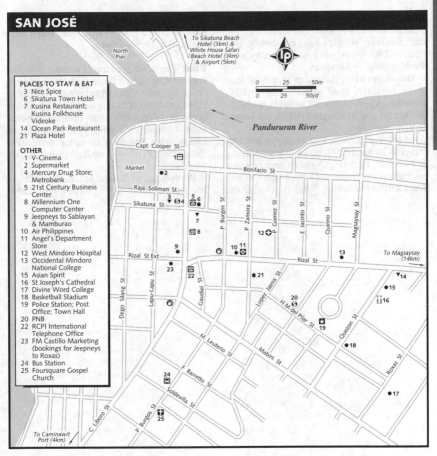

PLACES TO STAY & EAT
3 Nice Spice
6 Sikatuna Town Hotel
7 Kusina Restaurant;
   Kusina Folkhouse
   Videoke
14 Ocean Park Restaurant
21 Plaza Hotel

OTHER
1 V-Cinema
2 Supermarket
4 Mercury Drug Store;
   Metrobank
5 21st Century Business
   Center
8 Millennium One
   Computer Center
9 Jeepneys to Sablayan
   & Mamburao
10 Air Philippines
11 Angel's Department
   Store
12 West Mindoro Hospital
13 Occidental Mindoro
   National College
15 Asian Spirit
16 St Joseph's Cathedral
17 Divine Word College
18 Basketball Stadium
19 Police Station; Post
   Office; Town Hall
20 PNB
22 RCPI International
   Telephone Office
23 FM Castillo Marketing
   (bookings for Jeepneys
   to Roxas)
24 Bus Station
25 Foursquare Gospel
   Church

giant, two-room family suite faces the water. A big, American breakfast in a dining room overlooking an immaculately kept garden is P188. Bangka hire to offshore islands can be arranged for around P2000 per day. The White House is more like a rich relative's mansion than a hotel. Book at least one week in advance.

Places to Eat

Kusina Restaurant *(Sikatuna St; dishes P110; open 6.30am-11pm daily)*, directly opposite the Sikatuna Town Hotel, will look after you well, with generous servings of sizzling beefsteak, chop suey or barbecue chicken with Java rice. A Filipino breakfast is P60.

Nice Spice *(Sikatuna St; open 8.30am-7pm daily)* does a big Filipino breakfast with cof-fee for P45, and spicy fried chicken wings with rice for P55. *Halo-halo* (an ice, fruit and milk sweet) and other desserts are a speciality (P25 to P80).

Ocean Park Restaurant *(Rizal St; dishes P40-150; open 9am-10pm daily)*, in the eastern part of town, is a popular and fairly big place serving good Filipino dishes. Despite the name, it's not so big on seafood.

Getting There & Away

Air San José's airport is about 5km northwest of town (P10 by tricycle).

Asian Spirit (☎ 491 4151) has daily flights between San José and Manila (P1593 one hour); the office is near St Joseph's Cathedral. **Air Philippines** (☎ 491 4158; Rizal St) flies the same route (P1748, three weekly).

MINDORO

Bus & Jeepney Several buses ply between Mamburao and San José (P154, seven hours) each morning, but it's a bum-numbingly long stretch. This journey is best broken by a refreshing stop in Sablayan.

Buses between Sablayan and San José leave regularly until about midday (P77, three hours). Jeepneys run to Sablayan (P77, 3½ hours) and Mamburao (P154, six hours) until around 3pm.

In the dry season, two jeepneys per day travel to Roxas (P190, seven hours), leaving at 9am and 11am daily. You can reserve a seat on this very popular and very rough route at **FM Castillo Marketing** (*Rizal St*). During the wet season the road is impassable and you have to take a boat to Bulalacao and a jeepney to Roxas from there.

Boat The boats that travel to/from San José dock at Caminawit Port, 4km south of town (P10 by tricycle). **Montenegro Shipping Lines** (☎ 491 5502) has overnight passenger services (P260/400/1200 ordinary/air-con/suite, 12 hours, six weekly) to Batangas, on Luzon. **Viva Shipping Lines** has services to Batangas (P160/400 ordinary/air-con, six weekly).

Pumpboats to Bulalacao, Mindoro Oriental, leave at 11am (P150, three hours, daily).

The Visayas

The Philippines' main island-group is the Visayas. Situated between Luzon (and Mindoro) to the north, Palawan to the west and Mindanao to the south, the main islands and major sub-groups of the Visayas are Cebu, the Camotes Islands, Bohol, Negros, Siquijor, Panay, Boracay, the Romblon Group, Masbate, Samar, Leyte and Biliran. Scattered among these are numerous small islands – some inhabited, others not. Perfect for the adventurous island-hopper with plenty of time on their hands.

For those on a tighter schedule, there is a virtual navy of regular fastcraft and reliable bangka between the major islands, as well as several flights between many of the more popular destinations. For island-hopping ideas, see Suggested Itineraries in the Facts for the Visitor chapter.

Although most people are drawn to the Visayas for the quiet tropical islands, palm-fringed beaches and stunning reefs, the region is also fast becoming famous for its long list of outdoor activities, including trekking, camping, rock climbing, mountain biking and bird-watching.

Cebu

Cebu City is a major gateway to the Visayas and an attractive alternative to entering the country at Manila's manic airport, with many popular destinations both on the island or on nearby islands.

Cebu has a long, bare backbone of a central mountain range, but unfortunately logging has taken a heavy toll on the island's forests, making the beaches on the north and south coasts the best tourist options. To the north, the offshore island of Bantayan – with its sublime white beaches – and Malapascua – for lovers of the island life style and shark-diving – are increasingly popular backpackers' haunts, while to the south, Moalboal is *the* place for diving and budget hedonism. Divers and bird-watchers rave about Olango, a reef-ringed outcrop not far from Mactan.

Cebu's main cities are Cebu City, Toledo, Danao, Mandaue and Lapu-Lapu (on Mactan). All five are strapped around the island's waist in a broad belt.

Highlights

- Hunt for witches around Siquijor's caves and beaches
- Be eye-balled in the Boholano jungle by a tarsier
- Visit the ancestral homes of historic Silay and gorging on the city's speciality – coconut pie
- Trek around the beautiful Twin Lakes crater area and when done, take on the mighty Mt Kanlaon and the magical Mt Guiting-Guiting
- Dive off Malapascua Island to see thresher sharks, and off Apo Island to see flourishing protected reefs
- Sip a cocktail on board a *paraw* at sunset, off White Beach, Boracay – yes, perhaps it *is* the best beach in the world...
- Explore the strikingly beautiful and remarkably friendly islet of Biliran to experience what Camiguin was like two decades ago.
- Spook yourself with a tour through a colonial-era haunted house in the historic South Leyte port town of Malitbog

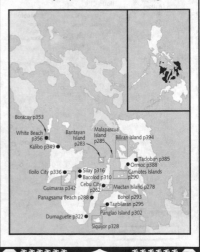

Boracay p353
White Beach p356
Kalibo p349
Bantayan Island p283
Malapascua Island p285
Biliran Island p394
Iloilo City p336
Silay p316
Bacolod p310
Cebu City p262
Tacloban p385
Ormoc p388
Camotes Islands p290
Mactan Island p278
Guimaras p342
Panagsama Beach p288
Bohol p293
Tagbilaran p295
Panglao Island p302
Dumaguete p322
Siquijor p328

Getting There & Away

You can wing or sail your way to Cebu – from destinations Philippine and abroad.

THE VISAYAS

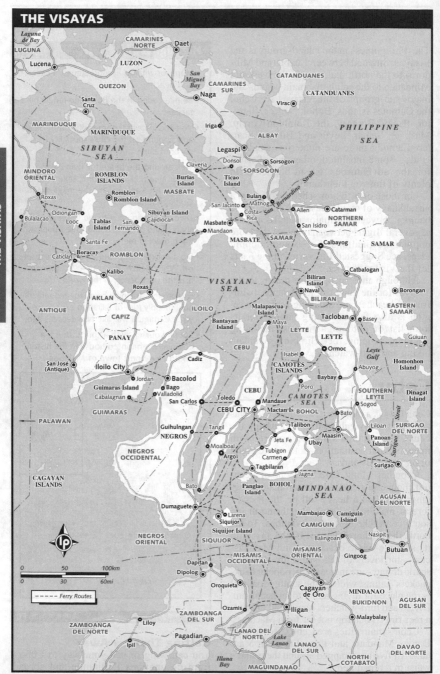

You'll find detailed transport information in the individual destination entries in this section. When planning your route from A to B, however, it's important to remember that schedules and fares change like the breeze. It's well worth checking ahead to make sure you've got themost up-to-date information.

CEBU CITY

☎ 032 • pop 718,800

Like an ageing screen siren, Cebu City somehow manages to seem young and innocent after all these years – just don't look too closely. To think, this place is older than Manila, has the nation's busiest port and a population nearing one million. But then again, what city wouldn't look good compared to Manila?

Chinese, Cambodians and Arabs are thought to have been wading ashore at Cebu as early as the 15th century, to trade gold, cotton, opium and slaves. So when European explorer Ferdinand Magellan turned up here in 1521, he was a late arrival.

Websites that may be helpful in planning your trip to Cebu City include ⓦ www.ce buisland.com and ⓦ www.esprint.com.ph/pointcebu.

Orientation

As far as most visitors are concerned, Cebu City is Manila minus the mayhem. Its traffic is chaotic, but not insane. Its size and layout can actually be understood, rather than merely endured. And – sigh – hardly any of the taxi drivers here are employed by Satan.

The city's centre has shifted inland in recent years, and locals now refer to the newer precinct around Fuente Osmeña as 'uptown' and the older district around Colon St ('the oldest street in the country') as 'downtown'. The boundary is blurry – for our purposes, we've divided uptown from downtown at Del Rosario St. Beyond the uptown area is Lahug, which includes the upmarket Beverly Hills.

Cebu City has a long history of changing its street names, with many of the old names living on, either in the minds of taxi drivers or on street signs yet to be removed. If you find yourself squinting up at a street sign with black lettering on a yellow background, it's an old sign – and the name *may* have since changed. Up-to-date signs are those with white, or reflective, lettering on a bright green

background. The most commonly confused streets are: Pres Osmeña Blvd (or simply Osmeña Blvd; formerly Jones St – jeepneys are still labelled 'Jones'); Gen Maxilom Ave (formerly Mango Ave); Manalili St (formerly V Gullas St); Maria Cristina St (formerly N Rafols St); Don F Sotto St (formerly Jasmin St, and referred to as DF Sotto St); Salinas Dr (formerly Cebu Airport Rd); and Osmeña St (formerly Second Ave 13th *and* MacArthur Blvd). There are also many streets, avenues, drives and boulevards using the same name, such as Osmeña, or Ramos – often all that differentiates them is a first name or initial (eg, J Osmeña St, S Osmeña St and so on).

Maps Decent enough tourist maps can be picked up free from the airport, the Department of Tourism (DOT) office in the LDM Building, and from most hotels. For something a bit more in-depth, pick up the blue cardboard-covered *Cebu City Street Map* (P140), with a 1:16 0000 scale, that takes in the city surrounds, including Mactan, and has reference pages for streets, hotels and other landmarks. It's sold at the National Bookstore (see Bookshops later) as well as at some of the better hotels.

For nautical and topographical maps and charts, set a course for the **National Mapping and Resource Authority** *(Namria; ☎ 412 1749; Room 301, 3rd floor, Osmeña Bldg, cnr Osmeña Blvd & Jakosalem St; open 8am-noon & 1pm-5pm Mon-Fri)*.

Information

See the Facts for the Visitor chapter for details of consulates in Cebu City.

Tourist Offices The **Department of Tourism** *(DOT; ☎ 254 2811; ground floor, LDM Bldg, Lapu-Lapu St; open 7.30am-6pm Mon-Fri)* is behind Amway. There are also counters at the international and domestic arrivals terminals at Mactan Airport *(☎ 340 8229/340, 340 2486/2450; open for all arrivals)*.

Immigration Offices The new **Bureau of Immigration Office** *(☎ 345 6442; cnr Burgos St & Mandaue Ave; open 8am-noon & 1pm-5pm Mon-Fri)* is behind the Mandaue Fire Station, opposite the Mandaue Sports Complex. You can extend a 21-day visa to 59 days here for a whopping P2020 (this includes a *compulsory* express fee). You only

THE VISAYAS

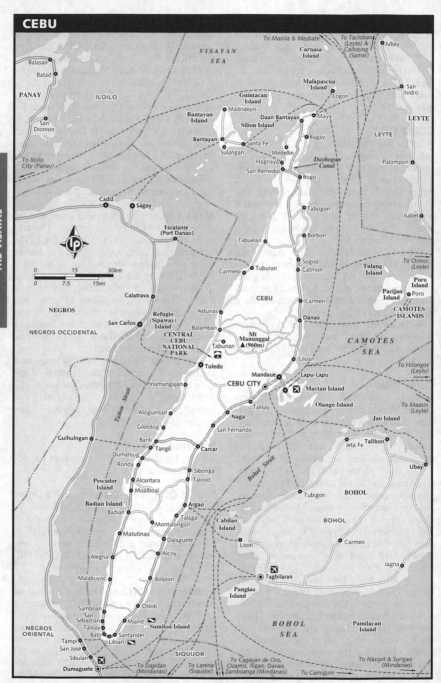

CEBU

need to produce your passport, and you should be out of there within an hour. For longer visa extensions, you will have to pay around P500 per month. See Visas & Documents in the Facts for the Visitor chapter for more details.

Some readers have commented that making an effort with appearance can help with manoeuvring through the immigration office's bureaucracy.

Money Bank hours are 9am to 3pm Monday to Friday. The **Equitable PCI Bank** has two branches that issue cash advances on major credit cards and Cirrus – these are outside SM City, and on the corner of Gonzales and Borromeo Sts, downtown. Many banks have credit card-friendly ATMs, but the most dependable is the one at **HSBC** (J Osmeña St). There's a 24-hour security guard on duty beside the machine, and cards accepted include Visa, MasterCard, Cirrus and Global Access. You can change travellers cheques here – you incur a P61 charge per cheque, but the rate is OK, and the service is sublime in comparison to other banks.

There are also ATMs at **Ayala Centre** (off Arch Reyes Ave, Cebu Business Park) and **SM City** (North Reclamation Area).

Post The city's main **post office** is in the downtown area, near Fort San Pedro, with another branch nearby at City Hall. Hole-in-the-wall sub-branches can be found at many of the universities around town.

Email & Internet Access You won't have to walk far to find an Internet café, especially in the busier streets uptown and around the universities. Cebu City is one of the cheapest Internet cities in Southeast Asia – especially uptown. You'll pay only P20 to P25 per hour in an air-con room on a Pentium III with coffee, drinks and light snacks on offer. Cheaper places aren't worth the savings for the slower connections and stuffy rooms. Business hours vary, but many are open through the night and most are open seven days a week. Evenings tend to be full of young guys playing the latest commando-type game, so best to go during the day, or take headphones.

If you're near the Ayala Centre, drop in to **Finn's@Lounge** (Gorordo Ave; open 10am-11pm daily), north of Gen Maxilom Ave, for a cool and spacious Scandinavian cyber-experience – Scandinavian newspapers, and a full bar specialising in Scandinavian liqueurs. You'll also find espressos, meals and a large cable TV screen. West of the Capitol Building, **Net Grill** (N Escario St) has food and modern terminals in a decent environment.

For those who have let both washing and contacting friends slip behind, do both at once at **Bubbles On Line** (F Ramos St • A Pond St).

If you want to log on over breakfast, two branches of **Bo's Coffee Club** (Osmeña Blvd • Ayala Centre; open 7am-midnight Mon-Sat, 8am-11pm Sun) offers a free connection with your espresso.

On F Ramos St, **Books and Brew Internet & Study Centre** (Raintree Mall; open 8.30am-5.30am daily) provides a cool quiet escape with terminals, snacks, study booths, second-hand paperbacks for P120, and weekly rental books on philosophy, psychology, religion and literature for P10 to P30.

Fulfil a few needs by dropping into **@Mix Internet Cafe** (☎ 255 5896; F Ramos St; open 8am-2am Mon-Thur, 8am-3am Fri-Sat, 2pm-2am Sun), next to Metrobank, where you'll find pool tables, terminals, snacks and a travel desk.

Subtle Graphix (☎ 255 0254; 147 Palaez St; open 9am-9pm Mon-Sat) also offers printing, scanning and computer repairs.

Elicon House, the budget hotel on Junquera St (see Downtown under Places to Stay – Budget later), is surrounded by Internet cafés. The best is **Cybernet Live Café** (☎ 254 8533, 416 8026; 151 Junquera St; open 24hr), which has fast connections, air-con, photocopier, scanner, snacks, toilets and very helpful staff.

Bookshops There are several outlets of the **National Bookstore** (Gen Maxilom Ave • SM City • Ayala Centre; ⓦ www.nationalbook store.com.ph; open 9am-9pm daily), all with stocks of local and international fiction and nonfiction, magazines, stationery and maps.

Newspapers The *Sun Star* newspaper lists what's on around town, movie guides, apartment rentals, shipping schedules and classifieds. Sunday's paper is particularly informative. The other main newspapers – the *Freeman* and the *Cebu Daily News* – are also OK. They can be bought from street

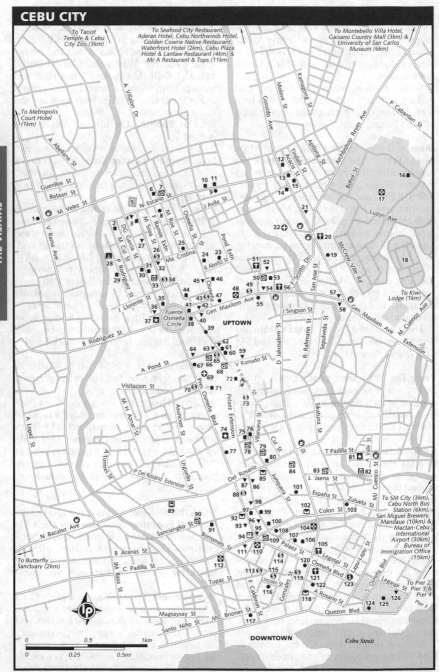

CEBU CITY

To Taoist Temple & Cebu City Zoo (3km)

To Seafood City Restaurant, Aderan Hotel, Cebu Northwinds Hotel, Golden Cowrie Native Restaurant, Waterfront Hotel (2km), Cebu Plaza Hotel & Lantaw Restaurant (4km) & Mr A Restaurant & Tops (11km)

To Montebello Villa Hotel, Gaisano Country Mall (3km) & University of San Carlos Museum (6km)

To Metropolis Court Hotel (1km)

To Kiwi Lodge (1km)

UPTOWN

Fuente Osmeña Circle

To Butterfly Sanctuary (2km)

To SM City (3km), Cebu North Bus Station (6km), San Miguel Brewery, Mandaue (10km) & Mactan-Cebu International Airport (30km) Bureau of Immigration Office (15km)

To Pier 2, Pier 3 & Pier 4

DOWNTOWN

Cebu Strait

0   0.5   1km
0   0.25   0.5mi

CEBU CITY

PLACES TO STAY
2 Villa de Mercedes
3 Jacinta Pension House
6 Mayflower Pension House
10 Cebu Pensione Plaza; LJ's Ice Cream; Shell Service Station
11 Cebu Grande Hotel; The Apartelle; Capitol Commercial Complex
12 Kukuk's Nest Pension House & Restaurant; Philippines National Bank (PNB)
13 The Golden Peak
14 West Gorordo Hotel; Family Choice Restaurant
15 Pensionne La Florentina
16 Marriott Hotel
23 Casa Rosario Pension House
24 C'est la Vie Pension
29 Dynasty Tourist Inn
30 Jasmine Pension House; Verbena Pension House
31 Travel Bee Bed & Breakfast
35 Shamrock Pension
38 Cebu Midtown Hotel; Robinson's Plaza; Aboitiz Express
41 Garwood Hotel; Philippine Airlines; Elegant Circle Hotel; Pizza Hut
44 Fuente Pension
46 NS Royal Pensione
53 Eddie's Hotel & Beverly Room Bar & Restaurant
60 Residencia Ramos; Swagman Travel; Velez General Hospital
61 Holiday Plaza Hotel
71 Pacific Pensionne
72 Diplomat Hotel & Diplomat Garden Restaurant; European Delicatessen & Butcher Shop Restaurant
75 Teo-Fel Pension House & Café Felicidad
76 Cebu Regal Pension House; LS Pension House
80 Elicon House & Elicon Café; Cybernet Café
91 Fortune Lodge
97 Cebu View Tourist Inn
99 Hotel de Mercedes; Javy's Café; Metrobank
100 Century Hotel; New Cinema Theater; Adult Cinema
106 Pension
107 Hotel Victoria de Cebu; Visayan Restaurant

PLACES TO EAT
4 Taj Mahal; Wheels Bike Shop
21 Royal Concourse
27 Bo's Coffee Club

32 KFC
36 Larsian
40 Jollibee; Century 21 Cinema; Mr Donut
42 McDonald's; Bank of the Philippine Islands (BPI)
45 Dish
52 KFC
54 Swiss Chalet Restaurant
57 Finns@Lounge
58 Lighthouse Restaurant; Hodge Podge
59 Jo's Chicken Inatô
62 Bo's Coffee Club
63 Abuhan Restaurant; White House Filipino Grill
64 McDonald's
86 Fruit Stalls
87 Jollibee; Santa Rosario Church
93 Snow Sheen Restaurant
95 Golden Crust Bakery
96 Pete's Kitchen
98 Our Place
111 Fruit Stalls; Bank of Philippine Islands (BPI)
126 Food Stalls

OTHER
1 Guadalupe Market
5 Capitol Building
7 Net Grill
8 Fruit Stalls
9 Fruit Stalls
17 Ayala Center Shopping Mall; Cebu Business Park
18 Hippodromo
19 24-Hour Convenience Store
20 Chapel of Our Lady of the Miraculous Medal
22 Perpetual Soccour Hospital
25 Scuba World
26 Equitable PCI Bank; Cebu Doctors Hospital
28 Philippine Chinese Spiritual Temple
33 Rizal Memorial Library & Museum; Red Cross
34 PNB
37 Fuente Police Station; Equitable PCI Bank
39 Raintree Mall; Books and Brew
43 HSBC & ATM
47 National Bookstore; Air Philippines
48 Mango Plaza; Ruftan's Supermarket
49 Metrobank
50 Internet Cebu
51 Redemptionist Church of Cebu City
55 Aboitiz Express
56 Iglesia Church

65 Equitable PCI Bank
66 Bubbles On Line
67 24-Hour Convenience Store
68 Bubbles on Line; 24-Hour Convenience Store
69 Metro Cebu Community Hospital
70 PNB
73 Metrobank; @Mix Internet Café
74 Police Station
77 Cebu State College
78 Compuserve Internet Café
79 Cybernet Live Café
81 Police Station
82 Casa Gorordo Museum
83 @netdepot
84 64MB Cafe
85 Post Office; San Carlos University
88 Bank of the Philippine Islands (BPI)
89 Cebu South Bus Station
90 Internet Cafés
92 Post Office; University of Cebu
94 Cinerama Cinema
101 Food Market
102 Post Office; University of The Visayas
103 Heritage of Cebu Sculpture; Palacio Shipping
104 Guisano Shopping Mall
105 Cebu Cathedral; Religious Souvenir Stalls
108 Colonnade Mall; Supermarket; Jollibee; Oriente Cinema; PLTD Calling Office; Fruit Stalls; Aboitiz Express
109 Microbagz; KFC
110 Gaisano Metro Shopping Mall; Jollibee
112 Gaisano South Shopping Mall
113 Equitable PCI Bank
114 Equitable PCI Bank
115 Equitable PCI Bank
116 Guitar Shops
117 Carbon Market
118 Post Office; Cebu City Hall
119 Equitable PCI Bank
120 Namria Map Office
121 Basilica Minore del Santo Niño; Religious Souvenir Stalls
122 Magellan's Cross; Bank of Philippine Islands
123 Department of Tourism (DOT) office
124 Cebu Port Authority; Food Stalls
125 Fort San Pedro; Public Toilets

THE VISAYAS

vendors, and inside and outside malls. Newspapers often sell out by the afternoon.

Medical Services Cebu's three main medical centres are in the uptown area. **Cebu Doctors Hospital** (☎ 253 7511; Osmeña Blvd) is near the Capitol Building. Farther south is the **Metro Cebu Community Hospital** (☎ 253 1901; Osmeña Blvd). The **Cebu (Velez) General Hospital** (☎ 253 1871; F Ramos St) is nearby.

Emergency For emergency tourist assistance, call the 24-hour **Task Force Turista** (☎ 254 4023) or **Cebu City Police Station** (☎ 253 5636, 116).

Basilica Minore del Santo Niño

This magnificent church and convent (Osmeña Blvd; admission free) is one hell of a survivor. Built in 1565 and burnt down three times, it was rebuilt in its present form in 1737. Almost makes you afraid to go near it, lest it burst into flame while you're busy admiring the heavenly ceiling murals and ornate altar. Holy souvenirs are available inside the church and also outside the main gate, on Osmeña Blvd.

Butterfly Sanctuary

The Butterfly Sanctuary (☎ 261 6884; admission by donation) is west of the downtown area, where you wouldn't expect butterflies to hang around. But hang around they do, from branches and leaves all over the garden of Julian Jumalon's home. You will receive a lecture and tour showing you butterflies in various stages of their lifecycle, butterfly collections and artworks made from damaged butterfly wings – even a presidential portrait! The best time of day for viewing is the morning, and the best time of year is from June to February. Ring first to make a booking.

To get there, catch a jeepney (P4) from N Bacalso Ave, which turns into Cebu South Rd, and hop off at Macopa St (after the second pedestrian overpass). Walk up Macopa St, and take the first left after Basak Elementary School. The sanctuary is on the corner at the end of this street. A taxi will get you there from downtown for around P65.

Casa Gorordo Museum

Downtown, not far from Pier 3, the Casa Gorordo Museum (☎ 255 5630; 35 L Jaena St;

admission P25; open 8.30am-noon & 1pm-5pm Mon-Sat) is one of the hidden gems of Cebu City. Originally a private home, it was built in the 1860s by the Gorordos, a merchant family. The lower part of the house has walls of Mactan coral stone, cemented using tree sap. The stunning upper-storey living quarters are pure Philippine hardwood (known as *tugus*), held together not with nails but with wooden pegs. Items on display include gorgeous wooden kitchenware, antique photos and a collection of *berso* (hand cannons) used for launching fireworks. Group tours can be organised through the museum.

Fort San Pedro

Built in 1565 to keep a lookout for pirates, Fort San Pedro (Legaspi St; admission P50; open 8am-noon & 1pm-5pm Tues-Sun) has since served as an army garrison, a rebel stronghold, a prison camp and the city zoo. These days, it's in retirement as a peaceful, walled garden and handsomely crumbling ruin.

Magellan's Cross

Magellan's cross? Wouldn't you be if you'd sailed all the way from Europe only to die in a soggy heap on the island of Mactan? Ferdinand's Catholic legacy, a large wooden cross, is housed in a stone rotunda (built in 1841) across from Cebu City Hall. The crucifix on show here apparently contains a few splinters from a cross Magellan planted on the shores of Cebu in 1521. A painting on the ceiling of the rotunda shows Magellan erecting the cross (actually, the locals are doing all the work – Magellan's just standing around with his mates).

Philippine Chinese Spiritual Temple

A colourful, multi-tiered maze of dragons, pergolas and carefully crafted gardens, this haven from the hustle and bustle is within surprisingly easy walking distance of uptown's busy Capitol Building area. Regular prayer meetings are held here. To find it, head west along J Avila St and look for the distinctive roof at the end of the street.

Rizal Memorial Library & Museum

A short walk from Fuente Osmeña, this regal-looking museum (Osmeña Blvd; admission by donation; open 8.30am-11.30am & 1.30pm-4.30pm Mon-Fri) is a good stopover for those interested in Cebu's and the nation's history. With an emphasis on the country's political heroes, the exhibition includes paintings, busts, coins, replica battle sword and books focusing on history and art. Underneath the building is the **Cebu City Public Library and Information Centre** (open 8am-noon & 1pm-5pm Mon-Fri).

Taoist Temple
Overlooking the city, in the ritzy Beverly Hills residential area, the magnificent Taoist Temple is a symbol of the city's large and influential ethnic Chinese population. To get to the temple take a Lahug or Calunasan jeepney and ask to stop at the Taoist Temple or Beverly Hills (P4) – you've then got a short walk uphill. Alternatively, take a taxi from uptown for about P65.

Tops Lookout Area
Nearby Mt Busay makes a mighty backdrop for Cebu City, but the best view is from the mountain itself, where you'll find the Tops Lookout Area (admission P50). Better known simply as 'Tops', this modernist, fortress-like viewing deck provides spectacular views, especially at sunrise or sunset. There are food stalls up here, but you can also wander down to the stylish Mr A (see Lahug under Places to Eat later). Many Lahug jeepneys get within about 500m of the lookout (take one on Osmeña Blvd, north of Del Rosario – you may have to change at Cebu Plaza Hotel – and ask for jeepney to Tops), and a taxi will go all the way from downtown for a negotiated price up to P500.

University of San Carlos Museum
Perched on the 5th floor of the university, the captivating collection of specimens at this museum (Archbishop Reyes Ave; admission P15; open 8am-noon & 1.30pm-5pm Mon-Fri) would be the envy of any museum. A mixture of marine biology, entomology and natural history, the collection features thousands of carefully bottled beasties, some positively alien bat species, and a morbidly fascinating six-legged kalabaw (native buffalo). There's also a fine collection of pottery from the archaeology department nearby. The university is east of the uptown area (P4 by University jeepney, P50 by taxi).

San Miguel Brewery
Free tours of the San Miguel Brewery (☎ 345 7246; cnr A S Fortuna & G Lopez Jaena Sts) happen at 9am every Tuesday and Wednesday. Although aimed at school students, anyone else is welcome to tag along and no bookings are needed. Tours cover the entire brewing process and take about two hours – yes, you have to wait that long for the free beer-tasting. The plant is in the city of Mandaue (G Lopez Jaena St is also known as Mandaue Hwy), which is fast becoming an outer suburb of Cebu City. It's roughly halfway between downtown Cebu City and the airport, so if your timing's right you could drop in for a beer on your way through. A taxi from downtown to the plant should cost around P70, alternatively, catch a Mandaue Hwy jeepney (P4).

Waterfront Hotel & Casino Filipino
If betting's your bag, then the Casino Filipino is the place to go. If not, the place is still worth a look at if only for the mechanical horse-racing betting machine, the fake night-sky of the main gaming room, and the spellbinding ceiling mural – a 50m-by-30m recreation of explorer Ferdinand Magellan's world map – in the foyer. For more details, see the Lahug entry in Places to Stay – Top End, later.

Carbon & Tabo-an Markets
The Carbon Market (MC Briones St) is Cebu City's biggest market – where racks of clothes and baskets snuggle cheek-by-jowl with stalls of fish, live chickens and drying intestines. Most jeepneys heading downtown go to Carbon (P4). Tabo-an Market (Lakandula St), off the extension of Sanciangko St, is a smaller, less chaotic, less stinky version of Carbon, but still with lots to muse over – especially for the photographer – including basket upon basket of dried fish, and also buso (hanging rice) weavers. Slightly less accustomed to tourists, this market may have better deals than others. The Labangon jeepney will get you here (P4).

Activities
Habagat Outdoor Equipment, one of biggest manufacturers of outdoor equipment in the Philippines, is based in Cebu. It has an outlet in SM City and also an office (☎ 253 6292;

DR Aboitiz St; open 2pm-9pm Mon-Sat) next to Casa Rosario Pension, full of enthusiastic outdoor guides. There are no formal packages, but rates can be negotiated. Speak to: Ramon Vidal about **rock climbing** and **caving** in Cantabaco on the west coast; Randy Su about minor **treks** in local hills; and Adrian Muaña about **mountain biking** – no rental, guiding only.

Baruto Paddlers *(☎ 253 9109, 0919 298 0200; 31 Sepulveda St)* runs kayaking lessons and tours in Cebu–Mactan channel and outlying islands such as Olango Island. Four-hour lessons cost P300, day trips start at P400, and overnight trips from P800.

Cebu is a popular place to organise local or further-afield **diving trips**. For details, see Mactan Island under Around Cebu City later.

Places to Stay

You certainly won't suffer from a lack of accommodation choices in Cebu City. Due to the pollution, crowds and poorer demographic of downtown Cebu, the better hotels (and restaurants) are located uptown and in Lahug. Unless you have particular reason to stay downtown, or have a penchant for carbon monoxide, adult cinema and general mayhem, you are more likely to find better accommodation and peace of mind uptown.

Places to Stay – Budget

Downtown The **Ruftan Internet Cafe & Pensione** *(☎ 256 2613; Legaspi St; budget/ better rooms P165/250)* is a glimpse of the future of low-end accommodation in Southeast Asia, with shabby, no-frills rooms without air-con or bathroom, but with email on tap in the foyer. There are also better, quieter rooms facing away from noisy Legaspi St. A favourite with budget backpackers.

Other OK cheapies include **Fortune Lodge** *(☎ 256 2214; Kilat St; double rooms P180-300)* and **Elicon House** *(☎ 255 0300/0400, 253 9189/0367, fax 253 0367; Junquera St; economy singles/doubles P198/288, standard rooms P450/575)*, near the corner of Del Rosario St, with the attached Filipino eatery **Elicon Café**.

Hotel Victoria de Cebu *(☎ 254 1331; V Gullas St; singles/doubles from P325/339)* isn't as grand as its name suggests, but it has large rooms with fan and cold-water bathroom. For P170 extra, you get air-con and hot-water bathroom. Try not to get a room

facing the noisy street. Good massage and shiatsu (P250) are available on the 2nd floor, and two doors up is the cheap-eat Visayan Restaurant.

Hotel de Mercedes *(☎ 253 1105, fax 253 3880; 7 Pelaez St; singles/doubles from P462/ 721)* is a little shabby around the edges but an excellent budget option, especially with the offer running when we visited of 20% discount for cash payments. It has big, bright rooms with air-con and telephone. For an extra P200, you get new red carpet. It's opposite Pete's Kitchen.

Cebu View Tourist Inn *(☎ 254 8333/9777; 200 Sanciangko St; singles/doubles from P500/600)* is another of the best new budget places to stay. Just around the corner from Hotel de Mercedes, this cool, clean place has tidy, welcoming rooms with air-con and telephone.

Uptown All rooms, unless otherwise mentioned, have cable TV and private cold-water bathroom.

Villa de Mercedes *(☎ 253 3320/2064, fax 255 5656; 99 Orchid St, Capitol Site; double rooms P450-600)* has some of the best views you'll find in budget accommodation – looking beyond the edge of town toward the northern hills. Standard rooms are large and no frills. Pay an extra P150 for hot water and cable TV. Children under 12 are accommodated for free.

Residencia Ramos *(☎ 253 6249; 301 F Ramos St; budget singles/doubles P449/505, premium rooms P561/617)*, tucked off the street, is an older-style place with a relaxed atmosphere and budget rooms. For hot water and cable TV, try the premium rooms.

Mayflower Pension House *(☎ 255 8000, fax 255 2700; e mayflower@cebu.weblinq .com; Villalon Dr; singles/doubles/triples with fan P230/300/380, with air-con P460/580/ 720)*, near the Capitol Building, has small, freshly painted rooms. Cheap deals are available for squashing up to seven in a room. There's a tricycle parking bay right outside.

Kukuk's Nest Pension House *(☎ 231 5180; e kukuks_nest80@hotmail.com; 157 Gorordo Ave; singles/doubles with fan & shared bathroom P200/300, doubles with air-con, bathroom & cable TV P400)* is a tired old meeting place offering simple rooms with bamboo furnishings. Although not the best bargain in town, it is loved by many for its Bohemian character, attracting a local arty crowd. There's a small library in the main building, and a popular outdoor bar-restaurant on the noisy street where the theme is beer.

Pensionne La Florentina (*☎ 231 3318, 232 6738; 18 Acacia St; singles/doubles P490/590*), an attractive older-style building on a quiet street around the corner from Kukuk's, is a better alternative for the less gregarious. Get an upstairs room facing the street, and you'll have nice views at top-value rates. The communal shady veranda out the front is a great place for a beer and a meal.

Jasmine Pension House (*☎ 255 4559/ 3757, fax 254 2666; cnr DG Garcia & DF Sotto Sts; singles/doubles from P400/500*) and its neighbour **Verbena Pension House** (*☎ 253 3430/0203, fax 253 3430; 584-A DG Garcia St; singles/doubles P390/450*), have basic, cheap rooms. Verbena will accommodate up to four in a room cheaply; cable TV costs P50, a fridge P70.

Travel Bee Bed & Breakfast (*☎ 253 1005/ 1556, fax 253 1556; e westside@mozcom .com; 294 DG Garcia St; doubles with fan/ air-con P400/600*) is opposite Jasmine and Verbena and has slightly larger rooms. The 'included breakfast' is nothing to rave about – coffee and toast with butter.

Shamrock Pension House (*☎ 255 2999/00, fax 253 5239; Fuente Osmeña; rooms from P500*) is perfect for those who want cheap accommodation in the thick of uptown. For an extra P50 you can have hot water and cable TV. Children under 12 are free.

Pacific Pension (*☎ 253 5271, 254 9216, fax 253 5217; 313-A Pres Osmeña Blvd; singles P498, doubles P554-700*) is on a quiet street off Fuente Osmeña, on the downtown side of Fuente Osmeña. It would be hard to find better for the price – standard rooms are clean, with a big window and have cold-water bathroom. There's a humble restaurant with a loud TV downstairs.

C'est la Vie Pension (*☎ 253 5266, 253 2376; Juana Osmeña St; double rooms P500*), near Aboitiz St, is on a quiet street and has very large, clean rooms.

Teo-Fel Pension House (*☎ 253 2482, ☎/fax 253 2488; Junquera St; singles/doubles from P400/600*), on a leafy, quiet stretch of Junquera St, offers smallish, aqua-coloured rooms with air-con, private bathroom, windows and rattan-furnishings. For an extra P150 to P200, you'll get cable TV and hot

water. On the ground floor is the little **Café Felicidad**, and there are PLDT phones in the sitting areas.

Places to Stay – Mid-Range

For mid-range and top-end hotels, it is worth asking about 'promotional rates', a reduction of up to 40%, which occur for extended periods throughout the year, making even the more expensive hotels very reasonably priced. Many of these hotels also offer free accommodation to children under 12 (but stress that the children *must* be accompanied by their parents!). Unless otherwise mentioned, all rooms have hot-water bathroom and cable TV.

Uptown The **Dynasty Tourist Inn** (*☎ 254 6372, fax 254 6372; e dynasty@htl.pacific.net .ph; DF Sotto St; doubles/twins P600/650*) has well-priced rooms with good views. You'll find it at the western end of DF Sotto St, where the road hits P Rodriguez St.

Fuente Pension House (*☎ 253 4133/6789, fax 254 4365; 175 DJ Lorente St; singles/twins P680/780*), just behind Fuente Osmeña, is not as schmick as other pension houses, but it is clean, and some rooms have windows. What makes it worthwhile are its central (yet quiet) location and its rooftop terrace bar where you can get tempura shrimp and a beer for P100 while enjoying a view of Cebu. Another bonus, which will suit late arrivals – check-out time is 24 hours after check-in.

Cebu Pensione Plaza (*☎ 254 6300/60/69; N Escario St; budget singles with shared bathroom P440, standard doubles P660-880*), near the Caltex service station, has plain, clean doubles with the usual conveniences, plus air-con and telephone.

The Apartelle (*☎ 255 6385; N Escario St; studios per day/month from P500/6000*), next to Cebu Grand Hotel, has excellent-value modest apartments, especially for the long-termer. All rooms have basic kitchen facilities, and for an extra P350, rooms have table and dresser.

Diplomat Hotel (*☎ 254 6341, fax 254 6346; e diplomat@cebu.pw.net.ph; 90 F Ramos St; doubles P700-900*) is a good choice for those who miss their culinary comforts – the hotel complex includes the Diplomat Garden Restaurant and the European Delicatessen & Butcher Shop (see the Uptown entry in Places to Eat, later). Rooms are spartan and in a rather cell-block complex, but it's kept very clean and secure and the staff are always 'at your service'. Standard rooms with air-con and telephone are well priced, and there are more-expensive swankier rooms.

Casa Rosario Pension House (☎ 255 0525, 256 2225, fax 2535134; 101 ER Aboitiz St; twins/triples P750/850), on a quiet street near Fuente Osmeña, has brightly painted large rooms at a good price. The upstairs rooms have small terraces, and the double with single room has a large window as well. It's a squeaky clean building with a restaurant and friendly service.

NS Royal Pensione (☎ 254 5358/62/64, fax 255 1556; Juana Osmeña St; doubles from P800) is another very clean, tiled and painted hotel. Standard rooms are decent, and for an extra P300 you can have a view of the mountains.

Garwood Park Hotel (Park Place Hotel; ☎ 253 1131/0110, fax 253 0118/19; W www .garwoodparkhotel.com; singles/doubles from P1400/1600) is on Fuente Osmeña. Standard swish rooms have no window, but for P200 to P400 extra, you'll command a good view. Rates include a buffet breakfast.

West Gorordo Hotel (☎ 231 4347, fax 231 1158; e wgorordo@skyinet.net; Gorordo Ave; singles/doubles P840/1030) is a squeaky-clean hotel, with freshly painted and tiled rooms with good views. Rates include breakfast, and other meals can be taken at next-door's **Family Choice Restaurant**, a very popular Chinese restaurant with – yes – families.

The Golden Peak (☎ 233 8111; W www .lexres.com; cnr N Escario St & Gordoro Ave; rooms from P1100) has good-value, large rooms with the usual affair plus bathtub, and buffet breakfast included. On the 7th floor a pool with a view was under construction at the time of writing.

Cebu Grand Hotel (☎ 254 6361/2, fax 254 6363; W www.cebugrand.virtualve.net; N Escario St; doubles from P1400), west of the Capitol Site, has freshly painted and carpeted rooms with good views. There's also a pool with a view on the 7th floor, a gym, and **Geraldo's** – a cosy bar off the marble foyer with karaoke and live bands. Buffet breakfast included.

Eddie's Hotel (☎ 254 8570–76, fax 254 8578; e clover@pacific.net.ph; F Manalo St; rooms P1480-1880) is just near the girlie-precinct. However, at the check-in, they assured us that visitors of hotel guests are not allowed to stay.

Rooms are recently renovated and have windows and wardrobes. The hotel's 24-hour **Beverly Room Bar & Restaurant** serves a decent steak.

Other City Options The **Kiwi Lodge** (☎/fax 232 9550; e kiwilodge@pacific.net.ph; 1060 G Tudtud St; rooms P790-980) is a 20-minute walk from town, on a quiet street, in the slightly industrial area between Ayala Centre and SM City.

Clean, light rooms are good value, especially the deluxe (P945), which has a view. The restaurant-bar on the ground level is a popular hang-out for businessmen and expats – they come for the pool tables, 'fish and chips' and Sunday roasts.

Aderan Hotel (☎ 234 0322, ☎/fax 414 7087; rooms from P800), on the way to Lahug, is a reasonably priced, mid-range place. The rooms range a lot in quality – some have carpet, TV and/or fridge – so if you're unhappy, ask to see other rooms. Tucked almost under the stairs is a small, shaded pool with a Warner Bros mural, and also a health club offering massage. A taxi from downtown should be around P50.

Montebello Villa Hotel (☎ 231 3681–89, fax 231 4455; Arch Reyes Ave; standard/deluxe rooms P1400/1800) has a wonderful, well-established garden, complete with birdhouses, two swimming pools and a tennis court. At these rates its rooms aren't as special as the surrounds, but if you can have a free breakfast at the poolside restaurant, who cares? The hotel is behind the big Gaisano Country Mall, full of shops and restaurants, a P50 taxi ride from downtown.

Metropolis Court Hotel (☎ 255 7541–48, fax 255 5060; V Rama St, Guadalupe; rooms from P1560), in the northern suburb of Guadalupe (a P20 to P30 taxi ride from Osmeña Blvd), is Mexican ranch meets Las Vegas. The entrance has old hacienda decor, with carved wooden doors, tiles and a stone-walled pool area. The standard rooms are large and modern, but if you're willing to double the price, the interior gets a bit more interesting. Theme rooms include Cavern (with rough clay walls and stalactites), Mobile (sleep inside a '50s car), Roman, Industrial and Alien.

Places to Stay – Top End

Uptown The **Marriott Hotel** (☎ 232 6100, fax 232 6101; W www.marriott.com; Cardinal Rosales Ave, Cebu Business Park; doubles from P2800) is set amid a little parkland, behind the Ayala Centre.

As you might expect, rooms are comfortably classy and with good views and on weekends the package includes buffet breakfast. Good deals are also often available to travellers on SuperCat, Delta Fast Ferry, WG&A, Trans-Asia, Sulpicio or Cebu Ferry. A ticket, with guest name appearing, must be presented upon check-in.

Holiday Plaza Hotel (☎ 254 9880, fax 254 7646; W www.holidayplazacebu.com; F Ramos St; singles/doubles from P2000/2300) has polished, well-maintained rooms with views of the city and bay. There's a rooftop restaurant and bakehouse.

Cebu Midtown Hotel (☎ 253 9711, fax 253 9763; e cmh@gsilink.com; Fuente Osmeña; singles/doubles from US$75/85) is the most central, upper-bracket option. The rooms have good views, as do the pool and bar on the 5th floor.

Lahug The **Cebu Plaza Hotel** (☎ 231 1231, fax 231 2071; Nivels Hills; rooms from US$80) is considered by most as the premiere hotel in Cebu. Ritzy five-star rooms have beautiful views towards the city or the mountains, and the grounds also provide pool, tennis courts and the exceptional Lantaw Restaurant (see Lahug under Places to Eat later). A peaceful retreat from town, and it's only a P60-odd taxi fare away.

Waterfront Hotel & Casino Filipino (☎ 232 6888, fax 232 6880; W www.water fronthotels.net; Salinas Dr; singles/doubles from US$145/165) is cheekily named, as it is more than 2km from the water, in the hilly eastern outskirts of the city centre. The Waterfront appeals to those taken by the thought of a 24-hour casino, 13 food-and-beverage outlets, discos, gyms, piano bars and ballrooms. See also the Waterfront Hotel & Casino Filipino entry earlier.

Cebu Northwinds Hotel (☎ 233 0311/ 12/13, fax 232 0597; e northwinds@cebu.pil net.com; Salinas Dr; rooms from P1280) is oriented towards the business crowd, offering business-centre and function facilities. The rooms are tastefully decorated and provide great views.

Places to Eat

Cebu has good, but not great, restaurants. And alas, for those hoping to find a culinary gem hidden down some quiet back street, many of the city's worthwhile eateries are to be found in hotel complexes or shopping malls. The invasion of fast-food outlets has taken a heavy toll on Cebu's home-grown cuisine.

There's a generous serving of street stalls set up at regular spots around town. The biggest stall of them all is the **Carbon Market** (see the Carbon & Tabo-an Markets entry earlier). Many stalls around town sell flame-grilled chicken kebabs (P20) and 'banana-Q' (grilled banana; two for P6), *lechon manok* (roast chicken; P100 to P120), *lechon baboy* (roast pork; P200 per kg), *bola bola* (meatballs; P6) and *buso* ('hanging rice' in woven pyramids; P2).

Still in snack mode, Cebu City is full of **bakeshops** (bakeries). These offer a reliable and intriguing source of fresh bread rolls, cakes and buns – the plain-looking 'coconut bread' (rolls; P1) are particularly good. For dessert, most restaurants will happily whip up a 'halo halo' ice-cream delight.

Downtown While truly great restaurants are rare in Cebu City, they're virtually non-existent in the downtown area. Fast-food joints and uninspiring Chinese and Filipino-style diners are the norm.

Golden Crust Bakery (Colon St) is a great place that doubles as a karaoke bar, making it one of the only bakeries in town that stays open late.

Snow Sheen Restaurant (☎ 255 7576; Osmeña Blvd; dishes around P70; open 7am-11.30pm daily) is typical of what's on offer in the downtown area restaurant-wise. It has OK, low-priced Chinese (specialising in *pansit canton* – Cantonese noodles) and Filipino food in vaguely cleaner and brighter surroundings than the other more anonymous restaurants in the area.

Pete's Kitchen (Pelaez St; dishes around P50, cakes P15), opposite Hotel de Mercedes, is actually two restaurants sharing *three* shopfronts. Brighter, breezier and busier than most, these twin eateries offer small, cheap Chinese and Filipino dishes, smorgasbord-style where the cooks wave flies away with custom-made swatters. There's very little for vegetarians here.

Visayan Restaurant (☎ 253 8631; Manalili St; dishes P50-180; open 8.30am-10pm daily), near Hotel Victoria de Cebu, offers big portions of good Filipino and Chinese food in cleaner and more comfortable surroundings than you'll find nearby. Vegetarians should note: the bean-curd soup has meat in it, the fried rice has meat in it...

Our Place (cnr Pelaez & Sanciangko Sts; meals P50-120; open late Mon-Sat), upstairs, is a favourite haunt of foreign blokes. It's a cosy, colourful, old-style place with ceiling fans, a well-stocked bar and a menu ranging from breakfast omelettes (P60) to hearty steaks (P120). The dinner menu is as anti-vegetarian as they come.

Uptown On a small lane off the western side of the circle, next to the Equitable PCI Bank, **Larsian** (off Fuente Osmeña Circle; barbecue from P3; open 5pm-5am daily) is a lively, smoky strip of hawkers offering barbecue – chicken sticks (P3 to P25), chorizo (sausage sticks; P10), whole fish (P25) – and beer (P18).

Taj Mahal (Persian Palate; ☎ 253 6745; N Escario St; vegetarian dishes P35-55, meat & seafood P85-145; open 11am-3pm & 5.30pm-10.30pm Mon-Sat), opposite the Capitol Building, dishes up generous helpings of good Indian and Middle Eastern food. Its menu includes a rarity in Cebu City – a large vegetarian section. Its front window advertises spicy food, but even the 'hot' curries are quite mild. If anything's going to have you sweating here it's the lack of air-con – just ask them to turn it on and they'll happily oblige. There are two other Persian Palate outlets, in the Ayala Centre, level 3, and at Crossroads (see under Lahug later).

Royal Concourse (☎ 231 3160; Gorordo Ave; meals P50-P200; open 10am-10pm daily) looks like a ritzy hotel, but when you get inside, it looks more like a food-court, serving Filipino and Japanese food, mixed grills, sweets and more. But wait, there's more – at about 10pm Friday and Saturday nights, a giant TV screen and sound system get arched up, turning this place into a disco. Upstairs has a more intimate, polished-wood interior.

Jo's Chicken Inatô (☎ 253 1862, 253 1863; V Ranudo St, behind Hospital Velez • ☎ 346 9805; H Cortes St, Mandaue; dishes P40-70; open 9am-10pm daily) is a large, breezy place with wooden tables and bamboo chairs. It serves cheap Filipino and Chinese dishes, specialising in chicken, grills and barbecues.

Ayala Centre (☎ 231 5342/0; off Arch Reyes Ave, Cebu Business Park; open 10am-8pm Mon-Thur, 10am-9pm Fri-Sun) is a shopping mall with a surprising array of decent food outlets, and by the time you've walked around this complex and found the restaurant areas, you'll have worked up a decent appetite. Try **Sizzling Chef** for well-priced, big steaks as well as traditional dishes, **Don Henrico's** for excellent pizzas and pasta, **Sol y Luna** for Spanish, **Tequila Joes** for Mexican and cocktails...the list goes on.

Diplomat Garden Restaurant, on leafy F Ramos St, serves Filipino and Chinese cuisine. This big, bright and friendly place, directly behind the Diplomat Hotel, is popular with large groups. It was being renovated at the time of writing.

European Delicatessen & Butcher Shop Restaurant (☎ 253 7088/12/74; ⓔ eurodeli@ cebu.i-next.net; 91 F Ramos St; meals P200-800; open 6am-11pm daily), in the foyer of the Diplomat Hotel, specialises in imported cold meats, cheeses and wine downstairs, and upstairs offers a menu you could get lost in.

The average backpacker may feel a little underdressed here, but as long as you can afford to pay the prices, you'll be most welcome.

Abuhan Restaurant (F Ramos St; meals P60-110; open 24hr), inside Kan-Irag Hotel, is a breezy place popular with locals. It has a large Filipino and Western menu with good breakfasts and vegetarian and seafood meals.

Lighthouse Restaurant (☎ 233 2383/6; Gen Maxilom Ave; meals P100-260; open 11.30am-2.30pm & 5.30pm-10.30pm daily) is a Spanish-style restaurant with a Filipino, Chinese and Japanese menu. Background live music (often Mexican) adds to the pleasant, if somewhat confusing, mix. There is a sister restaurant in Gaisano Country Mall.

Hodge Podge (☎/fax 232 5579, 0917 320 8503; Gen Maxilom Ave; dishes P100-200; open 11am-3pm & 6pm-11pm daily), next to Lighthouse, is a welcoming, loungey restaurant, which specialises in yakiniku (P300) – Japanese barbecue cooked at your table. For the six months a year when 'Mike', the Japanese chef, returns to Japan, the standard changes and the food gets a distinct Filipino flavour.

Dish (☎ 254 0567; Juana Osmeña St; meals P65-180; open 9am-midnight Mon-Sat), opposite NS Royal Pensione, is one in the new breed of slick, minimalist designer cafés. With smooth tunes and polished service, enjoy generous serves of pan-Asian meals – pad thai (P75), sago pudding with mango and coconut cream (P35) and sensational coconut-curried prawns (P140).

Bo's Coffee Club (F Ramos St • Osmeña Blvd • Ayala Centre; coffee P30-65, cakes P20-30; open 7am-midnight Mon-Sat, 8am-11pm Sun) is the Filipino version of Starbuck's, even down to decor, logo and cookies. One of the only places you'll find good espressos, and also a typical Americano range. Popular with young Filipinos, this is a good air-con escape from the streets. See Ayala Centre under Shopping for opening hours of that outlet.

White House Filipino Grill (☎ 253 5774/6597; F Ramos St; buffet breakfast P69, lunch & dinner P99; open 6am-11pm daily), a huge, white building opposite Bo's Coffee Club, has big, cheap Filipino buffets, with yummy specialities like grilled pork rack ribs, biko (sticky-rice dessert) and bottomless coffee (breakfast) and iced tea (lunch and dinner). It also serves some healthy rarities like fresh carrot juice (P55).

LJ's Ice Cream Café (☎ 255 0071, 0917 362 2311; N Escario St; coffees from P20, ice-cream scoops P10; open 10am-midnight daily), neighbouring Cebu Pensione Plaza, is a cool (in temperature, that is) retreat where you can enjoy homemade ice cream, espresso coffee, shakes, frozen coffees and meals. Sit back under the air-con, slurp up a piña colada ice cream, sway to the hits of the '80s and enjoy.

Lahug Considered by many to be Cebu's top seafood restaurant is **Seafood City** (☎ 253 7793/3795; Salinas Dr; seafood P20-410 per 100g; open 6pm-11pm daily). So one may well ask why they've decided to style the place on a supermarket. You wheel a trolley past displays of iced seafood, aquariums and a vegetable section, pick out your fancy, then a waiter comes to your table, collects your trolley and asks how you'd like everything cooked.

There's a long list of suggested preparations, as well as other Chinese-inspired dishes, and a good wine list. It's a P50 taxi ride from downtown.

Mr A (☎ 232 5200/5300; dishes P100-250; open 3pm-2am daily) can be reached by following the road past the Cebu Plaza Hotel, towards the lookout area known as Tops (see the Tops Lookout Area entry earlier). A favourite with the city's young professionals, it has a cool, open-air pub feel and fine Filipino and Western dishes. The views are fantastic.

AA's (Salinas Dr; open 5pm-late daily) is another very popular collection of barbecue stalls where you choose from fresh fish, chicken or pork, which is then barbecued. It's slightly higher in price and quality than Larsian (see Uptown earlier in Places to Eat).

Golden Cowrie Native Restaurant (☎ 233 4243/4670; Salinas Dr; meals P70-160; open 10.30am-2pm & 6pm-10pm daily), next to Cebu Northwinds Hotel, a slick native-style restaurant on busy Salinas Dr, serves reasonably priced tasty native and seafood dishes, presented on a banana leaf.

Lantaw Asian & Seafood Restaurant (☎ 231 1231/8316; Cebu Plaza Hotel grounds; meals P120-500; open 11.30am-2pm & 6pm-11pm daily) offers a superb dining experience in an open restaurant overlooking Cebu Plaza's manicured gardens and Cebu City. If you can't afford anything else at this lush establishment, it's worth popping in at least for a beer, just to see another side of Cebu. This is a great place to try native dishes at their best, such as sinigang (soup with meat/fish and vegetables soured with tamarind; P160, good for three). There's also live shellfish (pay by weight) and a Friday and Saturday night buffet.

Café Tartanilla (☎ 231 1231; buffet meals P375-465; open 6am-11pm daily), also at Cebu Plaza, does a lavish buffet three times daily. A taxi here costs around P65.

Crossroads (Gov Cuenco Ave) is a new congregation of great restaurants and bars in Banilad, just near the Waterfront Hotel. There's good Thai food at **Krua Thai** (☎ 032-233 9388; meals P100-150; open 11am-2pm & 6pm-10pm daily), Japanese at **Banri Noodle Bar** (☎ 234 0788; meals P100-250; open 11am-2pm & 5pm-10pm daily), an outlet of **Persian Palate** (☎ 234 2530; open 11am-11pm daily) and more.

The Village (Salinas Dr) opposite the entrance to the Waterfront Hotel, is another collection of restaurants and bars, with lots of outdoor seating.

Entertainment

Club H2O (☎ 233 7424/6; admission P100-150; open 9pm-late daily) is a popular disco beneath the Waterfront Hotel. People start rocking up around 11pm.

Ratsky (☎ 234 2554, fax 234 2113; Ayala Centre, ground floor; night-time admission P150; open 11am-4am daily) is a smooth bar where hip young things head out at night for a drink and a boogie to live music. Pasta, sushi, burgers and oysters are on the menu. Enter from the car park from the left of Ayala's main entrance if you want to avoid being lost forever inside Ayala. If Ratsky doesn't do it for you, there are many other bars in Ayala. Dress code applies.

Club Circus (Lahug; open 9.30pm-4am nightly; admission P50-100), on a quiet street in the hills north of town, is a little less slick than the others, but it does have a Saturday Night Fever dance floor and a window-wall view across to the city's lights. It kicks off around 10pm, but you can visit the adjoining quieter bar with pool tables earlier. Drinks here cost P50, and the admission charge includes getting reimbursed at the bar with a drink to the value of the admission cost.

As well as the **Ayala Centre** (see Ratsky earlier) two other popular places at night are **Crossroads** and **The Village** (see Lahug under Places to Eat earlier). All three of these venues have a range of nightlife, so the best idea is to just turn up and see what's happening on the night.

Shopping

Cebuanos certainly love their shopping centres and tend to do them in grand style. You can generally eat, bank, organise flights, and fulfil most of your consumer needs in these meccas, and all in the comfort of air-con.

Robinson's Plaza (Fuente Osmeña) is a small-time shopping mall, but handy if you're uptown. It has a department store, supermarket and a good cheap selection of meals in the food court.

SM City (North Reclamation Area; open 10am-8pm Mon-Thur, 10am-9pm Fri, Sun & holidays) is the pièce de résistance of shopping malls. You can organise travel, banking, and cover all other necessities in a place big enough to have its own government and currency. You'll also find very helpful information booths here to help you navigate your way.

Ayala Centre (☎ 231 5342/0; off Arch Reyes Ave, Cebu Business Park; open 10am-8pm Mon-Thur, 10am-9pm Fri-Sun), a six-storey dome, seems small in comparison to the more-upmarket SM City. However, you'll still find most banks, airlines and tour companies represented here. There are also European and American label boutiques, restaurants (see Places to Eat earlier), bars (see Entertainment earlier), health spas, cinemas, every fast-food chain imaginable, games halls and even a child care centre, which makes you wonder if some people never leave this place. And before you ask – yes, it also has a bingo stage.

Getting There & Away

Air If you've got the option and it fits your itinerary, flying into Cebu City rather than Manila has its advantages. Cebu City's **Mactan-Cebu International Airport** (MCIA; ☎ 340 2977) is second only to Manila in terms of air traffic, but way ahead in terms of user-friendliness.

Airport terminal fees are P100 (cash) for domestic flights and a hefty P550 for international flights.

The following airlines have offices either at MCIA on Mactan, or in Cebu City itself, or both:

Air Philippines (☎ 240 0920) MCIA
Asian Spirit (☎ 241 0225) MCIA
Cathay Pacific (☎ 240 3823, W www.cathay pacific.com) MCIA
Cebu Pacific (☎ 240 0422, W www.cebupacific air.com) MCIA
Malaysia Airlines (☎ 340 2978, 231 3887, 232 090, W www.malaysiaairlines.com) MCIA • 2nd floor, Export Bank Bldg, Gorodo Ave
Pacific Airways (☎ 340 3500, fax 232 2116) MCIA
Philippine Airlines (☎ 240 0422, W www.philip pineair.com) MCIA
SEAIR (☎ 341 3021/22, fax 341 3023, W www .flyseair.com) MCIA • (☎ 255 0801, 254 8232) Capitol Commercial Complex, N Escario St
Singapore Airlines (Silk Air; ☎ 243 1343, W www.silkair.com.sg) MCIA

Within the Philippines Asian Spirit has a daily morning flight to and from Tagbilaran (P515, 20 minutes).

PAL has daily flights from Manila to Cebu City (P2400, one hour) about every two hours from 5am to 4.30pm, with an extra evening flight. Cebu City–Manila flights run to a similar schedule.

Air Philippines flies between Manila and Cebu City (P2310) three times daily.

Cebu Pacific flies daily – on the hour, every two hours – between Manila and Cebu City (P2310). Manila–Cebu City flights go from 5am to 5pm. Cebu City–Manila flights run between 7am and 7pm. You get a discount of about P300 for taking the early morning flight from Manila to Cebu, or the evening flight from Cebu to Manila.

PAL flies to Davao (P2100, one hour) and returns, every morning and most afternoons.

Cebu Pacific flies from Cebu City to Davao (P2090) and back daily. It also flies to Zamboanga (P2090, one hour) and back four times a week.

Air Philippines also has a Zamboanga–Cebu City flight (P2090) four mornings a week, and return flights at noon. It also flies each morning to General Santos City (P2090, one hour), returning in the afternoon.

PAL and Cebu Pacific fly from Cebu City to Bacolod (PAL P1380, Cebu Pacific P1450, 30 minutes) and back every day.

PAL flies to Puerto Princesa via Iloilo (P2800, 2½ hours) and back, twice a week.

PAL flies between Iloilo City (P1600, 40 minutes) and Cebu City daily.

Cebu Pacific also has daily flights to and from Iloilo (P1600), departing Cebu in the late afternoon, and returning early in the morning.

SEAIR flies between Caticlan and Cebu City (P2290, one hour) six days a week.

Outside the Philippines Cathay Pacific has flights from Cebu City to Hong Kong (HK$1990/3700 one way/return, 2½ hours) twice daily with return flights the same day.

PAL has morning flights from Hong Kong (HK$2210/3560, 2½ hours) to Cebu City three times a week, returning usually on the same day.

PAL flies between Cebu City and Narita (JPY111,800/JPY176,700, four hours) five times a week; between Cebu City and Seoul (KRW644,700/1,048,400, four hours) twice a week.

Malaysia Airlines flies between Cebu City and Kuala Lumpur (via Kota Kinabalu; MYR320/640, five hours) twice a week.

Singapore Airlines' Silk Air flies between Cebu City and Singapore (SG$931/959, five hours) daily.

Bus The main bus lines servicing Cebu are **Ceres Bus Liner** (☎ 261 5008), **CBL Liner** (☎ 232 1850), **ABC Liner** (☎ 253 1668) and **Rough Riders** (032-232 9593).

The most popular destination outside Cebu City is the popular, southern dive-spot of Moalboal. The **Cebu South bus station** is a short taxi ride from downtown (around P30), otherwise take the Basak–Colon, Urgello–Colon or Labangon–Colon–Pier jeepney (P4). From here, there are buses leaving all day for: Argao–Dalaguete (P40, two hours); Bato (via Oslob; P100, five hours); Toledo (P56, three hours); Moalboal (P60, three to four hours); Lilo-an (P110, five hours).

If you're after a public bus north, the **Cebu North bus station**, servicing several bus lines, has rather inconveniently shifted out to Mandaue, a P65 taxi ride from uptown. A Mabolo–Carbon or Mandaue–Cebu City jeepney will take you there, and bring you back into town (P4). The station is on Wireless St, in the desolate Reclamation area of town. Although there are food stalls, there's very little to do out here if you've got a long wait for a bus.

Rough Riders buses to Maya, the gateway town for boats to Malapascua leave from here several times daily (with/without air-con P66/44, 3½ to five hours).

Here you'll find also find **Phil-Cebu Bus Lines** (usually called CBL) buses to Hagnaya, the gateway town to Bantayan. They leave four times daily, from 5.30am (P44/66, two to four hours), departing from the Ayala Centre before picking up more passengers at the northern terminal. If the bus only goes as far as Bogo, you can then take a jeepney to Hagnaya (P15, 30 minutes). If you are heading to Malapascua Island and your accommodation is uptown, it's easy to jump on one of these buses at the Ayala Centre, get off at Bogo and take a jeepney to Maya (P20, one hour). If you want to do some sightseeing along the coast, you can hop off on the way and wait for another bus to come. There are so many buses running each day, they're rarely packed out, and waving one down is not a problem.

For heading both north and south, there are also air-con L-300 vans (☎ 256 3813; N Bacalso), with terminals near the buses, making

Cebu Ferries

destination	operator	price (P)	duration (hrs)	frequency
Bantayan				
Santa Fe	Palacio Shipping	150	9	5/week
Bohol				
Jeta Fe	Lite Shipping	70	2	1/day
Tagbilaran	Cokaliong Shipping	105	5	1/day
	Lite Shipping	100	4	2/day
	Negros Navigation	120	3	1/week
	Palacio Shipping	100	3½	3/week
	Socor Shipping	380	1½	4/day
	SuperCat	370	1½	3/day
Tubigon	Lite Shipping	70	2	1/day
	Tubigon Shipping	50	2	every 1–2 hours, dawn to dusk
Ubay	J&N Shipping	100	6	2/day
Comotes Islands				
Poro	Palacio Shipping	95	1	1/day (midnight)
	Socor Shipping	360	1½	1/day
Leyte				
Hilongos	Socor Shipping	420	2	2/day
Maasin	Cokaliong Shipping	171	6	4/week
	SuperCat	400	2	1/day
	Trans-Asia Shipping	171	5	3/week
Ormoc	Cebu Ferries	190	5	3/week
	Socor Shipping	390	2	1/day
	Sulpicio	136	4	1/week
	SuperCat	460	2	3/day
Tacloban	Cebu Ferries	290	12–13	2/week
Luzon				
Manila	Negros Navigation	1285	18–22	1/week
	Sulpicio Lines	1140	18–22	most days
	WG&A Superferry	1265	18–22	most days
Masbate				
Masbate town	Trans-Asia Shipping	370	12	3/week

themselves very obvious to tourists. They have no schedules, but leave when the van is half to three-quarters full, so if you're the first seated, you may have to wait. Being air-conditioned and with fewer passengers, these are a faster, cushier way to get around. Rates are up to 30% higher than the bus.

Philtranco (☎ 234 1266; Reclamation Area, fronting SM City) runs daily morning 'overland' (bus-boat) trips to Ormoc (P149, eight hours), Tacloban (P149, nine hours), Butuan (P331, 14 hours), Cagayan de Oro (P400, 18 hours), Davao (P427, 24 hours), Legaspi (P368, 30 hours) and Manila (P610, 32 hours). Good luck.

Boat Cebu City's multipiered port throngs with boats heading to Philippine islands and to international ports. Larger passenger-ferry companies, such as Philippine Fast Ferry (operators of SuperCat), have high-speed ferries, known as fastcraft, to and from Cebu City every day of the year except Good Friday and New Years Day (it's generally business as usual on Holy Thursday, Black Saturday and Easter Sunday). Ticket prices for passenger liners quoted in this section apply to the cheapest fare, usually known as 'economy' or 'budget'. More expensive categories available are usually 'tourist', and 'cabin' (air-con), which cost around 20% and

Cebu Ferries				
destination	operator	price (P)	duration (hrs)	frequency
Mindanao				
Cagayan de Oro	Cebu Ferries	390	10–11	most nights
	Sulpicio	269	8½	4/week
	Trans-Asia	269	10	3/week
Dapitan	SuperCat	815	5½	1/day (via Tagbilaran and Dumaguete)
	George & Peter Lines	310	12	5/week
Davao	Sulpicio	985	33	2/week
Iligan	Sulpicio	304	10	1/week
	Cebu Ferries	390	10–11	3/week
Nasipit (Butuan)	Cebu Ferries	390	10–11	3/week
	Sulpicio	316	12	4/week
Ozamis	Cebu Ferries	390	10–11	4/week
	Sulpicio	306	8	1/week
	Trans-Asia	390	12	3/week
Surigao	Cokaliong Shipping	255	10–12	most nights
	Sulpicio	290	7	1/week
	Trans-Asia	255	12	3/week
	WG&A	365	7	1/week
Zamboanga	George & Peter Lines	685	30–36	2/week
Negros				
Dumaguete	Cokaliong Shipping	200	6	daily
	George & Peter Lines	205	6	daily
	SuperCat	480	2½	2/day (via Tagbilaran)
Panay				
Iloilo	Cokaliong Shipping	450	14	3/week
	Trans-Asia	380	16	daily
Samar				
Calbayog	Palacio Shipping	270	10	4/week
Siquijor				
Larena	Palacio Shipping	155	7	3/week
	SuperCat	630	3	daily (via Tagbilaran and Dumaguete)

30% more, respectively – and are often well worth it if you plan to get some sleep.

Most companies offer discounts to: students (15%), disabled travellers (20%), senior citizens (20%) and minors (50%). SuperCat also offers 'Skip Trip' package deals to islands (like Bohol) which include accommodation, sightseeing and return fare (for more details see the introductory Getting There & Away section to Bohol later).

All shipping information is very vulnerable to change – make sure you have the current schedules and fare information before you make your plans. Some passengers have complained that even tourist bureaus and the

individual companies' websites have not provided the latest schedules. The shipping guide in the *Sun Star* newspaper publishes a weekly schedule that is generally reliable but it is always good to double-check your schedules directly with the shipping companies. Also, some companies have several boats, leaving from different piers, so you will often need to telephone them to find out departure ports. A recorded information hotline (☎ 256 8102) for WG&A, SuperCat, Trans-Asia Shipping and Cebu Ferry will give you shipping details as well as the Chinese Horoscope.

Aboitiz Express (☎ 253 4663; Gen Maxilom Ave, opposite the Metrobank • Colonnade

Mall, cnr Legaspi & Colon Sts • Robinson's Place Plaza • Ayala Centre • SM City; open 9am-5pm Mon-Sat) is a booking office for WG&A Superferry, SuperCat and Cebu Ferries – it's handy to keep an eye out for these.

Bookings for most shipping companies can also be made at **The Business Box** and **All Lines**, both at *(Ayala Centre, 2nd floor)* and **The Travellers Lounge** *(SM City, in car park left of entrance 3)*.

The main Cebu City passenger-ship companies and their details are as follows:

Aleson Shipping Lines, Inc (☎ 255 5673, 253 1934, 255 7157, fax 255 6277) 117 R Palma St

Cebu Ferries (☎ 233 2611, 24-hour hotline 256 8102–05 local 225, fax 232 3436; W www.cebuferries.com) Pier 4, North Reclamation Area

Cokaliong Shipping Lines (☎ 232 7211, 231 6825, fax 231 6826) D Serging Osmeña Ave, North Reclamation Area; boats leave from Pier 1, Port Area

EB Aznar Shipping Corporation (☎ 233 5915–18, fax 233 2072) EB Aznar Building, T Padilla St

George & Peter Lines (☎ 254 5404/0679/ 5154/8479) Lim Building, ground floor, corner Jakosalem St and Quezon Blvd

Lite Shipping Corporation (☎ 253 7776/6857, 255 1721–26, fax 255 1724) corner GL Lavilles St and MJ Cuenco Ave

Maypalad Shipping (☎ 253 5435, 253 7004) 39 R Palma St

Negros Navigation (☎ 232 6235, 412 9985, fax 232 6255, 233 8456) 1L & 1K Sail Centre Complex, Humabon Ave, North Reclamation Area • SM City, lower ground floor

Palacio Shipping (☎ 255 4538/6630/4540, 253 7700, fax 256 0672) corner Mabini and Zulueta Sts

Socor Shipping Lines (☎ 255 7767/7560, 254 3867, 419 0646, fax 255 0115; e oceanjet@ skyinet.net) Pier 1, Warehouse Bldg, Port Area

Sulpicio Lines (☎ 232 5361–80, 233 1100) Sulpicio Go St, Reclamation Area

SuperCat (☎ 412 9386/87, 232 4511–16, information hotline 256 8102–85 local 220; W www.supercat.com.ph) Pier 4, North Reclamation Area

Trans-Asia Shipping Lines (☎ 254 6491 local 225, 254 9782, 255 7989, fax 255 7899) corner MJ Cuenco Ave and Quezon Blvd

WG&A Superferry (☎ 232 0421/90/99, 24-hour call centre 256 8102/03/04/05 local 224, W www.wgasuperferry.com) Pier 4, Reclamation Area and S Osmeña St, North Reclamation Area

Camiguin Cebu Ferries has a boat from Camiguin to Cebu City (P420, 10 hours) once a week, but no boat going the other way at this stage.

Getting Around

To/From the Airport After years of tourists complaining about the scams of airport taxi drivers, airport police have cracked down. Tourists are now handed a slip as they leave the terminal, with the registration of the taxi they are to enter, and a phone number of airport management, which passengers are encouraged to call with any complaints. Even if you bypass one of these officials, taxi drivers have been scared into honesty and will generally charge you the 'fixed price' of P150 to any destination in Cebu City – very reasonable in light of the traffic and distance.

Hire-car company supervisors are also milling around, handing tourists a similar card with the driver's registration and a fixed rate for trips between the airport and Cebu City (P195).

All in all, Cebuano taxi drivers are a gentler breed than their Manila counterparts. Most drivers really will stick to the metered price for anything other than the airport or out-of-town destinations.

Pursuing a cheaper option of getting into town requires a bit more effort. You must make it through the throng of taxi drivers and through the main gates, walk upstairs and past the Waterfront Hotel, then turn right down the main road (Airport Rd) until you reach the tricycle bay. From there, you can catch a tricycle to the jeepney terminal at MEPZ (pronounced 'meps') for around P20. From there you can grab one of the jeepneys pouring across to SM City (P8) or White-gold, where there are terminals with jeepneys travelling uptown and downtown (P4).

To/From the Pier At first, arriving at Cebu City pier seems startlingly similar to arriving at the airport – a throng of taxi drivers all desperately hoping you won't want them to use their meters. If they try the 'fixed-fare' line on you, just wander across to the other side of the road to find a cabbie who will switch on the meter – the *real* (ie, metered) rate into central Cebu City is P40 to P50.

Taxi Unless a big ship has just docked, or it's serious festival time, catching a taxi in Cebu City couldn't be easier. Flag fall is

P25 and then P2 for each additional 300m, and most drivers will automatically use the meter.

Around the uptown and downtown areas, P30 to P50 is a typical, fair fare. To reach fringe areas such as Lahug it can cost up to P80. If you want to see all the sights, touring in a taxi for a day is a perfectly sensible way to do it – and it's definitely cheaper than hiring your own car (see the Car entry later in this section). By the way, before you suspect your driver of taking the long way around, remember there's a huge number of one-way streets here, especially in the downtown area.

For many out-of-town destinations, taxis will fix a price that may seem way above what the meter would give. This is to cover petrol and the return drive for which the driver may not get a fare. So it often makes more sense to ask your driver to wait and negotiate a return fare – it may be no dearer than one way.

Jeepney Cebu City has no local buses, so jeepneys and taxis pretty much rule the road. As in Manila, most jeepneys have a set route, and this is displayed in the front window and along the side. You'll pay P4 to travel up to 5km within the city, and the longer journeys shouldn't cost more than P8. If in doubt, locals are always very helpful and well informed on these matters

One important thing to remember with jeepneys – they travel a circular route, so don't expect to take the same jeepney back the way you came. Also, if a jeepney has just passed a destination written on the side, it will have to do the full circuit before returning – a long way to get to a place that may only be a 10-minute walk.

Car Unlike in Manila, do-it-yourself driving here can be quite OK, but it's not cheap, nor common.

Local car-hire companies generally charge around P2000 to P2500 for 24 hours (no petrol included), with special deals for longer periods. A lot more common is to get a car with a driver, all petrol included (about P800 for first three hours, then around P200 per succeeding hour), an option we highly recommend.

Most hotels can arrange car hire for you, or you can contact **Friends Rent-A-Car**

(☎ 340 5729, fax 340 5954); **Avis Rent-A-Car** (☎ 340 2486/1141; Arch Reyes Ave • ☎ 340 2486/1141; MCIA); or **Thrifty Car Rental** (☎ 232 6888; Waterfront Hotel • ☎ 340 2486; MCIA).

AROUND CEBU CITY
Mactan Island
If you're flying into Cebu City, nearby Mactan is actually where you'll land. Connected to Cebu City by the Mandaue-Mactan Bridge (the 'old bridge') and Marcelo B Fernan (the 'new bridge'), this little island can certainly claim to have it all. Whether you *want* it all is another matter. There's an oil depot, a string of ritzy beach resorts, an export-processing zone, several guitar factories and, of course, an international airport. And it was here, on the Punta Engaño Peninsula, that the Portuguese explorer Ferdinand Magellan made the fatal mistake of underestimating the fighting spirit of Mactan's Chief Lapu-Lapu (see the boxed text 'Magellan's Last Stand' later).

Almost 500 years later, foreigners are still falling victim to Mactan, only these days it's their budgets that cop the beating.

One reader described it as 'a tourist hell-hole'. Its beaches are less-than-average by Philippine standards. However, they are only a taxi ride from Cebu City or the airport, and if you've got money to burn, there are some ritzy places to stay. Most of Mactan's charm lies beneath the surface. Mactan is bejewelled with reefs, as is its little neighbour, Olango Island (see that section later). Alas, great chunks of coral have been destroyed by dynamite fishing, and the coral-munching crown-of-thorns starfish.

For information on **diving** around Mactan, contact **Scotty's Dive Centre** (☎ 231 5060/1; W www.divescotty.com; Shangri-La's Mactan Island Resort); **Scuba World** (☎ 254 9554, fax 254 9591; W www.scubaworld.com.ph); or in Cebu City, **Seaquest Dive Centre** (fax 346 0592) or **Sea Explorers Philippines** (☎ 234 0248, fax 234 0245; W www.sea-explorers .com; 36 Arch Reyes Ave, Knights of Columbus Sq). Sea Explorers has six dive centres around the Visayas and offers great diving packages and island-hopping deals for those wishing to dive from more than one of their locations. All these dive companies make regular trips as far north as Malapascua and as far south as Cabilao, off nearby Bohol.

THE VISAYAS

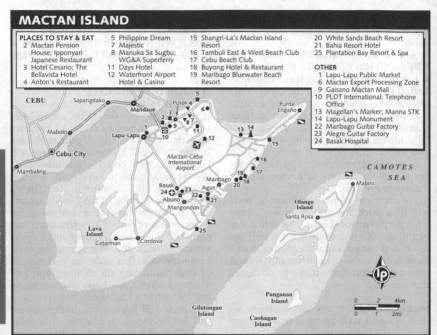

MACTAN ISLAND

PLACES TO STAY & EAT
2 Mactan Pension House; Ipponyari Japanese Restaurant
3 Hotel Cesario; The Bellavista Hotel
4 Anton's Restaurant
5 Philippine Dream
7 Majestic
8 Manuka Sa Sugbu; WG&A Superferry
11 Days Hotel
12 Waterfront Airport Hotel & Casino
15 Shangri-La's Mactan Island Resort
16 Tambuli East & West Beach Club
17 Cebu Beach Club
18 Buyong Hotel & Restaurant
19 Maribago Bluewater Beach Resort
20 White Sands Beach Resort
21 Bahia Resort Hotel
25 Plantation Bay Resort & Spa

OTHER
1 Lapu-Lapu Public Market
6 Mactan Export Processing Zone
9 Gaisano Mactan Mall
10 PLDT International; Telephone Office
13 Magellan's Marker; Manna STK
14 Lapu-Lapu Monument
22 Maribago Guitar Factory
23 Alegre Guitar Factory
24 Basak Hospital

For a peek at a **guitar factory**, ask a tricycle driver to take you to **Alegre** (☎ 340 4492; ⓔ alegreguitars@hotmail.com; open 8am-5pm Mon-Sat). Alegre is only one of several such places in **Abuno**, the 'guitar town' in the centre of Mactan.

There's an open-air workshop, and a show-room where you can have a play without too much hard sell from the staff. Alegre guitars range from the P2000 decoration 'cheapie' to the P60,000 'export quality', made from a German Spruce soundboard and a Brazilian Rosewood side and back. The guitar factories in this district also make mandolins, ukuleles and the cute little *cocolele* – a native ukulele with a brightly polished coconut shell for a body.

Places to Stay & Eat There are two distinct sides to Mactan's accommodation options – east and west – with nothing in between. The west is represented by the island's main metropolis of Lapu-Lapu City, a long, ugly stretch of road near the bridge to Cebu with plenty of shops and Japanese restaurants. It is, however, handy if you have an early morning flight.

Mactan Pension House (☎ 340 5524–27, fax 340 5528; ⓔ judithrojas_20@hotmail.com; ML Quezon National Hwy; twins from P690) has tidy rooms with centralised air-con, hot-water bathroom and cable TV.

Ipponyari Japanese Restaurant (☎ 341 2755, fax 341 1150; open 11am-2.30pm & 5.30pm-10.30pm daily), next door, has large plates of sushi, with tuna, caviar and shrimp for P280.

Opposite, **Gaisano Mactan** shopping mall has the usual **Jollibee** and **KFC** joints. Head west along G Y de la Serna St for the town centre and the vast **Lapu-Lapu Public Market**.

Hotel Cesario (☎ 340 0211, fax 340 0615; ⓔ xenios@mozcom.com; ML Quezon Hwy; doubles from P850), at the bottom of the new bridge, offers Mactan budget rooms with a great perk – you get free use of Bellavista Hotel's sauna and pool. With breakfast for one and airport transfers included, this is one of the better deals on the island.

The Bellavista Hotel (☎ 340 7821, fax 340 7823; ⓦ www.thebellavistahotel.com; ML Quezon Hwy; singles/doubles from US$98/108) is the upmarket version of its sister hotel (Cesario) next door. As rooftop bar, restaurant and healthclub are offered to the poorer neighbours, the extra $80-odd is just getting you a swankier room.

Philippine Dream (☎ 340 3888, fax 340 4090; e phildream@cebu.nexmil.com; Cebu Yacht Club, MEPZ1; doubles from P999) is for those who want the Love Boat experience without having to leave the shore. This permanently docked boat has close to a hundred rooms, a disco, karaoke, the **Baywatch** restaurant with live music, a folk and country music bar, and free shuttle to and from the airport.

Anton's Restaurant (☎ 340 0468, fax 340 2976; Airport Road, MEPZ1; meals P100-250; open 11am-2pm & 5pm-10pm daily) is just up from Cebu Yacht Club in the Ferry Terminal Building and has a menu big on seafood, Filipino and Chinese food. Plastic chairs and place mats, a wall-window view over the water to Cebu and easy-listening jazz combine to give a breezy, yachty feel.

Majestic (☎ 340 9714/15; Marina Mall; meals around P200; open 11am-10pm daily) is a favourite with locals who come for the 'live' seafood and Chinese cuisine. But if Sizzling Live Eel with Black Beans (P145/100g) is not your fancy, there's plenty of pork, chicken and tofu.

Waterfront Airport Hotel and Casino (☎ 340 4888, fax 340 5862; W www.waterfronthotels.net; Airport Rd; singles/doubles from US$145/165) is the sister hotel of the Waterfront Hotel in Lahug, Cebu City, and offers similar exclusivity at a similar price, right next to the airport.

Days Hotel (☎/fax 341 0476–78; W www.dayshotel.ph; singles/doubles from P2500/ 2700) is a slightly cheaper option near the airport. Rooms are large with a big screen TV, and for an extra P1100, you get a spa and fridge. Airport transfers, continental breakfast and a daily newspaper are included.

A dozen or so beach resorts have staked out Mactan's eastern coast. All have their own restaurants and diving facilities, and most provide free shuttle buses to and from the airport. It's not as easy as it looks on the map to browse the resorts along the eastern coast. The more expensive ones are walled in, with guards at the front gate, effectively cutting off the beach to casual strollers. A gate fee (around P50) applies to non-staying guests.

Bahia Resort Hotel (☎ 495 2352, ☎/fax 253 6597; doubles P1200, P75 per extra person up to 5), in the cheap and cheerful category, offers funny old rooms with hot-water bathroom, air-con, screened sunroom and loft. There's bedding for four to five people, making it the best budget deal for groups on the island. There's no beach here, but there is a private lagoon and a saltwater swimming pool.

Buyong Hotel and Restaurant (☎ 492 0119, 340 9942, 495 7380; Maribago; rooms with fan/air-con P500/1200), a bit shabby but the fanned rooms, with hot-water bathroom, are a Mactan bargain for one or two people.

Shangri-La's Mactan Island Resort (☎ 231 0288, fax 231 1688; W www.shangri-la.com; singles/doubles US$180/210), a vast and glitzy oasis at the northern end of the stretch of resorts, is considered the premiere hotel in Mactan. Enticements include a 350m private

THE VISAYAS

Magellan's Last Stand

A few sniggers must have gone around the royal palace when news reached Spain of Ferdinand Magellan's demise. It was 1521, and poor old Ferdinand had done the hard bit for his adopted country (he was Portuguese by birth). He'd sailed around the world. He'd quelled a mutiny. He'd landed in Samar and named and claimed the Philippines for Spain. And on Sugbu (modern-day Cebu), a vital trade centre, he'd carefully befriended all the scariest tribal chiefs – or so he thought. There was one chief, Lapu-Lapu of Mactan, who wasn't so easily impressed. So what did Ferdinand do? He ordered 60 of his most bloodthirsty soldiers to suit up, along with 1000 obedient Cebuano warriors, and in a huge flotilla he sailed to Mactan to have a word with this Lapu-Lapu fellow. In a rush of pure European blood, he even told the Cebuano warriors to sit back, relax, and learn how the civilised world dealt with troublesome natives. But Lapu-Lapu and his men defended their island with unimagined ferocity, and Ferdinand was soon back on his boat – fatally wounded by a spear to his head, a poisoned arrow to his leg and a mighty blow to his pride.

Mic Looby

beach cove, six-hole golf course, multilevel swimming pool, babysitting services, shopping arcade, and a complimentary shoeshine.

Better than Shangri-La for those who prefer polished wood to marble, **Plantation Bay Resort and Spa** (☎ 3405900/86, 1800 1888 7788, fax 340 9921; ⓦ www.plantationbay.com; Marigandon; doubles from US$145) is considered the other top option. The hotel and rooms front a 3.5-hectare artificial saltwater lagoon, big enough to house water sports, beaches and a floating restaurant. You'll need to make use of the hotel's 24-hour car service to get around this huge virtual paradise where the options for indulgence range from massage to archery lessons.

Other expensive beach-side resorts nearby are: **White Sands** (☎ 340 5960–63, fax 340 5969; ⓔ whitesands@cbu.skyinet.net; Maribago Beach; singles/doubles from US$116/137); **Maribago Bluewater Beach Resort** (☎ 232 5411–14, 492 0100, fax 492 0128; ⓦ www.bluewaterresort.com; Maribago; singles/doubles from US$130/140); **Cebu Beach Club** (☎ 340 7994–98, 1800 1888 0081, fax 340 9981; ⓦ www.tambuli.com; singles/doubles from US$70/80); and **Tambuli East and West Beach Club** (☎ 232 4811, 1800 1888 8228, fax 232 4913; ⓦ www.tambuli.com; singles/doubles from US$60/70).

Manna STK (known as 'Sutukil'; ☎ 340 6448, 0917 548 3868; Mactan Shrine; seafood at market price; open 11am-10pm daily) offers the freshest seafood on the island in quaint waterfront surroundings. At the entrance, a market stall offers you the day's catch, you choose what you'd like and how you'd like it, then take a seat and wait for your meal to arrive. Lapu-Lapu (grouper) goes for P350/100g, prawns P250/500g and lobster P400/250g.

Getting There & Away Jeepneys run all day to Cebu City from Lapu-Lapu City (P10). The going rate by taxi from Cebu City to Lapu-Lapu City or the airport is P150, and to the eastern beach resorts you'll pay around P250. Be prepared for a slow crawl through heavy traffic.

Olango Island

In 1998 the Philippine government classified 610,607 hectares of coastal resources under an environmental protection programme.

Of these, several choice ecotourism spots were deemed National Integrated and Protected Areas (NIPAs). One of these NIPAs is Olango Island.

About 10km off the coast of Mactan, **Olango Island Wildlife Sanctuary** (☎ 0919 390 9639; Santa Rosa; admission for non-Filipinos US$2, children under five, seniors and handicapped citizens free) takes in 1030 hectares of sandflats, mudflats and mangroves on Olango's southern shores. This is a vital refuelling depot for approximately 50,000 birds of 47 species (including the endangered Chinese egret *Egretta eulophotes* and Asiatic dowitcher *Limnodromus semipalmatus*) flying the east-Asian migratory route to Australia. The birds, who prefer Olango to neighbouring islands because of the abundant food and ideal nesting sites, arrive in late September and leave in early March, but the best times for twitchers is between November and February.

Included in the province of Olango Island is the **Marine Sanctuary** off neighbouring **Gilutongan Island** (admission P50). Around the outskirts of the sanctuary the reefs are endangered by commercial fishing fleets, with their dynamite, cyanide and – more recently – chlorine. However, the sanctuary itself is now well protected. Snorkelling equipment can be rented on Gilutongan Island, at Maribago Wharf or from dive shops (approximately P200 per day). Much of the reef on the western side of Olango has been blown to bits, but the lower part of the drop-off is still alive with coral and fish. The eastern side of the reef is even better, although currents make it dangerous for inexperienced divers.

Places to Stay & Eat At the time of writing, **San Vicente Community Village** (☎ 0919 390 9639; San Vicente; rooms P150) was under construction. The village will comprise five nipa huts with three rooms each; each room will contain three bamboo floor mats but no fan. Three basic meals are provided for between P200 and P400 (depending upon numbers), and there are also cooking facilities for rent if guests wish to bring their own food. Bottled water is available on the island, but it is more expensive than on Mactan.

Tents (☎ 0919 390 9639; P95) are available for rent at the Wildlife Sanctuary Office. Guests will have to bring their own food and water.

Arnold and **Efren** (Cao-oy; meals around P800) floating restaurants, on the southern tip of the island, offer pricey seafood meals.

Getting There & Away Most resorts on Mactan will organise a day trip for you, but if you want to put your time and money to better use, take the islander-run Olango Birds and Seascape Tour. It costs around P2300 per person (minimum of two people). This includes a local lunch, bird-watching and snorkelling guides, sanctuary entrance fees, island cruise, native cooking and fishing demonstration, transfers from Mactan and more. The tour is run by the **Suba Olango Multi Purpose Ecotourism Cooperative** (☎/fax 495 7951; W www.oneocean.org), a fishing-community association. Proceeds go towards the upkeep of the sanctuary, and the development of livelihood alternatives for Olango fishing communities.

For less money and a little more hassle, you can take the boat that runs between Angasil Wharf on Mactan and Santa Rosa on Olango (P10, 30 minutes). Boats run all day from 6am to 6.30pm. If you want to go island-hopping, visit the pumpboats at Maribago Wharf on Mactan. The going rate is P2000, but this price can be almost halved during quiet periods. A one-way or return trip between any of Santa Rosa Pier, the wildlife sanctuary and San Vicente, by tricycle will cost P60.

Toledo

The port city of Toledo, due west of Cebu City, presents a cheap and quick way to travel between Cebu and Negros. Once home to one of Asia's copper-mining giants, and currently home to a massive coal and oil power plant, this lush, relatively quiet city is far from being the industrial nightmare you might expect. Toledo's choice of food and accommodation is limited.

The city's landscaped central square – aglow with coloured lights at night – is watched over by the **Toledo City Parish Church**, which in turn is watched over by the statue of a giant monk, San Juan de Sahagun, to whom the church was dedicated.

Places to Stay & Eat Above a general store in a quiet residential area, **Aleu's Lodge** (☎ 322 5672; Poloyapoy St; rooms with fan & shared bathroom P100, with air-con, cable TV

& private bathroom P400) is a no-frills hotel. It has small shabby budget rooms, and slightly better standard rooms. It is about 1.5km from the pier (P4 by tricycle).

Springpark Mountain Resort (☎ 325 2044, ☎/fax 262 3851, 261 9511; camping P80 per person, dorm P120, cottages from P560), about 45 minutes inland from Toledo proper, is in the breezy cool of the nearby mountainous region of Cantabaco. There are three spring-water swimming pools, and a restaurant. To reach the resort, ring ahead to arrange transport from the Toledo pier area, or take the Toledo-Cebu v-hire van and ask to be let off at Springpark (P50 to P60).

In the centre of Toledo, there's no shortage of **bakeries**, and **fruit stalls** next to the pier.

Ran Ritch Café Bar & Restaurant (dishes P60-100; open 9am-9pm daily), on the street heading inland from the bus station, has OK Filipino food and imported wines.

Getting There & Away There are four boats daily from Toledo to San Carlos on Negros with **Aznar Shipping**: two fast (P85, one hour) and two slow (P70, 1½ hours). **Danila Lines** also has two slow boats daily for the same price as Aznar.

Buses run every hour or so daily between Cebu South bus station and the Toledo bus station (P56, 2¾ hours), near the pier. The first bus heads off around 5am, the last at around 4pm.

NORTH OF CEBU CITY

Once free of Cebu City's industrial fringe, the island's northern coast has many reasonable beaches and some great mountain views. The biggest metropolises are Danao, one of Cebu's bigger cities; and Bogo, which is on the verge of being officially recognised as a city. The most popular destinations, however, are the islands off the northern tip – Malapascua, which can be reached from Maya (a short ride from Daan Bantayan), and Bantayan, which can be reached from Hagnaya.

For buses heading north, see Getting There & Away under Cebu City earlier.

Danao

A thriving, seaside city it may be, but Danao is fairly rough around the edges. Danao is best known for its gunsmithery, which supplies cheap weapons for security guards throughout the Philippines. The backdrop to the town is a scenic mountain range, which includes **Danasan Plateau**, one of the few places on the island from where you can view both sides of the channel. A *hubel-hubel* (large-seat motorbike) will take you on the 40km journey (P150) or you can take the jeepney (P30), but make sure you don't miss the last jeepney returning in the afternoon.

A good person to chat to about venturing into the mountains, viewing nearby caves and seeing monkeys, is resident Hans Mueller. But Hans' fame in the area is not for his tour guiding. Rather, it's for his **German Delicatessen** (☎ 200 3440, 254 0553; Rizal St; meals P80-150; open 9am-midnight daily), opposite the old market, where he cooks up a delicious range of German treats – bread, sausages, pickles and hams – from which he supplies many of the major Cebu hotels.

The best place to stay in the area is **Intosan Resort** (☎ 200 3476; rooms P550-1200), a short tricycle ride from town (P4). Basic rooms are good value, with double bed, cable TV, hot water and a small balcony. The P1200 rooms have a kitchen. There's a pool table and swimming pool and a pretty average restaurant, but you are better off eating at Hans' place.

Buses running between Cebu City and the far north go via Danao (P20, 50 minutes). Pumpboats leave all day from the Danao City port for Poro town in the Camotes Islands (P40, two hours).

Sogod

The gently curving coastline of Sogod is about 70km north of Cebu City. It's a quiet town with attractive **beaches** nearby. To the south, you'll find the Vima Beach Resort, which rents out picnic shelters (P25) along a pleasant, palm-shaded beach.

Places to Stay & Eat About 5km north of Sogod is **Alegre Beach Resort** (☎ 254 9800/ 11/44, fax 254 9833; rooms US$240-576), the resort that put the town on the international tourist map. Alegre is highbrow and high security. If you manage to get inside, the leafy grounds include a huge swimming pool, a dive shop, a library, a putting green and a tennis court.

It's not quite as Disneyland as other top-end Philippine resorts, but the prices are equally as exorbitant. Sitting atop the re-

sort's very own white-sand beach is **Pavilion Restaurant & Bar**, which has prices to match the rooms – a buffet dinner goes for a hefty P650.

Buses pass through Sogod from Cebu City (P30, 1½ to two hours) throughout the day.

Bogo

The road north from Sogod heads inland through lush mountains before returning to the sea to meet up with Bogo, one of the country's fastest-growing towns. There's not a lot here for tourists, but there is an **Equitable PCI**, **PNB** and **Metrobank** in town, as well as **Ryan Marketing** at the roundabout, the last reliable Internet centre (P30 per hour) for those heading north.

Nailon Beach Resort (☎ 253 1097; rooms from P1200), just to the east of Bogo proper, sits at the end of a prominent point and features a swimming pool and rooms with air-con, cable TV and hot-water bathroom.

A regular/air-con bus from Cebu City to Bogo will cost you P44/66 and take around three hours. Nailon is a five-minute tricycle ride from the bus terminal (P5).

Daan Bantayan

About 130km north of Cebu City, in the thick of sugar-cane country, you'll reach the drab town of Daan Bantayan. In the village of Tapilon, about 5km from Daan Bantayan, pumpboats are available for trips out to the marine sanctuary of **Gato Island** (see Diving under Malapascua Island later in this chapter). If you want to stay here, the mayor's resort **Maria Luisa Vacation Resorts** (☎ 437 8798; cottages P1200, rooms P1500) has a wacky-shaped swimming pool and a view across to Gato Island. Cottages have air-con and cold-water bathroom, and rooms have hot water.

Maya

From Daan Bantayan, it's a 20-minute jeepney (P5) or hubel-hubel (P20) ride to Maya along a bad road. If you are heading to Malapascua and miss the last boat, you can stay at **Abba Family Lodge** (double with fan & shared bathroom P250), 100m from the pier, which has surprisingly clean rooms. As well as boats to Malapascua (see Getting There & Away under Malapascua Island later), there is a boat each morning from Maya to San Isidro, Leyte (P80, three hours).

Bantayan Island

Beautiful Bantayan Island, off the north-western coast of Cebu, has some exquisite white **beaches** and relaxed resorts on its southern coast around the wonderful little town of **Santa Fe**, and many green, shady roads and villages. It's used by most tourists as a peaceful retreat where the most harm that could come your way is to be hit on the head by a falling coconut. The island can also be used as a stepping stone to Negros.

The main activity on Bantayan seems to be sleeping. Second to that, you may see tourists flicking through the pages of a novel or taking a leisurely stroll through town. Most resorts can organise a bicycle for P150 per day, a motorbike for P500 a day, or snorkelling equipment for P100 a day. There is no decent snorkelling around the island, but boats can take you to **Silion Island** for P700 (4 pax) which has more to offer.

About 10km from Santa Fe (P10 by tri-cycle or jeepney), **Bantayan town** is the island's largest (and ugliest) town. There is an **Allied Bank** here where you can change trav-ellers cheques, a market and a slow **Internet connection** (*2nd floor, Veronica Bldg; P60*), behind the Allied Bank.

Bantayan is a popular place to be for the Holy Week celebrations but expect high prices to accompany the festivities.

Places to Stay & Eat All the resorts in Santa Fe have an excellent white beach.

Budyong Beach Resort (*☎ 438 9040; cottages with bathroom & fan/air-con P350/800*) has excellent-value nipa huts under palm trees on the sand, and balconies facing the water. The restaurant has good Filipino food.

Sugar Beach Resort (*huts with bathroom & fan P350*) has great budget beach shacks in the shade, set back from the beach. There is no phone and no restaurant, but the women minding the huts will happily cook up your meals.

Kota Beach (*☎ 254 2726; ☎/fax 254 5661; e kota@cebu.i-next.com; cottages with fan/ air-con P840/1200*), next to Budyong, has rea-sonable cottages with cold-water bathroom, and some are close to the beach. **Ding Dong Restaurant** (*meals P80-110; open 7am-10pm daily*) has very good Filipino food.

Santa Fe Beach Club (*☎ 438 0165; cottages with fan/air-con P900/2000; non-guests ad-mission P50*) has two resorts on the island.

The better of the two is the one housing the **Ogtong Cave**, a small cave with freshwater swimming. Standard cottages vary in size, but all are clean with fan and private cold-water bathroom. The air-con rooms have hot water, fridge and views of the beach. There is also a restaurant and swimming pool.

St Bernard Beach Resort (*☎ 0917 963 6162; e fhl@mozcom.com, w come.across.to/ bantayan; Alice Beach; cottages P450-650*) has very good cottages in the shade close to an OK beach. The menu is Filipino with some international additions, and plenty of salads (meals P100 to P180). The resort is wheel-chair accessible.

Moby Dick's Beach Resort (*☎ 352 5269; cabins P450-500*), on the road from Bantayan town to Madridejos in the north (turn left at San Pedro Chapel), is a rambling house/ resort full of character and family atmos-phere. Barry, the owner, cooks up great food in a restaurant full of his carved whales. There is no good beach, but there is a swim-ming pool and lovely view out to sea.

There is some good food to be had in Santa Fe.

Moby Dick's (*meals P110-200; open 10am-10pm daily*), known locally as Little Dick's, is a five-minute walk up the road heading north from town. It has tree-trunk chairs, carvings and an island feel. There is great homemade bread and speciality 'volcano'

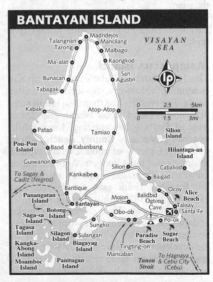

BANTAYAN ISLAND

dishes – mashed potato mountains with meat, shrimp or vegetarian filling – just to continue the whale and Dick motif.

D'Jungle (meals around P160; open 10am-late daily) has a great bar and international menu. The big breakfasts (around P150) come with a choice of brewed coffee or beer.

El Paso (dishes P130-180; open noon-10pm daily) is an attractive native-style restaurant serving fresh and tasty Thai dishes.

Tickety Boo Bar & Restaurant, next to St Bernard Beach Resort, is a popular nightly hang-out, with organ and singing most nights.

Getting There & Away For buses from Cebu to Hagnaya, see Getting There & Away under Cebu City.

Local airline **SEAIR** (☎ 0917 390 0375, 0917 690 2099; Santa Fe ● ☎ 341 3021/2, fax 341 3023; MCIA; ⓦ www.flyseair.com) flies between Cebu and Santa Fe three days a week (P1650, 25 minutes). Many resorts have free airport transfer, otherwise it's a P5-tricycle ride between Santa Fe and the airport.

Boats leave Hagnaya for Santa Fe three times daily (P67, one hour).

Bantayan town has boats every second morning to Cadiz on Negros (P120, four hours). Smaller pumpboats leave Bantayan for Sagay, also on Negros (P130, two hours), daily if public demand is strong enough. The schedule depends upon the tide – just ask at the pier.

Palacio Shipping has boats between Cebu City and Santa Fe (P150, nine hours) five nights a week.

Malapascua Island

This little island off Cebu's northern tip has everything the low-key, sun-seeking traveller needs. The island – less than 2 sq km in size, 8km northwest of Cebu Island, and 25km west of Leyte – has enticing, long, white **beaches** (especially **Bounty Beach**, where you arrive), plenty of good restaurants, and resorts to suit most budgets. Another major drawcard of the island is found underwater – the **thresher shark** (see the boxed text 'Thresher Sharks' and also Diving later).

All these factors have combined to make Malapascua the current buzz word in domestic tourism, a factor which pleases many of the developers who have already started earmarking plots for more resorts, and terrifies some of the locals who don't want to see the island become 'another Boracay'. Development may be restricted by the limited water on the island (which results in a rather brackish water supply) and the fervour of some of the locals and conservationists who are trying to create a strategy for managing the island in a way that will benefit the islanders and protect the island's environmental features.

The nearby main town (actually, everything on this compact island is nearby) of **Logon** is simple and friendly. It has some small eateries and general stores and is great to wander through on a stroll around the island. The island itself is often referred to by older locals as Logon. There is also the village church, which houses the **Virgen de los Desamparados**, the 'miracle' of the island, and the patron saint of the locals. She appeared as a piece of driftwood that wouldn't burn. After some time, locals decided it was an appearance of the Virgin Mary, and by the time they'd painted and dressed it, it did in fact look like the Virgin Mary.

There are no cars on the island, only a few bicycles and a network of walking tracks. These tracks wind past such attractions as the waterside town **cemetery**, with its sun-bleached graves (some of them are open, with skulls and bones on view), and the **lighthouse** on the island's northwest.

Paddle boats can be hired in front of Cocobana Resort for P250 to P300, and **beach volleyball** is also available.

Diving The most popular dive off Malapascua is Monad Shoal, to see the thresher sharks. The plateau where the sharks congregate is at 25m depth, 15 minutes by pumpboat from Bounty Beach, and the best time for sightings is early morning. Although dynamiting has mainly destroyed the closer reefs, macro-photographers will love the area around **Gato Island**, a marine sanctuary and sea snake breeding ground (from around February to September). There are also three wreck dives in the area.

There are five dive centres on the island, all offering standard rates – one dive US$20, equipment rental US$5 and open-water diving-certificate US$300. Dive centres are: **Sea Explorers** (☎ 437 0411, 0919 447 9030; ⓦ www.sea-explorers.com); **Bubble 07 Diver's Corp** (☎ 0919 322 9102, 0915 817 5340; ⓦ www.bubble07.com); **Philippine Island Divers** (☎ 340 7635, 340 5127, fax 340 7634;

MALAPASCUA ISLAND

PLACES TO STAY & EAT	12 Monte Luna Beach
2 Ging-Ging's Garden	Resort; Philippine
Restaurant	Island Divers
3 La Isla Bonita	13 Blue Corals Resort
4 Malapascua Exotic	15 Logon Beach Resort
Island Dive Resort	16 White Sands
5 Sunrise Beach Resort	17 Maldito's
6 Loida's Beach Club	
7 Sunset Resort;	OTHER
Tropical Beach Resort;	1 Malapasay Elementary
Bubble 07 Diver's Corp	School; Health Centre
9 Cocobana Beach Resort	8 Sunsplash Bar
11 Malapascua Bluewater	10 Sea Explorers
Resort; Divelink	14 Cemetery

W www.phildivers.com); **Divelink** (☎ 231 4633, fax 234 0584; e gary@cebu.weblinq.com); and **Exotic Divers** (for detailssee Malapascua Exotic Island Dive Resort under Places to Stay & Eat later).

Information The phones here are mobiles only – and not all the resorts can afford such luxuries. The island's electricity is supplied by a diesel-powered generator. It operates from 5.30pm to 11.30pm (sometimes later) daily, although some resorts, such as Cocobana, Blue Corals, Malapascua Bluewater Resort and Malapascua Exotic Island Dive Resort, have their own generators. This is great if you want air-con, not so great if you want tranquillity, although sometimes it's the neighbouring resorts

which suffer the most from generator noise pollution.

Places to Stay & Eat Most of the resorts are on the stretch along Bounty Beach. Room rates are extremely flexible, and many resort managers won't even wait for a reply before they begin trying to cut a deal with you. Low season and extended-stay bookings command the best bargaining power. Many resorts provide mosquito nets and you may well need them. Unless otherwise stated, all rooms have fan and private cold-water bathroom.

Ging-Ging's Garden Restaurant *(meals P50-70; rooms with shared bathroom P150; restaurant open 7am-10.30pm daily)*, 200m off the beach, not only offers the very best economy dining (budget travellers usually end up having all their meals here), it also has the cheapest rooms on the island *and* the cheapest beers (P25). Book meals ahead so that fresh ingredients can be bought.

White Sands *(nipa huts P300)* is on a quiet cove behind Bounty Beach, near the village. The brand new huts in the shade on the edge of the beach are a bargain.

Monte Luna Beach Resort *(rooms P350)*, at the western end of Bounty Beach, is a low-key place with no restaurant. It has run-down rooms on the beach.

Sunrise Beach Resort *(cottages P500)* has cottages on the quiet eastern end of the beach. There is no restaurant, and you'll have to hunt for the owner in the houses out the back.

Tropical Beach Resort *(cottages P500)* and **Sunset Resort** *(cottages P600)* have a similar setup to Sunrise, but on Bounty Beach.

Logon Beach Resort *(☎ 0918 913 7278, 0919 651 1015; w www.logonbeach.com; nipa huts P600)* is a friendly family-run place with a prime location, high on a rocky outcrop, overlooking a private cove. Nipa huts have balconies facing the sunset. Cheaper rooms with shared bathroom were being built when we visited. To get to the resort, find the beach in front of White Sands, turn left and follow the signs to Logon Beach Resort that take you up the hill.

Malapascua Exotic Island Dive Resort *(☎ 437 0983/84, 0918 774 0484, fax 437 0984; w www.malapascua.net; rooms with fan & shared bathroom P300, rooms with fan & private bathroom P650-850, beach cottage with air-con P2500)* is located on the quiet easterly beach and is a great self-contained

THE VISAYAS

Thresher Sharks

In the past, huge deep-water thresher sharks (*Alopias vulpinus* and *Alopias pelagicus*) were only very rarely sighted by divers. But their recent discovery at the underwater plateau of Monad Shoal, off Malapascua, where they visit each morning, has changed all that, bringing shark fanatics and underwater photographers from around the globe to ogle at these bizarre and ominous-looking creatures.

The thresher grows to approximately 6m, and is one of the most easily recognised of all sharks, because of its long scythe-like tail (after which it is named), which makes up about half the shark's body length. It can use its tail to tear through the water at great speeds and corral its prey – mainly schooling fish and squid – and possibly even stun them with its tail. When you see the thresher at Monad Shaol, however, it will be doing none of the above. While no-one knows why the threshers make their daily appearance at the plateau, it seems that the cold waters off Malapascua allow them to move up to shallower waters and be *cleaned* of external parasites by cleaner fish. Local dive centres can almost guarantee a sighting of this on an early morning dive. There is some concern that over-exploitation of this attraction will scare away the sharks and add pace to the already outrageous speed of development on the island.

So, if you do decide to take a peek at this magnificent creature, remember the following: you're extremely privileged to be doing so, dive in small groups and be careful not to disturb the shark's activity. No verified, unprovoked attacks of thresher sharks on humans have ever been recorded, although as one shark textbook tactfully recommends – 'its large size and powerful tail should invite respect'!

Sonia Orchard

resort, housing the oldest dive centre on the island, a restaurant/bar and a 24-hour generator. Accommodation-diving packages can be negotiated.

Malapascua Bluewater Resort (☎ *0918 919 9128, 0919 317 1804, ☎/fax 231 6124;* e *janetmalapascua@hotmail.com; rooms & cottages P600-800*) is a big place on spacious grounds with cottages on the beach and generator-infused cheaper rooms out the back. There is a 24-hour electricity supply, and a rather pricey restaurant.

Loida's Beach Club (☎ *437 1030, 0918 892 0291;* e *loida@gmx.de; rooms/cottages P750*) has a rather crowded conglomeration of cottages on the beach and stretching back, as well as 2nd-storey rooms. There is a restaurant with a lovely pergola on the beach.

Cocobana Beach Resort (☎ *437 1040/07, 0918 775 2942;* e *freddy.krummenacher@ bluewin.ch; single/double garden cottages with shared bathroom P480/660, garden cottage with private bathroom P800/960, beach cottage P900/1080*), Malapascua's first resort, is a well-oiled machine with 24-hour electricity, run by long-time resident, Freddy. The Cocobana has a bar right on the beach, a decent restaurant, and breakfast is included.

Blue Corals Resort (☎ *0919 653 3890; doubles P1100*) is a new resort built on the famous old rock lookout (great views) and the mixed response from locals. It's a bit of an eyesore as you approach the island, with its bright flashing lights, but it does have excellent rooms with views over the water, a pricey restaurant and 24-hour electricity.

La Isla Bonita (*set menus P220-300, pizzas P150, other dishes P130-180; open 8am-11pm daily*) has the best food on the island at some of the highest prices, in humble, breezy surroundings. Whether you indulge in Thai, Greek, German, Indian or Filipino, fish in coconut (P135) or baked with basil, tomato and mozzarella (P180), you will enjoy quality ingredients and scrumptious flavours. Order meals ahead of time.

Sunsplash Bar (*open 7am-late daily*) is an open bar and restaurant with pool tables and sofas. Despite the floating bar with a 2-for-1 Happy Hour, and 'drink for your country' shooter-drinking competitions, the place maintains a subdued, laid-back feel *most* of the time.

Maldito's is a controversial newcomer on the island. It is a well-designed 24-hour restaurant-disco that pumps out loud music and generator noise.

If you're desperate for moneychanging, Internet, a fax or international calls, venture here with deep pockets.

Getting There & Away There are public pumpboats from Maya to Malapascua (P50, 20 minutes to one hour) that leave whenever the boat is full. To avoid a possible several-hour wait you can hire a boat for a one-way trip at any time of the day (P400). If the tide is low at Maya, the larger pumpboats can't dock, and must ferry passengers to and from shore using smaller craft (P10).

To travel between Malapascua and Bantayan, you have to hire a pumpboat and pay 'special ride' rates of around P1300 to P1500.

It's possible to do a diving or boating trip (eg, to Leyte) through the Malapascua Exotic Island Dive Resort (see Places to Stay & Eat earlier) and continue on your island-hopping way afterwards.

SOUTH OF CEBU CITY

The west and east coasts south of Cebu City tend to be mostly pebbly or rocky affairs, but there's plenty of diving and snorkelling to be had. Moalboal is Cebu Island's premiere dive destination. For buses heading south, see Getting There & Away under Cebu City earlier.

Argao & Dalaguete

Spanish colonial-era buildings and limestone walls make Argao a little special, but it's the town's nearby **beaches** of Kawit, Mahawak and Mahayahay that draw the guests. Neighbouring Dalaguete is well known for its plaza and streets of flowering bushes. Its popular **Dalaguete Public Beach** has communal showers by the water and food and drink stalls.

Bamboo Paradise Beach Resort (☎ 485 8684; e paradise@maweb.de; singles P400, doubles P600-850, apartments P1000-1100), in Argao, is run by Irene and Gunther. This charming place has large, cosy rooms with bathroom and fan or air-con. There's some OK snorkelling at the nearby (200m) beach. The resort will take you 10km (P50 by tricycle) to the boat for Loon for free, and can also pick you up from Mactan airport for P1000.

Argao is about 65km from Cebu City, and plenty of Ceres Bus Liner and other buses (some of them air-con) stop here (P40, two hours) on the way between Cebu City and Bato, on Cebu's southern tip. From here, it's another 70km to Bato (P40, one hour).

Lite Shipping boats go from Argao to Loon (P50, three hours) two or three times daily. There are also cargo pumpboats leaving from near Bamboo Paradise for Cabilao Island (P50, one hour) twice a week, which will carry passengers.

Moalboal & Panagsama Beach

Diving, dining and drinking top the list of tourist activities on the beaches of Moalboal (hard to pronounce – try 'mo-all-bo-all'). About 90km from Cebu City, Moalboal proper is on the main road, with the lively tourist haunt of Panagsama Beach a short tricycle ride from town (day/night P20/50).

Poor coastal development has led to the beach of Panagsama Beach being washed away. In addition, many of the resorts have built walls jutting out to sea, making it impossible to walk along the ocean-side. Most of the accommodation, restaurants, bars and dive centres are on the water's edge and can be approached by the strip that runs along the back.

For those wanting a quieter retreat, **White Beach** – north of Panagsama Beach, and a P20 tricycle ride from either Panagsama or Moalboal – actually has a beach (and a great one at that) as well as relative tranquillity. There are no bars here and the eateries are limited to the three resorts.

Things to See & Do Moalboal's dive centres are all affiliated with resorts – for details, see Places to Stay later. The average price of a **dive** is US$15 (no equipment), equipment rental $5 and an open-water, diving certificate US$250 to US$300. The **snorkelling** here is good too, and most resorts rent out snorkel, mask and fins for around P200 to P300 per day.

An often-choppy, 3km boat ride from Moalboal's Tongo Point diving spot, tiny **Pescador** offers some of Cebu's most spectacular diving. With generally excellent visibility and depths of around 50m, the island's waters are usually teeming with fish – no dive trip around here is complete without a plunge at Pescador. Snorkelling is possible too; the best spot is said to be on the island's southern side.

There is a fee (P50) to dive at Savedra Reef, and a fee may soon be introduced at Pescador (see the boxed text 'From Dynamite to Diving Fees' under Bohol later).

For active travellers who are sick of diving and lazing on idyllic beaches, visit Jochen at

THE VISAYAS

Planet Action (☎ 474 0068; W www.action philippines.com) who's been leading some of the most exhilarating adventure tours in the Visayas for the last seven years. Trips cater for beginners through to advanced actioneers and include all equipment and meals. Some favourite trips are: **canyoning** – rappelling down 30m waterfalls; **horseriding** – view Bohol, Negros and Leyte from 1000m-high mountain trails; **caving**; and **river climbing**. Jochen also extends his adventure range into Negros, including: a two-day 'hard' **hike** to active volcano Mt Kanlaon (all-inclusive US$120 per person); and a two-day hike to beautiful Lake Danao – one of the crater lakes of Twin Lakes ($85).

If you're low on cash, rent a mountain bike from Jochen (US$7 per day) and ride to **Kawasan Falls**, inland from Matutinao, 20km south of Moalboal, or else take a bus (P15). Once you've had enough activity, unwind at the **orchid farm**, just outside Moalboal (tricycle P20; admission P20).

Places to Stay – Panagsama Beach

There's a wide range of accommodation on and around Moalboal's Panagsama Beach, from simple nipa huts through to luxurious air-con rooms.

Mollie's Place (Philippine Dive & Tour; ☎ 0917 254 7060; singles P100, doubles P125-600) has dirt-cheap, liveable rooms with fan and shared bathroom, and better ones with private, cold-water bathroom and air-con. The food is reasonable (try the papaya jam), and staff can arrange ticketing and diving through Savedra Dive Centre (see Savedra Beach Resort later).

Pacita's Nipa Hut (☎ 0919 210 8216; cottages P350-700) has a sea-view location and good prices. At the economy end, nipa huts are pretty run down, but have fan and cold-water bathroom. For P500, huts are better and have sea views, and for P700, they have air-con.

Quo Vadis Beach Resort (☎ 474 0020, 0919 825 6412; W www.moalboal.com; rooms P450-1550) is one of the best of the middle range options. Clean, standard rooms/cottages have fan and private cold-water bathroom. Top of the range rooms have air-con and hot water. There is a swimming pool, **Visaya Divers** (contact through resort), and the excellent Asian-European **Arista Restaurant** (☎ 032-474 0020).

Sunshine Pension House (☎ 474 0049; e sunshinepension@yahoo.com; cottages P400, twins/doubles P450), a short walk from the water, has well-priced, large rooms and cottages with fan and cold-water bathroom. The restaurant specialises in Swiss food.

Eve's Kiosk (☎/fax 0918 773 3730; W www .eveskiosk.com; cottages P350, rooms P650-750) has budget cottages with fan and cold-water bathroom, and rooms with air-con and hot water. There is a pool, an average restaurant and **Nelson's Diving School** (☎ 474 0087; W www.neptunediving.com).

Love's Lodge (☎ 474 0061, 0917 618 5456; e loveslodge@hotmail.com; standard/deluxe rooms P500/1200) has great rooms and excellent positioning on the quiet southern end of the beach. Standard rooms have fan, a

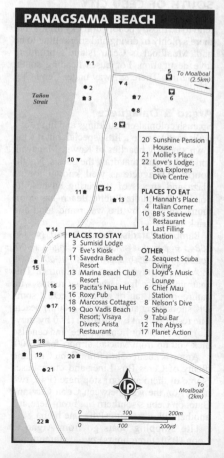

PANAGSAMA BEACH

Tañon Strait

To Moalboal (2.5km)

To Moalboal (2km)

PLACES TO STAY
3 Sumisid Lodge
7 Eve's Kiosk
11 Savedra Beach Resort
13 Marina Beach Club Resort
15 Pacita's Nipa Hut
16 Roxy Pub
18 Marcosas Cottages
19 Quo Vadis Beach Resort; Visaya Divers; Arista Restaurant
20 Sunshine Pension House
21 Mollie's Place
22 Love's Lodge; Sea Explorers Dive Centre

PLACES TO EAT
1 Hannah's Place
4 Italian Corner
10 BB's Seaview Restaurant
14 Last Filling Station

OTHER
2 Seaquest Scuba Diving
5 Lloyd's Music Lounge
6 Chief Mau Station
8 Nelson's Dive Shop
9 Tabu Bar
12 The Abyss
17 Planet Action

0   100   200m
0   100   200yd

cold-water bathroom and windows, and sparkling-clean deluxe rooms have hot water, air-con and breakfast included. Love's Lodge is affiliated with **Sea Explorers** (contact the resort; W www.sea-explorers.com).

Marina Beach Club Resort (☎/fax 474 0047, 231 4202; rooms & cottages P400-1300) has cheap huts with fan and cold-water bathroom and pricier ones with air-con. Big, clean, tiled rooms with hot water, fridge and coffee facilities start at P1000. Marina Beach is affiliated with **Submaldive Scuba Centre** (☎ 474 0046).

Marcosas Cottages (☎/fax 474 0064; W www.marcosas.com; cottages P550-1300) has cheap, slightly shabby cottages with fan and cold-water bathroom. The bonus is a basic kitchen, fridge and veranda looking out to sea. More-expensive doubles have air-con and huge hot-water bathroom.

Sumisid Lodge (☎ 346 9629, 345 4638, fax 346 0592; rooms P450-850) is a stylish but homely place up the northern end. Lovely native-style rooms with fan and shared bathroom are P450, those with air-con and private cold-water bathroom P850. Also included are a great breakfast (homemade bread and espressos) and the sound of the waves outside your window. It's affiliated with **Seaquest Dive Centre** (contact through resort).

Savedra Beach Resort (☎ 474 0372, ☎/fax 474 0011; e margit@cybercebu.com; rooms P1200) has rooms – with air-con and hot-water bathroom – facing the water. It's affiliated with **Savedra Dive Centre** (☎ 474 0014, fax 474 0011; W www.savedra.com).

Places to Eat – Panagsama Beach Most places to stay have good restaurants, although there are plenty of other eateries worth a look; most open for all meals. **Last Filling Station** (☎ 474 0068) is famous for its breakfasts (P75 to P100), while **BB's Seaview Restaurant** (☎ 480 5941; meals around P150) does fine, cheapish Filipino seafood. **Hannah's Place** (☎ 474 0091, 346 9629) aims for a more upmarket crowd, and **Italian Corner** (meals P100-150; open for dinner only) does good traditional Italian pizzas and other dishes.

Places to Stay & Eat – White Beach The **Asian-Belgian Resort & Dive Centre** (☎ 474 0106, 0917 744 7603; e eurodivers50@hotmail.com; doubles P600) has good native-style rooms with fan and cold-water bathroom.

There is a restaurant serving Euro-Asian food, and a dive centre offering cheap, open-water diving courses (US$250).

If you can't get in at Asian-Belgian resort, try **Dolphin House** (☎ 474 0073, fax 474 0074; singles/doubles from US$15/20).

Entertainment In Panagsama Beach, lively drinking holes include **Lloyd's Music Lounge**, **Chief Mau Station** and **Roxy Pub**. **Tabu Bar** has a disco every Saturday night.

Getting There & Away Buses leave throughout the day from Cebu South bus station to Moalboal (P60, three to four hours). To get from Moalboal to Bato (P40, 1½ hours) by Ceres Bus Liner bus, just wait by the main road and be prepared for standing room only. There are also air-con vans doing these routes for slightly higher fares. Most resorts can organise van hire for Cebu or Bato (P1200 to P1500).

Samboan

On the western side of Cebu's south coast, Samboan has great views across Tañon Strait from its impressive, 19th-century **Escala de Jacob stone staircase and watchtower** above the town. Halfway between Samboan and Bato (P4 by jeepney from either), **Fantasy Place** (☎ 0919 439 3013; doubles P800) is a modern, Spanish-style resort with plenty of light, colourful tiles and brilliant, white walls. Rooms have fan and one cold-water bathroom between two rooms. The resort has a buffet restaurant (dinner P200) and a pool looking out to the sea and mountains. They will take you free of charge to the nearby **waterfalls**, or arrange a **dolphin watching** tour (P1200).

Bato

Bato, on Cebu's southern tip, is a pretty port town with regular boats making the crossing to Dumaguete's Tampi port on Negros. Solid, old ferries sail to and from Bato (P27, 45 minutes) every 1½ hours or so, from 5.30am to 5pm daily. Buses from Bato to Moalboal take about 1½ hours (P40), and continue on to Cebu City (total trip P100, four to six hours).

Lilo-an & Sumilon Island

Like its nearby sister-town of Bato, Lilo-an is an attractive coastal town with boats that run all day to Sibulan on Negros (P27, 30 minutes). In the waters off nearby Lilo-an Point, manta rays are regular visitors between February and June. The town also offers easy access to the island of Sumilon, which has the country's first marine reserve and is slowly recuperating from years of abuse. Rumour has it that a luxury resort will be built here soon.

In Santander, Lilo-an, you can stay at **Cebu Lilo-an Beach Resort** (☎ *0919 796 8682; doubles/triples P800/1000*) – just turn left and stick to the coast when you alight from the boat from Negros. Standard rooms have fan and cold-water bathroom, and the more expensive rooms have a double and a single bed, hot water, air-con and veranda. There's diving available (including trips to Apo Island) and dive instruction upon request. It's P10 by tricycle from Bato.

There are Ceres Bus Liner buses and air-con vans (P110, five to six hours) running all day to Cebu.

Camotes Islands

Little more than an hour's boat ride from Cebu City, the Camotes are the most underrated islands in the Visayas, offering an authentic island life that many adventurous tourists crave. This group's two main islands,

Poro and Pacijan, are connected by a mangrove-fringed land bridge that enables visitors to explore the two by motorcycle, the main mode of transport here.

There are only a few places to stay on the islands, and besides local shops and markets, visitors must rely on these places for a basic menu.

There are also several 'resorts' that offer day-time beach shelters for a small fee.

Fishing and agriculture are the major livelihoods on the Camotes, as well as local tourism. As transport and communication are poor, few international visitors make this very worthwhile stop on their itinerary. The few that do will be welcomed warmly by the locals.

For more information on the Camotes Islands, drop into the tourist office on Poro Pier, just next to the Palacio and Oceanjet ticketing booths.

Getting There & Away

For information on boat services between Poro town and Cebu City, see Getting There & Away under Cebu City earlier. Several giant pumpboats operate between Poro town and Danao (P40, two hours), north of Cebu City. Others serve Isabel on Leyte. Pumpboat schedules and prices seem to vary from day to day, so ask for the latest information at the respective town piers.

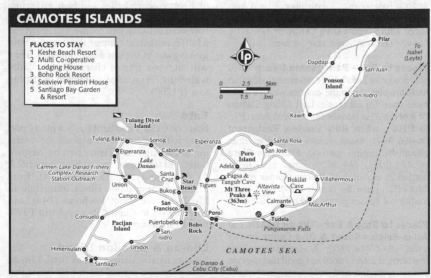

CAMOTES ISLANDS

PLACES TO STAY
1 Keshe Beach Resort
2 Multi Co-operative Lodging House
3 Boho Rock Resort
4 Seaview Pension House
5 Santiago Bay Garden & Resort

Getting Around

Getting around the Camotes Islands is usually on the back of an off-road motorcycle, and once you leave the Poro–San Francisco area you will find out why – most of the roads are so poor they would be impassable for any other vehicle. Nonetheless, most motorbike riders will happily take you and up to three other passengers, plus the weekly shopping on board. Jeepneys are scarce.

PACIJAN ISLAND
San Francisco

Bigger and denser than Poro town, 'San Fran', the main town on Pacijan Island, stands at one end of the long land bridge and mangrove forest that runs all the way across to Poro Island. San Fran has a lively market (to the left after the causeway, on the bay), a church, a giant basketball complex, a pretty little town square and plenty of colourful murals. Motorcycles and their riders can be hired for trips around the island, or across to Poro Island, from around the town square. From San Francisco to Poro town it's about P25.

Lake Danao & Danao Fisheries

The **Carmen–Lake Danao Fishery Complex/ Research Outreach Station** on **Lake Danao** is 15 minutes from San Francisco, in the town of Union (oon-**yon**). The fishery performs research on tilapia, a freshwater fish, to establish optimum growth conditions. The fish are farmed in outdoor fish ponds and in floating pens on the lake. A motorbike ride from Poro will cost around P130.

Esperanza

Esperanza is Pacijan's second largest town and has a main street lined with yellow-painted pot plants. The town runs along a white-sand beach strewn with fishing boats. Like most towns in the Camotes, Esperanza has a school, a church, shops and a basketball court. The road north from Esperanza takes you up to **Tulang Baku** where you can ask a fisherman to take you out to **Tulang Diyot** (P20 return). Esperanza is about half an hour from San Fran by motorbike (P150 one way).

Star Beach

Fifteen minutes north of San Francisco, a road from Santa Cruz takes you to **World Big 4 Golf Club and Marina**, an immaculately kept, grassed and terraced area where

you can rent mushroom cottages for P50 to P100, overlooking the water. Behind this popular picnic spot is the 'golf course' – but you'd have to supply your own clubs as no-one around had any idea where to find some when we were there. A motorbike from Poro costs P60.

Places to Stay & Eat

Keshe Beach Resort (Bakhaw Beach, Esperanza; nipa hut P800) doesn't offer any activities, but if you're after a romantic getaway, this is your place. Upon arrival, you get the distinct feeling that they are not used to guests, but once warmed up, you'll have half a dozen people cleaning your huge, spanking-new nipa hut (with private cold-water bathroom) and shopping for your dinner (meals around P140). Although the price is steep, it is the best tourist accommodation in the Camotes and you'll be treated like island royalty. From Esperanza, follow the beach south as far as it goes.

Santiago Bay Garden & Resort (☎ 345 8599, 420 3385, 0915 815 3849; Santiago; doubles with fan & shared bathroom P500) is the other beachey alternative, at the southern tip of the island (P150 by motorbike) and has a cheerful atmosphere with lots of locals and music. Rooms are small and strung in rows over what must be one of the best untouristed beaches in the Visayas. Popular with Cebuanos, this relatively new resort has a large restaurant (the lunch and dinner menu is simple – 'chicken or fish' – served with rice for under P100) with rattan furniture, and private tables and pergolas (the larger ones for day rent at P200), all perched over the stunning white beach.

Multi Co-operative Lodging House (San Francisco) is in a large building on the town square. Word has it that it offers cheap (around P100), basic rooms with fan and shared bathroom, but it was closed when we visited. For food in San Francisco, visitors must make do with the weekend market, general stores and bakeries.

PORO ISLAND
Poro Town

The pretty little town of Poro is a pleasant place to wander. Its curving main road takes in a basketball court built right on the water, and the marble-floored **Santo Niño de Poro Parish church**, overlooking a leafy town square. Most visitors arriving in Camotes will land at the port of Poro and be greeted by an onslaught of motorbike riders willing to take you anywhere on the island.

Altavista View & Mt Three Peaks

About 5km from Poro town, a very bumpy road takes you up to the lookout area known as Altavista View *(admission P3)*. The serene plateau has a 'comfort room', a small tree house and three other open cottages that you can sit in for P15 to P25. Whether you choose the rental options or the free benches, the views you will receive – Pacijan and Tulang Islands to the west and Leyte Island to the north – are nothing short of breathtaking. The three fairly tiddly peaks nearby – Mt Three Peaks – that make up Camotes' highest region are Elijan, Kaban-Kaban and Kantomaro. A return motorcycle trip from Poro town should cost around P60.

Bukilat Cave

Beside a bumpy dirt road about 6km inland from Tudela, is the well-hidden Bukilat Cave *(admission P2)*. The road you want heads north from Tudela, then east, passing the Calmante Elementary School about 4km along. A sign for the cave pops up once you're almost there. The entrance fee is payable at the nearby waiting shed or shop. Swallows nest among the stalactites, and one inky-black corner is apparently the start of a long passage, which can be explored properly if you can rustle up a guide and some torches (flashlights). A return motorcycle ride from Poro town should cost P120.

Just west of Tudela, a 1km walking trail inland takes you to **Panganuron Falls**.

Boho Rock Resort

On the southwestern tip of Poro Island, this 'resort' *(admission P3)* is an absolute gem of a swimming spot. You can see it from the Poro town pier, but to reach it by land you head about 2km west of Poro town, on the main road, until you see the turn-off to the resort. The entrance path takes you past the Camotes Electric Cooperative, and then down to a rocky islet that's been turned into a stunning **aquatic playground**. A 'mushroom cottage' (a thatched-roof shelter on the rock) can be rented for P15. A motorcycle ride to the rock, from Poro town or San Francisco, should cost around P15.

Places to Stay & Eat

Seaview Pension House *(Poro; twins P125)* is a run-down pension house on the water's edge. Rooms have a fan and window, and share a common, cold-water bathroom. Run by a devout family (there are 'Family of the Year' and 'Altar' awards displayed alongside crucifixes), you will feel most safe and welcome. From the pier, turn left down the main road and walk about 100m.

There are several general stores in Poro town; a couple of **bakeries** (including one that's open 24 hours!); and the tiny, pierside **Pantalon Café**, serving coffee and pastry (P10), and boiled eggs (P5). There's a small **market** behind the café.

Bohol

☎ 038

Bohol's (bo-**hall**) main attraction rests peacefully in the centre of the island – the Chocolate Hills. While this magical land formation draws the crowds, it also shines the spotlight away from some of the island's other excellent destinations and activities. The lush interior has jungle, rice terraces, an immense national park and a visitor's centre for the Philippine tarsier; the coast offers great diving and island-hopping opportunities; and a tour of the towns will reveal some of the country's best examples of colonial Spanish churches, many of which are made from coral stone.

As well as being well known for its quiet, friendly people, Bohol is also known for its *ube* or *ubi* (yams), the bright-purple sweet potatoes that give halo halo, the national dessert, its distinctive colour and flavour.

If you are interested in experiencing a slice of Boholano life, as well as helping out the locals, contact **Process-Bohol** *(☎ 411 3641; e process@mozcom.com)*, a non-profit, community-managed organisation that arrange homestays, demonstrations and tours.

Getting There & Away

Air There are daily flights both from Manila and Cebu to Tagbilaran airport and back again. See Bohol under Getting There & Away for those cities.

Boat Tagbilaran is Bohol's main port – other ports include Tubigon, Jagna, Ubay

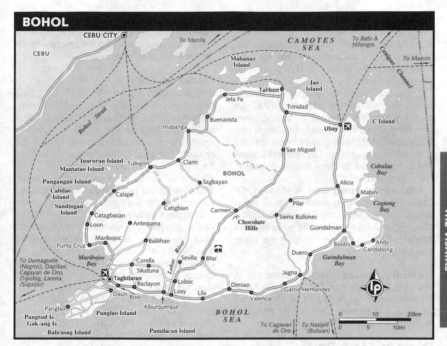

BOHOL

CEBU CITY
CEBU
To Manila
CAMOTES SEA
To Bato & Hilongos
To Maasin
Mahanay Island
Talibon
Jao Island
Jeta Fe
Trinidad
Buenavista
Inabanga
Ubay
C Island
San Miguel
Inaruran Island
Mantatao Island
Tubigon
Clarin
BOHOL
Cabulao Bay
Pangangan Island
Sagbayan
Alicia
Cabilao Island
Calape
Mabini
Sandingan Island
Catigbian
Pilar
Cogtong Bay
Catagbacan
Carmen
Sierra Bullones
Loon
Antequera
Chocolate Hills
Guindalman
Maribojoc
Balilihan
Basdio
Anda
Punta Cruz
Sevilla
Duero
Candabong
Maribojoc Bay
Corella
Bilar
Guindulman Bay
To Dumaguete (Negros), Dapitan, Cagayan de Oro, Dipolog, Larena (Siquijor)
Sikatuna
Jagna
Tagbilaran
Baclayon
Loboc
Dimiao
Garcia Hernandez
Dauis
Bool
Loay
Lila
Valencia
Panglao
Alburquerque
BOHOL SEA
Pungtud Is
Gak-ang Is
Panglao Island
Pamilacan Island
To Cagayan de Oro
To Nasipit (Butuan)
Balicasag Island

0   10   20km
0   5   10mi

THE VISAYAS

and Talibon and Jeta Fe. There are umpteen ways to get here from Cebu City (see Getting There & Away under Cebu City earlier) as well as connections to Manila, Leyte, Mindanao, Siquijor and Negros. Look under individual Getting There & Away entries in this section for information on boat travel between Bohol and other destinations in the Philippines.

If you're in Cebu City and short on time or patience, you should consider the popular two-day Bohol package deal offered by Aboitiz Express and SuperCat. Advertised as 'Skip Trips', the deals include a return fastcraft trip from Cebu City to Panglao or Tagbilaran, two days' accommodation at one of several local resorts, and some of the island's activities. For more information, contact **Aboitiz Express** (☎ 232 4511/636; W www.supercat.com.ph)

TAGBILARAN
☎ 038 • pop 78,000
Unfortunately, what little there is to see in the port capital of Tagbilaran (tag-bill-**are**-an) is often obscured by a fog of exhaust fumes due to the 2000-plus tricycles that comprise the

main form of transport. But this city has good accommodation, and it's a popular base for day trips to the many great sights nearby.

Orientation & Information
Carlos P Garcia Ave (known by locals as CPG; CP Garcia) is the main drag, but the M Clara St wharf is just as much a hive of activity in this busy port city.

There is a well-staffed **City Tourism & Information & Assistance Centre** (☎ 235 5497, 411 4559; W www.tagbilaran.gov.ph; cnr CP Garcia Ave & H Grupo St; open 8am-noon & 1pm-5pm Mon-Fri), on the southwest corner of Agora Market, which can assist with accommodation and transport inquiries and bookings.

The **main post office** (JS Torralba St) is opposite the city hall and **police station** (☎ 166).

There's a **PT&T office** (CP Garcia Ave) and an office of **Philippine Long Distance Telephone** (PLDT; Noli Me Tangere St) nearby.

Email & Internet Access Internet cafés have sprouted like cyber-mushrooms in Tagbilaran, particularly around Holy Name University (still known by many as Divine Word

College) on C Gallares St. **Slash Cybercafé** (☎ 411 3251; *Legase St; P10 per hr; open 8am-midnight daily*) must qualify as one of the world's cheapest Internet cafés, and also one of the noisiest due to the crowd of players on commando games.

If you can't stand the gunfire and testosterone, all other Internet cafés charge P20 per hour. Try **SynCom Internet** (*Lesage St; open 8am-10pm daily*), up the road, for a more studious atmosphere with good air-con, or any of the others on this strip. The **Internet Cathedral** (*MH del Pilar St; open 9am-midnight*) is also quite good.

Millennium Internet Cafe (☎ 4114024; *CP Garcia Ave; open 24hrs*) provides for all computing and desktop publishing needs. If the music is too loud there, try the squishy **Unix Internet Cafe** (*R Palma St; open 9am-late Mon-Sat*).

Medical Services Medical treatment is available at **Governor Celestino Gallares Memorial Hospital** (☎ 411 3324; *Miguel Parras St*) and at **Ramiro Community Hospital** (☎ 411 3515; *63 C Gallares St*).

Things to See & Do

In the heart of town, have a look at the huge **St Joseph the Worker Cathedral**, also known more simply as Tagbilaran Cathedral. It was built in 1767, and in 1798, Joseph must have had his back turned one day, as the cathedral burnt to the ground. It was rebuilt and enlarged in 1855. In the Bishop's Palace at the back of the Cathedral, you'll find the office for the **I love the ocean movement** (ask for Bondix), a local marine conservation group that runs eco-activities, and also **blind masseurs** who give great massages for a mere P50 for 30 minutes.

Special Events

Tagbilaran is the headquarters of the giant Bohol Fiesta, celebrating St Joseph, which runs throughout May every year. The town's own fiesta kicks off the proceedings on 1 May, with lead-ups from April 22nd.

In the first week of July, the Sandugo Festival celebrates the March 1565 blood compact (see Bool under Around Tagbilaran later). It is followed by a string of other festivals (such as an arts and culture festival and an agricultural fair) that have turned the whole of July into party month. For more information on Tagbilaran's festivals, visit the tourist office (see Orientation & Information earlier) or the Bohol government website (w www.bohol.gov.ph).

Places to Stay

Nisa Travellers Inn (☎ 411 3731; *CP Garcia Ave; singles/twins with fan & shared bathroom P140/160, with air-con & cold-water bathroom P500*) is the city's backpacker haven. Despite the closed-down look of the entrance (make a U-turn left up the stairs), it's a friendly, spacious and clean place with a lovely timber balcony area and restaurant. The P500 rooms facing away from the street are some of the only quiet rooms in town.

Charisma Lodge (☎ 411 3094; *CP Garcia Ave; single/twin with fan & shared bathroom P115/225, with cold-water bathroom P280, double with air-con & bathroom P490*), directly opposite Nisa Travellers Inn, isn't exactly charismatic, but it does have passable rooms if Nisa Travellers Inn is full.

Casa Juana (☎ 411 3331; *CP Garcia Ave; singles P180-300, doubles P375, family room P525*) is pretty cheap, dirty and dank, but it does have polished floorboards throughout, room service and a central location.

Windward Pension House (☎ 411 3599; *C Gallares St; singles P200-400, doubles P500*) offers a little sea breeze in its harbourside rooms, but you'll still be struggling with the street noise. Rooms are large and reasonably clean, with air-con and cold-water bathroom; the double has cable TV. The off-street rooms with fan are a good deal for singles.

Everglory Hotel (☎ 411 4969; *singles with fan & cold-water bathroom P350, doubles with fan/air-con P400/550*) is an optimistically named place, under the neon Timex sign as you walk up from the main wharf. If you can get a room looking out over the wharf (and you have a good set of earplugs), this is an excellent place to watch the world go by – if not, you're best off elsewhere. The 4th-floor restaurant has magnificent views.

Gie Gardens Hotel (☎ 411 3025; *MH del Pilar St; singles/doubles P490/590*), just off CP Garcia Ave, is a large hotel with stained carpets and old, wooden furniture. The rooms are cosy, comfortable and clean and have air-con and cold-water bathroom. Cable TV is P75 extra.

Chriscent Ville Pension House (☎ 411 4029/3070, fax 411 4028; *C Gallares St; singles/*

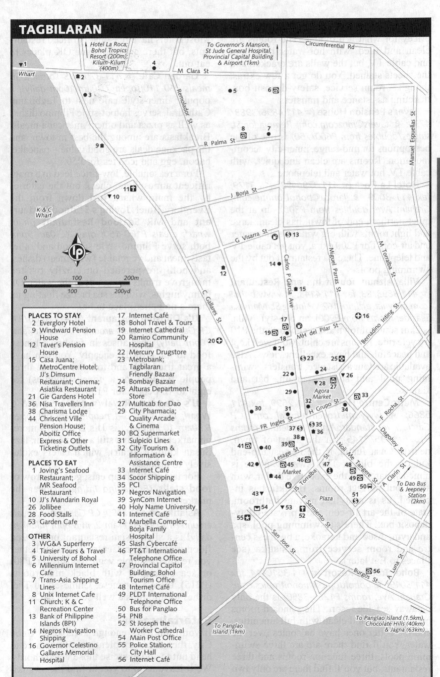

TAGBILARAN

THE VISAYAS

PLACES TO STAY
2 Everglory Hotel
9 Windward Pension House
12 Taver's Pension House
15 Casa Juana; MetroCentre Hotel; JJ's Dimsum Restaurant; Cinema; Asiatika Restaurant
21 Gie Gardens Hotel
36 Nisa Travellers Inn
38 Charisma Lodge
44 Chriscent Ville Pension House; Aboitiz Office Express & Other Ticketing Outlets

PLACES TO EAT
1 Joving's Seafood Restaurant; MR Seafood Restaurant
10 JJ's Mandarin Royal
26 Jollibee
28 Food Stalls
53 Garden Cafe

OTHER
3 WG&A Superferry
4 Tarsier Tours & Travel
5 University of Bohol
6 Millennium Internet Cafe
7 Trans-Asia Shipping Lines
8 Unix Internet Cafe
11 Church; K & C Recreation Center
13 Bank of Philippine Islands (BPI)
14 Negros Navigation Shipping
16 Governor Celestino Gallares Memorial Hospital

17 Internet Café
18 Bohol Travel & Tours
19 Internet Cathedral
20 Ramiro Community Hospital
22 Mercury Drugstore
23 Metrobank; Tagbilaran Friendly Bazaar
24 Bombay Bazaar
25 Alturas Department Store
27 Multicab for Dao
29 City Pharmacia; Quality Arcade & Cinema
30 BQ Supermarket
31 Sulpicio Lines
32 City Tourism & Information & Assistance Centre
33 Internet Café
34 Socor Shipping
35 PCI
37 Negros Navigation
39 SynCom Internet
40 Holy Name University
41 Internet Café
42 Marbella Complex; Borja Family Hospital
45 Slash Cybercafé
46 PT&T International Telephone Office
47 Provincial Capitol Building; Bohol Tourism Office
48 Internet Café
49 PLDT International Telephone Office
50 Bus for Panglao
54 PNB
52 St Joseph the Worker Cathedral
54 Main Post Office
55 Police Station; City Hall
56 Internet Café

twins from P650/750, doubles P1200) is a bit pricey for what it provides. The rooms are clean and tiled, with hot-water bathroom and cable TV, but the walls are cracked and the sheets stained. You do get a few extras, though – room service, safety-deposit box, ticketing assistance and transfers.

Taver's Pension House (☎ 411 4896/3983/ 4790; e tavers@mozcom.com; Remolador St; singles/doubles from P600/750) is one of the best options for mid-range, inner-city accommodation. Rooms are clean and quiet, with cable TV, hot water and telephone.

Hotel La Roca (☎ 411 3796–98, 411 3179, fax 411 3009; e laroca@bohol-online.com; Graham Ave; doubles from P800), up at the quiet northern end of town, has clean, large and light rooms with big windows, hot water and air-con. For P200 extra, you get cable TV and telephone. There's a restaurant out by the swimming pool.

Villa Alzhun Tourist Inn and Restaurant (☎ 411 3893/83, fax 411 4143; W www.bohol .com.ph/villa_alzhun; 162 VP Inting St, Mansasa Seaside; rooms from P900), an old-style villa, is 2km south of town and well worth the P10 tricycle ride. Rooms are chintzy but well kept and peaceful, and have excellent views. Also available are tour assistance, transfers, swimming pool and spa, restaurant, bar and karaoke.

MetroCentre Hotel (☎ 411 2599, fax 411 5866; W www.metrocentrehotel.com; CP Garcia Ave; standard/superior/deluxe rooms P1375/1595/2145), in the heart of town, next to Casa Juana, is the newest top-end kid on the block. This swanky place is aimed squarely at the executive dollar, with small but perfect rooms. Breakfast is included, as is a stylish private bathroom, state-of-the-art air-con, and a private safety-deposit box. There's a swimming pool, spa and gym, disco and karaoke, a business centre and room service from Asiatika (see Places to Eat later).

Bohol Tropics Resort (☎ 411 3510–14, fax 411 3019; e boholtropics@boholtropics.com; Graham Ave; rooms P1265-3850) is the only getaway seaside resort. The standard rooms here are large and clean with full amenities, and the better ones have balconies over the water. You'll find there are are three swimming pools, three function rooms and three restaurants, but you'll find there are only two dive shops.

Places to Eat

Most hotels have reasonably priced restaurants, but there are also some OK places to eat out.

Garden Cafe (☎ 411 3756; JS Torralba St; meals P60-110; open 7.30am-10pm daily), a popular diner-style café next to Tagbilaran Cathedral, serves hotpot-style Filipino dishes as well as pizza and other Americana meals. Breakfasts are among the best in town, and the package deals are good value – pancake, bacon, egg and iced tea for P50.

For a reasonable, low-price feed in a magnificent atmosphere, check out the eateries by the main wharf, just down from the Everglory Hotel. **Joving's Seafood Restaurant** and **MR Seafood Restaurant** (main wharf; meals P100-150; open 6.30am-9pm) both serve Filipino-style seafood and other tasty meat and vegetable (with meat) dishes, and both are perched on crazily twisted mangrove trunks rising out of the water. On balmy nights, with the sea breeze floating in, there's no better place to be.

JJ's Dimsum Restaurant (☎ 411 3306/31; CP Garcia Ave; meals around P50; open 7am-10pm daily) specialises in feeding Chinese food to the crowds, cheaply. You can have a great fried fish and tofu for two to three people for P90, or a pansit (noodles) for eight to 10 people for P130.

JJ's Mandarin Royal (☎ 411 3756; K & C Wharf; meals for 3-4 people P65-290; open 6.30am-10pm daily) is JJ's Dimsum's more-upmarket sibling (but still a plastic-chair, lazy Susan kind of affair), which caters exclusively to groups.

For late night cheap eats, go to the row of **food stalls** (Bernadino Inting St) near the market.

Asiatika (☎ 411 2599; CP Garcia Ave; meals around P150; open 11am-2pm & 6pm-midnight daily) is a slick Asian restaurant on the 2nd floor of the MetroCentre Hotel. Whether you're after a simple vegie teppanyaki (P80) or sea cucumber with black mushrooms (P215), there's Japanese, Chinese and Thai dishes to suit, plus a well-stocked bar.

Entertainment

If you didn't get enough karaoke in Cebu City, then there are plenty of places here to head out to and exercise those vocal chords. We'll leave it up to you to find the swankiest place with the best songlist, as they seem to change name and management as quickly as you can sing 'you've lost that lo-oving fe-eling...'

For live music, **Kilum-Kilum**, about 200m past Bohol Tropics on the left, has bands most evenings.

Getting There & Away
Most airline and ferry ticketing can be done at the **Aboitiz Express** (C Gallares St) and neighbouring ticketing offices near Chriscent Ville Pension House.

Air The **Asian Spirit** (☎ 411 5701/5503; Tagbilaran airport) flies back and forth from Manila (P2430, 2½ hours) every morning. You can also make bookings at **Tarsier Tours and Travel** (☎ 411 3615, 235 3541; Ma Clara St).

A subsidiary of PAL, **Laoag International Airlines** (☎ 411 2480; Tagbilaran airport) has return flights from Manila (P2440, two hours) daily. Students get 20% discount.

Asian Spirit has a daily flight to and from Cebu City (20 minutes).

Boat When you arrive at Tagbilaran pier, you will be received by an onslaught of taxi and jeepney drivers sent by the various hotels who will quote you 'set prices' for trips around town.

If you don't like what you hear, it's a short walk up the wharf to where you can take a tricycle to anywhere within the inner-city limits for P4.

There is a P11 terminal fee for departing Tagbilaran.

In Tagbilaran, there are ticketing offices for: **Cebu Ferries** and **WG&A** (☎ 411 3048/3651; C Gallares St); **Cokaliong Shipping** (main wharf); **Socor Shipping** (☎ 235 3562; main wharf); **Palacio Shipping** (☎ 411 3402; main wharf); **Lite Shipping** (☎ 411 4724/2874; 50 Soledad St); **Trans-Asia Shipping** (☎ 411 3234; R Palma St); **Negros Navigation** (☎ 411 5717; Digal Bldg, CP Garcia Ave) and **Sulpicio Shipping** (☎ 411 3079; H Grupo St). There are two offices of the super-efficient **SuperCat** (☎ 235 4008; main wharf • ☎ 235 4291; Dao bus station).

Cebu For boats servicing the route between Tagbilaran and Cebu City, see the 'Cebu Ferries' table in Cebu City's Getting There & Away section, earlier.

Luzon Negros Navigation sails from Tagbilaran to Manila (P1285, 27 hours) twice a week as does WG&A (P1185, 30 hours).

Mindanao The most popular route to Mindanao is covered daily by SuperCat, which has a boat every morning from Tagbilaran to Dapitan (P660, three hours) via Dumaguete on Negros, returning in the afternoon.

WG&A has a boat to and from Cagayan de Oro (P290, eight hours) once a week; and to and from Dipolog (P270, six hours) once a week.

Trans-Asia also has a boat to and from Cagayan de Oro (P238, nine hours) three times a week; Cebu Ferries services the same route (P290, eight hours) once a week.

Sulpicio has a boat from Tagbilaran to Dipolog (P182, three hours) and Iligan (P245, 15 hours) once a week.

Negros SuperCat leaves for Dumaguete (P400, 1½ hours) and back twice daily. WG&A sails to Dumaguete (P200, three hours) and back once a week.

Siquijor Palacio Shipping has a boat to Larena (P85, three hours) and back, three nights a week. SuperCat has a boat each evening to Larena (P525, 1¾ hours) via Dumaguete. It returns in the morning.

Bus Tagbilaran's new road-transport hub for buses and jeepneys is the **Dao** (dah-oh) **Integrated Bus Terminal** (☎ 235 4377; E Butalid St), at the end of C Marapao St, a P25 tricycle ride, or P40 taxi northeast of town. You can also take the multicab (small jeepney) from the northeast corner of the Agora Market (opposite Jollibee) for P4.

Daily buses leave from the station for destinations including Loboc (P14, 24km), Loon (P16, 27km), Tubigon (P31, 53km), Jagna (P37, 63km), Carmen (P53, 92km), Talibon (P66, 114km) and Ubay (P71, 123km). For Panglao Island, buses cost P2.50 to Dauis (4km) and P11 to Panglao town (18km). To avoid trekking out to Dao, the Panglao bus can be hailed down from A Clarin St (on the corner of Noli Me Tangere St, behind the PNB). Buses travelling further than 40km start their service at 3am and leave almost hourly until 5pm. Local buses start at 5am and travel approximately every 20 minutes until around 6pm.

THE VISAYAS

Buses are often overcrowded so it's wise to arrive at the terminal at least 10 minutes prior to departure, and carry as little luggage as possible.

Students receive up to 20% discount for jeepneys and buses.

Car Hotels in Tagbilaran can organise hire cars with drivers, particularly for trips to the Chocolate Hills (see Getting There & Away under Chocolate Hills later). A day-long island tour (from 6am to 6pm) skirting the entire coastline, and allowing for many small stopovers, will cost around P2000 for a car and driver – more for a van. Half a day will cost P1500. Call **NF Rent-a-Car** (☎ *411 4568, 501 7588, 0917 372 4116)* or **Lugod Rent-a-Car** (☎ *411 2244, 235 3326, 501 8907).*

Getting Around

The airport is a short tricycle ride north of town (P10).

Tricycles are the main public transport around Tagbilaran, and have a fixed-price for any short trip within the inner-city area (P4). Although buses and jeepneys will take you to most just-out-of-town destinations, taxis are a good, time-saving alternative. Many of the city's surrounding attractions are a short drive away on good roads, and most taxis go by their meters (within 30km of Tagbiliran). You can either pick a taxi off the street or call **Varescon** (☎ *411 2507, 235 5638).*

You can get from Tagbilaran to all the surrounding towns by jeepney (P4 to P30) – most jeepneys have a price list taped to the inside roof. For bus information, see that entry under Getting There & Away, earlier.

AROUND TAGBILARAN
Loon & Cabilao Island

The **church** at Loon (low-on) was built in 1855 and features what is claimed to be the country's longest stone staircase, at 154 steps. The stairs lead you from the church to Napo, the town's former administrative centre. The town holds its annual fiesta in early September.

Like Balicasag and Pamilacan Islands (see those sections later) to the south, the island of Cabilao in the waters off Loon is a startlingly rich **dive site**, with two community-run marine sanctuaries (diving fee P50). Cabilao's waters are home to seven species of shark and are full of micro-life. One of these miniature critters has become particularly famous in recent years, adorning the pages of many a diving magazine – the pygmy seahorse (*Hippocampus bargibanti*) – an 8mm-long seahorse that is almost perfectly camouflaged among the surrounding red gorgonian coral.

The celebrity seahorse can be found on the house reef (however, it takes a well-trained set of eyes to find one), but there is diving, for beginners to advanced, all around the island. The island's top reef is off the northwestern point, near the lighthouse.

Sea Explorers (☎ *0917 454 5897;* W *www .sea-explorers.com,* W *www.cabilao.com)* has one of its six Visayan dive centres on Cabilao. If you dive with these guys, ask to be led by Bobet – one of the most well-respected dive guides in the Visayas. He discovered the pygmy seahorse around the island and can almost guarantee you a sighting. For real budget travellers, Sea Explorers also offers pretty run-down **cottages and rooms** (*doubles with fan & cold-water bathroom from P250).*

Polaris Resort (☎ *0918 903 7187;* e *info@ polaris-dive.com; rooms with cold-water bathroom & fan P600-800, with air-con P1200)* is a better accommodation option. It offers diving (*US$20 per dive, open-water diving certificate US$290),* boat trips, good European, Asian and vegetarian meals (P80 to P130) and a boat-shaped 'sundowner' cocktail bar.

La Estrella (☎ *0912 502 0286;* W *www .laestrella.de; 2-person/4-person nipa hut from P625/1200)* has clean, comfortable huts with fan, cold-water bathroom and veranda. For P200 extra, doubles get a beach view.

Cabilao Beach Club (☎ *0917 454 5897;* W *www.cabilao.com; doubles with hot-water bathroom, fan & sea view P1200)* should hopefully be up and running by the time you read this. A slightly more upmarket resort on the northeastern tip of the island, this place is run by the Sea Explorers mob and will open up some relatively unchartered diving territory.

Getting There & Away Loon is 27km from Tagbilaran (P16 by bus or jeepney). To get to Cabilao Island, you must head several kilometres north and coastward of town (a good 20 minutes on a bumpy road) to Mocpoc. You can get there from Loon by bus or jeepney (P8) or motorbike (P40). From Mocpoc, it's a 15-minute pumpboat ride (P10 – but you'll have to wait until the boat is full or else pay for the empty seats) to the closest port (Talisig) on Calibao. A tricycle or motorbike will cost P15 to the resorts. A boat from Mocpoc directly to the resorts will cost P200. From either Panglao or Mactan Islands, it can take two to three hours.

For boats to Loon and Cabilao Island from Cebu Island, see Getting There & Away under Argao, Cebu Island.

Antequera

Antequera (ahn-**tee**-care-a) is about 20km from Tagbilaran (P11 by bus or jeepney). The town has its annual fiesta in early October, but comes alive every Sunday, when **basket weavers** from nearby hills bring their beautiful woven creations to market. If you want to pick up one of Bohol's best handicraft items, you should aim to get to Antequera by 7am or 8am to avoid the rush.

Just out of Antequera are **Mag-aso** and **Inambacan Falls**, as well as some of Bohol's best **caves**. Cave guides can be tracked down in Antequera itself, or in Tagbilaran.

Corella & Tarsier Visitors Centre

Corella (cor-**ell**-i-a) is an attractive, jungle-fringed town with a big garden of a central square. There's nothing in particular to see, but it's a good place to get lost. Fiesta fever hits Corella on the fourth Saturday of April.

The town is about 10km from Tagbilaran and jeepneys and buses head back and forth all day (P6, 20 minutes).

Beyond the town of Corella, near the village of Sikatuna, in a baryo known as Canapnapan, is the Tarsier Visitors Centre (☎ 0912 516 3375, 0919 874 1120; requested donation P20; open 8am to 4pm daily) where you can visit the tarsier, the world's smallest primate (see the boxed text 'Primatus stevenspeilbergias' later).

The centre, run by the Philippine Tarsier Foundation and dedicated to the conservation and research of the Philippine tarsier, includes information boards and audiovisual displays, a captive breeding programme, a wildlife sanctuary and a 12.5km hiking trail that takes you all the way to Loboc. The breeding areas are off-limits, but a small patch of forest beside the centre allows for guided walks and discreet ogling of several mature tarsiers. This is a much more sustainable and humane way to appreciate the tarsier than to pet the caged

animals run by tourist-orientated operations in nearby Loboc.

To get here from Tagbilaran, a taxi will cost around P200 for a return trip (20 minutes one way). You can catch a bus or jeepney to Corrella or Sikatuna (P6 to P10, 30 minutes), but tricycles from there to the centre can be scarce. You can also hike in from Loboc along the aforementioned trail.

Bool

At Bool (bo-**oll**), about 3km east of Tagbilaran, you'll find a monument to a blood-compact mateship ritual known as *sanduguan* (literally, 'one blood'). This is where, on 16 March 1565, Spanish conquistador Miguel Lopez de Legazpi and Boholano chieftain Rajah Sikatuna downed a cup of each other's blood in one of the first symbolic gestures of Western-Eastern accord in the Philippines.

Baclayon

About 6km from Tagbilaran (P4 by jeepney or bus), Baclayon was founded by a pair of Spanish Jesuit priests in 1595. **Baclayon Church**, one of the country's oldest, was built a year later. Baclayon is also where they make the delicious, little, macaroon-like biscuits called *polboron*. The town's fiesta is in early December, and boats go from here to nearby Pamilacan Island (see that entry later in this section) for P30. Pamilican Island Dolphin and Whale Watching Organisation can pick you up for their tours from here (see Pamilican Island later for details).

Alburquerque

This small coastal town is not the Alburquerque made famous by Bugs Bunny. It is well known however, for its magnificent **church** and belfry, built in 1886. There are also several **waterfalls** on the edge of town. Fiesta time is early May. Alburquerque is about 12km from Tagbilaran (P10 by jeepney or bus).

Loboc

The mighty Loboc River flows past the town of the same name, creating a thundering torrent for the popular **Tontonan Falls** (a river cruise to the falls costs P400) and the Visayas' oldest hydroelectric plant. Along the banks of the Loboc, you'll be invited to visit illegally run tarsier cages. You'll be

Primatus stevenspeilbergias

If you're wondering where Steven Spielberg got the inspiration for ET and many other of his freaka-zoid alien creatures, look no further than the Philippine tarsier (*Tarsius syrichta*). This crazy little primate can fit in your palm yet leap five metres; rotate it's head almost 360 degrees; move its ears in the direction of sound; and it has huge imploring eyes 150-times bigger than a humans, in relation to body size. If you needed more reasons to fall in love with this creature, try this – the tarsier is not only one of the world's smallest and cutest primates and the oldest surviving member of the primate group (a mere 45 million years old) – it is also an endangered species. The main threats to its survival are habitat destruction, introduced species, hunting and the pet trade. The Philippine tarsier is found in Bohol, Samar, Leyte and parts of Mindanao, but the province which is doing the most to promote awareness of the tarsier, attempting to ensure its survival – and also the most likely place visitors are going to see one of these guys – is in Bohol. If you would like to know more about the tarsier, visit the **Tarsier Visitors Centre** (see Corella & Tarsier Visitors Centre) for information and a peek at a tarsier in the wild, or by visiting W www.bohol.net/PTFI. Donations can be made at the centre, and larger donations can be made by contacting Mr Danny C Nazareno at the centre (e *tar sier@mozcom.com; Philippine Tarsier Foundation, Km 14, 6337 Canapnapan, Corella, Bohol)* or Fr Florante S Camacho, SVP, President of the **Philippine Tarsier Foundation** *(c/o Holy Name University, 6300 Tagbilaran City, Bohol)*.

Sonia Orchard

doing the entire species a favour if you reserve your tarsier viewing for the Tarsier Visitors Centre (see that entry earlier).

The town of Loboc is also home to the huge, 18th-century **San Pedro Church**. In late May to June, Loboc hosts the **Balibong Kingking Festival**, which honours Our Lady of Guadalupe.

Throughout the Philippines you'll hear travellers talking about **Nuts Huts** (W *www.groove-events.be/nutshuts/index.htm; dorm bed P165, nipa huts from P385)*, a jungle retreat perched among the greenery over the Loboc River, 3km north of Loboc. The friendly, Belgian-Chinese Nuts Huts team have created a wonderful, homely environment, with comfortable, private accommodation, excellent travel advice and great food – lots of vegetarian and Euro-Asian delights (meals P40 to P130) plus rarities such as brewed coffee and homemade bread and yogurt. Whether you're the active or contemplative traveller, you'll need at least a couple of days here – if you stay four nights, the last night is free. Make use of guided and/or mapped hikes, mountain bikes, volleyball, motorbike hire (P500 per day), river cruises, or simply the serenity of the surroundings. It's a perfect base to check out the Chocolate Hills, Tarsier Visitors Centre and Rajah Sikatuna National Park.

If you're coming by bus, jeepney or tricycle, ask to be let off at Nuts Huts (there's a big sign on the left of the main road), just after Loboc on the way to Carmen. From there, it's a 10-minute walk (you'll need a torch after dark). You can also catch a pumpboat up the Loboc River (P50 for two) from Sarimanok (a pumpboat company) to the resort.

Loboc is about 24km from Tagbilaran (P14 by jeepney or bus, about P300 by taxi). A motorbike can take you from Tagbilaran pier for around P400 to P500.

Bilar & Rajah Sikatuna National Park

About 40km east of Tagbilaran (P18 by bus), Bilar is popular for its public swimming hole, known as **Logarita Spring** *(P5; open Sat-Thur)* which is fed by three mountain springs and overlooks rice fields. Bilar's annual fiesta is held in mid-May. It's a P18 bus ride from Tagbilaran.

About 500m past the Bilar Town Hall on the right-hand side is the turn-off for Logarita Spring and Rajah Sikatuna National Park *(RSNP; non-Filipino admission fee P100)*, an immense 9000 hectares of **native molave forest** and grasslands. The park includes over 30km of poorly marked **trails**, over a hundred **caves**, a **camping area** *(per person P20)* at the nature centre, and basic **rooms** *(per person P50)* at the administration building near

Logarita Springs. The park is regularly frequented by naturalists from around the globe for its endangered and endemic species, especially bird-watchers who consider it one of the best twitching grounds in Asia. Mammals and reptiles that also call RSNP home are the Philippine tarsier, flying lemur, civet cat, monitor lizard and the Philippine monkey. However, for lack of funds the park is not managed or marketed as it deserves. It is definitely worth a visit though, and if you request a guide, ask at the Bilar College. The crew at nearby Nuts Huts (see Loboc earlier) may also suggest other walks.

Kitchen facilities are available at the administration building but not at the camping area. Visitors need to bring their own food, but there is plenty of fresh water available.

PANGLAO ISLAND

Two bridges connect Bohol to Panglao, an overnight success for diving-oriented beach resorts. From a virtually deserted beach in the early 1980s, Alona Beach has become a thriving tourism community just managing to keep commercialism at bay. But if you don't like diving, backpackery beach-bars and lazy, white beaches, Panglao may not be the place for you.

A good way to get around on Panglao is by motorbike – either get yourself a driver or rent one off the street for around P500 per day. Pumpboats can be rented off the shores to take you to nearby islands for around P1500 for half a day of island-hopping or dolphin- and whale-stalking.

Fiesta time in Panglao town is in late August. In Dauis, it's in mid-August.

Warning: diving is not only addictive, it is also expensive, and many of the Panglao dive centres accept cash only. You can change travellers cheques (with a 1% surcharge) at the tourist office just near Alona Kew, but if you want a cash advance on your credit card, you'll be charged a whopping 7% fee. Many of the resorts also affix this exorbitant credit card surcharge, so it's a good idea to cash up in Tagbilaran before arrival.

The **Bohol Island Cybernet Café** (P50 per hr) is the best emailing location, on the road up from Alona Kew.

Things to See & Do

The refreshingly cold waters of **Hinagdanan Cave** (admission P10), at Bingag, on the island's northern coast, with its mixture of fresh and salt water, is definitely worth a visit for its stalactite and stalagmite formations. **Diving** is the most popular tourist pursuit on Panglao. Apart from revelling in underwater paradises just south of Alona Beach (see Balicasag Island and Pamilacan Island later), divers also use Panglao as a base from which to reach Cabilao (see Loon & Cabilao Island earlier) to the north. You can probably score the best deal by combining accommodation with diving. The average prices are: one dive US$18, equipment rental US$5, open-water diving certificate US$300, snorkel-equipment hire US$6.

Places to Stay & Eat – Alona Beach

There's no shortage of resorts along Alona Beach. All either have dive centres or are closely affiliated to one, and usually also have restaurants and bars. The resorts are so closely packed together, shopping around for food or diving deals is no problem. Unless otherwise mentioned, all rooms have fan and cold-water bathroom.

Alonaville Beach Resort (☎ 411 3254; doubles with shared bathroom P200, nipa huts P500) is one of the good, budget deals. Rooms are small and run-down and the bar-scene might keep you awake, but you won't find much any cheaper or closer to the action.

Alona Pyramid Resort (☎ 502 9058, fax 502 9090; nipa huts P350) has two-storey huts with two double beds. It's affiliated with **Atlantis Dive Centre** and the popular Safety Stop Bar.

Peter's House (☎/fax 502 9056, 0918 770 8434; W www.genesisdivers.com; doubles for divers/nondivers P300/400) is aimed almost exclusively at the young budget diving crowd. Doubles with shared bathroom and great views are in a large nipa complex with a popular divers hang-out on the beach. Affiliated with **Genesis Divers**.

Alonaland (☎ 502 9007, 0917 304 0211, fax 502 9007; nipa huts & cottages P350-800) is a better budget option for those who can cope with a 50m walk to the beach (through Alona Tropical). Accommodation ranges from basic nipa hut to cottage with air-con and kitchen facilities.

Tierra Zul (☎ 502 9065, ☎/fax 500 0694; twin rooms with fan/air-con P600/1000) has large, clean, mid-range rooms on the western

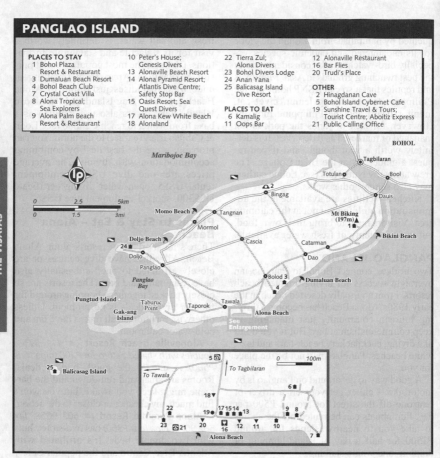

PANGLAO ISLAND

PLACES TO STAY
1 Bohol Plaza
    Resort & Restaurant
3 Dumaluan Beach Resort
4 Bohol Beach Club
7 Crystal Coast Villa
8 Alona Tropical;
    Sea Explorers
9 Alona Palm Beach
    Resort & Restaurant
10 Peter's House;
    Genesis Divers
13 Alonaville Beach Resort
14 Alona Pyramid Resort;
    Atlantis Dive Centre;
    Safety Stop Bar
15 Oasis Resort; Sea
    Quest Divers
17 Alona Kew White Beach
18 Alonaland

22 Tierra Zul;
    Alona Divers
23 Bohol Divers Lodge
24 Anan Yana
25 Balicasag Island
    Dive Resort

PLACES TO EAT
6 Kamalig
11 Oops Bar

12 Alonaville Restaurant
16 Bar Flies
20 Trudi's Place

OTHER
2 Hinagdanan Cave
5 Bohol Island Cybernet Cafe
19 Sunshine Travel & Tours;
    Tourist Centre; Aboitiz Express
21 Public Calling Office

THE VISAYAS

end of the beach, away from the bar scene. The restaurant, unfortunately, doesn't serve evening meals, but has a lovely view and the home-style management is very friendly. Attached is **Alona Divers** (☎ 502 9043; W www .nautilus-diving.com).

Alona Tropical (☎ 411 4517/2244, fax 235 3326; nipa huts with twins P800, double rooms with fan/air-con P1480/1800), at the quieter eastern end of the beach, is a good choice if you want something a cut above budget accommodation. It also has a deservedly popular restaurant. It's affiliated with **Sea Explorers** (W www.sea-explorers.com).

Alona Kew White Beach (☎ 502 9042/27, fax 502 9029; W www.bohol-info.com/alon akew.html; standard nipa huts P850-1000, with air-con & hot water P1900-2200) has

small nipa huts off the beach among some greenery.

Bohol Divers Resort (☎/fax 411 4983; e boholdiv@bohol-online.com; rooms with fan/air-con from US$12/40) is a quiet and popular diving resort. A restaurant with a good view, a swimming pool, safety deposit boxes and transfers are a part of the package.

Crystal Coast Villa (☎ 411 3796-98, 411 3179, fax 411 3009; 1-/2-/4-person villas from P980/1200/2400), on the attractive, raised point at the eastern end of Alona Beach, has units with great views and air-con. There's a swimming pool and a restaurant, which share the view.

Oasis Resort (☎ 502 9083, 346 9626, fax 3460592; singles/doubles from P1000/1200) has good shaded nipa huts, back from the

From Dynamite to Diving Fees

The illegal dynamite blasting of reefs is one of the biggest environmental problems in the Philippines. In Bohol – a province with over 640km of coast, and one of the top-10 fish-producing provinces in the Philippines – the consequences have been devastating. Over 20% of Bohol's working population are involved in the fishing industry, and seafood makes up over 50% of the Boholano diet. However, with the introduction of dynamite and other destructive fishing practices, the increase in pollution, and past bad coastal management, municipal fish catches in some communities are less than 10% what they were 30 years ago.

Dynamite fishing was inspired by the discovery of grenades, left by the Japanese after WWII. Today, Talisay City in Cebu is the capital of the booming dynamite industry, making caps out of soda bottles and fertilisers, and creating an economic and social crisis throughout many provinces.

However, in Bohol, the provincial government and NGOs are determined to reverse the situation, setting up community-based marine sanctuaries, mangrove reforestation projects and coastal law-enforcement councils. In order to support means of livelihood other than dynamite fishing, tourists are encouraged to patronise these community-based projects and not baulk at paying marine sanctuary diving and snorkelling fees. These fees help compensate the fisherfolk for loss of work, and encourage sustainable use of the reefs.

In communities where sanctuary infrastructure is not yet up and running, tourists can contact the village head (or head of the fisherfolks' organisation) and request permission to snorkel or dive, giving a donation (suggested P50) if permission is granted.

Sonia Orchard

beach around a pool. For P500 extra you get air-con and a rare commodity – hot water. It's connected to **Seaquest Divers**.

Alona Palm Beach Resort & Restaurant (☎ 502 9141, fax 502 9142; ⓦ www.alonapalmbeach.com; singles/doubles from US$87/92) is the new luxury resort on the strip. Hi-tech rooms are spacious with large screen satellite TV, dataport telephone, minibar, space-age bathroom and veranda. If the sea's not for you, there's a swimming pool. The restaurant has a rich Euro menu (mains P200 to P350).

Trudi's Place (2-course meal P110; open for all meals) is a lovely, open bar-restaurant where you can dine on the beach and enjoy very good cheap food.

Kamalig (meals P150-200; open 4pm-midnight Mon-Sat) is on the road that runs up between Alona Kew and Sunshine Travel. People come here for good Italian food.

Places to Stay & Eat – alternatives to Alona Beach

Dumaluan Beach Resort (☎ 502 9081/92; Bolod; huts from P595, rooms with hot water & air-con from P1500) is a good option if you want to avoid the hype of Alona without paying big bucks. A large range of accommodation meets the needs of most visitors, and

swimming pool, spa, diving and a good restaurant are available to all. Its only neighbour is Bohol Beach Club.

Bohol Beach Club (☎ 411 5222–24, 1800 1888 2227, fax 411 5226; ⓦ www.tambuli .com; Bolod; singles/twins from US$60/65) is one of the upmarket options, but with its floral curtains, plastic chairs and pebble-mix verandas, it feels a bit dated. However, it has all the resort extras you'd expect (water sports, transfers, swimming pool etc) and regulars seem to love it. Pick-up from Tagbilaran can be arranged through the resort for US$8 per person.

At remote Doljo Beach, **Anan Yana** (☎/fax 502 8101; ⓦ www.ananyana.com; rooms US$60) has stylish Filipino rooms on 3km of white, sandy beach. Tasteful, Asian-minimalist decor and architecture, a serene setting and no phone or TV make this the best romantic getaway. Swimming pool, diving and a good, Italian-influenced restaurant add to the luxury. Pick-up from Tagbilaran can be arranged through the resort for US$10 per person.

Bohol Plaza Resort & Restaurant (☎ 500 0882/1019, fax 500 0970; ⓦ www.bohol-island.com; Dayo Hill, Dauis; rooms from P1100) offers an option that most visitors haven't considered – to avoid the beach completely and be 200m up a mountain. Rooms are tiled, spacious, with hot-water bathroom, telephone and air-con. All rooms have great views and the price increases with altitude. There is a swimming pool, spa and mountaintop restaurant, and there are city shuttles available. You may be able to talk them into a cheaper deal if you are travelling with SuperCat. Even if you're not staying here, wander up for a sunset cocktail and watch the Tagbilaran lights come on across the water – the P25 admission is 'consumable'.

Entertainment

For those after nightlife, walk along Alona Beach around **Oops Bar**, **Safety Stop Bar**, **Alonaville Restaurant** and **Bar Flies**. It won't take long to work out where the action is.

Getting There & Away

There's an **Aboitiz Express** and **SuperCat** booking office next to the Alona Kew White Beach resort. Next door, **Sunshine Travel and Tours** can help with bookings. For buses from Tagbilaran, see that Getting There & Away section, earlier. The simplest way to reach Alona is to hire a tricycle from anywhere in Tagbilaran (P150, 30 to 45 minutes). Taxis from Taglibaran are around P250 to P300. Transport to resorts not on Alona Beach will command slightly higher fares. There are often jeeps or minibuses hanging around after dropping off passengers in Alona. You can usually commandeer one of these for around P200 for a quick trip back to Tagbilaran.

BALICASAG ISLAND

About 6km southwest of Panglao, Balicasag is a magnificent **diving** spot. Low and flat, the island is ringed by a reef that drops away to impressive **submarine cliffs** as deep as 50m. Soft and hard corals can be found around the cliffs, as can trevally, barracuda, wrasse and the occasional white-tip shark.

The pristine reef here has been declared a marine sanctuary.

Balicasag Island Dive Resort (☎ 502 6001; e ptabidr@bohol-online.com; cottages from P1400) has large cottages with fan, bathroom and veranda in duplex nipas. It has friendly staff, a good restaurant and a coral-sand island all to itself. It's run by the Philippine Tourism Authority (☎ 411 2192).

Balicasag is a 45-minute boat ride from Alona Beach – ring ahead for them to arrange

pick up. If you're just nosing around for the day, a return boat trip from Panglao will cost around P800.

PAMILACAN ISLAND

The tiny island of Pamilacan is about 23km east of Balicasag. The people from this island are descendants of three generations of whalers, who, since the 1992 ban on capturing cetaceans (whales and dolphins) have had to resort to other forms of livelihood. There are 12 cetacean species known to visit these waters. Many people are willing and wanting to take you out to see them, but the best group is the community-based **Pamilacan Island Dolphin and Whale Watching Organisation** (☎ 0917 9713101 or ask on the island for Leo Sumalpong), which uses the old converted whaling boats and a local crew. The trip includes a full day out on the water and transfers from Baclayon or Panglao – boats for three/eight people cost P2000/4000. The best time for spotting whales is between February and July, although dolphins are fairly common year-round.

There is no snorkelling gear on the island so if you want to look at the reef you'll have to rent gear from a Panglao dive shop.

There are three sets of nipa huts offered on Pamilican, all providing basic meals (best if vegetarians notify in advance, or bring supplies with them for the first day).

Nita's Nipa Huts (☎ 0918 824 9447; P400 per person) are the cheapest and most well established. They range from double to family sized – the double with views, on the water's edge, is the best positioned. All have fan and shared bathroom. Nita can organise a nighttime squid-fishing trip for visitors and arrange a pick-up from Panglao for P1000/2000, which is good for four/10 people.

The other huts are **Osite's** (☎ 0918 591 7171; P500 per person) and **C&C Nipa Huts** (☎ 0919 419 4684; P500 per person).

There are regular boats between Pamilacan and Baclayon (P30) or a private one can be arranged for P300. Boats from Panglao beach will take you to Pamilican for P1000.

TUBIGON

The ramshackle fishing town of Tubigon (to-**bee**-gon), in the middle of Bohol's lush northwestern coast, is well served by daily fastcraft to and from Cebu City. There's not a lot on offer here for travellers, although it does have a PNB, and it is a handy access point for cutting across Bohol if you're in a hurry to see the Chocolate Hills.

Places to Stay & Eat

Tinangnan Beach Resort & Lodging House (☎ 237 2267; rooms with fan & shared bathroom P200-250) is a 15-minute walk or five-minute tricycle ride (P5) north from the central bus and market area of Tubigon. Set upon stilts with a rickety bamboo floor amongst the intertidal mangroves, it also has a restaurant serving basic seafood meals (P50). Warning – mosquitoes abound.

Matabao Beach Resort (☎ 508 0027, 0918 770 3514; rooms with cold-water bathroom & fan/air-con P400/1000) is 6km along the road to Tagbilaran. It has native-style rooms that look out to the nearby islands. Staff will serve up seafood dishes if guests order in advance and videoke is always on tap. A motorbike from the pier will cost P75; if coming by bus from Tagbilaran, get off at Cahayan Market and take a tricycle to the resort (P5).

Getting There & Away

Tubigon Shipping goes to Cebu on the hour from 6am to 6pm (P50, two hours). Lite Shipping leaves once daily (P70, two hours).

Buses from Tubigon's market area (near the pier) pass through all day on the way to Tagbilaran (P31, 1½ hours) via towns such as Calape (P7, 15 minutes) and Loon (P16, 45 minutes). If you're heading straight for the Chocolate Hills from Tubigon, buses inland leave regularly for Carmen (P40, 1½ hours).

CHOCOLATE HILLS

Opinion is divided over the deliciously named Chocolate Hills (admission P10). While some can take them or leave them, other travellers will tell you the hills are the most surreal natural wonder on Earth. And at sunrise on a clear morning, with the sound of the forest waking, we tend to agree.

Legend has it that these 1268 near-identical hills, with sizes ranging from 40m to 120m, are the solidified teardrops of a lovelorn giant. Scientific explanations for this curious landscape are more mundane, with the boffins putting it down to uplifting of ancient coral reef deposits, followed by erosion and weathering. This national geological monument gets its name from the covering lawn-like vegetation, which roasts

to a rich chocolate-brown in the dry season (December to May). At any time of year, you can take great **motorbike tours** (see Getting Around later) along exhilarating, winding roads to the main viewing sites, as well as to the lesser-known wonders such as the **Eight Sisters Hillocks**.

The nearby town of Carmen is home to Fatima Hills. Pilgrims climb the steps up to the **Our Lady of Fatima statue** here every year on 13 May.

Places to Stay & Eat

Chocolate Hills Complex (☎ 0912 856 1559; dorm beds P75, other rooms from P350) is the sole occupant of the utterly spectacular lookout area. While grotty and dilapidated from the outside, this resort offers clean and comfortable rooms with sensational views. Strangely, the cheaper rooms with two and three single beds, fan and cold-water bathroom have the five-star views. Higher priced accommodation (P600/800), while having hot water, air-con and double beds, lacks the very sight that visitors have come to see. The only place to eat (and bringing your own food is strictly forbidden) has the standard Filipino affair (P80 to P100), and cheap sandwiches (around P25) for stopover guests.

Getting There & Away

Buses for Carmen (4km north of the Chocolate Hills) leave from the Tagbilaran bus depot hourly (P53, two hours). From Carmen there are also buses to and from Talibon (P50, two hours) and Tubigon (P40, 1½ hours).

Most hotels in Tagbilaran (see Tagbilaran earlier) can organise a hire car to take you to and from the Chocolate Hills. The average price for a standard air-con sedan with driver is P1500. If you have the luxury of choosing when to go, try to get there as the sun is rising or setting.

Getting Around

At the Chocolate Hills drop-off point (on the main road, at the base of the Chocolate Hills Complex hill), you'll find motorbikes are available to whisk you up the hill (P10 one way). Of course, you can also walk up the hill (20 to 30 minutes). The same bikers will take you to and from Carmen for P15 (one way). One of the finest ways to view these miraculous formations is to take a 20-minute motorbike ride *through* the hills (P150).

THE VISAYAS

BUENAVISTA

Ten kilometres before Jeta Fe, coming from Tubigon, Buenavista has a friendly and picturesque market on a mangrove inlet. From here, or at the river crossing 3km heading south on the main road, you can buy the local delicacy – urchin gonads.

In many countries, including Japan and the US, top dollar is paid for these treats. But for you – they're going cheap at P50 for a 375ml bottle of 'nads. At the Buenavista market, you can follow it up with a fresh syrupy waffle (P2) making a pretty special budget two-course meal. But for something even more special, go on a **Cambuhat Village Ecotour** (☎ 0919 296 3513). This includes a cruise up the mangrove-lined Daet River to the village of Cambuhat where you'll see an oyster farm, raffia weaving, nipa building and enjoy a delicious seafood lunch. The tour takes six hours, costs P650 (less for group bookings) and includes transfers from Tagbilaran. Call Segundo Aparece (☎ 0919 296 3513) for more information, or contact **Bohol Travel & Tours** (☎ 411 3840; Sarabia-Co-Torralba Bldg; CP Garcia St) in Tagbilaran.

JETA FE

Jeta Fe is a quiet town with the usual central church and plaza. From the pier, you can ask a boatmen to take you out for a tour of **Banacon Island** (P600 to P700, 2½ hours), southern Asia's biggest mangrove plantation. Jeta Fe offers yet another way to get to Cebu. Lite Shipping goes to Cebu every evening (P85, two hours), and other pumpboats travel over throughout the day. The best accommodation is in nearby Talibon.

TALIBON

pop 54,000

Talibon, on the north coast, is one of Bohol's busiest centres. Its long pier has regular boats to and from Cebu, as well as to Jau (how) Island nearby (P5). There is no accommodation on Jau at this stage. All transport leaves from the excellent market on the main street before the wharf.

Places to Stay & Eat

Sea View Lodge (☎ 515 0154; singles/doubles with fan & cold-water bathroom P75/150, with air-con P500), on the main street, is probably the best accommodation

in town. It's not well signposted – the entrance is to the right of, and behind, Chelsea's bakery.

Petong's Place (open 6am-6pm; meals P30), a couple of doors up from Sea View Lodge, has plenty of cheap and decent seafood meals – the only irregular thing about this place is the opening hours.

As there is not much on offer around Talibon, it is probably best if you come and eat up big over lunch.

Getting There & Away

See Bohol under Getting There & Away in Cebu City, for boats to and from Cebu.

It's a four-hour bus ride from Tagbilaran (P70), with the Chocolate Hills almost exactly at the halfway point (P50, two hours). You can also take one of the regular buses to Tubigon (P50, two hours).

UBAY

At the opposite end of Bohol to Tagbilaran, remote, overgrown Ubay is the island's largest metropolis after the capital, with a population of almost 60,000 people. It has a lively market on the sea, just near the wharf, selling everything from woven goods to ice cream. There are plenty of cheap and busy Filipino eateries on the water's edge. Way off most travellers maps, Ubay offers masses of uncharted tourism territory around nearby **President Garcia Island**. No official accommodation exists on the island at this stage, but it is a great place to meander through the mangroves, and organising **homestays** through the village captain is possible once on the island.

J&N Lodge (☎ 518 0014, 518 0048; Boyles St; doubles with fan per person P70, doubles with air-con P300-400) is a budget-priced place in the heart of town. While the cheaper rooms are a bit run-down, the more expensive rooms are recently renovated and have private bathroom.

Getting There & Away

J&N Shipping has boats to Cebu twice daily (P100, six hours).

Daily boats also run each morning to Maasin, Bato and Hilongos on Leyte (all P100, two to three hours).

Buses run between Ubay and Talibon, and Ubay and Jagna.

GUINDALMAN, ANDA, CANDIJAY & JAGNA

Now that the coastal road from Guindalman to Candijay is almost completely sealed, this remote mountainous headland is likely to entice more tourists. At Guindalman, you can ask the village head, Nestor Deloy, if he can arrange **snorkelling** or **diving** on the healthy coral reefs.

Anda has little more than a high school, church, municipal hall and police station, all situated on a stretch of sandy **beach**. Toward the main road from the beach there is a small **market** with **bakery**, **food stalls** and plenty of maize. As the hilly land is unsuitable for rice, the staple food here is corn and you'll see copious quantities growing and drying on the roadside.

There is no accommodation in Anda, but 3km before the town (P20 tricycle from Anda), there is a turn-off for **Dap Dap Beach Resort** *(twins/family huts P600/800)*, a resort with restaurant on an idyllic sandy cove, at the end of a 1km road. Next to Dap Dap, **Coastal Paradise** *(single/double huts P400/500)* is a slightly better deal with newer, well-shaded nipa huts. No menu is offered, but dinner can be organised at P25 per person.

On the top of the headland at Candijay, ask at the mayor's office for a tour of the **mangrove bamboo-boardwalk** *(donation suggested)*. There are 32 species of mangrove here and a thriving ecosystem full of mud crabs, oysters and birds.

Jagna (hahg-na) is a largish fishing village on Bohol's southern coast, about 63km east of Tagbilaran. It has vaguely sandy beaches and a colourful flower-filled market. **Garden Café** *(☎ 238 2398; rooms P300)*, behind the church in the centre of town, has clean, cell-like rooms, and serves food including Filipino dishes (P42) and pizza (P15 a slice). Jagna's fiesta kicks off on 29 September.

About 12km west of Jagna, **Valencia** (val-en-**she**-a) is home to **Badian Spring**, a popular public bathing spot with a couple of pools. The second Saturday of January is fiesta day in Valencia.

Cebu Ferries and WG&A both have boats between Jagna and Cagayan de Oro (P210, four hours), and between Jagna and Butuan (Nasipit port; P250, five hours), on Mindanao, once a week. A slower, cheaper alternative is the once-a-week Sulpicio boats for Nasipit (P211, six to seven hours) and Cagayan de Oro (P175, five hours).

There's an **Aboitiz Express** and **SuperCat** booking office beside the Cruztelco telephone office. Buses travel daily, from outside the Jagna church, to and from Tagbilaran (P37, one hour), Anda (P20, 1½ hours), Ubay (P35, 2½ hours) and many other coastal towns.

Negros

Wedged between the islands of Panay and Cebu, travellers too often treat Negros as a mere stepping stone. Surprisingly few stop to enjoy the laid-back charm of the southern university-city of Dumaguete and its surrounding beaches, or the time-capsule city of Silay – the 'Paris of Negros' – on the northwest coast.

The island's rugged interior is home to the grumpy old volcanic giant Mt Kanlaon and the beautiful Twin Lakes, great for hiking; the startlingly remote southwest coast has good beaches and diving; while some of the best reefs in the Visayas can be found around the southern island of Apo.

The Negrito people are made up of several distinct ethnic groups, most of which are nomadic, and range across not only Negros, but also the nearby islands of Panay, Guimaras and Masbate.

On Negros, the tribes include the Bukidnon (the southeastern interior), the Karolanos and the Ata (around the town of Mabinay), the Magahat (near Sipalay), and the Hiligaynon and Ati (areas to the west and southwest of Negros' central mountain range). Apart from English, Visayan dialects dominate on Negros: Ilonggo (spoken by around 80%), Cebuano and Hiligaynon.

Since 1890 the island has been divided into two provinces – Negros Occidental to the west, with Bacolod its capital; and Negros Oriental to the east, with Dumaguete its capital. In both the major cities, and in many smaller cities and towns, historic buildings have been maintained in uncommonly good condition.

The wealth and old architecture in Negros Occidental is largely descended from the booming sugar industry that put this region on the international map at the beginning of last century.

THE VISAYAS

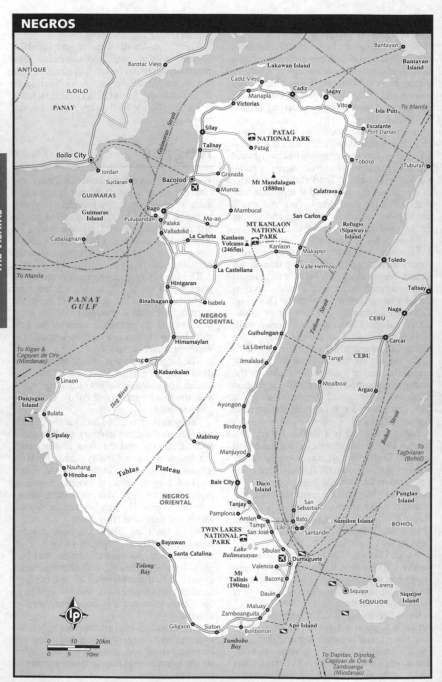

NEGROS

THE VISAYAS

Getting There & Away

Bacolod and Dumaguete airports are serviced by flights from Manila and Cebu City. See Getting There & Away in the Bacolod and Dumaguete sections later.

Negros' busiest ports are Bacolod and Dumaguete, but smaller settlements on the island are also accessible by boat. Major connections include ports on Bohol, Cebu, Luzon, Mindanao, Panay and Siquijor. See individual destinations' Getting There & Away entries later in this section for information on boat services.

Getting Around

Along the north and east coasts it's 313km between Bacolod and Dumaguete, which are at opposite corners of the island. The coastal route (via San Carlos) takes seven hours, and it's wise to take an express bus if you want to avoid the many small village stops. The inland route (via Mabinay) is shorter and faster (5½ hours), with wonderful views. Of course, hopping off anywhere along these routes is no problem.

BACOLOD

☎ 034 • pop 429,000

The earliest residents of Bacolod (back-**oll**-od) were from the nearby areas of Silay and Bago. From a small settlement of around 5000 people in 1770, it grew to become the capital of Negros Occidental in 1849. A bit of an acquired taste for most travellers, Bacolod does have some fine places of interest in its centre, and plenty of sights nearby.

Orientation

Jeepneys circle the central public plaza, which is surrounded by shops, and guarded by the scary old **San Sebastian Cathedral**.

Near the airport, about 3km from downtown Bacolod, the late-to-bed Goldenfield Commercial Complex is four blocks of restaurants, hotels and nightspots.

Information

There's a **tourist information office** (☎ 435 1001; San Juan St) opposite the public plaza. Other tourism-related queries can be taken to the **Provincial Tourism Officer** (☎ 433 2517/ 15, 709 8775; Provincial Capitol Bldg), next to the museum.

Bacolod's **post office** (Gatuslao St) is near the intersection with Burgos St.

Wherever you are in town, **Internet cafés** are never far away, especially if you're near the university area. For bar and pool tables thrown in, visit the cafés around 20th, 21st and 22nd Sts (off Lacson St); see Entertainment later. Rates are P25 to P30 per hour.

A couple of hotels also offer Internet access from their business centres.

Things to See & Do

The **Negros Museum** (☎ 434 5552, fax 433 4764; off South Capitol Rd; adult/child P40/20; open 9am-6pm Mon-Sat) is an impressive neoclassical 1930s building displaying artefacts from the region's sugar-growing industry, among other things. Dominating the main exhibition hall is the *Iron Dinosaur* steam train, which used to haul sugar cane.

Nearby is a remarkable living museum, the Negros Forests & Ecological Foundation Inc (NFEFI) **breeding centre** (☎/fax 433 9234; ⓔ nfefi@moscom.com; South Capitol Rd; adult/child P10/2; open 9am-noon & 2pm-5pm Mon-Fri) – home to endangered animals endemic to Negros. With 97% of the island's original forest wiped out, this could well be one of the most precious pieces of land in the Philippines.

Here you can meet Gerry, Sheila, Regina and the gang – Visayan spotted deer; Visayan warty pigs, *baboy talunon*; leopard cats, *maral*; and many other strange creatures. Donations are gratefully accepted and urgently needed.

Special Events

On the weekend nearest 19 October, the city goes joyfully crazy with the annual **MassKara Festival** (masskara means 'many faces'), which sees participants wearing elaborate, smiley face-masks, and dancing in the streets.

Held in April/May each year, the **Panaad Festival** (also known as Panaad sa Negros Festival) is held at Bacolod's Panaad Sports Stadium and Park, and has displays of crafts, art and architecture from the province's 30 major towns and cities.

Places to Stay – Budget

Unless otherwise mentioned, all rooms have fan and cold-water bathroom.

Pension Bacolod (☎ 434 7065, 433 3377; 11th St; singles/doubles with fan & shared bathroom P95/165, with fan & bathroom P185/ 228, with air-con & bathroom P310/375), on

THE VISAYAS

THE VISAYAS

BACOLOD

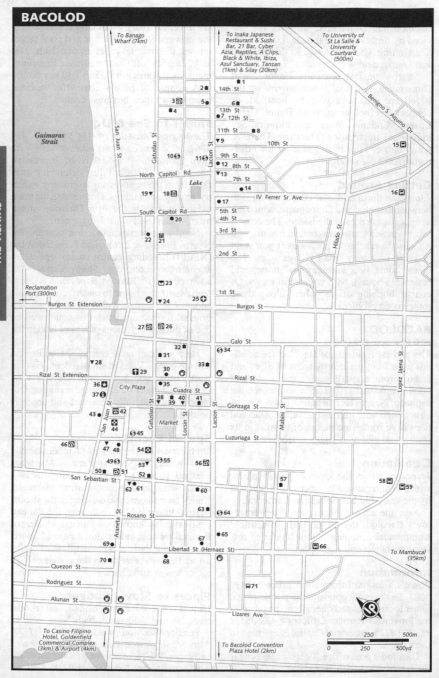

To Banago Wharf (7km)

To Inaka Japanese Restaurant & Sushi Bar, 21 Bar, Cyber Azia, Reptiles, A Clips, Black & White, Ibiza, Azul Sanctuary, Tanzan (1km) & Silay (20km)

To University of St La Salle & University Courtyard (500m)

Guimaras Strait

Reclamation Port (300m)

Benigno S Aquino Dr

San Juan St

Gatuslao St

North Capitol Rd

Lake

South Capitol Rd

Lacson St

10th St

14th St

13th St

12th St

11th St

9th St

8th St

7th St

IV Ferrer Sr Ave

5th St

4th St

3rd St

2nd St

1st St

Hilado St

Burgos St Extension

Burgos St

Galo St

Rizal St Extension

Rizal St

City Plaza

Gatuslao St

Cuadra St

Gonzaga St

Market

Locsin St

Lacson St

Mabini St

Lopez Jaena St

Luzuriaga St

San Juan St

San Sebastian St

Araneta St

Rosario St

Libertad St (Hernaez St)

Quezon St

Rodriguez St

Alunan St

To Casino Filipino Hotel, Goldenfield Commercial Complex (3km) & Airport (4km)

To Bacolod Convention Plaza Hotel (2km)

To Mambucal (35km)

Lizares Ave

0   250   500m
0   250   500yd

BACOLOD

PLACES TO STAY
1 Casa Bianca Pension
2 L'Fisher Hotel; L'Sea Dimsum & Noodle House
4 Jacqueline's Pension Apartelle
6 Royal Am Rei
8 Pension Bacolod
31 Las Rocas Hotel
32 Hotel Alhambra
33 Business Inn
39 Bacolod Pension Plaza; McDonald's; Cinema
41 Bascon Hotel
50 Baldevia Pension Plaza
52 Kings Hotel
57 Rosita's Hometel
60 Bacolod Executive Inn
63 Star Plus Pension House
70 Ester Pension

PLACES TO EAT
9 Kai Sei Japanese Restaurant
13 Cyber Heads Cafe & Bakery; Bank of the Philippine Islands (BPI)
17 McDonalds; Jollibee
19 Food Stalls
24 El Camino (Dos)
28 Manokan Country
38 Jollibee; Cinema
40 McDonalds
47 Gaisano Food Plaza & Gaisano Department Store

53 Food Stalls
62 El Camino (Uno)

OTHER
3 Internet Café
5 Shirmano's Wine Cellar
7 Mayfair Plaza; Kraa Thai Restaurant; Le Cafnet
10 PNB
11 PNB
12 ANP
14 Negros Navigation; Aboitiz Express
15 Ceres Liner Bus Station
16 Old Northern Bus Station
18 Negros Museum
20 Wildlife Breeding Centre
21 Provincial Capitol Building
22 Department of Environment & Natural Resources (DENR)
23 Main Post Office
25 CL Montelibano Memorial Regional Hospital
26 Internet Café
27 Internet Café
29 San Sebastian Cathedral; La Consolacion College
30 Cebu Pacific
34 Equitable PCI Bank; United Cocoplanters Bank
35 Negros Navigation
36 Police Station
37 Tourist Office

42 Equitable PCI Bank; PT&T International Telephone Office
43 WG&A Superferry; Negros Navigation; Cebu Pacific; Air Philippines; Internet Café
44 Plaza Mart City Mall; Negros Navigation; Food Court; Internet Café
45 PNB
46 Dot@One
48 City Hall
49 Bank of the Philippine Islands (BPI)
51 Internet Café
54 Gaisano Mall; Jollibee
55 Equitable PCI Bank
56 Capitol Institute of Technician's Internet Cafe; Aboitiz Express
58 Ceres Liner Southern Bus Station
59 Southern Bus Station
61 Aboitiz Express
64 Equitable PCI Bank
65 Morbai Maps & Charts
66 Jeepneys to Mambucal
67 Aboitiz Express; Cebu Pacific
68 Panaad Sports Stadium & Park
69 Bacolod City Public Library
71 Bus for Ma-ao

THE VISAYAS

refreshingly quiet and peaceful 11th St, offers excellent value for money and big, immaculate rooms. Little wonder indeed that it's often fully booked.

Ester Pension (☎ 23526; Araneta St; singles/doubles P150/200, with air-con from P300) has a dirty foyer but OK rooms. The double beds are on the small side and rooms facing the street are noisy.

Star Plus Pension House (☎ 433 2948/9; cnr Lacson & Rosario Sts; double with shared/private bathroom P260/335, with air-con from P385) is clean and well maintained. Room service is available from the café.

Rosita's Hometel (☎ 434 5136; cnr Mabini & San Sebastian Sts; doubles with shared bathroom P300, with air-con & bathroom P400) has plain, clean rooms.

Bascon Hotel (☎ 435 4071–73; Gonzaga St; singles/doubles from P300/400) has big cleanish rooms, most with cable TV.

Jacqueline's Pension Apartelle (☎ 434 8208, 709 8580; fax 433 1846; 13th St; twins/doubles P550/450) has OK rooms. Make sure you do get the hot (make that warm) water and cable TV that the brochure claims.

Places to Stay – Mid-Range

King's Hotel (☎ 433 0572/6, 434 4500/4600, fax 433 0572; cnr Gatuslao & San Sebastian Sts; twins or doubles P600-1200) has big clean rooms with air-con, hot water and Filipino breakfast. The rooms need a paint job, but otherwise are very good value for a central location.

Baldevia Pension Plaza (☎ 433 8107–09; San Sebastian St; single with cold-water bathroom & fan P418, standard twins or doubles P638-1210) is behind the shops near the corner of San Juan St. The standard rooms have hot water, cable TV, telephone and air-con.

Bacolod Pension Plaza (☎ 433 4547, fax 433 2203; Cuadra St; rooms P550-850) has good rooms with air-con, cable TV, telephone and hot water bathroom. They lack the executive slick of other mid-rangers but the 4th-floor 'budget-saver' room is good value.

The following four places have good clean rooms with professional staff. All rooms have hot-water bathroom, air-con, cable TV and telephone. Room service and other facilities are provided. Although geared towards a business crowd, they're a good deal for all tourists.

Business Inn (☎ 433 8877; W http://pop-web.i-next.net/-businn; 28 Lacson St; rooms P790-1790).

Bacolod Executive Inn (☎ 433 7401–04, fax 433 7442; W http://bcdexectutiveinn.com; 52 San Sebastian St; singles/doubles from P790/890).

Hotel Alhambra (☎ 433 4021–23, fax 434 5173; cnr Locsin & Galo Sts; singles/doubles from P795/895) aims for a more elegant edge.

Royal Am Rei (☎ 433 8881–84, fax 433 0222; e amrei@mozcom.com; 13th St, near Lacson St; rooms from P945) is an establishment that is modern in design.

Places to Stay – Top End

L'Fisher Hotel (☎ 433 3730–39, fax 433 0951; cnr 14th & Lacson Sts; singles/doubles from P1755/2195) is Bacolod's most famous ritzy place to stay. All rooms are plushly carpeted, with all the trappings you'd expect of a first-class hotel. The hotel's 24-hour **Café Marinero** looks out over the swimming pool.

Bacolod Convention Plaza Hotel (☎ 434 4551, fax 433 3757; cnr Magsaysay Ave & Lacson St; rooms from P1500), at the other end of town, has spacious, well-decked-out rooms. It also has a swimming pool, tennis court and the **Four Seasons Chinese Restaurant**.

Casino Filipino Hotel (☎ 434 8901–10, fax 434 8913; Goldenfields Commercial Complex; singles/doubles from P1600/1800), in the Goldenfields Commercial Complex, looks like it was built to withstand a nuclear attack, but inside is designed to depict the grandeur of the Negrenses golden age. Features include a large casino, a cockfighting pit and a chapel to repent in afterwards. There are good eateries and a swimming pool.

Places to Eat

If you are still excited by barbecue chicken when you reach Bacolod, you're in luck – the night-time streets are full of it.

Manokan Country, in the Reclamation Area, is a thriving outdoor row of restaurants offering barbecues (P30) and beers (P18), day and night.

El Camino (open 7am-midnight daily) is a chain of three restaurants and a favourite with locals. It's a noisy, busy, open-air, barbecue-o-rama. The most central is on the corner of San Sebastian and Araneta Sts.

Plaza Mart Food Court (Araneta St, near City Plaza) is a busy place dishing out all varieties of meals and cakes all day.

L'Sea Dimsum & Noodle House (☎ 433 3129; Lacson St; meals P45-105), next to L'Fisher Hotel, is a very popular place offering meat and rice dishes (P46) and generous noodle dishes.

University Courtyard (La Salle Ave), opposite University St La Salle, offers cafés, bars, pastry shops, Internet cafés as well as bookshops and clothing outlets.

Mayfair Plaza (Lacson St) a moderately-sized plaza, is a well air-conditioned retreat, and has **Le Cafnet** (Internet P30 per hr; open 9am-8pm Mon-Sat) for espressos, good cakes and Internet; and **Khaa Thai Restaurant** (☎ 432 2739; meals P50-100; open 11am-10pm daily) a low-key Thai eatery.

Inaka Japanese Restaurant & Sushi Bar (☎ 434 4045; cnr 21st & Lacson Sts; meals P85-220; open 10am-2pm & 6pm-10pm Tues-Sun) has excellent Japanese food, and is well worth the extra pesos, with plenty for both carnivores and veggos. It's up past L'Fisher Hotel, near the funky bar district.

Kai Sei Japanese Restaurant (☎ 433 5599, 434 7787; cnr 10th & Lacson Sts; set menus P100-200; open 11am-2pm & 6pm-9.30pm daily), a large Japanese eatery, has well-priced set menus and very good à la carte. The cheapie includes soup, tempura, sashimi and a soft drink (P100).

Stand-out eateries in the Goldenfield Commercial Complex include **Carlo's Ristorante Italiano** (☎ 435 4899, 703 0435; meals P100-200, pizza P100-160), which does good Italian food and great breakfasts; and **Asian Magic** (☎ 432 1275; opposite the Casino Filipino Hotel; meals P80-130) for a large range of pan-Asian dishes.

Entertainment

21 Bar (cnr 21st & Lacson St; open daily until late), opposite the wonderful Inaka Japanese Restaurant & Sushi Bar, is one of many popular bars and Internet cafés in the area where the young university crowd hang out. For other good options in the area, try 20th, 21st and 22nd Sts – **Cyber Azia**, **Reptiles**, **A Clips**, **Black & White**, **Ibiza**, **Azul Sanctuary** and **Tanzan** for beer drinking).

The **Goldenfield Commercial Complex** in the south of town is aimed at a more mature crowd. Apart from the **Casino Filipino**, there are several **pool halls**, **discos** and a 24-lane **10-pin bowling centre**. The Goldenfield Commercial Complex is a P50 taxi ride from the centre of Bacolod.

Shopping
For *Vogue Living*-style souvenirs, shop at **ANP** *(Lacson St; open 8am-noon & 1pm-5pm Mon-Sat)*.

Getting There & Away
Air Bacolod's airport has daily flights to and from Cebu City and Manila. Airline offices at the airport include **PAL** *(☎ 434 1596)*, **Cebu Pacific** *(☎ 435 2020–23, 434 2052, fax 434 2053)* and **Air Philippines** *(☎ 433 9210–12)*.

Cebu Pacific flies from Cebu City to Bacolod (P1450, 30 minutes) and back daily. PAL fly the same route twice daily (P1380). All three airlines have several flights daily to and from Manila (PAL P2148, Cebu Pacific P2034, Air Philippines P1651; one hour).

Cebu Pacific also flies from Bacolod to Davao (via Cebu; P2895, two hours) every morning, returning the same way.

Boat The Reclamation Port is a P4 tricycle from the City Plaza and services **SuperCat** *(☎ 434 2350/51, 441 0659)*, **Royal Ferry Services** *(☎ 432 0188)*, **Aleson Shipping** *(☎ 434 8404)* and the 'floating coffin' **Bullet Express** *(☎ 432 0188)*. Banago Wharf is about 7km north of central Bacolod – P10 by jeepney or P100 by cab – and services **Negros Navigation** *(☎ 245 5588)* and **WG&A Superferry** *(☎ 434 2053, 434 2020–25)*.

The most popular route from Negros to Panay is the regular Bacolod-Iloilo City boat service, but you can also go via Guimaras from the town of Pulupandan, 31km south of Bacolod.

Smooth and efficient SuperCat ferries run nine times daily from Bacolod to Iloilo City (P240, one hour) and back, between about 6am and 5pm. Royal Ferry Services cover the same route four times daily (P160, 75

minutes), as do Bullet Express (P140, 75 minutes), and Aleson Shipping twice daily (P75, two hours).

WG&A has two boats a week between Bacolod and Manila (P1335, 19 to 21 hrs), one a week between Bacolod and both Iligan (P1225, 14 hours) and Cagayan de Oro (P1270, 13 hours).

Negros Navigation has boats for Manila six days a week (P1345, 19 to 23 hours), and for Cagayan de Oro twice a week (P1260, 13 hours).

Bus & Jeepney The main bus company is **Ceres Bus Liner** *(☎ 434 2387)*, which has a terminal on the northern end of Lopez Jaena St (take a 'Shopping' jeepney from the city centre, P4). Other buses 'squat' outside the old defunct northern bus terminal, just near the Ceres Bus Liner terminal. There is another Ceres terminal on the southern end of Lopez Jaena St, servicing routes south; competition lines are stationed opposite.

The shortest trip between Bacolod and Dumaguete (P119, five to six hours) is via Mabinay – buses leaving every 45 minutes all day. There are also seven buses leaving daily for Dumaguete via San Carlos (P120, seven hours). Ceres Bus Liner also runs trips to Cebu City (with a ferry leg between San Carlos and Toledo; P115, 11 hours).

A plethora of bus lines travel the north coast, either all the way to San Carlos (3½ hours) stopping at the towns along the way, or terminating at towns closer to Bacolod. Prices are: Silay (P7, 15km), Victorias (P15, 34km), Cadiz City (P24, 65km), Sagay (P30, 83km), Escalante (P35, 100km) and San Carlos (P60, 144km). Air-conditioned buses are about 30% dearer. Buses also travel the west coast, stopping at places like Bago City (P9, 22km), La Carlota (P20, 45km) and Sipalay (P74, 178km). The other major bus line for these provincial trips is **Victorias Royal Transit** *(☎ 434 1691, 433 1506)*.

Many jeepneys also service the local routes. There are also jeepneys, not recommended for tourists, taking the quick route to San Carlos via the NPA stronghold town of Don Salvador.

Getting Around
A taxi from the airport to the city centre shouldn't cost more than P50. You can also catch a passing jeepney marked 'Libertad'

(P4). A taxi between downtown Bacolod and the Goldenfield Commercial Complex should cost P40 to P50.

PALAKA

Palaka, 30km south of Bacolod, is home to **Game Fishing Ventures** (☎ 433 9501, fax 433 9507), a fishing and recreational compound popular with families and business groups. On the main road, just south of the small city of Bago, this place has a one-hectare lagoon filled with sea bass, bangus, eel and crabs. At the entrance, you'll pay P10 for a fishing rod and worms are handed out for free. You may also be able to buy small fish from the marine biologists who are working in nearby research ponds, and try your luck with catching a bigger fish. If all else fails, there's an excellent **restaurant** (open 8am-11pm daily) serving seafood from the aquariums. Jeepneys and buses pass here on the way to and from Bacolod (P12, 45 minutes). Boats leave from the nearby town of Pulupandan, for Suclaran (P40, one hour).

LA CARLOTA

One of the six main cities in Negros Occidental, La Carlota lies about 45km south of Bacolod. With a particularly hyperactive population of around 57,000 people, the city is famous for fiestas.

It's also well known among nature lovers for its lusciously ferny Guintubdan Nature Camp (see Places to Stay later), an alternative to Mambucal as a starting point for hikes into Mt Kanlaon Nature Park (see that entry later).

La Carlota's annual **Kabankalan Sinulog** is a wild street party held on the second Sunday in January. Dancers are daubed in black in honour of the island's Negrito people, and a feast is held in honour of the child Jesus. On 1 May, the city holds its annual **Pasalamat Festival**, a fun-filled, three-day thanksgiving ritual to honour the year's harvest and hard labour. A Mardi Gras atmosphere and home-grown drumbeats build up to a closing ceremony with dazzling native costumes and huge parade floats.

The city's centre is home to the stunning, fortress-style, 19th-century **Church of Our Lady of Peace**, one of the country's best examples of Romanesque architecture. Another attraction is the **La Carlota Sugar Central sugar mill**. For the latest information

about visiting the mill, contact the Bacolod **tourist office** (☎ 435 1001).

Places to Stay & Eat

La Carlota itself is light on accommodation, but there are some good options nearby.

Guintubdan Nature Camp (☎ 460 2459 (mayor's office); twin/triple rooms with cold-water bathroom from P400/600, camping P150 for 6-person tent), a 15km jeepney ride (P20) east of town and up the mountain, has basic clean rooms and a communal area with magnificent views. You'll have to bring your own food and use the kitchen or the staff can cook for P50 per person. From here, guides can take you on excellent day-trips into Mt Kanlaon Nature Park (P50 per hour), including any of the seven nearby waterfalls (all within 1km to 2km) and to the mountain's crater (see Mt Kanlaon Nature Park, later).

Buenos Aires Mountain Resort (☎ 461 0540/0164, fax 461 0199; e bago@lasaltech .com; dorm beds P100, cottages from P300, rooms with air-con P1000) is about 20km east of Bago, past the town of Ma-ao. Built in the 1930s, this lush mountain resort situated on the edge of a river is famous for having housed President Quezon when he hid from the Japanese during WWII. Buses and jeepneys leave Bacolod for Ma-ao all day (P15, 1½ hours). From Ma-ao, take a tricycle to the resort (P80, 30 minutes). A taxi from Bacolod will cost P300 (one hour).

Getting There & Away

Jeepneys marked 'La Carlota' head off from Bacolod (P20, one hour) throughout the day.

MT KANLAON NATURE PARK & MAMBUCAL

With its dense forest and volcanic crowning glory, the 25,000-hectare Mt Kanlaon Nature Park is particularly popular with hikers and bird-watchers. The park's central highlands are rich in wildlife, including the perilously rare bleeding-heart pigeon and Philippine spotted deer. The central highlands are noted for several species of wild orchid.

Anything from day-hikes to week-long camping expeditions into the park can be arranged from Mambucal, just north of Mt Kanlaon, or from the other side of the mountain, Guintubdan Nature Camp. From Mambucal, the Wasay entrance station marks the start of the trail to Mt Kanlaon.

Before embarking, visitors *must* register and buy a permit from the Bacolod **Department of Environment & Natural Resources** *(DENR; ☎ 434 7769, 0919 525 6755, fax 433 3728; Capitol Area; permit per person P300)* – this is for your own safety. The DENR sometimes evacuates the area and enforces a clearance zone around the base if its daily monitoring suggests any threat of volcanic eruption. Trekkers wanting to walk to the summit will need to organise a guide at either of the resorts or mayor's offices' (approximately P400 per day; two days usually required) and should also allow a couple of days preparation. For a slicker package with all equipment and food included, contact Planet Action (for details see Moalboal & Panagsama Beach under South of Cebu City in the Cebu section earlier).

Places to Stay & Eat

Mambucal Mountain Resort *(☎ 433 8887, 703 0009, 710 0344; camp sites P50, rooms with cold-water bathroom from P350)*, a 24-hectare forest property in Mambucal, has creepy bubbling mud, boiling sulphur springs and quicksand. Less ghoulish attractions include a human-made warm sulphur bath (P30), natural springs and seven sets of waterfalls nearby. The restaurant sells basic meals.

Getting There & Away

Mambucal is about 35km from Bacolod, and jeepneys (P10, one hour) will take you all the way to the resort. You can also catch a bus from the east-coast city of San Carlos to the mountain town of Kanlaon (P75, four hours) and continue to Mambucal by jeepney or motorcycle.

SILAY

The city of Silay, about 14km north of Bacolod, is listed among the Philippines' top 25 tourist destinations. Silay is a remarkable living museum, with 31 ancestral homes, mostly built between 1880 and 1930. Two of the best are open to the public. Silay tasted sweet success when a French resident planted sugar cane in the 1850s, and its pier swiftly became an international port of call. A golden age dawned in the early 1900s, when Silay became *the* place for European musicians and intellectuals to hang out. But its reputation as the 'Paris of Negros' wasn't to last. The combination of growth in nearby Bacolod, the damaging effect of the WWII, and the ensuing development of the sugar industry overseas, resulted in a decline in Silay's cultural and industrial activity.

Information

The staff at Silay's **tourist office** *(☎ 495 4600/0061, fax 495 0587; e sil2@babysky.net .ph; 2nd floor, City Hall; open 8am-noon & 1pm-5pm Mon-Fri)* are extremely helpful. There are **Equitable PCI**, **PNB** and **BPI** banks in town.

Things to See & Do

Silay's past has been beautifully preserved in the form of two museums, both of which are former ancestral homes.

Built in 1908, **Bernardino Jalandoni Ancestral House** *(☎ 495 5093; Rizal St; adult/child P20/10; open 10am-5pm Tues-Sun)* is affectionately known as 'The Pink House'. Apart from the relatively new paint job, the building is said to be virtually unchanged from the days when it was home to the Jalandoni family. On display are Japanese government banknotes from the days of occupation, an ornate four-poster bed, a 1907 Steinway piano and many other intriguing objects. Admission includes an optional guided tour.

You can't miss the **Balay Negrense Museum** *(☎ 4954916, fax 495 0291; e balay 1898@hotmail.com; Cinco de Novembre St; adult/child P30/10; open 10am-6pm Tues-Sun)*. Also known as the Victor Gaston Ancestral Home, this spectacular house was built of balayong hardwood in 1901. Victor's father, Yves Leopold Germain Gaston, is credited with being the first to cultivate sugar cane commercially in the region. The house has been painstakingly restored, and furnished with period pieces donated by locals. However, the bevelled-glass windows and Chinese-carved, wooden ceiling and fittings are all original. Also on display are family photographs and letters, and costumed mannequins languishing around with martinis to give you a feel for hacienda-living. Entry includes an optional guided tour.

Another of the houses, **Hofileña Ancestral Home** *(☎ 495 4561; Cinco de Novembre St; visits by appointment with owner)* houses Silay's best art collection as well as antiques and items from the Hofileña family (which

THE VISAYAS

SILAY

To Barangay Hawaiian (10km), Victorias (20km) & Patag (32km)

Antonio Luna St

Burgos St

National Rd (or Rizal St)

Cinco de Noviembre St

Plaridel St

R Hofilena St

Gomez St

Zamora St

Zulueta St

Public Plaza

Eusebio St

Burgos St

Silay-Mambululac Rd

Dr Juan Valencia St

To Ang Kalubihan (600m)

To Palamunitan Sang Silay, José Locsin Provincial Hospital, Equitable PCI Bank (50m), Fortuna Pension House (1km)

0   150   300m
0   150   300yd

SILAY

PLACES TO STAY & EAT
5   Coffee Shop
7   Baldevia Pension House; Iolo's Cafe
27   Hestia
28   El Ideal Bakery

OTHER
1   Buses & Jeepneys to Barangay Hawaiian & Patag
2   Bernardino Jalandoni Ancestral House (The Pink House)
3   Market
4   Buses & Jeepneys to Victorias & Cadiz
6   Metrobank
8   Iglesia Ni Cristo Church
9   Akol Ancestral Home
10   Hofilenia Ancestral Home
11   Jalandoni House
12   Green House Ancestral Home & Culture Centre
13   Police Station
14   Tourist Office; City Hall
15   Church of San Diego
16   Cine Silay Cinema
17   Philippines National Bank (PNB)
18   Internet Café
19   PLDT Public Calling Office; Dunkin' Donuts
20   Buses & Jeepneys to Bacolod
21   Civic Centre
22   Silay Medical Clinic
23   Gamboa Ancestral Home
24   Balay Negrense Museum
25   Post Office
26   Buses & Jeepneys to Bacolod; Silay North Elementary School
29   Bank of Philippine Islands

includes a movie star, a ballet dancer and various musicians). The house is now owned by local personality Ramon Hofileña, a descendent of the original owner and the only Filipino to bless the front cover of *Reader's Digest*.

For almost 30 years, Ramon has also run the **Annual Cultural Tour Of Negros Occidental** (☎ 495 4561 *or the Silay tourist office; admission around P380*), which, according to the man himself, makes it the 'longest-running cultural tour in the world'. The three one-day tours are scheduled in December, and take in attractions from the nearby region.

Designed by an Italian called Verasconi, the silver-domed **Church of San Diego**, in the centre of town, is topped by a crucifix that is lit at night. On the fence around the church, several saintly statues stand guard.

No visit to Silay would be complete without sampling the delicacies of **El Ideal Bakery** (for details see Places to Stay & Eat).

Special Events

Silay has two week-long fiestas each year. The charter-day anniversary runs from 5 to 12 June. The fiesta in honour of San Diego,

who is said to watch over Silay, runs from 6 to 13 November and includes a colourful street-dance competition.

Places to Stay & Eat

Fortuna Pension House (☎ 495 3981/4109; e elleng@bacolod.worldtelphil.com; *rooms P400-1000*), one of the 31 recognised ancestral houses, has been converted, with minimal alteration, to accommodate guests. This stately home, with views across the plantation, offers a glimpse of hacienda-living, but with a friendly homely feel.

There's a range of accommodation, from simple rooms to entire floors, but most have good views, and hot-water bathroom. Only breakfast is available (P100). Fortuna is less than a kilometre south of the city – turn left at José Locsin, pass the José Locsin Provincial Hospital and follow the signs. A tricycle will cost P4.

Baldevia Pension House (☎ 495 0272/ 5140; e bph@babysky.net.ph; *Rizal St; rooms* with hot-water bathroom & fan P330, with air-con P495-1100) is conveniently positioned off the main drag, just near the bus and jeepney terminals. It has clean, tiled rooms some of which have views of the Church of San Diego. Attached to the hotel is **Iolo's Cafe**.

Ang Kalubihan (official name is 'Silay Manukan Garden'; barbecue pieces P7-30, other dishes P30-70; open 3pm-10pm daily) is a breezy outdoor eatery under a stand of coconut palms. On a warm clear night, this is a great place for a barbecue and beer.

Palamunitan Sang Silay (☎ 495 2804; e nicled@babysky.net.au; caught fish P80-260 per kg, meals P30-85; open 10.30am-10pm Tues-Sat) combines a quaint, picturesque setting with an innovative concept. The bamboo restaurant is built on stilts above a fishpond and guests are invited to sit on the bamboo pier, dangle a line (supplied by the restaurant) and catch their meal. If you're short on patience or luck, there are plenty of fresh seafood dishes to be enjoyed.

El Ideal Bakery (Rizal St; open 7am-6.30pm daily), in one of the ancestral houses just south of the public plaza, is the home and birthplace of many of the delicacies for which Silay has become famous, spawning culinary imitations across the country. The bakery was set up in 1935, during Silay's heyday, to provide snacks for the wealthy gamblers who couldn't drag themselves away from the table. Some of the bakery's famous creations include *lumpia ubod* (spring rolls filled with pork, shrimp and the juicy tip of the coconut palm) and *piaya* (flat bread sprinkled with brown sugar and sesame seeds). Our favourites were the *buko* (young coconut) and *guapple* (large guava) pies, served warm (P20 a slice). Delicious.

For cheaper imitations, go to the **public market** between 6.30am and 7.30am Monday to Saturday, and you'll see people bartering their baked goods with each other before heading off to sell them in Bacolod and neighbouring areas.

Getting There & Away

Both buses and jeepneys travel between Silay and Bacolod (P8, 30 minutes). In Silay, all buses and jeepneys heading north and south stop along Rizal St. From Silay, there are buses all day stopping at the coastal towns towards San Carlos (P52, three hours).

Getting Around

Walking around Silay is what it's all about – there's plenty of history to take in. If you're feeling lazy, short trips around town by tricycle are no more than P4.

AROUND SILAY

The sugar-cane capital of **Barangay Hawaiian** is only a 15-minute ride by jeepney (P4) north of Silay. To visit the **Hawaiian Philippine Sugar Company** (☎ 495 3200) or any other plantation, you'll need to call ahead or arrange a tour through the Silay tourist office (see Information under Silay earlier). Tours may include watching the harvesting process (October to April), chatting with workers and children, kalabaw-riding (P50), and even a homestay (approximately P200 per person including simple meals provided by a family). Another option is to take a 3km ride on a *bagoneta* (pedal-driven cart that runs along railway tracks; P5 for public bagoneta, P50 for private cart, 45 minutes) through cane fields, past fishponds, to the coastal village of Mambag-io, where you can purchase fish and oysters. These rides run in both directions all day, every day. The trips leave from Crossing Laguay, 3km north of Silay (P4 by jeepney or P15 by tricycle).

There's also historic sugar-cane paraphernalia on display at the huge Victorias Milling Company (Vicmico), the world's biggest mill during the '60s and '70s, in the town of Victorias, north of Silay. Book through the Bacolod tourism office (☎ 435 1001). Jeepneys run all day to Victorias from Silay.

Patag is a small village within **Patag National Park**, about 32km east of Silay (P20 by jeepney, one hour), the site of a horrendous battle during WWII. These days, great hikes are possible from Patag village into the national park, with several **waterfalls** along the way. The Silay tourism office can organise a local farmer guide (P150 a day) and a homestay (around P300). Even if you go it alone, the office requests that you contact them before departure (see Information under Silay earlier). The only other accommodation is in the old **Patag Hospital** building (donation only) or **camping**, but you'll need to bring your own gear.

NORTHEAST COAST

This region, full of sugar cane with a mountain backdrop, takes in Cadiz, Sagay and

THE VISAYAS

Escalante, all of which have several buses passing through to Bacolod or Dumaguete daily. Regular jeepneys also connect these places.

Cadiz

About 65km from Bacolod, Cadiz is an important fishing port and exit point for all that Negros sugar. The city's annual **Ati-Atihan Festival**, in honour of patron saint Santo Niño, is held on the weekend nearest 26 January.

Accommodation is limited. Your best options are to stay in a neighbouring town or find a homestay.

There are pumpboats every second day between Cadiz and Bantayan town (P120, 3½ hours) on Bantayan Island. Buses run from Bacolod to Cadiz (P24, 1½ hours), and from Dumaguete to Cadiz (P120, six to seven hours). There are also regular jeepneys to Sagay.

Sagay

Proclaimed a city in 1996, Sagay has wasted no time in becoming a dynamic regional hub with a population nearing 150,000 people. A combination of Old Sagay (on the coast) and New Sagay (on the National Hwy) – P10 by jeepney between the two – the city has seen a frenzy of bridge building, road works and construction projects. Sagay City's **Sinagayan Festival** (in honour of St Joseph) takes place in mid- to late March.

Sagay Sugar Central and Lopez Sugar Central are the city's two **sugar mills**. To view the mills' locomotives, contact the Bacolod tourist office (☎ 435 1001).

The city is the proud guardian of the 32,000-hectare **Sagay Marine Reserve**, established in 1999 to protect one of the only areas on Negros still teeming with marine life. The sanctuary is centred on **Carbin Reef**, about 15km northeast of Old Sagay (one hour by pumpboat). Also here is **Maca Reef**, where flocks of migratory birds are a common sight, and the nearby island of **Suyoc** can be reached on foot during low tide. To organise a boat, visit the **tourist office** (☎ 488 0101; City Hall; 8am-noon & 1pm-5pm Mon-Fri) or ask at the pier. A small boat will cost around P200 per person.

There is a daily pumpboat to Bantayan town, Bantayan (P130, two hours). Jeepneys run regularly between Sagay and Cadiz (P10,

30 minutes), and between Sagay and Escalante (P8, 30 minutes).

Balay Kauswagan (☎ 722 5994; e inquiry@ sagay-city.com.ph; dorm beds P150, twin rooms P500) is a convention centre but has decent rooms with air-con and private cold-water bathroom. There is a swimming pool but no restaurant.

Escalante & Around

Escalante is almost 100km from Bacolod, There is an **Equitable PCI Bank** in town.

The little **Isla Puti** (Enchanted Isle), also known as Bagumbanwa Island, is a 20-minute pumpboat ride from Escalante (also approachable from Vito Port, Old Sagay), and has some attractive white-sand beaches. Boats can be organised at the pier (P600, good for 10 people) or through the city's **tourist office** (☎ 454 0362/24; City Hall). There is accommodation on the island at **Jomabo Island Paradise Beach Resort** (☎ 434 3971/2, 454 0090; e jomabo@1speed com.com; camping P150 per tent, rooms and cottages P700-2800), which also has a restaurant, tennis court and water-sports facilities.

Several kilometres out of Escalante is **Bonista Beach Resort** (book through Escalante tourism office; singles/doubles P1200/1600), which has a good beach, swimming pool and restaurant. Rooms have air-con and hot-water bathroom.

Escalante celebrates two major **festivals**: one on 20 September, to remember the massacre of 20 sugar-cane workers by soldiers during an industrial dispute; and the other, on 30 May, when the town celebrates its patron, St Cruz, with a colourful street party.

Pumpboats go daily from Escalante's Port Danao to Tuburan on Cebu. Escalante is on the bus route between Dumaguete (five to six hours) and Bacolod (2½ hours). For more information see Getting There & Away under Bacolod earlier.

SAN CARLOS

San Carlos is the booming port city on the east coast that connects Negros to Cebu. Ferries run daily between San Carlos and Toledo, on Cebu's west coast. This place isn't overflowing with charm, but it's fine for an overnight stay. There's a **Metrobank** and an **Equitable PCI Bank** on the main drag, which runs in a straight line from the pier.

Refugio Island (also known as Sipaway Island), is a white-sand and coral outcrop about 4km off the coast of San Carlos. About 7km long and about 1.5km wide, the island has a couple of basic stores, a free public swimming pool, and some good walking trails. Regular pumpboats head for the island (P20, 20 minutes) from near the main pier in San Carlos.

The city is famed for its annual Pintaflores Festival, held from 3 to 5 November. This particularly frenetic street festival harks back to the days when Filipinos would welcome foreign visitors by dancing en masse.

Skyland Hotel & Restaurant (☎/fax 312 5589; Broce St; twins with fan/air-con P325/ 475, family rooms P450/575) has spotless rooms.

Getting There & Away

For boats to Toledo, see Getting There & Away under Toledo earlier.

There are daily buses from San Carlos' bus station (about 1km from the pier) to Dumaguete (P70, four hours), Bacolod via Silay (P60, three hours) and Bacolod via Kanlaon (P75, four hours).

SOUTHWEST COAST
Sipalay

About 200km from both Bacolod and Dumaguete, the remote city of Sipalay (population 64,000) is surrounded by rugged beaches, scattered islets and waters teeming with marlin, trevally and tuna. The area has only recently opened up to foreign tourism, offering relatively unexplored diving, game-fishing and the brilliantly managed Danjugan Island Marine Sanctuary (see the boxed text 'Danjugan Island Triumph' later). Boats can also be hired from Sipalay for exploring the marine paradises of nearby Maricalum Bay and Tinagong Dagat (Hidden Sea), and you'll find information about the indigenous Magahat people at the city hall.

Sipalay's annual Sacred Heart of Jesus Fiesta is held in late December.

A long, bumpy 6km out of Sipalay, Artistic Diving Beach Resort (☎ 098-281 0077, 0919 409 5594; W www.artisticdiving.com; twins/doubles P700) sits on a quiet beach and has good, clean rooms with fan and hot-water showers. The resort offers diving (one dive US$19, equipment rental US$6, open-water diving certificate US$285) on the nearby reefs, the two natural wrecks (including a US WWII warship), and at Danjugan Island Marine Sanctuary (if bookings permit). Also for rent are snorkelling gear (US$3 for two hours), motorbikes (US$3 per hour) and pumpboat-catamaran (US$1 per hour), and guides can be hired for trekking to nearby caves (US$5 for a half-day).

The easiest way to get to Artistic Diving is to go to Pats Restaurant in Sipalay where radio contact can be made with the resort which will send someone to come and pick you up for around P200. A cheaper alternative is to ask one of the many hubel-hubel to take you there (P100).

THE VISAYAS

Mine, All Mine

With the introduction of the Mining Act of 1995, foreigners have been encouraged to occupy the rich wildlife and tribal areas of southwest Negros through gold and copper mining firms. Successive governments have given their blessing to these poorly run operations despite the catastrophic copper-tailings dam failure in 1982 that released 28 tonnes of waste onto surrounding agricultural land.

Heartfelt pleas against corporate mining by church leaders, indigenous people and environmental groups seemed momentarily rewarded when Philex Gold and Maricalum Mining Corporation both announced closures of their open-pit mines, late in 2001. However, the celebration was not to last – one of Maricalum's copper-tailings dams was left open to dry, and months later, locals were hit with an epidemic of respiratory illnesses due to the dust storms rising off the dried dam. It seemed the palm fronds that the company threw down over the dam were not quite enough to mitigate the level of toxic waste.

At the time of writing, the local government was lobbying the mining giant, who has politely responded that the problem is too expensive to fix. Letters in support of the tightening of Philippine mining laws should be addressed to Secretary Heherson Alverez, Department of Environment & Natural Resources, Visayas Ave, Quezon City, Philippines.

Sonia Orchard

About 5km before Bulata, Antol is the launching pad for **Escape Tours** (e acler@ mozcom.com), which offers game-fishing trips using local fisherfolk in outrigger boats to take you 15km offshore to the teeming waters of the Sulu Sea. Day trips cost around US$90 per person and include boat, guide and food. Book well in advance for equipment hire. The best time of year is April until July. **Homestay** accommodation can be organised, or else visitors can stay at **Punta Bulata White Beach Resort** (☎/fax 433 5160; w http://puntabulata.tripod.com; rooms with air-con from P1000, tent with air-con from P800).

Getting There & Away Buses run between Sipalay and Bacolod (P74, 4½ hours) daily, and between Sipalay and Dumaguete (P120, seven to eight hours).

Danjugan Island

About 3km west of the little coastal town of Bulata, the 1.5km-long island of Danjugan (dan-**hoo**-gan) is within easy reach of Sipalay and Bulata. This 42-hectare island has six lagoons, a primary limestone rainforest, mangroves, and is home to over nine species of bat and 58 species of bird including the endangered white-breasted eagle and the grey-headed fishing eagle.

A **resort** was under construction on the island when we visited. When finished, it will

be rather spartan but very green, including composting toilets as well as solar cells to eliminate the need for a generator.

Bird-watching and diving will be available using local guides and boats. Room rates are likely to be approximately US$100 per person, including meals. In order to keep the guest list below 16 to 20 people, visitors must book before arriving on the island – you should contact the **Philippine Reef & Rainforest Conservation Foundation** (☎ 441 1658; e prrcfi@mozcom com).

DUMAGUETE
☎ 035 • pop 102,300

The capital of Negros Oriental, Dumaguete (doo-ma-**get**-eh) is a leafy port city dominated by the large Silliman University campus, founded in 1901, and a wonderful waterfront stretch of hotels and restaurants on Rizal Blvd. Known as the 'City of Gentle People', Dumaguete's residents do indeed match the city's breezy, open and attractive feel. Being a university city, Dumaguete is also loved for its young, hip crowd and good nightlife.

Information

The city **tourist office** (☎ 225 0549, 422 7105; e ctourism@mozcom.com; City Hall; open 8am-noon & 1pm-5pm Mon-Fri) will do their best to help with your queries and bookings.

Danjugan Island Triumph

After falling victim to dynamite fishing in the 1980s, Danjugan Island was bought in 1994 by a group of concerned divers from Bacolod called the **Philippine Reef & Rainforest Conservation Foundation** (☎ 441 1658; e prrcfi@mozcom.com), with help from the World Wide Land Conservation Trust and Coral Cay Conservation Society (British NGOs). They originally used the island to run environmental education programmes for children, using the profit from the wealthy city kids to fund the locals. In 2000, three areas of the surrounding reef were declared sanctuaries and have been since run by the island's community.

Apart from rainforest, reef and lagoons, Danjugan offers rugged, densely forested hills that reach a height of around 800m. It was here that Filipino researchers discovered the bare-backed fruit bat *Dobsonia chapmani* – formerly thought extinct – among the 10,000-or-so bats in the island's main colony. The British Embassy continues to fund environmental and social education as well as ongoing biological surveys on the island. However, at the time of writing, a small ecotourist resort was being built and it's hoped that this will enable the island community to become economically self-sufficient.

In early 2002, the Philippine government, through the DENR, declared Danjugan Island the best managed reef in the country – an award handed out every four years, and last given to Apo Island (Negros) in 1998.

Sonia Orchard

Money There are several banks in town, including two offices of **Equitable PCI Bank** and a **Bank of Philippine Islands** (BPI), all on the main drag *(Perdices Sts)*. Near the BPI (corner of Legaspi St), there is a plague of moneychangers.

Post & Telephone The main **post office** *(cnr Santa Catalina & Pedro Teres Sts)* is near Rizal Park. There's a **PT&T telephone office** *(Perdices St)*, and over the road next to Jollibee, a **Datcom** telephone office.

Email & Internet Access As you'd expect from a university city, there is no shortage of Internet cafés, especially on Perdices St and Rizal Blvd and around the university. The best setup is at **Why Not** *(Rizal Blvd; P35 per hr; open 8am-2am daily)* – the only place we've found where you can sit in your own private, coconut-wood booth and have mango daiquiris brought to you while you surf. Another good option is **Manson's Place** *(Perdices St; P20 per hr; open 8am-midnight daily)*, which has a plethora of terminals with good connections, serves cheap Filipino food (P25 to P50) and offers one hour free surfing for every five coffees consumed.

Medical Services The **Silliman University Medical Centre** *(☎ 225 0841/3563; V Aldecoa Rd)* is relatively well set up.

Things to See & Do
A must-see in Dumaguete is Silliman University's **Anthropology Museum & Centre for the Study of Philippine Living Culture** *(admission P5; open 8am-noon & 2pm-5pm Mon-Fri)*, in the central campus area. Enter from Hibbard Ave, the extension of Perdices St, head past the Silliman Cafeteria, and stroll to the old building with the staircase at the front. Displays include artefacts from Siquijor, as well as ancient Chinese bits-and-pieces dug up on a variety of Philippine islands.

Another university offering is the **Silliman University Marine Laboratory** *(☎ 225 2500; e mlsucrm@mozcom.com; admission P10; open 8am-noon & 2pm-5pm Mon-Fri)*, on the northern shore near the airport. Displays include shells, marine mammal skulls and bones, ecosystem aquaria and tanks of giant clams and lapu-lapu.

The Negros Island Tour Guide Association of the Philippines can take you on one of its full- or half-day **cultural tours** – it has a list of itineraries including the Wednesday Malatapay market (see Zamboanguita later), Silliman University, arts and craft tours, dolphin watching and Mt Kanlaon. Prices had not been set when we spoke to them, but inquiries can be made through **Eight Wonders Travel & Tours** *(☎ 225 5968; e 8wonders@ dgte.mozcom.com; La Residencia Al Mar, Rizal Blvd; open 9am-noon & 1pm-5.30pm Mon-Sat)*.

Also, **Dumaguete Scenic Tours** *(☎ 225 9838, ☎/fax 225 9122; Why Not, Rizal Blvd)*, run by Aussie George Robinson, offers: three-hour jeepney tours (P400 per person) to local destinations; overnight trips to Mt Talinis and Twin Lakes (see entry later; P1500 per person); and custom-made itineraries.

Even though the out-of-town resorts offer a more ambient place to stay and **dive**, if you are short on time, drop into **White Tip Divers** *(☎ 225 2381/2402, fax 225 7716; e whitetip@mozcom.com; Hibbard Ave)*, near Harold's Mansion, where PADI Staff Instructor Snoopy can arrange diving on any of the surrounding reefs, as far as Apo Island.

Other things to see within Dumaguete itself, include the **Bell Tower**, built 1754 to 1776, on the corner of Perdices and Colon Sts, and the large and lively **public market** on Real St.

What the locals and tourists spend most of their time doing is strolling along the 780m-long Rizal Blvd, a scenic walk by day and the centre of the town's nightlife.

Places to Stay
Vintage Inn *(☎ 225 1076, 422 9106; Legaspi St; singles/doubles with cold-water bathroom & fan P220/330, with air-con & hot water P330/495)*, opposite the market, is one of the few acceptable budget options. Jeepneys and buses heading north stop just around the corner from here.

Harold's Mansion Tourist Inn *(☎ 225 8000/01, 422 9000, fax 225 0439; e harolds mansion@yahoo.com; 205 Hibbard Ave; singles/ doubles with fan & cold-water bathroom P275/385, with air-con, hot water & cable TV P495/605)* looks less like a mansion and more like a giant pink icing-cake. It's a 10-minute walk from the main shopping area, but it does have very clean, well-priced rooms.

Paseo Rovira Guest House *(☎/fax 225 2194/7; Rovira Rd; twins with air-con P500;*

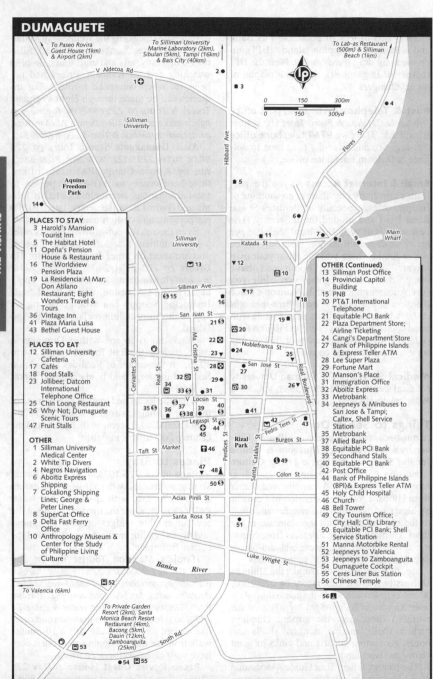

DUMAGUETE

To Paseo Rovira
Guest House (1km)
& Airport (2km)

To Silliman University
Marine Laboratory (2km),
Sibulan (5km), Tampi (16km)
& Bais City (40km)

To Lab-as Restaurant
(500m) & Silliman
Beach (1km)

V Aldecoa Rd

Silliman
University

Aquino
Freedom
Park

Silliman
University

Hibbard Ave

Flores St

Katada St

Main
Wharf

THE VISAYAS

PLACES TO STAY
3   Harold's Mansion
    Tourist Inn
5   The Habitat Hotel
11 Opeña's Pension
    House & Restaurant
16 The Worldview
    Pension Plaza
19 La Residencia Al Mar;
    Don Atilano
    Restaurant; Eight
    Wonders Travel &
    Tours
36 Vintage Inn
41 Plaza Maria Luisa
43 Bethel Guest House

PLACES TO EAT
12 Silliman University
    Cafeteria
17 Cafés
18 Food Stalls
23 Jollibee; Datcom
    International
    Telephone Office
25 Chin Loong Restaurant
26 Why Not; Dumaguete
    Scenic Tours
47 Fruit Stalls

OTHER
1   Silliman University
    Medical Center
2   White Tip Divers
4   Negros Navigation
6   Aboitiz Express
    Shipping
7   Cokaliong Shipping
    Lines; George &
    Peter Lines
8   SuperCat Office
9   Delta Fast Ferry
    Office
10 Anthropology Museum &
    Center for the Study
    of Philippine Living
    Culture

OTHER (Continued)
13 Silliman Post Office
14 Provincial Capitol
    Building
15 PNB
20 PT&T International
    Telephone
21 Equitable PCI Bank
22 Plaza Department Store;
    Airline Ticketing
24 Cangi's Department Store
27 Bank of Philippine Islands
    & Express Teller ATM
28 Lee Super Plaza
29 Fortune Mart
30 Manson's Place
31 Immigration Office
32 Aboitiz Express
33 Metrobank
34 Jeepneys & Minibuses to
    San Jose & Tampi;
    Caltex, Shell Service
    Station
35 Metrobank
37 Allied Bank
38 Equitable PCI Bank
39 Secondhand Stalls
40 Equitable PCI Bank
42 Post Office
44 Bank of Philippine Islands
    (BPI) & Express Teller ATM
45 Holy Child Hospital
46 Church
48 Bell Tower
49 City Tourism Office;
    City Hall; City Library
50 Equitable PCI Bank; Shell
    Service Station
51 Manna Motorbike Rental
52 Jeepneys to Valencia
53 Jeepneys to Zamboanguita
54 Dumaguete Cockpit
55 Ceres Liner Bus Station
56 Chinese Temple

Silliman Ave

San Juan St

Ma Cristina St

Cervantes St

Real St

Noblefranca St

San José St

Rizal Boulevard

V Locsin St

Legaspi St

Pedro Teres St

Burgos St

Taft St

Market

Rizal
Park

Santa Catalina St

Colon St

Acias Pinili St

Santa Rosa St

Luke Wright St

Banica   River

To Valencia (6km)

To Private Garden
Resort (2km), Santa
Monica Beach Resort
Restaurant (4km),
Bacong (5km),
Dauin (12km),
Zamboanguita
(25km)

South Rd

doubles with air-con & cable TV P700, kitchenette P1500) has clean rooms in the quiet northern part of town, near the airport.

The Habitat Hotel *(☎ 225 0833, 422 8458; Hibbard Ave; singles/doubles from P490/615)* has rooms with all the usual mod-cons plus a stereo. Free transfers are offered and there's a travel agency within the hotel.

Private Garden Resort *(☎ 225 0658; e pri vategardenresort@yahoo.com; Noreco Rd, Mangnao; double with fan & shared bathroom P250, rooms with hot-water bathroom, kitchen, cable TV & fan/air-con P500/700)* is a great budget option. It's on the coast, out of the hullabaloo of the city, but still within a P3.50 tricycle ride. Scuba instruction (open-water diving certificate US$330), rental motorbikes (P400 to P650 per day), Internet, pool tables, table tennis and even CD-burning facilities are available. Head 3km south from town and turn left at the Shell service station.

Opeña's Pension House *(☎ 225 5214; 27 Katada St; singles/doubles with air-con P460/ 558)* is alongside Silliman University and has reasonable rooms with private bathroom and cable TV.

The Worldview Pension Plaza *(☎ 225 4110–12, 422 8369; Perdices St; singles/ doubles P495/605)* has a great central location and is the best of the mid-range hotels. Rooms are sterile-clean with all the mod-cons, and the staff are very friendly. The food downstairs is best avoided, but there is OK food across the road at **Rosantes** and other options on nearby Silliman Ave and Rizal Blvd.

Plaza Maria Luisa *(☎/fax 225 7994; Legaspi St; singles/doubles from P650/850)*, overlooking the attractive Rizal Park, is often full. It has rooms with private hot-water bathroom, air-con, telephone and cable TV, and includes breakfast. There is a tour agency within the hotel.

Bethel Guest House *(☎ 225 2000, fax 225 1374; e bethel@mozcom.com; Rizal Blvd; singles/doubles/triples P700/900/1600)*, on picturesque Rizal Blvd, is a swish six-storey place offering spotless rooms with all the usual amenities, and very helpful, knowledgable staff who are well trained to serve a business crowd. The more expensive rooms have great views of the city and Rizal Blvd.

La Residencia Al Mar *(☎ 225 7100/01, 422 8449, ☎/fax 225 4724; e das@mozcom.com; Rizal Blvd; singles/doubles from P1150/1265)*

is a freshly renovated, Spanish-style place. Rooms have all the mod-cons and the dearer rooms have balconies and great water views. **Eight Wonders Travel and Tours** (see Things to See & Do earlier) and **Don Atilano** (see Places to Eat) are on the ground floor.

Places to Eat
One of the best and cheapest food options available is the nightly **food stalls** at the top end of Rizal Blvd, that serve excellent tempura fish and squid-balls with sweet chilli or sweet and sour sauce (P2.50 per stick).

Chin Loong Restaurant *(☎ 422 6933, 225 4491; cnr San José St & Rizal Blvd; special dinner P110; open 8am-11pm daily)* offers big servings of tasty Chinese and Filipino food. Particularly recommended is the 'special dinner' – bird's-nest soup, fried rice, chop suey, two mains and a soft drink.

Why Not *(☎ 225 4488; Rizal Blvd; meals & pizzas around P150; open 6am-2am daily)*, one block down from Chin Loong Restaurant, is the most popular day-and-night haunt for tourists and Dumaguete's large expat community. The establishment is an all-in-one including a snack-bar, diner, bar, pool hall, Internet café and disco. The vegetarian offerings are slim, but the pizzas are great, and the carrot cocktails (P65) and avocado shakes (P45) are less ridiculous than they sound.

Silliman University Cafeteria, *(entrance Hibbard Ave; open 6am-6.30pm Mon-Sat)*, within the Silliman University grounds, is a big, TV-focused eatery that is open to the public. Like most university cafés around the world, it serves reasonable, ultra-cheap food.

There are also several **cafés** opposite the university on Silliman Ave, serving espressos, pizza, pancakes and other light meals to the funkier student set.

Don Atilano *(☎ 225 7100/01; Rizal Blvd; meals P150-500; open 11am-2pm & 5pm-10.30pm daily)*, inside La Residencia Al Mar, is a glitzy restaurant serving imported meats and wines and the best steaks in town.

Lab-as Seafood Restaurant *(☎ 225 3536; Flores St; meals around P250; open 10am-10pm daily)* is nestled amongst a group of great restaurants on the water at the northern end of town. The seafood here is excellent, as is the sea breeze.

Santa Monica Beach Resort Restaurant *(☎ 225 0704, 420 1146; Banilad; meals around P200; open 6pm-10pm daily)* is 5km south of

THE VISAYAS

town (P100 by taxi or P30 by tricycle), but is worth it for what is considered by many as the best seafood in town.

Getting There & Away
Air There are two flights daily with **Air Philippines** from Manila to Dumaguete (P1948, one hour) and back again. **Cebu Pacific** does the same flight once daily (P1900).

Boat At the pier, you'll find the offices of the fastcraft operators **SuperCat** (☎ 225 5799/ 5811), **Delta Fast Ferry** (☎ 225 3128, 420 1111), **Cokaliong Shipping** (☎ 225 3588) and **George and Peter Lines** (☎ 225 2345).

Cebu & Bohol Cokaliong Shipping, SuperCat and George and Peter Lines all service the Cebu City–Dumaguete route. See the 'Cebu Ferries' table in Getting There & Away under Cebu City, earlier. The quickest, cheapest way to get to Cebu Island from Dumaguete is to take an easy-rider (small jeepney) from opposite Vintage Inn to Sibulan (ask to be taken to the pumpboat; P5, 15 minutes), then take one of the regular pumpboats across to Lilo-an (P27, 30 minutes). These boats run back and forth between the two ports from 6am until 5.30pm. There will usually be a bus waiting for you at Lilo-an pier that will take you straight to Cebu City (P110, five hours). A similar path can be travelled via the Negros port of Tampi, 25 minutes from Dumaguete by jeepney (P10), where boats go to and from Bato (P35, 45 minutes) on Cebu from 5.30am to 5pm daily.

Bohol SuperCat and **WG&A** (☎ 035-225 5799) both travel to Tagbilaran from Dumaguete. SuperCat leaves twice daily (P400, 1½ hours); and WG&A leaves once a week (P200, three hours).

Luzon Both **Negros Navigation** (☎ 225 6764/5, 420 1399) and WG&A service the Manila route. WG&A leaves twice a week (P1185, 36 hours) and Negros Navigation leaves once a week (P1285, 24 hours).

Mindanao George and Peter Lines has a daily morning boat to Dapitan (P130, four hours) and a boat to Zamboanga (P500, 16 hours) twice a week.

   SuperCat has a daily fastcraft between Dumaguete and Dipolog (P365, 1½ hours).

Cokaliong goes to Dapitan most mornings (P125, 3½ hours). WG&A goes to Cagayan de Oro once a week (P420, six hours).

Siquijor Delta fastcraft travel between Dumaguete and Siquijor town (P100, one hour) and return four times daily.

   SuperCat goes direct from Dumaguete to Larena (P160, 45 minutes) in the evening, and from Larena to Dumaguete in the early morning. Palacio Shipping services the same route (P60, 1½ hours) three times a week.

Bus & Jeepney For buses between Dumaguete and Bacolod, see Bus under Getting There & Away in the Bacolod section. The Ceres Bus Liner terminal is on South Rd, a short tricycle from town (P3.50 to P5).

   Buses and jeepneys leave from Real St for destinations north, such as San José, Bais and Tampi.

Getting Around
A tricycle into town from Dumaguete airport costs P5. There are tricycles everywhere and they charge P3.50 for trips around town – being a tourist, however, you should settle the price clearly before you take off. For slightly longer trips, you might want to offer P5.

   There are signs posted around town for motorbike rentals. **Manna Motorbike Rentals** (Santa Rosa St), next to OK Pensionne House, rents out motorcycles for P20 per hour.

   If you want to see the nearby attractions by rent-a-car (or van), ring **Boni Rent-a-Car** (☎ 225 4819, 422 8461) or **Menz Rent-a-Car** (☎ 225 1386, 422 4635, both of which rent out cars with drivers for P1000 for three hours, then P100 per succeeding hour.

AROUND DUMAGUETE
Valencia
Head 6km southeast from Dumaguete along a tree-lined road and you'll find yourself at the foot of **Mt Talinis** (which means 'pointed'). The mountain's twin peaks are also evocatively known as Cuernos de Negros (Horns of Negros). Valencia is a lovely, clean and leafy town with a large, grassed central square. About 2km from the town centre, in a baryo called Terejo (ter-**eh**-ho) is **Banica Valley**, a richly forested area ideal for **swimming**, **hiking** and overnight stays. Four kilometres from Valencia are the **Casa Roro**

Falls, 30m falls which will feel most refreshing after the climb down the 335 steps to get to them. The best way to get there other than walking is to hire a hubel-hubel from the market to take you to the steps (P80).

Places to Stay & Eat In baryo Terejo, **Banica Valley Swimming Pool** (admission P10) is a natural swimming hole that's been concreted and fenced in. The shop over the road has simple **rooms** (P200) with fan and shared bathroom. The owner will cook you up your meals. These are OK if you can't get in at The Forest Camp, just around the corner.

The Forest Camp (☎ 423 4017, ☎/fax 225 2991; **W** www.geocities.com/campforest; swimming/sightseeing (for nonguests) adult/ child P60/20; huts P1000) is on a choice stretch of river, with three landscaped pools and one natural, and Mt Talinis towering overhead. The stylish native-style huts have fan and private cold-water bathroom, and Filipino food is available at a small restaurant (P100 to P150). There's also a **camping ground** (per person P150), horse-riding (P20 per 20 minutes), and guided treks to Casa Roro Falls (P150, 1½ hours return), the falls halfway up Mt Talinis (P300, three hours), or to the lakes at the top of Mt Talinis (P600, six to seven hours) where there is a cottage available with floor mats (P50 per person). Forest Camp is one of the few places in the Philippines declared an alcohol-free zone.

Getting There & Away Jeepneys run all day between Dumaguete and Valencia (P5, 15 minutes). In Dumaguete, jeepneys for Valencia wait for passengers at the unnamed road just south of the Banica River. You can hire a tricycle from Valencia to Banica Valley or Forest Camp for about P20.

Twin Lakes National Park

About 20km northwest of Dumaguete, the twin crater lakes of Balinsasayao and Danao offer some of the most scenic hiking in the Visayas. The area is virgin forest and full of wildlife, from monkeys to rare orchids. It's also the traditional home of the indigenous Bukidnon people. If you want information on the park, or to arrange a guide, go to the Sibulan municipal building. Tour groups in Dumaguete run trips to Twin Lakes (see Things to See & Do under Dumaguete ear-

lier), as does Planet Action (see Moalboal & Panagsama Beach under Cebu earlier).

The entry point for the 15km hike to Twin Lakes is off the coastal road. From Real St in Dumaguete, catch one of several daily buses and jeepneys heading north and hop off about 2km before San José (P8 to P10), or take a tricycle from San José to the start of the 15km hike to the lakes.

Bais City

About 40km north of Dumaguete, Bias, home to some 68,100 people, is one of the country's top spots for **dolphin and whale watching**. More species of cetacean (including killer whales) have been seen in the waters of Tañon Strait, which separates Negros and Cebu, than anywhere else in the Visayas. Bais Bay is home to several mangrove-fringed islands making up a **bird sanctuary**, and the city's residents have built a network of raised walkways through the magnificent **mangrove forests**. While whale sightings are not to be depended upon, especially outside of their March-October migration season, spinner dolphins are quite common. Even if you're all out of luck, there is a 7km-long **sandbar** stuck out in the middle of the sea that boats can take you to frolic on; many tourists enjoy it as much as a cetacean visitation. **Bais City Tourism Office** (☎ 541 5161, 0919 820 9620, fax 541 5001) can organise a boat – P2500 for a 15-seater boat, P3000 for a 20-seater – as can most resorts.

Places to Stay & Eat Top of the range in Bais is **La Planta Hotel** (☎ 541 5755, ☎/fax 541 5756; Mabini St; prices on application) in the middle of town. This 1910 landmark hotel has large, bright, luxury twins and doubles with air-con, hot water, telephone and cable TV. The hotel has an excellent coffee shop and restaurant.

Bahia de Bais Hotel (☎ 402 8850; Dewey Islet Hilltop; rooms with bathroom & air-con P700-1000) is perfectly placed on the hilltop above nearby Dewey Islet, with gorgeous views of the bay. If you're going to stay here, it's worth paying the extra for the rooms with a view.

Getting There & Away There are buses and jeepneys running all day between Bais and Dumaguete (P20, one hour).

THE VISAYAS

SOUTHEAST COAST

Plenty of buses make touring this good southeast-coast road a breeze. The road winds past small towns with mangrove forests, sugarcane crops and dark-sand beaches with great views across to Apo Island. Accommodation options in some areas are limited, making day trips from Dumaguete a good idea.

Bacong

Bacong, about 5km from both Dumaguete and Valencia, has a wide, open central square with a couple of statues, a soccer pitch and a tennis court. Beside the square, facing Bacong's long black-sand **beach**, is **St Augustine Church**. Built in 1849, it has a wonderfully weather-beaten bell tower, and a pipe organ in the main chapel.

At the village hall nearby, get information about renting out the local **tree houses** that overlook the beach. At the time of writing, the tree houses were under repair. Next to the tree houses is the **Negros Oriental Arts & Heritage Workshop**, which churns out all sorts of stoneware for export.

Dauin

The market town of Dauin has a nice, 18th-century **church**, and is the administrative guardian of the beautiful divers' haven of Apo (see that section later). About 1km south of Dauin is the Marine Reserve of Masaplod Norte.

Atlantis Dive Resort (☎/fax 424 0578; W www.atlantishotel.com; singles/doubles from US$45/55) has luxury native-style rooms, a pool, restaurant and dive centre.

El Dorado Beach Resort (☎ 425 2274, fax 424 0238; W www.eldoradobeachresort.com; rooms US$25), has good native-style accommodation, a swimming pool and a good restaurant, and it runs a free shuttle bus from Rizal Blvd in Dumaguete four times daily. Breakfast is included. **Sea Explorers Dive Centre** (☎ 424 0094; W www.sea-explorers.com) is in the resort.

Zamboanguita

Zamboanguita (zam-bwang-**ghee**-ta) is best known by tourists for its huge and lively Wednesday **market** at Malatapay Beach, as well as being the departure point for Apo Island.

Hans and Nenita's Malatapay Cottages and Restaurant (☎ 0918 7400038; Malata-

pay; cottages P580) has very good standard cottages with doubles and fan. The beachside ones have better positioning as well as private cold-water bathroom.

Salawaki Beach Resort (☎ 225 1319; rooms P450), 2km from the centre of town (P4 by tricycle), has OK nipa cottages, if Hans and Nenita's is full.

Apo Island

Rugged and volcanic, the little 72-hectare island of Apo is fast becoming known for having some of the best **diving** in the Philippines. And if that's not enough for you, there are also some gorgeous white-sand **beaches**, great short walks, and a friendly village with an abundance of gregarious children. The island's **fiesta** is held 4 to 5 April.

The **Apo Island Marine Reserve & Fish Sanctuary** (part of the Negros Oriental Marine Conservation Park), a 15,000-sq-metre, NIPAP-protected area in the southeastern corner, is a vital marine-breeding ground and a favourite site among divers. A daily diving/snorkelling entrance fee of P150/75 for the sanctuary goes towards the community, which has run the sanctuary so well since its inception in 1986, that it received an award two years later for the Philippines Best Run Sanctuary, making Apo Island a model for sustainable ecotourism.

Places to Stay & Eat A time-worn **cottage** (P150) is available for rent in the island's southeastern corner, in front of the sanctuary. There is an electric lantern and mosquito net but not much else. Basic meals can be arranged in the nearby town of Apo, or else it's a five-minute walk to the resorts where you can pick up a good meal. When you get to Apo, ask for Damien's Place.

Liberty's (☎ 424 0888, 0917 603 9987; W www.apoisland.com; dorm room P200, doubles with fan & shared bathroom P500, with private bathroom P795), perched high above the beach and village, is the place that most divers head for. **Paul's Diving** (one dive US$16 to US$19, equipment rental US$6, open water diving-certificate US$275) – offers top instruction, which is one attraction, but the friendly, laid-back atmosphere and well-designed rooms with excellent views are equally as memorable. The food (Thai satay kebabs P150, baked prawns with cheese P250, pizza P110) is as excellent and varied as the music, which ranges from Meatloaf to Handel. Ring ahead for transfers from Malatapay (P125), and Dumaguete.

Apo Island Beach Resort *(☎/fax 225 5490; dorm P300, rooms/cottages P800-1000)* claims the best white sandy beach and completes the package with a quiet resort atmosphere. Stylish rooms and cottages have fan and private cold-water bathroom. The simple menu has good Filipino food with some international additions (P80 to P150). Transfer from Dumaguete can be arranged, as can a boat from Malatapay to Apo (P850 for eight people). Dive guiding (but no instruction) is offered by Mario, the village head and an instrumental person in the running of the sanctuary.

Getting There & Away Apo Island is about 25km south of Dumaguete. It can be reached directly by pumpboat from Dumaguete's Silliman Beach (1½ to two hours), or from the towns of Dauin or Zamboanguita (30 to 45 minutes). Another excellent option is to take a day trip over from Siquijor (see Diving under Things to See & Do in the Siquijor section later). The best departure point is from Malatapay Beach in Zamboanguita – just go to A La Butan restaurant and ask around. The best time to find a lift is 2pm, when the fisherfolk are returning. On a full boat, you shouldn't pay more than P150. For a 'special trip', you pay for the entire boat (P850).

Tambobo Bay

Ten kilometres southwest of Zamboanguita, as you enter this quiet fishing bay, the beach sand miraculously turns from brown to starch white. It's a screamingly serene getaway for landlubbers, and the protected waters also make it a favourite stopover for yachties.

Once you've suffered the long (but in actuality, very short) bumpy ride in, you'll see a turn-off for **Kookoo's Nest Beach Cottages** *(☎ 0985 405 114; W www.kookoosnest.com .ph; bamboo tree houses & cottages with shared/private bathroom P200/450, family beach-cottage with bathroom P500, fifth night accommodation free)*, a Robinson Crusoe-style setup, run by English couple Jamie and Nikki. Situated on a private white-sand cove, the four simple bamboo huts are perched above or near the water's edge.

The restaurant and dive centre are equally as primitive and idyllic. On offer are canoe

hire, day trips to Apo Island, and dive courses (one dive with equipment US$17 to US$20, open water diving-certificate $275).

Nikki has worked as a cook 'on tour' for seemingly everyone from Deep Purple to Gary Glitter, so will keep you and the drop-in yachties well fed and entertained with scandalous stories. The easiest way to get there is to call ahead for pick-up from Dumaguete (P100) or Zamboanguita (P50). You can also get there yourself from Zamboanguita by hubel-hubel (P30). Check their website for upcoming dive safaris to **Cagayan Islands**, 160km west of Negros, and **Sipalay** (see entry under Negros).

Siquijor

☎ 035 ● pop 81,600

Throughout the Philippines, Siquijor (see-kee-**hor**) has a reputation as a spooky place – its mountainous interior (around the village of San Antonio) being the traditional home of *mangkukulam* (healers). These days, Siquijor's healers can be found all over the island and their magic powers are mostly used to provide superb massage and herbal remedies.

However, the therapeutic effects of the island are not restricted to supernatural offerings – Siquijor is outrageously quiet, friendly and laid-back (even the jeepneys drive *really* slowly!).

The exceptions are the crazy Holy Week celebrations, when the local healers and revellers put the 'Mystique Island' on the festival map; plus May – a month of almost nonstop fiesta. For details see the entry for Lenten Festival of Herbal Preparation under Special Events in the Facts for the Visitor chapter.

Siquijor has a fine range of resorts, all of which are small and friendly enough to make you feel special. This is important, because there are not a lot of distractions on the island, and you are more or less stuck in your resort unless you pay for a way out. Most have their own restaurants, or can at least arrange food if given a little notice, and most also offer jeepney or motorbike tours around the island, up to the caves, or to the many beaches and offshore spots for diving.

An excellent, sealed 72km coastal road rings this picturesque coral-limestone island,

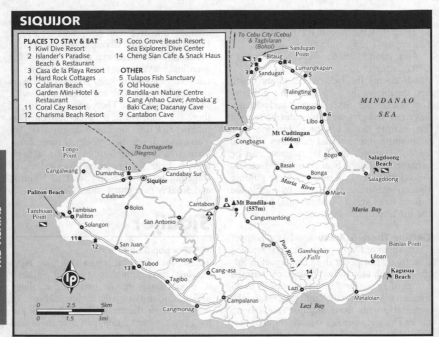

SIQUIJOR

PLACES TO STAY & EAT
1 Kiwi Dive Resort
2 Islander's Paradise Beach & Restaurant
3 Casa de la Playa Resort
4 Hard Rock Cottages
10 Calalinan Beach Garden Mini-Hotel & Restaurant
11 Coral Cay Resort
12 Charisma Beach Resort

13 Coco Grove Beach Resort; Sea Explorers Dive Center
14 Cheng Sian Cafe & Snack Haus

OTHER
5 Tulapos Fish Sanctuary
6 Old House
7 Bandila-an Nature Centre
8 Cang Anhao Cave; Ambaka'g Baki Cave; Dacanay Cave
9 Cantabon Cave

making it an absolute joy to tour. Larena is its main port, Siquijor town its capital. The only telephone land-line on the island runs between Larena and Siquijor town, with most resorts hooked up by mobile phone.

The great way to explore the island is by bike, or more simply to pick a point on the map and walk in any direction. If you are relying on jeepneys to pick you up and take you back to your resort, get started early, as many jeepneys stop for the day at around 3pm. As there is close to zero traffic on the island, it could be a long walk home if you hang around past mid-afternoon.

There's a tourism officer at the **Provincial Tourism Office**, next to the Elementary School in Siquijor town, and a **tourist office** (which seems to be open only rarely) in the Capitol Building in Larena. Being a small, compact island, most resort staff will be able to help you with most of your travel queries.

Getting There & Away
Siquijor is connected by boat to Cebu City (Cebu), Tagbilaran (Bohol) and Dumaguete (Negros). For details, see Boat under Getting

There & Away for those cities, earlier in the chapter.

Getting Around
Jeepneys and tricycles are the main means of transport. Jeepneys travel around the coastal road from Larena to Lazi (P15) via Maria (P10) and via Siquijor town (P8). They also do the Larena–Maria leg via Basak. Jeepneys start at about 5am and finish around 3pm, unless a late boat arrives, in which there will usually be a late trip from Larena. When you arrive at the pier, try to avoid getting into an empty jeepney as the driver may take off and you'll be asked to pay for the vacant seats.

Things to See & Do
One of the best ways to experience Siquijor is by following its coastal road in one big, fascinating circle. By car, motorcycle or tricycle, the 72km return trip takes the best part of an entire day, allowing for leisurely stops along the way. Resorts generally charge around P900 per jeep (for three people) for guided day trips around the island, and P400 for a motorbike tour; rental motorbikes are P300 to P500 per day, and rental mountain bikes P250

per day. From the central market area of major towns, you can organise a hubel-hubel tour (P300 to P400 for an afternoon). The road passes through the island's main settlements, and some glorious stretches of beach, especially those on the east coast.

Caving Siquijor's mysteries don't end with its mystic healers. The island's geography is just as intriguing. Limestone caves, many of which are yet to be fully explored, stretch deep into the island's dark heart. See Bandila-an Nature Centre & the Caves, later in this section.

Diving Diving is popular year-round, and favourite spots include **Paliton Beach** (three submarine caves), **Salagdoong Beach** (plenty of coral, and the odd mako shark), **Sandugan** and **Tongo Point** (colourful reefs). Nearby Apo Island (see Southeast Coast under Negros earlier) has a range of excellent dive sites, and many divers include this on their Siquijor itinerary.

There are two PADI dive centres on the island, which service the majority of the resorts: one at the northern tip **Kiwi Dive Resort** (☎ 0912 504 0596, ☎/fax 424 0534; W www .kiwidiveresort.com; Sandugan Beach; 1 dive including equipment US$18-22; open-water diving certificate US$290); and one of the six Visayan outlets of **Sea Explorers** (formerly Splash; ☎ 481 5007; W www.seaexplorerss cuba.com; Coco Grove Beach Resort, Tubod; 1 dive US$20, equipment rental US$5, open-water diving certificate US$300) on the southwest coast.

LARENA
pop 11,860
The lively little port-town of Larena is Siquijor's main point of entry for travellers. The port area has many small stalls and eateries and there's always plenty of transport available to whisk you away to one of the island's many peaceful resorts.

There's a **post office** here (and in Siquijor town), and if you really must, you can try sending emails from the **Larena Computing Services** (per hr P60; open 8.30am-6.30pm daily) in the main shopping street, opposite the **Allied Bank**. Emailing is offered from many of the resorts for exorbitant rates.

The Allied Bank in Larena will change travellers cheques if you've got all morning free. You're better off going to **Optimum** at **Belciña Pawn Shop** on the main drag, which will change cash or cheques at bank rates. The neighbouring Chinese shops will exchange, but at a lower rate.

Places to Stay & Eat
Luisa & Son's Lodge (singles/doubles P100/ 200), in Larena itself, opposite the pier, has no-frills rooms with fan and the eatery serves Filipino food. Having the pier and food stalls so close may be handy, but it can get very noisy and most travellers prefer the resorts out of town.

Garden Orchid Pension House (☎ 377 2048, 484 1002; Roxas St; singles with fan P185; family room with air-con P475) has reasonable rooms with shared bathroom. It cooks up well-priced, local food (around P50) and rents out motorbikes from P25 per hour.

Three resorts share the beach of Sandugan, 6km north of Larena. Although the beach isn't quite as blindingly white as some of the others (especially the east coast), Sandugan is the most popular tourist destination, especially for the younger, less resort-orientated crowd. A tricycle or jeepney from the pier will cost P5 to P6, but a 'special trip' will cost around P50.

Kiwi Dive Resort (☎ 0912 504 0596, ☎/fax 424 0534; W www.kiwidiveresort.com; dorm room with fan P175; cottages with fan & cold-water bathroom P390-590) is the most northerly resort, and the most popular with the budget diving crowd. But whether you're diving or not, hosts Bruce and Marithes will be dedicated to making your stay enjoyable. There are motorbikes, mountain bikes and jeeps for hire as well as maps, guidance and general travel advice.

The dorm rooms are sufficient, but if you've got the money, rent one of the well-designed cottages with blue stone floors, nipa roofs, balconies and pleasant but rare touches (like reading lamps and coffee and tea facilities). The communal area and bar are very welcoming. Guests can change foreign currency here at bank rates or get a credit card cash advance if they pay their bill by card. Free pick-up from the pier can be organised.

Islander's Paradise Beach & Restaurant (☎ 484 1058, 0918 775 2384, 0918 846 8509; e parabeech@aol.com; cottages P200-550) has great basic huts on the beach with fan and cold-water bathroom, and more spacious cottages with fridge. Life here is a little more rustic than at Kiwi, but just as laid-back and with ladles of great Filipino hospitality and very good local seafood meals with some interesting additions like red curry fish cakes (P120), pepper steak (P120) and curried eggplant (P70).

Casa de la Playa (☎ 377 2291, 0918 740 0079, 0918 771 4393; e laplaya@gmx.net; cottages P620-1100) is aimed at the esoteric traveller, offering healing massages, yoga and painting – among the jeep, paddleboat, mountain bike and motorbike rentals – and specialising in vegetarian food. The cottages are clean, spacious and moderately private, but make sure you ask for a mosquito net – you'll need it.

The P800 huts have air-con and others of similar price are on the beach. It's a large and leafy resort with friendly staff, only marred by slight over-pricing and rather aloof management.

SIQUIJOR TOWN
pop 21,200

The laid-back capital of Siquijor is Siquijor town, about 8km from the main port town of Larena. Siquijor town has a lively old **market** selling excellent fresh fish. A short walk from the pier, the town's **coral-stone church** was built in 1783, and dedicated to St Francis of Assisi. You can climb the fortress-like bell tower, up a creaky spiral staircase, for a porthole glimpse of the town's surrounds.

Places to Stay

Calalinan Beach Garden Mini-Hotel & Restaurant (☎ 0912 515 0370; room with toilet & fan P300; rooms with fan & cold-water bathroom P400-600), just 1km from Siquijor town, has pokey little rooms in a beachside villa. The place is run by Nicolaas, a hefty Dutch bloke who dishes up equally hefty American breakfasts, beef curries, homemade bread and other hearty dishes (P60 to P120).

BANDILA-AN NATURE CENTRE & THE CAVES

Almost 10km from Siquijor, past San Antonio is the Bandila-an Nature Centre, sitting atop Siquijor's highest point at 557m. It's a slow climb up there, peering down into jungle ravines with occasional reef glimpses. At 6km, you'll pass San Antonio, home to many of the healers, and centre of the ceremonies at Holy Week. The nature centre isn't comprised of a lot, but it's a good starting point for a 20-minute circuit walk to the Bandila-an peak (where you should theoretically be able to see the entire island and beyond, if it weren't mostly obscured by trees), past some natural springs, a creepy Balete tree, and be bedazzled by butterflies as they flutter about you. In the nature centre itself, there is a butterfly collection and some information on the 244-hectare park. There are 187 known floral species in the area, 27 bird and 103 butterfly species. The last remaining grounds for the possibly extinct race of the hanging lorikeet *Loriculus philippensis siquijorensis* are thought to be in this area. **Camping** is offered for free at the centre and, although cooking facilities and water are supplied, you'll have to bring everything else.

Within a few kilometres of the nature centre are a series of caves. The best known of these is **Cantabon Cave**. It's easy to find a guide in the nearby mountain village of Cantabon (can-**tah**-bon) – if possible, find a guide who can supply safety helmets and torches (a must). Tours should cost around P300. The caving here is no picnic, often involving narrow, vertical climbs, waist-deep water, bats and high humidity, but it's all worth it.

Other great caves in this area include **Cang Anhao Cave**, **Ambaka'g Baki Cave** and **Dacanay Cave**.

The best road to Bandila-an Nature Centre and Cantabon from the main ring road heads up from Siquijor town from beside the Siquijor Central Elementary School. A rougher route (OK on motorbike) can be taken from San Juan.

PALITON BEACH

There's nowhere to stay on Paliton Beach, but it's one hell of a place to be stranded! About 1km from the main road (take the turn-off at the little church in Paliton village, near the island's western-most point) along a disintegrating dirt track, this beautifully stunning white-sand beach has several simple huts and the sun-bleached shell of a failed hotel. The water is clear as glass and there are also wonderful views out to Apo Island. Following the dirt track in, you first pass a small beach with about a dozen tall palm trees. You'll find the main beach a little farther on.

SAN JUAN

The little town of San Juan is blessed with its own **natural spring swimming pool**. The main road takes a scenic dog-leg around the pool, set in a landscaped enclosure known as Calipay's Spring Park.

About 500m past San Juan, heading southeast, you'll encounter the **San Juan Cemetery**. Creep through the central passageway between the graves (on the inland side of the road) and you'll quickly reach a dead-end – in more ways than one. Piled in a big concrete box, open to the elements, are assorted skulls and bones.

Places to Stay

Coral Cay Resort (☎ 481 5024, 0919 269 1269; e scoralcayresort@yahoo.com; rooms P500-800, cottages P800-1650) is on a lovely stretch of beach at Solangon, about 3km from the town of San Juan. All rooms are clean and comfortable, with bamboo furniture and bathroom. Cheaper rooms have fan and cold water, more-expensive ones have air-con and hot water.

There are jeepney tours, a swimming pool, a small thatched-roof open-air gym, mountain bike rental, pool tables, plenty of palm trees and more. There's also a long, well-stocked bar and a restaurant serving fresh fish (from P150), big breakfasts (P120) and imported wines.

Charisma Beach Resort (☎ 481 5033; e resortcharisma@yahoo.com; doubles with fan P500, with air-con P700), 100m towards San Juan from Coral Cay, is a humble, well-tended and friendly resort with basic rooms, all with cold-water bathroom. There is a pool, and a small beach restaurant serving Filipino food with some popular Anglo additions (meals P100 to P150).

Coco Grove Beach Resort (☎ 481 5008, fax 481 5006; w www.coco-aporesorts.com; cottages P850-1550) is in a stunning spot on the beach at Tubod, about 3km southeast of San Juan. Behind a wall of local beach-stone, there's a picture-perfect world of shady tropical gardens, pool, beach and cottages. Even the cheapest rooms have polished wooden floors, air-con, minibar, veranda and a marble bathroom with hot

water. Sea Explorers Dive Centre (see Diving under Things to See & Do earlier in this section) is on the resort's premises, along with a list of free toys and activities.

LAZI
pop 18,300

The quiet southeastern town of Lazi (lah-si) is bisected by the island's only major river, the Poo (po-oh). The town is home to the stylishly time-worn, coral-stone **San Antonio de Padua Church**, built in 1857. Over the road is the oldest **convent** in the Philippines, a magnificent timber villa, creaky with age and eerily serene. Donations from visitors are welcome – look for the 'Love Offering Box' in the entrance hall.

Just out of Lazi, turn right at the Caltex service station, and amble up several kilometres to the refreshing **Gambughay Falls** on the Poo River. Just before the falls, there's a parking bay on your right for your jeep (P10) or motorbike (P5), then continue up the road another 500m until the second well-worn path to your right. Steps will take you down to this popular swimming spot.

Another 1km along the main road past the Caltex station, there's a signed turn-off for **Cheng Sian Cafe and Snack Haus**, where you'll find the best meals in the area.

Between the towns of Lazi and Maria, **Kagusuan beach** is reached via the pretty village of Minalolan – look for the turn-off for Barangay Nabutay and travel past the old limestone mine. A good road leads from the village down to Kagusuan, where steep concrete steps take you down to a string of beautiful, secluded coves.

MARIA

The **church** in the little town of Maria has a great belltower, but it's more well known for being the home of the infamous statue of Santa Rita – a black-clad, evil-eyed woman who killed her husband and holds his skull in her hands. She's the spookiest statue you're ever likely to see – or not see. Tourists love terrifying themselves with the sight of her, so when the small replica of the statue was stolen, the priest removed naughty Rita from the church and now keeps her under lock and key in the neighbouring convent. So if you want a glimpse of this moribund figure, you'll have to track down the priest.

SALAGDOONG BEACH

Billed as the island's most picturesque beach, a few kilometres past Maria, Salagdoong has pristine, white-sand coves and a rocky outcrop with a pagoda. The buildings here are a mixture of old and new, with several picnic shelters (P30 to P50) and barbecues for hire (P150) as well as a **kiosk**.

The bumpy old turn-off road to Salagdoong is almost 2km long, and winds its way through a stand of molave trees, much loved by Siquijor's **fireflies**.

LIBO

The oldest house on Siquijor is right by the road near Libo, on the east coast. Home to one of the oldest women on Siquijor, it's an amazingly durable timber building, perched on high posts and gazing out to sea.

TALINGTING

The sleepy town of Talingting (formerly called Enrique Villanueva, but recently returned to its original name) has a beautiful, sweeping **boulevard** skirting the beach and some magnificent old trees.

Just north of the small town is the **Tulapos Fish Sanctuary** – follow the signposted turn-off left towards the beach from the main road (300m). Opened in 1986, the sanctuary covers 14 hectares of prime sandflat, beach, mangrove forest and reef. Of particular interest for divers and snorkellers are large schools of great barracuda, large potato groupers and the occasional black tip shark. Visitors should check in at the guardhouse (or at least see if there's a guard on duty), and obey the sacred rules about not pinching shells, fish or anything else in the sanctuary. If you wish to go swimming, snorkelling or diving, you will have to get permission from the Tulapos barangay captain, Cesario Alcala, or else, contact the Manila DENR, Special Concerns Office (☎ 02-926 8346). Fees to snorkel in the sanctuary are P25, to dive P50 to P100. The best diving is March to December.

Hard Rock Cottages (☎ 480 3389, 0918 740 5158; Bitaug, Talingting; cottages P400) in Bitaug, 2km east of Sandugan, is a basic setup, comprising two large clean huts perched 6m above the water on a private beach. Huts have bamboo verandas, toilet and cold-water bathroom, and access is only by concrete stairs from above, making them two of the most secluded rooms on the island. The owner will arrange pick-up from the pier if you call in advance.

Panay

The tiny show-pony island of Boracay has stolen much of Panay's limelight. However, if you stick around for long enough on this large, triangular island you'll stumble across a number of decaying forts and watchtowers, some interesting

Spanish churches, adventure sports (particularly mountain biking, trekking, kayaking and rock-climbing), great seafood, handicrafts and one hell of a party spirit. The amazing Ati-Atihan Festival, held in Kalibo in January, is the most famous fiesta of its kind in the Philippines.

Much of Panay's festive tradition can be traced back to its indigenous tribal groups, namely the Ati and Ata (see the boxed text 'Atis & Parties' later). There are communities of both groups on the mainland. For information about anthropologically minded tours of these tribal areas, read about Panay Adventures Tours in Things to See & Do under Iloilo City later.

Panay is made up of five provinces: Iloilo, with its capital city Iloilo City, the main port on the island; Guimaras, a large separate island, nestled between the mainland and Negros; Antique, whose capital is San José; Capiz, whose capital is Roxas; and Aklan, proud keeper of the island of Boracay on the northern tip, but whose capital city is Kalibo. The provincial borders loosely coincide with the island's mountain ranges.

Getting There & Away

Air Apart from the main airport in Iloilo City, there's a string of domestic airports along Panay's north coast whisking people to and from Boracay. These are in the towns of Caticlan, Kalibo and Roxas. Connections are to Manila, Cebu City, Davao on Mindanao and Puerto Princesa on Palawan. See the Iloilo City, Caticlan, Kalibo and Roxas sections later for more information on air transport.

Boat Iloilo City has links to Negros, Cebu, Luzon, Mindanao and Palawan. Other ports service the popular routes to Manila and Cebu City. Roxas offers a connection with

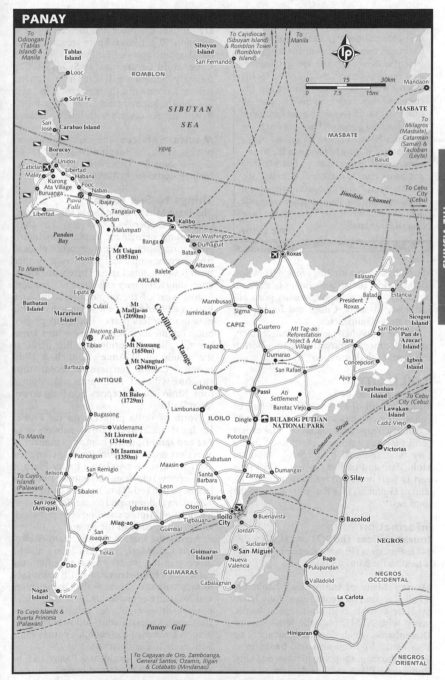

Atis & Parties

One of the all-time favourite legends of the Philippines concerns a bunch of Malay *datus* (chiefs) of Borneo, who packed up their families and followers in 1250 and sailed for the greener pastures of Panay. Once there, the chiefs somehow convinced the aboriginal Ati tribe that the rich lowland area of Panay was a fair swap for a gold necklace and a hat. The generous Ati even agreed to get out of the newcomers' way by heading into the mountains, but not before holding a fantastic song and dance ritual to seal the deal. To this day, the Ati live in Panay's mountain regions and their legendary party is re-enacted every year with the Ati-Atihan Festival in Kalibo, and several other towns.

Mic Looby

Masbate, Kalibo with Sibuyan and Romblon Islands, and Caticlan with Tablas Island and, of course, Boracay. Other smaller ports are San José, Estancia, Culasi and Jordan and Suclaran on Guimaras.

See the individual Getting There & Away entries for more information on transport to and from each destination.

ILOILO CITY
☎ 033 • pop 365,820

Iloilo (ill-o-ill-o) City is the main hub of Panay. The city has wide, attractive streets and its curving riverside layout makes it a good place to explore. 'Downtown' Iloilo City is surrounded by three old suburbs: Molo, Jaro and La Paz (la-pass). The city's port is well protected by the wonderful island of Guimaras (see that entry later) to the southeast.

Information
Tourist Offices The DOT (☎ 335 0245, 337 5411; Bonifacio Dr; open 8am-5pm Mon-Fri) is next to the Museo Iloilo.

Money Many of Iloilo City's **banks** are huddled around the central area along Iznart St. Here you have all your regular banks, many with ATMs, plus the lesser-known **Queenbank**, which does cash advances on Visa cards. You can also find **banks** in or around the main shopping plazas – SM City, Robinson's Plaza and The Atrium.

Email & Internet Access Internet cafés are all over the place and the going rate is around P30 per hour. There are cafés in all the shopping plazas, near the university, and **Cyberworld Centre**, next to St Joseph Elementary School on Iloilo Diversion Rd, which is open until the wee hours and also has food, a bar and pool table. Some hotels have business centres with Internet access.

Medical Services The most central hospital is **St Pauls Hospital** (☎ 337 2741–49; General Luna St). Otherwise, try **Iloilo Doctor's Hospital** (☎ 337 7702; West Ave).

Things to See & Do
The large **Museo Iloilo** (Bonifacio Dr; adult/child P15/5; open 9am-5pm daily) has some fascinating permanent displays, including prehistoric relics of Panay, treasure plucked from sunken ships, and jewellery unearthed from Spanish burial sites. There's usually an interesting temporary exhibition of some sort.

Just west of the city centre is the area known as **Molo**. Once a separate town, it's now more or less part of Iloilo City proper, but it retains its independence with a large, central plaza. Overlooking the plaza is the wonderful **St Anne's Church**, a 19th-century, Gothic renaissance, coral-stone structure with tall, twin spires and a domed roof. Molo is a P4 jeepney ride from downtown Iloilo.

North of Iloilo proper, over the Forbes Bridge (Bonifacio Dr) are the suburbs of **La Paz** and **Jaro**. Both are home to a number of ancestral houses and impressive churches. Well worth a visit is Jaro's **Belfry Plaza**, a P4 jeepney ride from downtown (look for jeepneys marked 'Jaro' or 'Jaro and Liko'). The plaza is dominated by the **Belfry Tower**, a lonely, old figure standing high and handsome on the edge of the square.

Across the road is the huge **Jaro Metropolitan Cathedral**, the seat of the Catholic diocese in the western Visayas. Climb the cathedral's front steps and you'll come face to face with the Shrine to the Divine Infant and Nuestra Señora de la Candelaria, which is neon-lit at night. An annual feast and fiesta (see Special Events following) is held here in honour of the church's patron saint, Señora de la Candelaria.

Tours around Iloilo and Panay can be arranged for all tastes and budgets through

Panay Adventures Tours (☎ 329 2737, 0918 778 4364, 0918 526 3401; e d_yanson@hot mail.com), run by Daisy and Reuel Yanson. Daisy, a history and anthropological researcher and writer, specialises in eco-cultural tours to the tribal groups around Panay and Guimaras like the Aetas and Bukidnon. Both Daisy and Reuel are keen mountainbikers and can equally cater to more energetic itineraries. An out-of-town day in the van with Daisy's fascinating narrative costs P3000, petrol included. They also offer cheaper car tours and customised camping trips. Bookings can also be made through Iloilo DOT office.

For the more adventurous, Iloilo has a big, welcoming community of action-jacksons, ready and willing to take you **scuba-diving, rock climbing, mountaineering, mountain biking, kayaking, caving**. If there's a way to manoeuvre over any of the earth's surfaces, these guys are doing it. Some of the possibilities on offer are: climbing Mt Madja-as, kayaking around Tibiao, rock climbing and caving in Bulabog Puti-An National Park, scuba-diving and mountain biking around Guimaras – see individual sections for details.

If you're low on cash and high on flexibility, contact **Art Tajanlangit** (☎ 320 6946, 0919 556 6929; e tribuoutdoorshop@hotmail.com), who can hook you up with the various outdoor clubs in Iloilo featuring the whole of Panay in all of the above activities. If you join a club-organised trip, you'll only be pooling the cost of permits, food, petrol and any other basic overheads.

If you drop into his shop, **Tribu Outdoor Shop & Climbing Gym**, on the ground floor of the Amigo Terrace Hotel shopping mall (see Places to Stay for details), you'll also find posted notices of up-and-coming events, and you'll probably meet one or two of the local actioneers enjoying a cuppa at the adjoining coffee shop.

If you've only got limited time to be as hard-core as possible, **Real Adventures** (☎ 320 1272, 0918 940 3400, fax 337 3970; e real-adv@iloilo.net, e dast@iloilo.net; 88 Rizal St, La Paz) is the answer. It specialises in two-day multiple-activity trips where all equipment, guides, food, accommodation and permits are covered.

Activities include the above-mentioned sports (plus more) and its playgrounds include Guimaras, Tibiao (Antique) and Bulabog Puti-An National Park. It will happily tailor trips to your liking, and prices start at around US$100 per person, all-inclusive.

Special Events
Iloilo City is famous for its mardi gras–style **Dinagyang Festival**, held in the fourth week of January. Celebrating Santo Niño (Child Jesus) with outrageous costumes and dances, this three-day frenzy of imagination takes the form of a street party, capturing perfectly the fun-loving nature of the Ilongos – not to mention their stamina.

On 2 February every year the Jaro Metropolitan Cathedral hosts the **Nuestra Señora de la Candelaria** (Feast of Our Lady of Candles). As much a religious ritual as it is a good, old-fashioned street party, this event includes the blessing of all sorts of candles, and a spangly procession headed by the year's Jaro fiesta queen.

Also in February, on the third Sunday of the month, is the exciting **Paraw Regatta**, a race from Iloilo City over to Guimaras, in traditional sailing outriggers called *paraw*. Dating back to the 16th century, the race is a high-speed version of the trip supposedly taken by Panay's ancient Malay settlers on their journey to the island from Borneo.

Several outer suburbs and towns around Iloilo City proper hold annual **kalabaw races**. One such event is held in early May in Pavia, about 5km north of Iloilo City.

Places to Stay
There are a lot of accommodation choices on General Luna St, which is a great location if you plan to get around by jeepney.

Places to Stay – Budget
Castle Hotel (☎ 338 1021; Bonifacio Dr; singles/doubles with air-con P500/550) and **River Queen Hotel** (☎ 335 0176; Bonifacio Dr; singles with fan P320, doubles with air-con P650-750) have both seen better days, but they're cheap, central, and air-con rooms have cable TV and private cold-water bathroom.

Family Pension House (☎ 335 0070; General Luna St; budget singles/doubles with fan P250/325, standard doubles with air-con from P525) is a lively and popular place with clean, well-priced budget rooms. Standard rooms are OK.

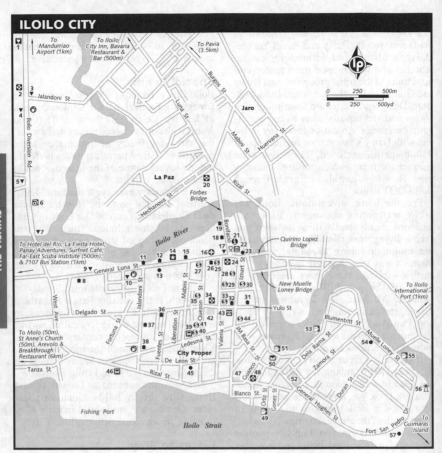

ILOILO CITY

Eros Traveller's Pensionne (☎ 337 1359; *General Luna St; singles/doubles with fan P230/295, with air-con P325/395*) is down a laneway opposite St Paul's Hospital. A favourite with students, this casual establishment offers very clean simple rooms with private bathroom. Cable TV is P50 extra.

Fine Rock Hotel (☎ 336 9075, fax 336 9080; *Jalandoni St; singles/doubles P420/560*) has good-value, clean, tiled rooms with air-con and hot-water bathroom. There is a 24-hour coffee shop downstairs.

Places to Stay – Mid-Range

Pensione del Carmen (☎ 338 1626; *General Luna St; singles/doubles/twins P550/650/700*) is a rather well-to-do, old, family-home owned by the gracious and elegant Carmen.

Rooms are great value with hot-water bathroom, air-con and cable TV. Beakfast is offered (P65 to P95) and guests can make use of Carmen's kitchen and fridge. There is a large communal guest balcony, overlooking the river.

Four-Season Hotel (☎ 336 1070; *cnr Fuentes & Delgado Sts; singles/doubles from P680/830*) is one of Iloilo's best. It looks far pricier than it is, with sparkling standard and deluxe rooms with air-con, cable TV, phone and hot showers. The swanky lobby also features a good restaurant, business centre and travel assistance.

Iloilo Midtown Hotel (☎ 336 6888, 336 8888, fax 338 0888; *Yulo St; singles/doubles P732/854*), on the eastern extension of Delgado St, is a six-storey place also known as

ILOILO CITY

PLACES TO STAY		
8	Barceló Sarabia Manor Hotel; Al Dente	
11	Residence Hotel; Waterfront Terrace Restaurant	
12	Pensione del Carmen	
15	Family Pension House	
18	Castle Hotel	
19	River Queen Hotel	
26	Eros Traveller's Pensionne; PNB Bank	
31	Iloilo Midtown Hotel (Summer House)	
32	Amigo Terrace Hotel; Amigo Terrace Restaurant; Amigo Plaza Shopping Center; Tribu Outdoor Shop & Climbing Gym; Far East Bank; Queenbank; BPI Bank	
36	Four-Season Hotel	
37	Fine Rock Hotel	
38	Centennial Plaza Hotel	

PLACES TO EAT		
3	Jalandoni Seafood Stalls	
4	Nes & Tat's Manokan & Seafoods	
5	Calzada Grill; Fiesta Ilongga	
7	Marina	

9	Ocean City Seafood & Restaurant; Metrobank; 58rio; Hot Spot Bar & Billiards	
10	Barrio Inasal	
17	Tibiao Bakery	

OTHER		
1	Barracks	
2	SM City	
6	Cyberworld Centre	
13	University of San Agustin	
14	Police Station	
16	St Paul's Hospital	
20	Gaisano City Shopping Mall	
21	Department of Tourism	
22	Museo Iloilo	
23	Provincial Capitol Building	
24	The Atrium Shopping Mall (Supermart); McDonald's; Days Hotel	
25	PNB	
27	Bank of Philippine Islands (BPI)	
28	Bank of Philippine Islands; United Cocoplanters Bank	
29	Equitable PCI Bank	
30	Bank of Philippine Islands	
33	Metrobank	
34	SM Mall; Jollibee	

35	Equitable PCI Bank	
39	Jeepneys to Miag-ao & San Joaquin	
40	Metrobank	
41	Equitable PCI Bank	
42	Marymart Mall; McDonalds	
43	RCPI International Telephone Office; Equitable PCI Bank; Internet Café	
44	Equitable PCI Bank; Dunkin' Donuts	
45	Robinson's Supermarket & Plaza	
46	Ceres Bus Terminal	
47	Central Market	
48	Gaisano Department Store	
49	Boats to Jordan (Guimaras)	
50	Post Office; Immigration Office	
51	Boats to Jordan (Guimaras)	
52	Plaza Libertad	
53	Boats to Bacolod; Negros Navigation; WG&A SuperFerry	
54	Sulpicio Lines	
55	Boats to Buenavista Wharf (Guimaras)	
56	Lighthouse; Rotary Park	
57	Foreign Pier; Trans-Asia Shipping	

the Summer House. It's central and good value for money, with large, clean, light rooms with windows overlooking the street and the usual amenities. There's also a coffee lounge in the lobby of the hotel.

Residence Hotel (☎ 337 2454; *General Luna St; singles/doubles P600/790, with river views P760/980*) looks like the dusty old set of a James Bond movie. All rooms come with hot water and cable TV, but all amenities seem to be on their last legs. Its magnificently positioned riverfront restaurant serves average food.

Iloilo City Inn (☎ 320 6290, 329 0078, fax 329 2139; W *www.nagarao.com; 113 Seminario St, Jaro; singles/doubles/triples with fan P350/410/510, with air-con P540/600/700*) is in the northern suburb of Jaro, above the Bavaria Restaurant & Bar (see Places to Eat). The clean rooms are excellent value, all with private hot-water bathroom and cable TV.

Centennial Plaza Hotel (☎ 337 2277, fax 337 2299; e *cenplaza@i-iloilo.com.ph; Jalandoni St; singles/doubles from P900/1050*) has new, large and light rooms with minibars and views of the city.

Places to Stay – Top End

Hotel del Rio (☎ 335 1171, fax 337 0736; *MH Del Pilar St; standard singles/doubles P1045/ 1210, deluxe P1320/1540*), on the western extension of General Luna St, has comfortable furnished rooms, and larger carpeted rooms with views of the water. There is a restaurant, swimming pool, business centre, travel centre and on-call shiatsu-ist.

La Fiesta Hotel (☎ 338 0044, fax 337 9508; W *users.iloilo.net/lafiesta/; rooms from P1210*), directly opposite, has equally swish rooms.

Barceló Sarabia Manor Hotel (☎ 335 1021, fax 337 9127; W *www.barcelo.com; General Luna St; singles/doubles from P2634/3134*) is a large, well-run place. There is a pool, gym, hair salon and the excellent Al Dente Restaurant (see Places to Eat).

Amigo Terrace Hotel (☎ 335 0908, fax 337 0144; e *amigo@iloilo.net; Iznart St; singles/ doubles P1800/2000*) was the city's first modern, high-class hotel. The place is looking a little tired these days, but the rooms are large and clean with views over the city towards Guimaras Island.

Days Hotel (☎ 337 3297, 336 8801, fax 336 8000; W *www.dayshotel.com.ph; General Luna*

THE VISAYAS

St; rooms from P2409), within The Atrium (Supermart) shopping mall, at first glance, doesn't present as 1st class. Head to the 4th floor of the complex and you'll find a reception desk worthy of a hotel charging these rates. All rooms have good amenities, breakfast and the daily newspaper, while better rooms have views.

Places to Eat
There's some excellent eating to be done in Iloilo – especially for seafood-lovers – often accompanied by fine views. There are also plenty of *manokan* (barbecued chicken) houses, especially on General Luna St and Iloilo Diversion Rd. The latter, known simply as Diversion Rd, has become the restaurant strip – between the river and SM City – offering a good range of options and prices. To get there, catch a Leganes or Santa Barbara jeepney from General Luna St (P4).

Amigo Terrace Restaurant, on the ground floor of the hotel of the same name, serves barbecues (P120) and buffets (P350) and 'mad-cow-free roast beef'. On the ground floor of the hotel's shopping mall, you'll find Tribu Outdoor Shop and Climbing Gym (see Things to See & Do earlier).

Jalandoni Seafood Stalls *(Iloilo Diversion Rd; meals P25-100; open 7am-midnight daily)* is a row of street stalls selling good, cheap, barbecued seafood including prawns for P120 per kg.

Nes & Tat's Manokan & Seafoods *(☎ 321 2571, 509 3112; Iloilo Diversion Rd; meals P55-100; open 8am-11pm daily)*, opposite the Caltex, is a popular, open-air restaurant on the river, with a sumptuous display of Filipino seafood dishes. Just point to the display dishes – crumbed prawns, barbecued catfish, crab or salad – and they'll cook you up a replica.

Calzada Grill *(Iloilo Diversion Rd; set meals P40-70; open 6pm-3am daily)* is a popular place for Filipino food, live music and 24-hour pool tables.

Fiesta Ilongga *(☎ 321 2812; Iloilo Diversion Rd; meals P90-140, all-you-can-eat P200; open 11am-3pm & 6pm-10pm daily)*, next to Calzada, with colourful marine-inspired murals, is a popular hang-out with the local divers. The menu offers mainly seafood, and the all-you-can-eat meals include sushi, tempura, barbecue and grilled fish.

Marina *(☎ 320 1225, 320 1230; Iloilo Diversion Rd; meals P35-150; open 8am-midnight daily)*, just over the northern side of the bridge, is an open-air, nipa restaurant on the river, offering authentic Filipino food with a strong seafood emphasis. Favourites are the seafood in coconut and chilli (P155), char-grilled *bangus* (milkfish; market price) and *beef ampalaya* (beef and horseradish soup; P115).

Barrio Inasal *(☎ 337 2482; meals P40-100; open 11am-2pm & 5pm-10pm daily)* is a wildly popular eatery serving Filipino dishes, especially barbecue, in a garden setting.

Al Dente *(☎ 336 7813; Barceló Sarabia Manor Hotel, General Luna St; pasta P80-140, pizza P140-200; open 11am-midnight Sun-Thur, 11am-2am Fri-Sat)* is a cool, smooth café-restaurant, run by Pauline, a New York–trained chef. The Italian and European dishes, cakes (P40 a slice) are large and tasty, and Pauline will happily customise dishes. One day a week, all-you-can-eat meals are great value (P150).

Ocean City Seafood & Restaurant *(☎ 336 9272, 336 0118; General Luna St; meals for 3 people P100-190; open 10am-11pm daily)* is a popular restaurant, with a few speciality foods such as clam, abalone, Peking duck (P600 for half) and pan-fried pigeon (P200 a piece).

Peppy Thai *(☎ 321 2735; Iloilo Diversion Rd; meals around P80; open 10am-2pm [at latest] Mon-Sat)*, at the northern end of Diversion Rd (in the suburb of Jaro) has some of the best authentic Thai food that you'll find outside Thailand. The restaurant is a humble, streetside affair with a small array of dishes such as fried 'paper' squid, spicy coriander noodles, green curry and fried pork dumplings with sweet chilli sauce. Arrive early before the food runs out.

Bavaria Restaurant & Bar *(☎ 320 6290; 113 Seminario St, Jaro; meals P80-200; open 8am-midnight daily)*, below Iloilo City Inn, is a popular haunt for German travellers who can soothe any homesickness with the alpine murals and decor, and Euro-German meals, wines, beers and spirits.

Breakthrough Restaurant *(Arevolo; fish meals around P100; open 7.30am-9pm daily)* is an open-air, beach restaurant catching the sea breeze in the northwest suburb of Arevolo. The day's catch, including lobster, crab and oysters, is displayed for you to peruse. The chef will cook up your purchase for an additional P10 to P25. Get here by Calumpang jeepney (P5) or by taxi (P50).

Tibiao Bakery *(cnr Bonifacio Dr & General Luna St)*, opposite The Atrium (Supermart) shopping mall, is a big place with good baked munchies.

Entertainment

Many of the popular restaurants roll on into the night. There are also several bars that attract a young crowd.

Barracks *(☎ 321 2295/6; Iloilo Diversion Rd; meals P60-150; open 6.30pm-late daily)*, cashing in on the American military obsession, looks like a set from MASH – a large open barracks with wooden mess-tables, 40-gallon drums, sandbags, a heli-pad and khaki-clad staff ('sergeant' to you). There's cheap, meaty, pub grub and live music every night.

58rio *(General Luna St; open 6pm-1am daily)* is a well-located restaurant-bar on the river; and **Hot Spot Bar & Billiards** *(☎ 338 2736; General Luna St; pool tables per hr P80; bar food P25-85; open 2pm-2am Mon-Sat, 5pm-2am Sun)*, next door, is a modern, two-storey, licensed pool hall.

Shopping

The main shopping centre in town is **SM City** *(Iloilo Diversion Rd)* and is open 9am to 8pm daily. It costs P4 by Santa Barbara or Leganes jeepney to get there. **Robinson's Plaza** and **The Atrium** are much smaller, but will service most basic shopping or ticketing needs.

Getting There & Away

All of the shopping plazas – The Atrium (Supermart), SM City, Robinson's Plaza and Guisano City Shopping Mall – have ticketing offices open 9am to 8pm daily.

Air Airline offices at Iloilo's **Mandurriao airport** *(☎ 320 8048)* include **Cebu Pacific** *(☎ 320 6889)*, **PAL** *(☎ 320 3030/3131/7151)* and **Air Philippines** *(☎ 320 8048/49/52)*.

PAL flies from Cebu City to Iloilo City once daily, and has two return flights (P2143, 30 minutes). Cebu Pacific flies to Cebu City every morning (P1944).

PAL has four return flights daily from Manila to Iloilo (P2843, one hour), Cebu Pacific has three flights to Manila from Iloilo (P2544) and Air Philippines has four one-way flights (P2543).

Cebu Pacific flies daily from Iloilo City to Davao (P3184, two hours) via Cebu City in the early morning. PAL (P3043) and Air Philippines (P2990) fly the same route several times a week.

PAL flies from Iloilo to Puerta Princesa (P2568, one hour) and back four times per week.

Bus The main destination outside Iloilo City is Caticlan (as a launching pad to Boracay). Buses and vans run continually all morning to Caticlan (nonair-con/air-con P112/123, 5½ hours), slowing down or stopping service around 1pm. Other destinations include Kalibo (P68, four hours), Roxas (P47, three hours), and Estancia (P52, 3½ hours). These are serviced by a variety of bus lines, including **Ceres Bus Liner** *(☎ 321 2491/2371, 337 0456)*, with buses starting before dawn and running every 30 minutes until around 4pm. Air-con buses are up to 30% more expensive.

Also servicing the route to Caticlan (and several other major destinations) are privately operated (and usually air-con) L-300 minibuses that, when full, head off along standard bus and jeepney routes for around 25% above the usual bus fare. Drivers tout for passengers – especially foreigners – at most of the main bus stations. For direct trips to Caticlan (P130) or Kalibo (P100) from Iloilo City, these can cut down travelling time by about half an hour, and are a more cushy way to travel. There are jeepneys running all day every day to towns west of Iloilo; they may terminate in these places, or simply drop you off and keep going. Possible destinations include Tigbauan (P20, 22km), Guimbal (P4.50, 29km), Miag-ao (P15, 40km) and San Joaquin (P20, 53km).

Boat Iloilo City is serviced by these lines:

Aleson Shipping Lines *(☎ 337 3108/9)*
Bullet Express *(☎ 338 0618/0619/0620)*
Cokaliong Shipping Lines *(☎ 336 3322/1122/ 3333)*
Negros Navigation *(☎ 337 9882/9759, 320 3430)*
Milagrosa J-Shipping *(☎ 335 0955, 337 8627)*
SuperCat *(☎ 336 8290/1316)*
Sulpicio Lines *(☎ 337 9051/6261)*
Trans-Asia Shipping *(☎ 337 2247/5323, 336 2413)*
WG&A Superferry *(☎ 337 2567, 335 0375)*

THE VISAYAS

There are plenty of daily ferries and pump-boats between Iloilo City and Guimaras' main ports of Buenavista Wharf and Jordan. See Getting There & Away under Guimaras later for more information.

Cebu & Negros See the Panay entry under Boat in Cebu City's and Bacolod's Getting There & Away section, earlier in this chapter, for information on boat services between Iloilo City and Cebu City, and Iloilo City and Bacolod.

Luzon Negros Navigation goes to Manila most days (P1345, 17 to 22 hours). Sulpicio leaves for Manila twice a week (P895, 20 hours, or via Estancia 30 hours). WG&A has boats to Manila three days a week (P1245, seven hours).

Mindanao Negros Navigation has a once weekly boat to Cagayan de Oro (P1260, 14 hours); to Zamboanga (P765, 17 hours), which continues on to General Santos (P1270, 33 hours); and to Ozamis (P1215, 14 hours), which continues on to Iligan (P1215, 20 hours).

Sulpicio goes to Zamboanga/General Santos four afternoons a week (P548/930, 13 to 16 hours), and to Cotabato (via Zamboanga; P779, 48 hours) once a week.

WG&A has a once weekly trip to General Santos (P1200, 24 hours); to Davao (P1200, 34 hours); to Cagayan de Oro (P1190, 13 hours); to Iligan (P1145, 14 hours); and to Ozamis (P1145, 18 hours).

Palawan Milagrosa has a boat twice a week for Cuyo Islands (P220, 12 hours) that continues on to Puerta Princesa (P495, 36 hours), before returning to Iloilo City.

Getting Around

To/From the Airport The airport is about 4km out of town and a taxi there costs about P100. Taxi drivers (and their meters) are quite reliable here.

Car Hire-car companies, as in other Philippine cities, usually provide drivers for a similar price to cars without drivers. Rates within the city's limits for hire cars are around P500 for the first three hours then P150 for succeeding hours; and for air-con vans, P850 for the first three hours then

P200 per hour. Companies include **Sarabia Manor Hotel** (☎ 335 1021) and **Lexus Rent-A-Car** (☎ 033-335 1171) at the Hotel del Rio. **Panay Adventures Tours** (see Things to See & Do earlier) has comparable rates, with optional tour-guiding thrown in.

Jeepney The ever-reliable jeepney offers a great way to explore Iloilo. For the standard P4 around-town rate, jeepneys marked 'La Paz', 'Jaro' and 'Liko' will take you north of central Iloilo; and 'Molo' and 'Arevalo' will take you west. Of course, they'll also bring you right back to where you started. For a little more you can get to Guimbal (P4.50), Tigbauan (P7), Oton (P8), Miagao (P15) and San Joaquin (P20).

BULABOG PUTI-AN NATIONAL PARK

About 33km north of Iloilo is this 854-hectare park, home to monkeys, wild chickens, native orchids, 18 species of bat, and the endangered bleeding-heart pigeon. When you arrive at the base, you'll be asked to log in, give a donation, and on the weekends you'll have to show a permit. These are free for anyone who makes the trek to the faraway DENR office in Barotac Viejo. A better alternative is to visit the park from Monday to Friday, or contact Tribu Outdoor Shop (see Things to See & Do under Iloilo City earlier) to organise a permit.

There are about 35 **caves** within the park, eight of which are within 3km of the base – just ask someone at the base to guide you (suggested tip P50). For those who get their rocks off clambering up sheer cliff-faces, some of the best **rock climbing** routes in the Philippines have been set up in the park by the local enthusiasts. More advanced climbers can enjoy 50m routes and can even help peg new ones if they wish. Beginners are also encouraged to come along for a lesson. Contact Tribu Outdoor Shop for more details.

Visitors can stay in the empty **cottage** (P250) at the base for or pitch a tent among the mahoganies. There's nearby swimming (P7) and plenty of drinking water, but you'll have to bring your own food. The guys at the base sell soft drinks and will cook for you (suggested tip P50).

Buses and jeepneys run between Iloilo and the nearby town of Dingle (ding-leh) until late afternoon (P25, 45 minutes). From

Dingle, it's a P10 tricycle ride to the park base and an extra P5 to the rock-climbing area.

GUIMARAS
☎ 033 • pop 14,1500

The 'world's sweetest mangoes' are only one of many draw cards on the island-playground of Guimaras (gim-**are**-ass with a hard 'g'). This quiet, mountainous island is strapped by a handful of scenic, winding roads with well-signed attractions, making it perfect touring country and a hot favourite with mountain-bike riders (see Special Events later). On the coast, island-hopping opportunities abound, with some of the best areas being on the west coast, around Alubihod Beach in Santa Ana Bay and Baras Beach in Lawi Bay.

San Miguel, the island's laid-back capital, is not much more than a wide, main street. It has a PT&T telephone office, ticketing office, bakeries and other eateries.

There's a helpful **tourist office** (☎ 503 0328; W www.guimaras.gov.ph; open 8am-4.30pm daily) at Hoskyn Port.

Things to See & Do

The time-ravaged **Navalas Church** is about 7km from Buenavista (bwen-a-vis-ta) on the northern end of the island, near a beachside boulevard of coconut trees. Built in the 17th century, the limestone church is fronted by some beautiful, big trees and a squat, roofless belltower. Head down the coconut boulevard from Navalas Church, towards the water, and you'll reach the 1910-built summer retreat of the wealthy Lopez family, known as **Roca Encantada** (Enchanted Rock). From the beaches here you can often hire pumpboats to explore the strange cluster of seven islands to the north, known as **Siete Pecados**, or the 'Islands of Seven Sins'.

To see the source of Guimaras' famous mangoes, try **Oro Verde mango plantation** (☎/fax 0912 520 0354), near Buenavista. A vast, mouth-watering stand of more than 50,000 trees (some more than 100 years old), the plantation is a very busy place come harvest time in April and May (see Special Events later). The soil in this area is reddish and acidic, which is just how mango trees like it. Contact the plantation directly to make an appointment for a visit.

If you want to take a more educational tour, just outside San Miguel on the road to Lawi, you'll find the **National Mango Research & Development Centre** (open 8am-noon & 1pm-5pm Mon-Fri), which is dedicated to developing cost-effective and environmentally friendly mango production. There is information available on mango varieties, current projects and research, mango product processes and even a few recipes.

Macopo Falls (doubles with shared bathroom P200; picnic shelters per day P50; daytrip admission P10), 1.5km from San Miguel (look for the hand-painted sign that says 'Farm Tourism'; P15 by tricycle from San Miguel), offers hiking, swimming, great views and cheap accommodation all in the one spot. At the bottom of a steep precarious hill trail among young mahoganies and other carefully labelled trees, is a refreshing pool beneath the falls, which snake through pristine, rocky terrain high above. Four-room native-style **cottages** with shared balcony and panoramic views are perched halfway down the trail, as are some thatched-roof daytime shelters. There are no stores or eateries here, so you should stock up on food in San Miguel and staff will happily cook (P50 per meal), and even shop, if you don't feel up to it.

Our Lady of the Philippines Trappist Monastery, on the main road south of San Miguel, looks to have landed a lucrative sponsorship deal with God. This immaculate complex includes a turreted accommodation-and-seminar building, a modern church with blindingly well-polished tiles, and some prime farmland. A surprisingly humble store opposite the church sells carved souvenirs, sweets, cookies and preserves (a 320g jar of delicious calamansi (citrus) marmalade, guava jelly or mango jam for P50) – all 'religious made with prayerful hands'. There is also some of the cleanest **accommodation** (☎ 0917 240 0329, 0912 520 1538; rooms with fan P350, with air-con P500; prices include all meals) you're likely to find available for reverent guests, but you'll have to book well in advance with Brother Stephan Peralta. You can get here from San Miguel by jeepney (P6) or tricycle (P50).

One of the best ways to enjoy the sites of Guimaras is by taking a mountain-bike trip. Several resorts in Guimaras rent out OK mountain bikes (around P300 per day), but for a better bike, and trail guides, contact Boyz Jamandre of the **Iloilo Mountain Bike**

THE VISAYAS

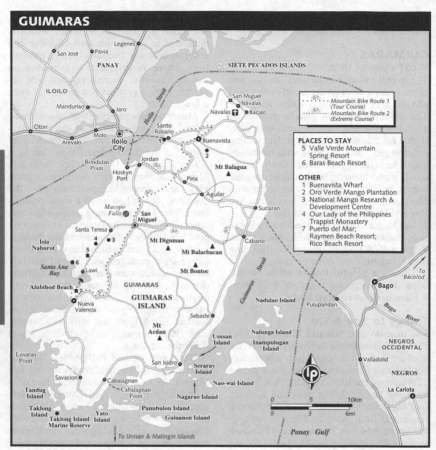

GUIMARAS

Mountain Bike Route 1 (Tour Course)
Mountain Bike Route 2 (Extreme Course)

PLACES TO STAY
5 Valle Verde Mountain
   Spring Resort
6 Baras Beach Resort

OTHER
1 Buenavista Wharf
2 Oro Verde Mango Plantation
3 National Mango Research &
   Development Centre
4 Our Lady of the Philippines
   Trappist Monastery
7 Puerto del Mar;
   Raymen Beach Resort;
   Rico Beach Resort

To Unisan & Malingin Islands

Panay Gulf

Association (*IMBA; ☎ 3201272, 0918 940 3400, fax 337 3970; e real-adv@iloilo.net; 88 Rizal St, La Paz, Iloilo City*); bikes from here cost around US$15 to US$20 per day. IMBA also runs monthly fun rides that attract more than 300 riders, as well as an international mountain bike festival (see Special Events).

Special Events
The **Ang Pagtaltal Sa Guimaras** draws big crowds to Jordan (hoar-**daan**) every Good Friday (late March to April) to watch the re-enactment of Jesus Christ's crucifixion. Unlike the blood-spattering re-enactments in other parts of the country, the Guimaras presentation usually sees an amateur 'Christ' roped rather than nailed to his cross.

The island's much admired mangoes are honoured every May (just after harvest time) with the **Manggahan Sa Guimaras fiesta** (Mango Festival). It's held on the lawns in front of the Provincial Capitol Building in San Miguel. For more information, contact the tourist office (☎ 503 0328) at Hoskyn Port.

Every February or May (coinciding with the Manggahan Sa Guimaras fiesta) the island hosts the **Guimaras International Mountain Bike Festival**, a three-day event centred on a 45km, off-road-circuit. For more information, contact Boyz Jamandre from IMBA.

Places to Stay & Eat
Valle Verde Mountain Spring Resort (*☎ 336 9535, 0918 730 3446; doubles P250, rooms for 5 persons P350*) is halfway between San

Miguel and Lawi, on one of the island's highest points, peering over the valley rainforest and nearby reefs of Lawi Bay. You'll be greeted by the forever-smiling Luisa and shown to a basic hut, and pointed the way down the 311 steps to a spring-fed swimming pool and picnic hut (P15 entry to pool for nonguests).

The generator brings electricity in the late afternoon, and delicious local dishes can be prepared with prior notice (around P50 a meal). You can get here by jeepney from Jordan (P10) or San Miguel (P4) if you don't mind the 500m walk to the resort, or by tricycle (P100 from Jordan). Mountain bikes (P400 to P500 per day) and motorbikes (P500 per day) can be organised.

Puerto del Mar (*☎ 336 5457/1710; rooms with fan/air-con P700/900; admission nonguests P20*) is hidden behind a steep hill, next to Alubihod Beach. Follow the path around the hill, over bridges, through mangroves, to Villa Corazon, the resort's main eating area. Beyond is a private cove with a miniature beach, and nipa huts perched on steep hills on either side. The balconied huts have private bathroom and some have great views. From here, you can hire pumpboats for trips around the nearby islands and islets (P200 per hour for two people).

Raymen Beach Resort (*☎ 0912 520 8691; Aludihod; doubles with fan & shared bathroom P500, with private bathroom P600, family rooms with air-con P900*) has reasonable rooms and picnic huts (P75 to P300) on this popular beach. There is a restaurant with Filipino food (P50 to P100), and staff can arrange jeep tours (P1800) and island-hopping trips (P200 per hour).

Alubihod Beach can be reached by jeepney (P15) or tricycle (P150 to P200) from Jordan.

Rico Beach Resort (*hut with shared bathroom P450*), next to Raymen, is a very basic setup, with no restaurant – only elevated huts with lovely views.

Baras Beach Resort (*☎ 0917 241 1422, 0917 945 0838, 0917 940 1501; ⓦ http://baras.willig-web.com; doubles/twins P650-750, family P900*) is a thoroughly secluded place on a sublime beach, a short ride by pumpboat from Alubihod Beach. Food is good and well priced, with seafood a speciality (breakfast P100 to P150, lunch P195, dinner P220). On a hillside in a narrow

cove, the resort's nine private cottages have million-dollar views above a central white-sand beach. Each cottage is unusually spacious, with fan, private bathroom, and a highly seductive balcony. Some have kitchen, fridge and furnishings.

The beachside entertainment area includes a bar, pool tables and table tennis. You can rent snorkelling gear (P150 per day), any one of the large fleet of boats (P200 to P350 per hour with crew) and good fishing gear (P150 per day).

The simplest way to get here is to arrange to be picked up by the resort's 18m pumpboat from Iloilo (P1100 per boat, one hour). Otherwise, you can make your own way to Lawi, on the northern shore of Santa Ana Bay, or to nearby Alubihod Beach, and then hire a pumpboat around to the resort (P250 per boat, 15 minutes). Day-trippers are charged P50 to hang out.

There is also **accommodation** available at both the Macopo Falls and The Trappist Monastery (see Things to See & Do earlier).

Getting There & Away

There are pumpboats and ferries between Iloilo City and Jordan (Hoskyn Port) every day from around 5am to 6.30pm (P7.50, 15 minutes). They leave Iloilo at Ortiz boat station, at the southern end of Ortiz St (take a Mandurriao jeepney – P4). Small ferries service the same route (P7.50, 30 minutes) every hour.

Pumpboats to Buenavista wharf (west of Buenavista town) leave from Iloilo's Parola boat station, on Muelle Loney St (P8.50, 20 minutes).

A hired pumpboat from between Iloilo City and Guimaras (P1500 per boat) can be organised from any of the ports, or from anywhere you see a pumpboat.

Pumpboats run daily between the west-coast Negros town of Pulupandan and the northeastern Guimaras town of Suclaran (P40, one hour).

Getting Around

Tricycles roam all over Guimaras, on very good roads, and cost around P150 per hour or P900 a day. This price easily includes waiting time at the various places of interest. The tourist office at Hoskyn Port can organise this for you and inform you of the going rate for any destination.

THE VISAYAS

Jeepneys are a common sight, mostly on the sealed road routes between the main towns. The average short-trip price is P6 (eg, from Jordan to San Miguel). Pumpboats are also available for hire at port towns and many beaches. The average price per boat is about P300 for the first hour then P100 per succeeding hour.

SOUTHWEST COAST
☎ 033

The southwest coast is dotted with many towns and low-key resorts. The beaches have dark sand that won't appeal to all, but if you like checking out old Spanish churches, or are after a quiet getaway or picnic location, there are plenty of choices.

Tigbauan

Only 22km from Iloilo City, the small town of Tigbauan (tig-**bow**-an) is an unassuming place centred on the baroque-fronted **Tigbauan Church**, the site of the country's first Jesuit school for boys, established in 1592.

Guimbal

Guimbal (**gim**-bal with a hard 'g') is 29km from Iloilo. It has one of the prettiest town plazas in the region, and on the western side of this plaza is the mighty sandstone landmark known as the **Guimbal Roman Catholic Church**. Down by the water, you will find several incredibly solid, creeper-covered 17th-century *bantayan* (watchtowers) squeezed in among the houses along the waterfront, built by the Spanish for keeping out marauding Moro (Muslim) pirates.

From Guimbal, you can take a jeepney to Igbaras (**igg**-bar-ass; P10, 15 minutes) and ask someone to set you on the 30-minute walk to **Nadsadjan Waterfall** (nad-sad-han), a 15m-high torrent with a deep swimming hole at the base.

From Igbaras, take the street from the plaza towards the mountains, past Jocelyn Store, along a glorious, very rough road through a deep valley. You should cross the river three times, and pass through the rice-terrace village of **Igtalongon**, before finally arriving at the falls. Jeepneys do make the bumpy trip out to Igtalongon (and sometimes beyond), but you definitely shouldn't count on them.

Places to Stay & Eat Right on the water just west of Guimbal proper, **Shamrock**

Beach Resort (☎ *508 8561; cottages or rooms with fan P450, with air-con from P850*) offers big, clean hotel-style cottages with private cold-water bathroom. Day-time picnic shelters are available (P150) and the breezy restaurant does big serves of Filipino food with a few extras (curry, teriyaki) for P60 to P100. There are also darts, pool tables, volleyball and chess. Check-out time is 10am.

Bantayan Beach Resort (☎ *512 0013, fax 315 5006;* @ *bantayan@iloilo.net; 2-/6-person cottages P750/1200, 2-/6-/10-person rooms P750/850/1200*) is a vast property about 1km west of the Shamrock. A popular and laid-back place on the water, it has cottages, and large tiled rooms with balconies. Check-out time is a positively unfair 9am, but, as with the Shamrock, this is only enforced at peak times.

Racso's Woodland (☎ *315 5003, 512 0014;* @ *racsos@iloilo.net; nonguest adult/child P50/ 30; rooms from P900*) is a large property opposite Bantayan Beach Resort with a miniature woodland, a plant nursery and a miniature bird and fish zoo, with some creatures in less-fortunate conditions than others. There are big, hotel-style rooms with cable TV and private hot-water bathroom, a huge pool and a poolside restaurant.

Miag-ao

The attractive town of Miag-ao (mee-**yag**-ow) occupies a hill 40km from Iloilo City. Taking pride of place at the top of this hill is the imposing **Miag-ao Church** (officially known as Santo Tomas de Villanueva), one of four Philippine churches to have made Unesco's World Heritage list. Built between 1787 and 1797, the church served as a fortress against Muslim raiders and was damaged by revolutionary fighting in 1898, fire in 1910 and earthquake in 1940. Seemingly indestructible, this prime example of Philippine rococo was restored to its former glory in 1962. Its bas-relief facade depicts St Christopher strolling through a tropical forest with baby Jesus.

On the west side of town is the Visayan campus of the University of the Philippines.

There are plenty of destinations for day trips from this town including **Sinuhutan Cave**, **Danao Lake**, interesting **rock formations** and cool **fern forests**, all surrounding the town of La Consolacion, a jeepney ride from Miag-ao (P20, 45 minutes). **Bugsukan Falls** and **Tabay Falls** can also be reached by Bacolod–Delije Rd jeepney (P20, one hour) and then by foot (one hour). If you're light on time and energy, take a tricycle to Cabang (P10) to see **pottery making**, as well as **loom-weaving** in Indag-an.

Unfortunately, the accommodation in town isn't great – you may have to make do with **Villa Marina Beach Resort** (rooms from P350), near the university. Double rooms are small and very basic, but do have aircon and private cold-water bathroom. The beach is nothing to get excited about but the picnic shelters have good views (P120).

San Joaquin

About 53km from Iloilo you'll come to San Joaquin (san-ho-kwin), famous for its *kalabaw* fights, held every January. At the eastern end of town is the very spooky **Municipal Cemetery of San Joaquin**.

Tiolas

The pretty little town of Tiolas (t-yoll-ass), 60km from Iloilo, is where the coast road forks. The main road – to San José (Antique) – heads inland through some spectacular mountain country and rice terracing, while a rough, mostly unsealed road follows the rugged coast to the remote town of Anini-y, on Panay's southwestern tip. Along the inland road you'll find **stalls** selling excellent, locally made peanut brittle (P5 to P10).

Places to Stay & Eat – Inland (Northern) Road from Tiolas Just north of Tiolas proper, **Rest Along The River Restaurant** (dishes P50-75; open 7am-7pm daily) is an inviting open restaurant with native-style decor. A cool place to sip the juice from a coconut and enjoy good local dishes like *chicken tino-on* (chicken and spices steamed inside a banana leaf).

San Bernadino Mountain Resort & Restaurant (☎ 0917 497 3806; meals P70-120; rooms & bungalows with air-con & cold-water bathroom P400) is about 10km from Tiolas at the top of a steep hill, just before the Iloilo–Antique border. Freddy and Wilma (famous, not for their past in Bedrock, but for running Batanga resthouses Sweet Inn and Seaview Lodge), offer a family atmosphere and meticulously kept rooms, restaurant and gardens, all with

great views over the nearby valley. There's very good Filipino and Western food at the open-air restaurant – try the Hungarian goulash and huge fresh salads. There is also a small swimming pool and plans for horse riding and van tours.

Places to Stay & Eat – Coastal Road to Anini-y This bumpy road, south of Tiolas, meanders along the coast past pebbly, palm-lined beaches, waters dotted with fisherfolk and views back to the mountainous coast. There are several almost identical resorts, all with basic (usually bamboo) huts with fan and cold-water bathroom, positioned so close to the water that you'll feel like you're about to sail away during the night. Shady picnic shelters are also available for rent along these beaches.

The resorts don't have restaurants so you'll have to bring your own food and they will cook for a small fee if you don't feel up to it. If you give good warning they can probably organise meals. The luxuries aren't in abundance but the hospitality certainly is.

The first in line from Tiolas, and a fine choice if you decide to look no further is **Basang Basa Beach Resort** (☎ 0917 252 3754, 0917 467 3651; cottages P500-1000), followed 2km south by **Tobog Beach Resort** (cottages P600-1000) and **Bogtong Bato Beach Resort** (cottages P600-700) right next door. Another 5km brings you to **Lawigan Beach Resort** (☎ 337 0008; cottages P550-700), 17km before Anini-y.

Anini-y & Nogas Island

There are two roads to Anini-y (ah-nee-nee) – one from Tiolas, the other from San José (Antique), but both are unsealed and the going can be pretty tough. About 80km from Iloilo, Anini-y is a lonely little place with some big attractions, as well as a handful of basic day-time **cottages**, and a couple of small **eateries**. The attractions include **sulphur hot springs**, in the town itself, and **Nogas Island**, with a marine sanctuary and one of Panay's best and most pristine coral reefs, just off shore.

For diving, contact Real Adventures (see Things to See & Do under Iloilo City earlier; prices are available upon application). The only place to stay is **Cazeñas Lodging House** (☎ 358 9346; rooms with fan & shared bathroom per person P70).

THE VISAYAS

SAN JOSÉ (ANTIQUE)
☎ 036 • pop 48,300

On the west coast, about 96km from Iloilo, this largish port town doesn't draw a big crowd. Being one of several places in the Philippines called San José, most people refer to it as San José Antique. Antique, by the way, is pronounced an-**tee**-kay.

On the street leading straight inland from the Provincial Capitol Building is a **PT&T telephone office**, a **Metrobank** and a **PNB** bank. Opposite the town's central plaza there's an **Equitable PCI Bank**.

Places to Stay & Eat
Marina Lodge (☎ *0919 539 8606; rooms with fan & cold-water bathroom P250, with air-con P600*) is a rough and ready place about 200m from the pier (on the right when you're facing inland), accessible from the beach or by the road. The beach isn't much to speak of, but the beach shelter is a serene spot with a good view across the bay. The entrance is signposted off the main street, down a private driveway.

There are some small eateries at the pier and in the town.

D'Reyeses Batchoy & Restaurant & Pizza House (*meals P22-50, pizzas P55-90; open 5.30am-7.30pm daily*), a low-key, airy restaurant opposite the city plaza is good for *buko* (coconut) pie (P10) and for Tagalog Mills & Boon novels.

Regina's Restaurant (*meals P50-130; open 7am-9pm daily*), down the street from D'Reyeses, has Chinese, Filipino, Indonesian, seafood and steak, and chintzy decor.

Getting There & Away
Ceres Bus Liner buses (and other companies) leave every 30 minutes, between San José and Iloilo City (P60, 2½ hours), and San José and Libertad (P60, five hours). Air-con vans service the same route; prices are around 25% more expensive.

The town's pier serves **MBRS Shipping Lines** (☎ *0919 286 4712*), which sails to Manila three times a week (P710, 17 hours), and Cuyo Islands (Palawan) once a week (P190, four hours). Buy your tickets at the Trade Town Building in the public market.

TIBIAO & AROUND
Near the town of Tibiao (tib-*ee*-ow), north of San José, the mighty **Tibiao River** has plenty of white water and some excellent **kayaking** spots. There's no commercial accommodation in Tibiao, but Romeo Reyno, at the municipal tourist office in the centre of town can organise a **homestay** for you.

Bugtong Bato Falls (*admission P10*) is a 6km walk from Tibiao. Head off from the main road near the municipal tourist office. Altogether there are seven levels of waterfalls (but it's only possible to scramble above the third), sprawled across a steep, 14km stretch of river. The first and second falls are the only safe swimming areas – falling rocks elsewhere make exploring too dangerous. The second waterfall is reached via a rope.

Inland from Tibiao, in the rice, mango and coffee country of barangay Tuno, is the **Whitewater Kayak Inn** (☎ *02-821 6706, 823 2725;* Ⓦ *www.tribaladventures.com/kayakinn .htm; huts P400*), peering over the Tibiao River. The bamboo huts are exquisitely basic – just a lantern and sleeping mats – but the landscape, hospitality and *kawa* (fire-heated woks used as hot baths) create a primitive paradise. Edwin, the guide, will help you with hiking (eg, to Bugtong Bato Falls, 3km), kayaking, mountain biking, cooking and anything else.

The kayaking is grade 3+, but can get quite low in the dry season, so it's a good idea to contact the inn beforehand if you plan on kayaking.

You can either bring your own food (the Culasi market is a good place to pick up fish), or call ahead to organise food.

If travelling from Caticlan, get a jeepney to Crossing Nabas (P20, 30 minutes), and another towards Tibiao (P45, three hours). Jump off before the town at barangay Importante, and either walk or find a motorbike (P20) to take you the 7km to the inn. If you've come from Iloilo (P68), you're probably best off going to the vice-mayor or tourist office and ask to arrange a lift. There are buses every 30 minutes leaving San José for Libertad via Tibiao (P26, two hours).

Alternatively, Tribal Adventures (see Boating & Other Water Sports under Boracay later) runs trips to Kayak Inn from Boracay.

ROXAS (CAPIZ)
☎ 036 • pop 126,350

On the island's north coast, the city of Roxas (**raw**-hahs) claims to be the 'seafood capital of the Philippines'. A big claim, but there are some excellent cheap and fresh sea critters to be consumed and mountain-loads of the dried form being shipped out daily.

The home town of the Commonwealth's first president, Manuel Roxas, the city has an attractive central district based around the Metropolitan Cathedral and belfry on Rizal St, on the banks of the Panay River. It makes a good alternative transport hub to the more crowded Kalibo, as it has two nearby ports, an airport, and buses to and from Iloilo City.

Information
There's a PNB branch (Magellan St) with an ATM near the cathedral, and a Metrobank (Burgos St) two blocks away. Just over the bridge from the cathedral is a BPI branch with an express teller. A little further south, still on Roxas Ave, there is an Equitable PCI Bank, where you can get credit card cash-advances, and also another Metrobank.

BayanTel international phone office (Arnaldo St) also has an Internet service. There's an Islaphone international phone office at the Culasi Port gate.

Things to See & Do
Ang Panublion (Roxas City Museum; Arnaldo St; open 8.30am-noon & 2.30pm-6pm Tues-Sat) is near the cathedral. Originally built as a water-storage tank, this 1910 heritage building houses period furniture, local artefacts and a shell collection.

Diagonally opposite the cathedral, the Local Products Centre, beside the river, has quite a range of souvenirs and artworks. Running along the belfry side of the cathedral, small eateries and religious-souvenir stores line the mall.

Baybay Beach, just north of downtown Roxas, towards Culasi Port, is a hugely popular long, brown-sand beach lined with eateries and picnic shelters. This is the best place to pick up fresh and cheap oysters and seafood. These goods can also be seen at the city's wet market at Teodoro Arcenas Trade Centre.

Pan-ay Bell is the largest bell in Asia and is found in a church in the town of Pan-ay, just outside of Roxas, which is a 20-minute ride from Roxas, in Pan-ay. The beautiful bell, made entirely of coins during the Spanish period, is more than 2m tall. To get there,

take a tricycle (P20 to P25), or a Pan-ay jeepney from Banica St (P5, 20 minutes).

Guisano Mall (Arnaldo Blvd) is the city's shopping plaza, and the best place to head for fast food, cinema, Internet access, super-market and general shopping.

Special Events
Not yet rivalling nearby Kalibo's famous fiesta, Roxas' Sinadya Fiesta is pretty wild nonetheless. A colourful, four-day event held in early December, it culminates in the celebration of the Immaculate Conception of the Virgin Mary.

Places to Stay
City Lodge (☎ 621 3716; Plaridel St; rooms P350-650) and Capiz Lodge (☎ 621 2076; Plaridel St; singles/doubles with fan P350/450, with air-con P550/650) have near identical rooms and location. Rooms with fan and bathroom are clean and good budget options. Plaridel St is down the southern end of town. Head east off Roxas Ave at the Cocoplant Inc building, then take the next left.

Plaza Central Inn (☎ 621 3061; P Gomez St; singles with fan & bathroom P370, singles/doubles with air-con & cable TV from P470/530), on the plaza, is a bit noisy, but has well-kept rooms with polished, wood floors and artificial flowers.

Halaran Plaza Hotel (☎ 621 0649; P Gomez St; twins with bathroom & fan/air-con P400/600), next to Plaza Central, beside the river, is a good-value hotel. Like its neighbour, it has rooms with timber floors and furnishings. Downstairs is a breezy, riverside café with Chinese and Filipino food (P20 to P90).

Julieta's Hotel (☎ 621 2089; Arnaldo Blvd; singles/doubles P600/750), north of Guisano Mall, has well-priced big, clean, tiled rooms with hot water, cable TV and air-con.

Baia Norte Beach Club (☎ 621 2165, 621 4920; Baybay; room with cable TV, air-con & cold-/hot-water bathroom P880/1200) is on the eastern end of Baybay Beach.

Roxas President's Inn (☎ 621 0208; cnr Rizal & Lopez Jaena Sts; singles P950, twins/doubles P1150/1300) has stylish rooms with timber floor, hot-water bathroom, quiet air-con and cable TV. Pokey single rooms are a little pricey – blame it on the central location. Rates include breakfast at the fine restaurant, which specialises in local dishes (eg, sizzling squid, P120).

THE VISAYAS

La Hacienda Hotel (☎ 621 5129; Arnaldo Blvd; rooms from P1597), next to Guisano Mall, is Roxas' classiest hotel – a quiet place with white walls and marble floors. Rooms are big and light, fitted out with cable TV, air-con, hot-water marble bathroom, fridge and coffee bar. There is a swimming pool and the fine Squatter's Restaurant Huts (☎ 621 1626; meals for 3 people P150-300; open 6am-11pm daily).

Places to Eat

In the centre of town, there are several manokan (chicken houses) and other eateries, but the best dining is in Baybay, where 'resorts' – comprising a string of nipa barbecue huts – line the beach. Grilling starts at some stalls in the late morning, and by dinner time, it's beers and barbecues all round. Borda's Beach Resort, Baybayon (or Marc's Beach Resort) and Barbasa Beach Resort are all left (towards Culasi Wharf) of Arnaldo Ave, and serve baskets of oysters (approximately 15 to 20 shells for P25), which they open upon purchase. A variety of fish and squid (starting at about P40) fill the ice-boxes of the restaurants and can be barbecued and served with rice (P10).

The Wayfarer (☎ 621 1479; Baybay; open 8am-midnight daily; seafood around P100, steaks around P140), next to Baia Norte Beach Club, is a slicker, pricier Baybay option, with pool table and bar.

Getting There & Away

Air There is a PAL (☎ 621 0618) and an Air Philippines office at the airport, and PAL ticketing outlet at Roxtta (☎ 621 2344; Altavas St). Cebu Pacific (☎ 621 0307; Legaspi St) is on the street that runs behind the cathedral.

The Roxas–Manila route is serviced daily by Cebu Pacific (P1310, one hour), PAL (P1300) and Air Philippines (P1400).

Bus & Jeepney Buses for Iloilo City leave from the Ceres Bus Liner terminal, on the southern end of Roxas Ave, opposite the Caltex service station. There are no Ceres Bus Liner buses going direct to Kalibo, but you can take one to Sigma, then change for Kalibo (P50, two hours). Much easier is to take an L-300 van direct (P70, 1½ hours) – they leave all day until 5pm from the main Albar terminal (P5 by tricycle from the

cathedral), just near the Ceres Bus Liner terminal. There are other signposted L-300 terminals around town with drivers making themselves very obvious.

There is also a large jeepney terminal at Guisano Mall with vehicles that head for Estancia (P50, one hour) and Pan-ay (P15, 10 minutes).

Boat There is a boat terminal on either side of Roxas. To the west, the large Culasi Port has boats going to Manila. To the east of town, the little Banica wharf serves pumpboats to Masbate. Jeepneys from town will take you to both Culasi/Banica for P5/10.

Negros Navigation (☎ 621 3822; Roxas Ave), WG&A Superferry and Moreta Shipping (☎ 621 0283, 621 5044, 621 6053) all have boats to Manila and offices at Culasi Port. Negros Navigation has boats three times a week (P955, 18 hours), including once via Estancia. WG&A has a boat to Manila most days (P845, 17 hours) and one a week to Dumaguit Port (Kalibo; P90, 1½ hours). Moreta Shipping has a boat to Manila twice a week (P600). There is an Aboitiz Express booking office (☎ 621 3822; Rizal St) near the plaza.

Tourists can also take the PPA (☎ 621 2008) cargo pumpboat that travels between Roxas and San Fernando (Sibuyan Island; P120, five hours) three times a week.

Roxas' Banica wharf services pumpboats to Masbate, with trips to Mandaon, Milagros (P170, six hours) and Balud (P80, four hours) twice a week, and to nearby Ulatayan (P20, 30 minutes) daily.

Getting Around

The Roxas City airport is a five-minute ride by tricycle (P15) north of central Roxas.

KALIBO

☎ 036 • pop 62,440

Kalibo is thought to have been founded around 1250 by Malay settlers from Borneo. The town's residents have long been known for both their religious and festive zeal, which still bursts forth each year in the form of the Ati-Atihan Festival (see Special Events later).

Information

Kalibo Tourism Centre (☎ 262 1020, 268 4110; Burgos St; open 8am-noon & 1pm-5pm Mon-Fri) is just around the corner from the Municipal Hall. For international phone calls, try the **Kalibo Public Calling Office** *(Burgos St)*. **Internet cafés** are easy to find except after 8pm when they all close shop. Connections are expensive (P40 to P50 per hour) and precarious.

Things to See & Do

Five minutes from town in New Buswang (P25 by tricycle) is the **Bakhawan Eco-tourism Centre & Mangrove Park** (☎ 262 3059, 262 7013), the base for a 70-hectare mangrove reforestation area. The area was originally mangrove, but due to bad land-use it deteriorated to mudflats. Now, more than 13 years after being replanted, the area has been naturally 'reclaimed' by the land and is a thriving ecosystem, providing the community with many valuable dietary and economic resources.

Run by the Kalibo Save the Mangrove Association (Kasama), a community co-operative, there is now a laboratory for researching crustacean and fish cultures and even a crab-fattening project. Visitors can check out the plantation and intertidal ecology from a bamboo boardwalk (P2). There is also a bird-viewing platform, and binocu-lars and local tour-guides are available. **Accommodation** *(dorm beds with air-con P200, twins with air-con & cold-water bathroom P500)* is available at the centre as are Filipino **meals** *(breakfast P50, lunch & dinner P100)* and there are also several restaurants nearby.

Kalibo is the centre for many fine crafts such as: **pinya cloth weaving** – an 8th-century tradition that produces fine cloth from silk and pineapple-leaf fibres woven on a bamboo handloom; **abaca weaving** – from banana seda, a member of the banana family, producing a stiff cloth; and **nito weaving** – a sturdy vine that is woven into stiff baskets and mats. The *pinya* cloth is still used for producing *barong* (traditional formal wear), but all methods are employed for producing modern designs popular with the European market (we perused some cushion covers being made up for Calvin Klein).

For viewing the *pinya* weaving process, visit **Heritage Arts & Crafts** (☎ 268 5270; **w** *http://popweb.i-next.net/~heritage; workshop on General Luna St, extension of Luis Barrios St; open 9am-4.30pm Mon-Fri)* and **Dela**

THE VISAYAS

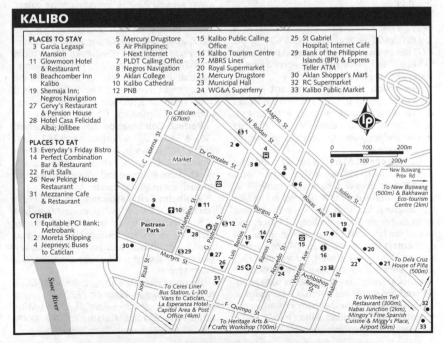

KALIBO

PLACES TO STAY
3 Garcia Legaspi Mansion
11 Glowmoon Hotel & Restaurant
18 Beachcomber Inn Kalibo
19 Shemaja Inn; Negros Navigation
27 Gervy's Restaurant & Pension House
28 Hotel Casa Felicidad Alba; Jollibee

PLACES TO EAT
13 Everyday's Friday Bistro
14 Perfect Combination Bar & Restaurant
22 Fruit Stalls
26 New Peking House Restaurant
31 Mezzanine Cafe & Restaurant

OTHER
1 Equitable PCI Bank; Metrobank
2 Moreta Shipping
4 Jeepneys; Buses to Caticlan

5 Mercury Drugstore
6 Air Philippines; i-Next Internet
7 PLDT Calling Office
8 Negros Navigation
9 Aklan College
10 Kalibo Cathedral
12 PNB

15 Kalibo Public Calling Office
16 Kalibo Tourism Centre
17 MBRS Lines
20 Royal Supermarket
21 Mercury Drugstore
23 Municipal Hall
24 WG&A Superferry

25 St Gabriel Hospital; Internet Café
29 Bank of the Philippine Islands (BPI) & Express Teller ATM
30 Aklan Shopper's Mart
32 RC Supermarket
33 Kalibo Public Market

Cruz House of Piña (☎ 262 3267; e dchpina@kalibo.i-next.net; New Buswang; open 9am-5pm Mon-Sat). For sales, the Heritage Arts and Craft's **shop** (1476 Datu Bangkaya St – extension of Maagma St) specialises in pinya and abaca products, and Dela Cruz has mainly nito and pinya.

Special Events
In January is the fantastic **Ati-Atihan Festival**, the nation's biggest and best mardi gras, which possibly dates back to the days of the Borneo settlers. A week-long street party raging from sun-up to sundown and peaking on the third Sunday of January, the festival offers prizes for the best costumes and dancers.

And if this just isn't enough, similar festivals are held in January in the neighbouring towns of Batan (late January), Ibajay (late January), Makato (15 January) and Altavas (22 January).

Places to Stay
To see the huge Ati-Atihan Festival from close up in Kalibo, you should book a hotel at least a month in advance and expect to pay from two- to five-times the regular listed price.

Gervy's Restaurant & Pension House (☎ 262 4190; Pastrana St; singles/doubles with fan P200/400, with air-con P430/600; meals P37) has clean rooms with shared bathroom. Good cheap Filipino food is served downstairs at the restaurant.

Glowmoon Hotel & Restaurant (☎ 262 3073; S Martelino St; singles/doubles with fan & shared bathroom P250/300, with air-con, hot-water bathroom & cable TV P650/750) has similar budget rooms to Gervy's, and decent air-con rooms.

Garcia Legaspi Mansion (☎ 262 5588, 262 3541; 3rd floor, 159 Roxas Ave; singles with fan P350, doubles with bathroom, cable TV & air-con or hot-water P650, doubles with cable TV, air-con & hot water P850), on the town's main thoroughfare, is a cheerful place, and one of the best mid-range deals in town.

Shemaja Inn (☎ 268 7626; 647 Mabini St; singles with fan & shared bathroom P250; rooms with private bathroom from P500), a few blocks away, has large rooms with cable TV and hot-water bathroom. Get a room at the back, away from the games room.

Hotel Casa Felicidad Alba (☎ 268 4320; Arch Reyes St; twin/family rooms P500/700)

has clean rooms with air-con, cable TV, cold-water bathroom and a terrace overlooking the street.

La Esperanza Hotel (☎ 262 3989, ☎/fax 262 5658; Osmeña Ave; rooms from P700), next to the Ceres Bus Liner and minivan terminals, and on the way to the airport, is a good choice for stopover guests and those desiring slick service. For P700, you get air-con, cable TV and telephone; for another P200, rooms have hot water; and for P1300, you get a bath tub.

Beachcomber Inn Kalibo (☎ 036-262 4846, fax 268 4765; e bcombinn@kalibo.i-next.net; Roldan St; rooms P950-1500), near Shemaja Inn, has small, marble-decked, furnished rooms with the usual mod-cons. For P1100, rooms have a drinks fridge and large window. This is a friendly place with a business office and ticketing assistance. Breakfast can be provided, and a local Filipino–Chinese restaurant can deliver other meals.

Bakhawan Eco-tourism Centre & Mangrove Park (for details see Things to See & Do, earlier) has peaceful accommodation.

Places to Eat
New Peking House Restaurant (Martyrs St; meals around P80) is an unassuming eatery serving fine Chinese food.

Mezzanine Cafe & Restaurant (☎ 262 3077, 268 4104; Luis Barrios St; meals around P50, pizza P75, steak P140; open 10am-10pm Mon-Thur & Sat, 10am-2am Fri) has up-tempo decor and a permanently set-up stage for the Friday night live-music. The dishes are good and cheap and include noodles, burgers, pizza and Filipino and Chinese dishes.

Perfect Combination Bar & Restaurant (Mix & Match Bar & Restaurant; ☎ 262 5131, 268 4240; L Barrios St; meals for 3 people around P200; open 7am-9pm daily) has a good, cheap Filipino and Chinese menu and specialises in group meals.

Willhelm Tell Restaurant (☎ 262 1903; Roxas Ave; dishes P65-200; open 11am-2pm & 5pm-midnight daily) is a little place specialising in meaty European dishes and steaks. Families should be warned – sleazy videos are shown on the adjoining karaoke room screen.

If you're out at the airport, the best places to eat are **Miggy's Place** (☎ 262 1649; meals around P80; open 8am-8pm daily) and **Mingoy's Fine Spanish Cuisine** (☎ 262 4877; meals P140-200; open 7am-9pm daily).

Everyday's Friday Bistro (cnr Arch Reyes & L Barrios Sts; open 5pm-midnight daily) is a good place for a drink, game of pool, music, and no videoke.

Getting There & Away

Air There are offices at Kalibo airport for **PAL** (☎ 262 3260/3), **Cebu Pacific** (☎ 262 5406, 268 7190), **Air Philippines** (☎ 262 4444/ 5555) and **Mindanao Express** (☎ 268 5005/ 7150/7151).

The first three have daily flights to and from Manila (PAL P1751, Cebu Pacific P1644, Air Philippines P1644; one hour).

Cebu Pacific flies to Cebu City return three mornings a week (P1293, 40 minutes); and Mindanao Express flies the same route four afternoons a week (P1491).

Bus & Jeepney There are **Ceres Bus Liner** (☎ 268-4026; Osmeña Ave terminal) buses leaving all day for Iloilo City (P68, five to six hours). There are also buses five times daily from Iloilo City to Caticlan that pass through Kalibo (P50, 1½ hours from Kalibo). L-300 minivans to Caticlan (P120, 1½ hours) run all day, whenever the vans are full, from this same area, as well as buses and vans for Roxas – for details see Getting There & Away under Roxas (Capiz), earlier.

Air-con buses and minivans meet Manila flights at Kalibo airport, taking passengers to Caticlan (P150, or P175 including the boat transfer to Boracay, 1½ hours).

Boat Manila and Cebu are serviced by boats from Kalibo's nearby ports of New Washington and Dumaguit. Jeepneys to the ports (P20, 30 minutes) leave from Maagma St, near the Caltex service station on the corner of Mabini St.

Negros Navigation (☎ 262 4943, 268 4903; C Laserna St) has boats to Manila (P955, 17 hours) twice a week.

Moreta Shipping (☎ 262 3003; Roxas Ave) has one boat a week to Manila (P650, 16 hours).

WG&A Superferry (☎ 268 4391; cnr A Reyes & Acevedo Sts) has boats to Manila (P845, 14 hours) and Roxas (P90, 1½ hours) three days a week.

MBRS Lines (☎ 268 6850; Roxas Ave) has a boat to Cajidiocan (Sibuyan Island; P280, three hours) and on to Romblon Town (Romblon Island; total trip P310, five hours).

CATICLAN

Caticlan is little more than a departure port for Boracay. Buses arriving here carry passengers straight to the wharf and guides lead the throngs through a smart pavilion onto outrigger boats. For details, see Getting There & Away under Boracay. Boats also leave from here to Tablas Island.

Should you decide to stay overnight in Caticlan, there's the very basic **Casimero Lodging House** (☎ 036-288 7027; 4-person room with fan & shared bathroom P200, twins with fan & bathroom P300), a short walk from the port. At the time of writing, **Barnacle Bells Restaurant & Lodging House**, next to the airport, was being built. It should have better rooms with air-con.

Getting There & Away

Air There's a small airport servicing the ever-popular flights from Manila and Cebu, 2km from the port. Tricycles charge P30 for the journey.

Asian Spirit (☎ 02-851 8888; Manila • ☎ 032-341 2555; Cebu) and **SEAIR** (☎ 02-891 8708, fax 891 8711; Manila • ☎ 032-341 3021/2, fax 341 3023; Cebu; ⓦ www.flyseair .com) both have daily small aircraft servicing the ever-popular route to Cebu (Asian Spirit P2150, SEAIR P1990; one hour). Asian Spirit also flies to and from Manila several times each day (P2350, one hour). For the larger Asian Spirit flights, there is usually airport–wharf transfers included.

Bus & Jeepney As soon as you exit the port at Caticlan, a throng of bus drivers will launch upon you, yelling out destinations and signalling for you to follow. For buses to Iloilo City and Kalibo, see Bus under Getting There & Away in those sections, earlier.

Boat For the Caticlan–Boracay boat service, see Boat under Getting There & Away in the Boracay section later.

There are also daily morning boats to and from Santa Fe (P100, 2½ hours) and Looc (P100, three hours), both on Tablas Island, as well as to and from San José on Carabao Island (P30, one hour).

The MBRS Lines' MV Virgin Mary and MV Mary the Queen ply the Manila–Odiongan (Tablas Island)–Caticlan–Lipata (Panay) route. See Boat under Getting There & Away in the Romblon section later.

THE VISAYAS

Boracay

☎ 036

Delicately poised between paradise and pandemonium, the internationally renowned island of Boracay is the best-known tourist spot in the Philippines. Often so crowded it's a wonder its famous **White Beach** is still above sea level, little Boracay remains a glorious playground for sun worshippers.

Boracay is little more than a speck off the northwestern tip of Panay (about 9km long, and only 1km wide at its narrow midriff) – yet it manages to be a world within itself. White Beach, the main boat drop-off point from Caticlan on Panay during high-season, is where the action is. Here, lazing and browsing for food, drinks and souvenirs are the main activities. More-active tourists will enjoy the huge range of water sports.

In just 15 minutes you can escape the heavily touristed White Beach on the east coast to the surprisingly quiet **Bulabog Beach** to the east. Wilder and windier, the east coast is a favourite windsurfing spot and host of the **Boracay International Funboard Cup**, the fourth leg of the annual Asian Windsurfing Tour (see Windsurfing under Activities later). Also on the east coast, the **Mt Luho View Deck** (admission P20) offers magnificent views. Just climb the stairs near the main road near Lapuz-Lapuz.

The electricity supply is notoriously unreliable and brownouts are a daily occurrence, so at night it's wise to always keep a torch (flashlight) within reach. Water is nonpotable so guests will have to purchase drinking water unless they are staying at one of the resorts with piped-in drinking water. The ice, however, is produced on the island and is safe for consuming in shakes and daiquiris.

Orientation & Information

White Beach is the centre of Boracay's tourist area, and three 'boat stations' are stretched out across its sands. These can be hard to spot, being only patches of beach with waiting sheds set back. The beach is dominated by a sandy pedestrian highway – the White Beach Path – where motorised vehicles are banned and it's almost compulsory to go barefoot.

The *E-Z Map*, published annually, is on sale at the Boracay Tourist Centre for P80.

Tourist Offices The Boracay Tourist Centre (*most desks open 9am-10pm daily*), including an office of the **Filipino Travel Centre** (*☎ 288 3704/5; Tourist Centre; open 9am-6pm daily ● ☎ 02-528 4507–09, fax 528 4503; @ travelct@skyinet.net; Ramona Apt Bldg, 1555 M Adriatico St, Ermita, Manila*), between boat stations two and three, is a hive of tourist-related activity. From behind a long row of desks, helpful staff offer postal and telephone services, general Boracay information, moneychanging, and ticketing. Convenient though it may be to have all services in one place, the tourist centre isn't the cheapest place for shopping and postal services. It does, however, offer the best and fastest Internet connection (P60).

There is also a **DOT office** (*☎/fax 288 3689; open 8am-noon & 1pm-5pm Mon-Fri*) in D'Mall. Although it doesn't handle bookings, it has a list of all accommodation (with prices) on the island, as well as dive centres and transport options, and staff are most helpful with inquiries.

The *Boracay Bulletin* is a free publication that you can pick up at outlets all along White Beach. It includes 'what's on' information, local gossip and news, classifieds and ads.

Money Two major banks on the island, **Allied Bank** and **The Land Bank** (*open 9am-4pm Mon-Fri*), change money and travellers cheques. Many resorts and the tourist centre will also change both; the tourist centre foreign-exchange desk is open 9am to 10pm daily. Money-changing rates and efficiency are excellent on Boracay, so there's no need to cash up before arriving.

Post, Telephone & Fax There's a postal counter at the Boracay Tourist Centre which charges a P5 service fee and a **post office** at the northern end of the Main Rd.

Several resorts have phone and fax facilities, but the rates are ridiculously high – you are better off going to the Boracay Tourist Centre or one of the many international calling offices. There are also international phone booths on the sand and dotted along the path, including a PLTD one in D'Mall.

For local phone calls, only the last five digits of the phone number need to be dialled. Many resorts and restaurants will let you make these calls for free.

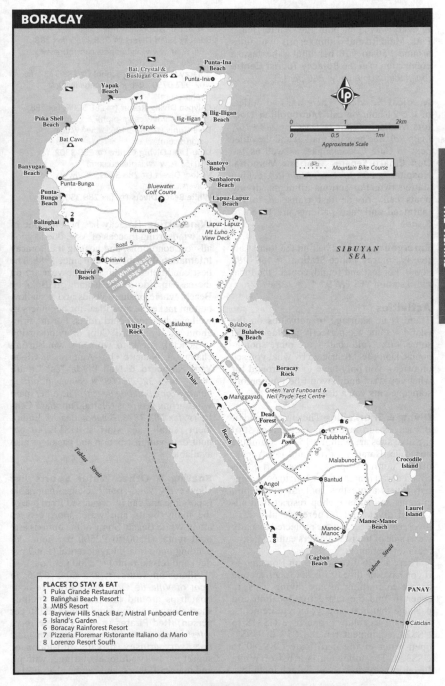

BORACAY

Punta-Ina Beach
Punta-Ina
Bat, Crystal & Buslugan Caves
Yapak Beach
Puka Shell Beach
Ilig-Iligan
Ilig-Iligan Beach
Yapak
Bat Cave
Santoyo Beach
Banyugan Beach
Punta-Bunga
Sanbaloron Beach
Punta-Bunga Beach
Bluewater Golf Course
Lapuz-Lapuz Beach
Balinghai Beach
Pinaungan
Lapuz-Lapuz
Mt Luho View Deck

SIBUYAN SEA

Road 5
Diniwid
Diniwid Beach

Approximate Scale

0 ----- 1 ----- 2km
0 --- 0.5 --- 1mi

.... Mountain Bike Course

Willy's Rock
Balabag
Bulabog
Bulabog Beach

Boracay Rock
White
Green Yard Funboard & Neil Pryde Test Centre
Manggayad
Dead Forest
Fish Pond
Tulubhan
Tablas Strait
Malabunot
Crocodile Island
Bantud
Beach
Angol
Laurel Island
Manoc-Manoc Beach
Manoc-Manoc
Tablon Strait
Cagban Beach

See White Beach map - page 356

PANAY

Caticlan

PLACES TO STAY & EAT
1 Puka Grande Restaurant
2 Balinghai Beach Resort
3 JMBS Resort
4 Bayview Hills Snack Bar; Mistral Funboard Centre
5 Island's Garden
6 Boracay Rainforest Resort
7 Pizzeria Floremar Ristorante Italiano da Mario
8 Lorenzo Resort South

THE VISAYAS

Email & Internet Access Internet access is everywhere, on both the White Beach Path, Main Rd and within resorts, with rates around P50 to P70 per hour. The fastest connection is at the **Boracay Tourist Centre** (open 9am-10pm daily; P60 per hr).

Medical Services There are two outlets of the 24-hour on-call **Metropolitan Doctors Medical yClinic** (MDMC; ☎ 288 6357; Main Rd), one near the market and the other next to Café Cocomangas, as well as the **Don Ciriaco Senares Tirol Snr Memorial Hospital** (☎ 288 3041; off Main Rd), behind station two. For serious ailments, diving boats can provide fast transport to the mainland and then patients are taken to Kalibo.

Emergency Located behind the tourist office is **Boracay Police Station** (☎ 166, 288 3066). For lost and found, contact the local radio station **YES FM 91.1** (☎ 288 6107).

Activities

There is no shortage of activities on the island – some are perfectly packaged, and some – like volleyball – are more spontaneous. Don't feel restricted by what you see on offer – you only have to ask around for what you want and it won't be long before someone cuts you a deal.

Diving & Snorkelling The entire island of Boracay is surrounded by reef and most of the dive sites are within a 15- to 20-minute boat ride. Boracay's pride and joy, Yapak, off the northern tip, is a sheer soft-coral-covered wall running from 30m to 65m. Big-fish lovers adore this spot, though depth, currents and surface chop restrict it to advanced divers only. There are also drift dives, cave dives, and the protected (usually west) side of the island offers calm, shallow reefs for beginners.

There are 26 dive centres on Boracay, so if you have the time, it's best to shop around before committing to any diving trips, in order to find the instructor, location and package that best suits your requirements. Prices are as follows: one dive US$18 to US$24, equipment rental US$2 to US$7, open-water diving certificate US$280 to US$320. The following is a list of White Beach's many dive shops, which include:

Aquarius Diving (☎ 288 3132, fax 288 3189; e aquarius@boracay.i-next.net)
Boracay Safari Divers (☎ 288 3260, fax 288 6476; w www.skybusiness.com/boracay divelodge)
Boracay Scuba Diving School (☎ 288 3327, fax 02-922 9750; e boracayscubadiving@ yahoo.com)
Calypso Diving Resort (☎ 288 3206, fax 288 3478; w www.calypso.ph)
Dive Gurus (☎ 288 5486; w www.dive gurus.com)
Lapu-Lapu Diving Centre (☎ 288 3302, fax 288 3015; w www.lapulapu.com)
Victory Divers (☎ 288 3209; w www.victory divers.com)
White Beach Divers (☎/fax 288 3809)

Windsurfing Boracay has become one of the windsurfing meccas of Asia, due to good all-year conditions, and hosting the **Boracay International Funboard Cup** since 1988. The best conditions for most of the year are on the eastern side of the island, off Bulabog Beach, where onshore winds and a shallow bottom make the area ideal for beginners as well as advanced board riders. For inquiries about the Funboard Cup, or windsurfing in general, speak to women's windsurfing champion, Nanette Graf-Aguirre, at **Green Yard Funboard & Neil Pryde Test Centre** (☎ 288 3449/3207/3208; w www.windsurfing boracay.com; Bulabog Beach). The other main windsurfing centre is **Mistral Funboard Centre** (☎/fax 288 3876; Bulabog Beach). Equipment rental rates start at US$12/40 per hour/day, with instruction and packages also available.

Boating & Other Water Sports Just about every water-sport package imaginable is possible and can be organised from one of the many boats and water-sport centres along White Beach. Some of the options are: **boat rental** (P300 to P2500 per hour, depending upon boat), **kayak rental** (P500 per day) and **jet-ski rental** (P2000 per hour).

Allan Fun Tours (☎ 288 6069/6195; in front of Villa de Oro) has daily five-hour boat trips around the island that include snorkelling gear, food and drinks (P350 per person). **Red Pirates** (☎ 288 3561; e redpi ratesboracay@hotmail.com; Bom Bom Bar) does very cruisey, private, full-moon or sunset *paraw* (traditional outrigger with jib and mainsail) tours, and can be chartered to take you to many of the great spots around northern Panay (P350 per hour, P2500 for full day, food included).

Tribal Adventures (☎ 288 3207, ☎/fax 288 3449; ⓦ www.tribaladventures.com) offers one- to three-day mountain biking, walking and kayaking trips to Whitewater Kayak Inn (see Tibiao & Around earlier) and to near Tibiao in northern Panay (P840 to US$235), as well as daily equipment rentals.

Horse Riding Offering a variety of scenic horse rides around the island, **Boracay Horse Riding Stables** (☎ 288 3311; ⓔ hors estable@yahoo.com) caters for all levels of experience (P490 to P890, one to two hours). The stables are off the main road, north of the post office. Lessons and children's rides are also available.

Massage If you're only up to a massage, **Fausto's Shiatsu** (☎ 288 3305; 1 hr P300; open 9am-7pm daily), near boat station three, is conducted by one of the best blind-masseuses on the island.

If you have the bucks, you'd be pressed to find a more luxurious and soul-reviving service than that offered by **Mandala Spa** (☎ 288 5858; ⓔ info@mandalaspa.com; treatments US$31-137; open 10am-10pm daily). Tucked away into lush inland forest, this first-class German-Filipino operation offers restorative and indulgent packages (eg, foot bath, papaya body wrap, floral bath and massage, US$71, 2½ hours) conducted in your own private, native-style villa with capiz French doors, and windows looking out into overgrown gardens. Everything is performed with a professional but loving touch, and the small details, such as the 'calamansi (citrus) slush' you are given to sip in the bath, are divine.

Places to Stay

Boracay accommodation rates are ruled by the high (or 'regular') season (1 December to 31 May) and the low (or 'lean') season (1 June to 30 November). During low season, prices are halved. Many resorts pump their rates up by around 20% at peak season during the periods of 23 December to 3 January, Chinese New Year and Easter. The rates quoted here apply to the standard high season.

The long, beautiful White Beach is a fun place to stroll, but if you're looking for accommodation it can became more of a trudge. Most of the cheaper, simpler places are south of the Boracay Tourist Centre. Having said that, many of the good food and bars are north. If you have a clear idea of your budget and priorities (ie, diving, dining, bar-hopping), it's straightforward to hone in on an area and you'll be soaking up the sun and the cocktails in no time.

And if it's all too much on White Beach, seek out the solitude of lovely Diniwid Beach's low-key resorts just to the north.

White Beach – South of Boracay Tourist Centre One of Boracay's pricey landmarks, **Lorenzo Resort South** (☎ 02-928 0719, 926 3958, fax 926 1726; ⓔ lorenzo@e-boracay.com; rooms US$128-140) is the most popular of the three 'Lorenzo' resorts. The resort has its own slice of beach and stylish native rooms with seaward balconies.

Ki's Cottages (Tin Tin's; huts with fan & bathroom P300) has excellent-value huts with terrace, only 20m down a path from the beach south of boat station three.

Jazzed Up Café (☎ 288 5170, ☎/fax 288 5171; ⓦ www.jazzedupcafe.com; doubles with air-con, hot-water bathroom & cable TV P2500), above a café where Brian, the owner, sings jazz tunes each night, has well-priced rooms considering its beach position and amenities.

Villa Camilla (☎ 288 3354, fax 288 3106; ⓦ www.aaow.com/villacamilla; rooms with fan & cold-water bathroom P1600, with hot water & fan/air-con P1900/3200), is a low-key complex with swimming pool.

Angol Point Beach Resort (☎ 02-522 0012; double huts with fan & bathroom P2000) has lovely large shady grounds on the beach and excellent private nipa huts that use the local architectural style (often combining woven abaca walls, nipa roofs and bamboo furnishings).

Moreno's Place (☎ 288 3611; nipa huts with fan & bathroom P400), down the lane next to the PAL office, has good-value roomy huts with terrace, basic marble bath, veranda and hammock.

Mountain View Inn (☎ 621 0547, fax 621 0259; rooms with fan & bathroom P600-700, with air-con P2000) is 300m from the beach on a quiet and spacious grassed area at the foot of the hills. The ranch-like resort has big clean rooms with veranda and an open communal kitchen area.

Melinda's Garden (☎ *288 3021; nipa huts from P900-1400*), in the laneway down from the PAL office, is a leafy garden with simple nipa huts with capiz lamps, basic marble bathroom and hammock. There's a small bar-restaurant here, too.

Orchids Resort (☎ *288 3313/5079, fax 288 3012;* ⓦ *pny-web.i-next.net/~orchids; rooms P600-1000*), a popular budget choice, is a well-maintained nipa building, on the lane past Melinda's Garden.

Attractive, native-style rooms share a balcony with neighbours.

A-Rock Resort (☎ *288 3201/62,* ⓔ *arock@ boracay.i-next.net; nipa & concrete rooms with bathroom & fan/air-con P500/1500*), down the lane at Boracay Dive Lodge and built around a garden, has good-value budget rooms.

La Isla Bonita Resort (☎ *288 3501; nipa huts with bathroom & fan/air-con P800/ 1800*), on the beach, has good-value nipa huts with veranda and hammock. The air-con rooms have marble floors.

Oro Plaza Beach Resort (☎ *036-288 3303; nipa duplexes with fan & bathroom P700*) has decent nipa rooms set back from the beach.

Mona Lisa – White Sand Beach Resort (☎ *036-288 3205;* ⓦ *www.monalisaresort .com; huts with bath & fan US$48, with air-con US$60-75*) has slick, shaded nipa huts with balcony. The air-con huts have hot water and cable TV.

Michelle's Bungalows (☎ *288 3920/3086;* ⓦ *www.mbungalows.com; nipa rooms with fan & bathroom P600-1000*), down a lane near the market, is a small friendly nipa compound. Rooms range in size and the biggest ones have basic kitchen.

Casa Pilar Beach Resort (☎ *288 3073,* ☎/*fax 288 3202; nipa huts with fan & bathroom P1500-2200, rooms with air-con & hot water P2800-3800*) has spotless huts and hotel-style rooms.

Bamboo Beach Resort (☎ *288 3109/5067, fax 288 5047; rooms with fan/air-con P800/ 1800*), 50m down a lane, has reasonable, clean rooms.

White Beach – North of Boracay Tourist Centre For some reasonably priced central options, all off the lane north of the tourist centre, try: **Morimar Boracay Resort** (☎ *288 3120;* ⓦ *www.pacific.net.ph/~mori mar/mori2.html; nipa duplexes with bathroom*

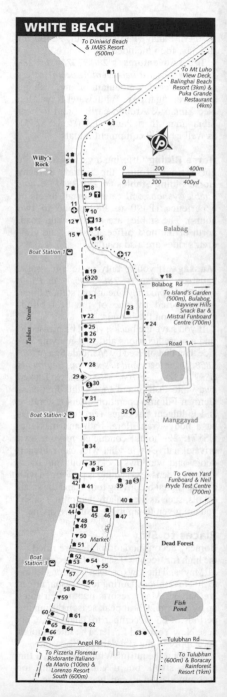

WHITE BEACH

PLACES TO STAY
1   White Beach Terraces Resort
2   Friday's Boracay; Cottage
    Queen Beach Resort
4   White House Beach Resort;
    Sea Wind
5   Pearl of the Pacific; Waling-
    Waling Beach Hotel Boracay
6   Villa Regina
7   Boracay Plaza Beach Resort;
    Serina's Place Annexe
19 Ban's Beach Resort
21 Fiesta Cottages; Serina's Place
    Steakhouse Boracay
23 Frendz Resort
26 Galaxy Beach Resort
27 Crystal Sand Beach Resort;
    Red Coconut Beach Hotel
34 Boracay Regency; Tirol & Tirol
    Cottages; El Centro Island
    Beach Resort
36 Sunset Beach Resort; PT&T
    International Telephone Office
38 Ati-Atihan Beach Resort
39 Benross Cottages
40 Rainbow Villa Resort;
    Shangri-la Oasis Cottages
41 Villa de Oro; Allan Fun Tours
46 Morimar Boracay Resort
47 St Vincent Cottages
49 Bamboo Beach Resort;
    Shanghai Restaurant
51 Casa Pilar Beach Resort;
    Restaurante Banza
52 Mona Lisa White Sand Beach
    Resort; Michelle's Bungalows

53 La Isla Bonita Resort; Oro
    Plaza Beach Resort; RCPI
    BayanTel Calling Office;
    Allied Bank
56 A-Rock Resort
61 Mountain View Inn
62 Melinda's Garden;
    Orchids Resort
64 Moreno's Place
65 Angol Point Beach Resort
66 Villla Camilla; English Bakery;
    Outer Space Bar & Shaanti
    Restaurant
67 Jazzed Up Café; White Beach
    Divers; Ki's Cottages

PLACES TO EAT
10 Mañana Mexican Cuisine
12 Café Cocomangas;
    Beachcomber Bar
15 Jonah's Fruit Shake &
    Snack Bar; Dejà Vu
18 English Bakery
22 Café Sun Thai; Tribal
    Adventures
24 Blue Lotus Bakery
28 Real Coffee & Tea Café;
    Sea Lovers Bar & Restaurant;
    Bom Bom Bar; Red Pirates
31 True Food Indian Cuisine;
    Lapu-Lapu Diving Center;
    Summer Place The Bar
33 Restaurant de Paris Resort;
    Seoul Korean Restaurant
35 Siam House; Victory
    Divers

48 La Capinnina Italian Restaurant
    Café & Wine Bar; Caffé 1920
50 English Bakery; Vinjo Indian
    Cuisine; Boracay Scuba Diving
    School
55 Honey Bee Restaurant; Lolit's
57 Sulu Thai Restaurant
59 Cocoloco Bar & Restaurant

OTHER
3   Boracay Horse Riding Stables
8   Main Post Office
9   Church
11 Metropolitan Doctors Medical
    Clinic; True Home Hotel
13 Moondog's Shooter
14 Boracay Safari Divers
16 YES FM Radio Station
17 Boracay Medical Center
20 Allied Bank; Landbank
25 Aquarius Diving
29 D'Mall
30 DOT (information); Hey Jude;
    Caffé 1920
32 Don Ciriaco Senares Tirol Sr
    Memorial Hospital
38 Allied Bank
42 Charlh's Bar
43 Boracay Tourist Center
44 Calypso Diving Resort;
    The Wreck Bar
45 Police Station
54 Fausto's Shiatsu
58 Star Fire General Store
60 PAL; Dive Gurus
63 Mandala Spa

& fan/air-con P500/1200); **Shangri-La Oasis Cottages** (huts with fan & bathroom P300); **Rainbow Villa Resort** (☎ 288 3700; rooms with bathroom & fan P500-800, with bathroom & air-con P1000-1500, with air-con, cable TV and hot water P1800-2000); and **St Vincent Cottages** (☎ 288 6265; nipa huts with fan & bathroom P400).

Villa de Oro (☎/fax 288 5456; nipa huts with fan & bathroom from P1200, with air-con from P2500) is a big place with a range of native huts. There's a buffet-style restaurant out the front.

Sunset Beach Resort (☎ 288 3648; rooms with fan & bathroom P800), 20m down the laneway north of Villa de Oro, has both native-style and tiled rooms with a small terrace.

Ati-Atihan Beach Resort (☎ 288 3226; nipa huts with fan & bathroom P400) and **Benross Cottages** (☎ 288 3503; nipa huts with bath-

room & fan/air-con P500/1800), 300m down a lane, both have basic huts.

El Centro Island Beach Resort (☎ 288 6352, ☎/fax 288 6055; duplexes with air-con, hot water & cable TV P2000-2600) and **Tirol & Tirol Cottages** (TNT; ☎ 288 3165; huts with fan & bathroom P1000, with hot water, air-con & cable TV P2300-2800) both have swish, native-style huts in leafy grounds. The more expensive huts front the White Beach Path.

Boracay Regency (☎ 288 6111–15, fax 288 6777; ⓦ www.boracayregency.com; rooms from P5280), a huge pink building with a pool, dominating the central White Beach landscape, has ritzy rooms with the works. Prices include breakfast.

Crystal Sand Beach Resort (☎ 288 3149, fax 288 3087; ⓔ crystal@boracay.i-next.net; rooms with air-con, hot water, cable TV & phone P2950-4800) is a fancy place with hotel-style rooms. The upstairs ones have views.

Red Coconut Beach Hotel (*02-522 1405/4748, fax 522 4795;* w *www.redcoconut .com.ph; singles/doubles with fan P2211/ 2607, with air-con P3036/3432),* just north of D'Mall, is another towering complex around a pool. Prices include breakfast.

Galaxy Beach Resort (*288 3130; cottages with fan & bathroom P800-1000, with air-con from P1500)* is a big place, with huts that increase in quality with price.

Frendz Resort (*288 3803;* w *www .frendzresort.com; nipa rooms with fan & bathroom P700),* down the laneway next to Aquarius Diving, has good-value nipa rooms with terrace; some have a private, leafy view. This quiet and friendly place has a shared kitchen and pool table.

Serina's Place (*288 6100/3088; huts with fan & bathroom P1000)* has basic nipa huts on the beach.

Fiesta Cottages (*288 3818/6064; cottages with fan & bathroom P500-1000, with air-con P2000),* behind Steakhouse Boracay, has garden cottages, which vary from basic to quite slick.

A big open place, **Ban's Beach Resort** (*288 3837; cottages P900)* has basic nipa huts with balconies.

All resorts from this point are north of the White Beach Path and front the beach directly with little public traffic. This creates a more island-paradise edge, which you will, indeed, pay for.

Boracay Plaza Beach Resort (*/fax 288 3702;* e *bplaza@boracay.i-next.net; rooms with fan/air-con P1500/2000, with air-con & hot water P3000)* has tiled, rooms with balcony. Nearby is the resort's annexe, **Villa Regina** *(cottages with fan/air-con P1000/ 2000),* which has roomy cottages in a high-walled compound. Prices include breakfast.

True Home Hotel (*288 3784,* */fax 288 6517;* e *truehomehotel@yahoo.com; air-con rooms P2650-4150)* is a small hotel with homely furnished rooms. The pricier ones are beachfront. Prices include breakfast.

Waling-Waling Beach Hotel Boracay (*032-288 5555–60, 896 9457/8, fax 02-896 9456;* w *www.waling.com; rooms US$100-240)* provides all you'd expect from such a pricey hotel. Views start at US$140.

Pearl of the Pacific (*02-926 0162, fax 924 4482;* w *www.pearlofthepacific.com.ph;*

rooms US$120-200) is a huge native-style place with luxury rooms.

Set back from the beach among coconut palms, **Sea Wind** (*288 3091, fax 288 3425;* w *www.seawind.com.ph; rooms P3500-4500)* has all the mod-cons at a better price than some of its neighbours.

White House Beach Resort (*288 3064, fax 288 3675;* e *lat-whb@philwebine.com; standard room US$40, mountain-view cottage US$50, deluxe rooms US$65-70, beach house US$150),* an unpretentious place, has OK standard and good mountain-view rooms with mod-cons and furnishings. The real bargains are the two four-person beach houses each with a kitchen, sunroom, and veranda/balcony facing the beach. Each occupy one floor – the upstairs one has excellent views – and rented together, they make a fantastic deal for groups.

Cottage Queen Beach Resort (*288 6293; nipa rooms with fan & cold-water bathroom P800)* is a basic, friendly family-run place, strangely stuck among the high-rollers. There is no hype and no restaurant here – just a simple *sari-sari* store.

Friday's Boracay (*288 6200, fax 288 6222;* w *www.fridaysboracay.com; singles/ doubles US$155-180),* the favourite of many a moneyed visitor, has staked out the finest stretch of White Beach. A beautifully designed native-style resort, with plush rooms, this is also the home of the top restaurant on the island (for details see North of Boracay Tourist Centre under Places to Eat, later).

White Beach Terraces Resort (*288 4000, fax 288 3596;* e *foxpit93@yahoo.com; twins & doubles P4320)* has the best location, tucked against a rocky point at the far northern end of the beach, with almost zero traffic. If you can overlook the ugly green architecture, the large rooms (some with excellent views) with air-con, minibar, sound system, cable TV and huge bathroom are good value.

North of White Beach If you take the narrow concrete path around from the White Beach Terraces Resort's restaurant (see White Beach – North of Boracay Tourist Centre under Places to Stay earlier), you get to Diniwid Beach (which is also accessible by tricycle from the main road back at White Beach). Around the next rocky outcrop, you find Balinghai Beach, which is best approached inland by tricycle, or by boat.

JMBS Resort (☎ 288 3934; Diniwid Beach; double-storey 2-bedroom beach shack P500, studio loft P800) has low-key, excellent-value accommodation, both with fan and cold-water bathroom.

Balinghai Beach Resort (☎ 288 3646, fax 288 6028; W www.boracay.cc; double/family rooms with cold-water bathroom & fan US$60-65/75) is an exquisite, eccentrically designed resort built into the cliff with coral architecture and twisting overgrown staircases. Built by Otik, and Julia, his Swedish artist wife, the rooms have king-size beds made from polished tree-trucks, capiz doors that open up to excellent views, private verandas and top-view bathrooms. Otik and Julia will happily organise candlelight dinners on the private beach and other island activities. Nonguests are most welcome to book meals here.

Bulabog Across Boracay's narrow middle from White Beach is the far-less-peopled Bulabog Beach, where you'll meet plenty of serious windsurfers who call this place home for many months a year.

Island's Garden (☎ 288 3161; W www .biancagarden.com; rooms with fan & bathroom P300-500, with air-con P1300) has cheap nipa huts. This places gets pretty marshy during the wet season.

Bayview Hills Snack Bar (☎ 288 3379; nipa hut with fan, bathroom & cable TV P900) has one big, well-kept bungalow with a good view. Ask at the snack bar for other locals who have similar huts for private short- and long-term rent.

Tulubhan Built into the top of the cliff, above a small beach, **Boracay Rainforest Resort** (☎/fax 621 1772; e rainforest@roxas_on line.net.ph; rooms with cold-water bathroom & fan/air-con P1800/2500) has huge native huts with bamboo floors and terrace views. The open-air Filipino restaurant has the best view on the island, overlooking a huge expanse of reef, Bulabog Beach, the southern part of the island and Caribao Island in the distance. Even if you're not staying here, it's worth coming up to check out the vista.

Places to Eat
The White Beach Path is one big restaurant-resort strip – half the fun of dining is taking a walk around sunset and checking out the

sites, smells and menus along the path. In this highly competitive market, even the over-the-top resorts are forced to keep their restaurant prices relatively low. Funny thing is, few places manage to offer truly outstanding food. Many places tempt customers with generous set meals or buffets (from P150 to around P200 per person). Think twice and scrutinise well before being seduced by the displays – many of the seafood lies out in the heat for hours on end, resulting in numerous cases of food poisoning.

For breakfast and snacks, nearly every eatery here does good fruit-shakes, pancakes and set breakfasts. For bread, **English Bakery** (with three outlets) is popular, and the cheaper, new **Blue Lotus Bakery**, offering excellent Filipino baked goods, is where many of the restaurants buy their small baguettes (P7).

If you are on a tight budget, the market has **turo-turo** (point-point) **pots** (dish with rice P35) where you peek inside the display pots then point to the one you like. Other neighbouring **eateries** (meals for 3 people P275) offer cheap set meals (including seafood barbecue). For a real budget option, buy a fish from the market and cook it up if your resort has a communal kitchen, or ask around for a local to help you out.

Unless otherwise mentioned, all restaurants are on White Beach and open between 7am and 8am and close between 10pm and 11pm daily. Those restaurants with bars close between 1am and 3am.

South of Boracay Tourist Centre Although vegetarians have better options elsewhere, **Sulu Thai Restaurant** (noodles & soups from P160, meat dishes P165-200) claims one of the two Thai chefs on the island and serves good Thai food.

Pizzeria Floremar Ristorante Italiano da Mario (pasta P120-150, pizza P110-160, other meals P120-200) is a small restaurant with a big following.

Outer Space Bar & Shaanti Restaurant (☎ 288 5180; meals P80-130; restaurant open 2pm-1am daily) is a funky bar offering vegie food and electronic music.

Restaurante Banza (☎ 288 5167; e bora cay_98@yahoo.com; meals P240-450; open 8am-4pm & 6pm-11pm daily) is one of the best restaurants on the island. Convivial Portuguese owner/chef Antonio, serves the freshest seafood, with an emphasis on quality, flavour, oil and garlic. There's plenty to choose from, but the simple meals are some of the best, like the mouthwatering, garlic tiger prawns (P330). If you have a sweet tooth, the coconut and cinnamon cakes (both P100) are to die for.

Vinjo Indian Cuisine *(meals P150-300)*, above Boracay Scuba Diving School, has an Indian chef who cooks up huge portions of delicious, spicy, traditional Indian cuisine. The atmosphere is as good as the food.

Shanghai Restaurant *(Filipino dishes with rice P85, pasta P60-80)*, in the first laneway south of Calypso Diving, is a long-time favourite with budget diners. Breakfasts, from Hawaiian to Scottish, (P65 to P85) are great value and the shakes (P35 to P50) and beer (P25) are about the cheapest around.

Caffé 1920 *(ice cream P90, cake P70-90)* has two outlets (the other is just south of D'Mall) and has the best homemade Italian ice cream and cake on the strip.

La Capinnina Italian Restaurant Cafe & Wine Bar *(☎ 288 3259; e canyon37@hotmail.com; pasta P150-250, pizza P160-300, other meals P190-300)* is run by Gino, an Italian and long-time-resident restaurateur and outdoor enthusiast. It specialises in creative Italian cooking, and will cater to most tastes and requests. Gino's regularly updated specials include dishes such as squid-ink pasta with creamy seafood sauce (P250). Pastas and pizza crusts are freshly made, and the desserts, such as the mango and amaretto pannacotta (P120), are great. Also, if you're interested in finding out about hiking around north Panay, Gino's your man.

North of Boracay Tourist Centre Vegetarians and those preferring nonspicy food are also well catered for at **Siam House** *(set meals P90-200)*, which boasts a real Thai chef and some good, spicy Thai curries.

Seoul Korean Restaurant *(☎ 288 3240; dishes P150-300, set menu P300)* is the place to come for really spicy Korean meals.

Restaurant de Paris Resort *(☎ 036-288 3233; e deparis@boracay.i-next.net; set meals P160-190)* is a hodge-podge restaurant with red tablecloths and pool tables, serving French and Asian cuisine. With little competition, its French food remains quite popular.

Summer Place The Bar *(all-you-can-eat Mongolian barbecue P195; open 5pm-3am,* food to 11pm daily) is one of the favourite places for the ridiculously prevalent Mongolian barbecue. Its popularity may have less to do with the food and more with the native-style bar that spills onto the beach.

True Food Indian Cuisine *(meals P125-330)* has a great, Far Eastern ambience and a good vegetarian menu.

Hey Jude *(pizza P125-180, other meals P160-300; open 9.30am-1.30am daily)* is a small slice of the city right on the beach. For a slick café-bar with clean lines and smooth music, it has surprisingly good food.

Sea Lovers Bar & Restaurant *(meals P20-150; open 24hr)* has OK cheap food, better known for the fact that it never closes.

Real Coffee & Tea Café *(all-day breakfast P30-100, cakes & cookies P35; open 8am-7pm daily)*, next to Bom Bom bar, is the best place to go for strong, fresh coffee and delicious light meals. Run by the friendly mother and daughter team of Lee and Nadine, this cosy shack has great all-day breakfasts, from the humble cinnamon toast (P30) to omelettes with toast and pesto (P100). After a big night, the papaya, banana and calamansi zinger drink (P55) does the trick.

Café Sun Thai *(meals P140-180)*, at Sandcastles Resort, doesn't have the best Thai food, but with its cruisey beach bar and sand-seating, this place does have the best atmosphere.

Steakhouse Boracay *(dishes P150-300)* serves good German sausages (P90 to P120), steaks (P185 to P295) and other European dishes. Good music and a 2nd-storey view create a cruisey atmosphere.

Jonah's Fruit Shake & Snack Bar *(shakes P50-75)*, amid plenty of competition, proudly boasts the best shakes on the island. After trying one of its huge, creamy, banana-peanut numbers (P55), we're inclined to agree.

Dejà Vu *(meals P200-600)* has pricey but good French food, such as homemade pâté with chicken liver and hot baguette (P220) and baked oysters (P250).

Mañana Mexican Cuisine *(paella P400, other meals P140-300; open 11am-11pm daily)* serves big, tasty dishes and drinks on Mexican terracotta plates and blown glasses. What this restaurant misses out on in location, it makes up for in bright decor.

Café Cocomangas *(seafood P150-280, large pizza P270)* is more well known for its wild parties and shooters, but it does serve decent food.

Friday's Boracay (☎ 288 6200; brunch buffet P462, Friday evening buffet P690, à la carte P370-640, kids meals P180) has the most-expensive food on the island, but also the best. The brunch buffet – with order-to-make salads, soups, Japanese, Italian, Asian, pastries and more – is particularly famous. If you can't afford any of the above, its bar has a 4pm to 7pm happy hour with P20 beers and free bar snacks, and is a beautiful place to watch the sunset.

Puka Grande Restaurant (Puka Beach; meals P50-150; open 7am-6pm) has good, well-priced seafood, and makes for an excellent dining excursion from White Beach. It's at the northern end of the island, near Yapak Beach.

Entertainment

White Beach is one very long liquor shelf. Most places have a happy 'hour' starting at 4pm or 5pm and finishing at 7pm, 8pm or even 9pm. Most bars wind up when the people leave, usually between 1am and 3am.

The Wreck Bar, at Calypso Diving Resort, just south of the tourist centre, can be quite a lively, cruisey bar.

Charlh's Bar is a little shack right on the sand. It has live music, usually quite loud, usually quite late.

Summer Place The Bar (see Places to Eat) has a huge, open, native-style bar that offers a very pina-colada experience.

Hey Jude (see Places to Eat) is popular with those feeling homesick for the urban bar experience.

Bom Bom is a hip little rustic bar with an African edge, cool staff and a large following. Jam sessions with local drummers often start up around 11pm.

Café Cocomangas (see Places to Eat) and **Moondog's Shooter** is a sprawling, tropical nightclub with plenty of drinking challenges and entertainment, including pool, chess and backgammon.

Beachcomber Bar, over the road from Moondog's, can get just as lively after dark.

Getting There & Away

Air The swiftest way to Boracay from Manila is by air to Caticlan (see Getting There & Away in that section earlier) – but you won't be alone trying to book this flight

362 Romblon – C
and you can
ince if y
tele- co
Fo
all

during the hig...
are the airport...
where it's an e...
to Caticlan. F...
vidual Air er...
Away for Ka...
Panay sectio...

Boat A fleet of pumpboats shuttle people back and forth between Caticlan and Boracay every 15 minutes from 6am and 6pm (P19.50, 15 minutes), and then as the need arises between 7pm and 10pm (P30). A special trip costs around P300 to P400.

The boats arrive on White Beach, Boracay, stopping at one or more of the three boat stations. During the southwestern monsoons (June to November), the sea on the White Beach side can get too rough for outriggers. During this period they dock on the east coast, at or near Bulabog, a P20 tricycle ride from White Beach. Be prepared to get your feet wet upon arrival in Boracay.

A new jetty is under construction in the south of the island at Cagban Beach, near Manoc-Manoc, in order to reduce the traffic on White Beach. When complete, Caticlan boats will dock here and ferries will carry passengers around the island.

Getting Around

This compact island is perfect to explore on foot or mountain bike. Along the main street behind White Beach, a short tricycle ride costs P5. Beyond the main strip, trips rise in P5 increments. Mountain bikes can be hired for around P50/400 per hour/day and motorbikes for P150/1000 per hour/day.

Romblon

☎ 042 • pop 264,400

A great little grab-bag of islands, the Romblon group produces world-class marble (Romblon Island), and nurtures forests of unique creatures (Sibuyan Island).

The small group of islands north of Panay stretches the name 'Romblon' a long way. Romblon is the name of the province comprising these islands, *and* the name of one of the islands *and* the provincial capital city on that island.

The communication system in the province is rather archaic and confusing,

only call directly into the prov
...u are using RCPI or BayanTel
...munications.

...all other phone companies (including
...verseas carriers), you must call a Manila
...perator (☎ 02-412 2864 to 67) and ask to be
connected to the 'local' number, which will
consist of the last four digits of the phone
number.

Getting There & Away
Laoag International Airlines has a flight to
Tablas at 10.30am Tuesday, Thursday and
Saturday.

MBRS Lines (☎ 02-921 6716, 921 6721,
243 5886/8; Manila) has three boats servicing the area (one was out of service at the
time of writing). Three times a week, either
MV Virgin Mary or MV Mary the Queen
ply the following route: Manila to Odiongan (Tablas Island; P450, 10 hours), then
on to Caticlan/Hibino (Aklan, Panay; P180,
three hours), then to Lipata (Antique, Panay;
P150, three hours) and returning the way
it came.

Once a week, MV Mary the Queen also
sails from Manila to Romblon town (P450,
10 hours), then to Cajidiocan (Sibuyan Island; P160, two hours), then to Dumaguit
(Kalibo port; P280, three hours) and returning the way it came.

Shipshape Shipping (☎ 02-723 7615;
Manila) boat MV Princess Colleen departs
Batangas three times a week for Odiongan
(P250, eight hours), then on to Romblon
town (P170, two hours) and returning along
the same route.

Shipshape's MV Princess Camille departs Batangas three times a week for San
Agustin (Tablas Island; P310, 10 hours)
then on to Romblon town (P60, one hour)
and Magdiwang (Sibuyan Island; P160, two
hours), and returning along the same route.

Viva Lines' MV Penafrañcia III services
the same route as MV Princess Camille, but
without the stop in San Agustin, three times
a week.

On all these boats, the fare is reduced
when travelling more than one leg.

Several big, wooden cargo boats service
Romblon Province. They are less reliable,
less comfortable and often hard to get
schedules for – try the respective piers.
Nevertheless, they're a cheap way to get
around.

Kalayaan 7 and Kalayaan 9 both have
a weekly trip between Romblon town and
Lucena (Luzon; P280, 14 hours). There is
often a stop in Magdiwang. Another of the
Kalayaan fleet travels between San Fernando, via Romblon, to Lucena (P350, 15
hours) twice a week.

Gavina usually leaves Romblon town for
Cebu City (via Magdiwang) every fortnight
(P350, 14 hours). Its schedule depends upon
cargo.

Once a week, Del Rosario leaves Lucena
for Magdiwang (P280, 12 hours), then on to
Romblon (P110, two hours), then to San
Agustin (P110, one hour), then to San Fernando (Sibuyan Island; P110, four hours),
then to Cajidiocan (P110, one hour) and
then returning the way it came.

Looc and Santa Fe on Tablas Island, and
San José on Carabao Island, all have con-
nections with Caticlan on Panay; Looc and
Odiongan have connections with Roxas,
Mindoro; Odiongan has a connection with
Batangas; San Fernando (Sibuyan) has a
connection with Roxas, Panay; and Cajid-
iocan has a connection with Mandaon,
Masbate. See individual Getting There &
Away sections for more information.

CARABAO ISLAND
Situated less than 10km north of Boracy,
Carabao Island (known as 'Hambil' by
locals) has become more a novel day trip or
diving destination for Boracay visitors than
a travel destination in its own right. But
with its quiet streets, brilliant **white
beaches** and surrounding **reefs**, the island
offers some great exploring, quiet meandering or simply a retreat from the Boracay
hullabaloo.

The island is only 6km wide (from San
José to Lanas) and less than 10km long and
is home to about 12,000 residents, 5000 of
whom live in the main town of **San José**, on
the east coast. Although this side is blessed
with a long, soft-sand, white beach, during
the dry season (November to May) it is
often hammered by winds, making the
lesser (but still good) beaches on the west
coast the better option. In any case, a trip
from one side of the island to the other will
only take 15 minutes by motorbike, so there
is always a protected beach nearby.

San José has little more than a municipal
hall, plaza, church, school, district hospital,

a public long-distance calling office and basic shops. The market has meagre supplies of fruit and vegetables and when fish and meat arrive, a bell is sounded, summoning people onto the street. There is also a **tourist office** (open 8am-noon & 1pm-5pm Mon-Fri), near the port, where you can pick up a map of the island.

The narrow streets of the island – some sealed, mostly not – are so quiet that on a long walk past rice fields, over hills and through shady coconut and nipa stands, you may only pass the odd *kalabaw* (carabao). Motorbikes, though few and far between, do exist, and are available for hire if you ask around (with/without driver P200/100 per hour). They're a great way to get around the island – a coastal trip, stopping at beaches and visiting **Ngiriton Cave** to the north and **Angas Cave** to the south should take about two hours.

Another more leisurely transport option is to hire a horse (P200 for two hours, P100 for guide) – again, ask around or at the tourist office. Mountain bikes, though a perfect mode of transport for this island, are not available, but short-term visitors arriving from Boracay can arrange to bring bikes over from there.

Accommodation is available at **Carabao Lodge** (e carabaolodge@yahoo.com; *Sinongtan; 10-day packages, meals included US$500, other packages available on request*), on the west coast, less than 1km north of Lanas. Brand new nipa huts have fan, marble cold-water bathroom and verandas facing the

THE VISAYAS

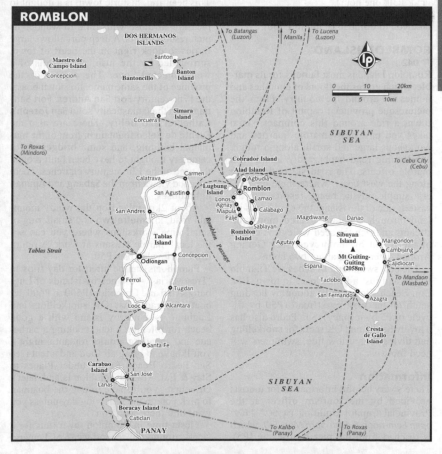

ROMBLON

beach. A motorbike ride to the resort from San José will cost P30. The resort offers diving, horse-riding and bicycle hire. Guests must book via email.

The only other option is a **homestay** *(P150)*, which can be easily organised at the tourist office.

White Beach Divers on Boracay (see Diving under Boracay earlier) runs dive trips to the reefs around Carabao (two dives and lunch on the island US$50), and Michael Parvus, at the dive centre, can organise mountain-bike hire, transport to the island, and accommodation at Carabao Lodge.

There is a daily morning boat arriving and leaving San José from/to both Caticlan (P30, one hour) and Santa Fe (Tablas Island; P30, one hour).

Private boats can be hired on Boracay to take you to Carabao (P500 to P700).

ROMBLON ISLAND
☎ 042

Romblon Island is most famous for its **marble**, which graces the floors of churches and homes all around the country. From the picturesque provincial capital of Romblon town, a ride around this compact island takes you past dusty marble quarries and workshops large and small, along a rough, exhilarating road haphazardly inlaid with marble offcuts. The road skirts the shore along the west coast, where there are several simple, idyllic **beach resorts**. On the eastern side of the island, the road heads inland through coconut-covered mountain, streams and rice-terraced valleys. A circuit of the island by motorcycle (see Getting Around, later) takes about two hours.

The best **swimming beaches** are Tiambin Beach and just a little closer to town, Bon Bon Beach. Both can be found by heading south on the west coast road (P50 by tricycle or P5 by jeepney). San Pedro also has a lovely beach, and OK reefs for **snorkelling** and **diving**, but at low tide, swimmers will need footwear.

Information
There's very helpful information for tourists provided by the **tourism officer** at the Provincial Capitol Building *(☎ 507 2101; open 8am-noon & 1pm-5pm Mon-Fri)*, which is reached from the pier by tricycle (P5).

Around the small triangular town plaza beside the dock in Romblon town, you'll find three **international telephone offices** (RomblonTel, BayanTel and PT&T). Also here is the **post office**, facing the water, and a **police post** on the opposite corner. Opposite Jak's Restaurant (see Places To Eat) is the **Romblon International Business Centre** *(per hr P90; open 8.30am-9pm daily)*, which has the latest whiz-bang computers, and incongruously fast Internet connection.

Several shops near the triangular town plaza are crammed with good-quality cane products, along with lots of home-grown, marble items (mortars and pestles are a favourite).

Romblon Town
This beautiful, historic town, is a delight to approach by sea, and offers an even greater pleasure to those with time to wander its picturesque streets. A deep port allows large ferries to dock right in the heart of town, surrounded by the lush, green hills of a well-protected cove. The capital of the province of the same name, this town boasts the 17th-century **Fort San Andres**, **Fort Santiago** and the fantastically solid **San Joseph's Cathedral** and **belfry**. There are also the **Fuente de Belen** fountain in front of the municipal building, and some **bridges** and a **cemetery** thought to have been built around the time of the 17th-century churches. There are good views from the **Sabang** and **Apunan lighthouses**.

About 2km inland on the windy mountain road, **kilometre two** is a smattering of small nipa workshops where you can see the local marble artisans at work. A return trip by tricycle costs P50.

Pumpboats can be hired for **day trips** to 'Tres Marias' – the nearby islands of Lugbung, Alad and Cobrador (P500 to P600 per boat). Cobrador has OK snorkelling, and Lugbung is a nearby island with a good beach for pitching a tent, cooking a barbecue and spending a quiet romantic night – you'll have to bring all food and a tent (see San Pedro Beach Resort under Places to Stay & Eat, Around Romblon Island, later). Of course, you'll have to pay the boatman to pick you up the following day unless you want him there with you.

Fiesta time in Romblon town runs for a week, around the second week of January;

you may need to book accommodation well in advance for around this time.

Places to Stay & Eat

Romblon Town Where the San Agustin boats dock, **Bayview Mansion** (☎ 507 2408; *doubles/twins with air-con, cold-water bathroom & fan P500, with harbour views P550, master bedroom P1000*) is not exactly a mansion, but it is excellent accommodation. All rooms are very clean, and the P550 rooms have million-dollar harbour views. The vista is shared by the rooftop terrace and master bedroom. There is a communal sitting area and kitchen on the ground floor (again with – yes – views) and staff will happily cook up meals (breakfast P50, lunch or dinner P150).

Romblon Plaza Hotel (☎/fax 02-413 9544; *Manila* • ☎ 507 2269; e RPHreservation@usa .net; Romblon town; standard rooms P400, with air-con P600-1100, penthouse P3000) is Romblon's 'classiest' hotel, situated one block from the pier. A big, clean and bright hotel, adorned with plastic flowers and plants, with good, spacious, standard rooms with fan/air-con, private cold-water bathroom, furnishings and a small balcony; better rooms have cable TV and views. There's a bar and a rooftop **restaurant** (*meals P30-80; open 7am-midnight daily*) serving a variety of food from Filipino and barbecues to spaghetti and burgers. Even if you're not hungry, it is worth dropping in here for a drink, just to enjoy the best views in town.

Muravian Hotel (☎ 507 2505; *twins/ doubles with fan & cold-water bathroom P300, rooms with air-con and cable TV P500*), near Romblon Plaza Hotel, is a new hotel with good clean rooms and views across to the sea. The rooftop terrace has views of the town, mountains and water. There is no restaurant, but staff can cook meals (breakfast P50, lunch or dinner P100).

Jak's Restaurant & Bar (*meals P65-125; open 8am-9pm daily*), behind the town plaza, is a well-run place offering a regularly updated menu, cool tunes and friendly service. The food ranges from Filipino regulars such as *pansit* (noodles; P65), to Western dishes such as fisherman's pie (P120) and pizza (P125 to P175). When you arrive or leave by boat, this nearby place is a great stopover for real coffee and a decent bite to eat.

Romblon Shopping Centre Eatery (*Filipino dishes P40; open 5.30am-9pm daily*),

behind Jak's, facing the triangular town plaza, has average Filipino fare, but it's a good place to sit and watch the world go by.

Cozy Jr (*barbecue from P5; open 3pm-9pm daily*), next to the Shopping Centre Eatery, is one of several streetside barbecue houses where you can get a tasty fresh tuna stick (P5) with rice (P7).

L Machon Bakery (*open 4am-6.30pm daily*), on the plaza, just up from the pier, has the usual baked goods as well as donuts (P1), brownies (P2.50) and excellent coconut macaroons (P1).

Around Romblon Island There are several good beach resorts south of Romblon town, on the island's west coast. From town, the first of these is **Tiamban Aqua Club Beach Resort** (☎ 02-723 6710; w www.emc .com.ph/tiambanp; rooms & cottages P700), which has good native-style rooms and huts with fan and cold-water bathroom. There is a shady garden, perfect for dining, and a good beach. The resort offers all-inclusive, half-day, island-hopping tours (P400), fishing trips (P300), overnight camping trips to Bangud Island (P500), as well as snorkelling and mountain-bike hire. They can also arrange scuba diving.

Palm Garden Beach Resort (e atoymor tos@hotmail.com; nipa huts with fan & cold-water bathroom P350) is a low-key alternative next to Tiamban. Mangroves surround the small beach. Atoy, the owner, can help out with motorbike rentals. A tricycle to either of these resorts will cost P50, or you can take a jeepney for P5.

In Ginablan, about 10km south of Romblon town (P10 by jeepney with a 30-minute walk, or P150 by tricycle), are two of the island's best beach resorts.

Marble Beach Resort (*Ginablan; cottages with fan & cold-water bathroom P250-P350*) has lovely, balconied, bamboo cottages and more-substantial, marble-floored ones. The cottages and **Big Bantoy Scuba Diving Centre** (e bigbantoy@yahoo.com) are perched on a rocky headland with a small private beach; the welcoming restaurant on the sand is rustic and laid back. There is no menu but meals (P150) are cooked upon request. Yvan, the dive centre's one-and-only, has one of the cheapest diving setups in the Philippines (one dive US$15, equipment rental US$5, open-water diving certificate US$260).

THE VISAYAS

The resort is lucky to have a marine sanctuary in front of it and stretching for 5km along the coast, so some of the best dives are on the house reefs. North of Romblon Island, there is a WWII Japanese wreck, and on nearby Tablas Island, the Blue Hole dive – the inside of an old volcano – is favoured by advanced divers. Yvan also knows plenty of good walks to do around the island.

San Pedro Beach Resort (☎ 507 2102, 02-633 7946/7, fax 02-631 3080; e cest@moz com.com; *cottages with fan & cold-water bathroom P350*), next door, is in a beautiful, grassy clearing beside a gorgeous little beach. Cottages with balcony, on a rise above the water, are spotless and marble-floored. There's a small restaurant beside the beach serving big meals including plenty of vegetables and fruit (P150). The kind, obliging and cultured Mina Mingoa, one of the three sisters who own this resort, will make you feel most at home, and help out with any tourist-related queries. She can organise camping trips, tricycles, motorbikes, snorkelling gear (P20) or diving.

Buena Suerte Resort (☎ 507 2069; *3-/10-person cottages P300/500*) is 10km southeast of Romblon town (P20 by jeepney), on the mountainous eastern side of the island. Take the signposted turn-off in the small village of Tambac, and a 1km rough road will take you inland to this sloping, garden retreat set around a large, marble-floored swimming pool.

The basic cottages have fan and cold-water bathroom. A canteen beside the pool serves simple meals. The resort has seen better days and the service is a bit slovenly, but it is quiet and secluded.

Getting There & Away

The port phone number is ☎ 507 2455. Daily pumpboats leave San Agustin on Tablas Island for Romblon town in the morning and early afternoon (P55, one hour). Romblon town–San Agustin boats leave at the same time. In Romblon town these boats come and go from *next* to the dock.

A daily pumpboat leaves Romblon town in the early afternoon for Magdiwang (P120, 2½ hours) on Sibuyan Island. Magdiwang–Romblon town boats leave in the morning.

A pumpboat leaves Romblon for Banton Island (P100, four hours) twice a week, returning the following day.

For more shipping information, see the introductory Getting There & Away section to Romblon (province) earlier.

Getting Around

Romblon town is such a charming place that the best way to get around is by foot, although tricycles can be hired from near the dock for short trips (P5). A circuit of the island by tricycle is pretty much impossible on the steep, rocky road. You're much better off hiring a single motorcycle (with/without driver P500/250-350 per day). You shouldn't have any trouble finding someone in town – if so, Atoy at Palm Beach Garden Resort (see Around Romblon Island under Places to Stay & Eat earlier) has several bikes.

BANTON ISLAND

Remote Banton Island is a small rock island with some good, white-sand **beaches**, a cone-shaped mountain, plenty of coconut palms, a crumbling, 18th-century **Spanish fort**, and some great **diving**. You can rent motorbikes to tour the island on the Spanish-laid cobblestone coastal road, but as the island is so small, getting around on foot is more than adequate. The strong currents, which restrict diving to the advanced, bring in sharks, barracuda and other big pelagic fish. Even better diving can be found in the **marine sanctuary** off the **Bantoncillo Island** to the southwest. As there is no dive centre on the island, divers will have to take a live-aboard from Boracay (see Diving & Snorkelling under Boracay earlier) to enjoy the underwater delights.

Recently, the mayor turned the fort into **accommodation** (*rooms with fan & shared bathroom P100-300*). Visitors can stay there in simple rooms with beds and mosquito nets and get basic food from the local eateries. Being in open seas, you're only likely to get a smooth crossing to the island between March and May.

There is a pumpboat service between Romblon and Banton Island (P100, four hours) twice a week.

TABLAS ISLAND
☎ 042

Tablas, the largest of the Romblon Group, is a three-hour boat ride from Mindoro's east coast. Its largest town is Odiongan. Few tourists come here except as a stepping stone to Romblon and Sibuyan Islands. However, the local government is trying to make this a more-attractive tourist destination so there may be more accommodation and transport options available for tourists soon. At the moment, it is virtually impossible to travel from Panay to Romblon without spending a night on Tablas. The best stopover option is Looc, then Odiongan, and San Agustin is also OK.

The best **beaches** are in Ferrol, in between Odiongan and Looc, and also at Alcantara. There are also **waterfalls** at San Andres and near San Agustin and **mangroves** at Roda Beach near Looc. There is also a **marine sanctuary** near Looc.

Daily pumpboats connect Tablas Island to Carabao Island and Caticlan (Panay); as well as between San Agustin (see later) and Romblon town. Odiongan is connected to Mindoro and Luzon. See those individual entries for boat information and details.

Looc

About 25km from Odiongan, Looc (lo-oc), is a calm and quiet place – except when the Fiesta Sa Dagat rolls around. week-long fiesta rolls around in late April.

The Looc **tourist office** (*open 8am-4.30pm daily*) is at the southern corner of the town plaza, but there are plans to move it to the fishing port. The ground floor of the Marduke Hotel building has a **BayanTel international telephone office**, and an Asian Spirit ticket office.

The main attraction in Looc is the **Looc Bay Marine Refuge & Sanctuary**, a 48-hectare coral reef protected area, 10 minutes by pumpboat from Looc. A boat can be organised at the town's tourist centre to take you to the sanctuary's moored bamboo raft, where you can snorkel (P100 per person for three hours, including snorkelling gear). **Buenavista Marine Sanctuary**, a little further north, is only two hectares, but is located around an islet where tourists can wander about. The tourist office can also organise trips to **Agojo Beach**, a white beach, 30-minutes away by pumpboat.

Taking place in late April, the week-long **Fiesta Sa Dagat** (Festival of the Sea) includes a boat parade, boat races and a fishing competition. The **Talabukon Festival** (the town fiesta) – which celebrates the legend of the giant who defended the area from pirates

by strangling them, giving the town its name Looc ('to strangle') – is at the same time.

Places to Stay There is no sign for **Plaza Inn** (*Grimares St; per person P75*) – just look for a white building between Gonzales St and the Marduke Hotel. It has very basic rooms with thin mattresses, a fan and vinyl slapped down on the floor. Strangely, you pay no extra for a private bathroom.

Roberto's Bar (*☎ 509 4031; nipa huts with fan & shared bathroom around P200*), the town's favourite eatery, has brand new nipa huts in its garden. Prices had not been set when we visited, but they're likely to be reasonable, with food and accommodation packages looking attractive.

The only bummer is the restaurant's nightly videoke, but guests are requested to 'sing, not yell', and the machine is switched off, strictly at 10pm.

Morales Lodging Inn (*per person P100, plus P25 with fan*), near the tourist office, is a cheap, eccentric lodging house with bottom-dollar rooms – twin beds with mangy, thin mattress and a shared bathroom. Run by the energetic Modesto Morales, there's a bar of sorts, a pool table, tourist information, and plenty of kids and locals hanging out.

Marduke Hotel (*☎ 098 199 2037; Grimares St; singles/doubles/triples P400/500/600*) is the rather grand, large, white place peeking over its shorter neighbours beside the market and town plaza (behind the Koop Drug Store). It has five big rooms with air-con and private bathroom. The charming proprietor, Honourable Amando Martinez, will personally see that you avail yourselves of the free, brewed coffee and fresh mangoes, and he may even cook you breakfast.

Roda Beach House (*rooms with bathroom & fan/air-con P250/500, picnic cottages P150*), about 3km from Looc proper (P10 by tricycle or P20 for a 'special trip' – a private tricycle), is a good out-of-town alternative. Rooms are reasonable, facing the beach and the southern coastline across the water. Except for light meals, you'll have to order ahead. The videoke, however, you can count on.

Places to Eat Conveniently located facing the town plaza, is the bright and friendly **Pacific Garden Restaurant** (*meals for 2 P80-100; open 7am-9pm daily*) offering good Filipino and Chinese food. The specialities are *lomi* (noodle, meat, shrimp, egg and vegetable soup; P40) and *tapsilog* (fried rice with fried egg and meat; P85 for two). It also has a well-stocked bar and no videoke.

Toril's Restaurant *(Tirol St; meals P25-50; open 6am-9pm daily)*, close to the market and Marduke Hotel, serves light snacks and pre-cooked Filipino dishes.

Roberto's Bar *(☎ 509 4031; meals P40-80; open 9am-midnight daily)* is a friendly night-time oasis two blocks from the town plaza, on the same street as the Looc Foursquare Gospel Church. This place is one long, deep and green garden, furnished with rock-slab benches and tables, with an open-air, native-style bar and restaurant.

Good Filipino, Chinese and seafood dishes are available until late, as are wine and champagne. In between videoke tracks, the atmosphere is very soothing. There are nipa huts for overnight stays (see Places to Stay earlier).

Getting There & Away Looc's Fish Port, on the sea side of the market, services boats to Caticlan (P5 by tricycle from town). Port Malbog, a 10-minute tricycle ride south (P15), has boats for Roxas (Mindoro).

Jeepney & Tricycle Jeepneys from Looc to Odiongan (P23, one hour), Santa Fe (P15, one hour) and San Agustin (P60, 2½ hours) run until about 4pm. There are morning jeepneys for San Agustin that will get you to the pier in time for the boats to Romblon town. A motorbike on the rough old road between Looc and Santa Fe will probably cost no less than P150.

Boat There are daily morning pumpboats between Caticlan and Looc (P100, three hours).

Larger pumpboats ply between Looc and Roxas, on Mindoro (P150, 3½ hours), twice a week.

Alcantara

Alcantara, 9km from Looc, is a small town with an OK beach. There is accommodation here and the jeepney from Looc to San Agustin passes through, making this an alternative overnighter for tourists heading up to San Agustin.

Dranville Beach Resort *(huts with bathroom P250)* is a restaurant and picnic area

with two new bamboo huts. The beach has grey sand but is fairly clean and good for swimming. The restaurant has a bar and videoke and will only make light snacks unless given an advance order.

You can get here from Looc by jeepney (P8) or public tricycle (P10). From town, a tricycle can take you to the resort (P15). To San Agustin, it's P50 by jeepney.

Odiongan

The clean, green, port town of Odiongan (oh-**d'yong**-ahn) is a mix of brightly coloured houses and neatly trimmed hedges, with a busy market bang in the middle. Odiongan's **fiesta** is held in early April.

There used to be a helpful tourist office in town, but it was in the process of moving when we visited and nobody could tell us where to find it.

There's a **PNB bank** *(cnr M Formilleza & JP Laurel Sts)*, a few blocks from the market. Opposite the bank is a **PLDT international telephone office** and an **RCPI telephone office** next to Shellborne Hotel.

There is a no-name **Internet café** *(Manuel Quezon St; per hr P50; open 9am-9pm daily)* not far from the market.

Near the village of Tuburan, 7km from town, is an impressive, multitiered *busay* (waterfall) known simply as **Busay**. You can get there by tricycle or motorcycle for around P200 return (including waiting time). There's a 500m-long walk up from the rough road to the falls.

Places to Stay On the 3rd floor of an anonymous building next to the Golden Gift Convenient Store & Snack House, near the central market is **Shellborne Hotel** *(rooms per person with shared/private bathroom P150/200, singles/doubles with air-con P500/700)*. If you can rouse anyone in the little information booth at the top of the stairs (on the right), you'll get a very average room.

Poctoy Beach Inn *(☎ 508 5386; doubles with cold-water bathroom, air-con and cable TV P600)* is on the road into town from the pier. The beach, hidden beyond a stone wall, is crap, but the rooms are OK.

Haliwood Inn *(☎ 508 5292; Barangay Liwayway St; rooms from P850-1750)* is the town's classiest affair. Rooms have cold-water bathroom and a choice of two to five beds, and a combination of amenities including air-con and cable TV.

The restaurant serves well-priced Filipino and Chinese dishes (P50 to P150) along with videoke.

Places to Eat The **market**, in the centre of town, is huge, well stocked and friendly. You can buy baked goods (try the *ube jam* – sweet potato and coconut-milk cakes; P10), peanut butter (P30), barbecued sweet corn (P5) and loads of fruit and nuts.

Bistro *(meals P40-100; open 5.30pm-midnight daily)*, on the same street as the PNB, PLDT and Haliwood Inn, is an outdoor eatery and videoke bar serving Chinese and Filipino dishes.

Lyn's Snack Bar & Restaurant *(snacks P25-30; open 7am-10pm daily)*, on the plaza, is an immaculately clean air-con diner serving Filipino dishes, burgers and hot dogs.

Getting There & Away Jeepneys run up until about 4pm from near the market, as well as from the pier, to and from towns north and south of Odiongan. The main destinations are Looc (P23, one hour) and San Agustin (P50, two hours).

Montenegros Shipping Lines has boats from Odiongan to Batangas (P250, 10 hours) and back again, three times a week.

Pumpboats leave from Odiongan for Roxas (P100, three hours) three times a week.

For more options, see the introductory Getting There & Away section to Romblon (province) earlier.

San Agustin

With a backdrop of high, rugged mountains and a deep, palm-fringed harbour, the serene town of San Agustin (san-ah-goos-**tin**) is a lovely place to miss a boat.

There's a **PLDT international phone office** in town on Mangoba St and a very friendly well-stocked **market**.

If you have a few hours to kill before your boat departs, you can take a 30-minute walk (P50 by motorcycle) to the **Dubduban Busay waterfalls**.

Places to Stay & Eat Built into a sandy cove, 5km before town, **Kambaye Beach Resort** *(☎ 02-416 7923; single nipa huts with cold-water bathroom & fan P200)* is looking a bit worse for wear since being hammered

by a recent typhoon. The huts only have single beds, but Joe, the owner says that most guests like to sleep on the huts' large balcony, listening to the waves. He also assured us that renovations were underway and that soon there would be new huts, a cliff-top restaurant and swimming pool. Great news if this is true, but seeing is believing.

Kamilla Lodge *(doubles with fan P250)*, a short walk from the pier, on the northern edge of the plaza, has very clean rooms with marble bathroom, and very friendly staff. Next door's evening videoke can be a bit grating.

Most of the food options exist within the market – several **stalls** *(meal with rice P15-30; open 7am-5pm daily)* serve decent Filipino dishes. When we visited, an out-of-place, new, peachy-white **commercial complex** had just been built on the edge of the market. Most of the stalls had not been filled when we were there, but there were a couple of **eateries** open, and one – **Ruzzel's Restaurant** *(meal with rice P35; opening 10am-10pm daily)* serves night-time Filipino food, beer and videoke.

Getting There & Away Jeepneys travel between Looc and San Agustin (P60, 2½ hours).

Pumpboats to Romblon town (P55, one hour) leave from *next to* San Agustin's long, concrete pier twice daily, in the early morning and early afternoon.

For boats travelling further afield, see the introductory Getting There & Away section to Romblon (province) earlier.

Santa Fe

About 23km from Looc, Santa Fe is a small, drab town with a main street running along the waterfront. Few tourists ever return here, and now that all the lodging houses have been closed down, there is even less reason to risk it. Those determined to spend the night can ask the mayor to organise a **homestay**.

A regular pumpboat travels between Santa Fe and Caticlan (P100 plus P10 shuttle boat service to/from the shore, two hours) every morning.

If you accidentally board the wrong boat in Caticlan and end up here, don't despair, jeepneys for Looc meet every boat arrival (P15, one hour). Motorbikes also do this trip (P150), but it's a tough ride.

SIBUYAN ISLAND

Wearing the massive Mt Guiting-Guiting (2058m) like a saw-toothed crown, Sibuyan Island (see-**boo**-yan) is blessed. While countless neighbours are being stripped bare, Sibuyan Island's natural resources are being protected and nurtured, largely thanks to the dedication of Dr Art Tansiongco, an ex-mayor of Magdiwang, who pushed for protected area status of the mountain, which was granted in 1996.

Biologically, Sibuyan is the Galapagos Islands of the region, having been cut off from all other land masses during the last Ice Age. In pristine isolation, with 60% of the densest forest cover found in the Philippines, the island is home to five **unique mammal species** – including the bizarre tube-nosed fruit bat. No other island of its size in the world is known to have that many, and it is believed that more flora and fauna species will be discovered with further exploration.

Technically there are entry points into the park from the three municipalities of Magdiwang, Cajidiocan and San Fernando, but, as guides and permits are compulsory, visitors must first proceed to the **Magdiwang visitors centre** where information and the necessary arrangements can be made.

At the time of writing, Sibuyan Island was still suffering the aftermath of a generator blow-out in the previous year. The island's main electricity supply is only delivered from around 6pm to 6am, but this will hopefully soon be rectified.

San Fernando

This town, near the banks of the mighty **Cantingas River**, is one of the three entry points onto the island. Although a quiet town, caught almost off guard by visitors, the accommodation here is scenic and relaxed, and there is plenty of water to play in, either on or off the island.

For a real getaway, private pumpboats can take you to **Cresta de Gallo**, a small white-coral sand island off the southern tip of Sibuyan. You can skip around the island in about half an hour and see little but your own footsteps. There is some OK snorkelling, but you will have to bring your own gear. While you're at it, pack plenty of water and a wide-brimmed hat as there is little shade on the island. The trip takes about 40 minutes and a boat for the day will cost around P1000.

On the coastal side of town, **Sea Breeze Inn** *(singles/twins with fan & shared cold-water bathroom P150/300, doubles with private bathroom & stereo P400)* has more than adequate bamboo huts with verandas, facing out to sea. There is a common kitchen, or visitors can make use of the newly built **Sea Breeze Cafe** *(meals P50-100)* which only opens for visitors and will adapt to accommodate most palates, supplies permitting. This family-run affair offers great Filipino hospitality.

About 6km out of town (P10 by tricycle), **Cantingas River Resort** *(twin bunk room with fan & bathroom P300, bunks for 4 with off-site bathroom P500; nonguest admission P2)* is a government-owned, casually run guesthouse offering little except a great location. Built on the banks of the river, visitors will have plenty of splashing around and exploring to do during the day, but will have to buy and cook their own food in the basic kitchen.

There are slim pickings in terms of **eateries** in town. The three options are based in the market area, and seem to be aiming at a nonexistent nightclub crowd. Two of them open at 4.30am and close at noon, while the other opens at a bizarre 3am and stays open until 6pm. Filipino meals cost around P30.

Tourists can catch the cargo pumpboat that travels between Roxas (on Panay) and Azagra port in San Fernando (P120, five hours) three times a week. For the most reliable information about this trip, ring the **PPA office** (☎ 036-621 2008) at the Culasi Port terminal in Roxas. In San Fernando, ask at the pier.

Kalayaan Shipping has a boat from San Fernando (via Romblon) to Lucena (P350, 15 hours) twice a week.

Private MB *Godspeed* leaves San Fernando for Boracay (P300, 2½ hours) once a week, staying overnight before returning. For details, ask for Mr Yul Garcia (San Fernando), or visit Laura's Shop (outside Cajidiocan – see entry under Cajidiocan later).

Whenever there's an early boat arrival, jeepneys leave San Fernando for Magdiwang at 4.30am (P70 plus P5 to the pier, two hours), wait for the morning boats and then return with passengers. In addition, three jeepneys run between San Fernando and Magdiwang before early afternoon. Tricycles can be hailed for a lift to Cajidiocan (P50 or P100 for 'special trip').

THE VISAYAS

Magdiwang

The gateway to Mt Guiting-Guiting Natural Park (see that entry following), Magdiwang (mag-**dee**-wang) is a friendly, no-frills port town. Its pier, 2km from the town, is lined with picture-perfect little houses on stilts, decorated with flowering pot plants. Mangroves thrive in the clean, clear waters around the pier.

The town is 3km from the pier (P10 by tricycle) and has three **international telephone offices**, but the nearest **bank** of any use to foreign tourists is in Romblon town, on Romblon Island. There are plenty of half-day trips from town, including to **Lambingan Falls** (P50 by tricycle), but most nature lovers here tend to go straight to the Mt Guiting-Guiting Natural Park.

About 12km from Magdiwang (4km past the turn-off to Mt Guiting-Guiting Natural Park Visitors' Centre) is the beautiful **Lambingan Falls** and swimming hole. Tricycles can take you from Magdiwang to the visitors centre (P40, 20 minutes) and to the falls (P50, 30 minutes).

Places to Stay & Eat Officially a homestay, tricycle drivers bring all travellers from the pier straight to **Vicky's Place** *(MH del Pilar St; rooms per person P150)* without asking questions. This lodging house has been welcoming guests since 1993. Upstairs there are homely, timber-floored rooms that come with fan and immaculate shared bathroom. Vicky, the mastermind behind the whole smoothly run operation, cooks wonderful Filipino and Western meals – she'll discuss with you what you feel like during the day, then whip up a huge meal based on creative inspiration and her ever-expanding repertoire (breakfast P50, lunch or dinner P70 to P120). Alcoholic and soft drinks are available, and there's also a laundry service. Vicky can arrange motorbike hire and carries a wealth of helpful travel information. Every tricycle driver knows the house – it's just off National Rd, opposite the school.

Roger's Place *(José Rizal St; rooms per person P100)*, run by ex-vice-mayor Roger, is the new kid on the block. It carries the prestigious title Mt Guiting-Guiting Parkview Inn, but everyone knows it as Roger's Place, or 'the lodging house above the RCPI building'. While Vicky's Place overflows with a family feel, at Roger's Place you'll be totally left alone to enjoy to the wonderful views of the mountain. Rooms are simple, and there is a communal sitting area with cable TV and a stove-top for making use of the free coffee. Roger can organise meals from the nearby café he conveniently owns (breakfast P70, lunch or dinner P100 to P150). Roger has a 24-hour generator, which is great for electricity, not so great for peace and quiet.

Getting There & Away There are three jeepneys daily between Magdiwang and Cajidiocan (P30, one hour) and an early morning jeepney from San Fernando to the pier at Magdiwang most days (P75, two hours), in time for the first boat arrival, which returns to San Fernando after picking up passengers.

Pumpboats travel between Romblon town and Magdiwang (P120, two hours) once daily.

For shipping options taking you further afield, see the introductory Getting There & Away section to Romblon (province) earlier.

Mt Guiting-Guiting Natural Park

The great 15,000-plus-hectare natural park is not only the dominant feature of the island, it is also one of the Philippines' natural treasures. A biologist's wonderland, the island has been cited as one of the centres of plant diversity in Asia and the Pacific, being home to an estimated 700 plant species, some of which are only found on the island. Such extraordinary diversity and endemism is also represented in the animal kingdom. The island is home to 130 bird species, and a long list of rare and endangered mammals and reptiles.

About 8km from Magdiwang (heading east along National Rd, then inland) is the sparkling new **Mt Guiting-Guiting Natural Park Visitors Centre**, the main entry point for the park (P50 by tricycle from Magdiwang). From here, you can gather information, organise permits and (compulsory) guides to take you up the trail to the 2058m-high mountain peak that stands before you. Although there are other trails throughout the park, this is the only one that takes you to the summit. It's a very challenging, 10-hour climb one way, so you definitely need three days if you plan to go the distance.

The standard **trek** involves a six- to eight-hour walk to the base camp area of Mayo's Peak, where you can pitch a tent, and collect

THE VISAYAS

fresh water (depending upon the season), and drop your heaviest gear. Then you can tip-toe across the knife-edge ridge to the rocky face of Mt Guiting-Guiting itself. From there, you follow an extremely steep trail up jagged rocks to arrive at a bonsai forest on a breathtaking summit, before returning to Mayo's Peak for a well-earned sleep.

Very ratty **tents** are available free of charge from the visitors centre but you'd be advised to bring your own. You'll also need to organise a guide (P350 per day) and an optional porter – and bring food for yourself and your guide. If you plan to conquer the summit, you must bring mountaineering attire (eg, cold weather gear, and no sandals!). The trek is an extremely rewarding but advanced climb, and visitors are advised to allow time for organising the guide and equipment.

Cajidiocan & Around

Cajidiocan (cah-ee-**d'yo**-can) is Sibuyan Island's access point for boats to and from Masbate. It's also an alternative base to Magdiwang for trips into Mt Guiting-Guiting Natural Park. However, visitors should check in at Magdiwang first. From the 'Residential Ranger Station' just outside town, you can do a one-day trek to some excellent **caves** within the park. **Cawa Cawa Falls** (cawa means cauldron, as the falls pool into two huge swimming holes), an excellent swimming spot, are 8km from town, but a motorbike or tricycle (P50 one way) can take you most of the way, then you just walk for half an hour.

The town's main street, Ramon Magsaysay St, includes **RCPI** and **PLDT international telephone offices**. On the right-hand side, **Marble House** (per person P150) has no signposting but is known by all the locals. It's as the name tells – a big marble house – with rooms with fan and large windows onto the street or towards the mountains. The shared bathroom is large and, of course, marble. On the next corner (E Quirino St), **Gladys Point Eatery and Snack House** (meals P20-40; open 6am-10pm daily) serves Filipino food and hamburgers.

About 3km toward San Fernando (P20 by tricycle), Laura's Shop is the front piece of a recently established community. Though known by locals as 'the German Village', and being, at this stage, only German and

German-Filipino families, the community aims for assimilation and welcomes all nationalities to drop in to the Filipino shop/eatery **Laura's Shop** (meals P20-50; open 7am-9pm daily), or stay in their **accommodation** (doubles P400) for short-term rent or long-term lease. The stone-walled, nipa-roofed duplexes come with ceiling fan and a shared (between the two sides) kitchen and marble bathroom.

A similar community exists 5km further along the road, in Otod. One resident, Uwe Goehler, has recently set up a dive centre, **Sibuyan Asian Diver** (w sibuyan-asian-diver .com), and offers diving (1 dive with equipment US$17-27, open-water diving certificate US$300) around the island, including to the sand islet **Cresta de Gallo**, which is off the southern tip .

There are two pumpboats between Cajidiocan and Mandaon (Masbate; P150, four hours) twice a week.

For other boat options, see the introductory Getting There & Away section to Romblon (province) earlier.

There are three jeepneys daily from Cajidiocan to Magdiwang (P35, one hour) and back, finishing in the early afternoon. Tricycles to San Fernando cost P30, or P100 for a special trip.

Masbate

☎ 056

Broad, lumpy hills dominate this most uncharacteristic of Philippine island-provinces. Grassy green and sparsely inhabited, the island is ideal for cattle grazing – which is what Masbate is best known for, apart from its annual rodeo (see Masbate Town later). The island was once heavily forested and provided timber for the building of Manila Galleons. Masbate has a few stunning, unspoiled, white-sand beaches (see Bagacay later), and provincial officials are hoping to lure visitors by providing infrastructure. As yet, most of Masbate's best beaches have no formal accommodation and are difficult to get to.

A poor island-province even by Philippine standards, Masbate (mas-**bah**-teh) has long been known for the ruthlessness of its local politics. As with the plantations on other islands in the Philippines, Masbate's

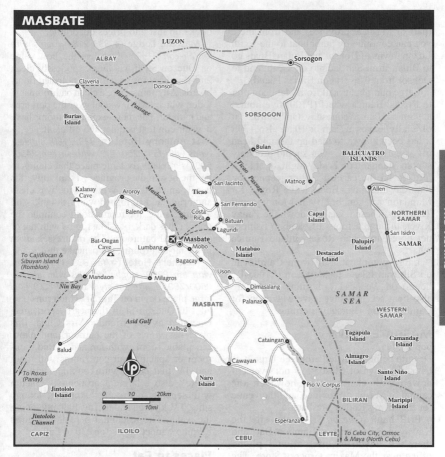

MASBATE

vast cattle ranches are owned by a handful of rich families.

The majority of the population struggles to make the most of their marine and agricultural resources. Masbate's fisherfolk have long made do with antiquated equipment, while also competing with farmers forced to live off the sea by chronic unemployment on the land. A shining light in all this is the provincial government's Fishery Development Program, aimed at improving Masbate's fishing industry through sustainable technology, conservation, tougher fishing laws and loans for local cooperatives.

Getting There & Away

Air Masbate isn't too well served by airlines. PAL, Air Philippines and Cebu Pacific have all overlooked the place, so it's up to the smaller operators. See Getting There & Away under Masbate town for more information.

Boat *Our Lady of Sacred Heart,* operated by **WG&A**, leaves Manila from pier 14 Tuesday nights at 11pm, and arrives at Masbate around 6pm the following day. From Masbate to Manila the same ship leaves every Thursday at 4pm and arrives at Manila the following day at around noon. Fares range from P445 for a bunk bed on a covered deck (meals not included) to P2800 for a posh stateroom that sleeps two.

From Cebu, **Trans Asia** leaves every Monday and Wednesday at 6pm.

Regular morning pumpboats sail from the busy pumpboat area at Masbate town's pier to the nearby islands of Ticao and Burias (part of Masbate province) and from there you can continue by pumpboat to the south Luzon towns of Donsol and Bulan. Boats go to Bulan from San Jacinto on Ticao, and to Donsol from Claveria on Burias Island.

Large pumpboats sail from Mandaon pier to Roxas' Banica wharf (P100, five hours) at 9am or 10am Wednesday. On Saturday, it officially leaves at 9am or 10am also – but it has been known to load up fast and head off as early as 7am – you should probably stay in Mandaon on Friday night, or at least turn up on the earliest bus or jeepney on Saturday morning. Boats leave Roxas for Mandaon at 9am or 10am Monday and Thursday. These boats sail down the Panay River, through a forest of bamboo fishing-net poles, to reach Roxas' inland Banica wharf.

Large pumpboats sail from Cajidiocan on Sibuyan Island to Mandaon (P100, 4½ hours) on Wednesday morning. There are also boat services that leave Mandaon for Cajidiocan on Thursday morning.

MASBATE TOWN
pop 71,441
Despite being sprawled around a large harbour, the town of Masbate is not over-endowed with charm. It is, however, the capital of Masbate Province, and the venue for the rowdy Rodeo Masbateño.

PNB bank *(Quezon St)* is opposite the Kawayan Restaurant & Bamboo Bar, and there's a **BayanTel international phone office** near the Maxim Grocery Store. The **post office** is nearby also. There's a **police station** beside the pier, below Quezon St. Call ☎ 166 in the event of an emergency.

Rodeo Masbateño (also known as Rodeo Filipino, or Rodeo Pilipino) is usually held in April or May. This five-day event attracts cowpokes from all over the country, and features men's and women's lassoing, barehand cattle wrestling and – the crowd favourite – bull riding. The festivities begin with a colourful parade that makes its way to the Rodeo Arena, Minchs Annexe. For more information call ☎ 333 2120.

Places to Stay
Most of Masbate town's accommodation is on Quezon St, running in an arc above the port area. Keep in mind that during the week-long Rodeo Pilipino, accommodation books up fast and prices quadruple.

Masbate Lodge *(☎ 333 2184; rooms with fan/air-con P150/500)* offers the best value on Quezon St. It has large, spotlessly clean 2nd-storey rooms with lovely, polished floorboards. All rooms share a clean bathroom and toilet, which has views out over the port area and harbour. The more-expensive rooms have new air-con that is quiet and efficient.

St Anthony Hotel *(☎ 333 2180; singles/twins with fan P250/300, with air-con P450/500)* is a relatively large place that claims to be 'the best in the province'. Thankfully, this is only an idle threat. While the lobby is clean and bright and furnished with fish tanks and a lounge suite, the rooms don't continue the trend. It has dark, box-like rooms with fan or air-con and bathroom. The mattresses, even in the air-con rooms, are pancake thin.

Rancher's Hotel *(☎/fax 333 3931; rooms with fan P250, singles/doubles with air-con P500/700, apartment-style room P800)* is a large place down on Tara St, which runs parallel to Quezon St in the nearby port area. Operated by the friendly Mrs Chua, this place has views of the harbour, and plain, acceptable rooms with fan and shared bathroom or spacious air-con rooms with bath and TV that come with cooking facilities. There's also a large, apartment-style setup with separate bedroom, bathroom, lounge suite, TV, kitchen and narrow balcony facing the water. The restaurant here serves good Filipino budget meals for P30 to P50.

Places to Eat
The Quezon St strip has plenty of cheap, lively eateries.

L & M Martinez Enterprises *(dishes around P20)*, at the far end of Quezon St, opposite the Shell service station and the bus station, is a street-side foodhouse with local dishes.

A few blocks towards the town centre, **D'San Restaurant** and **Elm's Snacks** do sit-down Filipino meals from P30 to P60.

Kawayan Restaurant & Bamboo Bar *(dishes around P100)*, a couple of blocks further, opposite the PNB bank, is a new nightspot and eatery serving plenty of traditional beef and pork dishes.

Situated on either side of St Anthony Hotel, **Ronnie's Restaurant** and **JRF Sizzling Chicken** offer good local fare for P50 to P100.

Nearby Ibañez St, which runs off Quezon St (with Maxim Grocery Store on the corner), is a lively **food street**, especially at night. Stalls and small cafés offer freshly cooked chicken pieces, spring rolls and other snacks from P10 to P35. Among these eateries is the aqua-coloured **Xiamen Fresh Water & Restaurant**, where tasty mushrooms with shrimp balls cost P50 and spectacular sizzling beef costs P90. The fresh water is a sideline business – the restaurant delivers water to households not connected to town water.

La Concha Cakes & Bakes (Quezon St) is a well-stocked, sit-down eatery with baked goods and groceries, opposite the church.

In the port area, near Rancher's Hotel on Tara St, cheap eateries include the Chinese-flavoured **Peking House**, towards the pier.

Entertainment
Masbate town shuffles off to bed pretty early, but a few places do stay up.

Kawayan Restaurant & Bamboo Bar is always good for a late-night drink. **Ronnie's Inn** often has live bands.

Getting There & Away
Air Masbate town's airport is a P10 tricycle ride from Quezon St.

Asian Spirit flies from Manila to Masbate town (P1950, one hour) daily at 6am. The same plane returns to Manila at 7.30am.

Bus & Jeepney Small minivans travel between Masbate town and Mandaon (P100, two hours), as do regular buses and jeepneys, which run from around 6am to around 2pm. In Masbate town, the minivans drop passengers at the Shell service station, at the end of Quezon St, though if you tell the driver the name of your hotel they will usually take you there after dropping off other passengers.

Most buses and jeepneys terminate next to the market in the pier area.

The scenic Masbate town–Mandaon route is sealed and smooth from Masbate town to the small town of Milagros, but from there to Mandaon it's unsealed and crumbly.

Boat The Masbate town pier is near the market, below Quezon St. There's a rustic **WG&A ticket office** (☎ 333 2373, 333 2342) near the pier, opposite the Shell service station. The thronging pumpboats here offer regular connections (usually around 9am or 10am) to Costa Rica and Lagundi on Ticao, and Claveria on Burias Island. You can also hire these boats for 'special rides' (see Ticao & Burias Islands, later). You'll find information on other boat services under Boat in Masbate province's introductory Getting There & Away section.

BAGACAY
About 14km from Masbate town, **Bituon Beach Resort** (☎ 333 2242; huts/cottages/rooms P350/500/1500), in Bagacay, is easily the best place of accommodation on Masbate. With a white-sand, coral-crumbed beach in a stunning, secluded cove, this place is an idyllic mini-village offering a wide range of accommodation. There's a long, sun-bleached row of small, tidy nipa hut-style rooms with bathroom and shared balcony, palm-shaded, concrete duplex cottages right on the sand with bathroom, wall-mounted fan and small balcony, and more-lavish rooms next door with big balconies and air-con. The thatched-roof restaurant serves good Filipino and international breakfasts for P95 to P125, and main meals for not much more. The **swimming pool** (adult/child P30/50) here pales in significance to the turquoise waters of the beach, but it's a good place to dump the kids. The beach's proximity to Masbate town makes it a popular getaway on weekends, and it can get a bit crowded and littered during and just after holidays.

The resort is a P100 tricycle ride from Masbate town (30 to 45 minutes), 7km past the town of Mobo, at the end of an unpromising dirt road.

MANDAON
pop 31,572
A knobbly, green hill provides an unusual backdrop to the port town of Mandaon (mandah-ohn), 64km from Masbate town. **Batongan Cave** is about half an hour by jeepney or bus, near the main road between Mandaon and Masbate town. Look for the high, rocky hill that seems so out of place it might have fallen out of the sky.

West of the gold-mining town of Aroroy, about 40km by road from Mandaon, day trips can be made to the **Kalanay Cave**, which has yielded some interesting archaeological relics. There's also a decent beach nearby.

THE VISAYAS

A particularly scenic connection if you can make it is the five-hour pumpboat trip between Mandaon and Roxas' Banica wharf, on Panay (see Masbate province's introductory Getting There & Away section earlier). Boats in either direction go via several islands off Masbate, including the stunning, high-peaked island of **Cagmasoso**, about an hour's sailing from Mandaon.

Places to Stay & Eat
Mesa's Lodging House & Eatery (rooms per person P100), beside the pier, has small, tidy rooms upstairs (watch your head!) with fan, ancient shared bathroom and a cosy little common lounge area. Rooms are above the eatery, which does good local dishes.

4-K's Restaurant & Lodging House (rooms P150), across the road from Mesa's, is a less cosy option with large, plain rooms upstairs with fan and shared bathroom. It also pumps out loud videoke favourites most nights. Filipino food here is around P30.

Mommy's Bread House is a good bakery near the pier.

Lina's Store, at the nearby bus station (via the market from the pier), is run by the friendly Lorna Manuel, who has fresh food available virtually 24 hours a day. She also has a two-way radio and can keep you posted on the boat, bus and jeepney situation. Opposite the square, you can while away the waiting time at the 4-K's Billiard Hall.

Getting There & Away
Ordinary (ie, nonair-con) buses and jeepneys run back and forth between Mandaon and Masbate (P40 to P50, two hours) up until about 1pm or 2pm. After that, you have to rely on 'air-con buses' (P70, two hours), which make their last runs around 3pm or 4pm. In Mandaon, the buses and jeepneys collect passengers at a square (locally known as 'the terminal') about 300m from the pier. Don't wait at the pier for these vehicles, they're often full by the time they pass by. Lorna Manuel, at Lina's Store is a great source of information on boats, buses and jeepneys. Jeepneys tackling the particularly bad road to Aroroy (P50, around three hours) leave from the station. There are two per day, more on weekends, heading off at between 7am and 9am.

TICAO & BURIAS ISLANDS
The islands of Ticao (tee-**cow**) and Burias (boo-**ree**-ahs) are wild and enticingly unexplored, with plenty of potential for free-form hiking. Good accommodation is nonexistent on either island – they are best explored as day-trip destinations from Masbate town.

For information about the unpredictable pumpboat schedules and prices for Ticao and Burias Islands, ask at the security-guard booth at the Masbate town pier's gate.

Ticao Island
On Ticao's rugged west coast, **Costa Rica** is a lonely little fishing village with a long, brown-sand beach. Not exactly an island paradise, it at least makes for a good boat trip – sometimes **dolphins** and **flying fish** are spotted along the way. Daily pumpboats go from the Masbate town pier to Costa Rica (P10, 45 minutes), Lagundi and several other villages and towns on Ticao. A hired 'special ride' pumpboat will cost P500 for the return trip.

Burias Island
In February 1999, in the town of **Claveria** on Burias, a **cave** of truly cathedral-like dimensions was uncovered by a visiting official. Thought to have been a prehistoric burial ground, the cave shows signs of relatively recent habitation in the form of scrawlings on the gravestones, as well as small shards of Ming Dynasty porcelain. Known to locals for years, the cave has a well-hidden, narrow entrance. Guides may be found in sitio Macamote, barangay Boca Enganyo, just outside Claveria proper. Expect to pay about P100, and make it clear that you only need one guide or you'll find half the village tagging along.

Further out than Ticao, remote Burias is still a worthy day-trip destination if you start out early. Pumpboats from Masbate to Claveria take about three hours and cost about P800 to P1000 to hire for the day.

Samar

The island province of Samar still has many wild and beautiful places intact, and it remains relatively undeveloped for tourism. It has a narrow coastal plain, and a mountainous and heavily forested interior. Travelling to Samar by road, you cross the scenic San Juanico Strait by the 2km-long bridge linking it with the neighbouring province of Leyte. Try to do this in the daytime, so you can enjoy the great view of coastline and busy waterways.

Flying to either Catarman or Calbayog, you'll see a mass of small offshore islands, wide river estuaries and millions of coconut palms.

Historically, Samar is interesting – Magellan first set foot in the Philippines here in 1521, at the island of Homonhon in the south. During the Philippine-American war, Samar was the scene of some of the bloodiest battles. Tales of brutal combat wove their way into US Marine Corps folklore, and for years after the war American veterans of the

campaign were toasted in mess halls by their fellow marines with, 'Stand, gentlemen, he served on Samar'. Perhaps because it was sparsely settled before the US colonial period, Samar has a handful of towns and villages founded by or named after Americans: Allen, Taft, Wright, MacArthur and the tiny village of Washington.

As with so many places in the Philippines, copra is a major product here, and it's often quite a feat for drivers to dodge the ubiquitous piles of coconut meat drying along the narrow roadsides. Fishing and subsistence farming of rice, maize and root crops are the two other major economic activities. Samar also produces export-quality shell-craft, plus abaca and rattan products.

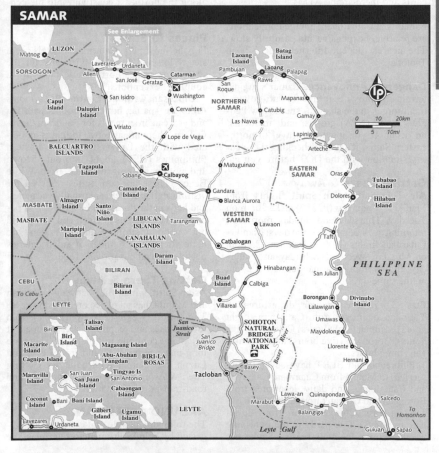

Waray is the language commonly spoken on Samar, and the traditional dance of welcome – the *kuratsa* – is, astonishingly, patterned after the courtship movements of chickens. Could this be why the DOT in Borongan includes *hinihigugma kita* ('I love you') on its list of useful Waray phrases for tourists?

Very little English is spoken on this island and even Pilipino (Tagalog) is much less likely to be understood than in other parts of the Visayas.

Information

There are **PNB** branches in Catarman, Calbayog, Catbalogan, Borongan and Guiuan. They will only change US dollars. It is not yet possible to get cash advances on credit cards and there are no ATMs.

The only public access to the **Internet** on Samar is at Catbalogan, but the connections are relatively expensive and painfully slow. The nearest decent Internet access is in Tacloban.

Dangers & Annoyances Samar's rugged terrain still provides refuge for anti-government forces in the shape of small New People's Army (NPA) groups, and 'incidents' do occur. If you intend to travel in northeastern Samar it's worth checking the security situation with the DOT before you go.

Getting There & Away

Air There are **Asian Spirit** flights from Manila to Calbayog (P2380) at 12.30pm on Tuesday, Thursday and Sunday mornings, returning at 14.35pm the same days. Manila–Catarman flights (P2400) leave at 12.30pm on Monday, Wednesday, Friday and Saturday; flights from Catarman leave at 2.25pm on the same days.

Bus There are regular departures to Tacloban on Leyte from Catarman (eight hours), Guiuan (eight hours) Calbayog (five hours), Borongan (five hours) and Catbalogan (three hours).

Philtranco and BLBT have several daily services to Manila from Catarman, Calbayog and Catbalogan, and daily departures from Borongan and Guiuan (around P600/450 aircon/'1st class', 26 to 30 hours from all departure points). Due partly to the punishing weather during the rainy season, Samar has some of the worst roads in the Visayas – huge potholes can make for very slow going.

Boat A boat leaves Calbayog for Cebu City (P275, 10 hours) on Tuesday, Thursday and Saturday evenings. The boat from Cebu City to Calbayog departs on Monday, Wednesday, Friday and Saturday evenings. There are daily boats from Allen to Matnog (P50, one hour) on Luzon, with six departures starting at 4am. There may also be a boat between Matnog and San Isidro.

CATARMAN
pop 67,671

A small and rather ramshackle town, Catarman is the point of air entry to northern Samar, and is a stopping-off point for trips along the northeast coast and into the centre of the island.

Places to Stay

For the most part, Catarman's hotels are a sleazy lot, and seem to exist only for the short-time trade. Fortunately, there are a couple of exceptions.

Diocesan Catholic Centre *(DCC; rooms P100)* has spartan but clean rooms with fan and you can order meals for P60 from the refectory. There are also two **lodgings** associated with the University of the Eastern Philippines (UEP), about 3km out of town and within walking distance from White Beach. These are sometimes reserved for visiting staff, but there are usually vacancies, and beds in the dorm can be had for P50 per person. The campus is green and nicely laid out – good for strolling, and the students are quite friendly. A number of small eateries outside the campus provide food.

Getting There & Away

Asian Spirit, which flies between Catarman and Manila, has an office on Magsaysay St. The airport is 2km (P20 by tricycle) from town. Buses and jeepneys meet the boats at Allen and continue to Catarman. There are long-distance buses to and from Leyte and Luzon. See Samar's introductory Getting There & Away section earlier, for flight and road-transport information.

AROUND CATARMAN

The following couple of day trips were suggested by helpful Frumencio Lagrimas, the tourism officer for northern Samar. You can find him at the Provincial Capitol Building by the airport (☎ 055-354 1233).

Take an early jeepney to Rawis/Laoang (one hour) then transfer to a jeepney to Catubig (one hour). From Catubig make a trip upriver by pumpboat to **Las Navas** (one hour) and return the same way. It's possible to go by boat all the way from Laoang to Las Navas, but it's about a three-hour trip one way. The mayor in Las Navas will help you find accommodation if you want to stay overnight. **Pinipiskan Falls** is a three-hour hike from Las Navas, and from there there's a **jungle track** that continues to Matuguinao and takes a couple of days to walk. This beautiful and rugged area was part of the setting for the 1999 'Elf Authentic Adventure', an international skilled endurance competition, so you have been warned!

Alternatively, you could go to the **Biri-Las Rosas Islands**. These undeveloped islands are a marine-protected area and home to fishing communities. There is good **snorkelling** and **diving** at Biri, and occasionally good **surf**, but you'll need your own equipment. You can make a return trip by hiring a boat from Lavezares (P500 to P700 return, one hour each way). There is no commercial accommodation. If you're interested in exploring this area you may want to check with the DENR in Catarman. It may have more-current information than the DOT. Also quite generous with information about trips to this part of the island are the students at UEP.

The road from Laoang along the north east coast is open as far as Lapinig. It is an undeveloped area of **surf beaches** and **rock formations** along the coast. Of note in Laoang is the US-built lighthouse near the ferry landing – a picturesque structure that has been withstanding typhoons since 1907.

ALLEN
pop 20,066
This is a small port town for boats to Luzon. If you need to stay overnight here you could try **Laureen's Lodging** (rooms P100-150), right at the wharf, with a restaurant attached. It's clean, if basic and noisy, and is handy to the boats.

Mary Ann Lodge, by the jeepney stand in town, has the same sort of rooms as Laureen's for the same price.

Manila-bound buses go via Allen. Allen is 1½ hours from Calbayog, 3½ hours from Catbalogan and one hour from Catarman.

See the introductory Getting There & Away section to Samar earlier, for information on boats to and from Luzon. Philtranco buses meet each boat and depart for Tacloban on Leyte (P211/157 air-con/'1st class', five to six hours).

BALCUARTRO ISLANDS
This group of islands is just below the north-western point of Samar. The largest is **Dalupiri**, also called San Antonio, and has good beaches and clear water; but beware of the zillions of spiky sea-urchins and swim in reef shoes. Stay at **Flying Dog Resort** (cottages P500), the only commercial accommodation on the island. The setting is a beautiful landscaped garden right on the beach, but the pretty cottages are under-maintained and tatty. There is electricity from 5pm to midnight only, so rooms are fanless and can be hot if there is no breeze.

You can hire a boat to the island of **Capul** to the west, which was a galleon staging post during Spanish days and has a ruined watchtower where sentries once combed the horizon for Moro pirates.

Take a tricycle from Allen to San Isidro (P20/50 regular/hire), or get off northbound buses in San Isidro. You may have to hire a boat to Dalupiri (P150, 15 minutes) if there are no other passengers. To return to San Isidro, stand on the beach and wave down a passing passenger boat (P20).

CALBAYOG & AROUND
pop 147,187
The pretty road from Allen to Calbayog hugs the coast, passing through villages and river estuaries framed with nipa palms, and has a backdrop of mountains. Calbayog has a busy and colourful wharf area that is full of painted cargo, fishing and passenger boats, and is walking distance from the town centre and hotels.

Tourist information is available from the City Information Office at City Hall. The one and, so far, only **museum** in Samar is in the College of Christ the King and is open during school hours Monday to Friday. It houses a collection of artefacts from around the province, as well as ancient ceramics, beads and coins.

THE VISAYAS

Nearby are the **waterfalls** of Bangon, Mawacat and Larik, the **Guinogo-an cave system**, and **Mapaso Hot Springs** (where, remarkably, small red crustaceans called *pokot* survive in the scalding water). All these attractions are between one and two hours' drive, plus between 15 and 40 minutes' walk, from the city.

Calbayog comes alive for the annual **fiesta** on 7 and 8 September, with parades, outdoor performances and re-enactments, cultural displays and huge street markets.

Places to Stay & Eat
San Joaquin Inn and **Central Inn** offer rooms for P100 to P500. Neither is particularly appealing.

Eduardo's Tourist Hotel (☎ 055-209 1558; *rooms P600-1200*) is the best hotel in town. All rooms have air-con and TV. The attached **Chinese restaurant** is probably the best in town. There is a selection of **food stalls** at the bus station. Better are the food stalls that set up nightly along the west side of Nijaga Park near Rosales bridge.

Getting There & Away
Asian Spirit flies to and from Manila three times a week for P2380.

There are many regular daily buses between Calbayog and Catarman via Allen (P48, four hours) and between Calbayog and Catbalogan (P35, two hours). Jeepneys ply the coastal road, but it's faster to take a bus between the major towns. All jeepneys from Allen depart from and terminate at the Capoocan bus terminal north of Rosales bridge. From there it's a P10 tricycle ride into the town proper.

CATBALOGAN
pop 84,180
This is the provincial capital of western Samar, but this port town has little to encourage a lengthy stay. It is the place to catch a bus over to the east coast, and you may need to stay overnight here.

Places to Stay & Eat
Fortune Hotel (☎ 055-251 2147; *rooms P150-450*) is in the noisy centre of town and has a good range of rooms. The attached restaurant has a varied and reasonable menu.

Maqueda Bay Hotel (☎ 055-251 2386; *rooms P500-700*) has great sunset views.

A few minutes by tricycle south from the centre of town, it has air-con rooms with bathroom. The restaurant has enormous windows looking directly onto the water.

Getting There & Away
Although Catbalogan is a port town, there are presently no passenger vessels operating.

There are daily buses between Calbayog and Catbalogan (P30, two hours). There are also jeepneys, but it's faster to take a bus. There are also daily bus services to Borongan (P60, three hours) on the east coast and to Tacloban (P50, three hours) on Leyte. Buray, about half an hour out of Catbalogan, is the junction for Borongan–Tacloban buses, so there are more services to the east coast from Buray than from Catbalogan.

BORONGAN
pop 55,141
The road joining the east and west coasts rises over Samar's central range of mountains, passing through forested country before reaching the Pacific coast at Taft. This road is quite scenic, especially the views of the river during the approach to Taft. There have been confirmed sightings of the **Philippine eagle** in the Taft Forest, where this rare bird is protected by law. The small town of **Taft** – named after the first US Governor General of the Philippines, William Howard Taft – is set among some picturesque scenery, but has no formal accommodation.

From here the road turns south towards Borongan. There is the possibility of good **surf** along the coast from Borongan to Umawas, but it's fickle at best – December to May can be good, but surfers need to be prepared to wait for days or weeks for the right conditions. There are marlin and sailfish offshore and you can go **fishing** with locals if conditions are right.

Borongan town is the jumping-off point for the island of **Divinubo**, a pretty spot 10 minutes offshore, with a lighthouse built by the Americans in 1906. It has been converted from gas power to electricity and is still in use, beaming out every 15 seconds. Divinubo has good snorkelling, caves and forested slopes.

Places to Stay
There are several basic lodgings in town costing P100 to P200 per night, but, unless

you are really pinching your pesos, they're best avoided as they are uniformly run down and dreary.

Domsowir Hotel *(rooms P500-700)* is centrally located on the river bridge.

Pirate's Cove *(nipa cottages P800-1200),* near the port, offers low-key and very stylish accommodation, with nipa cottages with a difference. Check out the mosaics and shell mirrors. There is a sea pool at low tide, good snorkelling and breezy pavilions out over the water. You can arrange day trips inland, fishing and boat hire from here.

Getting There & Away

Regular buses run daily from Borongan to Catbalogan (P60, three hours) and Tacloban (P150, five hours) on Leyte via Basey. There are also buses to Manila (see Samar's introductory Getting There & Away section). Jeepneys make the journey to Guiuan (P40, 2½ hours) every hour from 7am until 6pm.

GUIUAN
pop 38,694

The relaxed and easygoing township of Guiuan (ghee-won), in a beautiful natural setting on the southeastern tip of Samar, has a great range of historical attractions spanning the period of first colonisers from the days of the final liberators. Visit the 16th-century **church** and fabulous carved Spanish doors and altar, which the rather mercenary Imelda Marcos was (luckily) prevented from buying in order to bulk up her already huge personal antique collection. Walk up to the **weather station** for wide, sweeping views across the Pacific Ocean and Leyte Gulf. Drive along the huge crumbling **WWII runway** and soak up the historical atmosphere. Go across the bay to the island of **Tubabao**, where a few traces remain of the period when White Russian emigres lived here – most had been living in Shanghai and Canton after fleeing the Russian revolution. The White Russians took refuge here after the newly communist Peoples Republic of China sent them packing. The former camp was set up under the auspices of the International Refugee Organisation.

Places to Stay & Eat
Tanghay Lodge *(rooms P260-780),* on the waterfront, 1km or so from the town centre, is by far the best option in town. It has a swimming

area in the bay and great sunset pavilions set out over the water. There is good food here, as well as at **Sporks Restaurant**, in town.

DJ's Singalong, about 2km away from Tanghay Lodge at the other end of the waterfront, is a great bar built on stilts out over the water and is open till late for beer and snacks.

Kevin's Pension and **Blue Star Lodging** are just passably clean, but what can you expect for P100 to P150?

Getting There & Away
Bus & Jeepney Buses to Tacloban leave every night at around 8pm but you should think twice about taking the coast and mountain road after dark. Regular jeepneys run to Borongan (P40, 2½ hours) and you can connect to daytime buses to Tacloban and Catbalogan from there. The road northwest to Basey via Marabut is under construction and some stretches are particularly rough. This route has also been the site of NPA ambushes, the most recent in 2000, so inquire at DOT before heading out.

The potentially hazardous ride may be worth it, though, as the scenery north of Marabut is quite spectacular (see Marabut Islands later). No public transport runs all the way from Guiuan to Basey, due to the bad condition of the track, especially after rain. It may be possible to hire a jeep to drive to Tacloban along this road, but it will cost you around P2500.

Boat There's a nightly boat to Tacloban (P100 to P150, eight hours), leaving around 10pm. This route has been unlucky, with one boat sinking and one burning up on the journey.

AROUND GUIUAN
The island of **Homonhon** is where Magellan first landed in the Philippines on 16 March 1521. The island has blowholes, white-sand beaches and a freshwater cascade and creek. You can get a public bangka from Guiuan (P20, two hours) during daylight hours and depending on the tide. Be prepared to stay overnight in the old **hospital building** if necessary.

Suluan, an hour beyond Homonhon, has a derelict lighthouse. The 500 steps up to it are good exercise and the reward is a fantastic view across the islands of Leyte Gulf and the Pacific Ocean. There are also coastal caves that are accessible at low tide. If you want to stay overnight on Suluan, the barangay captain will help you. Also around Guiuan is **Sulangan Beach** for swimming, snorkelling and beachcombing for the beautiful **golden cowrie** shell. But be warned – these shells are protected by law, and are therefore illegal to collect. WWII historians will also want to see the remains of **Navy 3149 Base** at nearby Ngolos.

Balangiga
pop 10,662

This small town, between Basey and Guiuan, was the scene of an infamous incident known as the 'Balangiga Massacre'.

Throughout September of 1901, Filipino guerillas, many of them dressed as women, infiltrated the town. By smuggling weapons hidden inside coffins which they claimed contained the corpses of cholera victims, the guerillas were able to stockpile weapons in the local church. On the 28th the guerillas then attacked and killed most of the US garrison stationed there. A terrible revenge was subsequently taken by relieving US forces, which were instructed to 'kill anyone capable of bearing arms', including all boys aged 10 years and over. The commanding officer was later court-martialled. There is an annual re-enactment and commemoration on that date.

Sohoton Natural Bridge National Park

This is Samar's premier natural attraction, a protected area of **caves** and **forest**, and home to at least six of Samar's endemic birds. Access is via Basey which, given the current state of the road linking Basey and Guiuan, is easiest to access from Tacloban on Leyte. Check to see if the road condition is passable when you visit. For further information see Sohoton Natural Bridge National Park under Around Tacloban in the Leyte section, later.

Marabut Islands

Located off a stretch of coastline between Basey and Marabut, this mini-archipelago of jagged limestone islands is a magical place, with picturesque views reminiscent of Thailand's Ao Pang-Nga and Vietnam's Halong Bay. Until recently there were no places of accommodation that would allow you to explore the islands, but the newly

opened **Marabut Marine Park Beach Resort** (rooms P2100) has changed all that.

The resort features five duplex bungalows of wood, bamboo and palm thatch (10 rooms total), each with fan and private bathroom. The resort restaurant does excellent, if a bit pricey, seafood. There are also kayaks and snorkelling gear for rent. Reservations and transportation arrangements can be made by contacting the **Leyte Park Hotel** (☎ 053-325 6000, fax 325 5587; Tacloban). The resort is most easily accessed by hiring a pumpboat from Tacloban (P1000, one hour). It's also possible to take the passenger boat from Tacloban to Basey (P15, one hour) and then a jeepney from Basey to the resort (P10, one hour). Or you can take a jeepney from Tacloban to Basey (P20, one hour), and then transfer to another jeepney for the remaining 15km to the resort.

Leyte

The island of Leyte has a relatively narrow and fertile coastal strip that gives way to a rugged, mountainous interior. The staple crops are rice, maize and root vegetables with fishing, coconuts, abaca and tobacco providing cash income. Cattle are ranched in the hills of northern Leyte. Forestry is still a major industry, though it is now regulated more efficiently following the devastating Ormoc floods of 1991, which were caused largely by excessive deforestation above the city.

During the Japanese occupation, Leyte was the base of a formidable fighting force of Filipino guerilla units, led by local hero Ruperto Kangleon. Assurance of strong guerilla support was instrumental in MacArthur's choice to use Leyte for the liberation landings, and it remains a centre of WWII memorials and commemorative events. For travellers, Leyte offers pre-colonial, colonial and WWII historical interest; great natural beauty, with national parks and hiking trails; and exceptional diving and whale shark spotting in the waters off the southern coast.

Special Events

There are several popular annual festivals on Leyte. The **Pintados**, or 'painted', festival in Tacloban on 29 June celebrates the traditional tattooing practised here before

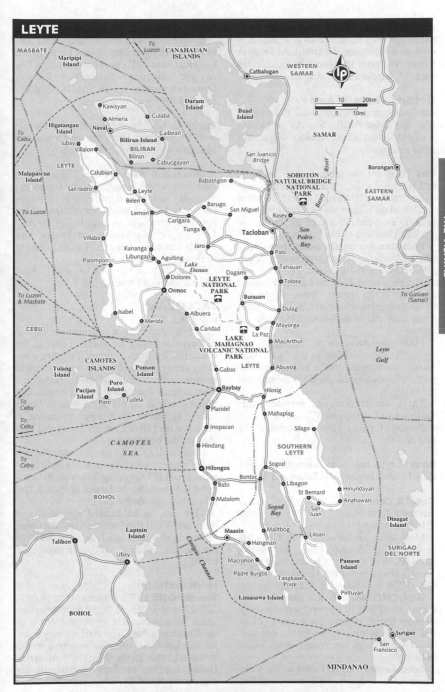

the Spanish arrived; nowadays water-based paints are used for the festival's body decoration. In Calubian, the **Lubi-Lubi Festival**, which celebrates the town's namesake, the coconut, happens on 15 August.

Getting There & Away

Air Tacloban is connected with Manila by **PAL** and **Cebu Pacific**. See Air in Getting There & Away under Tacloban later, for more information.

Bus There are bus services between Leyte and Biliran, Luzon, Mindanao and Samar.

Several daily buses run between Tacloban and Naval on Biliran, via Lemon (P80, three hours). You can also take an Ormoc to Tacloban bus and change at Lemon.

Philtranco has regular buses from Tacloban to Manila (26 hours), with several departures between 6.30am and 11.30am, one departure around 4pm, and another around 11.30pm. Buses depart Ormoc for Manila (P760/900 regular/air-con, 26 hours) three times daily. All Manila-bound buses go via Samar.

Philtranco runs from Tacloban and Ormoc to Davao (P560 to P705) on Mindanao, via Surigao, in the afternoon – departure times depend on the incoming bus arrival time.

There are regular bus services from Tacloban to Catbalogan (P70, three hours), Calbayog (4½ hours) and Borongan (P100, five hours).

Boat Leyte has boat connections with Bohol Cebu, Luzon, Mindanao and Samar.

Bohol & Cebu There's a daily boat service that sails from Maasin to Ubay on Bohol (P160, three hours).

Most boat connections with Cebu are to Cebu City. A boat leaves Baybay for Cebu (P210 to P140, six hours) each night. There's also a boat from Hilongos to Cebu City (P350, two hours) each morning.

SuperCat/SeaAngels has three Ormoc–Cebu City (P500, two hours) services daily. Regular ferries run the same route (P120, five hours). **Sulpicio Lines** leaves late Sunday evening, and San Juan Ferries leaves each night.

Cebu Ferries leaves Tacloban for Cebu (from P290, 13 hours) on Tuesday and Sat-

urday at 4pm. In the opposite direction, boats depart from Cebu for Tacloban Monday and Friday at 6pm. Boats from Ormoc to Cebu (from P210, six hours) leave on Friday and Sunday at midnight. From Cebu to Ormoc departures are on Sunday, Wednesday and Friday at 1pm.

Luzon A boat leaves Baybay for Manila weekly. **Sulpicio Lines** leaves Ormoc for Manila via Masbate once a week.

Mindanao & Samar From Maasin **Trans Asia** leaves for Surigao (P300, 1½ hours) Thursday at 8pm and Friday at 6pm. Regular boats leave Maasin for Surigao (five hours) every night. A boat leaves Baybay for Surigao via Maasin on Friday, and there's a morning ferry daily from Liloan to Surigao (five hours).

The daily boat from Tacloban to Guiuan takes about eight hours.

TACLOBAN
pop 178,639

This busy and compact town is the capital of Leyte, and hugs the southern edge of the beautiful San Juanico Strait. Tacloban's activity centres on the bustling wharf area and market in the middle of town. Tacloban's most famous daughter is Imelda Romualdez Marcos, whose family home is at Tolosa, a little way south; the family's influence in the town is evident in street names and various public buildings.

Historically, Tacloban is better known as the place to which General MacArthur returned with US liberating forces on 20 October 1944 (actually, he landed at Palo, a few kilometres outside the city).

This date is celebrated annually, and there are WWII memorials around the town, including moulded reliefs on outer walls of the Capitol Building that commemorate the landing.

Information

Tourist Offices The tourist office (☎ 053-321 2048, fax 325 5279; ⓔ dotr8@mozcom .com; Senator Enage St; open Mon-Fri) is in the Children's Park. The staff are very helpful and knowledgeable. If you arrive on the weekend, the Leyte Normal University House (see Places to Stay later) usually has a good supply of DOT brochures.

Mural depicting Lapu-Lapu slaying Ferdinand Magellan, Cebu City – the Visayas

Baskets for the Sunday market, Antequera, Bohol – the Visayas

Orchid plantation, Bacolod, Negros – the Visayas

Chocolate Hills, Bohol – the Visayas

White Beach, Boracay – the Visayas

Money The **PNB bank** *(cnr Santo Niño & Justice Romualdez Sts)* changes US dollars. The **Equitable PCI Bank** *(Rizal Ave)* will advance cash against Visa cards and the branch on Salazar St gives cash advances on Visa and MasterCard.

Email & Internet Access Internet cafés have hit Tacloban in a big way. They're mostly along Ave Veteranos and charge P40 per hour. Try **Internet Continental** *(225 Ave Veteranos; open 8am-10pm daily),* or **3M** *(open 9am-9pm Mon-Sat)* opposite Alejandro's.

Things to See & Do

Take a sunrise climb along the **Stations of the Cross** to the top of Calvary Hill for wide views across the San Juanico Strait and some decent bird-watching. Spare a thought for the people living in the huts at the top as they carry water up the steep steps. Visit the chaotic and colourful **market** early, as much of the fresh produce (including the gorgeous flowers) is gone by 7am and the meaty section grows decidedly smelly. The latter is not for the faint-hearted.

A must is the **Santo Niño Shrine and Heritage Center** *(admission P200; open 8.30am-11.30am & 1pm-4.30pm daily),* an enormous palatial residence and opulent guesthouse built to Imelda Marcos' orders and *never slept in!* It houses an extraordinary collection of antiques and *objets d'art* from across the world, including personal gifts from Mao Tse Tung.

THE VISAYAS

TACLOBAN

San Juanico Strait

San Pedro Bay

Wharf

To Buddhist Temple, Paseo de Legaspi & San Juanico Bridge

Market

Calvary Hill

Children's Park

Plaza Libertad

Magsaysay Blvd

Trece Martires St

Senator Enage St

Jones St

Lopez Jaena St

MH del Pilar St

Justice Romualdez St

Claudio St

Torres St

Rizal Ave

Salazar St

Gomez St

Zamora St

Burgos St

Ave Veteranos

Santo Niño St

Paterno St

Juan St

Real St

PLACES TO STAY
2 Leyte Park Hotel; San Pedro Bay Restaurant
12 Manhattan Hotel
13 Primrose Hotel
20 Manobo Lodge
21 Asia Stars Hotel
22 Tacloban Plaza Hotel
27 Alejandro's Hotel
28 Welcome House Pension
29 Cecilia's Lodge
31 Leyte Normal University House

PLACES TO EAT
15 Jollibee
16 Alpha Bakery
18 Shakey's Pizza
19 Yamyam Foodlane

OTHER
1 Tourist Office
3 Hospital
4 Provincial Capitol Building; Small & Medium Enterprise Development Crafts
5 Post Office
6 WG&A Shipping Line
7 Cebu Pacific Airways
8 Air Philippines Office
9 Bus & Jeepney Terminal
10 Stations of the Cross
11 Equitable PCI Bank
14 Equitable PCI Bank
17 Gaisano Department Store
23 PNB
24 City Hall
25 Santo Niño Church
26 3M
30 Internet Continental
32 People's Center & Library; Santo Niño Shrine & Heritage Center

0 250 500m
0 250 500yd

To Agus Restaurant (1.5km), Greenhouse Kitchen Inn (2km), Philtranco Bus Station (2.5km), Airport (10km) & Palo & MacArthur Park Beach Resort (12km)

There are some fabulous Russian icons, 18 of which were stolen in 1998 because of the lack of effective security. The centre is sadly under-curated, decaying almost before your eyes, but it's well worth the entry fee for a guided tour. This fee covers up to six people.

See the exhibition of **WWII photographs** in the beautiful old part of Alejandro's Hotel and read the absorbing history of the building, used variously by Japanese troops, displaced Filipinos and liberating forces – while always being home to Alejandro's family.

The helpful leaflet *Do-it-yourself tour of Tacloban and Environs* from the tourist office includes most of these places and more, and describes an informative self-guided **walking tour** of points of interest in the city.

Places to Stay – Budget

There is a range of budget accommodation in town.

Manobo Lodge (☎ 035-321 3727; *Zamora St; rooms P250-450*) is tatty but spotlessly clean; it's also just off the main road and quieter than many places in town. A bathroom is shared between two rooms.

Cecilia's Lodge (☎ 053-321 2815; *Patermo St; rooms P200-600*) is a rabbit-warren of rooms and doors.

Leyte Normal University (LNU) House (☎ 035-321 3175; *Paterno St; rooms P400*) offers the best value for money. It's a little beyond the town centre, and is spacious and airy; it even has a grassy area outside. All rooms have air-con and bath, and there is a restaurant and tea room open during school hours on weekdays.

Places to Stay – Mid-Range

Manhattan Hotel (*Rizal Ave; singles/doubles around P500/750*), next to the market and wharf, is getting a bit tired and needs some maintenance, but is still good value. All rooms have air-con, bathroom and TV. Rates vary depending on whether you pay by cash or credit card. Its central location makes it very noisy though; all the other mid-range lodgings are quieter.

Tacloban Plaza Hotel (☎ 053-325 5850; *Justice Romualdez St; rooms P500-650*) has good rooms and all include air-con, TV and bathroom.

Welcome House Pension (☎ 053-321 2739; *rooms with fan from P200, with air-con,* *bathroom & TV P600-1500*), at the end of Santo Niño St, is a small, new and bright place.

Primrose Hotel (☎ 053-321 2248; *Zamora St; rooms with fan/air-con P300/700*) was recently renovated and the new rooms are fine, with either fan and bathroom or air-con, bathroom, TV and fridge.

Places to Stay – Top End

Leyte Park Resort Hotel (☎ 053-325 6000, *fax 321 1099;* e *leypark@tac.weblinq.com; rooms P2000-4600*) still can't be beaten for location, as it is right on the waterfront and has beautiful grounds. Rooms with a view of the sea are the most expensive. Day use of the good-sized pool for nonguests costs P100. The Leyte Park offers nightly entertainment (also open to nonguests) which, depending on the day, may be a disco, for ballroom dancing or a sing-along. There is live music every evening in the open-air bar at the entrance to the hotel's grounds.

Alejandro's Hotel (☎ 053-321 7033, *fax 523 7872; Patermo St; rooms P950-1365*), opened in 1999, is built around the beautiful 1930s home of Alejandro Montejo. The rooms are nothing special, but the common areas of the old building – especially the veranda on the 2nd floor – make up for them. The attached restaurant and coffee shop is also a plus.

Asia Stars Hotel (☎ 035-321 4952; *Zamora St; rooms P750-1350*) has big rooms and pleasant staff.

Places to Eat

The city's famously delicious cakes and sweetmeats are favourite *pasalubong* (souvenirs) for visiting Filipinos to take home. Try *binagol*, a sticky confection wrapped in banana leaves, and something else that's yummy, which comes baked in half a coconut shell. There are good shops selling these on Zamora St, near the waterfront.

Seafood in Tacloban is good. For fish dishes, try **San Pedro Bay** restaurant at Leyte Park Resort Hotel; and **Agus Restaurant**, 1km or so along the airport road.

For breakfasts, **Alejandro's Coffee Shop** at the hotel of the same name, offers excellent Filipino and American breakfasts for P100. There is also a selection of imported wines to go along with lunch and dinner selections.

Greenhouse Kitchen Inn, about 500m beyond the Agus Restaurant, serves Filipino food with a welcome spicy touch.

Yamyam Foodlane has excellent Filipino fast food, is clean and cool and has spotless – and functioning – Western-style toilets.

Shakeys Pizza *(Zamora St)* is good for a splurge if you're burnt out on local fare. About 1½ blocks to the northwest, where Zamora St intersects with Rizal Ave, is a **Jollibee**.

More traditionally, cruise the **lechon stalls** along Real St for slices of whole pigs on spits and barbecued chicken, or visit the **food stalls** around the market. There are good bakeries all over town; try **Alpha Bakery** *(cnr Rizal Ave & Zamora St)*, for example.

Shopping

Tacloban is famous for the quality of its abaca products, so check out the handicrafts at **Small & Medium Enterprise Development (SMED)**, in the old jail next to the Capitol Building.

Getting There & Away

Air From Tacloban, **PAL** flies to Manila daily, and has an office at the airport. **Cebu Pacific** also flies from Tacloban to Manila daily, and its office is on Senator Enage St.

Bus & Jeepney The Philtranco station is about 2km south of the city on the airport road. Long-distance buses leave from here northbound to Manila and southbound to Mindanao.

Regular daily buses and jeepneys from other parts of Leyte and Samar use the station by the market in the town centre. Examples of routes and fares from Tacloban include: San Isidro (P70, 3½ hours), Ormoc (jeepney P65, 2½ hours; air-con bus P300, two hours) and Maasin (P100, five hours).

Getting Around

The airport is about 12km south of the centre of town. A jeepney will cost P5, or you can hire a tricycle for P80.

AROUND TACLOBAN
Palo

This is the place to immerse yourself, if so inclined, in WWII history for half a day. The township of Palo, 12km from Tacloban, is the site of **Red Beach** where, on 20 October 1944, MacArthur fulfilled his vow to return and liberate the Philippines from the occupying Japanese forces (see the boxed text 'I Shall Return' in the Around Manila chapter).

At Red Beach itself, 1km or so from Palo town, there is the moving (though macho) **Leyte Landing Memorial** which, as you approach, gives a strong impression of figures walking out of the sea. Compare it with the photos of the actual event in the MacArthur Park Beach Resort. There's also a **rock garden** where many international tributes were set in stone in 1994 to commemorate the 50th anniversary of the Leyte landing.

Visit Guinhangdan Hill, known then as **Hill 522**, the scene of fierce fighting. The beautiful, 16th-century **church** was turned into a hospital from October 1944 to March 1945.

Places to Stay Just beyond the Red Beach monument, **MacArthur Park Beach Resort** (☎ 053-323 3015, fax 323 2877; rooms P1500-2000) is the only place to stay at Palo. The location of this place is stunning. There are usually 'promotion' rates that can discount the published rate, so be sure to ask. The resort facilities, including the swimming pool, can be used for P100 per person.

Getting There & Away Take a jeepney from the market in Tacloban for P10, or hire a tricycle for P100 per hour. Ask the driver to drop you off at Red Beach, on the Tacloban road about 1km before Palo township. Tricycles are available locally to travel the short distance between each site.

Sohoton Natural Bridge National Park

Although Sohoton Natural Bridge National Park is on Samar, it is easiest to access it from Tacloban, which is why it's included here. The park contains a series of **caves** under limestone outcrops. There are enormous, sparkling stalactites and stalagmites, with **cascades** and **swimming holes** along the cave system. It's reached by boat, with forest and small villages on the riverbanks on either side. The forest in this area is home to at least six species of Samar's endemic birds, monkeys and other **wildlife**. You should check conditions before you head off – after heavy rain the caves may be inaccessible.

Getting There & Away Take a jeepney (P20 per person, one hour) or boat (P15 per person, one hour) from the market in Tacloban across the San Juanico Strait to Basey.

In Basey call into the Community Environment & Natural Resources Office (Cenro) and ask for Francisco Corales or his assistants. They will organise transport and a guide. On the weekend they can be found around the market in Basey. (By the way, Basey is renowned for mat weaving, so you might want to check out the market if you have time.) From Basey to Sohoton takes 1½ hours by boat.

The pumpboat will hold about five people, and rental will cost around P500. You pay a US$2 (or peso equivalent) park entry fee at Basey. Rent a kerosene lamp for P50 or take a good torch (flashlight).

The tourism department in Tacloban recommends starting early (leave by 7am). Take a packed lunch, and if you miss the last transport back in the late afternoon, you can stay at **Distrajo's Place** in Basey.

SOUTH OF TACLOBAN
Burauen

Burauen (boo-**rah**-wen) is 44km from Tacloban (P30, one hour by jeepney). It was the home of Justice Romualdez, Imelda's great-great-grandfather, a renowned composer of Filipino songs. The location of his house is slated to be recognised as a historical site. The township also has a Japanese war cemetery. It is one of the starting points – the other is Ormoc – for the Leyte Mountain Trail.

Lake Mahagnao Volcanic National Park & Leyte Mountain Trail

If you wish to visit this national park – site of former volcanic activity – or to hike the 40km mountain trail, you need first to visit the mayor in Burauen for information.

The trail takes in **rainforest**, **lakes** and **waterfalls** as it crosses the mountain range in the centre of Leyte. It finishes near Ormoc, at either Lake Danao National Park (see that section under Around Ormoc, later), or at the volcanically active Tongonan National Park. The DENR in Tacloban sets up the trail, so you can get information and look at route maps there.

THE NORTHWEST

Calubian and San Isidro are in the northwest of Leyte. **Calubian** is home to the Lubi-Lubi Festival, celebrating its namesake (the coconut) on 15 August each year. **San Isidro** is a small township on the coast with boat connections to Cebu. Each of these places has basic **lodgings** and can be reached by bus from Tacloban (3½ hours) and Ormoc (4½ hours).

ORMOC

☎ 053 • pop 154,297

This busy port town has a bustling wharf area – which is where all the bus and jeepney stations and shipping offices are located – and an attractive grassy promenade along the waterfront. Like much of Leyte, it has strong historical connections.

Ormoc is believed to be one of the early Malay settlements in the Philippines and its name probably comes from a spring called 'Ugmok', settled by Malays long before the Spanish conquest. More recently, it was a centre of WWII activity, with some of the bloodiest battles on Philippine soil taking place over three days in 1944, between the allied US and Filipino forces, and the retreating Japanese. Yamashita's Gold, a quasi-mythical treasure-trove named after the Japanese commander and left behind by the fleeing Japanese, is believed by some to

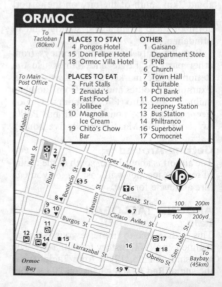

ORMOC

PLACES TO STAY	OTHER
4 Pongos Hotel	1 Gaisano
15 Don Felipe Hotel	Department Store
18 Ormoc Villa Hotel	5 PNB
	6 Church
PLACES TO EAT	7 Town Hall
2 Fruit Stalls	9 Equitable
3 Zenaida's	PCI Bank
Fast Food	11 Ormocnet
8 Jollibee	12 Jeepney Station
10 Magnolia	13 Bus Station
Ice Cream	14 Philtranco
19 Chito's Chow	16 Superbowl
Bar	17 Ormocnet

be hidden in the hills outside Ormoc (see the boxed text 'Gold-Diggers' in the Facts for the Visitor chapter).

The town has recovered well from the appalling effects of the typhoon of 5 November 1991, which brought down huge flash floods from the mountains behind the town. About 8000 people died and tens of thousands were made homeless.

The flooding was exacerbated by logging operations that had left the hillsides bare of stabilising vegetation. Logging operations have since stopped.

Information

The **PNB** (Bonifacio St) will change US dollars. **Ormocnet** (offices open 8am-11pm Mon-Sat) has public Internet access points on Bonifacio St, by the bus station and on San Pedro St, by the Ormoc Days Hotel. Rates are P40 per hour.

Golf

Visitors to **Leyte Golf & Country Club** (☎ 255 0282) are welcome. It is 7km outside Ormoc and there are overnight cottages and a swimming pool.

Places to Stay

Pongos Hotel (☎ 255 2540; Bonifacio St; singles with fan P250, doubles with air-con P650) has a selection of rooms in its old and new buildings, ranging from an ordinary single with fan to a double with air-con.

Don Felipe Hotel (☎ 255 2460, fax 255 4306; rooms with fan/air-con from P220/420) is comfortable and good value. It's on the waterfront and it's fun to watch the world go by from the hotel coffee shop.

Ormoc Villa Hotel (☎ 255 5006, fax 561 4065; e villa@ormocnet.net.ph; Obrero St; rooms around P3000) is a recent and lavish addition to Ormoc's accommodation; there is often some sort of promotion that can halve prices, so ask at reception. Nonguests can use the pool for P100.

Places to Eat

The coffee shops in **Don Felipe Hotel** and **Ormoc Villa Hotel** are good; expect to pay from P200 for interesting and tasty food.

For cheaper meals, try **Zenaida's Fast Food** (Rizal St) and **Chito's Chow Bar** on the waterfront. There are plenty of **bakeries** and **fruit stalls** in town.

For burgers and other fast food, there's also a **Jollibee** near the corner of Rizal and Aviles Sts.

Getting There & Away

There are regular buses to and from Tacloban (about P70, 2½ hours) and to and from Maasin in the south of Leyte. You can also take buses northwest to Palompon and San Isidro on Leyte.

There is a huge selection of vessels heading daily from Ormoc to Cebu. See Leyte's introductory Getting There & Away section earlier.

AROUND ORMOC

From the Ormoc waterfront you can see the Camotes Islands (see that section earlier).

Lake Danao National Park

Lake Danao is a beautiful body of fresh water in the hills above Ormoc. You can swim and picnic for the day, or camp overnight. Regular jeepneys run from Ormoc (P20, one hour). It is also one starting point for the Leyte Mountain Trail; the other is in Burauen (for details of the trail see the entry under South of Tacloban, earlier in the Leyte section).

If you plan to start hiking from this end, contact the DENR field office at Lake Danao. Local guides can be hired from the small barangay at Lake Danao.

BAYBAY

pop 95,630

The south-bound road from Ormoc to Maasin passes through Baybay (bye-bye). This small township has boat connections to Cebu, Manila and Surigao (see Leyte's introductory Getting There & Away section earlier). Baybay is known for its smooth but potent *tuba* (palm wine).

Ellean's Lodge (Bonifacio St; rooms with fan & shared bathroom per person P100, room with bathroom P300), 50m from the wharf, is in a nice, old, wooden house, but its room partitions don't quite reach the ceiling, so it's not too private and can be noisy. All rooms but one have shared bathroom.

Visayan State College of Agriculture (Visca; rooms from P200) is passed by the road 7km north of Baybay. It's set on a large, rural block of land. There is a small guesthouse here with rooms (when available). Buses and jeepneys will drop you there.

SOUTHERN LEYTE

There are a number of reasons why Southern Leyte, a separate province from the northern two-thirds of the island, deserves to become a major destination for visitors to the Philippines.

For one, it's safe. Despite what looks on the map to be a disturbing proximity to Mindanao, the shipping lanes of the Canigao Channel make it highly unlikely that Southern Leyte's resorts would be the target of kidnappers looking for foreign hostages.

The province, which is wrapped around the deep-water Sogod Bay, has some excellent dive sites for both beginners and experienced divers. Local waters are filled with many species of coral and fish, including a population of *ihotiki* (local Cebuano language for whale shark) which can be spotted from boats or from an island viewing station near Liloan.

For history buffs, the town of Malitbog has a number of evocative old structures dating back to the Spanish and American colonial periods. Last but not least, the Cebuano-speaking southern Leyteños are more laid back and hospitable than their Waray-speaking neighbours who inhabit the northern part of the island.

There are dive sites in Sogod Bay and around Limasawa, with rich reefs and dropoffs. Wall and cave diving is possible at Lungsodaan in Padre Burgos. At Son-ok in Pintuyan, on the southernmost point of Leyte, local people are managing the area as a fish sanctuary and there has been a resulting increase in the population of *ihotiki*, dolphins and whales. Peter's Dive Resort (☎ 053-573 0015; W www.whaleofadive.com) in Padre Burgos is the most reliable dive operator in the area.

MAASIN
pop 71,163
This is another small and bustling port town, and is the provincial capital of southern Leyte. There's a beautiful old **church**, built in 1700, and a huge image of Our Lady of Assumption on a hill behind the town. Built to commemorate an old legend about an angel that descended from the heavens to turn back a typhoon, the image is lit up at night and looks like some benevolent apparition floating in the sky. Maasin or it's nearby resorts are the best place to base yourself while

checking out the attractions in Southern Leyte. Visit **Cagnituan Cave** and the **Guinsohoton Waterfall** with its swimming hole, a welcome cool-off after hiking the 6km in.

Information

The very knowledgable Rio Cahambing, tourism officer with the provincial government, can give information on diving and whale-shark spotting in Southern Leyte. Find him at the **Provincial Planning Development Office** *(PPDO; ☎ 053-570 9017, fax 570 9018; ℮ diverio_2000@hotmail.com, ℮ scuberph@yahoo.com)* in the Provincial Capitol Building.

Mr Cahambing suggests that visitors email ahead to ensure that there are vacancies in accommodation in Maasin or at nearby resorts – Southern Leyte has much tourism potential but as yet little infrastructure. Emailing ahead is also a good idea to ensure that an excursion to spot whale sharks can be arranged.

There is a PNB in town that can change US dollars.

Public Internet access can be found at **Country Mouse** *(Demeterio St; open 9am-9pm, Mon-Sat).*

Places to Stay & Eat

Verano Pensionne *(rooms per person P80)*, at the budget-end of the scale, is a family house with small rooms.

GV Pensionne *(rooms P300)* is new and adequate. Just opposite is the **Ampil Pensionne** *(rooms P300)* with complimentary breakfast (don't expect much at this price). Both places get a good share of ambient street noise, so try to get a room at the back if you're a light sleeper.

Maasin Country Lodge *(☎ 053-381 2102; rooms with air-con from P650)*, a few minutes' tricycle ride from the town centre, is the best accommodation in the town proper. It has good-value rooms with air-con and TV. There is a restaurant here, with seating outdoors on the riverbank.

Southern Comfort Pensionne *(rooms with air-con P550-700)*, in the centre of town, is another mid-range hotel. It's quite noisy though.

Residence Beach Resort *(huts P150)* is 17km south of Maasin at Buscayan village, about 500m off the main road toward the shore. This superb little stretch of beach has clean sand – real sand, not coral pebbles – and is shaded by coconut palms.

The three bamboo huts (more were under construction when we visited) are very basic and share a toilet and bathrooms. Food can be bought in the village or, better yet, bring food from Maasin. It's a P100 tricycle ride from Maasin.

Getting There & Away
Regular buses run to Maasin from Ormoc (P60, 3½ hours), and to Padre Burgos (P50, 45 minutes). There are also regular buses to Liloan (P80, four hours), the ferry port for Mindanao.

Maasin has good sea connections to Mindanao (see Leyte's introductory Getting There & Away section earlier). There is no longer a boat connection to Cebu – the nearest boat landing from Cebu is at Hilonggos, about 37km north of Maasin.

PADRE BURGOS
pop 8926
This township has good **beaches** with offshore **snorkelling** and **dive sites**, including Tangkaan Point, to the south of town. The point is reached via a steep stairway that leads to a pebble beach and a boulder on which is perched a whimsical equestrian statue of St James the Apostle.

Padre Burgos is also the starting point for excursions to see **whale sharks**, which sometimes congregate across Sogod Bay in Liloan Bay near the bridge that connects Panaon Island to Leyte. Boats dock at Puyaw Islet, an observation station that has a comfortable bamboo pavilion. Note the picturesque natural bonsai tree growing out of a rock on the islet – and ask about the Japanese tourist who tried to buy it! If whale sharks are spotted, a bangka can be rowed out to get a closer look.

Nearby Buyog Islet, which has an ancient burial site – possibly left by Arab traders in the 12th century – can also be visited if the tide is favourable. Package tours to view the whale sharks cost the peso equivalent of US$12 per person and accommodate seven to 10 people.

There is no guarantee that whale sharks will be spotted, though the best time of year to see them is November and February to May. They are usually spotted in the late afternoon between 3pm and 5pm. Package tours last all day and include snorkelling and a picnic lunch on Puyaw Islet. Bear in mind that you still must pay for the tour even if no whale sharks are seen.

Because this activity is newly established in the province, you'll have to contact Rio Cahambing (see Information under Maasin earlier) at least a few days in advance so that a boat can be arranged.

For those interested in **diving**, Peter's Dive Resort (see Places to Stay & Eat) in town, charges around US$22 for two boat dives including equipment, or US$19 for shore dives. It can also organise dive trips to the islands of Limasawa and Panaon.

Places to Stay & Eat
Peter's Dive Resort (☎ 053-573 0015; rooms P250-700; ℮ infodesk@whaleofadive.com) is on a coral-pebble beach and features comfortable rooms made of wood and bamboo. The cheapest rooms, located above the dive shop, share a bathroom but have individual verandas. Two cottages on the beach have private bathroom – one of them can accommodate a family. Peter's can arrange for guests to be picked up at the pier in Hilonggos or Maasin.

Davliz Travel Lodge (cottages with aircon P400-800), on a cliff above the beach, though the concrete cottages are rather dank and airless.

Getting There & Away
Regular jeepneys run from Maasin to Padre Burgos (P20, 45 minutes) and from there you can get a boat to the islands of Limasawa and Panaon.

MALITBOG
pop 19,320
Due to its location near abaca plantations and on the edge of the deep-water Sogod Bay, Malitbog had almost a century of prosperity that lasted from the mid-19th century until WWII. During that time a number of interesting edifices were built that still stand. Typically, the town boasts a beautiful old church, the **Santo Niño Parish**, constructed of coral blocks in 1857. There's also a **watchtower** built in 1862, the ground floor of which still serves as the city jail. Take a peek inside the front door to get a view of the cells (no occupants when we visited). Along the embarcadero near the

THE VISAYAS

Spanish Ghosts

In the past decade or so conservationists in the Philippines have been trying to raise public aware-ness about the importance of preserving outstanding examples of historic residential architecture. The results have been mixed. Every year old mansions from the Spanish and American colonial periods continue to fall to the wrecking ball, but an encouraging number have been saved and turned into museums. While some of these are quite good and worth a visit, as with all homes that have been extensively restored and renovated, they often fail to convey the spirit of the time that they are trying to evoke. Rooms are spotless and devoid of the patina of age. Objects are often labelled, making it hard to imagine the lives that once revolved around them.

Not so the Villa Margarita. Located in Maltibog, an old port town in Southern Leyte, this moulder-ing mansion is still owned by the Filipino-Spanish *mistiso* heirs of the man who built it. The house was constructed in 1922 by Agustin Escaño, born in Malitbog in 1870, the son of Don Fernando Escaño, who arrived in the Philippines from Spain in the mid-19th century. Using the best hardwoods from nearby Surigao Island, Agustin laid out the design himself, importing fixtures from Europe and fur-nishing the house with locally made furniture of the finest hardwoods. He named the house Villa Mar-garita, after his Filipina wife, and to this day the people of Malitbog refer to it thus, or as simply Villa.

What differentiates this old residence from other colonial-era houses that are open to visitors is that Villa Margarita was sealed up decades ago and has become a virtual time capsule. Very little has been touched since the Esaño family moved into a smaller house nearby.

Upon entering the main doorway, the pungent smell of hoary antiquity wafts over you. Walk up the sweeping staircase, its banisters flanked by graceful statuettes clad in verdigris, and into the spacious *sala* (livingroom). The walls, water-stained by 80 years of monsoon rains, were ornately painted by Agustin himself (his thumbprints can still be seen in the whimsical floral patterns). Upon the walls, in Art Nouveau frames, are the faded portraits of moustachioed Spanish grandees and their Filipina señoritas draped in lace. Cobwebbed chandeliers hang from the ceilings, and heavy teak furniture and glass cabinets stacked with dusty porcelain fill the rooms. Aficionados of the colours and textures that can only be created by decades of benign neglect will find the interior of the Villa Margarita a magical place.

The only thing missing are the resident ghosts – or are they? Don Ramon Escaño, the son of Agustin and caretaker of the Villa Margarita, claims that even back when the house was inhabited by the Escaño family, there were no shortage of unexplained occurrences.

Explaining in a quaint mixture of English and Spanish, Don Ramon told us of the old days when lavish parties were thrown in the elegant sala: 'During the parties we would have to go to the kitchen and set aside plates of food for the spirits. If we ever forgot to do this, after the party was finished and the guests had departed and we had all gone to bed, we would hear the sounds of plates and glasses being smashed in the middle of the night'.

Steven Martin

watchtower are a row of old *bodegas* (ware-houses) for storing abaca and copra.

A few grand old mansions, once the homes of the merchant-class elite, can also be seen around town. One of these, the **Villa Margarita**, is open to visitors (see the boxed text 'Spanish Ghosts').

Unlike many of the old architectural gems to be found in the Philippines, the Villa Margarita, a residence built in 1922, has not been restored. Instead, it has been left as a time capsule of sorts. There are 20-minute tours given on an appointment

only basis, and cost the peso equivalent of US$3 per person.

Email the Southern Leyte governor's of-fice (e nodecom@digitelone.com) at least one week in advance so it can arrange a tour for you.

Appointments can be made for any time between 9am and 4pm daily, but Sundays are preferred as the owner of the house, Don Ramon Escaño, must take time off from work to give tours. While a visit to the Villa Margarita may take a bit of planning, it's fully worth it. Hollywood and 10 million bucks couldn't build you a spookier haunted house!

Getting There & Away
Jeepneys from Maasin to Malitbog cost P30 and take about one hour.

LIMASAWA
pop 5157

Limasawa is historically significant in the Philippines as the first place in which the Spanish celebrated mass, on 31 March 1521, thereby starting the Christianisation of the country. A pumpboat makes the journey from Padre Burgos daily (P20, one hour) and lands at barangay Magellanes. There you need to contact the mayor and arrange to stay at the two-room **guesthouse** (rooms P300-400) overnight.

The site of the first mass and its commemorative marker is a half-hour hike away in barangay Triana, and a local person will probably offer to walk with you. The island also has beautiful beaches for **swimming**, **snorkelling** and **diving**. The daily boat to Padre Burgos leaves Limasawa around 6am.

The boats do not run if the sea is rough, so be prepared to wait for calm weather.

Biliran Island

This small and quiet island province takes its name from borobiliran, an abundant native grass. Biliran became a province separate from Leyte in 1992, and a short bridge connects the two.

The island is about 32km long and 8km wide, and is packed with natural attractions such as waterfalls, hot and cold springs, and rice terraces. Offshore islands with white-sand beaches offer good snorkelling. You'll need to bring your own snorkel gear though, as the island is only geared towards very low-key tourism. It's a great place for nature lovers, but not for nightclubbers.

Biliran is lush and it can rain anytime, with most rainfall in December and the least in April. This climate allows three rice harvests annually, and some rice is exported. There is little else in the way of exports or industry though, and most people are subsistence farmers or fishers. They generally speak Cebuano on the west coast and Waray-Waray on

the east. Literacy is high, at 92%, and many people speak English. This is a friendly, relaxing and clean place to spend a few days. If you've been to Camiguin and enjoyed the amicable atmosphere, you'll find Biliran similar but with far fewer foreign visitors.

Information
Call in to see the helpful staff at the **Provincial Tourism Council** (2nd floor, Capitol Bldg). Take a motorised tricycle there from Naval for P10.

You can change US dollars only, and only at the **PNB** in Naval. There are no credit card facilities.

Biliran now has direct dialling within Naval, but calls to other parts of the island go through the **Biliran operator** (☎ 053-541 9881), who will connect you if there is a relevant local number. At the time of writing there was no Internet access on Biliran.

Getting There & Away
You can get to Biliran from Cebu, Leyte, Luzon and Samar.

Bus There are regular bus services from Naval to Ormoc (P100, two hours) and to Tacloban (P120, three hours). Nonstop air-con megataxis run between Naval and Tacloban (P150, two hours) every 1½ hours throughout the day.

Philtranco and **PP Bus Company** buses leave Naval early each morning for Manila (P690 to P790, 25 to 30 hours).

All buses and jeepneys arrive and depart from a terminal near the embarcadero.

Boat Boats to Cebu leave Naval on Tuesday, Thursday and Sunday (P160 to P220, 11 hours). This line has some substandard boats, so check out what you're buying into before handing over the cash. It's much faster (and safer) to take a boat from Cebu to Ormoc, and then a bus to Naval.

Getting Around
Buses and jeepneys make regular daily trips from Naval north to Kawayan (P15, one hour), and south and east to Caibiran (P30, 1½ hours) via Biliran town. Motorised and pedal tricycles operate in the towns. The flat fee for short local trips is P5.

The round-island road is very bumpy, slow and dusty. Public transport does not run

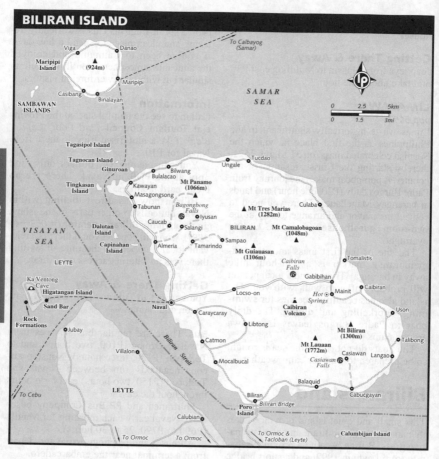

BILIRAN ISLAND

along the coast road between Kawayan and Caibiran, or along the cross-country road between Naval and Gabibihan. You can charter a multicab for these stretches for around P1000 to P1500 per day, or hire a motorcycle with driver for around P1000 per day.

If you can afford it, the motorcycle ride – and the views of the lush scenery along the way – is highly recommended.

NAVAL

Naval (nah-**bahl**), the provincial capital, is a low-rise, easy-going harbour town. There are flowers everywhere and the narrow streets are a great place to stroll around and soak up the amiable atmosphere. Naval is also a handy base for day trips to Higatangan and to the waterfalls to the east.

Places to Stay

Budget hotels in Naval are very cheap but fairly grotty. On the other hand, most of them are family run and friendly.

Marvin's Place (rooms P600) is by far the best option. It's fairly new, bright and clean, with big air-con rooms with bathroom. There is a breezy balcony and garden overlooking the ocean.

Take a pedal tricycle for P5 (give a bit more if you have heavy bags) or a motorised tricycle for P20 to barangay Atipolo, 2km south of town.

Rosevic Lodge (Vicentillo St; rooms with fan/air-con P250/500) is marginally better, with a courtyard and outdoor sitting area. Small rooms have either fan and shared bathroom or air-con and bathroom.

LM Lodge (Vicentillo St; beds P80-120) redefines the word 'basic', but the sheets are clean. Look for big grey gates with LM embossed on them; there's no other sign.

Brigida Inn (Castin St; dorm beds from P100, rooms with air-con P450) still sports its old 'Bay View Lodge' sign. It's cramped and dark, with OK dorm beds and poor-value, air-con rooms.

None of these lodgings has a restaurant, but meals can be ordered at all of them.

Places to Eat

Most eating places are on Inocentes St, the main street, leading from the market, jetty and terminal area.

Goldilocks has a good selection of Filipino food. **Armelan's**, next to Goldilocks, has less choice but better Filipino breakfasts.

Geebees does simple budget meals of meat or fish with rice, vegetables and soup during the day, and in the evenings turns into a foodless, singalong bar.

There are plenty of eateries and barbecue places at the terminal.

NORTH OF NAVAL

This pretty stretch of coast is the only part of the island that is easy to explore by public transport.

About 2km beyond Almeria is **Agta Beach Resort** (dorm beds P100; rooms with air-con P450) with spartan dorm beds and big, good-value, air-con rooms with private bathroom. It's on a stretch of beach with swimming at high tide only, and is busy with locals on the weekend. The resort is a good base for visiting **Dalutan**, an island with white sand and good snorkelling. Hire a bangka for P50 and paddle yourself across in 30 minutes.

Walkers may want to visit **Bagongbong Falls**. These are a two-hour hike from Caucab, where the barangay captain will help you find a guide. You should pay the guide about P100.

The **rice terraces** of Sampao, Iyusan and Salangi are each about 5km off the main road and you'll need to walk in unless you charter a vehicle. They're nowhere near as steep as the famed terraces at Banaue, but they're quite pretty and worth a look if you can't get up north to northern Luzon.

At **Masagongsong cold spring** (admission P5; open daily), the water has been tapped to fill a good-sized pool. Opposite the pool, on the main road, is the new **Villa Antonio** (rooms with air-con P600). This also has a spring-fed pool on a terrace overlooking the sea. Day use costs P80 for nonguests and there are good air-con rooms. Simple food can be ordered.

In Kawayan you can hire a bangka for around P300 to take you to **Ginuroan**. The island has a steep and rocky foreshore, but the offshore **coral gardens** are good.

You can walk around pretty and undeveloped **Maripipi Island** in less than a day, or hire a motorcycle for P100 per hour. There is a ruined, pre-Spanish **watchtower** by the primary school in Maripipi township, and in several barangays women make **terracotta pottery**. Offshore, the uninhabited **Sambawan Islands** have white sand and good snorkelling. There is no commercial accommodation on Maripipi Island, but the barangay captains will arrange homestays. You can charter a bangka to Maripipi (P300 one way, 20 minutes) from Kawayan. There are sometimes passenger boats from Naval to Maripipi Island (P50, 1½ hours), but this depends on how many passengers turn up. It's best to check the night before – if not enough passengers want to make the trip, departure is postponed until the following morning.

EAST & SOUTH OF NAVAL

Caibiran Falls is a steep 20-minute hike off the cross-island road. It is quite undeveloped and, if the water's not flowing too fast, there are two big **swimming holes** at its base. Nearby, **Caibiran Volcano** can be climbed in a steady 1½ hours. Check with the tourist office for directions to these as they are not signposted; you will need to charter a vehicle and guide. The volcano is active, so get advice before setting out.

Mainit hot spring is a series of small cascades with sitting pools, exposed on a riverbank beside rice fields. **Tomalistis Falls** pour from a cliff face and are only accessible by boat. They are reputed to pour the sweetest water in the world, and passing ships once used them to replenish their drinking water. To visit **Casiawan Falls** you need to drive 20 minutes on a track off the south coast road, and then walk for 10 minutes. Due to the El Niño/La Niña weather phenomenon, rainfall was less than usual in 2002, making the falls less spectacular.

WEST OF NAVAL

Due west of Naval is **Higatangan Island**. A shifting, white sandbar is good for **swimming** and **snorkelling**, and you can walk to the **Ka Ventong Cave**, with its reputed snake population – nothing like poking around a cave full of snakes to get that adrenaline flowing! On the western side of the island, accessible by boat only, is a series of interesting **rock formations** with small, sandy bays between them. Former President Marcos, along with fellow resistance members, reportedly took refuge on the island in WWII, and Marcos Hill is named in his memory.

The only accommodation is **Limpiado Beach Resort** *(rooms P200-300)*, near the sand bar, with simple rooms. There are five boat trips from Naval (P20, 45 minutes) daily, and the boats return the following morning. A one-way charter costs around P500.

Mindanao & Sulu

The bulky island of Mindanao, comprising around 20 provinces, lies to the south of the Philippine Archipelago and has a landmass of almost 95,000 sq km. Its landscape is lush and varied, encompassing coastal plains and swamps, fertile volcanic plateaus and river valleys. A backbone of rugged forested mountains runs north to south and the Philippines' highest peak, Mt Apo, dominates the skyline of Davao City. There are numerous offshore islands.

Mindanao's two big river systems are the Agusan, which feeds wildlife-rich swampy plains to the east, and the Rio Grande de Mindanao – also known as the Pulangi – flowing from the centre southwards to Cotabato City. It was to the mouth of this river in 1475 that Mohammed Shariff Kabungsuan brought Islam to the Mindanao mainland.

To the south, the hundreds of islands of the Sulu Archipelago stretch towards Indonesia.

In the Sulu Archipelago, only Bongao Island in the Tawi-Tawi Group was considered relatively safe for travel at the time of publication.

Highlights

- Hang out with a rum crowd on the scenic island of Siargao, a laid-back surfers' haven off the northeast coast of Mindanao
- Check out the hiking and snorkelling possibilities on the amiable and remarkably picturesque island of Camiguin

Mindanao

Christianity is the major religion in Mindanao, though there are more Muslims in the province than elsewhere in the Philippines. Predominantly Muslim areas include Marawi city and the area around Lake Lanao, and Cotabato city. There is a sizeable Muslim minority in Zamboanga.

Mindanao remains home to many indigenous people and it's still possible to have encounters with different cultures on their own terms and on their ancestral land. Rather than taking a 'tribal people tour' – and there are plenty of those – wander around, say, the T'boli heartland of Lake Sebu on market day and be as much of an observer or participant as you choose.

Mindanao's economy rests largely on agriculture, and there are vast plantations of pineapples, bananas, maize, coconuts and citrus fruits.

There are also large cattle ranches. While there is legislation in force to prevent the excessive logging operations of the past,

forestry is still both an industry and an environmental issue. Outside the cities, most local people are subsistence farmers or fishers.

For a detailed photographic journey through Mindanao in all its geographic, historic and cultural variety, you can't do better than read *Mindanao – a portrait*. It's a beautiful coffee-table book of photos and essays published in 1999. It's much too heavy and expensive to carry around, but some tourist offices have it in their library for visitors to browse through.

Getting There & Away

You can get to Mindanao from Bohol, Cebu, Leyte, Luzon, Negros, Palawan, Panay and Siquijor in the Philippines, and directly from Indonesia, Malaysia and Singapore. Specific travel information is given under the relevant destinations in this chapter.

Transport schedules and prices should be taken as guidelines only. While this is true for all the Philippines, Mindanao's security issues intermittently affect some transport routes.

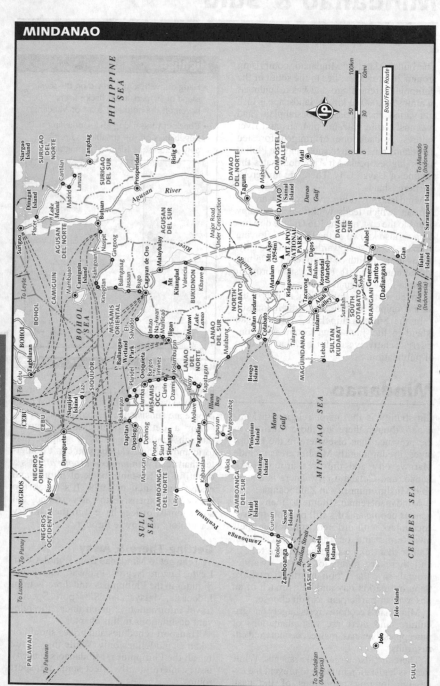

MINDANAO

Warning

At the time of writing both the Department of Tourism (DOT) and foreign embassies in the Philippines were actively discouraging travel to Mindanao and the Sulu Archipelago. During the interval between this edition and the last, the militant Islamic group Abu Sayyaf had targeted both Filipinos and foreigners for kidnapping. Scores of Filipinos and foreigners have been held for ransom, and a number have been executed when demands were not met. Besides the Abu Sayyaf, members of the radical Moro Islamic Liberation Front (MILF) and the communist New People's Army (NPA) are still actively engaged in armed opposition against the government in some parts of Mindanao. In March 2002, American and Philippine armed forces began operations against Abu Sayyaf on Basilan island off the coast of Zamboanga. Needless to say, Basilan was strictly off limits to visitors at the time of writing.

Terrorist bombings have also become more common in Mindanao since the last edition of this book was researched. Attacks against transportation and commercial targets (buses, ferries, shopping malls etc) have resulted in significant losses of life. In February 2000 a bomb planted on an inter-island ferry that was about to dock in Ozamis killed at least 45 people. In April 2002 at least 15 people were killed in a blast in a shopping mall in General Santos City. News of these attacks rarely attracts much attention in the international media, so don't assume things are safe just because you haven't heard any bad news about a place. Check with your embassy before venturing into any potentially dangerous areas.

Potential visitors to Mindanao and Sulu should contact their embassies in Manila before venturing into the provinces of western and southern Mindanao and all of the islands of the Sulu Archipelago. Islands and areas that were unaffected (that is, considered safe) at the time of writing included Camiguin Island, Dinagat and Siargao islands near Surigao, and the northeastern corner of Mindanao.

Long-distance bus fares are subject to fluctuating fuel prices. It's better to travel air-con on, say, the endless Manila–Davao run (around P1200, 48 hours) as the bus stops less frequently and the drivers are more likely to stay alert (even if you're not sitting close by and nervously poking them every time their heads nod).

Normally boat routes change less frequently than do their schedules and prices. Perhaps the region's troubles are affecting travel between Mindanao, Sulu and the rest of the archipelago, because routes seem to be less certain than usual.

Do travel by bigger, newer, faster boats where possible. Sea safety issues are being addressed, but change is slow with the older boats, and filling in your name and nationality on a passenger list in case of an accident or sinking is hardly the most reassuring way to start a journey.

Air There are flights from Manila to Butuan, Cagayan de Oro, Cotabato, Davao, Dipolog, General Santos and Zamboanga; from Cebu to Davao, General Santos and Zamboanga; and from Panay to Davao.

Bouraq Airlines and Air Philippines fly between Davao and Manado in Indonesia.

Silk Air flies from Singapore to Davao via Cebu City.

Bus There are buses from Manila to Davao via Surigao. Manila–Davao buses also ply the route via Calbayog and Catbalogan on Samar and via Tacloban on Leyte.

Boat There are boats from Manila to Cagayan de Oro, Cotabato, Dapitan, Davao, General Santos, Iligan, Nasipit (Butuan), Ozamis, Surigao and Zamboanga.

On Bohol there are boats from Tagbilaran to Cagayan de Oro and Surigao, and from Jagna to Cagayan de Oro and Nasipit (Butuan). Boats run from Cebu City to Cagayan de Oro, Dapitan, Iligan, Nasipit (Butuan), Ozamis and Surigao. There is also a boat from Maasin on Leyte to Surigao.

On Negros, there are boats from Bacolod to Nasipit (Butuan), and from Dumaguete to Cagayan de Oro, Dapitan, Ozamis and Surigao. Boats also run from Iloilo on Panay to Cagayan de Oro, Cotabato, Nasipit (Butuan) and Ozamis, from Palawan to Cagayan de Oro and Nasipit (Butuan) and from Lazi on Siquijor to Iligan.

To Indonesia and Malaysia, there are boats from Davao and General Santos to

Manado in Indonesia, and boats from Zamboanga to Sandakan in Malaysia.

SURIGAO

☎ 086 • pop 118,534

Surigao is the capital of the province of Surigao del Norte, the entry point to northern Mindanao. It is a crowded, busy and dusty city, with not much to hold a traveller's interest, but you may need to stay overnight here and cash up with pesos before heading off island-hopping.

If you are in Surigao for a couple of days, attractions close to the city include **Silop Cave**, 7km away, with its 12 entrances leading to a big central chamber. **Day-asin**, a floating village, 5km from the city, and **Mati**, to the south, where the Mamanwas people

have created a 'village' to showcase their culture. There are OK **beaches** around the city.

Information

The **Surigao City Tourist Office** is opposite the city hall, on the corner of the children's park.

For information about travel elsewhere in the region, the provincial **Department of Tourism** (*DOT; Rizal St*) is located by the city grandstand.

The **Equitable PCI Bank** (*San Nicolas St*) will advance cash against MasterCard and Visa credit cards. The **Philippines National Bank** (*PNB; Rizal St*) changes US dollars. There are no facilities for changing money on the offshore islands, so make sure you take enough.

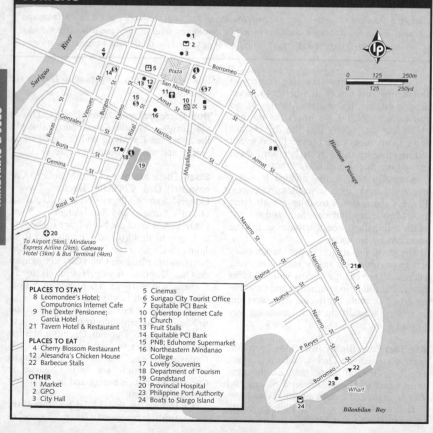

SURIGAO

PLACES TO STAY
8 Leomondee's Hotel;
  Computronics Internet Cafe
9 The Dexter Pensionne;
  Garcia Hotel
21 Tavern Hotel & Restaurant

PLACES TO EAT
4 Cherry Blossom Restaurant
12 Alesandra's Chicken House
22 Barbecue Stalls

OTHER
1 Market
2 GPO
3 City Hall
5 Cinemas
6 Surigao City Tourist Office
7 Equitable PCI Bank
10 Cyberstop Internet Cafe
11 Church
13 Fruit Stalls
14 Equitable PCI Bank
15 PNB; Eduhome Supermarket
16 Northeastern Mindanao
  College
17 Lovely Souvenirs
18 Department of Tourism
19 Grandstand
20 Provincial Hospital
23 Philippine Port Authority
24 Boats to Siargo Island

There are several Internet cafes in town, including **Computronics** on Borromeo St, below Leomondee's Hotel, and **Cyberstop** on Magallanes St.

Places to Stay & Eat

Dexter Pensionne *(San Nicolas St; rooms P150)* is a budget option, with basic rooms.

Garcia Hotel *(☎ 231 7077)*, next door, has similar rates. These two are pretty noisy, though the Garcia is friendlier.

Tavern Hotel and Restaurant *(☎ 231 7300, fax 231 7301; Borromeo St; old-wing rooms from P150, new-wing rooms up to P600)* also has cheap rooms in its old wing near the kitchen, which is a bit smelly. There are brighter, cleaner rooms in the new wing. It's pleasant, light restaurant overlooks the sea.

Leomondee's Hotel *(☎ 232 7334; Borromeo St; rooms P200-1000)* is a newish place; ask for a room at the back, off the noisy main road.

Gateway Hotel *(☎ 826 1283, fax 826 1285; rooms from P620)*, about 3km from the wharf and along the airport road, is the best hotel in Surigao. The good-value big, bright rooms have air-con, bathroom and cable TV. It has a good **restaurant** *(meals around P200)*.

Cherry Blossom *(San Nicolas St)* has been around for a while and is popular in the evening, though it looks a bit tired on the outside. There are some Filipino fast-food places on the streets around the city plaza, including the popular **Alesandra's Chicken House**, and masses of **barbecue stalls** along the wharf. **Fruit stalls** are opposite the cinemas on San Nicolas St.

Shopping

Lovely Souvenirs *(Rizal St)* has a good selection of Filipino basketwork and other crafts. **Eduhome Supermarket** next to the PNB is a decent supermarket.

Getting There & Away

Air Asian Spirit flies (P1300) from Cebu to Surigao at 10.15am on Monday, Thursday, Saturday and Sunday, and in the opposite direction on the same days at 11.15pm.

Bus Very regular buses run daily to Butuan (P50, two hours) and Cagayan de Oro (P135, six hours), along the west coast, to Davao (P275, eight hours) in the south and to Tandag (P126, around six hours) in the east.

Boat For Manila, WG&A leaves twice weekly, while Cebu Lines and Sulpicio Lines have a regular weekly service.

For Cebu City, Trans Asia has boats leaving twice weekly; Cokaliong Lines has regular trips three times weekly; and Sulpicio Lines also makes the trip three times a week.

To get to Negros, ask at the Port Authority about possible boats to Dumaguete.

Boats run regularly to the offshore islands of Dinagat and Siargao. Sulpicio Lines runs a weekly boat to Davao. Check schedules wherever possible.

Getting Around

From the wharf, public utility vehicles (PUVs) and tricycles run along Borromeo St towards the bus terminal, which is about 5km out of town towards the airport. These cost P3 anywhere along this route. A special trip by tricycle will cost P20 to P40, depending on distance.

SMALLER ISLANDS

There is a group of islands within easy day-tour reach of Surigao city. These seem to have erratic accommodation facilities, so check the situation with the city tourist office if you want to stay overnight.

The islands include **Hikdop Island**, 45 minutes away by a public bangka (pump-boat) that leaves at around 10am. It has good beaches and the beautiful **Buenavista Cave**. **Nonoc Island** was formerly a nickel mine and its vegetation is sparse, but it is at one end of an extraordinary 391m footbridge that links it with Sibale Island.

There is a shade-house in the middle of the bridge where you can rest during your walk across! Nonoc is 30 minutes from Surigao by pumpboat.

Tiny and uninhabited **Raza Island** is locally known for simultaneously having high tide on one side of the island and low tide on the other. **Bayanagan Island** is reached through mangrove swamps, and was the site of an early scientific expedition in 1887; many marine species collected here at the time remain unclassified.

SIARGAO

The relaxed island of Siargao is a haven after the dusty and crowded capital city Surigao. It is well known on the surfing trail for the 'Cloud Nine' surf break. The Siargao

AROUND SURIGAO

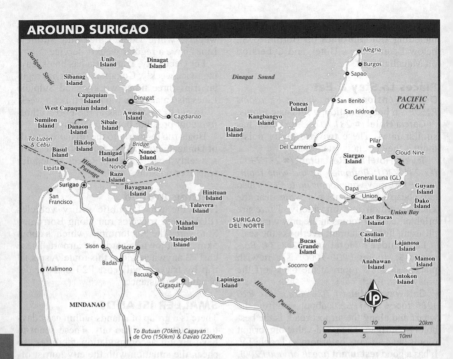

Cup surfing competition is held in late September or early October every year. Surfing can be good from April to October and is great on the northwest coast during the northeast monsoon, but like many places in the Philippines, surf can't be guaranteed. Surfers call the country the 'Ficklepines' and fickle the surf can be, so be prepared to wait for the right conditions. Surfboard rentals can be found in General Luna.

Siargao has plenty of natural attractions for nonsurfers too, with beaches and rock pools, extensive mangrove swamps, inland forest, waterfalls and nearby islands. This is not the island for people seeking an active nightlife, but there are enough places to meet people and have a quiet drink or two.

The port is in the main township of Dapa. On arrival you'll probably want to head straight over towards General Luna (known locally as GL) and the east coast, where the low-key beach resorts are located.

General Luna
pop 12,347

General Luna (or GL) is a small township on the southeast coast. Eat at **Maridyl's Eatery** on the main street or at **The Pub** near the school; the owner of the latter is generous with information about attractions in the area.

Some of the earliest established resorts on Siargao are to the south of the township, and most have loyal return visitors every year. They're also quite popular with the locals, drawing large groups of students and budget conventioneers.

The accommodation can become quite crowded and noisy at times.

Nearest to the township going south is **Maite's Beach Resort** (cottages P350 per person), which has rather characterless concrete cottages. Its rates get you basic accommodation and all meals daily.

Jade Star and the newer **N and M Resort** come next and are next door to each other, with simple bamboo cottages and gardens on the beach. They both charge P150 to P200 for rooms, and meals are around P100 each.

BRC Beach Resort (rooms P100 per person, full board P350), a little further along, has a big grassy garden leading to the beach and very simple rooms of bamboo and thatch. Bathrooms do not have running water – use the scoop.

A couple of kilometres further along the coast is the low-key but very beautiful, stylish and private five-star **Pansukian Tropical Resort** (e *travelvision@skyinet.com; full board US$150-210 per person*). Weary travellers in need of a treat can buy sheer luxury here, all meals included. Rates also include use of snorkelling equipment, windsurfboards and kayaks. If you really want money to burn, the resort can arrange transport via helicopter from Manila or Cebu.

Cloud Nine

This surf break is about 6km north of GL. The newer resorts and surf camps here are mostly run by some seriously laid-back expat Australians. Stay at **Cloud 9 Resort** (*cottages P400-800*), with its cottages on the beach facing the surf break, and an indoor/outdoor restaurant and pool table. (This is where drivers will drop you if you just ask for 'Cloud Nine', so say if you want to go somewhere else.) Further along is the **Green Room Resort**, and next door to that is the **Jungle Reef Resort** (*rooms P250-500*).

All resorts have big bamboo pavilions for hanging-out over the water, and in front of Cloud 9 Resort there is a long public walkway out over the reef, great for rock-pool watching at low tide. Eat at any of the resorts – Cloud 9 has the best food of the three – or walk up the beach to **Snag Miguel's Beach Club Restaurant** (no that isn't a spelling mistake) for good fresh Western and Filipino food in a prime sunset setting.

All the resorts can help organise day tours and boat trips, and they prefer to use the boats and skills of local people as guides when possible.

Elsewhere on Siargao

Visit barangay (small village or neighbourhood) **Pilar**, largely built on stilts over mangrove flats – you can hire a pumpboat from Cloud Nine or rent a motorcycle (P500 return) and go yourself. You'll have to pay someone to guard your bike, though, while you explore the village.

Take a boat around to the mangrove swamps of Del Carmen and look for **crocodiles** (but don't hold your breath!) – you can hire a bangka for P100 to P200, depending on how deep you want to go into the mangroves and how long you want to stay out.

Take a motorcycle around the island and up to **Burgos** on the northeast coast to a small resort built by Richard, a craftsman who also makes surfboards finished in bamboo.

Islands Near Siargao

Visit the tiny white-sand-and-palm hummock of **Guyam** (a classic Robinson Crusoe desert island); the bigger **Dako**, with its beautiful beach, snorkelling and diving; and **Bucas Grande**, with the Sohoton Lagoon hidden from the sea.

You can hire a bangka from the pier at GL. Prices depend on which islands you visit and how long you want to stay.

Getting There & Away

SEAIR has a flight from Cebu to Siargao at 11.10am every Saturday (P1990), and in the opposite direction on the same day at 12.15pm.

Siargao is serviced by at least two fast boats every morning. The companies are Fortune Jet, Askha Queen and New Frontiers Express, and their offices are opposite the main entry to the wharf on Borromeo St in Surigao. Check times at the wharf though, as schedules can change or boats may be out of service. The same boats return to Surigao daily. There are also slower boats running; check at the wharf for current details.

Getting Around

Jeepneys run from Dapa to GL (P10, one hour). Alternatively you can hire a motorcycle and driver to take you there (P100, 25 minutes). The going rate for motorcycle hire is around P300 for half a day to P800 for the day depending on your destination. These motorcycles are big enough to seat large families at one hit and are known locally as *hubel-hubel*, a choice phrase for copulating pigs. Having ridden groin-to-groin with the driver and a complete stranger, plus several bags, this writer well understands the associations of intimacy.

DINAGAT

☎ 085 ● pop 9883

This large island is accessible by daily boat from Surigao, and is home to several fishing communities. The northwest coast of the island is quite rugged and picturesque – featuring jungle-clad karst formations jutting up out of turquoise waters. It's possible to explore the island as an (expensive) package tour with Pansukian Tropical Resort (e travelvision@skyinet.com) on Siargao, otherwise you can try your luck with hiring a boat from the wharf in Siargao. There doesn't appear to be a set boat schedule, so check at the wharf.

BUTUAN
☎ 085 • pop 267,279
If you're interested in history, don't let Butuan's chaotic appearance put you off spending at least a day here. The city has been a major port to a greater or lesser degree since at least the 4th century AD.

Butuan is widely recognised as the earliest known place of settlement and sea trade in the Philippines. In 1976 the oldest boat in the Philippines was discovered here – a carefully crafted *balangay* (sea-going outrigger) that has been carbon-dated to AD 320.

This find, along with discoveries of extensive wooden coffins of tribal peoples who practised skull deformation, has made Butuan a centre of archaeological and ethnographical importance. Visit the **museum** *(open 9am-noon & 1pm-4.30pm Mon-Sat)*, 1km or so from the town centre, with its small but excellent collection. It stands in a quiet garden of lily ponds; take a picnic and enjoy the surroundings.

Towards the airport, at barangay Libertad, is the **balangay discovery site** *(open 8.30am-4.30pm Mon-Sat)*, where the remains of the several boats discovered are on display, along with coffin burials. Confusing spellings these, but the word *'barangay'* in fact derives from *'balangay'*, as the boats were big enough (around 15m long and 2.5m wide) to move whole communities of settlers in one journey.

A tricycle will take you to the discovery site for P100 per hour, which should be enough time to look around. The ride out here is worthwhile in itself.

There is also a **Diocesan Ecclesiastical Museum** *(admission free)* at the cathedral convent (you just walk into the cathedral compound and ask around for someone to unlock the museum – it's all very informal), commemorating missionary work in the region. Butuan, like Limasawa in Leyte, claims the honour of the first mass held by Magellan on Philippines soil at nearby **Magallanes**; a memorial marks the spot.

Orientation & Information
Several key streets have changed their names recently but shop signs carry the old street names. Concepcion St is now E Luna St; Juan Luna St is now AD Curato St; and Zamora St is now JC Aquino St.

There is a **PNB** for changing US dollars and the **Bank of the Philippine Islands** (BPI) will advance cash against your MasterCard. Both banks are on Montilla Boulevard.

There are several Internet cafes. Most central is the **Cybercafe** *(JC Aquino St)*, underneath the Urios College Gym.

Places to Stay & Eat
Butuan has many eateries and a range of accommodation to suit all budgets. Some of the cheapest hotels seem to be rather buggy.

BUTUAN

PLACES TO STAY
2 Imperial Hotel
4 Emerald Villa Hotel
5 Hensonly Plaza Inn
22 Embassy Hotel

PLACES TO EAT
6 New Mansion House
9 Shakey's Pizza
11 New Narra Restaurant
12 Jollibee

OTHER
1 GPO
3 PAL Agent
7 WG&A Shipping Lines Agent
8 Negros Navigation Agent
10 Bank of the Philippine Islands (BPI)
13 Otis Department Store
14 Cinemas
15 Crown Thrift Market
16 MJ Santos Hospital
17 Urios College
18 Urios Gym; Cybercafe
19 St Joseph Cathedral
20 Greenwich Supermarket
21 Police Station
23 PNB

Hensonly Plaza Inn (☎ *342 5866, fax 225 2040; San Francisco St; rooms with fan & shared bathroom P90, singles with fan & bathroom P250, rooms with air-con & bathroom P450)* is good value. It's old and tatty but spotlessly clean.

Imperial Hotel (☎ *341 5309; rooms with shared bathroom & fan P100, rooms with air-con & bathroom P400)* is OK – what more can you expect for the price? – but take a room with bathroom, as the shared bathrooms are smelly and grubby.

Embassy Hotel (☎ *342 5883; rooms with air-con & bathroom P300-600)*, in the mid-range, isn't bad but it's on a noisy road. There's a restaurant and videoke bar attached.

Emerald Villa Hotel (☎ *225 2141, fax 342 5378; rooms P350-650)* offers better value. If you can afford a couple of hundred pesos extra, stay here and you'll find you can actually sleep with the lights out.

All rooms have air-con, bathroom and TV, and are clean and bugless. The attached restaurant does very good American breakfasts (P80).

There's one top-end hotel at mid-range prices worth recommending.

Balanghai Hotel (☎ *342 3064, fax 342 3067; rooms from P750)*, beside the museum, has a large, clean swimming pool overlooked by the restaurant. Rooms all have air-con, bathroom and TV. The hotel offers a flexible (but pricey) range of day-tour options, including tours to the region's marsh and forest habitats.

New Narra Restaurant (*E Luna St)*, around the corner from Rizal Park, has good Filipino food. The *adobong manok* (chicken cooked in garlic and vinegar) is tasty, but get here early as it's cooked mid-morning and then left out. Better yet, ask for the menu and order something unadventurous, such as the chicken fried rice.

Getting There & Away
Air AirPAL and Cebu Pacific both fly from Manila to Butuan and back daily. The **PAL office** (☎ *341 5257)* is at the airport and there is a ticket agent in town on Villanueva St, opposite the Veterans Bank.

Bus There are services between Butuan to Surigao (about P60, 2½ hours), Cagayan de Oro (P70, four hours) and Davao (P120, six hours). These times and prices are for or-dinary services; the less frequent air-con buses run direct and are much faster.

Boat Butuan's main port area is at Nasipit, about 10km west of town. Jeepneys run between Nasipit and Butuan (30 minutes).

WG&A has boats running twice a week between Manila and Nasipit (36 hours). The Negros Navigation boat to Manila runs once a week. For details about boats from Manila, see Boat under Getting There & Away in the Manila chapter.

Cebu Ferries has boats to Jagna on Bohol once a week. For Cebu, WG&A has boats twice weekly.

Negros Navigation has a weekly service to Negros. It also has boats going via Cebu to Palawan once a week.

Getting Around
The airport is 10km out of town. A jeepney ride costs P5 and a taxi will cost around P70.

The bus terminal is about 1km from the city centre. Jeepney and tricycle rides cost P5; a special ride by tricycle will cost P100 per hour.

AROUND BUTUAN
Inland and a little south from Butuan is the floodplain of the Agusan River and the Agusan marshes. There are villages of houses floating on bamboo poles and tree trunks around the township of Bunawan, and the swamps around Talacogon are a prime habitat for bird life. The forested area north of the Agusan River remains the habitat of the tarsier, the tiniest primate in the world.

Unless you have the time (and assistance) to go about hiring transport and a guide for the trip – which could take several days to arrange – you're best off going through the Balanghai Hotel in Butuan (see Places to Stay & Eat in the previous Butuan section). Philguides Maps series includes Agusan del Norte and Agusan del Sur maps, which cover these areas. They are available at National Book Store outlets.

BALINGOAN
pop 8197
This is a blink-and-you'll-miss-it township about two-thirds of the way from Butuan, heading south towards Cagayan de Oro. With the 1999 cancellation of the Fast Ferry service from Cagayan de Oro to Camiguin

Island, this is now the only port serving Camiguin Island by ferry (see the Getting There & Away entry for Camiguin later).

There are extremely basic **lodgings** at the wharf above the eatery. Regular bus and jeepney services run between Cagayan de Oro and Balingoan (P40, 1½ hours).

CAGAYAN DE ORO
☎ 088 ● pop 461,877

You know you're approaching a comparatively large and wealthy city by the number of new car lots on the northern access road from Butuan, and the vast Limketkai and Gaisano shopping malls on the edge of the city centre. The 'Oro' part of Cagayan's name comes from the Spanish discovery of gold in the river here.

Today, much of the city's economic activity centres on the vegetable gold of the Del Monte pineapple processing plant a few kilometres north of town, and the company's plantations in the hills above Cagayan.

It is also a university town, and the Xavier University maintains a **Folk Museum** (*Corrales Ave; open 8.30am-11.30am & 2.30pm-5pm Tues-Fri, 8.30am-11.30am Sat*) at its campus. Beside the tourist office and sports complex, the Public Library houses a good **shell collection**. You may need to ask the library staff for access.

Information
The **DOT office** (ⓔ *dot10@cdo.weblinq .com; Velez St*) is at the front of the Pelaez Sports Center. Most banks will change US dollars. The **BPI** (*cnr Velez & Borja Sts*) and both branches of the **Equitable PCI Bank** will advance cash against MasterCard and Visa credit cards.

Cagayan has some Internet cafes. Try **Cyberlink** (*Velez St*) between T Chavez and Hayes Sts. Most charge around P35 per hour.

Places to Stay – Budget
City Plaza Hotel (☎ *2272 3788; General Capistrano St; singles with fan & shared bathroom P140-240*) is good value, if noisy. It's a bit worn but very clean.

Parkview Lodge (*rooms P220-500*) overlooks Friendship Park and is good for the price. The higher priced rooms have a TV but are otherwise almost identical to the cheaper rooms.

Nature's Pensionne (*T Chavez St; rooms P470-670*) has good-sized rooms, all with air-con and bathroom.

Places to Stay – Mid-Range
VIP Hotel (☎ *2272 6080, fax 2272 6441; Velez St; rooms with bathroom P660-990*) is great value, with very well-furnished, comfortable rooms; make sure you ask for one with a proper window (opening onto daylight rather than onto the inner building-well). There's a good coffee shop that's serves breakfast all day and is open late.

Ramon's Hotel (☎ *2272 4738, fax 2272 2578; rooms from P500*), relatively new and centrally located, has a great setting, with some rooms overlooking the river as well as a balcony (with river view) attached to the restaurant. All rooms have air-con, bathroom and TV.

Grand City Hotel (*Velez St; rooms from P690-1260*) is getting a bit old and tired but still has OK rooms. The corridors and lobby are dark and narrow; ask for a room well away from the room-service food lift that beeps loudly and often.

Coconut Beach Resort (☎ *855 2702; cottages from P680*), about 10 minutes' drive north of town, is very pleasant and quiet, with fine air-con cottages with bathroom and TV. Discounts are sometimes given Monday to Thursday, but weekends can be very busy. It's on the beach and also has a good-sized swimming pool. A taxi from town will cost around P80, or pay about P7 for a jeepney ride.

Places to Stay – Top End
Dynasty Court Hotel (☎ *857 1250; cnr Tiano & Hayes Sts; rooms from P950*) is right in town. Rates include breakfast and lunch, but be warned that the standard rooms have no windows. There is a fine coffee shop and restaurant.

Pryce Plaza Hotel (☎ *858 4536, fax 2272 6687;* ⓔ *prycepht@cdo.philcom.com.ph; rooms*

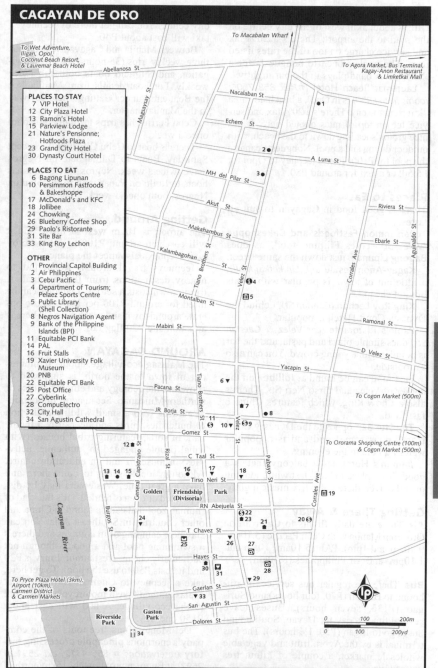

CAGAYAN DE ORO

To Wet Adventure,
Iligan, Opol,
Coconut Beach Resort,
& Lauremar Beach Hotel

Abellanosa St

To Macabalan Wharf

To Agora Market, Bus Terminal,
Kagay-Anon Restaurant
& Limketkai Mall

PLACES TO STAY
7 VIP Hotel
12 City Plaza Hotel
13 Ramon's Hotel
15 Parkview Lodge
21 Nature's Pensionne;
    Hotfoods Plaza
23 Grand City Hotel
30 Dynasty Court Hotel

PLACES TO EAT
6 Bagong Lipunan
10 Persimmon Fastfoods
    & Bakeshoppe
17 McDonald's and KFC
18 Jollibee
24 Chowking
26 Blueberry Coffee Shop
29 Paolo's Ristorante
31 Site Bar
33 King Roy Lechon

OTHER
1 Provincial Capitol Building
2 Air Philippines
3 Cebu Pacific
4 Department of Tourism;
    Pelaez Sports Centre
5 Public Library
    (Shell Collection)
8 Negros Navigation Agent
9 Bank of the Philippine
    Islands (BPI)
11 Equitable PCI Bank
14 PAL
16 Fruit Stalls
19 Xavier University Folk
    Museum
20 PNB
22 Equitable PCI Bank
25 Post Office
27 Cyberlink
28 CompuElectro
32 City Hall
34 San Agustin Cathedral

Nacalaban St

Echem St

A Luna St

MH del Pilar St

Akut St

Riviera St

Makahambus St

Kalambagohan St

Tiano Brothers St

Velez St

Ebarle St

Montalban St

Mabini St

Ramonal St

D Velez St

Yacapin St

To Cogon Market (500m)

Pacana St

Tiano Brothers St

Velez St

Pabayo St

JR Borja St

Gomez St

To Ororama Shopping Centre (100m)
& Cogon Market (500m)

Magaysay St

Corrales Ave

Aguinaldo St

12

C Taal St

Rizal St

13 14 15

General Capistrano St

16

17

18

Corrales Ave

Golden Friendship
(Divisoria) Park

Tirso Neri St

RN Abejuela St

22
23

21

20

Burgos St

24

T Chavez St

25

26

27

Hayes St

30

31

28

29

Cagayan River

To Pryce Plaza Hotel (3km),
Airport (10km),
Carmen District
& Carmen Markets

32

Gaerlan St

33

San Agustin St

Riverside
Park

Gaston
Park

Dolores St

34

0   100   200m
0   100   200yd

MINDANAO & SULU

from P3000), a five-star property on Carmen Hill, is about 3km west of the city centre on the road to the airport. There's a 20% tax and service charge on top of the rates listed here. The pool is open to nonguests for a P100 fee. A band plays in the bar nightly.

Lauremar Beach Hotel (☎/fax 858 7506; rooms from P950) is in Opol, a beachside area 7km from the city. There's a 20% tax and service fee on top of rates quoted here. It has nice grounds leading down to the beach, with outdoor dining and a pool. Nonguests can use the pool for P100. Take a jeepney to Opol for P5.50, or a taxi for around P80.

Places to Eat
There is good food in Cagayan to suit all tastes.

Persimmon Fastfoods and Bakeshoppe (Velez St) serves Filipino food, as does **Bagong Lipunan**, just down the same street.

Kagay-Anon Restaurant (Limketkai Mall), a little out of town, is popular with locals but not cheap.

King Roy Lechon (Gaerlan St), behind the Dynasty Court Hotel, is popular.

Paolo's Ristorante (cnr Velez & Gaerlan Sts) does simple pizza and pasta, and the bar is popular with a young crowd. You can also eat outside.

Fast food can be found at **Jollibee** on the corner of Velez and Tirso Neri Sts. There's also a **Chow King**, which features Chinese fast food.

The Site Bar, opposite the Dynasty Court Hotel, does some food and is a popular watering hole in the evening.

Ramon's Hotel has a balcony that is a good shady place to breakfast while looking over the river; there's also live music nightly.

Getting There & Away
Air There are daily flights to Cagayan de Oro from Manila with Cebu Pacific (5.10am, 9.30am and 1pm), PAL (5.10am, 10am and 1.10pm) and Air Philippines (8.40am).

Bus There are regular bus services northbound to Butuan (P70, four hours) and Surigao (P136, seven hours). Buses leave several times a day for Davao. Southbound buses go to Iligan (P50, 1½ hours). The bus terminal is by the Agora fruit and vegetable wholesale market, a couple of kilometres out of town.

Boat Macabalan Wharf is 5km from the city centre. You can get there by jeepney; a taxi will cost about P40.

Between Manila and Cagayan WG&A has three weekly trips (35 hours); Negros Navigation and Sulpicio boats both run twice weekly. For boat details from Manila, see the Boat entry under Getting There & Away in the Manila chapter.

Cebu Ferries has trips to Jagna on Bohol once a week.

There is boat to Cebu City nightly, except Saturday. Boats to Dumaguete on Negros leave twice a week. Negros Navigation has boats to Iloilo on Panay, and to Bacolod on Negros, both once a week.

Getting Around
The airport is 10km west of town, and it will cost you around P100 to get there by taxi. Jeepneys also meet the planes.

Jeepneys travel around town and to nearby destinations from the terminal. A trip in town costs a set P4. Tricycles can be hired for around P100 per hour. These operate around town and are metered. There is an automatic P20 flag fall.

AROUND CAGAYAN
The **Malasag eco-village**, about 20 minutes out of town to the north, is supposed to showcase the ecology and ethnic cultures of northern Mindanao. Set in acres of botanical gardens with a small wildlife collection of butterflies, birds and deer, it is a theme park of sorts, featuring tribal houses (with tribal people engaged in 'authentic' activities), a museum and an education centre. Although locals seem to come here and have a great time, Westerners may be disappointed or even offended – it's the kind of 'human zoo' that can be found in China and other countries in Southeast Asia. You can stay here camping or in cottages and there's a swimming pool and a good – though not particularly cheap – restaurant. Entry is P20 and it costs P50 to use the pool. To get here, take a jeepney to Cugman and get off at Malasag, then take a motorcycle up the hill to the eco-village. A taxi will cost about P150 one way.

Del Monte offers free tours of the company's enormous **pineapple processing factory** (reservations ☎ 855 4312, ext 2591 or 2592) at Bugo, approximately 15km north of

Cagayan, between 8am and 1pm on Saturday. You need to call a day or so in advance to book. The pineapple plantations, all 95 sq km of them, are about 35km north and east of Cagayan, on the Bukidnon plateau at Camp Phillips. There are pineapples as far as the eye can see (an extraordinary sight) and some really weird-shaped harvesting equipment. Jeepneys run to Camp Phillips (P10, one hour) but the plantations lie behind the complex, so it's best to hire someone on site there to drive you on a looping back road through the plantations to the Del Monte Clubhouse and Golf Course about 5km away. You can then pick up a bus to Malaybalay or back to Cagayan from the main road there. A special return trip by taxi will cost around P500.

It was to the Del Monte plantation airfield that MacArthur fled after the battle of Corregidor in 1942.

The **Makahambus Cave** is about 14km out of Cagayan beyond the airport. The cave marks the spot of a violent encounter between (victorious) local people and US forces in the 19th century; there's a small shrine and beyond the cave chamber a viewing deck over the Cagayan River. Take a torch (flashlight). From here you can walk down 150 steps to the gorge and see large ferns; depending on the depth and force of the river, you may be able to cool off in plunge pools. To get there take a jeepney marked Dansolihon/Talakag. A return taxi ride will cost P200 to P300.

MALAYBALAY
pop 123,672
Note: At the time of research the road between Cagayan de Oro and Malaybalay was considered unsafe. Depending on the current situation, foreign travellers may be turned back at police or military roadblocks.

This small city is the capital of Bukidnon province. It is in the mountains above Cagayan de Oro and can be cool at night. For three days in early September Malaybalay is the setting for the annual **Kaamulan Festival**, a celebration of unity between the tribal people living in the area. Seven tribal groups are represented and activities include dance, song, storytelling, local food and wine, and ritual enactments. The festival is held in the pretty Pines View Park.

Thanks to Gail Cockburn of Ontario for the following information on hiking in the **Impalutao reforestation centre**:

For great hikes in one of the only untouched forests in the area, go to the Impalutao reforestation centre (it also has natural growth forests) about 40 minutes north of Malaybalay (between Kisolon and Malaybalay). Waterfalls and rivers throughout the reserve offer a cool place to swim and get away from people. Take a bus from Cagayan to Malaybalay but ask the conductor to let you know where to get off. Locally it is known as Gantugan – you may have to ask people on the bus for help if the conductor is not from the area.

Just north of Valencia (south of Malaybalay) off the highway is the **Monastery of the Transfiguration**. Even for nonreligious types this is a gorgeous drive into the hills, which are planted with coffee by the monks. On Sunday at 8am there is an English service with a lovely boys' choir, and you can buy the coffee and peanuts grown by the monks. You will need a motorcycle or a friend to take you as there is no public transport.

Driving up to Malaybalay from Cagayan you'll see the impressive 3000m **Mt Kitanglad** in the distance, one of the highest mountains in the Philippines and still a habitat of the Philippine eagle. There is apparently good **bird-watching** at Lalawan Dalwagan, at the base of the mountain 6km from the highway.

Places to Stay
Savers Plaza Lodging Inn (rooms P150-275) has budget rooms. **Haus Malibu** (☎/fax 841 2714; Bonifacio Dr; rooms P160-700) has a range of rooms. **Pine Hills Hotel** (☎ 841 3211; rooms P972-1290), on the highway, is at the top of the scale. It has good food, as does the Zion Ranch on the plaza.

Getting There & Away
Malaybalay is on the Cagayan to Davao and Cotabato run, and buses travel regularly every day. The journey normally takes about two hours.

CAMIGUIN
The pear-shaped volcanic island of Camiguin lies off Mindanao's northwest coast. While it's small enough to become familiar within just a few days, the landscape is lush and varied, with active volcanoes, pockets of forest,

CAMIGUIN

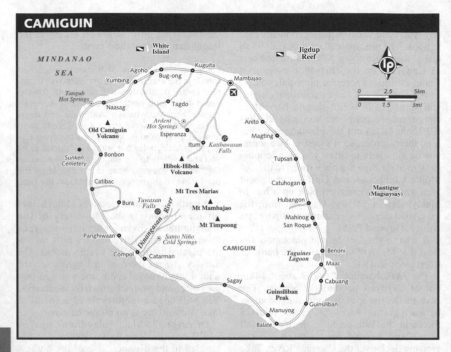

clear waterfalls, hot and cold springs, and an alternately black- and white-sand coastline.

The waters surrounding Camiguin are not bad for **diving**. Professional divers have located over 10 sites of note, including Jigdup Reef, with a coral-covered slope and wall to explore, and 'Old Volcano', an eerie moonscape of sunken lava flows. The best diving is probably off White Island, a tiny islet off Agoho. Diving around the island's best sites can be arranged in Agoho or Mambajao.

Mention the name Camiguin to just about any Filipino and they'll say 'Ah! Lanzones!', as Camiguin is widely recognised for having the sweetest *lanzones* in the archipelago. The annual **Lanzones Festival** takes place around the third week of October, when you can join in with everyone else and make an unashamed glutton of yourself on these truly delicious fruit.

Camiguin is a relaxed place to stay, although a decade of tourism has certainly given the welcome mat some wear.

Many of the 70,000 islanders are fishing folk and, although tourists are increasingly important to the economy, so far tourism is still pretty low-key and based around the island's natural attractions; no wild nightlife here, and no-one seems to mind.

Besides sitting on the beach, the main diversions for travellers seem to be hiking around the island and diving or snorkelling.

Getting There & Away

SEAIR flies from Cebu to Camiguin on Sunday at 11.15am, and in the opposite direction Friday at 1.15pm. The fare is P1300. The airport is near Mambajao.

There have been boats from Manila to Camiguin in the past, though it's uncertain whether or not they'll start this service again. Check with the tourist office in Manila or Mambajao.

The Fast Ferry service from Cagayan de Oro to Camiguin stopped operating in December 1999. Check if it's started again, but if not, you need to cross from Balingoan, about 80km north of Cagayan de Oro, to Benoni. At least eight boats make this trip and they run about hourly throughout the day.

Buses travel about every 15 minutes between Cagayan and Balingoan (P30, 1½ hours) and Butuan and Balingoan (P40, 2½ hours).

Getting Around

The road around the island is 64km long, so it's possible to make the circuit in a few hours if you have to. There are jeepneys, but they are few and far between. For ease of travel and access to places that jeepneys don't go, think about hiring a motorcycle (P500), or multicab that can comfortably seat about six people (P1000) and take you around for a day.

Benoni

pop 1487

Benoni has an artificial lagoon to the south of its wharf and is a fish-breeding area. You can stay at **J and A Fishpen** (☎ 387 4008; rooms P500), which has some air-con rooms out over the water. It also has a restaurant, where it's nice to eat perched out over other parts of the fishpens. Of course, the fish is fresh.

Between Benoni and Mambajao you'll see **Mantigue Island** – sometimes called Magsaysay – offshore. A few fishing families live here and there's still good coral. From the Islet Beach Resort at Mahinog a return trip to the island will cost P500.

Public jeepney or multicab rides from Benoni to Mambajao cost P20. A special ride to Mambajao costs P150; to the resorts north of Mambajao you'll pay P250. There is a flat rate of P3 for local rides.

Mambajao

pop 30,806

This is the capital of Camiguin, about half an hour's ride from the port at Benoni. There are a few places to stay here, but you may prefer to stay closer to the northern beaches.

There is a **tourist office** on the 2nd floor of the Provincial Capitol Building. The staff here have a list of homestay accommodation if you prefer to stay with a local family.

You can change US dollars at the **PNB**.

Camiguin Action Divers maintains an office here in Mambajao, so you can sign up for a course here, though the dive expeditions depart from its dive shop at Yumbing.

Places to Stay & Eat Budget accommodation is available at **Tia's Pension House** (☎ 387 0103; rooms P100), with very simple rooms in the family home.

Tia's Beach Cottages (☎ 387 1045; cottages P300) are just out of town in a sizeable but low-key setting. It's a popular venue for local seminars and the food is great. Bicycles are available for hire.

Casa Grande (☎ 387 2075; rooms P800), in town, has four rooms in a high and airy old house with lots of polished wood floors. Its attached restaurant has a varied menu.

Tarzan Nest (☎ 387 0273; rooms P250-350), off the main road about 3km southeast of Mambajao, features tree-house-style rooms built around a huge old hardwood tree. There's also a pool and restaurant. Look for the sign and turn south off the main road when you reach Balbagon.

Bahay Bakasyunan Resort (☎/fax 387 1057; rooms P1700), just out of town, is one of the top resorts in Camiguin. Cottages are made of woven bamboo and other natural materials, set on well-landscaped grounds shaded by coconut palms. Nonguests can use the pool for P100. Rates don't include tax.

Around Mambajao

Hibok-Hibok Volcano last erupted in 1951. About 500m off the main road is the Philippine Institute of Volcanology & Seismology (Philvolcs) station, which monitors the volcano's activity. A hired motorcycle or multicab will take you there to see the equipment and memorabilia of past eruptions. It's possible to climb the volcano, but be warned that it's a steep climb and you should be reasonably fit. Most resorts have a list of local guides who will take you up the trail; aim to leave around daybreak if you want to get up and down in a day.

Less energetic is the trip to **Katibawasan Falls** (admission P10). This is a beautiful clear stream of water dropping about 70m to a plunge pool. You can swim here but the changing rooms and picnic tables have seen better days.

A special trip by jeepney or multicab from Mambajao will cost about P300 return; from the resorts around Agoho it's about P350 return.

Nearby are the **Ardent Hot Springs** (springs & grounds open 6am-10pm daily). These are HOT hot springs – about 40°C – so head out late afternoon when the air temperature has cooled down a bit. The **big pool** (admission P20) is emptied for cleaning on Wednesday and takes the best part of the day to refill. The springs are in a lush setting. There is a good **restaurant** here, and attractive **dorms and cottages** (rates P150-1000);

guests can swim all night after closing time. The springs get very busy on weekends.

About 1km from the springs, going towards the highway, is **Abu's Nature Camp**, a pleasant collection of cottages in a pocket of forest.

Kuguita, Bug-ong, Agoho & Yumbing

These are the most developed of the northern beaches. A handful of dive shops have set themselves up in Bug-ong, Agoho and Yumbing. The German-run **Action Divers** (☎ 387 1266; ⓔ *camiguinaction@sni.ph*) is one of the better organised operations. It also offers PADI diving courses – up to US$700 to be certified as a divemaster. If you're already a diver, expect to pay about US$20 for a boat dive. Snorkelling equipment is rented out for P250 to P300.

Camiguin Action Divers (ⓔ *camiguinac tion@sni.ph*) is at Secret Cove in Yumbing, but it maintains a small office in Mambajao.

Going west from Mambajao, you first reach Kuguita, where there is the **Turtles Nest Beach resort** (☎ 387 9056; *rooms P300*). It's a bit dilapidated and loses its beach completely at high tide, but there's good coral about 100m offshore and nonguests can access it from the bar if you do! You should probably at least buy a drink at the bar if you do!

At Bug-ong, **Jasmine by the Sea** (☎ 387 9015; *rooms P400-500 high season, P250-350 off season*) continues to be excellent value. The good roomy cottages have balconies. There are mountain bikes for hire for P100 per day, and both the Western and Filipino food is very good, with home-made sugar-free breads and salads. Next door is **Morning Glory Cottages** (☎ 387 9017; *waterfront/non-waterfront rooms P400/200*), with rooms directly on the waterfront and some just behind. There is no restaurant, but you can cook for yourself or order food from the staff.

At Agoho, the **Caves Resort** (☎ 387 9040; *rooms P300-700*) has OK rooms and a big, airy restaurant and bar on the waterfront.

The **Camiguin Seaside Resort** (☎ 387 9031; *cottages P400*) has lots of roomy cottages and a big restaurant area, and is popular with group travellers. Opposite, check out the small restaurant **Sagittarius Serve Food**; it comes highly recommended. Between Bug-ong and Agoho is **Paradiso**

Restaurant *(mains around P150)*, with a good menu featuring fish and fresh pasta.

In Yumbing there are three mid- to top-range lodgings. **Secret Cove** (☎ 387 9084; *rooms P500-600*) has decent rooms. It's also the headquarters of Camiguin Action Divers. **Para's Resort** (☎ 387 9008; *rooms from P1275*) has clean rooms and reliable amenities (rates exclude tax), a good restaurant and a pool overlooking the water. Nonguests can use the pool for P50. Just up the road is **Camiguin Beach Club** (☎ 387 9028; ⓔ *pcr bank@skyinet.net; rooms from P650, 4- to 6-person rooms with shared bathroom & air-con P1200*), which also has a good-sized pool open to nonguests.

All these resorts give easy access to tiny **White Island**, a pure, white-sand bar a few hundred metres offshore. A return trip should cost around P200, but will cost considerably more from the more expensive resorts.

Tangub Hot Spring is a completely undeveloped spring that wells hot under the sea bed, a few metres offshore at Tangub, just beyond barangay Naasag. At low tide it's HOT; at high tide you'd never know it was there. It's fun to sit in the water at low-ish tide as cold sea water and hot spring water mix. You can also dive here – there's a smattering of soft corals and giant sea fans.

Bonbon
pop 1263

Just before Bonbon you pass the Old Camiguin Volcano, the slopes of which have been turned into a steep and beautiful **Stations of the Cross**. There are great views from the top. Between the hillside and Bonbon you'll see an enormous white cross floating on a pontoon in the bay; this marks the spot of the **Sunken Cemetery**, which slipped into the sea following the earthquake of 1871. It's possible to dive the cemetery – it's got quite a population of fish. The same earthquake destroyed the 17th-century **Spanish church** in Bonbon; its quiet ruins still stand, with grazing cattle and a makeshift altar inside.

Catarman
pop 15,386

About 10km further along the island road from Bonbon is Catarman. At the vice-mayor's office in the Municipal Hall there's a small display of **antique ceramics** *(office* *open Mon-Fri, closed noon-1pm).* You can stay in Catarman at **SRJ Inn** *(rooms P300-800)*, but there's only a small pebbly beach and it's quite noisy due to the attached open-air restaurant.

Near Catarman is the undervisited and unspoiled **Tuwasan Falls**. The road here is impassable after rain, but if it's dry a jeepney or multicab can take you to the start of the path. From there it's about a 15-minute hike to the falls, walking twice through the river (this is also not possible after heavy rain as the river is too high).

The falls thunder into a plunge pool, which may be too rough to plunge into, but it's nice to see the tree ferns and rainforest created by the spray. This area is slated for tourism development along the lines of horse rides and overnight camping; check how it's progressing with the tourism office if you're interested.

Also near Catarman is the **Santo Niño Cold Spring** *(admission P10; open 8am-noon & 1pm-5pm daily, closed for cleaning 8am-10am Mon)*, a terrific huge pool, 40m long, filled by the spring. And cold it is!

Guinsiliban

This is an alternative port to Benoni, and some ships from Cagayan de Oro dock here. At the time of writing all shipping was going through Benoni, except for the Sunday boat from Mambajao to Cebu. Behind the elementary school by the wharf are the remains of an **old Spanish watchtower**, used to watch out for possible Moro invaders from the mainland. A pretty shrine is maintained here.

ILIGAN
☎ 063 • pop 285,061

The first impression of Iligan as you arrive by road is of industrial plants, with the road passing endless cement and food-processing factories. The harnessing of water from Lake Lanao, in the hills above the city, to provide hydroelectricity has allowed for major development, and the city is busy.

Along with the provision of hydroelectricity there are also, inevitably, plenty of waterfalls, and the city prefers to market itself to tourists as the 'City of Magnificent Waterfalls'.

Late September is **Ang Sinulog fiesta** time, when the streets into town are lined with fantastic bamboo and *nipa* arches to honour San Miguel, the city's patron saint. The main day of celebrations is 29 September, when the *sinulog*, a fight-dance, and passion plays are performed, and groups of young people dressed in traditional costume go from house to house and serenade the occupants.

Information

The **DOT** *(☎ 221 3426, fax 517 602; ABC Bldg, Quezon Ave; open Mon-Fri)* is just below City Hall.

The **PNB** *(cnr B Labao & San Miguel Sts)* will change US dollars, and the **Equitable PCI Bank** *(Luna St)* will advance cash on MasterCard and Visa credit cards.

There are several Internet cafes in Iligan. Try the **Computer Cafe** *(MH del Pilar St)* beside the Equitable PCI Bank.

Things to See & Do

Tinago Falls *(admission P30)* is more beautiful and more accessible than the Maria Cristina falls; the falls thunder down into a big plunge pool (there are about 300 steps down to it!), and there is a beautiful pocket of rainforest created by the constant spray. Above the privately owned falls is a resort with a good swimming pool and a not good minizoo with, among other animals, a full-grown lion and a tiger in small concrete pens. It's pretty bizarre to hear the lion's roar echo through the gorge. You can get to the falls by taking a jeepney to Burun (P5, 30 minutes) and connecting with another up the hill to the falls.

A taxi from Iligan will cost about P100 one way. Expect to find this place very crowded on weekends.

On the highway, a little before the Tinago turn-off, the cold **Timoga Springs** *(admission to most pools P20)* have been tapped to fill several swimming pools, all of which have attached facilities. Jeepneys go there for P5; a taxi will cost P100 one way.

Places to Stay

Iligan Star Inn *(☎ 221 5272; Quezon Ave; rooms with fan & shared bathroom P220, with bathroom & air-con P420)* is a budget hotel in the centre of town (there's also a side entrance on Jorge Ramiro Sr St). The cheaper rooms and the common bathrooms are less than spotless; the others are OK.

Maria Cristina Hotel *(☎ 221 3352, fax 221 3940; rooms P560-950)* is close to Iligan Star

MINDANAO & SULU

ILIGAN

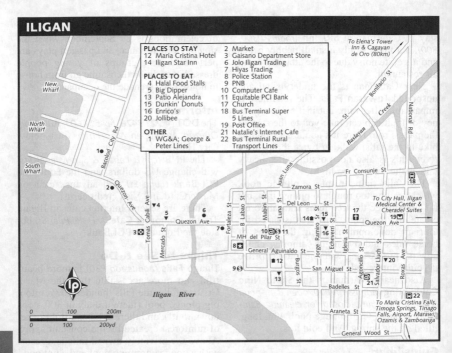

PLACES TO STAY	2 Market
12 Maria Cristina Hotel	3 Gaisano Department Store
14 Iligan Star Inn	6 Jolo Iligan Trading
	7 Hiyas Trading
PLACES TO EAT	8 Police Station
4 Halal Food Stalls	9 PNB
5 Big Dipper	10 Computer Cafe
13 Patio Alejandra	11 Equitable PCI Bank
15 Dunkin' Donuts	17 Church
16 Enrico's	18 Bus Terminal Super
20 Jollibee	5 Lines
	19 Post Office
OTHER	21 Natalie's Internet Cafe
1 WG&A; George &	22 Bus Terminal Rural
Peter Lines	Transport Lines

Inn. For a long time this was the best hotel in Iligan but it now needs some maintenance.

Elena's Tower Inn (☎/fax 221 5995; rooms P600-1200), just off the main drag, offers a better standard of comfort and cleanliness in its very pink rooms.

Cheradel Suites (☎ 223 8118, fax 221 4926; Jeffery Rd; rooms from P1000), five minutes east of town, is the best place to stay, as suggested by the price. It's a very comfortable, with a private pool and about 10 tasteful rooms with great bathrooms. If you're after more personal accommodation, the tourism department keeps a list of quality **homestays**, several with pools, starting at around P700.

Tinago Residence Inn (rooms & cottages from P700) at Tinago Falls has pretty rooms and cottages – lots of bamboo and *nipa* – with balconies, air-con and private bathroom. You'll hear the lion roaring on and off. It has a good restaurant overlooking the falls.

Places to Eat

Big Dipper (Quezon St) has Chinese food. It's around the corner from a good line of **halal food stalls** on Tomas Cabili Ave, if you're sick of the sight of pork.

Good Filipino food is served at **Patio Alejandra** and at **Enrico's**, one of the oldest restaurants in Iligan.

Shopping

This is a good place to look for Muslim crafts, especially if you are not going to the market at Marawi. Both **Jolo Iligan Trading** (Quezon Ave) and **Hiyas Trading** (Fortaleza St) have a good selection of weavings, traditional motif batiks and brassware.

Getting There & Away

The nearest airport is at Cagayan de Oro, from where Iligan is 1½ hours by road. There are very regular bus services north to Cagayan de Oro (P60, 1½ hours), but this road has been the scene of occasional ambushes. There are also buses south to Pagadian. Ozamis is 1½ hours away (P45).

There are two bus terminals on Roxas Avenue serving the same destinations, one for Super 5 Lines and its associates and one for Rural Transit.

WG&A has boat services twice weekly for Manila (46 to 53 hours). Cebu Ferries departs for Cebu twice weekly (11 hours).

George & Peter Lines has boats leaving once a week for Lazi on Siquijor (five hours).

Getting Around

The flat fare around town by jeepney is P2.50. No tricycles are allowed in the city centre, but there are plenty of taxis.

MARAWI & LAKE LANAO
pop 131,090

Marawi is the centre of Muslim culture in the Philippines. The Islamic City of Marawi, as it is properly known, is about an hour's drive south of Iligan and it's like driving into another world. At the border of Lanao del Sur the churches disappear and the spires of mosques appear on the skyline, women wear headscarves and there are signs in Arabic.

The city sits prettily in a bowl of hills and on the shore of Lake Lanao. Places to visit include the **Aga Khan Museum** (open 9am-noon & 1pm-4pm daily) on the campus of the Marawi State University (MSU); the **market** for fabrics and brassware crafted in the township of Tugaya across the lake; **Dayawan weaving village** outside the city proper; and the ceremonial wooden **Torongan** buildings.

Warning

Having whetted your appetite for cultural diversity, here comes the bad news. It's not too strong to say that most Filipinos you'll come across, both in Iligan and Marawi, are paranoid about travel in this area, as Marawi has long been a crisis area, even though trouble only flares up occasionally. It is not forbidden to visit the city unaccompanied, but the local tourism offices and hotels advise against it. Women travelling alone may feel particularly uncomfortable. Your four options are:

• to check the current situation in Iligan before coming and then decide whether or not to go;
• to hire a car and driver (ask the tourism department in Iligan for help with this – many drivers are too scared to make the trip) and make a day trip, calling in at the tourism office in Marawi to pick up a local city guide;
• to ignore all advice, take a jeepney and see what happens; or
• to not go.

Information

The **tourist office** (open Mon-Thur & possibly Sun) is located in the City Hall.

Places to Stay

Marawi Resort Hotel (☎/fax 520 981; cottages P850-1000) is the only hotel in Marawi. It is on the MSU campus and has huge grounds, lots of trees, a pool, restaurant and a good view of the lake. The cottages have balconies, but the bathrooms leave a lot to be desired.

Getting There & Away

Jeepneys and buses run regularly to/from Iligan. A return trip by taxi (if you can find a driver to take you), with a couple of hours waiting time, will cost at least P2000.

OZAMIS
☎ 088 • pop 110,420

While Ozamis is not the provincial capital of Misamis Occidental, it has a capital city feel to it and is bigger and busier than the capital Oroquieta.

It has a busy port area and compact central commercial area, but not much else to hold a traveller's interest.

Places to Stay & Eat

There are several lodgings in Ozamis, some with restaurant attached.

The Country Lodge (Ledesma St Extension; rooms with bathroom & fan P100-200, with air-con P350) is in the budget range. It's simple and a bit tatty but clean as a whistle.

Soriano Pension (Mabini St Extension; rooms with bathroom & fan P100-180, with air-con P350) is fine for the price, very clean and owned by a nice family.

Palace Hotel (☎ 521 0573, fax 521 3240; rooms P500-900) is a new mid-range place that has decent rooms with air-con, bathroom and TV.

Royal Garden Hotel (☎ 521 2888, fax 521 0008; rooms from P750) is the best choice in town, with a good restaurant and Filipino fast-food outlet attached.

Getting There & Away

Buses run every 15 minutes to/from Iligan (P45, 1½ hours), Pagadian, Dipolog and Oroquieta (P35, 1½ hours). All buses go from an integrated transport terminal, which is a tricycle ride (P10) from the port.

All the shipping agents are located at the wharf. Ferries run constantly between Kolambugan (an hour's drive south of Iligan) to Ozamis, and all buses use this service. The cost of the boat ride (P8.50, 25 minutes) is in addition to the bus fare and is collected on board the ferry. Negros Navigation boats leave for Manila via Iloilo, Panay, once a week (43 hours). Cebu Ferries depart for Cebu daily (11 hours), except Monday and Friday.

OROQUIETA
pop 59,843

Oroquieta is a sleepy riverside town and seems an unlikely setting for the provincial capital of Misamis Occidental. The **market** comes alive in the late afternoons, when the fishing fleet has delivered the day's catch.

Places to Stay

Sheena's Hotel (☎ 531 1158; Barrientos St; rooms with fan/air-con from P250/650) has plenty of character. It's a rambling old house with a garden and restaurant, but is on a very noisy stretch of road.

Casa Kristina Hotel (☎/fax 531 1272; Barrientos St; rooms P400-600), 200m further along from Sheena's, is a new place with bright rooms. The hotel has direct river frontage and a good restaurant with a balcony over the water.

Getting There & Away

All buses from Ozamis to Dipolog (and vice versa) go via Oroquieta (P30, one hour). Get off the bus at the petrol station in town on the way through, rather than at the bus terminal on the outskirts. Boats run from Manila and Cebu City to Ozamis. On Negros, there are boats from Bacolod to Ozamis, and boats also run from Iloilo on Panay to Ozamis.

Getting Around

There is a flat rate of P3 anywhere in town by public transport. A special ride by tricycle to Sheena's or Casa Kristina costs P10.

BALIANGAO WETLAND PARK

This small but great spot is way off the beaten track, with mangrove-lined river estuaries to explore, good snorkelling offshore beside the marine protected area, and white-sand beaches a short boat ride away. The only noise you'll hear is birdsong and the occasional fishing boat.

Excuse all the acronyms, but this is a community-based sustainable tourism (CBST) initiative, in which several local barangay are being supported by nongovernment organisations (NGOs) and the DENR (Department of Environment & Natural Resources) in a very low-key development. It consists of four simple bamboo and *nipa* cottages and a meeting and eating shelter, all powered by solar energy (not a radio or TV in sight), with septic tanks for sewage, and rainwater collection for showers and drinking. If you like your creature comforts, you may wish to just make a day trip, and overnighters should be prepared for lots of mosquitoes (nets are provided in the cottages).

There are four **cottages** (P300, or P75 per person) that sleep up to six people each. There's also a cleared **camp site** (P20 per person) where you can pitch a tent – you have to bring your own tent though. A boat to go snorkelling (bring your own equipment) costs P150 for half a day; a 30-minute tour upriver costs P150; and a boat ride to Sunrise Beach for swimming costs P200 for half a day. Staff live on-site but they need to make a trip to town to get provisions for visitors, so it's best to ring a day or so ahead, especially as the cottages can occasionally be full of students on field trips. Contact the **NGO PIPULI** (Ozamis; ☎ 521 1928, weekends ☎ 0918 490 2476, fax 521 1992).

Getting There & Away

Get a bus from Dipolog (P30, 1½ hours) or Oroquieta (P25, one hour) to Calamba. Here, it's easiest to take a special trip by tricycle to the park which, with a couple of hours waiting time, will cost about P200 return. Tell the driver to head towards Baliangao and as he may not know where you want to go watch the kilometre markers carefully; just after the '4km to Baliangao' marker a track goes right, with a faded signpost to the park. It's about two bumpy kilometres down this track; impassable to vehicles when wet. At the end of the track walk a delightful 400m or so along a series of boardwalk bridges through mangrove forest to the park buildings.

DIPOLOG
☎ 065 ● pop 99,862

Dipolog (dee-**poh**-lohg) is the capital of Zamboanga del Norte, and has a busy town centre just off the waterfront. If you're in an

VERONICA GARBUTT

VERONICA GARBUTT

Muslim dancers, Lanao – Mindanao

Beach near Zamboanga – Mindanao

JOHN BORTHWICK

Fast boat to General Luna, Siargao – Mindanao

Port Barton – Palawan

Underground River, Sabang – Palawan

Bangka ride – Palawan

energetic mood you can climb the many, many steps of the **Stations of the Cross** to Linabo Park. At 486m above sea level, this lookout gives a good view of Dipolog and its neighbouring city of Dapitan. **Sicayab Beach** is a fine grey-sand beach about 4km from town, and further out is the **Pamansalan Oisca Forest Park and Waterfall**.

Information

The **DOT** (☎ 212 2485; Rizal St) is in the City Hall. It's a good idea to stop here and ask about the current situation before going overland south from the city.

There are plenty of Internet cafes in town. Try **Cyberspot** (Ramos St) just off General Luna St, or the **Goodwill Internet Cafe** (General Luna), near the Top Plaza Hotel.

The **PNB** will change US dollars.

Places to Stay & Eat

There is a range of accommodation and eateries in town.

Ramillo Pension (☎ 212 3536; Bonifacio St; rooms P100-350) is a budget option that is fine for the price. The 2nd-floor rooms have a nice veranda but fan rooms on the ground floor are cooler. If you can afford it, the aircon rooms on the 2nd floor are the best.

Hotel Arocha (☎/fax 212 3197; rooms P200-700) is similar in standard to Ramillo Pension. The budget rooms are fine, but the more expensive ones are not good value when compared with other hotels in town.

CL Inn (☎ 212 3216; Rizal St; rooms P400-800) is central but quite noisy and a bit worn; its budget rooms are fine but the more expensive ones aren't. It has an OK but gloomy restaurant serving Filipino fast food.

Hotel Camila (☎/fax 212 3008; rooms from P500), a few hundred metres along General Luna St, heading out of town, is good value. The rooms are well furnished and comfortable, with air-con, bathroom and cable TV, but make sure you have a room on the opposite side from the church: early mass is broadcast over loudspeakers from 4.30pm to 5.15am every day. A **Sunburst Chicken Restaurant** is attached.

Top Plaza Hotel (☎ 212 5777, fax 212 5788; rooms P825-1540) is at the top end of accommodation. The hotel has a good restaurant and a **Top Diner** fast-food outlet attached.

Pizza Deli (Festival Shopping Arcade), in the fruit and vegetable market of this arcade, has a 'real' pizza oven and lots of tourist information on the walls.

Micki's (Rizal St) is bright and clean, and serves chicken, burgers and spaghetti-style dishes.

Getting There & Away

Air PAL flies from Manila to Dipolog at 10.05am on Monday, Tuesday, Wednesday and Friday (returning to Manila at 12.35pm), and on Sunday at 2.45pm (returning to Manila at 4.55pm).

SEAIR flies from Cebu to Dipolog on Wednesday at 9.45am and Saturday at 6.15am. In the opposite direction, Dipolog to Cebu flights leave on Friday at 10.50am and Saturday at 3.20pm. The fare is P1690.

Bus Regular buses link Dipolog with Ozamis via Oroquieta (P85, 3½ hours). They drop off right in town on General Luna St. Southbound buses to Zamboanga (non-air-con/air-con P180/220, eight to 10 hours) leave from the Satellite bus terminal on the southern edge of town, next to the post office.

Boat Dipolog's Palauan Port is technically in the nearby city of Dapitan, though geographically it's halfway between the two. Details of boats are in the Dapitan section of this chapter.

Getting Around

The airport is about 3km out of town and a tricycle there will cost about P20.

The flat fare in town for tricycles is P4. RBS Minivan has a stand on General Luna St opposite the high school; you can charter an air-con van for P250 an hour or P1800 per day (negotiable).

AROUND DIPOLOG

There is a pretty stretch of coast south of Dipolog, pleasant for day tours. Off the highway, about an hour from Dipolog (though

> ### Warning
>
> At the time of writing it was absolutely suicidal to take public transport overland from Dipilog to Zamboanga. For alternative routes and means of transport to Zamboanga see Getting There & Away in the Zamboanga section later in this chapter.

MINDANAO & SULU

it'll take closer to two hours by public transport), is the **Villaester/Villavalle Mountain Resort** *(admission P15)* at Carupe. This is a family-run property in the foothills of the mountains, where a spring has been tapped to fill a fair-sized pool. The surrounding scenery and vegetation is lush and damp (take a mosquito coil) and the 6km dirt road there, through small villages, gives a good glimpse of rural life off the beaten track. The pool is closed for cleaning on Thursday. There are very basic **cottages** *(P500)*; bring sleeping mats and mosquito nets. You can order food from the owners. To get there take a multicab from Dipolog to Villa Ramos (P12, 45 minutes) and then a van or extended motorcycle (P15) to Carupe, 6km off the highway. A special trip by RBS Minivan will cost around P250 an hour. The road will probably be impassable after heavy rain.

Another 8km down the highway on the coast at Punta Blanca is **Crystal Beach Resort**, where a spring fills a clear 20m pool and there is a small beach and day cottages for hire; bring your own food. Pool use costs P30 and you can overnight in a simple and breezy **cottage** *(P300)* right over the water. Catch a multicab or bus from Satellite terminal in Dipolog (P20, one hour) and get off at the entrance to the small resort.

DAPITAN
pop 68,178

This really is a clean, green and peaceful city on the edge of a wide bay; you may choose to stay here rather than in Dipolog if you're spending a few days in the area.

Dapitan's most famous temporary resident was the national hero José Rizal, who lived in exile here from 1892 until shortly before his death in 1896. During that time he designed the town's waterworks, fashioned a **grass relief map** of Mindanao that can still be seen opposite the **old church** in the town plaza, practised as a doctor and natural scientist, and taught school to local boys. The **Rizal Museum** *(open daily)* is at Talisay, just over the bridge in Dapitan. It is where Rizal lived. The main building houses a collection of Rizal memorabilia, and in the grounds are beautifully crafted, life-size, bamboo and *nipa* replicas of the house, clinic, school and chicken house where Rizal lived. There is a good stand of natural forest in the grounds, with boardwalks and paths along

the water. The museum is a fine memorial to a fine man. Rizal's **landing site** is marked by a memorial on the waterfront.

Aliguay Island, a white-sand island with good coral, is a 45-minute bangka ride from Dapitan.

Places to Stay & Eat

There are several places along Sunset Blvd to stay and eat, all overlooking the bay.

Aplaya Vida Lodge *(rooms P450)* consists of simple air-con rooms in a nice old wooden house. Across the road is a seafood restaurant affiliated with the lodge.

Casa Patricia *(rooms P300-450)*, close by, rents rooms with fan and shared bathroom, though the house is a bit dark and dreary. One air-con room has an attached bathroom.

Dapitan City Resort Hotel *(☎/fax 213 6542; rooms from P1200)* has full water frontage and all rooms have balconies. There is a pool that nonguests can use for P75, and a nice-looking restaurant.

Corazon de Dapitan has very good Filipino dishes and cakes (try the fantastic *bibingka*), which are served on the ground floor of a beautiful, old two-storey building on the corner of the plaza. There's a clean, flushing, Western-style toilet that even has a seat!

Dakak Park Beach Resort *(☎/fax 212 5932; rooms P8000-12,000)*, on Dakak Bay, about 15 minutes from Dapitan by road or 40 minutes by boat, is the absolute top of the range. It offers a private beach, golf course, horse riding, water sports and diving, comfortable rooms and cottages. Its standard is indicated by the room rates. Guests are transferred to the resort by hotel transport, but other visitors need to ride an extended motorcycle (P100 return, depending on waiting time) from Dapitan. Nonguests can have day use of the resort beach – but not the swimming pools – for P200.

Getting There & Away

Minivan From Dipolog catch an RBS minivan (P12, 30 minutes) from the RBS stand on General Luna St, opposite the high school.

Boat Palauan Port is halfway between Dipolog and Dapitan, about 2km off the highway. Ask the RBS minivan to drop you at the turn-off, and then take a tricycle (P5) to the port. The tricycles wait interminably for a total of eight – yes eight! – passengers, so you might want to pay for an extra couple of places so that you can get going.

To Manila, WG&A and Sulpicio Lines have boats once a week. The journey takes between 30 and 40 hours.

Delta Fast Ferries services, George & Peter lines and SuperCat leave daily for Dumaguete and Negros. SuperCat has connecting boats to Cebu.

DAVAO
☎ 082 • pop 1,147,116
Sprawling at the foot of Mt Apo, Davao (dah-**bow**, and sometimes spelt 'Dabaw') is the fastest-growing city in Mindanao. While predominantly Christian, it has an interesting and eclectic mix of Muslim, Chinese and tribal influences.

The tribal cultures are showcased during the second week of August each year, during the **Kadayawan sa Dabaw Festival**, with costumed street parades, dances and performances, along with fantastic displays of fruit and flowers.

Davao also has a long-standing Japanese history, which is associated with early abaca-processing warehouses in the area and, less happily, with WWII, when the thriving Japanese community dispersed. There are still strong ties between the mother country and 'little Japan', as Davao is also known.

Outside the city, export quantities of pineapples, bananas and citrus are produced, and plantations can be visited. For the natural history enthusiast, there are **walking tracks** around nearby Mt Apo and there's a breeding programme for the endangered Philippine eagle at nearby **Eagle Conservation Center**.

The nearby islands of **Samal** and **Talikud** offer clear water, good corals and wreck-diving.

Orientation
A couple of key streets have changed names but are still confusingly referred to by both old and new names. These are F Inigo St (formerly Anda St) and Pelayo St (formerly Legaspi St).

Information
The **regional DOT office** (☎ 221 6955; e dotr11@mozcom.com; open 8am-noon & 1pm-4.30pm Mon-Fri) is at Magsaysay Park.

The Philippine eagle (haribon) is a truly magnificent bird and, sadly, very rare.

The **City Tourism Office** is in City Hall opposite San Pedro Cathedral.

The **PNB** opposite the cathedral will change US dollars. The **Equitable PCI banks**, on Monteverde St near Santa Aña Wharf, and on Claro M Recto Ave heading towards the Aldevinco Center, will advance cash against MasterCard and Visa credit cards.

The **Indonesian Consulate** (☎ 229 2930; fax 297 0139; Ecoland Dr) is in the Ecoland Subdivision near the southern bus station.

There are many Internet cafes in town. Try **Gatesway Café**, off Claro M Recto St near the Hotel Maguindanao, or the **Weblink Cafe** (A Pichon St) behind City Hall.

Things to See & Do
You can easily fill a pleasant half-day in the north of the city towards the airport. Coming from the city, take a jeepney in the direction of Sasa and get off at the **Long Hua Temple** (Cabaguio St; open 7.30am-4.30pm), 2km to 3km from the city centre.

It's an easy landmark, a huge Chinese Buddhist temple with beautiful wooden floors and carved walls and doors. Walk also behind the main temple to see the smaller altar behind. Walking back towards the city for a couple of hundred metres, you'll see a sign on a small side street on the right to the **Taoist Temple**, with its fantastic red pagoda. Ring a bell on the gate if you want to go

MINDANAO & SULU

DAVAO

PLACES TO STAY
15 Marco Polo Hotel
22 Manor Pension House;
   Aljem's Inn 1
26 Le Mirage Family Lodge
28 Aljem's Inn 2
30 Royale House

31 Hotel
   Maguindanao
35 Grand Men Seng
   Hotel
36 El Gusto Family
   Lodge; Sunny Point
   Lodge

PLACES TO EAT
4 Harana Restaurant;
   Mongolian Garden;
   Nikkei Oriental;
   Ajmura; Sushi Rikki;
   Pescadero
12 Eateries

20 Calzada
23 Tsuru Japanese Restaurant
24 Prims
25 Kusina Dabaw; New
   Sunya Restaurant
27 Claude Cafe
37 Eateries

To Long Hua & Taoist Temples,
Puentaspina Orchid Garden,
Hagar's, Insular Century Hotel,
Dabaw Museum, T'boli Weaving
& Airport

Santa Aña
Wharf

Magsaysay
Park

Muslim
Fishing
Village

Davao
Gulf

Davao River

OTHER
1 Victoria Plaza
2 University of South-
   Eastern Philippines
3 Zirkle Disco
5 Gaisano Mall
6 Agdao Market
7 WG & A Lines
8 Sulpicio
9 Tourist Office;
   Immigration Office
10 Equitable PCI Bank
11 NCCC Department Store
13 Post Office
14 Madroza Fruit Center
16 Aldevinco Center
   Extension
17 Aldevinco Shopping
   Center
18 Equitable PCI Bank
19 Spam's Disco
21 Buses to Calinan
   & Eagle Camp
29 San Pedro Cathedral
32 PNB
33 Tourist Office; City Hall
34 Weblink Internet Cafe

To Bankerohan
Market

To Shrine of Holy Infant
Jesus of Prague, Calinan
& Eagle Camp

To Ecoland
Bus Terminal

0   100   200m
0   100   200yd

inside. Back on the main road, walk another 500m or so south and turn left into Bolcan St. At the end is the **Puentaspina Orchid Garden** (admission free; open daily). It's more of an orderly nursery than a garden, but it has some great specimens on show, including the gorgeous *waling-waling*, endemic to Mindanao.

Continue north by jeepney or taxi to the **Dabaw Museum** (admission P20; open 9am-5pm Mon-Sat), next to the Insular Century Hotel. It has a good collection of local historical interest, and a selection of tribal weavings and artefacts from most of the Mindanao tribes.

Walk through the grounds of the Insular Century Hotel to the **T'boli Weaving Centre**, to the left of the hotel jetty. There is a small collection of weavings and T'boli handicrafts, and, if you're lucky (or if any of the sales staff deign to notice you), you'll see weavers working complicated textiles on backstrap looms.

West of Davao, in the hillside barangay of Matina, is the **Shrine of the Holy Infant Jesus of Prague**.

From here there's a good view of Davao Gulf and the city. Take a jeepney from Bankerohan Market to Matina and then a tricycle to the shrine. A taxi there will cost about P50.

Places to Stay – Budget
Le Mirage Family Lodge (☎ 226 3811; San Pedro St; rooms with fan & shared bath/air-con & bathroom P150/400) is fine for a central lodging. Its rooms are noisy, but it's clean and secure.

Sunny Point Lodge (☎ 221 0155, fax 244 0562) and **El Gusto Family Lodge** (☎ 227 3662) are close to each other on A Pichon St and offer much the same standard, with rooms from P150 to P600. El Gusto has a central courtyard, which makes it lighter and brighter. Sunny Point, on the other hand, has a nice café on the ground floor.

Places to Stay – Mid-Range
Manor Pension House (☎ 221 2511; rooms P525-630), just off A Pichon St, has been newly renovated. The rooms are good value, and rates include breakfast.

Aljem's Inn 1 (☎ 221 3060, fax 221 3059; rooms P500), next door, is a little cheaper, but older and darker.

Aljem's Inn 2 (J Rizal St; rooms P560-750), newer than its counterpart, offers reasonable rooms.

Royale House (☎ 227 3630, fax 221 8106; Claro M Recto St; rooms P590-850), near the cathedral, has rooms that are expensive and ordinary at these prices, but there's often a promotion happening, cutting the rooms by up to 40%. This makes them good value!

Hotel Maguindanao (☎ 222 2894, fax 221 8121; rooms from P745), opposite the cathedral, is an older, good-quality hotel with comfortable rooms.

Places to Stay – Top End
Grand Men Seng Hotel (☎ 221 9040, fax 221 2431; e grand@menseng.com.ph; A Pichon St; rooms P1500-2800) is the best value in this range, with 1st-class rooms, a lively lobby and coffee shop, and good-sized pool. Rates don't include tax and service. Nonguests can use the pleasant pool and surrounds for P100.

Marco Polo (☎ 221 0888, fax 225 0111; Claro M Recto St; rooms P3200), opposite the Aldevinco Center, is a newish place that has 1st-class rooms and prices to match; rates don't include tax and service. Nonguests can use the 25m lap pool for P150.

Insular Century Hotel (☎ 234 3050, fax 235 0915; rooms from P3000) is a superbly landscaped property about 8km out of town on the way to the airport. It has extensive grounds, a swimming pool and a private beach with water sports, diving facilities and a jetty. Ask about promotions that can drop rates by 30%.

Places to Eat
Kusina Dabaw and **New Sunya Restaurant** on San Pedro St serve good Filipino fast food and are always busy.

Tsuru (Pelayo St; Japanese meal from P200), around the corner, is a restaurant where you'll get an authentic Japanese meal.

Prims (Pelayo St) is a cheap, cheerful and lively barbecue place that does good fish, has lots of tables and a band at night.

Calzada (Duterte St) is the local hard-rock café.

The **eateries** around Santa Ana Wharf and the Muslim Fishing Village have a strong emphasis on fish; they're lively – especially in the early evening – and cheap.

Claude Café (Rizal St; meals from P200) is a French restaurant with an extensive menu and good food.

On F Torres St, off Laurel St, is a line of international restaurants if you want to browse before eating. **Harana Restaurant** has Filipino and barbecued food; next door is the long-established **Mongolian Garden**; a little further along on the left is **Nikkei Oriental** (selling Chinese food despite the name); and then **Ajmura** and **Sushi Riki** Japanese restaurants, followed by **Pescadero** for seafood.

Entertainment
Most of the top-end hotels offer live music nightly and ballroom dancing at least once a week (try the 7th floor of the **Hotel Maguindanao** if you want to trip the light fantastic), with discos usually on Friday.

Dance at **Zirkle Disco** *(JP Laurel Ave; open nightly)*, behind Victoria Plaza, or at **Spam's** *(Palma Gil St)*. These are the 20-somethings' scenes. There's also dancing at **Calzada** restaurant.

If you need a dose of Western company and food, there are a couple of expat bars around town, including: **Hagar's**, a block before the Insular Century Hotel (coming from the direction of the city), which is famous for European sausages, salamis and cheese.

There's good bar food, a restaurant upstairs and live music on Friday.

Shopping
If you're looking for handicrafts, shop around at the **Aldevinco Mall** (also known as the Aldevinco Shopping Center). It's a rabbit warren of stalls with fabric, batik, weavings, carvings etc. Bargain and look carefully before you buy; some stuff is of very poor quality. Take your time – the vendors can be pushy, especially on slow days (almost every day). The stallholders are also very keen to change your US dollars or Japanese yen – again, take your time and shop around.

The **T'boli Weaving Center** at the Insular Century Hotel has some beautiful (and pricey) artefacts and fabric. The **New City Commercial Center** (NCCC) and **Gaisano Mall** are the big department stores in town.

Locals tell you that once you eat Davao durian you'll always come back to the city, and when it's in season there are plenty of stalls selling this strange and delicious fruit. You may have to work at acquiring the taste for it. It's in season from September to December, and when it's out of season they say durian ice cream has the same effect!

Getting There & Away
Air From Manila, PAL flies to Davao at 5.10am, 11am and 4.30pm daily. Air Philippines has daily flights from Manila to Davao at 5am and 8am, while Cebu Pacific flies at 5am, 9am, 11am and 4pm daily.

Air Philippines, Cebu Pacific and **PAL** (☎ 221 5641) fly several times a day to Davao from Cebu.

The current Brunei, Indonesia, Malaysia, Philippines East Asian Group Area (BIMP-EAGA) initiatives have made travel to/from Indonesia theoretically simpler. Presently **Bouraq Airlines** (☎ 233 0016) and Air Philippines fly between Manado and Davao once weekly.

Silk Air (☎ 221 6430) flies to Davao from Singapore via Cebu on Tuesday, Thursday and Saturday.

Bus There are buses between Davao and Cagayan de Oro, Butuan and Surigao (around P220, eight to 10 hours to each destination), south to General Santos (P95, 3½ hours) and west to Cotabato City. All these services run several times daily and all long-distance bus transport is based at the Ecoland terminal 2km south of Davao City centre. Manila-bound buses also leave from here. Keep your eyes open at the terminal; several bombs, thought to have been placed by disgruntled former bus line employees, exploded here during late 1999 and early 2000.

Buses to Eagle Conservation Center at Calinan leave from a small terminal on the corner of San Pedro St and Quirino St.

Boat Big interisland boats use the terminal at Sasa, by the Caltex tanks 8km north of town. This is also where boats to Paradise Island Beach Resort on Samal Island leave. Jeepneys run here, or take a taxi for around P70.

Other boats to Samal and Talikud islands go from Santa Aña Wharf in town.

WG&A has vessels leaving for Manila at 11pm Monday and Wednesday (P1680 to P5840, 31 hours); in the opposite direction boats leave Manila for Davao at 2pm on Monday and 10am Saturday.

To Cebu City, Sulpicio Lines has boats going via General Santos at 8pm on Sunday, and via Surigao at 7pm Wednesday.

WG&A has boats going to Zamboanga at 11pm on Wednesday.

There is a scheduled boat from Davao to Indonesia via General Santos every Friday from Sasa Pier, but details change often; check with the city tourism office at city hall.

Getting Around
The airport is 12km north of the city. A taxi to the city will cost around P70. From the city, jeepneys in the direction of Sasa go towards the airport; you'll then need to take a tricycle to the terminal.

The station for long-distance buses is at Ecoland, 2km south of the city centre. A taxi there will cost about P50, a jeepney about P5.

AROUND DAVAO
Samal Island
Samal is a sizeable island lying off Davao. Pearls are again being cultivated on a small scale near the site of a once-lucrative pearl farm near Kaputian, but most island communities rely on fishing for their livelihoods. There are a few resorts and settlements along the west coast, along which a rugged road runs. Extended motorcycles will take you around.

The island makes an easy day-trip from Davao, with Paradise Island Beach Resort (entry fee P30) a comfortable budget base. For those in need of pampering, the five-star Pearl Farm Beach Resort is a luxurious alternative; a day trip from the Insular Century Hotel, including boat transfers, use of the resort's facilities and a superb buffet lunch, will cost P1000. There's **snorkelling** and **diving** around the island – including two Japanese wrecks just off Pearl Farm beach – but you need to take local advice on the best and safest places to go, as Samal is on a busy shipping channel and there are some strong currents.

Places to Stay The **Paradise Island Beach Resort** (cottages from P750) offers overnight cottages; be warned it can get very busy and noisy on weekends. There's a good, reasonably priced restaurant.

Pearl Farm Beach Resort (☎ 221 9970, fax 221 7729; ℯ pearldav@weblinq.com; rooms US$110-600) has, as you'd expect from a five-star resort, tasteful and comfortable accommodation set in lush grounds, with private beaches and swimming pools, and

diving and other water-sports facilities. Ask about promotional specials.

Samal Island Casino Resort (rooms from P1200) is a newish place further south. Rooms are reasonably priced, but the restaurant is relatively expensive.

It is a favourite venue for seminars and group meetings.

Getting There & Away Pumpboats go regularly to Paradise Island Beach Resort from the big Caltex tanks near Sasa Pier (P5, 10 minutes). The other resorts organise transfers for their guests from Santa Aña Wharf in the city.

Talikud Island
This is the little island off the southwest point of Samal. It is much less developed than Samal, and has some spectacular coral gardens off its west coast that have regenerated well since dynamite and cyanide fishing stopped about 10 years ago.

Places to Stay The **Isla Reta** (cottages P400-500), on the east coast of the island, will appeal to budget travellers. There are simple bamboo cottages, and you can get equally simple food (or bring your own and the staff will cook it for a small fee).

There are extensive grounds and beaches to explore, and a fish sanctuary for snorkelling just offshore.

Pacific Little Secret (☎/fax 227 8216; rates US$100 per person per day, minimum 2 people), an exquisite and private resort just north of Isla Reta, will appeal to travellers chasing luxury. It sleeps a maximum four people in two beautiful breezy houses decorated with ethnic art.

There is a gazebo on the edge of the water, and secluded sitting areas and verandas. Rates include speedboat transfers to/from Davao, all meals, and use of a pumpboat and boat driver on call.

MINDANAO & SULU

Getting There & Away Boats run to Talikud five times a day from Santa Aña Wharf, Davao (P20, one hour). The first boat usually leaves at around 7am. The tiny township and jetty at Santa Cruz is a couple of hundred metres from Isla Reta, though most boats will drop off at the resort.

Eagle Conservation Center

A must for nature lovers, Eagle Conservation Center (☎ 221 2030; admission P25; open 8am-5pm daily), at Malagos, 36km from Davao, is the headquarters of the Philippine Eagle Foundation, which is dedicated to conserving these fantastic and endangered birds, also known as Monkey-Eating Eagles. Here you can see the results of the captive breeding programme – there have been several successes – along with other rare and endemic species of birds and animals such as Philippine deer and the wonderfully named Philippine warty pigs.

The camp is set in a pocket of native forest, and there are enough wild birds flitting around to keep the most avid bird-watcher happy. There is an informative video about eagles in the wild and the threats they are facing.

Volunteer guides are around at weekends to answer questions. Donation boxes are strategically placed throughout the grounds to help further the foundation's work. It gets *very* busy though, and if watching animals among hordes of noisy groups isn't your thing, plan to get here at opening time to beat the crowds.

A couple of kilometres before the camp as you drive up from Calinan is the **Malagos Garden Resort**, which is open for day use and has a swimming pool and garden with orchids; stop and cool off on the way back. Again, you might find that the centre can get very busy at the weekend.

Getting There & Away Take a bus to Calinan (P15, 45 minutes) from the bus terminal on the corner of San Pedro and Quirino Sts in Davao. Buses leave every 20 minutes. Jeepneys going in that direction (southbound) can be caught anywhere along Claro M Recto Ave or Pichon St. In Calinan, take a jeepney or tricycle (P5, 10 minutes) to Eagle Conservation Center at Malagos.

A special ride up to the camp from Calinan will cost around P80.

Mt Apo

At 2954m Mt Apo is the highest mountain in the Philippines and, most mornings, is clearly visible towering above Davao from unexpected points around the city. There are recommended climbing routes up the mountain, but these are not mere strolls – you need to be pretty fit to tackle them.

The trek takes in forest, waterfalls, volcanic craters, the possibility of Philippine eagles in the wild along with other animals & birds, and exotic plants such as orchids and carnivorous pitcher plants. Travellers not wanting to make the full climb can still camp at the start of the trail and walk in the foothills.

Current information on the state of the trail, guide hire, security issues etc can be found at the regional tourism department in Davao, but for better and more local information contact the **Kidapawan Tourism Council** (☎ 238 1831) in Kidapawan. A good brochure is available from both these offices detailing transport to the region, suggested routes, guide and porter fees, and recommended equipment.

This is the minimum three-day suggested schedule for trekking, starting from Kidapawan.

Day One Morning registration and briefing at Kidapawan Tourism Council at the Museum Building on Laurel St, Kidapawan. The registration fee is P50 for 'foreign' trekkers. Then take a jeepney to Ilomavis and Lake Agko. Arrange porters and overnight at Lake Agko.

Day Two Early start to hike to Lake Venado. Packed lunch on the way. Arrive at Lake Venado mid-afternoon and camp.

Day Three Dawn trek to the summit (leave camp at 6am). Reach summit by 8.30am; eat snacks and spend a couple of hours. Back at Lake Venado by 11.30am for lunch. Start hiking back by noon to Lake Agko; arrive at camp at 5pm and take jeepney back to Kidapawan.

Getting There & Away From Davao, take a bus from the Ecoland bus terminal to Kidapawan. Buses leave every 30 minutes (P45 to P63, two hours).

From Cotabato, take a bus from Magallanes St terminal to Kidapawan. Buses leave every 30 minutes (P54 to P72, three hours).

To jump-off points for the trek, take a jeepney from Kidapawan bus terminal to Ilomavis, 17km away (P30, one hour, or special trip P500).

DAVAO DEL NORTE

This province lies between Davao City and the Compostela Valley, and is little developed for tourism. Using Tagum as a base, you can visit the **Santo Tomas Penal colony** 40km northwest; this unlikely sounding tourist attraction consists of a plantation worked by the prisoners and an outlet for their carvings and other handicrafts. You can also visit the Tadeco banana and abaca plantations at Panabo, 25km east of the city, and the Hijo banana, cacao, coconut and guava plantation 10km away. The latter has a **guesthouse**. There are several lodgings in Tagum, the best of which is probably the **Molave Hotel** *(Osmeña St)*.

COMPOSTELA VALLEY

This area, to the north of Davao City, split from Davao del Norte and became a separate province in 1998. It is little visited and little developed, and more adventurous travellers may wish to explore it, using Maragusan township, 76km northeast of Tagum, as a base. There is a community of indigenous Mansaka people here, and the wildlife-rich **Bagong Silang Cold Spring area** where tarsiers (locally called *amagu*) and *maral* (wild cat) can still sometimes be seen. In **Mainit National Park**, near the provincial capital of Nabunturan, two rivers, fed by one hot and one cold spring, meet in a large swimming area believed to have curative powers because of its high sulphur content. Stay at the **Agwacan Inland Resort** *(rooms P350-800)* in Maragusan.

GENERAL SANTOS (DADIANGAS)

☎ 083 • pop 411,822

Formerly Dadiangas, the city was renamed in 1965 in honour of General Paulino Santos who, with accompanying Christian Visayans and Tagalogs, established a settlement here in 1939. Prior to this time, the area was inhabited mostly by Maguindanao Muslims and B'laan tribespeople. The city's history is showcased in two small museums: at the Notre Dame Dadiangas College (NDDC) is a **museum of memorabilia** about General Santos (the person); and at the Mindanao State University (MSU) campus near the airport is a **museum of Muslim and tribal culture**. Both are open during school hours. The annual cultural event, the **Kalilangan Festival**, takes place from 22–27 February. The festi-

val includes demonstrations of local dance, arts and cooking, as well as a 'trade fair' where locally produced handicrafts are sold.

A fast-growing city, General Santos is the centre of a big tuna fishing and canning industry (seven of the 12 canneries in the Philippines are based here), and is surrounded by asparagus farms and cattle ranches. The tuna in all its glory is celebrated annually in the **Tuna Festival** from 1–5 September when, among other things, there is – we kid you not – a competition for the best-dressed tuna. The **fishing boats unload** and sell their catch at the fishing port near Makar Wharf from about 5am to 9am and it's fun to watch.

About 8km out of town on the road to Koronadal (Marbel) is the Lagare Springfield Resort and the Olaer Spring Resort. **Cold springs** have been tapped into small falls and big pools, and there are day-use facilities from P10 to P30.

Weekends are very busy and it's probably wise to steer clear of the inevitable parties of men drinking beer.

Information

The very helpful **tourist office** *(☎ 554 3097, fax 552 8385;* e *gemgsc@mozcom.com; National Hwy)* is in the Department of Trade & Industry.

The **PNB**, by the city hall, will change US dollars. There's an **Equitable PCI Bank**, next to the Sydney Hotel, which will advance cash on MasterCard credit cards. Another **Equitable PCI Bank** *(Ireneo Santiago Ave)* will advance cash on Visa credit cards.

There are **Internet cafés** along Sergio Osmeña St, and near the church on Osmeña St.

Places to Stay – Budget

South Sea Lodge II *(☎ 552 5146; cnr Magsaysay & Salazar Sts; rooms with fan/aircon & bathroom from P240/590)* has good, clean rooms.

Warning

In April 2002, 15 people were killed in three separate bomb blasts in General Santos City, one of which happened in a busy shopping mall. Travellers should check the current situation with their embassy before travelling to General Santos City.

GENERAL SANTOS (DADIANGAS)

PLACES TO STAY
1 Tierra Verde 1
2 T'boli Hotel
5 East Asia Royale Hotel
20 Sydney Hotel
22 Vince's Pension House
25 South Sea Lodge II
25 Hotel Sansu & Wok 'n'
    Chow Restaurant
26 Matutum Hotel

PLACES TO EAT
17 NR Lechon House
21 Billabong Café

OTHER
3 Doctor's Hospital
4 Dept of Trade and
   Industry; Tourist Office

6 St Elizabeth
   Hospital
7 NDC College
   Museum
8 Mindanao State
   University
9 Nenita's Internet
10 Bula-ong Terminal
11 Police Station
12 City Hall
13 PNB
14 Post Office
15 Internet Cafe
16 White Tip Divers
18 Church
19 PCI Bank
24 Equitable Bank
27 Philippine Airlines
    & Air Philippines

Vince's Pension House (☎ 553 5983; *Magsaysay St; rooms from P220*) is tatty but clean. It has lots of luminous flashing Sacred Heart pictures which can be reassuring or disturbing, depending on your frame of mind.

Matutum Hotel (☎ 552 4901; *Pedro Acharon Blvd; rooms from P200*) is OK, but it's noisy and the bathrooms need some serious maintenance.

Places to Stay – Mid-Range
There are some good mid-range hotels in General Santos.

T'boli Hotel (☎ 552 3042; *National Hwy; rooms P450-650*) is the best in the mid-range. The good-sized, quiet rooms have private sitting rooms. There is also a restaurant.

Tierra Verde 1 (☎ 552 4500; *rooms P410-810*), next door to T'boli Hotel, has reasonable, clean and simple rooms. It has an outdoor bar and decent-sized swimming pool, which nonguests can use for P50.

Hotel Sansu (☎ 552 7219, fax 552 7221; *rooms from P350*) is certainly central, but it's also very noisy.

Cambridge Farm Hotel (☎ 553 6310, fax 554 5614; *rooms P400-1000*), an extraordin-

ary place, gets full marks for originality. The rooms are cluttered with knick-knacks and each is individually furnished.

The bathrooms are a treat; there is a garden bar and restaurant, a good-sized pool (day use is P25) and – not so great – a mini-zoo. The hotel is about 10 minutes out of town on the road to Koronadal. Taxis to/from town cost about P50, and about P150 from the airport.

Places to Stay – Top End
East Asia Royale Hotel (☎ 553 4119, fax 553 4129; e *royale@gslink.net; rooms from P1500*), recently opened, is a 1st-class business hotel with the sort of comfortable rooms you'd expect, but no pool. Service and tax are extra.

Sydney Hotel (☎ 552 5479, fax 552 5478; *rooms from P1184*), in the centre of town, has very pleasant rooms, but those overlooking the park and traffic circle are VERY noisy; ask for somewhere quiet.

Places to Eat
NR Lechon House (*Quirino St*) does good barbecue meals.

Fiesta sa Barrio, near the Gaisano Mall, is a seafood place specialising in Filipino fish dishes. In the same area is the **Ni-moshi-be**, a good Japanese restaurant.

Billabong Café, beside the Sydney Hotel, bakes good sugar-free 'Australian' bread and serves Filipino food.

Getting There & Away

Air PAL flies from Manila to General Santos at 6.30am daily. Air Philippines also has flights from Manila at 8am, returning daily (via Cebu) at 11.20am.

Bus There are regular bus services between General Santos and Davao (P95, 3½ hours), Cagayan de Oro (eight to 10 hours), Koronadal (Marbel; one hour) and Butuan (eight to 10 hours). The bus terminal for all services is at Bula-ong, on the western edge of town.

Boat Negros Navigation has boats bound for Manila via Zamboanga and Iloilo on Panay, leaving at 10pm on Thursday.

Sulpicio Lines boats leave for Manila on Friday at 6pm, and for Cebu City on Monday at 10am.

EPA Shipping Line (☎ 380 3591) has boats leaving Monday and Thursday for Bitung (Manado). Schedules change, so check with the shipping line; its office is inside the port compound at Makar Wharf. The journey takes about 36 hours. Officially, there is no problem with foreigners making this trip, but you may wish to check with the tourism office first. You will need to finalise any Indonesian visa requirements with the consul- ate in Davao before leaving.

Getting Around

The passenger airport has relocated to an area beyond Makar Wharf. A taxi to town will cost about P100.

Boat Makar Wharf is 4km from town. A taxi will cost about P50 and a tricycle P20. The shorter road there can be very busy and slow, but there is an alternative route along the National Hwy. This is a distance of about 10km and will cost about P60.

Jeepney, Tricycle & Taxi There is a flat fare (P3) around town by jeepney and tricycle. There are plenty of taxis and the flag fall is P20. The integrated bus and jeepney terminal is at Bula-ong on the western edge of town, about 1km from the town centre.

AROUND GENERAL SANTOS

There are white-sand beaches and areas for good snorkelling and diving around Maasim and Glan on the edge of **Sarangani Bay**. Take an L300 minibus from Bula-ong terminal to either town (P35, one hour).

Further south are **Sarangani Island**, **Balut Island** and **Ulanbani Island**, presently undeveloped but with good dive spots. The *Tropicana Express* boat (☎ 552 7628) leaves Makar Wharf in General Santos on Monday, Wednesday, Friday and Sunday for Balut and Sarangani (P200 one way, three to four hours). There was no commercial accommodation at the time of writing.

It might be possible to climb **Mt Matutum** in either two or three days, and camp at the top. In March 2002 trekking up the mountain was discontinued due to the extremely dry weather caused by the El Niño phenomenon, but if you're interested in doing the climb, check with the **Sarangani Bay Area Outdoor Club** (SBAOC; ☎ 522 3861) in General Santos. To get to Mt Matutum, take a jeepney or motorcycle to Polomolok and from there take another up to Lemblisong in the foothills.

LAKE SEBU

Beautiful Lake Sebu, ancestral home of the T'boli people, sits at an elevation of about 300m in a bowl of hills and forests. Enjoy the cool evenings at this altitude, where the thick woven T'boli clothes suddenly make sense. The annual **Lem-Lunay Festival** takes place in the second week of November and is a celebration of T'boli culture, culminating with horse fights – the sport of royalty in local culture – when two stallions fight over a mare in heat. (It's neither as bloody nor as fatal as cockfighting.)

Try to visit in time for the **Saturday market**, when tribespeople come in from the surrounding communities. Don't expect to see anybody wearing their traditional costumes, though. Except during special occasions, the T'boli dress is no different from any other Filipino's. Visit the **T'boli Museum** (admission P5; open 7am-5pm daily) on the road to Punta Isla. It has a small but good collection. A weaver is usually there, dyeing abaca with vegetable dyes and weaving the dyed fibre

Warning

Lake Sebu has been the scene of some security alerts in past years. There have been no major problems since 1996, but it's wise to check the current situation with the tourist offices in General Santos, Koronadal (Marbel) or Cotabato before setting off.

on a backstrap loom. Take a **boat trip** on Lake Sebu, **bird-watch**, and hike to either (or both) **Seven Falls** and **Traankini Falls**. A motorcycle will take you to within about a half-hour walk of each.

Places to Stay & Eat

Punta Isla (*dorm beds P75, cottages P300*) is a pretty resort on the lakeside, with a restaurant specialising in fresh-cooked tilapia fish caught from the lake and great views. It has good cottages and dorm beds. During the day, music booms from every day-use cottage, which detracts somewhat from the peaceful outlook.

On the same road, and offering facilities for about the same price, are **Estares Resort** and **Artacho Resort**. Both are nicely located on the lake, but have less attractive cottages than Punta Isla. Weekends are very busy.

Gono Lembong Lodge (*dorm beds P60, rooms P300*), 1km or so further along the main lakeside road, is managed by the local tourism department. The view is good, but the grounds aren't attractive.

Lakeview Tourist Lodge (*double P100*), near the jeepney terminal, has one very basic double room, with a small souvenir shop attached.

All the resorts have **restaurants** and there are **eateries** at the terminal.

Shopping

Lake Sebu is a good place to buy T'boli handicrafts – brassware and beads particularly – and weavings. Try **Mindanao Etnika** about halfway along the lake road, and browse in the many roadside souvenir stalls.

Getting There & Away

Koronadal (Marbel) is the junction for trips to Lake Sebu. Get there by bus from Cotabato or General Santos (P33, one hour).

Buses drop off in Koronadal on General Santos Dr at their respective terminals; from there make your way to the L300 minivan terminals near the junction of General Santos Dr and Alunan Ave.

You can take an L300 minivan (P15, 45 minutes) or a jeepney to Surallah. At the terminal in Surallah take a jeepney (P25, 45 minutes) or hire a motorcycle (P120, 30 minutes) to Lake Sebu.

Getting Around

Motorcycles are the public transport in Lake Sebu. Rides to the local resorts cost between P5 and P10 depending on distance. You can negotiate special-trip rates of between P75 and P100 per hour.

SURALLAH
pop 66,208

You pass through Surallah on your way to Lake Sebu from Koronadal (see Getting There & Away in the previous Lake Sebu section). If you need to overnight go to **VIP Trading** (*Camia St*), just opposite the L300 terminus, and take a simple room there with the Lagamayo family (*P200-250*). If you want to make any special trips by jeep, they can put you in touch with the Fernandez family, who may be willing to hire out their private car and driver.

KORONADAL (MARBEL)
pop 133,786

While Koronadal has been the official name of the provincial capital of South Cotabato since 1947, many people still refer to it as Marbel – a B'laan word meaning 'murky waters' – and that is the word you will see on most public transport vehicles heading there. Historically, it's linked to the animist B'laan people and Maguindanao Muslims, though now the population is predominantly Christian. The small **museum** (*Alunan Ave*) in the Gymnasium and Cultural Centre showcases primarily T'boli culture (and devotes much wall- and shelf-space to the museum's benefactors). Koronadal is the jump-off point for trips to Lake Sebu.

Information

There's a **tourist office** in the Vice-Mayor's department in the City Hall. The **PNB** opposite the Ramona Plaza Hotel will change US dollars.

For email, **Weblink** (*Alunan Ave*) is opposite the Cultural Centre. The server is long-distance though, which makes it a comparatively expensive P75 per hour.

Places to Stay & Eat

Alabado's Home *(cnr Alunan Ave & Rizal St; rooms with fan & bathroom P175, doubles with air-con & bathroom P450)* is in the budget range. It's on the main road and pretty noisy, but cheaper rooms are fine value. Small and dismal rooms with air-con are not such good value.

Ramona Plaza Hotel *(☎ 228 3284, fax 228 3151; General Santos Dr; rooms from P500)* offers good mid-range accommodation. Rooms have air-con, bathroom and cable TV.

Marvella Plaza *(☎/fax 228 2063; General Santos Dr; rooms P550-950)* is the best hotel in town. Rooms are OK but in need of some maintenance. There's also a swimming pool.

The Ramona Plaza and Marvella Plaza both have good **coffee shops** attached.

Getting There & Away

There are regular bus services from General Santos (P40, one hour) and from Cotabato (three hours). Make a connection here for Lake Sebu via Surallah.

COTABATO

☎ 064 • pop 150,450

This city of Maguindanao people lies on the Rio Grande de Mindanao, often called the Pulangi River. 'Maguindanao' is a compilation of the local words for kin, country and lake, so literally they are 'people of the lake country', from the floodplains around this great river. Islam is the oldest religion here, introduced in 1475, with Christianity a comparatively recent arrival, brought in by Jesuits in 1871. Cotabato City does not hold a great deal of interest for travellers, though the **Araw ng Kutabato Festival** in mid-June, with its mammoth dance parades, is a cultural highlight.

In December the **Shariff Kabungsuan Festival** commemorates the arrival of Islam in the region and involves river parades of decorated boats. Around the city itself, head up **Piedro Colina Hill** for good views of the city and coast and note the American-designed **old Provincial Capitol** building. At the foot of the hill lies **Kutawato Cave**, which is, bizarrely, right in the middle of a busy road intersection; inside are saltwater pools, an underground river and bats.

The **Cotabato City Hall** has an interesting facade of mostly Muslim influence.

A couple of kilometres out of town you'll find the **Regional Autonomous Government Centre**, which houses a museum and is the seat of government for the Autonomous Region of Muslim Mindanao.

Information

The **tourist office** *(☎ 421 7804, fax 421 8969)* is located in the old Provincial Capitol Building on Piedro Colina Hill.

The **PNB** will change US dollars.

Infotech *(S Pendatun Ave; open 8am-8pm)* provides Internet access for P30 per hour.

Places to Stay & Eat

El Corazon Hotel *(Makakua St; rooms with fan & bathroom from P260, with air-con, bathroom & TV from P560)*, in the centre of town, is OK.

City Plaza Hotel *(☎ 421 9148; Makakua St; rooms P300-700)* is newer and brighter than El Corazon Hotel, but a bit noisy.

Hotel Castro *(☎ 421 7523, fax 421 6404; Sinsuat St; rooms P550-850)* has small rooms, but friendly staff and a small, quiet coffee shop. There is a good Filipino fast-food restaurant on the ground floor and there are fruit stalls opposite.

Estosan Garden Hotel *(☎ 421 6777, fax 421 5488; Governor Gutierrez Blvd; rooms from P1440)* is the best hotel in town – well, it's a couple of kilometres out of town, next to the Regional Autonomous Government Centre.

There is a pool that nonguests can use for P100 and a pleasant coffee shop.

Mami King *(Don Rufino Alonzo St)* has tasty Filipino fast food, with a good bakery attached.

Getting There & Away

Air PAL *(☎ 421 2086)* flies daily to/from Manila.

Bus & Minivan Regular buses run daily between Davao and Cotabato (P170 aircon, five hours). There are no direct buses from General Santos and Koronadal. You have to take a bus to Tacurong (P20, 45 minutes) and then an L300 minivan to Cotabato (P70, 1½ hours).

Boat There are two wharf areas in Cotabato. Boats to Pagadian go from the wharf right in the centre of town. Interisland boats, and boats to Zamboanga, leave from Polloc Pier, 24km away. A jeepney there costs P15.

Boats to Zamboanga leave several times a week.

Boats to Pagadian (P110, five to six hours) leave around 7pm nightly, depending on the tide.

A Cebu Ferries boat leaves for General Santos at 6am Saturday (15 hours).

Getting Around
The airport is about 10km south of town. A jeepney going to Awang will take you there for P5, or a taxi will cost around P100.

ZAMBOANGA
☎ 062 • pop 606,794
There are three possible derivations of Zamboanga's exotic-sounding name. It may come from the 16th-century Malay word *jambangan*, meaning 'land of flowers', or from *samboangan*, a 'docking point', identified in an early Spanish map. Its origin may also lie in *sabuan*, the wooden pole used by local tribespeople to navigate their *vintas* – shallow draft sailboats – over the coastal flats. Take your pick!

Zamboanga has been a trading post for centuries and this, together with its closeness to the island of Borneo, has given the area an interesting and eclectic mix of inhabitants and cultures. Islam is strong here, as is Christianity, while animist beliefs and practices are still subscribed to by many of the people of the Sulu Archipelago. The most commonly spoken language is Chavacano, a Spanish-Creole language made up of Malay grammar and unconjugated Spanish verbs. Spanish speakers will find themselves understanding most of what they hear.

The city's main festival is the **Fiesta de Nuestra Señora Virgen del Pilar**, taking place from 10–12 October. It is a Christian festival, but is also a great opportunity for street parties, parades, dances, markets and food fairs, and enjoyed by all the community. It also has a big regatta that brings *vintas* with traditional brilliantly coloured angular cloth sails out on the water.

The city requires more energy and patience than many other Filipino cities. There are groups of lounging, aggressive youths on street corners and in the plaza, which may be intimidating, and lots of persistent and demanding beggars, many of whom are distressingly disabled.

Zamboanga is the headquarters of Southcom, the Philippine Army's Southern Command post, and the military and police presence is noticeable.

Information
The **tourist office** (☎ 991 0218; ⓔ dotr9@ jetlink.com.ph; Valderoza St) is next to the Lantaka Hotel. It has a small but good library

---

Warning

Zamboanga has a reputation among Filipinos from other areas of being a place of kidnappings, robberies and Muslim insurgency. This reputation is also fostered by the international media, which often uses Zamboanga as its dateline when reporting on anything that happens in the Sulu Archipelago.

At the time of writing, both the city of Zamboanga and the surrounding areas, including the roads north, were extremely dicey. A bomb blast in the city killed five people in October 2001, and in February of 2002 several people were injured when a bomb exploded at a cinema. Check the current situation with your embassy before setting out for Zamboanga.

The hinterland is definitely out of bounds to all but the most adventurous (or foolhardy) traveller. Kidnappings of both locals and foreigners do occur, there are regular shooting incidents between government forces and anti-government groups, and buses are bombed on the road. Road travel to Zamboanga from other parts of Mindanao is not advisable; not all buses are bombed or robbed of course, but the number that are is significant enough to be an issue. If you decide to come, it's safer to arrive by boat or plane.

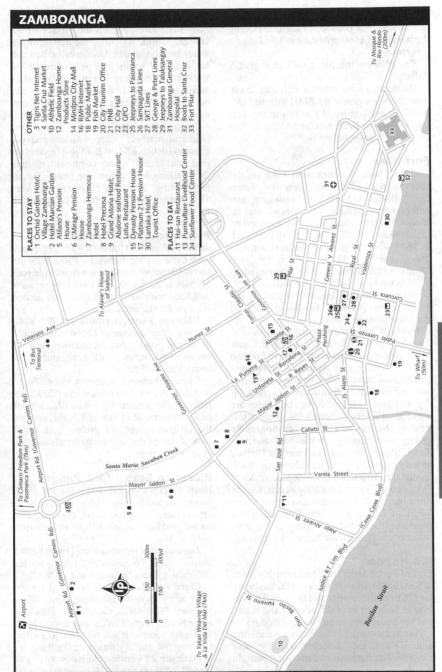

of books about the Philippines that travellers are welcome to browse through, including the wonderful 1999 publication *Mindanao – a portrait*.

The **PNB** on the plaza will change US dollars.

There are many Internet cafes in town. Near the town centre try **RMH Internet** *(Almonte St; open daily)*. If you're staying near the airport, use **Tigris Net** *(open Mon-Sat)*, at the top of Mayor Jaldon St.

Fort Pilar

Spend an hour or two at Fort Pilar (at the southeastern end of town near the waterfront). It's a solid and squat building, partially and sympathetically restored, and its chequered history reads like this: founded by the Spaniards in 1635; attacked by the Dutch in 1646; deserted in 1663; reconstructed in 1666; rebuilt in 1719; stormed by 3000 Moros in 1720; cannonaded by the British in 1798; abandoned by the Spaniards in 1898; occupied by the US in 1899; seized by the Japanese in 1942; and, finally, claimed by the Philippines in 1946.

Inside is a **museum** *(open 9am-noon & 2pm-5pm Sun-Fri)*, with two impressive galleries. One is a **marine exhibit** where you can learn everything you wanted to know (and much, much more) about marine ecosystems and animals. The information may be a bit dry and dusty for laypeople, but there are some good displays. Across the inner courtyard of the fort is a terrific **ethnographic gallery** concentrating on the boat-dwelling Sama Dilaut (otherwise known as the Badjao, or sea gypsies) of the Sulu Archipelago. Walk around the **ramparts** for 360-degree views of Zamboanga City and the busy ocean. On the fort's outer wall is an altar and shrine to the Virgin of Pilar and masses of candle sellers providing the individual 'bunches' of thin, coloured candles that are burned at the shrine.

Rio Hondo

East of Fort Pilar is the Muslim stilt village of Rio Hondo; its mosque is a clear landmark visible from the ramparts of the fort. The village is built out over the edge of the water, and the houses are joined by foot bridges.

Ask at the tourist office before wandering around Rio Hondo. Local reactions to your presence can range from curious to outright hostile.

The Waterfront

Spend late afternoon on the **terrace of the Lantaka Hotel**, watching the action on the water and the sunset. Unobtrusive hawkers lay beautiful shells and pearls on the sea wall of the hotel to tempt guests, but be sure you know what you can legally take out of the Philippines – and to your destination – if you want to buy marine products.

Beyond the hotel are the chaotic and colourful **markets**. Keep walking and you come to **Justice RT Lim Blvd** just beyond the main port area. It's busy at sunset with families walking, kids swimming, people fishing and boating, and food stalls and hawkers. This is where *vinta* regattas take place during fiesta.

Places to Stay – Budget

Atilano's Pension House *(☎ 991 0783; rooms with fan & shared bathroom P200, with air-con & bathroom P400)*, on a quiet side road off Mayor Jaldon St, is a rambling series of buildings with sections of grass and garden. It's fine for the price.

L'Mirage Pension House *(☎ 991 3962; Mayor Jaldon St; rooms P220-400)* is simple, clean and good value. Ventilation slats between rooms mean you'll hear your neighbours loud and clear.

Dynasty Pension House *(☎ 991 4579; Almonte St; rooms with fan/air-con P250/500)*, right in the centre of town, offers good budget rooms with fan and bathroom, but the air-con rooms are grubby and small; look at one of the mid-range hotels if this is your price range.

Places to Stay – Mid-Range

Hotel Preciosa *(☎ 991 2020, fax 993 0055; Mayor Jaldon St; rooms P680-1000)*, near the city centre, has good-sized, clean, if dull, rooms, and lazy catfish drifting in the atrium pool.

Zamboanga Hermosa Hotel *(☎ 991 2040; Mayor Jaldon St; rooms P650 & P750)* has OK rooms, but a bit small and stark.

Grand Astoria Hotel *(☎ 991 2510, fax 991 2533; ℮ info@grandastoria.com; Mayor Jaldon St; rooms P650-4200)*, the newest of the mid-range hotels, is good value (and always busy) with neat rooms. It's a hit with journalists covering the military action on Basilan.

Platinum 21 Pension House *(☎ 991 2514, fax 991 2709; Barcelona St; rooms from P600)* is a bit old and tatty in comparison with the other hotels in this price range.

Places to Stay – Top End

Marcian Garden Hotel (☎ 991 2519, fax 991 1874; rooms from P660), near the airport, has a nice garden and pool area, and rooms are big and good value. But it's really noisy, being on the main road, with all rooms overlooking the function centre and, at time of writing, a construction site behind.

Orchid Garden Hotel (☎ 991 0031, fax 991 0035; rooms from P1200), near Marcian Garden Hotel, is an international-standard business hotel with good facilities including a big pool, but not much character.

Lantaka Hotel (☎ 991 2033, fax 991 1626; rooms from P1150), ageing but full of character and on the waterfront, is the best of the lot. It has big rooms with balconies, a refreshingly nice garden and pool, and great views everywhere.

Official rates are given here, but ask about any current promotional offers. If you can afford it, stay here. If you can't afford it, at least treat yourself to a drink on the terrace at sunset.

Places to Eat

Zamboanga is packed with eating options. For extremely cheap and tasty Filipino food, eat at the food stalls of the **Puericulture Livelihood Center** (La Purisma St). There's a great selection with lots of fresh fish and vegetable dishes.

Sunflower Food Center, near city hall on the plaza, serves good Filipino fast food and great desserts.

Village Zamboanga, next to the Hotel Orchid Garden on the airport road, has Filipino-style outdoor eating in a decent beer garden with live music.

Lotus Restaurant, within the Grand Astoria Hotel, serves passable Chinese food, but is rather upscale – not the sort of place for a quick bowl of noodles.

Other good seafood restaurants include **Alavar's House of Seafood** (Toribio St), a long-established restaurant recently relocated to Toribio St, and **La Vista del Mar**, about 7km out of town near the Yakan weaving village, with good sea views as its name suggests.

Hai-San (San José St), in town, serves Japanese-style seafood.

Lantaka Hotel does good Sunday all-you-can-eat buffet brunches in the terrace dining hall overlooking the harbour.

Shopping

The **market** on the waterfront has cheap clothing and batik from Malaysia and Indonesia. The **Zamboanga Home Products store** (cnr San José & Mayor Jaldon Sts) sells lots of rather ordinary souvenirs and some interesting, good-quality carvings, basketwork and woven fabrics. A good shopping mall in the town centre is the **Mindpro City Mall**.

Getting There & Away

Air PAL flies from Manila to Zamboanga at the ungodly hour of 4.50am daily, and there is another flight at 2.35pm daily, except Saturday and Sunday when flights leave at 3.30pm. Other flights are with Cebu Pacific at 6.20am daily, and Air Philippines at 11.40am.

Air Philippines flies to/from Cebu on Tuesday, Thursday, and Saturday.

Cebu Pacific flies to/from Davao on Monday, Wednesday, Friday and Sunday.

Bus If you must travel by road, buses to Zamboanga run several times daily until late morning from Dipolog (P220 air-con, eight hours) and Iligan (12 hours). But it really is not advisable to travel to Zamboanga by road (see the boxed text 'Warning' earlier in this section).

Boat WG&A has boats leaving for Manila twice a week. Depending on the route, journey time is around 48 hours.

Negros Nagivation and Sulpicio Lines boats leave for Manila once weekly, going via Iloilo on Panay. The trip takes about 32 hours.

George & Peter Lines leaves for Cebu City via Dumaguete on Negros once weekly, and to Cebu weekly via Dapitan on Mindanao and Dumaguete.

WG&A has weekly runs to Davao and Cotabat. Smaller boats also run daily to Cotabato.

There is a daily service to Pagadian (four hours), and Sulpicio Lines has boats leaving for General Santos weekly.

Aleson Lines has boats leaving Zamboanga for Sandakan in Malaysian Borneo twice weekly (17 hours).

Sampaguita Lines (☎ 993 1591) boats leave for Sandakan twice weekly (17 hours).

Getting Around

To/From the Airport The airport is 2km from the centre of Zamboanga. Walk out of the arrivals hall and catch a public tricycle for P5, or take a special trip for P20. Taxis cost around P50. From town you can take a jeepney marked 'Canelar-Airport' for P3.

Tricycle, Jeepney & Bus The flat fare around town is P3 by tricycle and jeepney. Special trips by tricycle cost around P100 per hour.

If for some reason you're determined to travel north by bus, the terminal is near the Santa Cruz market on the outskirts of town.

AROUND ZAMBOANGA
Pasonanca Park & Climaco Freedom Park

These public park areas are in the foothills of a nearby range, and offer opportunities for walking, getting a sense of green and space, and hearing birdsong.

In Pasonanca Park there are three big landscaped public swimming pools, an amphitheatre where conventions are held, and a permanent camp site, where squads of cadets train. Just opposite this site is a pretty, well-equipped treehouse, which you can ask the Mayor's office for permission to stay in, but be prepared to be on very public display if you do.

Climaco Freedom Park, named in honour of Mayor Climaco who was murdered by unknown assailants in the 1970s, is beside Pasonanca Park and has the Abong-Abong River running through it. It is the site of the former mayor's well-tended grave. There is a steep walk up a Stations of the Cross hillside, and good views out across the city and ocean.

Jeepneys to Pasonanca, which is 7km from the city, run from Campaner St off the plaza. Be prepared for a fair bit of hiking once you get there, as public transport is erratic inside the park. It's easier – but more expensive of course – to hire a tricycle for a couple of hours.

Yakan Weaving Village

Also 7km out of Zamboanga, but heading west, is the Yakan Weaving Village (open daily). Village is the wrong term really; it's no more than a collection of six or seven stalls selling some good Yakan weavings, a little brassware, and lots of very ordinary Indonesian and Malaysian mass-produced batik. Yakan are the indigenous people of nearby Basilan island, and their woven designs are characterised by bright colours and geometric designs. You can find wall hangings, table runners and place mats here, and there is a backstrap loom set up on which a weaver works, except at Friday prayer times.

Taluksangay
pop 6783

This is a Muslim settlement about 20km northeast of Zamboanga City. Like Rio Hondo in town, it's built partially out over the water and a mosque dominates the skyline. The same sort of unwritten rules for visitors apply here; wear appropriate clothing and ask if you want to take photos. Taluksangay is on the organised day-tour route from Zamboanga, so local people are used to visitors and can be quite forceful in asking for money. Jeepneys for Taluksangay leave from Pilar St in town.

Santa Cruz & Sacol Islands

Great Santa Cruz Island is just 15 minutes off the Zamboanga waterfront, and is home to small fishing communities. Visitors come to see the pinkish beach, so coloured from coral washing ashore.

You can swim here, but it's on a busy shipping channel and currents are strong. Boats for the island leave from the waterfront between the Lantaka Hotel and Fort Pilar; a return trip costs about P300 in a pumpboat seating four people.

Little Santa Cruz Island is a military base that is occasionally open to the public as a public relations exercise.

Taluksangay mosque

Sacol Island is not generally visited by tourists and is undeveloped except for fishing villages. There are security concerns about active NPA and MILF groups in the island's hills. The beaches are often guarded by armed soldiers.

Sulu Islands

The 500 or so islands of the Sulu Archipelago stretch some 300km from Basilan to Borneo, separating the Sulu and Celebes seas. The archipelago is divided into two provinces: Sulu, with its capital of Jolo (ho-**lo**), and Tawi-Tawi, with Bongao as its capital. It is further subdivided into the Jolo, Tawi-Tawi, Tapul, Papiantana and Pangutaran and Sibutu Groups of islands.

The isolated Cagayan de Tawi-Tawi Group lies off the coast of Borneo, mid-way between Palawan and the Sulu Archipelago. These are still dangerous waters for sailors, less because of the elements than because of pirates and smugglers. Smaller passenger vessels as well as cargo boats are regularly plundered in these seas.

About 94% of the archipelago's population is Muslim, and this area is part of the Autonomous Region of Muslim Mindanao (ARMM). The people of Sulu were the first in the Philippines to be converted to Islam in the 14th century. It remained a stronghold of Islam during the Spanish era and, in the early 20th century, it was the scene of pitched battles between US forces and the tough local Tausug people. Later, during WWII, local people joined with the US liberating forces against occupying Japanese troops. During 1974 the Moro National Liberation Front (MNLF), opposed to the imposition of martial law, fought fiercely against government forces in and around Jolo.

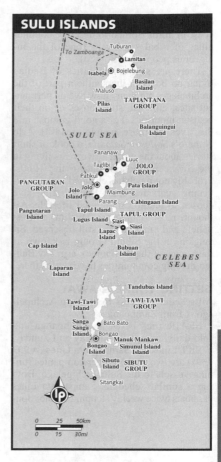

Warning

Travellers should be very cautious about travelling around the Sulu Archipelago, and should take seriously any current travel advice from the DOT in Zamboanga. As we went to press, the whole Sulu Archipelago was considered too dangerous for foreign tourists. We do not recommend that you go before consulting your embassy in Manila.

The town was destroyed and hostilities continue, to a greater or lesser degree, throughout the region.

Culturally the region is dominated by the Tausugs, or 'people of the current'. In and around Tawi-Tawi, the Samal people live in stilt houses by the coast. Terminology for the people of the region can be confusing. Samal is a generic term covering four distinct groups of people, sharing the Sama language, who inhabit the islands south of the Jolo Group. These are the Sama Talon, Sama Gimba, Sama Laut and Sama Pala-u peoples. The Sama Laut, meaning 'sea Sama' and often referred to in English as 'sea gypsies', are generally referred to as Badjao, though they themselves do not use this term. However 'Badjaw', from which

Badjao is derived, is a word used along the coast in north Borneo to describe communities of tribal sea Dyaks (one of the indigenous peoples of Borneo).

There are still communities of Badjao living on boats in the southern part of the archipelago, but many now live on permanent sites, either in stilt houses or on their boats at moorings. For a good glimpse into the lives of these people, read H Arlo Nimmo's *Songs of Salanda*, a book of short stories about the writer's two years living in the Sulu Archipelago during the 1960s. Probably not much has changed in the intervening years for those Badjao who have chosen to retain a traditional lifestyle. Although most Badjao are Muslim, animist beliefs and practices are still observed. Sitangkai, in the Sibutu Group, is known as the Venice of the Philippines, as many Badjao floating communities have settled there.

GETTING THERE & AWAY
All scheduled access to the Sulu Archipelago is from Zamboanga.

SEAIR flies between Zamboanga and Jolo daily, except Wednesday and Sunday.

SKT Lines and **Sampaguita Lines** (☎ 993 1591) are two of the bigger companies running vessels to the Sulu Archipelago. Both run a similar schedule. Sampaguita Lines has boats twice weekly stopping at Jolo, Bongao, Siasi and Sitangkai, and twice weekly for Jolo and Bongao only.

TAWI-TAWI GROUP
Bongao, the capital of Tawi-Tawi province, derives its name from the Tausug word *bangaw*, meaning heron. Today Bongao's wildlife is less famous for herons than for monkeys in great numbers on **Mt Bongao**, a sheer mountainous outcrop behind the township. There's an hour's hiking trail to the summit at 314m, with a **royal Muslim burial site** at the top (dress appropriately if you want to visit) and good views across the island chain. This sacred mountain is the site of a **festival** celebrated by Muslims and Christians alike in the second week of October. There is a small **museum** in the **old Spanish fort** near Bongao. Local people were instrumental in helping American forces to land and liberate the area from the Japanese in WWII, and Westerners here are called 'Milikan', a local distortion of 'American'.

Places to Stay
There are several simple lodgings in Bongao. **Southern Hotel** (*rooms P350*) is near the harbour. **Kasulutan Beach Resort** (*rooms P350*) is 2km out of town.

Beachside Inn and Restaurant (*rooms P350*) is 3km from town on the way to the airport.

Palawan

This long sliver of an island province deserves its exotic 'last frontier' aura. Stretching from the Mindoro Strait down to the tip of Borneo, it's a magnificent, coral-fringed range of jungle-clad mountains jutting up dramatically from the Sulu Sea. The flora and fauna in Palawan is quite unique to the island, and is said to have more in common with that of Borneo than with the rest of the Philippines. Due in equal parts to its rugged topography, its small population and its distance from other islands in the archipelago, Palawan has managed to stay largely pristine. You could spend a lifetime discovering new islands, beaches and reefs, particularly in the northern regions around El Nido and Busuanga Island.

As many other parts of the Philippines have received much promotion and subsequent tourism, the danger is that Palawan will also start to suffer from too much attention. A passionate local environmental movement and strong ecotourism ethics may help Palawan buck the trend and get as much out of tourism as tourism gets out of it. Sadly, local activists may not be enough to keep Palawan's underwater wonders intact. There are many challenges and threats, such as an increase of illegal fishing by Chinese trawlers plundering local waters – including Tubbataha Reefs National Park – almost at will.

Activities
Being a sparsely populated island has meant that forests and reefs are in a better state than in the rest of the archipelago. Not surprisingly, most activities centre around checking out the natural surroundings: hiking the Monkey Trail near Sabang, exploring the nearby limestone caves of the Underground River, or diving the many reefs that ring the island. You can contact W www.palawan.com for more information.

Diving & Snorkelling The waters surrounding Palawan are said to have nearly 40% of the total coral reef concentration in the Philippines. This makes for good diving, and Palawan has become one of the world's premier diving destinations. In the channel between Busuanga and Culion Islands there are also a number of WWII-era wrecks – the

Highlights

- Dive the coral-clad wrecks of a sunken Japanese fleet in the turquoise waters off northern Palawan's Busuanga Island
- Explore the stunning natural beauty of Unesco World Heritage–listed Underground River and surrounding lush jungle near Sabang
- Sense the history of Taytay, a 17th-century fortress town littered with the relics of Spanish rule
- Relax on a shimmering beach at El Nido, surrounded by breathtaking views of jagged limestone mountains and islets

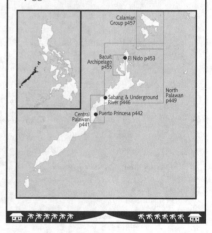

relics of an attack on a Japanese fleet by American planes in 1944. The wrecks are now covered with marine growth and teeming with fish.

Dive shops with rental equipment and instruction can be found in Puerto Princesa, Taytay, Port Barton and Coron. Boat dives, including equipment, should cost US$20 to US$30. To rent snorkelling equipment should cost no more than P300.

For those interested in serious diving, the Tubbataha Reefs, almost midway between Palawan and Jolo Island, have some of the world's richest dive spots. Live-aboard excursions to Tubbataha can be arranged in Puerto Princesa. Expect to pay from US$200 to US$300 per person per day, including

PALAWAN

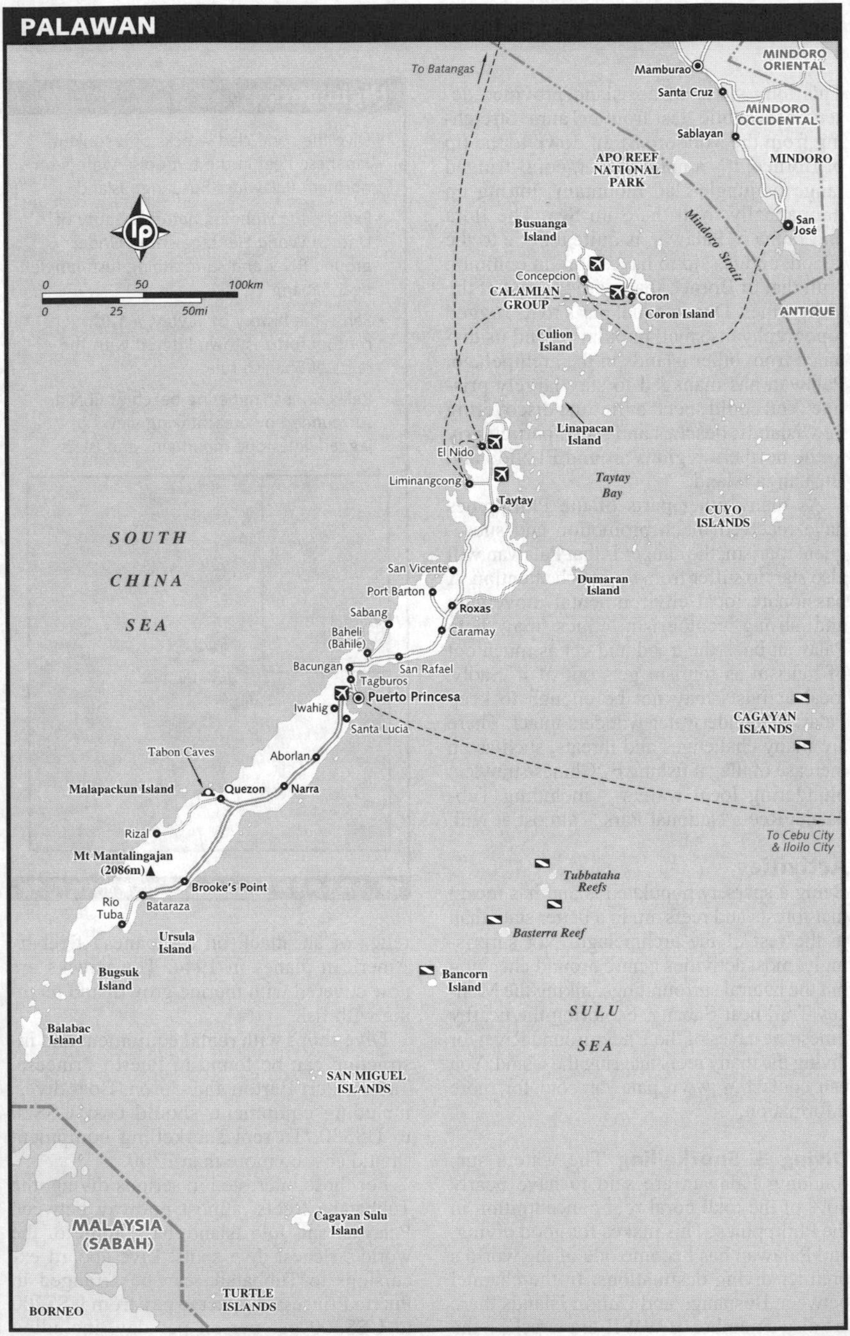

PALAWAN
To Batangas
Mamburao
MINDORO ORIENTAL
Santa Cruz
MINDORO OCCIDENTAL
Sablayan
MINDORO
APO REEF NATIONAL PARK
San José
Mindoro Strait
Busuanga Island
Concepcion
CALAMIAN GROUP
Coron
Coron Island
ANTIQUE
Culion Island
Linapacan Island
El Nido
Liminangcong
Taytay
Taytay Bay
CUYO ISLANDS
SOUTH CHINA SEA
San Vicente
Port Barton
Dumaran Island
Roxas
Sabang
Caramay
Baheli (Bahile)
Bacungan
San Rafael
Tagburos
Puerto Princesa
Iwahig
Santa Lucia
CAGAYAN ISLANDS
Tabon Caves
Aborlan
Malapackun Island
Quezon
Narra
Rizal
To Cebu City & Iloilo City
Mt Mantalingajan (2086m)
Tubbataha Reefs
Brooke's Point
Rio Tuba
Bataraza
Basterra Reef
Ursula Island
Bugsuk Island
Bancorn Island
Balabac Island
SULU SEA
SAN MIGUEL ISLANDS
MALAYSIA (SABAH)
Cagayan Sulu Island
TURTLE ISLANDS
BORNEO
0 50 100km
0 25 50mi
PALAWAN

Warning

Both local officials and frequent visitors to the Philippines had long assumed that Palawan was too far from the ethnic and religious tensions in Mindanao to be considered unsafe. That false sense of security was shattered in May 2001 when the Dos Palmas Resort, on Honda Bay northeast of Puerto Princesa, was the target of a kidnapping raid by the militant Islamic group Abu Sayyaf. Twenty guests and staff of the resort, three of them foreign tourists, were taken hostage. At the time of writing, some of the victims had been executed by the militants, while others were still being held hostage on the island of Basilan, south of Zamboanga, Mindanao.

In April 2002 several bombs were discovered planted in public places in Puerto Princesa, although authorities were able to defuse them before they exploded.

While the Department of Tourism (DOT) tends to downplay these incidents as isolated, officials at Western embassies in the Philippines warn that visitors to Palawan should exercise caution, particularly those planning to visit the southeastern coast of the island where resorts are sometimes located on isolated stretches of beach that are lacking in government security. The result of these tragic incidents on the island's tourism infrastructure has been predictable. Many of the larger resorts that have a beach or island to themselves have seen occupancy drop dramatically. Some of these places seem to be in a state of hibernation, operating on a skeleton crew while waiting for the storm clouds to pass. Other establishments have beefed up their security. It should be noted that at least one resort on Palawan made a point of publishing the following disclaimer in its brochure: 'The Resort shall not be responsible to its guests for incidents and occurrences due to circumstances beyond its control'.

At the time of writing, the security situation on Palawan is certainly far better than on Mindanao. Still, we think it's a good idea to check with your embassy to assess the current situation before going.

---

equipment and meals. Best visibility is usually between March and May.

Getting There & Away

Air Palawan's main airport is in Puerto Princesa, but Palawan also has some small airports in the north, with regular flights to/from Manila and Puerto Princesa. On Busuanga Island, there's an airport in the southern town of Coron and the YKR airport to the north near San José. On the Palawan mainland, there's the Lio airport north of El Nido, and another airport at Sandoval, about 20km southeast of El Nido.

Manila Flights from Manila to Puerto Princesa (one daily) are available with **PAL** (☎ 02-879 5601) and **Air Philippines** (☎ 02-551 7505). **SEAIR** (☎ 02-891 8709, 01-851 5555 in Manila) also charters flights to several destinations on Palawan.

For the diving resorts of Coron on Busuanga Island, **Asian Spirit** (☎ 02-853 1957 in Manila) has flights from Manila (four weekly), as does Pacific Air (P1650, one daily).

Mindoro There are no scheduled flights between Mindoro and Palawan, but flights can

be chartered between Calapan and Coron, El Nido and Puerto Princesa.

Pacific Air (☎ 036-288 3162) can organise a charter flight for you between Calapan and Coron on Busuanga. Give a few days' notice. Flights are subject to aircraft availability.

Visayas There are no flights between Cebu and Palawan – a great pity for travellers. Ask around though, as there's a possibility that this route will be picked up again.

Boat Shipping lines serving Palawan include **Negros Navigation** (☎ 02-245 5588 in Manila) and **WG&A** (☎ 02-528 7000 in Manila). **Sulpicio Lines** (☎ 02-245 0616 in Manila) is chiefly a cargo operator in Puerto Princesa, although you might be able to arrange a berth to/from Luzon or elsewhere on one of its ships.

Manila A WG&A/SuperFerry liner sails from Manila to/from Puerto Princesa via Coron (P1275 to P4220, 28 hours, one weekly). Negros Navigation also has boats going from Manila to/from Puerto Princesa (22 hours, one weekly).

Several ships also sail from Batangas to Coron town (around P300, 18 hours, two weekly). There are also weekly ferries between Liminangcong and Manila via Coron town.

Mindoro A bangka sails from Mindoro's San José to Concepcion, on Busuanga Island, twice weekly. This can be a particularly rough voyage, even in mild weather.

Visayas Negros Navigation used to have a route that went once a week from Cebu City to Iloilo city, then on to Bacolod and finally to Puerto Princesa. The route was discontinued, but may be reinstated in the future.

Getting Around

Air Palawan seems to have a disproportionately high number of tiny airlines offering flights around northern Palawan. The good news is that flights can be a relatively inexpensive and convenient way to see the island. The bad news is that these airlines seem to change their schedules, fares and even routes with bewildering frequency. Be sure to shop around before buying tickets, and it won't hurt to ask the locals which airlines have the best reputations and why before making a decision.

Road Heavy-duty road trips are the norm in Palawan, and these trips are made by jeepney/bus hybrids (overgrown jeepneys with the seats facing forward). On these long-distance juggernauts, it's a good idea to sit on the right – you'll swallow less dust from the oncoming traffic. If you've got the cash it's certainly worth hiring a private van or jeepney to cover long stretches. Not only will you be able to see more of the scenery, you'll be in a better frame of mind to actually appreciate the view.

Of course, some people want it all – cheap fare and great view. If you do decide to ride the roof of a passenger vehicle, know that the risks of injury are much higher during even minor mishaps (such as the vehicle coming to a rapid halt due to deep mud) when you're riding on the roof.

Boat Palawan's waters tend to be far smoother than its roads (and its waters aren't exactly smooth – especially off the eastern coast), making trips north from Puerto Princesa much more enjoyable if taken by boat rather than bus or jeepney.

Keep in mind that pumpboat schedules are not chiselled into stone. If you're planning on taking a pumpboat somewhere, check at the pier (or appropriate agent) the day before you intend to depart.

Two rival groups of resorts operate regular boat trips between Sabang and El Nido (via Port Barton) four times a week each. For simplicity's sake, we'll call them Group A and Group B. Both groups have daily aircon minibuses between Puerto Princesa and Sabang (P250, two hours), but these aren't necessarily timed to meet boats, so you may have to spend a night in Sabang.

Group A has its headquarters at the **Trattoria Inn** (☎ 048-433 4985) in Puerto Princesa. Ticket offices are at Sabang pier in Sabang, Swissippini Lodge & Resort in Port Barton, and El Nido Boutique & Art Café in El Nido.

Group A's boats travel from Sabang–Port Barton–El Nido (P850, eight hours, two weekly). The Sabang–Port Barton leg takes 2½ hours and costs P350. The Port Barton–El Nido leg takes five hours and costs P500. Boats make the reverse trip twice weekly.

Group B is based at the **Sabang Beach Resort** (☎ 048-434 3762) in Sabang. Ticket offices are at the Sabang Beach Resort office in Puerto Princesa, and at Lucing's Restaurant in El Nido.

Group B's boats go Sabang–Port Barton–El Nido (P850, seven hours, two daily). The Sabang–Port Barton leg takes two hours and costs P500. The Port Barton–El Nido leg takes four hours and costs P500. Boats make the reverse trip twice weekly.

Central Palawan

PUERTO PRINCESA
☎ 048 • pop 161,912

The carefree capital of Palawan is generally regarded as little more than a step-off point for excursions elsewhere on the island. Often overlooked as an attraction in its own right, this underrated town has some mighty fine hotels and excellent restaurants. 'Puerto', as the locals call it, is touted to be the safest and cleanest city in the Philippines, and you're likely to believe it if you've just stepped off the plane from Manila.

While you're here you could check out the **Palawan Museum** (admission P5; open 9am-5pm Thur-Tue), which is housed in the

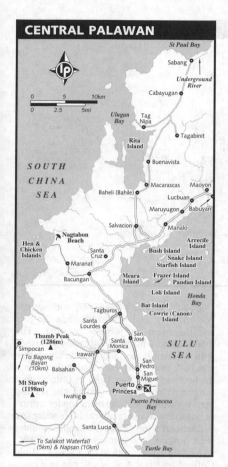

CENTRAL PALAWAN

St Paul Bay

Underground River

Sabang

Cabayugan

Ulugan Bay

Tag Nipa

Tagabinit

Rita Island

SOUTH CHINA SEA

Buenavista

Baheli (Bahile)

Macarascas   Maoyon

Lucbuan

Maruyugon   Babuyan

Salvacion

Manalo

Nagtabon Beach

Arrecife Island

Hen & Chicken Islands

Santa Cruz

Bush Island

Snake Island

Starfish Island

Maranat

Bacungan

Meara Island

Frazer Island

Pandan Island

Loli Island

Honda Bay

Bat Island

Tagburos

Cowrie (Canon) Island

Santa Lourdes

San José

SULU SEA

Thumb Peak (1286m)

Santa Monica

Simpocan

Irawan

San Pedro

To Bagong Bayan (10km)

Balsahan

San Miguel

Mt Stavely (1198m)

Iwahig

Puerto Princesa

Puerto Princesa Bay

Santa Lucia

To Salakot Waterfall (5km) & Napsan (10km)

Turtle Bay

0   5   10km
0   2.5   5mi

---

pier through the city centre, past the market and main bus and jeepney terminal, and past the front doorstep of the airport.

Maps The brochure-sized *E-Z Palawan* map features both a map of Palawan and the islands around it as well as a detailed map of Puerto Princesa. Copies can be purchased for P80 in many businesses that cater to travellers.

Information

The staff are helpful at the **city tourist office** (☎ 433 2983) at the airport. There's also a **provincial tourist office** (*Rizal Ave*) in the Provincial Capitol Building.

There are several big banks with ATMs along Rizal Ave, as well as moneychangers. The **Development Bank of the Philippines** (DBP) has an ATM accepting Visa credit cards, as does the nearby **Equitable PCI Bank**. The **Go Palawan** travel agent next door to the Trattoria Inn & Restaurant (see Places to Stay later) gives cash advances on major credit cards (with a hefty 10% commission).

The **main post office** (*Burgos St*) is just off Rizal Ave. A number of **telephone offices** can be found along Rizal Ave.

Near the market is **Kawing Internet** (*open 9am-7pm daily*). Several Internet cafés can be found on Rizal Ave, between the airport terminal and the Jollibee restaurant. The **Trattoria Inn & Restaurant** has an in-house Internet service, as do several other resorts and hotels around town.

Places to Stay

Duchess Pension House (☎ 433 2873; *107 Valencia St; small singles/doubles P120/ 220, doubles with fan P300*) has tiny rooms with common bathroom, and more liveable doubles with fan and bathroom.

Casa Linda Inn & Restaurant (☎ 433 2606; e *casalind@mozcom.com; Trinidad Rd; rooms with fan P350/450, with air-con P600/700*), with its manicured garden courtyard and pergola, is behind the Badjao Inn, down little Trinidad Rd. The rooms are a tasteful mix of hotel-style luxury and *nipa* hut-style character. A shoes-off-at-the-door rule ensures blissful silence and gleaming floorboards. The staff are friendly and efficient and, not surprisingly, this place gets rave reviews.

Backpackers Cafe, Bookshop & Inn (*dorm beds/singles/doubles P100/150/220*),

---

old City Hall building adjacent to Mendoza Park. It has exhibits on Chinese trade pottery and Spanish relics that were found in the province, as well as prehistoric artefacts from Tabon Cave. There's also a small collection of native musical instruments.

First held in April 1999, the **Kamarikutan Pagdiwata Arts Festival** has become a regular event on the nation's cultural calendar. It features the work of traditional and contemporary Filipino artists through exhibits, performances and workshops in various Puerto Princesa venues.

Orientation

Puerto Princesa is really an overgrown country town, with the main street of Rizal Ave its long, straight spine. Rizal Ave runs from the

PALAWAN

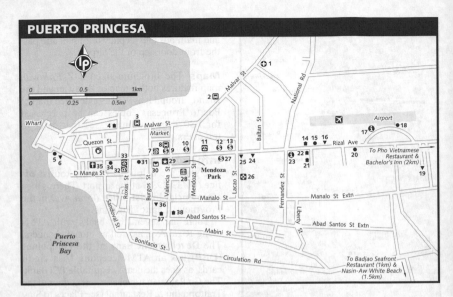

PUERTO PRINCESA

a relaxed and friendly hang-out, is diagonally opposite the Duchess. It has basic rooms and a dorm (or four-bed room). It also does good pancakes (P40), tasty bargain curries (P50) and a generous *tom yam* seafood soup (P90). Mountain bikes can be hired for P100 per day, and the big range of second-hand books cover seven languages. Happy hour (25% off drinks) is from 4pm to 5pm Monday to Friday, and there's plenty of indepth information about things to see and do in Palawan.

Trattoria Inn & Restaurant and **Swiss Bistro Garden** (☎ 433 2719, fax 433 8171; ⓦ www.palawan.net/trattori/palawan.htm; 353 Rizal Ave; singles/doubles with air-con, cable TV & bathroom P490/590) is a very popular place with Germans. Rooms have been recently renovated and are clean and comfortable. There's also a 'suite' with a small kitchen and fridge for P750. Arrangements for diving can also be made here.

Badjao Inn (☎ 433 2380; 350 Rizal Ave; ⓔ badjao@pal-onl.com; dorm beds P300, rooms with fan P800, with air-con P1350, with TV P1750) is just over the road. The dorm is a nice addition and, although the rooms are big and spotless, they're perhaps a bit overpriced. However, there are nicely landscaped grounds.

Puerto Pension (☎ 433 2969, fax 433 4148; ⓔ ppension@pal-onl.com; Malvar St; singles/doubles with semi-private bathroom P225/

342, with bathroom P463/477, with air-con P662/675) is well placed between the pier and the main bus/jeepney terminal. The rooms come with wide balconies furnished with wooden tables and chairs. This place was built from indigenous materials and has the best views in town from its little rooftop restaurant/bar. Even if you're not staying here, it's worth the climb to the top for a drink or bite to eat. Major credit cards are accepted.

Bachelor's Inn (Palay Rd; singles/doubles with air-con, TV & bathroom P490/590, suites P790), just south of the Palawan Bible College on Rizal Ave, is situated in a quiet neighbourhood. Rooms are clean and comfortable, and the two 'suites' have their own kitchens. It's a short walk away from some great Vietnamese noodle restaurants.

Places to Eat

Puerto has quite a few good little eateries catering to visitors, but prices are a bit higher than on other islands as some commodities must be shipped in. The best value meals in town are the small Vietnamese-run restaurants specialising in *pho*, a tasty noodle dish that will fortify you for less than P50.

Café Kamarikutan & Galeri (Rizal Ave), just past the airport, is good for breakfast or a light lunch, and serves an incredible range of coffees – all in a huge, airy bamboo mansion with an enormous oasis of a garden.

PALAWAN

PUERTO PRINCESA

PLACES TO STAY		26	Jollibee		16	WG&A SuperFerry
4	Puerto Pension	27	Vegetarian House		18	City Tourist Office; Palawan
15	Trattoria Inn & Restaurant;					Treasures & Gift Shop
	Swiss Bistro Garden; Go	**OTHER**			19	PAL
	Palawan Travel Agent	1	Provincial Hospital		21	Air Philippines
22	Casa Linda Inn &	2	Jeepney Terminal		24	Provincial Tourist Office;
	Restaurant	3	Buses, Minibuses; Jeepneys			Provincial Capitol Building
23	Badjao Inn; Negros		to North, South Palawan		27	NCCC Supermarket &
	Navigation Office	5	Milagrosa Shipping Lines			Department Store
38	Backpackers Cafe, Bookshop	7	Petron Service Station		28	DBP Bank
	& Inn	8	Kawing Internet, WG&A		29	Museum
39	Duchess Pension House		SuperFerry		30	Air Philippines; Police
		9	PNB Bank			Station
PLACES TO EAT		10	Jeepneys to Iwahig		31	Main Post Office
6	Bahay Kubo	11	Equitable PCI Bank		32	Morbai Maps & Charts Office
17	Ka Lui Restaurant; Island	12	RCPI International Telephone		33	Piltel International Telephone
	Divers		Office			Office
20	Café Kamarikutan	13	Allied Bank; Metrobank;		34	Hexagon Internet Café
	& Galeri		BPI Bank		35	Sulpicio Lines Office
25	Rodeo Grill	14	Equitable PCI Bank		36	Cathedral

Bahay Kubo *(Rizal Ave)* is an unpretentious place with good traditional Filipino specialities, including a delicious and refreshing *halo-halo* (crushed ice, coconut jelly, jackfruit, corn, sweetened condensed milk, and about 10 other seemingly incongruous ingredients). It's near the Customs House at the far west end of Rizal Ave.

Backpackers Cafe, Bookshop & Inn has great fresh-fruit pancakes (along with an ever-changing lunch and dinner menu).

Puerto Pension *(breakfast around P80)* has a rooftop restaurant/bar that serves breakfast with great views.

Kalui Restaurant *(Rizal Ave)*, east of the Trattoria Inn, has delicious, reasonably priced seafood. The menu is a choice of two set dinners, and while this might sound a bit limited, both choices are excellent value and it seems to get many repeat customers.

Vegetarian House *(cnr Burgos & Manalo Sts)* is a rarity of a restaurant in the meat-mad Philippines. But don't expect hippy decor or organic muffins here.

In simple and spotlessly white air-con surrounds, you're offered a big range of tasty mock-meat dishes (with gluten used as a meat substitute).

Badjao Seafront Restaurant off Abueg Rd and, as the name indicates, on the sea, is impressively done up with lots of wood and woven bamboo, and affords great views. The menu stresses seafood, and it's not as expensive as the atmosphere would have you believe. It's run by the same people who own the Badjao Inn.

Rodeo Grill *(Rizal Ave)*, between Lacao and Fernandez Sts, is the place if you're craving hearty Western meat dishes. If you're in the mood for a burger, **Jollibee** is just a few metres down Rizal to the west.

Ka Lui Restaurant is a brilliant place nearby serving sophisticated Filipino seafood set meals, including a succulent (no, really) seaweed appetiser. The giant P275 set meal should be enough for two people. A smaller P100 set meal is also quite good. It's open nightly except Sunday.

There is a handful of **Pho Vietnamese Restaurants** in town which specialise in *pho,* delicious and cheap bowls of noodles garnished with fresh mint. The most authentic of these eateries is about 2km past the airport on Rizal Ave Extension.

Getting There & Away

Air Air Philippines and PAL both fly between Manila and Puerto Princesa once daily.

PAL *(☎ 433 4575)*, **Air Philippines** *(☎ 433 7003; Rizal Ave)* and **Pacific Air** *(☎ 433 4872)* have offices at the airport. Pacific Air offers charter flights in three-seater planes from Puerto Princesa to Sandoval, El Nido, Cuyo, Culion and Coron town.

Bus & Jeepney Malvar St, near the market, is crammed with buses, jeepneys and minivans (three terminals in all). For buses

PALAWAN

Beneath the Veneer

For most visitors to the Philippines, first impressions of a culture thoroughly Hispanicised and Americanised are lasting impressions. At a glance, the islands seem as though they've drifted from somewhere off the coast of Latin America and come to rest incongruously in Southeast Asia. Indeed the veneer of Spanish and American culture seems thick, but in the end it is just that – a veneer.

A mixture of factors conspires to give outsiders this mistaken impression. The most obvious are Catholicism, the preponderance of Spanish and English loan words in use in all of the lowland dialects, and the ubiquity of Spanish surnames and place names. A less obvious factor can be found in the character of the Filipinos themselves: they are unparalleled imitators. This is nothing new. American soldiers engaged in fighting Filipino guerrillas during the 1899 to 1902 war noted with surprise that their Filipino prisoners of war were often quick to pick up on and imitate their captors' mannerisms and even slang. Of late, this talent for keen observation and skilful mimicry has become politically incorrect, a source of national shame that is sometimes denounced as 'colonial mindedness'. But this unique characteristic in the Filipino psyche is far from dead, as the musical dexterity of Filipino cover bands will attest.

Given these factors, first-time visitors to the islands can be forgiven for thinking that there is little to link the lowland cultures of the Philippines to the rest of Southeast Asia. But for those who spend an extended period of time in the Philippines learning one of the lowland dialects and absorbing the customs, the ties to the rest of the region become quite apparent. Language is the most obvious link. Despite the heavy influx of loan words, a speaker of Tagalog, Cebuano or another lowland dialect will find that these languages share a surprising amount of vocabulary with Malay as it is spoken in Indonesia and Malaysia.

Less obvious are ancient folkways that thrive in rural lowland areas. In some of the Visayan islands rural men wear the *habak,* a waist-cord talisman believed to protect the wearer from accidents and bad spirits – a custom that is also found in rural Thailand, Laos and Cambodia. As with the rest of rural Southeast Asia, shamanism and animism also flourish in lowland Philippine cultures. *Barangan* are Visayan shamans versed in putting hexes on foes, such as a curse that causes the victim's stomach to bloat painfully with each high tide.

Ancient animist beliefs that predate the arrival of Western colonisers manifest themselves in ways that may go unnoticed to the casual observer. Large banyan trees growing alongside roads are sometimes thought to host an animist spirit – drivers will honk their horn in passing to warn the spirit or pay respect. Even in the provinces around Manila, men trekking through the jungle take particular care not to offend forest spirits. When nature calls, men will gently warn away any spirit that might be nearby by saying *'Tabi-tabi po'* (Move aside, sir) before urinating.

Steven Martin

and jeepneys to the popular northern destinations of Port Barton, Taytay and El Nido, it's a good idea to turn up early and book a seat. Considering the gruelling trip ahead, you should then pass the time with a stiff drink at the rooftop restaurant/bar of the nearby Puerto Pension.

Oversized jeepneys go from Malvar St to El Nido via Roxas and Taytay (P300, 12 hours, one daily). This is a particularly torturous journey, and the winches on the front of these jeepneys aren't just for looks. During the rainy season, jeepneys doing this run are sometimes towed over the worst sections by bulldozers.

If you'd prefer to get to El Nido in gentler stages, take a bus or jeepney from Puerto Princesa to Taytay (P150, around 7½ hours, two daily) and stay overnight. A more leisurely way to reach El Nido is to take the jeepney to Port Barton (P100, five hours, one daily), and from there take a boat; see Boat under Getting Around at the beginning of this chapter for details.

Buses and jeepneys from Puerto Princesa to Roxas (P100, four hours) leave from the Malvar St terminals from 6am to around 9am daily. Roxas–Puerto Princesa buses and jeepneys leave from the bus terminal in the middle of town from around 6am to 9am daily.

From Puerto Princesa to Sabang, jeepneys (P50 to P70, 2½ to three hours) and buses (P150, 2½ hours) go several times a day from the Malvar St terminals. Air-con minibuses go from the Trattoria Inn & Restaurant in Puerto Princesa to Sabang (P250 to P300, two hours, one daily), and from Sabang to Puerto Princesa (one daily).

Minivans head off two or three times daily from the Malvar St terminals to the southern towns of Quezon (P150), Brooke's Point (P200) and Rio Tuba (P250).

Boat The **Negros Navigation office** (*Roxas St*), just off Rizal Ave, usually has a monthly and/or weekly schedule posted on a board out the front.

The office of **Sulpicio Lines** (*☎ 433 2641; Rizal Ave*) is nearby, and the **Milagrosa Shipping Lines office** is to the left of the pier gate (on the outside of the enclosure).

For boat trips between Sabang, Port Barton and El Nido, see Getting Around at the beginning of this chapter.

Getting Around
Tricycle feeding frenzies are the norm in Puerto Princesa, especially around the market and bus terminals, the pier, and the strolling tourist.

Unless you're happy to pay extra for being a *kano* (Westerner), insist on the official tricycle fare rate of P5 for every 2km.

For motorcycles, try **Hidalgo Motorbike Hire** (*☎ 433 7721*), which has bikes for P500 per day that can be hired through various hotels.

Mountain bikes can be hired from the **Backpackers Cafe, Bookshop & Inn** for P100 per day (see Places to Stay earlier).

AROUND PUERTO PRINCESA
From crocodile farms to underground rivers, there's a great range of attractions within an easy day trip of Puerto Princesa. For more extended excursions into areas less travelled, you can take the long roads into the far-flung reaches south of the capital.

Irawan
Palawan Wildlife Rescue & Conservation Center (*PWRCC; open 1.30pm-5pm Mon-Fri, 9am-5pm Sat*) is principally a breeding centre for the Philippines' two endangered crocs – the estuarine crocodile and the Philippine crocodile. Formerly (and still popularly) known as the Crocodile Farming Institute, its expanded its role to include rescuing and caring for other species of rare and endangered wildlife that are indigenous to Palawan. Don't expect 'crocodile wrestling' or other circus-like diversions. The crocs spend most of their time sunning themselves or half-submerged in ponds – except during feeding times – which are Monday and Thursday at noon. Guided tours are provided every hour on the hour. Entry is free. To get there from Puerto Princesa, catch a south-bound jeepney or bus to Irawan (P10, 30 minutes), or grab a tricycle (P100).

Iwahig
Far more pleasant than it sounds, the **Iwahig Penal Colony** was set up in 1905 and is claimed to be the biggest institution of its kind anywhere in the world. Effectively a model prison, it chains newly arrived prisoners for a few months before allowing them to roam relatively free and mix with an integrated community of convicts and their families.

The place actually looks more like a model farming community than a prison, and the inmates and their families are free (and eager) to chat with visitors. **Handicrafts** produced here are mostly carvings made from Philippine mahogany and baskets. Bring lots of small banknotes if you plan on buying souvenirs – the inmates aren't exactly rolling in change.

Jeepneys marked 'Iwahig' leave throughout the morning from Manalo St in Puerto Princesa, returning to town around 1pm.

Honda Bay
On the way out to Sabang, Honda Bay is dotted with small islands that are ideal for **snorkelling** and island hopping. Perfect for day trips, the islands include the dazzling, aptly named **Snake Island**, a winding strip of white sand that changes shape with the tides.

Snorkelling gear and boats can be hired at Santa Lourdes Pier, just north of the town of Tagburos (P15 by bus from Puerto Princesa). Easier but a bit more expensive is to go on a snorkelling package tour with one of the many tour agencies in Puerto. Expect to pay about P750 per person for an all-day excursion, including lunch and transport to/from your hotel.

SABANG & UNDERGROUND RIVER

Sabang is a beautiful little beach settlement on the edge of the **Puerto Princesa Subterranean National Park**, home to an underground river that empties into the sea and can be explored by boat. The national park was included on the Unesco World Heritage List in 1999, and is unique because of its diverse ecosystems within a relatively small area. The limestone cave that the river passes through is thought to be the longest navigable river-traversed tunnel in the world (though a similar underground river recently discovered in southern Laos is perhaps longer). The underground river can be explored by boat, and exiting the dark tunnel at its jagged mouth, which opens onto breathtakingly beautiful tropical vistas, is an unforgettable experience. Passengers on the boats are required to wear helmets and life vests.

From the beach in Sabang you can either take a boat to the mouth of the river (P500), or walk there over the **monkey trail** through the beautiful jungle of the national park – it takes about two hours. The trail is aptly named – there are plenty of monkeys – but beware as they can be very aggressive if they think you're carrying food. Also, parts of the trail are occasionally flooded, making it impossible to walk the entire length. Ask at the information office next to the pier before

heading off. You'll only get to see about 2km of the river's 8km total, because most of the river is off-limits for research purposes.

While you may save a little bit of money if you do the trip from Puerto yourself, it's much easier if you get a package tour through one of the many agencies in Puerto Princesa. Expect to pay about P1000 per person, which should cover transport, lunch and park permit.

If you're not on a package tour, you should pick up a national park permit (P150) at the information office next to the pier.

Day-trippers take note: the bumpy trip to/from Puerto Princesa and the sheer beauty of Sabang and national park area may have you wishing you'd brought your luggage from Puerto Princesa after all.

Places to Stay & Eat

Mary's Beach Resort (*cottages with/without bathroom P300/200*) is the best place. This simply idyllic resort is at the opposite end of Sabang Beach to the pier. Hidden just around the point, it has a giant shady tree with hammocks right on the sand and its very own beach (and island!). It has no-frills cottages and cottages with bathroom, as well as a basic little restaurant.

Sabang Beach Resort (☎ 048-434 3762; *cottages with bathroom & balcony P500-700, family cottages P1000*), near Mary's Beach

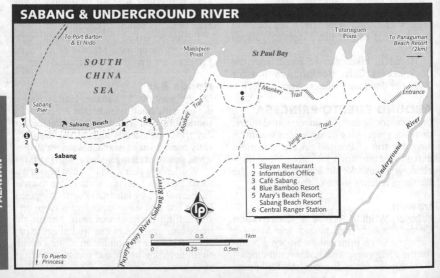

SABANG & UNDERGROUND RIVER

1 Silayan Restaurant
2 Information Office
3 Café Sabang
4 Blue Bamboo Resort
5 Mary's Beach Resort;
   Sabang Beach Resort
6 Central Ranger Station

Resort, has small, OK cottages with bathroom and balcony, and large, family cottages. The bungalows are arranged in a lush garden setting. The restaurant serves Filipino cuisine and seafood.

Blue Bamboo Resort (cottages P200-400) has a collection of charmingly rustic cottages built from bamboo and palm thatch, each with its own bathroom and veranda. Some cottages sleep up to four people. An equally rustic restaurant serves some delicious seafood. The nearby beach isn't spectacular, as it has coral pebbles instead of fine sand. There's also a dive shop on the premises.

Panaguman Beach Resort (rooms P500, cottages P750), beyond the Underground River, is a reclusive place offering big rooms with common bathroom or cottages with attached bathroom. The rooms are upstairs from the restaurant so there's a little ambient noise. The resort's boat leaves from the Sabang pier at 1pm daily. For more information, contact the Trattoria Inn & Restaurant in Puerto Princesa (see Puerto Princesa Places to Stay earlier).

Silayan Restaurant is a tiny hut of a place with some surprises on the menu. Try the chicken curry if you've had your fill of the usual grilled fish.

Café Sabang, on the main road into Sabang, about 500m from the beach, offers good food in a nice setting.

Getting There & Away

It's a pretty nasty old road out to Sabang (P300, two to 2½ hours) – even by air-con minibus – but it's well worth it. The Trattoria Inn & Restaurant in Puerto Princesa operates air-con minibuses to/from Sabang (one daily).

There are also jeepneys that operate between Puerto Princesa and Sabang (P80). In Puerto Princesa, they leave from the Malvar St terminals. The last jeepney for Sabang leaves at 3pm.

Boats travel to/from Sabang and El Nido via Port Barton (P850, 7½ to eight hours, two weekly). For more information see Getting Around at the beginning of the chapter.

SALAKOT WATERFALL & NAPSAN BEACH

The falls themselves are not so spectacular, but the ride out here passes through some awesome mountain scenery. In fact, it's best to make the falls a stop on your way to the beachside town of Napsan, on the west coast of Palawan about 15km beyond the falls. There are some pools at the base of the falls that are perfect for a refreshing dip, but don't come on a weekend or you'll have lots of company – Salakot Waterfall is a popular day-trip destination for families and students from Puerto Princesa just 58km away. There are bamboo cottages nearby too, if you want to overnight here, but the termites are making quick work of them – they may be piles of sawdust by the time you see them.

Places to Stay & Eat

Kiao Sea Lodge (☎ 048-433 3500; rooms P900, including meals), about 1km south of Napsan, is a collection of tidy cottages made of wood, bamboo and thatched roofs, shaded by coconut palms and adjacent to a long stretch of clean beach. All rooms have attached bathroom and a small veranda. The whole operation is well run and friendly, but things may change as the lodge was undergoing a major change of management at the time we visited.

Getting There & Away

Not surprisingly, the road from Puerto to Salakot Falls and Napsan is quite rough. Many travellers find that riding on the jeepney's roof is vastly preferable to being crammed into the passenger compartment. While the views are spectacular, drivers tell us that more than a few travellers have slid off the roof and been injured. Take a jeepney from the Malvar St terminals (P50, three hours) to the turn-off for Salakot Waterfall, then walk the remaining 500m to the falls. Napsan is about 15km beyond the turn-off to the falls. The Kiao Sea Lodge (See Places to Stay & Eat) sometimes has a shuttle service (P250), so try calling first if you don't want to hassle with public transport.

South Palawan

In contrast to the north, Palawan's southern region has little to offer the average traveller. Tourism infrastructure is almost nonexistent, though if you don't mind roughing it and can speak enough Tagalog to have the barangay captain arrange basic accommodation for you, there are enough caves and waterfalls

PALAWAN

down here to keep you exploring for weeks. **Quezon**, about 100km from Puerto Princesa, is the nearest major town to the archaeologically interesting **Tabon Caves**. This massive network of caves has recently yielded remnants of prehistory in the form of crude burial grounds (for more information see Way, Way Back under History in the Facts about the Philippines chapter). The caves are a half-hour boat ride from Quezon.

Places to Stay
Tabon Resort (cottages P150-450), near Quezon on Malanut Bay, is a relaxing place with well-built cottages and a restaurant built over the bay. The same owners operate **Malapackun Island Resort** (cottages P150-250), which features simpler cottages on nearby Malapackun Island.

Getting There & Away
Daily buses travel between Puerto Princesa and Quezon (P90, three hours). Air-con minivans head off two or three times daily from Puerto Princesa's Malvar St terminals to Quezon (P150), Brooke's Point (P200) and Rio Tuba (P250).

Boats to Tabon Caves can be arranged at the pier in Quezon. Expect to pay around P500 for the return trip and a few hours at the caves.

North Palawan

ROXAS
pop 47,242
The uninspiring town of Roxas (**roh**-hahs) is 135km from Puerto Princesa and specialises in roadside cafés for the steady stream of buses and jeepneys stumbling to/from Puerto Princesa. To tourists, Roxas is best known as the coastal gateway to a cluster of comely deserted islands, along with Coco-Loco, home of the Coco-Loco Island Resort.

Places to Stay
Coco-Loco Island Resort (☎ 048-433 3877; e cocoloco@pal-onl.com; rooms US$25-45 per person per night) is situated on a corner of its own island and has a collection of bungalows built from wood, bamboo and thatch that are basic but have some charm. Rooms have attached bathroom and 24-hour electricity. The most expensive room rate includes all meals and transport from Roxas. Prices drop in US$10 increments if you decide you don't want lunch or dinner, but there's really no other place to eat so you may as well go for the 'full board'. There's a good restaurant specialising in – what else? – seafood. Cruises to nearby Stanlake and Green islands can be arranged.

Getting There & Away
Plenty of buses and jeepneys cool their wheels in Roxas on their way north or south, but if you're planning to catch a ride in one of these vehicles, be prepared for a tight squeeze – they're nearly always packed.

Buses and jeepneys from Puerto Princesa to Roxas (P120, four hours) leave from the Malvar St terminals. Roxas–Puerto Princesa buses and jeepneys leave from the large bus terminal in the middle of town from around 6am to 9am daily.

A couple of jeepneys go from Roxas to Port Barton between 6am and 9am daily (P50, two hours). From Port Barton to Roxas, jeepneys also head off between 6am and 9am daily.

PORT BARTON
pop 4140
On the west coast, the refreshingly quiet town of Port Barton is a low-key tourist haunt. The town itself is on an attractive beach well accustomed to spectacular sunsets, but better beaches can be found on the islands scattered throughout the sheltered bay. Quite a few travellers show up here and find just the right mix of laid-back travel scene and local colour to keep them here for a few days. Just outside the bay is **Cacnipa Island**, on which the Coconut Garden Island Resort is located (see Places to Stay & Eat following).

Places to Stay & Eat
Swissippini Lodge & Resort (beachside/non-beachside huts P600/400) is the best of the several beachside cottages in Port Barton. This central resort has big A-frame balconied huts shaded by coconut palms. Rooms have fan and attached bathroom. There's a seafood restaurant and a dive shop on the premises. Swissippini accepts major credit cards, changes money and travellers cheques, and organises boat trips to/from Sabang and El Nido.

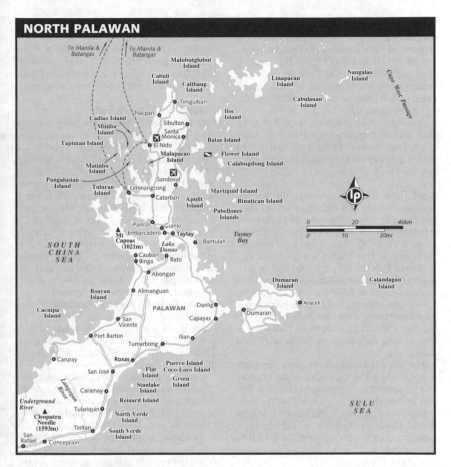

NORTH PALAWAN

To Manila &
Batangas

To Manila &
Batangas

Malubutglubut
Island

Cabuli
Island

Calibang
Island

Linapacan
Island

Nangalao
Island

Cabulauan
Island

Tiniguiban

Nacpan

Iloc
Island

Cadlao Island

Sibultan

Miniloc
Island

Santa
Monica

Batas Island

Tapiutan Island

El Nido

Malapacao
Island

Flower Island

Calabugdong Island

Matinloc
Island

Sandoval

Pangalusian
Island

Tuluran
Island

Liminangcong

Maytiguid Island

Catarban

Apulit
Island

Binatican Island

Pabellones
Islands

Pancol

Guinlo

Mt
Capoas
(1021m)

Embarcadero

Taytay

Taytay
Bay

Lake
Danao

Bantulan

SOUTH
CHINA
SEA

Cauban

Binga

Bato

Abongan

Boayan
Island

Alimanguan

PALAWAN

Danlig

Dumaran
Island

Calandagan
Island

Araceli

Cacnipa
Island

Dumaran

Capayas

San
Vicente

Ilian

Port Barton

Tumarbong

Caruray

Roxas

Puerco Island
Coco-Loco Island

San José

Flat
Island

Green
Island

Caramay

Stanlake
Island

Underground
River

Tulariquin

Reinard Island

SULU
SEA

Cleopatra
Needle
(1593m)

North Verde
Island

Tinitan

South Verde
Island

San
Rafael

Concepcion

0   20   40km
0   10   20mi

Elsa's Beach Cottages *(huts P300, 3-person huts P400)*, a few doors along from Swissippini, has good little huts.

El Busero Inn *(rooms/huts P150/300)* has simpler cottages and tawdry rooms. All cottages have private bathroom. There's also a dive shop associated with the inn.

El Dorado Sunset Cottages *(front/back rooms P300/275)* is over the creek at the north end of town. All cottages have private bathroom. The establishment is aptly named – the sunsets are really spectacular from here, especially over a cold beer. All the places mentioned so far have restaurants and bars attached.

Filipiniana Restaurant, opposite Elsa's Beach Cottages, would put the fanciest of resorts to shame with its wonderful fish curry.

Coconut Garden Island Resort *(2-person tents P200, cottages P200, with bathroom P500-550)* is on a lovely white-sand beach on Cacnipa Island, about 15km from Port Barton by boat. This place has attractive A-frame cottages with balcony and shared or private bathroom. It also has a lodging house with rooms, and two-person tents are available as well. There are good discounts for long stays (three days or more).

The food menu at the Coconut Garden Island Resort includes good Western and Filipino food, including some vegetarian dishes. Some excellent island-hopping jaunts are offered, and snorkelling and jungle walks are also popular here. A chartered 'special ride' from Port Barton to Cacnipa Island costs P500 per boat.

PALAWAN

Getting There & Away
Bus & Jeepney A jeepney runs from Port Barton to Puerto Princesa (P100, five hours, one daily). It heads off from the waiting shed at the beach end of Ballesteros St and cruises through town picking up passengers. From Puerto Princesa's Malvar St terminals, a jeepney heads daily for Port Barton.

A couple of jeepneys go from Roxas to Port Barton between 6am and 9am daily (P50, two hours). From Port Barton to Roxas, jeepneys also head off between 6am and 9am daily.

Boat There are eight pumpboat trips a week between Sabang and El Nido via Port Barton. But take note: unless you've made prior arrangements, or they have passengers or cargo to drop off, these boats won't necessarily *stop* at Port Barton. Fares between El Nido and Port Barton are P500 (four to five hours). Fares between Sabang and Port Barton cost P350 to P500 (two to 2½ hours). Every day, except Friday, these pumpboats pass Port Barton either heading south to Sabang or north to El Nido (with boats heading in both directions on Wednesday and Thursday).

For more detailed information, see Getting Around at the beginning of the chapter and/ or contact the Swissippini Lodge & Resort in Port Barton.

Between Port Barton and nearby Cacnipa Island (Coconut Garden Island Resort), there's a shuttle service most days (P100, 30 minutes). A chartered special ride should cost about P500 per boat.

TAYTAY
☎ 02 • pop 53,657
Taytay (**tye**-tye) is a quiet coastal town dominated by the centuries-old **Santa Isabal Fort**, and graced with some evocative Spanish architectural relics – reminders of the town's glory days as the capital of Palawan. Built in 1667 by the Spanish, the fort encloses an attractive chapel and public garden. Also worth checking out is the venerable **Santa Monica Church**, constructed with coral blocks in the 17th century. On a hill overlooking the cemetery is the site of the original wooden fortress built by the Spanish in 1622.

The site affords a fine view of the town. Fiesta time is early May, when the town honours its patron, the Miraculous Lady of Santa Monica.

For an excellent day trip, take the 30-minute jeepney ride from Taytay proper to **Lake Danao**, a picturesque freshwater lake surrounded by some good forest hiking trails.

Places to Stay & Eat
Pem's Pension & Restaurant *(singles P150, small cottages P250, large air-con cottages P500-600)* backs onto the water and has a garden courtyard, complete with a feasting table and views of the nearby fort. There are small single rooms with common bathroom, small, solid cottages for two with fan and bathroom, and larger cottages with air-con. The restaurant does basic Western-style breakfasts and standard western and Filipino mains for around P100.

Publico's International Guest House *(singles/doubles with fan P100/150, with fan & bathroom P300)*, in the middle of town, has basic rooms around a courtyard.

Casa Rosa Cottages & Restaurant *(cottages P250)*, perched on the hill above the town, has a few comfortable cottages with great views, and an excellent restaurant. There are delicious Western and Filipino dishes – try the pizza.

Casa Rosa is easy to spot from town, and is a short walk up from Taytay's main street, behind the Town Hall. It can also arrange accommodation on and snorkelling trips to Flower Island.

Rainbow Lodging Inn *(rooms P250-300)* and **Parenas Hotel** *(rooms P300)* are both family-run places with decent rooms for the price.

Getting There & Away
Boat For boats to/from El Nido, Liminangcong and other east-coast towns, you must use the pier at Embarcadero, a scenic 8km tricycle ride west of Taytay (P100, 30 minutes). The quiet little inland pier has a small eatery. Boats to/from Coron town in the Calamian Group moor in the bay at Taytay.

Bangka go from the Embarcadero pier to Liminangcong between 9am and noon daily (P100, 1½ to two hours). Boats from Liminangcong to the Embarcadero pier also leave between 9am and noon daily. Like many boat rides in this region, it is a beautiful trip. The route passes through the Malampaya Sound, a brackish bay in which a pod of rare

From Bamboo Poles to Corinthian Columns

When the Spanish arrived in the Philippines in the 16th century, local architecture was sensibly limited to structures of split and woven bamboo with roofs of palm thatch – cool and breezy in hot weather and easily repaired if damaged by typhoons. The first Spanish structures were similarly built – forts with wooden palisades and churches of rough hardwood. Over decades, as the Spanish entrenched themselves in the Philippines, these structures were rebuilt in more permanent materials: blocks of stone and coral. When earthquakes of disturbing frequency caused the Spanish buildings to collapse, the Spanish redesigned them to withstand the violent temblors. A grand and imposing church was an important symbol of the new religion that the Spanish were then introducing to their new colony. It wouldn't do if that symbol frequently collapsed, taking Christian lives with it. In areas where the earth was most volatile, such as northern Luzon, churches were built in a squat, fortress-like style that today is colourfully referred to as 'Earthquake Baroque'. Within the walled cities of the archipelago, Spanish citizens of means constructed houses of stone that took architectural cues from their homeland.

By the 19th century, Filipinos who could afford to do so were building hybrid structures that incorporated both local and Spanish design. Depending on the availability of materials, the walls of the bottom floor of a house might be made of stone or coral blocks, sometimes 50cm thick. The second storey was made of wood and decorated with wooden gingerbread ornamentation and ornate wrought-iron grillwork. Windows were as tall as doors, the bottom half being lined with lathe-turned wooden balusters topped with a windowsill wide enough for a person to lounge comfortably taking advantage of cooling breezes. The top half of these door-sized windows were usually fitted with capiz-shell window panes – perhaps the most unique and striking feature of these composite Philippine structures. As panes of glass were an expensive luxury throughout much of the archipelago, a local substitute was needed. The capiz shell *Placuna placenta,* a bivalve that is found in the coastal waters of the Philippines, is thin and almost flat. Window panes were made by cutting the almost translucent capiz shells into squares, roughly 8cm by 8cm in size, and then fitting the shells into a wooden lattice-like frame that held them in place. The result was a sturdy windowpane that could withstand typhoon winds and rain. Above doors and windows were transoms of filigreed wood that allowed air to flow even when doors and windows were closed.

During the American colonial period, roofs of palm thatch were replaced with sheets of corrugated tin, which made for hotter interiors but greatly reduced the risk of fires. Daniel Burnham, an American architect who was sent to the Philippines by the US government to study local architecture and advise the public works department, was impressed by the Philippine-Spanish hybrid design. Among other things, he decreed that minor public buildings – schools, libraries and police stations – would incorporate indigenous architectural styles, such as capiz-shell windows, into their design. As with the Spanish, the Americans too used architecture to symbolise an idea being introduced to their colony, not a new religion but a new form of government: democracy. Neoclassical structures imitating the classic style of Greece were erected around Manila and in the provincial capitals. Which is why you can stroll through a town like Bacolod, Negros, and come face to face with an imposing building that would not look out of place in Washington DC.

Steven Martin

Irrawaddy dolphins was recently discovered. If the season's right (early to mid-year), you may sail through great trails of pink and purple jellyfish.

Irregular pumpboats between Taytay (Embarcadero pier) and El Nido may leave any time from around 7am to noon (P200, 3½ to four hours). Special ride pumpboats can be arranged from the Embarcadero pier or El Nido for P2500 per boat.

Large pumpboats from Taytay to Coron (P450, eight hours, two daily) often travel via Linapacan Island.

These boats go from Coron town to Taytay twice weekly.

Bus & Jeepney Jeepneys travel from Taytay to El Nido between 7am and 9am daily (P150, 2½ to three hours). From El Nido, one or two jeepneys go via Taytay on their way to Puerto Princesa, leaving El Nido at 7am or 8am.

Despite valiant attempts, no bus or jeepney has ever managed to maintain a regular link between Taytay and Liminangcong. You'd be much better off catching a boat (see the previous Boat entry for details).

APULIT ISLAND

Less than 2km long, the very private paradise of Apulit Island is home to the exclusive Club Noah Isabelle. The resort organises pumpboat and kayak tours of the island's many natural wonders, including Puerto del Sol Beach and several caves and swimming holes.

Places to Stay & Eat

Club Noah Isabelle (☎ 02-845 1976, fax 845 2380; ℮ info@clubnoah.com.ph; cottages US$195-215) is one of the places in Palawan that has taken up the ecotourism mantra. It has an upscale (and pricey) restaurant and a row of well-built 'water cabanas' built directly over the water. These cottages have both air-con and ceiling fans, and attached bathroom. There is 24-hour electricity. Discounted rates are given to Filipinos and Balikbayans.

Getting There & Away

Club Noah Isabelle has a regular shuttle service between Sandoval airport and Apulit Island, the fares of which are included in the room rates. The resort can also organise a boat for you between Taytay and Apulit Island (one hour).

You can also get to the island from El Nido, via Sibultan (see the following entry for Flower Island).

FLOWER ISLAND

The diving around Flower Island is quite good, with giant clams and sea turtles often spotted.

The peaceful, utterly beautiful Flower Island is home to the **Flower Island Beach Resort** (cottages P1000), with comfortable cottages with bathroom. The restaurant is quite good, and meals are included in the rates. There's also diving and snorkelling equipment available for rent. The resort was for up sale when we visited, however, so things might change.

The best way to get to Flower Island is from El Nido. Jeepneys go daily from El Nido to Sibultan on a surprisingly good road (P60, 1½ hours). Boat hire from Sibultan to nearby Flower Island is P500 to P600 per boat.

Pumpboats can also be hired from Taytay for the scenic trip to Flower Island (P1000 per boat, 2½ to three hours). You can also arrange trips through Casa Rosa Cottages & Restaurant in Taytay (see the Taytay section earlier).

ICADAMBANUAN ISLAND

Icadambanuan Island is located at the south end of Taytay bay and is yet another little island paradise for those looking to do nothing more than swim, sunbathe and eat seafood.

Dilis Beach Resort (rooms P800, cottages P1200) is the only accommodation option on the island. Rooms have attached bathroom and are located in a breezy house on a hill. Cottages, also with bathroom, are on the beach. There's a restaurant on the ground floor of the house, and meals are included with the price of the rooms.

Pumpboats can be hired at Taytay for P400 per boat for the one-way trip. Once at the island, Dilis staff will arrange for your return to Taytay in the resort's pumpboat.

LIMINANGCONG

A ramshackle fishing village with a jaunty charm, Liminangcong's not a bad place to get stuck on your way between Puerto Princesa and the northern extremes of Palawan. If you happen to be here during late February, the **village festival** will keep you drunk and diverted for a few days.

Places to Stay & Eat

Kaver's Inn (rooms P300), on the main street near the main pier, is a big old colonial place that is friendly and has lots of charm. It has ageing, timber-floored rooms with tidy common bathroom, no fan and balcony. There's a restaurant and bar, as well as a battered but browse-worthy bunch of books in the family room/reception area.

Puerto Paraiso Inn & Restaurant (singles/ doubles P150/200) is the best place in town for dinner. This dock-side eatery is not much to look at from the main street, but it leads through to an open-air platform overlooking the harbour. Cheap and hearty meals include fried fish and rice (P50), vegetable curry (P70) and pork dishes (P70). Rooms are OK and have common bathroom.

Getting There & Away

Liminangcong's harbour is crammed with four piers. The main pier in the village (for boats to Manila, Batangas etc) is next to the Petron petrol station.

Pumpboats go daily from here to El Nido and Taytay.

EL NIDO
pop 27,029

In the northwest reaches of Palawan, a beautiful bay jealously guards El Nido. This increasingly popular little town is hemmed in by jagged cliffs and a lovely beach.

It's not easy to get to, but most travellers find it's well worth the effort. A boat trip to the islands of the **Bacuit Archipelago** is an absolute must.

Information

Power in El Nido officially cuts out at midnight (and unofficially at any other time).

The **RCPI Calling Office** *(Tabangka St; open 8am-noon, 1pm-5pm & 6pm-9pm Mon-Fri)* is open long hours.

There are no banks here, but there are several moneychangers (dealing mainly in US dollars), including the friendly **El Nido Boutique & Art Café** near the pier.

Things to See & Do

El Nido Boutique & Art Café *(Palmera St)* has everything you'll need for making the most of the area. From here, you can design your own diving and snorkelling trips, book boats to Busuanga or Puerto Princesa, reconfirm flights, add your name to upcoming island-hopping tours, hire mountain bikes and other sports gear, stock up on souvenirs, or just have a chat and a coffee.

Places to Stay

Bayview Lodging House *(Palmera St; rooms P200-400)*, near the pier, has largish rooms. It also sports a big, broad balcony on the 2nd floor facing the beautiful bay.

Cliffside Cottages *(huts P350-450)*, set back from the beach at the foot of the spooky cliffs, is a popular choice, with separate huts with bathroom.

Marina Garden Beach Cottages *(cottages with shared bathroom P300, beachside cottages P500)*, back on Quezon St (which the locals may still refer to by its old name, Calle

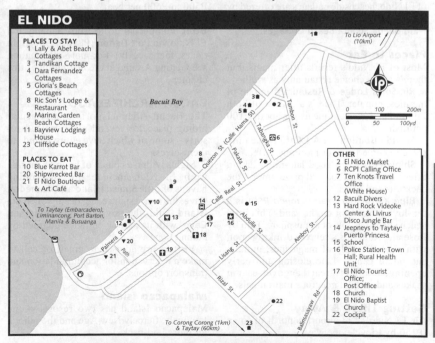

EL NIDO

PLACES TO STAY
1 Lally & Abet Beach Cottages
3 Tandikan Cottage
4 Dara Fernandez Cottages
5 Gloria's Beach Cottages
8 Ric Son's Lodge & Restaurant
9 Marina Garden Beach Cottages
11 Bayview Lodging House
23 Cliffside Cottages

PLACES TO EAT
10 Blue Karrot Bar
20 Shipwrecked Bar
21 El Nido Boutique & Art Café

OTHER
2 El Nido Market
6 RCPI Calling Office
7 Ten Knots Travel Office (White House)
12 Bacuit Divers
13 Hard Rock Videoke Center & Livirus Disco Jungle Bar
14 Jeepneys to Taytay; Puerto Princesa
15 School
16 Police Station; Town Hall; Rural Health Unit
17 El Nido Tourist Office; Post Office
18 Church
19 El Nido Baptist Church
22 Cockpit

Bacuit Bay

To Lio Airport (10km)

To Taytay (Embarcadero), Liminancong, Port Barton, Manila & Busuanga

To Corong Corong (1km) & Taytay (60km)

PALAWAN

Hama), has cottages with common bathroom and fancier cottages on the beach.

Ric Son's Lodge & Restaurant *(upstairs rooms from P300)* is a two-storey timber villa a few doors along from Marina Garden. It has airless but cheap rooms with common bathroom upstairs. The restaurant has the best beach views in town, and is a good choice for breakfast. On our last visit the rooms were not being rented out but this was said to be temporary.

Clumped together on Quezon St you have **Gloria's Beach Cottages** *(cottages P400, 4-person cottages P600)*, with shady, balconied cottages and a bigger four-person cottage with bathroom. We've received reports of thefts here, so take precautions. Nearby is **Dara Fernandez Cottages** *(cottages with bathroom P400-500)* and **Tandikan Cottage** *(cottages with bathroom P500)*.

Lally & Abet Beach Cottages *(waterside rooms P350, bungalows P700-800)*, at the far end of town from the pier, has roomy, balconied bungalows with bathroom and rooms with shared bathroom right by the water. There's also a decent restaurant.

In Corong Corong, a P5 tricycle ride south of El Nido, beachside cottages are offered by the peaceful **Dolarog Beach Resort** and El Nido **Buena Suenta Beach Cottages**.

Places to Eat

Most of El Nido's resorts offer meals, but there's a few choice restaurants as well.

Ric Son's Lodge & Restaurant is one of the most popular. There's a choice of both Filipino and Western meals for about P100 per dish.

El Nido Boutique & Art Café is the only place to come for your morning coffee.

Shipwrecked is a good late-night haunt, offering good seafood and pizza among the cocktails and beers.

Blue Karrot Bar *(mains around P60)* is a fun-loving bar right on the sand. This little beach shack has lots of atmosphere. Run by Rose and Rudi, it's a relaxed drinking spot, with a good supply of magazines, guitars, and board games. Late closing and early opening, it offers great hangover-easing shakes and simple, generous main meals.

Getting There & Away

Air El Nido's Lio airport is north of town (P150 by tricycle one way).

From El Nido to Manila, **Soriano Aviation** (☎ 02-804 0408) has a charter service requiring four days' notice from Manila and one day's notice from El Nido. In El Nido, you can book at the Ten Knots travel office (also known as the White House; Calle Real St).

Bus & Jeepney El Nido's Puerto Princesa-bound jeepneys head off from in front of the tourism office and post office at around 7am daily. The regular ones are called 'Souvenir', 'Sweetie' and 'Virgin Chaser'. It's a good idea to book a seat the night before – ask at the tourist office.

A new jeepney terminal has been built in nearby Corong Corong to serve El Nido, but so far nobody's taking much notice of it. Corong Corong is 1km south of El Nido (P5 by tricycle).

For more information on jeepneys between El Nido and Puerto Princesa, see the earlier Getting There & Away entry for Puerto Princesa.

Jeepneys go daily from El Nido to Sibultan on a surprisingly good road (P50 to P60, 1½ hours). Boat hire from Sibultan to nearby islands such as Flower Island costs P500 to P600 per boat.

Boat Pumpboats go to/from Sabang and El Nido via Port Barton (P850, 7½ to eight hours, four weekly). For more information see Getting Around at the beginning of this chapter.

BACUIT ARCHIPELAGO

The Bacuit Archipelago is a spectacular hiding place for several classy island resorts – some of which have entire islands to themselves.

Sights within a couple of hours' boat ride from El Nido include the snorkelling havens of little **Simisu Island** and **Cathedral Cave**, the rocky sightseeing beauty of **Snake Island**, and the mysterious **Cudugman Cave**, with its narrow entrance guarded by human bones.

Visitors are advised to email or call to make a reservation for accommodation and transport options.

Malapacao Island

Malapacao Island has two resorts – one famously, fiercely New Age and the other a lot more laid-back.

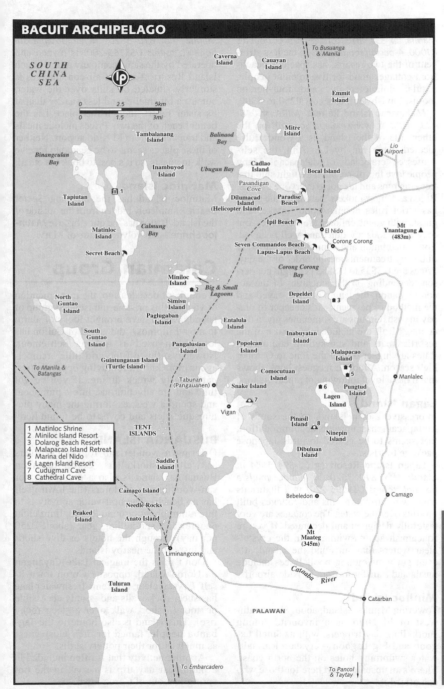

BACUIT ARCHIPELAGO

SOUTH CHINA SEA

0   2.5   5km
0   1.5   3mi

To Busuanga & Manila

Caverna Island

Cauayan Island

Emmit Island

Lio Airport

Binangculan Bay

Tambalanang Island

Balinaod Bay

Mitre Island

Inambuyod Island

Ubugun Bay

Cadlao Island

Bocal Island

Pasandigan Cove

Tapiutan Island

1

Calmung Bay

Dilumacad Island (Helicopter Island)

Paradise Beach

Ipil Beach

El Nido

Corong Corong

Mt Ynantagung (483m)

Matinloc Island

Secret Beach

Seven Commandos Beach
Lapus-Lapus Beach

Corong Corong Bay

Miniloc Island

2 Big & Small Lagoons

Depeldet Island

3

North Guntao Island

Simisu Island

Paglugaban Island

Entalula Island

Inabuyatan Island

South Guntao Island

Pangalusian Island

Popolcan Island

Malapacao Island

4

5

Guintungauan Island (Turtle Island)

To Manila & Batangas

Tabunan (Pangauanen)

Snake Island

Comocutuan Island

6 Lagen Island

Pungtud Island

Manlalec

Vigan

7

Pinasil Island

8

Ninepin Island

1 Matinloc Shrine
2 Miniloc Island Resort
3 Dolarog Beach Resort
4 Malapacao Island Retreat
5 Marina del Nido
6 Lagen Island Resort
7 Cudugman Cave
8 Cathedral Cave

TENT ISLANDS

Dibuluan Island

Saddle Island

Bebeledon

Camago

Camago Island

Needle Rocks

Anato Island

Peaked Island

Mt Maateg (345m)

Liminangcong

Cataaba River

Catarban

Tuluran Island

PALAWAN

To Embarcadero

To Pancol & Taytay

PALAWAN

Marina del Nido (☎ 02-831 0597 in Manila, fax 831 9816; cottages P2500, doubles P1000, 4-person rooms P2000), the less stringent of the two resorts, has spacious beachfront cottages good for five to eight people, regular double rooms and four-person rooms. Lavish set meals cost P250 to P300.

Malapacao Island Retreat (MIRA; ☎ 048-433 4829; ⓦ www.malapacao.com), on the other side of the island, is a wonderfully located place run by Lee Ann, the self-confessed 'crazy lady of Malapacao'. Many people love this place, but it's a tight ship that Lee Ann runs and it's not to everyone's tastes. Billed as a 'nonsmokers' paradise', the resort has strict rules about alcohol intake, and guests with young children are welcome – but only if the kids are quiet and well behaved. Yoga, meditation and a mind-boggling array of beauty treatments are the order of the day. Prices are US$35 to US$82 per night per person, depending on the amenities of the accommodation, the length of time stayed and the method of payment – it's cheaper to prepay in cash. Groups are sometimes given discounts. Meals are included, as are use of the resort's boats and snorkelling equipment. Rates are higher during the June to October high season. A look at its guest book shows that it has a loyal following of repeat visitors.

Lagan Island

Impressive Lagen Island, to the south of Malapacao, has upscale accommodation, that seems to be geared towards Japanese package tourists.

Lagen Island Resort (☎ 02-894 5644 in Manila, fax 810 3620; ⓔ elnido@mailsta tion.net; rooms US$195-270) is a luxurious place with air-con rooms and cottages built on stilts over the water. The cottages are very tastefully designed and decorated. If you're squeamish about swimming in the crystal-clear waters that surround the island, it's even got a swimming pool! Prices include meals and transfer to/from El Nido airport.

Miniloc Island

Towering Miniloc Island, about 8km southwest of El Nido, is a favourite among snorkelling day-trippers, with its **Small Lagoon** and **Big Lagoon** – crystal clear saltwater swimming holes on the north coast. There's an upscale resort here for those who can afford it.

Miniloc Island Resort (☎ 02-894 5644 in Manila, fax 810 3620; ⓔ elnido@mailsta tion.net; rooms US$165-200) is owned and operated by the same company as the Lagen Island Resort. A row of air-con cottages is similarly situated on stilts over the water, but are a bit smaller and less snazzy than at its sister resort, though this place has the better beach of the two. Prices include meals and transfer to/from El Nido airport. Neither of these places seems to be geared to receive walk-in guests, so it's best to book via email.

Matinloc Island

Matinloc Island has the amazing **Secret Beach**, completely hidden from the outside of the island. It also has the quite bizarre **Matinloc Shrine** – a revolving statue of Mary.

Calamian Group

A couple of decades ago, the mere mention of visiting this pristine and isolated group of islands would have brought looks of alarm to most Filipinos – the island of Culion has long been used as a leper settlement. Nowadays, this off-the-grid little archipelago is more known for diving opportunities, particularly wreck diving. If you've got time and are adventurous, hire a pumpboat and spend a week exploring the many picturesque islets and coves to be found here.

BUSUANGA ISLAND

Offering a wonderland for wreck divers as well as snorkellers, **Coron town** on Busuanga Island is also a great base for sun-worshipping explorers (the town itself has no beach). The best-value activity is to hire a pumpboat (around P1000, limit eight people) and snorkelling gear (about P250 per day) through the hotels or dive shops and inspect the nearby islands.

Don't miss the magical **Lake Cayangan** on Coron Island, opposite Coron town itself. Crystal clear, this semi-freshwater lake has sheer rock walls and is only accessible on foot (a short walk over a steep rocky rise). This island is also home to the **Tagbanua people**, famed for their elusiveness as much as for their pottery skills.

Another activity that is often included in a pumpboat day trip is a soak in the **hot spring** just out of Coron town.

CALAMIAN GROUP

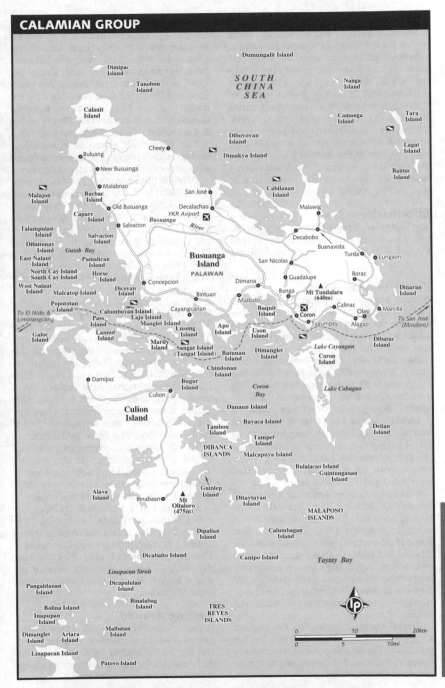

SOUTH CHINA SEA

Dumungalit Island

Dimipac Island
Tanobon Island
Nanga Island
Calauit Island
Camanga Island
Tara Island
Lagat Island
Bantac Island

Cheey
Diboyoyan Island
Dimakya Island
Buluang
New Busuanga
Malabnao
Malajon Island
Bacbac Island
Old Busuanga
San José
Decalachao
YKR Airport
Busuanga River
Cabilauan Island
Malawig
Capare Island
Salvacion
Talampulan Island
Salvacion Island
Decabobo
Buenavista
Dibutonay Island
Gutob Bay
Busuanga Island
PALAWAN
San Nicolas
Turda
Lungaon
East Nalaut Island
Pamalican Island
Borac
North Cay Island
South Cay Island
Horse Island
Concepcion
Dimana
Guadalupe
Mt Tundalara (640m)
Dinaran Island
West Nalaut Island
Dicoyan Island
Bintuan
Malbato
Banga
Malcatop Island
Baquit Island
Calinac
Olasi
Marcilla
Popototan Island
Calumbuyan Island
Cayangcanan
Apo Island
Coron
Tagumpay
Alagao
To San José (Mindoro)
To El Nido & Liminangcong
Pass Island
Lajo Island
Manglet Island
Uson Island
Dibatuc Island
Galoc Island
Lamud Island
Lusong Island
Marily Island
Sangat Island (Tangat Island)
Batunan Island
Dimanglet Island
Lake Cayangan
Coron Island
Chindonan Island
Damipac
Bugur Island
Culion
Coron Bay
Lake Cabugao
Culion Island
Danaun Island
Bayaca Island
Delian Island
Tambon Island
Tampel Island
DIBANCA ISLANDS
Malcapuya Island
Bulalacao Island
Guintungauan Island
Alava Island
Binabaan
Mt Oltaloro (475m)
Guinlep Island
Ditaytayan Island
MALAPOSO ISLANDS
Dipalian Island
Calumbagan Island
Dicabaito Island
Canipo Island
Taytay Bay
Linapacan Strait
Pangaldauan Island
Dicapululan Island
Bolina Island
Binalabag Island
TRES REYES ISLANDS
Inapupan Island
Dimanglet Island
Ariara Island
Malbatan Island
Linapacan Island
Patoyo Island

0   10   20km
0   5   10mi

Diving – and **wreck diving** in particular – is the other great pastime in this area. There are at least 10 wrecks around Busuanga, Japanese warships and merchant ships that were sunk by American fighter planes during WWII. The depths at which the wrecks are found vary from very shallow waters to quite deep, so there are diving opportunities for beginners as well as experienced divers. There are several dive shops in Coron, most of which offer some sort of wreck-diving package, sometimes including an overnight stay in a resort on one of the small islands nearest the wrecks. Diving instruction is also usually offered.

Information

The **Swagman Travel** office just up from the pier now offers email facilities, as well as the usual money-changing and telephone services.

Places to Stay & Eat

A short tricycle ride (about P5) from the Coron town wharf will bring you to the market area, the centre of Coron town, half of which is perched on bamboo stilts. Places to stay include the following.

Bayside Divers Lodge & Restaurant (dorm beds P150, rooms P750) has dorm rooms and big rooms with a view and bathroom. It's very friendly and quite popular. As the name implies, diving packages are arranged here.

L&M Pe Lodge Sea Lodge & Restaurant (rooms P250-350) has an interesting location, built out over the water just west of the market. Rooms are basic but have some charm, with walls and ceilings panelled with wood and woven bamboo.

Kokosnuss Garden Resort & Restaurant (rooms P400-800) is a 20-minute walk up the sloping main road past the Swagman Travel office (or grab a tricycle for about P10). This is one of the best places if you don't mind the relative isolation. Cottages and *nipa* hut-style rooms in this large garden compound range from the cheapest (with possibly the fanciest common bathroom in Southeast Asia) to big rooms complete with bathroom murals.

Krystal Lodge (doubles P300) is another very good place just out of town by the waterside. The double rooms look over the water. A friendly, family-run place, it also serves up great pancakes.

Kalamayan Inn (rooms P850-1250) is a new place in the centre of town, with spotless air-con rooms in a family home. American or Filipino breakfast is included with the room rates. Its restaurant also includes a cosy bar.

All places to stay have their own restaurants, and while the food won't exactly entrance your taste buds, you'll experience the tastiest dishes at the **Bayside Divers Lodge & Restaurant** (which does a great pizza).

The islands off Coron have started to sprout resorts – nearly all of them upscale and with wreck diving as the principal activity.

Divelink Resort (☎ 02-412 0644 in Manila, fax 372 6031; e info@divelink.com.ph; cottages US$258-378) is located on Uson Island, just off the coast of Coron, and has comfortable cottages in different sizes and with varying amenities that sleep up to six people. There's a swimming pool (used mostly to train beginning divers) and a poolside bar. The resort is just a brief pumpboat ride away from Coron.

Getting There & Away

SEAIR and Asian Spirit serve the little YKR airport on the north side of Busuanga Island (about a one-hour bumpy jeepney ride from Coron town). There are flights to/from Manila (P2300, daily), and flights from Puerto Princesa (P2200, three weekly). Ask at travel agents in Puerto Princesa about other airlines that offer charter services. There's an Air Ads office in Coron town, next door to the Bayside Divers Lodge & Restaurant.

MBRS Lines has temporarily discontinued its big passenger/car ferry doing the Manila–Coron–Liminangcong–Coron–Manila trip each week. Service was set to resume by the time you read this book.

Sulpicio Lines has a weekly boat between Manila and Coron.

Viva Lines has solid little wooden ferries sailing between Batangas and Coron town. They leave Coron on Friday (P400) and the trip takes 17 hours – up to 22 hours if the ship's heavily laden. From Batangas, they leave Wednesday.

Getting Around

If you're game, you can hire 125cc Suzuki motorcycles from the Blue Heaven Hang-Out Bar on the road to the Kokosnuss Garden Resort & Restaurant. The usual charge is P500 per day, without petrol.

DIMAKYA ISLAND

North of central Busuanga Island, the glorious little Dimakya Island is a pocket-size tropical playground. It has a long, white-sand beach, plenty of reef and a Japanese WWII wreck just offshore, and wildlife on view via several hiking trails. Equally idyllic islands are within easy reach of Dimakya, and boat trips can be organised through the island's resort, Club Paradise.

Places to Stay & Eat

Club Paradise (*☎ 02-893 8280 in Manila, fax 894 5725; singles/doubles with fan & bathroom US$100/130, with air-con US$110/140*) has standard cottages, rooms with fan and bathroom, and marble-bathroomed air-con quarters. The prices here include three daily meals at the large, local-food restaurant. Also on offer is a swimming pool, tennis court, library and heaps of water-sports equipment.

Getting There & Away

Club Paradise organises transfer trips from Busuanga Island's YKR airport to Dimakya Island by jeepney and boat (one hour). The cost of this trip is included in the price of your room.

CALAUIT ISLAND

The Club Paradise resort on Dimakya Island specialises in safari tours to Calauit Island, the rather surreal home of around 500 imported African animals. If you want to make arrangements for your own visit here, you will need permission from the **Conservation & Resources Management Foundation** (*☎ 02-705 001*).

SANGAT ISLAND

The **Sangat Island Reserve Swagman Travel office** (*☎ 02-523 854, fax 522-3663; cottages per person from US$65, with 4 diving trips per person US$95*) is part of a chain of 'bio-resorts'. This place offers quite stylish beachside cottages, which include bathroom and balcony. For those wishing to do some underwater exploring, you can hire your diving gear for US$7 per dive. The prices include a boat transfer to/from Coron town and meals.

Language

Pilipino (also known as Tagalog) is one of two official languages of the Philippines. The other is English and, along with Pilipino, it's used for most business, government and legal transactions.

Tagalog ranks as the principal regional language out of around 100 languages or dialects spoken in the Philippines. It belongs to the Malayo-Polynesian language family whose members extend from Madagascar to Tonga.

In 1937 Tagalog was declared the official national language, a choice based on the fact that, as the dialect spoken in Manila, it was already understood and spoken by most Filipinos. Historically, it was also the language used by the leaders of the Philippine revolution against Spanish rule, since most were from Tagalog-speaking regions. After debate over the elevated status of Tagalog it was decided to call the official national language Pilipino, with the view to making the new name (and language) more acceptable to Filipinos from non-Tagalog regions.

Most Filipinos can speak and understand both Pilipino and English, so foreign travellers will find that getting around isn't difficult, even beyond the cities.

Pronunciation

English speakers should have little trouble with Pilipino pronunciation. Words are generally pronounced as they are written and vowels and consonants have a consistent pronunciation.

Vowels

a	as in 'far'
e	as in 'get'
i	as the 'ee' in 'beef'
o	as in 'more'
u	as in 'June'

When several vowels occur in a sequence, each vowel is pronounced separately, eg, *panauhin* (visitor) is pronounced 'pana-uhin'.

Some Pilipino vowels are pronounced with what is called a glottal stop. This is done by making the sound of the vowel, then abruptly stopping it, as heard in the 'tt'

Body Language

Most Filipinos signify 'Yes' by raising the eyebrows or lifting the head upwards slightly. They also do this when they greet friends.

You can hiss to gain attention, for example, when calling a waiter in a restaurant. When you want to pay the bill, make the figure of a rectangle in the air with your index finger and thumb.

It's considered impolite to pass between people conversing or facing one another. If you must do so, the Filipino polite way is to extend an arm or two arms with the hands clasped and pointing downwards either without saying anything or murmuring *iskyús*.

Touching, especially women, is not taken well by Filipinos. You'll notice that a Filipino man will extend his hand to shake yours but a Filipino woman will not readily do so. When being introduced to a couple or greeting them, you shake hands with the man and smile with a nod of the head to the woman.

---

in the Cockney pronunciation of 'bottle'. Glottal stops often occur on a word-final vowel.

Diphthongs

There are a few diphthongs (combinations of vowel sounds) in Pilipino:

ay	as the 'uy' in 'buy'
aw	as the 'ou' in 'mount'
ey	as in 'they'
iw	produced by making the sound 'ee' and continuing it to 'oo'
oy	as the 'oi' in 'noise'
uy	produced by making the sound 'oo' and continuing it to 'ee'

Consonants

Most Pilipino consonants are pronounced in the same way as their English counterparts, with the exception of the following:

g	always hard, as in 'good'; never as in 'gentle'
h	as in 'haste'; always aspirated
ng	as in 'sing'; can occur at the beginning of a word, eg, *ngayon* (now)

What Are They Speaking?

Ang manidyer ay nagmaneho papunta sa palengke upang bumili ng alak. (The manager drove to the market to buy liquor).

A simple Tagalog sentence – but within it are words that vividly demonstrate the Philippines' long, rich history of trade and cultural exchange. Let's break the sentence up and see what we come up with. A keen ear would easily catch the English-loan word *manidyer* (manager). Indeed, were it to appear in a publication, it might even retain its English spelling. It is estimated that modern Tagalog is made up of about 20% English loan words – and the number is growing. Not surprising when you consider that a 1980 census revealed that over half the population of the Philippines claimed that they spoke English as a second language.

Perhaps less easy for the unaccustomed ear to catch is the word *nagmaneho*, from the Spanish *manejar* (to drive). Spanish loan words make up at least 15% of Tagalog vocabulary. While Tagalog is liberally peppered with these relics of Spanish rule, the two languages are far from mutually intelligible. As very few Filipinos received a formal education in Spanish during colonial times, loan words from Spanish often mutated and took on a slightly different pronunciation, making them unintelligible to visitors from Spanish-speaking countries. The Tagalog words *bandila* (flag) and *litrato* (photograph) are derived from the Spanish *bandera* and *retrato* respectively. Sometimes loan words have altered meaning completely: *seguro* means 'sure' in Spanish – the Tagalog *siguro* means 'maybe'! A census taken in 1990 showed that the number of Filipinos who spoke Spanish as a first language numbered only 2658 – limited to some of the old-money families of Spanish descent who reside in Manila.

Back to the sample sentence. The word *palengke* may seem familiar to visitors who have travelled in Mexico, where it is spelled *palenque* and means 'cockfighting ring'. Originally a Maya word meaning 'gathering place', its near-identical Tagalog equivalent means 'market'. It's likely that the Spanish in colonial Mexico borrowed the word from the Maya to describe any gathering of *indios* (as the Spanish called both the Filipinos and the Native Americans of the New World), and then introduced the word to the Philippines during the 250-year Galleon trade between Mexico and the Philippines.

Of course, contacts with outsiders didn't begin with the Spanish. Evidence of trade with India and Arabia has also been found in the Philippines and, not surprisingly, the Tagalog language reflects this. The word *alak* (liquor) shares a lineage with the Malay *arak* and was derived from the Arabic *araq*.

With the advent of Pilipino – the modified version of Tagalog intended to become the predominant language of the Philippines – a few feeble attempts were made to rid the language of 'foreign influences'. In some cases English loan words were replaced with Spanish ones that had fallen out of everyday usage. There were even attempts to invent new 'Pilipino' words to replace Spanish loan words. One such word was *salipawpaw*, meant to replace the Spanish-derived *eroplano*. It's no surprise that the doomed salipawpaw never got off the ground!

Steven Martin

---

r   rolled to produce a faint trill
s   as in 'sun', never as in 'his'

Word Stress

Word stress is marked by an acute accent over the vowel on which the stress falls, eg, *masayá* (happy). If stress falls on a word-final vowel with a circumflex accent (^), the vowel is pronounced with a glottal stop, eg, *masamâ* (bad).

Greetings & Civilities

Pilipino has polite and informal modes of address. It's better to use the polite form for adults you don't know well. When you use the formal mode with friends or younger adults, you'll more than likely get the comment: 'Don't use *hô/pô* with me. I'm not that old yet'. Where both the polite and informal are given in this guide, they are marked 'pol' and 'inf' respectively.

Use the title *mamà* for a man who is a stranger or *ale* for a woman. You may also use *misis/mis* (Mrs/Miss) for adult female strangers. Use *sir* for a professional man or *ma'am* for a professional woman. The more friendly and familiar term *páre* (for a man) or *brad* (for a younger adult, if you are yourself one) may also be used for a man who is a stranger, eg, *Iskyús lang, páre* (Excuse me, my friend).

Good morning.	*Magandáng umaga hô.* (pol)
	Magandáng umaga. (inf)
Good morning. (response)	*Magandáng umaga naman hô.*
Good afternoon.	*Magandáng hapon hô.*
Good evening.	*Magandáng gabí hô.*
Hello.	*Kumusta hô.*
Goodbye.	*Paalam na hô.*
Bye.	*Sige na muna.* (inf)
Yes.	*Ohò/Opò.*
No.	*Hindi hô.*
Excuse me.	*Mawaláng-galang na nga hô.*
Sorry.	*Iskyus/Sori hô.*
Thank you (very much).	*(Maráming) salámat hô.*
You're welcome.	*Waláa hong anuman.* (lit: 'it's nothing')
What's your name?	*Anóng pangalan ninyó?*
My name is ...	*Akó si ...*
May I take your photo?	*Maári ko ba kayóng kunan ng litrato?*

Language Difficulties

Do you speak English?	*Marunong ba kayóng mag-Ingglés?*
Does anyone here speak English?	*Meron hô bang marunong mag-Ingglés dito?*
Do you understand?	*Náiintindihán ba ninyó?*
I understand.	*Náiintindihán ko hô.*
I don't understand.	*Hindî ko hô náiintindihán.*
Please write it down.	*Pakisulat niyó ngâ yón.*
How do you say ...?	*Papáno hô ba sabihin ...?*
What does ... mean?	*Ano hô ang ibig sabihin ng ...?*

Getting Around

Where is the ...?	*Násaán hô ang ...?*
bus station	*terminál ng bus*
nearest LRT station	*ang pinakamalapit na istasyón ng LRT*
Metro station	*ang istasyón ng Metro Tren*

Signs

Most of the signs in airports and stations are in English, so you shouldn't encounter any major problems getting around.

Maínit/Maginaw	Hot/Cold
Pasukán	Entrance
Lábasan	Exit
Bawal Pumasok	No Entry
Bawal Manigarílyo	No Smoking
Bukás/Sará	Open/Closed
Bawal	Prohibited
CR	Toilets

| train station | *istasyón ng tren* |
| road to ... | *daán papuntáng ...* |

What time does the ... leave/arrive?	*Anóng oras hô áalís/dáratíng ang ...?*
boat	*bapór*
bus	*bus*
plane	*eropláno*
train	*tren*

| Where can I buy a ticket? | *Saán hô maaring bumilí ng tiket?* |

I'd like a ... ticket.	*... tiket nga hô.*
one-way	*isáng one-way*
return	*isáng round trip*
1st class	*1st class*
2nd class	*2nd class*

How do we get to ...?	*Papano hô namin marárating ang ...?*
Is it far from here?	*Malayò hô ba dito?*
Is it near here?	*Malapit hô ba dito?*
Can we walk there?	*Puwede hô bang lakarin?*
Can you show me (on the map)?	*Puwede hô ba niyóng ipakita sa mapa?*

What ... is this?	*Anó hô bang ... itó?*
province	*probinsya*
street	*kalye*
town	*bayan*
village	*baryo*

Go straight ahead.	*Tulóy-tulóy lang hô.*
Turn ...	*Liko hô ...*
to the right	*kanan hô/lang* (pol/inf)
to the left	*kaliwâ hô/lang* (pol/inf)
at the next corner	*sa súsunod na kánto*
at the traffic lights	*sa ílaw*

behind ...	*sa likód ng ...*
in front of ...	*sa haráp ng ...*
opposite	*katapát ng*
north	*norte/hilagà*
south	*sud/timog*
east	*silangan*
west	*kanluran*

There are designated bus stops for regular buses, but you can often get off anywhere, depending on the mood of the driver and the traffic situation – just say *Para!* (Stop!) loudly.

Where is the bus stop?	*Násaán hô ang hintúan ng bus?*
Which bus goes to ...?	*Alíng bus hô ang papuntá sa ...?*
Does this bus go to ...?	*Papuntá hô ba itóng bus na itó sa ...?*
I want to get off at ...	*Bábabâ hô ako sa ...*

What station is this?
  Ano hóng istasyón itó?
What's the next station?
  Anó hô ba ang susunód na istasyón?
Does this train stop at ...?
  Humíhintô hô ba ang tren na itó sa ...?
The train is delayed/cancelled.
  Náhulí/Nákanselá hô ang tren.
How long will it be delayed?
  Gaano katagál hô mahúhulí?

Is this taxi free?	*Bakánte hô bang taksing itó?*
Please take me to ...	*Dalhín nga niyó akó sa ...*
Stop here!	*Para na hô dito!*
Where does the boat leave from?	*Mulá hô saán áalis ang barkó?*
How long does the trip take?	*Gaano hô katagál ang biyahe?*
Is that seat taken?	*May nakaupô na hô ba diyán?*
Where can I rent a car?	*Saán hô maáring umupa ng awto?*
Where can I hire a bicycle?	*Saán hô puwedeng umarkilá ng bisikleta.*

Accommodation

I'm looking for a ...	*Nagháhanáp hô akó ng ...*
campground	*kampingan*

guesthouse	*bahay para sa mgáturista*
hotel	*otél*
motel	*motél*
youth hostel	*youth hostel*

What's the address?
  Ano hô ang adrés?
Could you write the address, please?
  Pakísulat niyó ngâ ang adrés.
I'd like to book a room, please.
  Gústo ko hong magreserba ng kuwarto.
Do you have any rooms available?
  May bakante hô ba kayó?

How much is it for ...?	*Magkano hô para sa ...?*
one night	*isáng gabí*
a week	*isáng linggó*
two people	*dalawáng táo*

Does it include breakfast?
  Kasama na hô ba doón ang almusál?
Do you have a room with two beds?
  May kuwarto hô ba kayó na may dalawáng kama?
Do you have a room with a double bed?
  May kuwárto hô ba kayó may kamang pangdalawahan?

I'd like ...	*Gústo ko hô ...*
a single room	*ng pángísahan na kuwarto*
to share a dorm	*na makísunong sa isáng malakíng kuwarto*

May I see it?	*Maarì ko hô bang tignán?*
Where is the bathroom?	*Násaán hô ba ang banyo?*
It's fine. I'll take it.	*Sige hô. Kukunin ko.*

air-conditioning	*erkon*
bathroom	*banyo*
bottle of water	*bote ng tubig*
clean	*malinis*
key	*susì*
mosquito coil	*katól*
shower	*dutsa*
soap	*sabón*
toilet	*kubéta/CR/toilet*
toilet paper	*tisyu*
towel	*tuwalya*
water (cold/hot)	*(malamíg/mainit na) tubig*

Around Town

Where is a ...?	*Saán hô may ...?*
bank	*bangko*
consulate	*konsulado*
embassy	*embahada*
market	*palengke*
museum	*museo*
police station	*istasyón ng pulís*
post office	*pos opis*
public telephone	*teléponó*
public toilet	*comfort room/CR/ pálikuran*
town square	*plasa*

I want to change ...	*Gústo ko hong magpapalít ng ...*
cash/money	*pera*
travellers cheques	*travellers check*

aerogram	*aerogram*
air mail	*ermeyl*
envelope	*sobre*
letter	*sulat*
stamps	*sélyo*

I want to call ...	*Gústo ko hóng tawagan ...*
Where can I use email?	*Saán hô kayâ akó makakagamit ng email?*
I need to check my email.	*Kailangan ko hóng tignán ang email ko.*
I want to send a fax.	*Gústo ko hóng magpadalá ng fax.*
What time does it open/close?	*Anóng oras hô itó nagbúbukás/ nagsásará?*

Shopping

general store	*tindahan*
bookshop	*tindahan ng libró*
chemist/pharmacy	*botika/parmasya*
market	*palengke*

Where can I buy ...?	*Saán ako makakabili ng ...?*
I'd like to buy ...	*Gústo ko hóng bumili ng ...*
I don't like it.	*Ayoko nitó.*
Can I look at it?	*Maarì bang tignán?*
I'm just looking.	*Tumítingín hô lang akó.*
How much is this?	*Magkano hô itó?*
Do you accept credit cards?	*Tumátanggáp ba kayó ng credit card?*

I think it's too expensive.	*Ang mahál-mahál namán.*
Can you lower the price?	*May tawad hô ba iyán?*

big	*malakí*
small	*maliit*
more	*mas marami*
a little bit	*katitíng*
many	*marami*
too much/many	*masyadong marami*
enough	*sapát*

Health

Where is the ...?	*Násaán hô ang ...?*
chemist	*botíka*
doctor	*doktór*
hospital	*ospitál*

I'm sick.	*May sakít hô akó.*
My friend is sick.	*May sakít hô ang kasama ko.*
I need a doctor who speaks English.	*Kailángan ko hô ng doktór na marúnong mag-Ingglés.*
Could I see a female doctor?	*Puwéde hong magpa- tingín sa babáeng doktór?*
I'm pregnant.	*Buntís hô akó.*
I feel nauseous.	*Naalibádbarán/ Nasúsukâ hô ako.*
I have a headache.	*Masakít hô ang ulo ko.*
I have a stomach- ache.	*Masakít hô ang tiyán ko.*

I'm ...	*May ... ako*
diabetic	*diabitis*
asthmatic	*hikà*
anaemic	*anemya*

I'm allergic to ...	*Allergic ako sa ...*
antibiotics	*antibiyotiká*
penicillin	*penisilín*

antiseptic	*antiseptiko*
aspirin	*aspirina*
bandage	*benda*
Band-aids	*koritas*
condoms	*kondom*
painkillers	*gamót na pang- pakalma ng kirót*
sanitary napkins	*tampon*
soap	*sabón*
sunblock	*sunblock*
tampons	*tampon*
toilet paper	*tisyu/papél sa kubeta*

Emergencies

Help!	Saklolo!
Watch out!	Ingat!
Call the/a ...!	Tumawag ka ng...!
police	pulís
doctor	doktór
ambulance	ambulansiya
I've been raped!	Ginahasà akó!
I've been robbed!	Ninakawan akó!
Thief!	Magnanakáw!
Fire!	Sunog!
Go away!	Umalís ka!
Where are the toilets?	Násaán hô ang CR?

Time, Dates & Numbers

The Pilipino counterparts of 'am' and 'pm' are *n.u.* for *ng umaga* (in the morning), *n.t.* for *ng tanghalì* (at noon), *n.h.* for *ng hapon* (in the afternoon) and *n.g.* for *ng gabí* (in the evening/at night)

What time is it?	Anong óras na?
It's (five) am.	Alas (singko) n.u.
It's (seven) pm.	Alas (siyete) n.g.

'Half past' is expressed by the word *imédya*, eg, It's half past (six), *Alas (seis) imédya.*

Monday	Lunes
Tuesday	Martes
Wednesday	Miyérkolés
Thursday	Huwebes
Friday	Biyernes
Saturday	Sábado
Sunday	Linggó
January	Enero
February	Pebrero
March	Marso
April	Abríl
May	Mayo
June	Hunyo
July	Hulyo
August	Agosto
September	Setyembre
October	Oktubre
November	Nobyembre
December	Disyembre
morning	umaga
afternoon	hápon

night	gabí
now	ngayón
today	ngayón araw
this morning	ngayón umága
this afternoon	ngayón hapon
tonight	ngayón gabí
tomorrow	bukas
this week	ngayóng linggó
this month	ngayóng buwán
yesterday	kahapon

There are two sets of numbers: the native Pilipino and the Spanish, written the Pilipino way. Spanish numbers are used for times, dates and prices which have both the high and low denomination or are above 10 pesos. English numbers are also widely used to express prices. For example the price 'P1.50' is *uno singkuwenta* or *one fifty*, but 'P1.00' is simply *piso* in Pilipino.

	Spanish	Tagalog
1	uno	isá
2	dos	dalawá
3	tres	tatló
4	kuwatro	apát
5	singko	limá
6	seis	ánim
7	siyete	pitó
8	otso	waló
9	nuwebe	siyám
10	diyes	sampû
11	onse	labíng-isá
12	dose	labíndalawá
13	trése	labíntatló
14	katórse	labíng-ápat
15	kínse	labínlimá
16	disiseis	labíng-ánim
17	disisiyete	labímpitó
18	disiotso	labíng-waló
19	disinuwebe	labínsiyám
20	beynte	dalawampû
21	beynte uno	dalawampu't isá
30	treynta	tatlumpû
40	kuwarenta	ápatnapû
50	singkuwenta	limampû
60	sisenta	ánimnapû
70	sitenta	pitumpû
80	otsénta	walumpû
90	nobenta	siyamnapû
100	siyento	sandaán
1000	isang mil	isáng libo/sanlibo
one million		
	isang milyon	isang angaw

1st	*úna*
2nd	*ikalawá*
3rd	*ikatló*

FOOD & DRINKS

breakfast	*almusal/agahan*
lunch	*tanghalian*
dinner	*hapunan*
snack	*meryenda*

I'm a vegetarian.	*Gulay lamang ang kinákain ko.*
I don't eat meat.	*Hindî akó kumákain ng karné.*
Please bring ...	*Pakidalá nga hô ...*
Is service included in the bill?	*Kasama ba ang serbisyo sa kuwenta?*

fork	*tinidór*
glass	*baso*
knife	*kutsilyo*
plate	*plato*
spoon	*kutsara*
serviette/napkin	*sirbilyeta*

Main Dishes

Names of dishes often describe the way they are cooked, so it's worth remembering that *adobo* is stewed in vinegar and garlic, *sinigang* is sour soup, *ginataan* means cooked in coconut milk, *kiliwan* is raw seafood, *pangat* includes sauteed tomatoes and *inihaw* is grilled meat or fish. The word for 'spicy' is *maangháng*.

adobo – often called the national dish; salty stewed chicken or pork, marinated in vinegar and garlic

adobong pusit – cuttlefish in vinegar and coconut milk soup

arroz caldo – Spanish-style thick rice soup with chicken, garlic, ginger and onions

aso – dog; eaten with relish (or just plain) by northern Luzon's hilltribes

baboy – pork

balut – boiled chicken egg containing a partially formed embryo

bangus – milkfish; lightly grilled, stuffed and baked

calamares – squid

carne – beef

crispy pata – crispy fried and seasoned pig skin

gulay – vegetables

lechon – spit-roast baby pig with liver sauce

lumpia – spring rolls filled with meat or vegetables

mami – noodle soup; similar to *mee* in Malaysia or Indonesia

manok – chicken

menudo – stew with vegetables, liver or pork

pansit bihon – thick or thin noodle dish

pochero – mix of beef, spicy sausage and vegetables

pusit – cuttlefish

tocino – pork dish made with saltpetre (also used in the recipe for homemade gunpowder)

Basics

bread	*tinapay*
butter	*mantikilya*
cheese	*keso*
coconut milk	*gatá*
cooking oil	*langís panluto*
eggs	*itlóg*
flour	*arina*
honey	*pulút-pukyutan*
milk (fresh)	*(sariwang) gatas*
yogurt	*yoghurt*

Meat & Poultry

beef	*karnéng-baka*
chicken	*manók*
duck	*pato*
goatmeat	*karnéng-kambing*
ham	*hamón*
meat	*kárné*
pork	*karneng-baboy*
turkey	*pabo*
venison	*karnéng-usa*

Seafood

clams	*tulyá*
crabs	*alimángo* (large, with dark, thick shell)
	alimasag (spotted, thin shelled)
	talangká (small)
lobster	*uláng*
mussels	*tahóng*
oysters	*talabá*
sea crabs	*alimásag*
shrimp	*hípon*

Vegetables

vegetables	*gulay*
beans	*bataw*

bean sprouts	*toge*
bitter melon	*ampaláyá*
cassava/manioc	*kamóteng káhoy*
Chinese string beans	*sítaw*
eggplant	*talóng*
lima beans	*patáni*
mild radish-type vegetable	*singkamás*
onions	*sibuyas*
peppers (capsicum)	*sili*
ramie leaves	*salúyot*
spinach-like vegetable	*kangkóng*
squash	*kalabasa*
sweet potatoes	*kamote*
onion	*sibuyas*
tomatoes	*kamatis*

Fruit

fruit	*prutas*
avocado	*abokado*
banana	*saging*
cantaloupe (rockmelon)	*milón*
custard apple	*atis*
lime	*dayap*
mandarin	*dalanghita*
mango	*manggá*
orange	*dalandan*
papaya/pawpaw	*papaya*
pineapple	*pinyá*
pomelo	*suhà*
Spanish plum	*sinigwélas*

star apple	*kaimíto*
watermelon	*pakwán*

(*calamansi* is a small citrus fruit used for juice)

Spices & Condiments

garlic	*bawang*
ginger	*lúya*
pepper	*pamintá*
saffron	*kasubhâ*
salt	*asin*
small hot chilli peppers	*labuyo*
soy sauce	*toyò*
sugar	*asukal*
vinegar	*sukà*

Drinks

water	*tubig*
boiled water	*pinakuluáng tubig*
cold water	*malamíg na tubig*
hot water	*mainit na tubig*
mineral water	*mineral water*
(cup of) tea	*(isang tásang) tsaá*
ginger tea	*salabat*
cocoa	*tsokolate*
coffee	*kape*
avocado drink	*abokádo dyus*
lemonade	*limonáda*
mango drink	*mango dyus*
with/without ice	*may/waláng yelo*
with/without milk	*may/walang gátas*
with/without sugar	*may/walang asúkal*

Glossary

arnis de mano – a pre-Hispanic style of stick-fighting (more commonly known simply as arnis)

bagyo – typhoon
balisong – fan or butterfly knives
bahala na – you could almost call this the 'national philosophy'; in the days before the advent of Christianity, god was called 'bathala' by ancient Filipinos; the expression 'Bahala na' is derived from this word and expresses faith in god (God will provide) as well a kind of fatalism (Come what may); it's somewhere between an Australian 'no worries' and Kurt Vonnegut's 'so it goes', but less individualistic than either: all things shall pass and in the meantime life is to be lived – preferably in the company of one's friends and – most importantly – family
bahay na bato – stone house
balangay – artfully crafted sea-going outrigger boat
balikbayan – an overseas Filipino returning or paying a visit to the Philippines
balisong – fan or butterfly knife
bangka – (or banca) a wooden boat, usually with outriggers and powered by a cannibalised automotive engine; a pumpboat
barangay – village, neighbourhood or community, the basic sociopolitical unit of Filipino society
barong – a generic term to describe the Filipino local dress (for women) and shirt for men that is the 'national costume'; it usually has a heavily embroidered or patterned front
Barong Tagalog – traditional Filipino formal shirt (the *barong* originally was for men only; it refers only to the shirt), with elaborate embroidery or patterning down the front; made of *jusi* or *pinya*
baryo – (from Spanish: barrio) district or neighbourhood
bas-relief – style of sculpture that stands out from a surrounding flat stone background
butanding – whale shark

fronton – *jai alai* court

guyabano – soursop

haribon – the Philippine eagle, an endangered species; haribon literally means 'king of birds'

jai alai – a fast-paced ball game, and one of the more popular sports in the Philippines
jeepney – a brightly painted vehicle that looks like an extended jeep, fitted with benches, adorned with everything but a kitchen sink and crammed with passengers
jusi – fabric woven from ramie fibres; used to make a *barong*

kalabaw – (or carabao) water buffalo
kalesa – horse-drawn carriage
kundiman – a melancholy genre of song originating in Manila (and the Tagalog region); one of the country's most-loved musical idioms

lahar – rain-induced landslide of volcanic debris; in other words, mud from volcanic ash
lapu-lapu – groper (also spelled grouper)

mestisos – Filipinos of mixed descent, specifically Eurasians or Amerasians; a Filipino of mixed Asian ancestry is not called a mestiso
Moro – Spanish colonial term for Muslim Filipinos, once derogatory but now worn with some pride

nara – a hardwood tree, the Philippine national tree
nipa – a type of palm tree, the leaves of which are used for making nipa huts, the typical house in rural areas

pansit bihon – thick- or thin-noodle soup
paraw – traditional outrigger with jib and mainsail
pasyon – Christ's Passion, sung or re-enacted every Holy Week
Pilipino – the national language; created out of Tagalog, the language in Manila and surrounding provinces
Pinoy – a term Filipinos call themselves
pinya – (or piña) fabric woven from pineapple fibres; commonly used to make a *barong*

poblasyon – town centre

sabong – cockfighting
santo – religious statue
sari-sari – small neighborhood store stocked with all kinds of daily necessities; sari-sari literally means 'assortment'

Tagalog – the dominant dialect of Manila and surrounding provinces, now the national language called Pilipino
tamaraw – an endangered species of native buffalo, found only in Mindoro; one of the most endangered animals in the world
tapsilog – a modern compound combining three words *tapa* (dried beef), *sinangag* (garlic fried rice) and *itlog* (fried egg); usually eaten for breakfast
tanigue – tuna steak, usually grilled (also known as tanguigue)
tinikling – Philippine national folk dance

tricycle – a Philippine rickshaw, formerly pedal-powered but now predominantly motorised

ACRONYMS
CBST – Community-Based Sustainable Tourism
DENR – Department of Environment & Natural Resources
DOH – Department of Health
DOT – Department of Tourism
GROs – 'Guest Relation Officers' are officially glorified waitresses; unofficially they are sex workers
MILF – Moro Islamic Liberation Front
MNLF – Moro National Liberation Front
NPA – New People's Army
Philvolcs – Philippine Institute of Volcanology & Seismology
PNP – Philippine National Police
VFA – Visiting Forces Agreement

Thanks

Many thanks to the travellers who used the previous edition and wrote to us with helpful hints, useful advice and interesting anecdotes:

Peirpaolo Abba, Jody Aboitiz, Dr B Abtmaier, Thomas Abtmeier, Denis Acheson, Lolita Adaro, Marc Aerts, Neil Agustin, Erik Akpedonu, Mariam Al Sarraj, Richie Aldez, Marin Aldrich, Ralph Alejandrino, Shaheed Ali, Nichola Alleman, Bob Allen, Tim Allen, Vittorio Z Almario, Eliane Cavalcante de Almeida, Cathy Alvarez, Mary Alvarez, Kannan Amaresh, Maria & Mark Anderson, W E Anderson, Patrick Andrivaux, Mary Ann Weber, Abby Antonio, Francesca Araneta, Michael Archibald, Sam Arie, Paul Arpin, Karina & Daniel Arsenault, Martiua Asclierl, Julie Ashcroft, Erlinda & Michael Astle, Toby Atkinson, Bard Atle-Lovehaug, John & Esther Atwell, Donald Austin, Brigitte & Matthew Awty, Carlo B, Phil Baarda, Gio Bacareza, Wong Bacareza, Stefan Backes, Christine Bader, Joanna Badura, Marie Balangue, Chris Bale, Jazmin Banal, Julie Bancilhon, John Banks, Walter Barnes, Marileth Barrios, Richard Bastain, J D Bate, Ferdinand Batoy, Chris Battye, Ross Baua, Johannes Bauch, David Beales, Ronald & Lisa Beames, A Belevitch, Graham Bell, Julien & Alexandra Bello, Shua Ben-Ari, Nick Benbow, Claire Benedicto, A M Benner, Scott Bennett, Andre Benning, Pierre Benoit, Theresa & Don Benoit, Russell Benton, George Beraman, Alexander Berkhout, Michael Berner, Gunter Bernert, Walter Bertschinger, Gemma Bigby, Ralph Bird, Chris Bisbee, Micheal Bishop, Helen Black, William Blaney, Michael Blaxland, Dory Blobner, Martje Bloot, Dik de & Cora Boer, Sanne Boessenkool, Karsten Bohm, Harry Boin, Richmod Bollinger, Lorcan Bolster, Michael Bolton, Helga Boom, Wee Boon Leong, George Boraman, Andrew Borlace, Jef Bos, Lars Bosteen, A & J Boutin, Steve Bovard, Kevin Braend, Christian Brauns, Geoff Breach, Siobhan Breslin, Lauraine Brin, Rune Bringgard, Bee Brink, D E Brock, Justin Brock, Martine Broeders, Bart van den Broek, John J Bromley, Nigel Brooks, Andrea Brugnoli, Karen & Annette Brunner, Patrick Brunner, Tony Brunschwiler, A M Bunker, Michael Burden, M D Burke, Lachlan Burnet, Thom Burns, S E Burris, Harald Busch, S B Butler, Paula Buur, Tom Byloos, Sheryl Cababa, Juan Antonio Caceres, Lyndsey Cal, George Campbell, Eric F Canzier, Peter Capostosto, Edmund Carew, Bo & Lucy Carlson, Jason Carmichael, John Dennis Carpio, Yenda Carson, Richard Carter, Rusty Cartmill, Alfafara L Catalino, Lucinda Cawley, Matt Chabot, Chris Chan, Julian Chan, Tim Chapman, Jeffrey Chase, Peter Chidgey, Anthony Shun Fung Chiu, Peter Chong, N D Chow, Susanna Chow, Henriette Noer Christensen, Ricco Christensen, W Chua, Jesse Chua-Reyes, Toto Cinco, Len Clampett, Jean Claude, K Cloostermans, Brian Clowes, Gail Cockburn, Nissim Cohen, Michelle Cohen-Peak, Lorna & Bill Collings, Chuck Collins, Lucy Colton, Alan Colville, David Coombes, Mel Copen, Rommel E Coquilla, Francoise Core, Bruce Cornfoot, Ernesto Corpuz, Tina Cortez, Karel Corthals, Kerem Cosar, Inna Costantini, Dan Coultas, Peter D Cowell, Garry Cowley, Anthony Cramer, Keith A Crandall, Geert Creffier, Dante C Cruz, Eduardo Cruz, Percy Cruz, Rogelio Dela Cruz Torres Jnr., Linda M Cummings, Tony Cummins, Daniel Cuneo, Rochelle Cuyco, Tomasz Czyzewski, Andy Dams, Olivier Darrigol, Glenn Davidson, Phil Davies, Steve Davies, Ray Davis, Rob de Groot, Joy de Guzman, Paul de Vries, Luc Deconte, Don & Helen Delaney, Robert DeNike, Bob Denny, Robert Diamond, Eliza Diana Iliescu, Jacqueline Dimeen, Sheila & Paul Doherty, Marnie Dolera, Elmer Domingo, Frederic Dominioni, C Donaghy, Stephen Donaldson, Gaye & John Dopper, J Dorman-Tiejada, David Douglas, Paul Doumitt, Dennis Drake, Rocky Drake, Brian Dudden, Weng Dumlao, S E Durnien, Paul Echague, K Edward Moore, Becky Eisses, Mike Elliott, Rob Erickson, Alfred Espedido, Hernando & Celia Esquivel, K H Evans, Neville Ewers, Joel Fagsao, Millie Fairhall, Norman Faner, Darina Farrell, Robert Farrington, J Fellenios, David Felts, Pierre Ferlov, George Fernandez, Michelle Fernandez, Shirley Fernandez, Annabel Ferrer, Hanne Finholt, Ulrich Fischer, Mika & Gary Fishman, Sean Fitzgerald, Roland Flageollet, Malin Flood, Carmen Flores, Daisy Flores, Johan Forsberg, Michael Fox, Scotty Fox, John Francis, Jean-Pierre Franck, Dale Franco, Duncan Frearson, Harold Frederick, Jeff Freeman, Peter Freeman, Sietse Fritsma, Lucy Fuchs, Reca Fucsok, Andrew Fuller, John Funk, Prof Per Gade, Sarah Gaitanos, Marta Galindo, Jack Gallagher, Dr Pablo Ortega Gallo, Don D Garcia, Marichit Garcia, Helmut Gartenhaub, Harold Gary, Ron Gaul, Julie A Gaw, Rebecca Giles, Walter W Glaser, Ophir Glezer, R J Gnanalolan, Steve Golik, Steve Gonsalves, Joseph Goodall, Gary Grady, Letty T Graham, W A Graham, J K Gray, Mrs & Mr Gray, Sammy Grieve, Heather Griffin, Ron Griffin, Oystein Grimstad, Frits Groenewegen, Cristina Gunn, Tuesday Gutierrez, Nina Haaland, Susanne Haas, Dan Habb, J Hagelgans, Bertil Hagnell, Danny Hahn, M J Haines, Robert Haines, Kenneth Hall, Steven Hall, Tanja Haller, James Halsema, David Han, Pauwels Hans, Elisabeth Hansen, Jonas Hansson, Chris Hargreaves, Don Harris, Brad Harsch, Dale Harshman, Glenn Hartell, Paul Harvey, Peter Harvey, Scott Harvey, Oliver Harwood, Fumiko Hattori, Celia & Pete Hawe, Don Hearn, Daniel Hebb, Louie Hechanova, John B Hee, Ingrid Heiss, Laurent Hendrichs, Luke Hendricks, Harold Hendry, Judy Hicks, Scott Hildebrand, Ceci & Frits Hillenaar, Jerry C Hizon, Yiu-yin Ho, Henk & Wil Hoekstra, Cristy & Harlan Hoffas, Anja & Rob Hofman, David Hofman, Sue Holdham, Judy Hong, Gwalgen Hops, Soren Horn, Ray Hossinger, F Van Hoyweghen, Khoo Hsu Jenn, Marshall Hughes, Adriaan Huijsing, Kenn Hunter, A Hutchinson, A & G Hutchinson, Brenton Ian Bart, Jamie & Nikki Ingram, Joshua Inman, Ulrich Iseli, Amala Ishaya, Cheiko Ishikawa, Brigitte Jacobs, Kenneth Jademo, Ian James, Steve James, Tom Janssens, Thomas Jansson, Jan Jasiewicz, Esmyra Javier, Terry Jellicoe, Kim Jen, F Jenneskens, Kurt Jensen, Ove Jensen, Benoit Joguet, Barclay Johnson, Leo Joki, Bo Jonsson, Henrik Josephsen, J S Kacskos, Gilad Kahn, Line Kallstad, Christoph Kalthoff, Mark Kanning, Tomasz Kasprzycki, Iwakami Katsuhiko, Dr Jay D Kaufman, Denis Kearney,

Julia Kedgley, Arthur Keefe, L Keith Bland, Terry Kempis, Joseph Kennedy, Helen Keraudren, Christof Kerber, Bjorn Kessler, Joisy & Davy King, Lisa King, Steve Kinsman, Hugh Kirley, Hilmar Kjartansson, Cassandra Klayh, Mark Kleiber, Dr Thom Kleiss, Steve Knaggs, Michael Kohn, Sarah Kokot, Lee Kokpiew, Joke Koppen, Klaudia Krammer, Alana Krider, Anne Kristiansen, Gedelita Kruger, Jane Kruuk, Christine Kruyfhooft, Susanne Kullberg, Krista Kuppens, Krzysztof Kurdowicz, Gerardine Laffan, Andreas Laimboeck, Kam Lam, Cecile Lambermont, Karel Lamboo, S Lane, Jonathon P Lang, Emma Langstaff, Age Langved, P Lantela Richard Lapin, Alistair Lathe, Fredy Lauener, Jeannine Laurens, Ino Laurensse, Tere Lauron, Winnie Law, Arlene Lawson, Pascal Lays, John Leach, Kevin & Debbie Leafe, David Lee, Eileen Lee, Jamie Lee, Eric Leeou, Eileen Legaspi-Ramirez, Michael Lehman, Boris Lelong, Mikelson Leong, Eric Lepelaar, Didier Lhulillier, Agnes Lim, Donna May Lina, Dan Lindfield, Rebecca Lineham, Ian Lloyd, Stuart Lloyd, Tim Lloyd, Emma Lobban, Kathrina Lobo, Andreas Loew, Christian Lohlein, Jose Lomas, Searle Loughman, Jim Louie, Joy Loyola, Mike Lu, Clare Lucas, Meynardo Luna, Cindi Lundy, Itay Lusky, Brendan Luyt, Don MacAdam, Mag Alexander Macalka, Ray MacDonald, Daniel Machanik, Malcolm MacKellar, Emma M Malabanan, Ben Mallorca, Stephen Malone, Prof Dr Manfred Malzahn, Rhea Manalo, Peter Mancuso, Mylene Manlogon, Lydia Mapua, Ato Mariano, Will Markle, Charles R Marks, Steven Marlborough, Conor Martin, Toby Martin, Andreas Mattheiss, Neil McBain, Brian McCauley, Geordie McConnell, Greg McCormick, Kenneth McCutcheon, Christopher McDaniel, Steven McGuigan, Vince Mcguire, Malcolm McLucas, Laurie McMahon, Shane McNamara, The McNamara Family, John D McRae, J Medhurst, M Meijer, Jan Mellaerts, Silvia Merli, Joseph Meyer, Ophir Michaeli, Vivi Mikkelsen, Jonathan Miller, Claudio Milletti, Lindsay Milne, Clio Minihan-Crane, David Mobbs, Justin Mog, R Moller, Joey Montalvo, Marc Montangero, Recelie G Montas, Dean Moore, K Edward Moore, Eve Mora, Yen Morris, Roger Mueller, Edan Mumford, B W Munro, Donald Munro, Allan Murphy, Joseph Murphy, Roy Myren, Geir Naess, Charles Nagel, Michael Narciso, Robert Navon, Gordon Neech, Dan Neisner, Wolfgang Neudahm, Georg Nicca, Preben Nielsen, J Nygren, Marwan Obeid, Analyne Oehler, Ziga Ogrizek, Tara O'Leary, M L Oliveros, Lennart Olsson, K O'Neill, Gal Oren, John Orford, Yan & Lorena Ottesen, Ruth Overstreet, Ian Owen, Rob Owens, Marianne Pamintuan, Charles Pantlin, Carol Parkin, Jeffrey Parrott, Steven Parsa, Melvin S Pascual Jr., Colin Paskins, Huy B Passage, Laurent Pater, Calvin Patterson, N Patterson, Rudolf Paul Maierhofer, Ralph Pauly, Patrik Persson, Wayne Peterken, Rikke M & Karsten Petersen, Morten Pettersen, Angela Phillips, Carl Pickin, M Pierre Benoit, Jean Pierre Marsac, Harold Pijke, John P Sevilla, Anne Place, Ahrni G Planco, Roland F Playford, A Pometta, Leesa Pope, Juliet Porritt, John Power, Adam Preece, Sandrine Presles, Dina Priess, A Proctor, A Pulola, Andrew Purdy, Cynthia Pyle, Jaime Quejada, Micheal Quilding, H Quinn, Jimmy Quinn, Talya & Rick Rabern, George Rady, Giacomo Rambaldi, Michael Ramos, Restituto R Ramos, Stella A Ramos, Chris Rea, Ted Reader, Edith Rebulado, Ken Reed,

Sofia Rehn, Allen Reilly, Jim Revell, Douglas Reynolds, Pete Rhodora, Stu Richel, Julie Riddle, Allan Rimmington, Neil Ring, Heiko Rippke, Stefan Ritz, Sylvia Robertson, A Robinson, Jon Robinson, Kevin Robinson, Isabelle Rochard, Aurelia Rogers, John & Aurelia Rogers, B K Roper, Roseanne Rostock, Martin Rowe, Peter Ruark, Melanie Rubenstein, Adam Rubin, Seamus Ryan, H H Saffery, Ronald Sakamoto, Charmaine D Sales, Tess Salvador, Moira Sambey, Ronnie Samuel, Clarence Samuels, Ewa Samvik, John D Sanchez, Gregory Sarno, Catherine Scherer, Dan Schlichtmann, Frank Schmidt, Michael Schmidt, Frederic Schneider, Mark A Schneider, James Schones, M & W Schramme-Argyropoulou, Guido Schrijvers, Marcel Schrijvers, Frank Schrolkamp, Kevin Scott, Noranne Scott, P Screach, Eric Seaman, Richard Selby, Alon Seren, Lee Shackelford, Rew Shearer, Betty Sheets, Paul Sheppard, Clyde Shoebridge, Robert Shung, Amy Siak, Anna Siepert, Ruth Simon, Joel Simons, Andrew Simpson, Nikki Singh, A F Siraa, Bryan S Siy, J Slikker, Ken Sloane, Sue Smith, R Smits, Tim Snowden, John Soar, JoJo & Louise Solacito, Laz Solang, D Somera, Tiki Sonderhoff, Carol Sosito, Brian Souter, D Speakman, J D Spector, Jillian Spencer, Peter Sprenger, Margo Stack, Edward Stanton, Jacqueline Stanton, Lilian & Russell Stapleton, Steve Starlight, Robert F Stauder, Doug Stevens, Rae Stevenson, Vibeke Stobakk, Richard Stokes, Sarah Stokoe, L D & P F Stonehouse, Ellen Stuiver, Martin Stummer, R W Le Sueur, Enmi Sung, Colin Sweeney, Greg Sweetnam, Odette Tabobo, Roderika M Taduran, Sam Talbert, Andrea Tan, Drei Tan, Jessie Tan, Iain Taylor, Trevor Taylor, Livvy Tee, Joel & Julia Tejada, Jo Tenten, Paul Tetrault, Kelly Theil, Anne Thomas, Marc Thomas, David Thompson, Roger Thompson, Ross Thompson, Rupert Thompson, Mike Thomsen, A L Threadgill, Tierney Thys, M H Tiba, J Tiejada, Edgar Tieman, Bradford Tiffany, Johan D Timp, Michelle Tinsay, Frank Toelle, Liam Toner, Justin Tooth, Anthony Tosti, Henning Tousted, Russell Trounce, Scott True, David & Bridget Trump, N J Turner, Rob Turner, David Twine, Dan Unger, Leon D Urbain, Patrick Uy, Carol Valdez, Rammal Valenzuela, B Vallet, Pascal van Bergen, Roger Van Den Berghe, Joyce van Dijk, Ron van Mastrigt, Paul Mike van Reenen, Victor van Straten, Jan van Zadelhoff, Antony Van Zalk, Del Vanhook, Rick Vaughn, Mark Vawdrey, P Vazquez, Fernando Vega, David Vera, Frank Verhagen, Dirk Verschueren, Jan Verweij, Karen Vidler, Kathy Villalon, Adrian A Villanueva, Don Villanueva, Maria & Otso Reunanen Virtanen, Elma & Alex von Essen, Lars von Lampe, Jason Vorderstrasse, Susan Voss-Rothmeier, Hans-Christian Wagner, Laszlo Wagreer, Jay Walder, Clive Walker, Ron Walker, R Wallis, Tim Watt, Philippa Wealands, Nah Wee Kee, Don Welch, Conrad D Wenham, Irene Wertenbroeke, Roy White, Thelma White, Winston White, Alan Whitlock, John Wickham, Danielle Wieggers, Benny Willems, Eden Williams, Timothy Willis, Andrea Wilson, Deanna Wilson, Max Wiman, Rudi & Carmencita Winger, Alexander Winter, Leah Wiste, Walter Witt, Stefan Wochinz, Brain Wolf, Casey Wong, Kyle Wood, Jacqueline Woodand, Emma Woodard, Rim Woodward, Hans-Peter Wunde, Gabriel Yap, Jocelyn Yoma, Diana H Youell, Anson Yu, David Yu, Noel Yuseco and Pieter Zegwaart.

Index

Text

Bold indicates maps.

Bold indicates maps.

Bold indicates maps.

Boxed Text

MAP LEGEND

CITY ROUTES

Freeway	Freeway	Unsealed Road	
Highway	Primary Road	One Way Street	
Road	Secondary Road	Pedestrian Street	
Street	Street	Stepped Street	
Lane	Lane	Tunnel	
	On/Off Ramp	Footbridge	

REGIONAL ROUTES

Tollway, Freeway
Primary Road
Secondary Road
Minor Road

BOUNDARIES

International
State
Disputed
Fortified Wall

HYDROGRAPHY

River/Creek
Canal
Lake
Dry Lake/Salt Lake
Spring/Rapids
Waterfalls

TRANSPORT ROUTES & STATIONS

Train
Underground Train
LRT
MRT
Cable Car, Chairlift
Ferry, Transport
Walking Trail
Walking Tour
Path
Pier or Jetty

AREA FEATURES

Building
Park, Gardens
Market
Sports Ground
Beach
Cemetery
Campus
Plaza

POPULATION SYMBOLS

✪ CAPITAL	National Capital	● CITY	City	● Village	Village
◉ CAPITAL	Provincal Capital	● Town	Town		Urban Area

MAP SYMBOLS

▲	Place to Stay	▼	Place to Eat	●	Point of Interest

Airfield, Airport	Dive Site/Surf Beach	National Park	Stately Home
Bank	Embassy/Hospital	Pagoda	Swimming Pool
Bus Terminal	Garden/Golf Course	Petrol Station	Telephone
Cave/Shipwreck	Internet Cafe	Police Station	Temple
Cathedral/Church	Library/Museum	Post Office	Tourist Information
Cinema	Lighthouse/Lookout	Pub/Bar	Volcano/Mountain
Cycling	Monument/Fountain	Shopping Centre	Zoo

Note: not all symbols displayed above appear in this book

LONELY PLANET OFFICES

Australia
Locked Bag 1, Footscray, Victoria 3011
☎ 03 8379 8000 fax 03 8379 8111
email: talk2us@lonelyplanet.com.au

USA
150 Linden St, Oakland, CA 94607
☎ 510 893 8555 TOLL FREE: 800 275 8555
fax 510 893 8572
email: info@lonelyplanet.com

UK
72-82 Rosebery Ave, Clerkenwell,
London, EC1R 4RW
email: go@lonelyplanet.co.uk

France
1 rue du Dahomey, 75011 Paris
☎ 01 55 25 33 00 fax 01 55 25 33 01
email: bip@lonelyplanet.fr
www.lonelyplanet.fr

World Wide Web: www.lonelyplanet.com *or* AOL keyword: lp
Lonely Planet Images: www.lonelyplanetimages.com